Essential Solitude

H. P. Lovecraft

ESSENTIAL SOLITUDE

THE LETTERS OF H. P. LOVECRAFT AND AUGUST DERLETH: 1932–1937

Edited by David E. Schultz and S. T. Joshi

Hippocampus Press

New York

Essential Solitude: The Letters of H. P. Lovecraft and August Derleth
Published by Hippocampus Press
P.O. Box 641, New York, NY 10156
www.hippocampuspress.com

Cover Design by Barbara Briggs Silbert.
Hippocampus Press logo designed by Anastasia Damianakos.

First Paperback Edition
978-1-61498-061-2 (Volume 2)
978-1-61498-062-9 (2 Volume Set)

Contents

1932

[242] [ALS][1]

[Postmarked Boston, Mass,
2 January 1932]

Extra! Special! Are you suddenly dead? We've just had a vision of you as a decomposed corpse hanging head downward in a Romanesque crypt! If this is a correct telepathic impression, let us know at once by special delivery air mail! ¶ Have made a museum day of it—doing all the Cambridge group: Germanic, Semitic, Peabody, Agassiz, & Fogg. Your friend Schorer would know all about these. Tomorrow we do the Gardner Palace in the Fenway, & the good old Fine Arts. Regards—Grandpa H P

W. Paul Cook

Notes

1. Front: Windings of the Trail and River, Mohawk Trail, Mass.

[243] [ALS]

Boston—Jan 2, 1932

Dear A.W.:—

Such has been the genial trend of the weather, that I am in Boston spending a long week-end with W. Paul Cook—making the rounds of the museums & discussing things in general. We had expected H. Warner Munn down, but obstacles to his coming intervened at the last moment. Cook has just presented me with "The Omnibus of Crime", & I think the first thing I shall read will be the much-discussed "Green Tea", by Le Fanu. I am also looking over the collected M. R. James, & reading the 4 tales not in the old editions.[1]

As for "Innsmouth"—it seems like cruelty to children to let you try to decode the smudged & interpolation-riddled rough draught, but unless I get around to typing it within the next fortnight I guess I'll send it along. I have a sort of hazy notion of trying to type the damn thing as a sort of obituary to my present fictional period—but we'll see.

Hope Bates takes the Magnolias. I think he'd be quite an editor if Clayton would only let him alone. But that old boy is the arch-Philistine of them all. Glad to hear of your recent work, & hope "The Panelled Room & Others" will find a typographical haven in time.

Yes—H S sent me one of those snaps of himself in full sacerdotal regimentals, & he certainly does cut an imposing figure.[2] The likeness is splendid—for Canevin surely is about as distinguished-looking an individual as I've seen in a good while. He seldom wears this ecclesiastical regalia—snappy sport clothes being his characteristic costume. During sermon hours on Sunday he dons a dark suit & back-side-to collar; but always gets them off again as soon as possible. I never saw him in the mediaeval frills, & fancy he wears them only on special ceremonial occasions.

Hope *Strange Tales* keeps up to the present standard. Cook has just shewed me the new W.T. with Wandrei's "Tree Men", I shall purchase my own copy when next I strike a news stand.

Glad you have had some congenial musical opportunities of late. Cesar Franck is a favourite of another Wisconsin-bred friend of mine—Alfred Galpin of Appleton, (now of Chicago, & at present travelling in Europe) who plans to become a composer. Hope you hear from STRA<u>U</u>CH. Note the spelling—which my hieroglyphics probably failed to convey last time. I am enclosing a letter from the other Penn. youth, with some typical bits of Lehigh Valley folklore. I must get hold of "The Lady Who Came to Stay"—praise for which is echoed by little Shea.

As for the controversy—I still hold to my original position regarding evidence. When there is no evidence to suggest explanations for certain phenomena, we cannot arbitrarily concoct some improbable notion based on irrelevant folklore & then maintain that the chances of this notion's truth are *even*. As a matter of fact, the chances in this direction are *very slight—since it could only be through rare & improbable coincidence* that the real state of things would in any way happen to resemble the unauthorised guess of someone who had no means of getting at the truth. And when, in addition, the guess is not only extremely improbable according to general cosmic laws but is palpably suggested by some wholly unrelated & non-informative idea-forming process, we may consider the chances of its truth as reduced to a very slender minimum. Think this over—using common sense instead of attenuated theoretical logic—& you can't fail to get what I mean. If certain alleged evidences & indications did not bear the earmarks of having been suggested by processes of wholly irrelevant & non-informative nature, they would be admissible at a higher face value; but when we know that these alleged evidences & indications would inevitably be put forward in any case—irrespective of truth or falsity—we cannot any longer consider them as genuine evidence.

I also continue to see a flaw in your contention that the *sheer bulk* of the Fort-Flammarion stuff forms any indication of the truth of any of it. Remember that once a natural myth-process gets started, its ramifications, repetitions, variants are well-nigh infinite & eternal. The one shout subdivides & protracts itself in a million echoes—the one story passes from mouth to mouth & subdivides into a million yarns of roughly cognate type. Often when Fort collects 100 cuttings hinting at a certain anomaly, he is really collecting only 100 echoes of some single typical folk myth. But more than this—what Fort & his kind collect is not any one body of coherent data all pointing the same way. It is, rather, a hodge-podge of all sorts of heterogeneous extravagance without any connecting thread. All this junk does not build up any one definite case for anything. The principle of selection is simply the scooping in of all items which lack a satisfactory explanation. Well—we know in the first place that the inevitable result of slipshod human nature is to create myriads of imperfectly transcribed or casually invented reports of alleged happenings outside the radius of the clearly explicable. We would know that thousands of such blunders & extravagances must inevitably exist, & without any foundation in truth, even if nobody had ever bothered to collect & publish them. All that such an array of freakish items means, is that extravagant misreporting is a common tendency of the human race, (which indeed we knew before) & that somebody has been patient enough to collect a few of the more interesting & sensational canards of the past few years. We may be sure that there is just as much of this irresponsible stuff still floating around uncollected—casual mistakes, & multiplying echoes of dozens of typical myths—as there is between the covers of any Fort or Flammarion book of marvels. We don't need to investigate *every* mistake & echo personally, because we know the general types of delusions to which they all belong. Just as a cannery inspector tests only certain cans chosen at random from the whole limitless output, so need the marvel-inspector choose only a typical & random array of alleged miracles to run to earth. If virtually every one reveals itself as a delusion or deception—as is the case—the verdict of common sense on the whole myth cycle is easy to imagine. As for your telepathic claim—I told you in the first place that I have no facilities for making a real investigation. All that I can say is in the nature of mere suggestion—& you'll notice that I did not definitely exclude actual telepathy as a remotely possible factor.

But you are all off in fancying that anybody can positively discriminate between dream & reality. All the elaborate reflections & precautions in Schorer's case are as typical of certain vivid dream-types as of objective reality. I've had just such reflections on alternatives—& such sober analyses of conditions—in states later revealed conclusively as belonging to dream. Nor is my point about the anomalousness of Schorer's writing you merely "my own idea". It is simply a common sense conclusion based on the way all sober sceptics regard their dreams. Certainly, if one person has an especially vivid dream about another he is apt to tell that other about it the next time they meet—or write about it the next time he happens to be inditing a letter to the other fellow. But to send a special-delivery letter in frantic haste . . . . . if this doesn't mean an initial predisposition toward gullibility regarding the bizarre, I greatly miss my guess! I've had many dreams of the grave illness or death of members of my family—dreams that were frightfully vivid & painful while they lasted, & from which I awaked with the most infinite relief. But did I forthwith write alarmed letters to the persons concerned? Don't make me laugh!

About memory—even the best & most accurate of memories can occasionally suffer transposition or interpolative suggestion under the right emotional conditions. Most of us don't realise how completely our whole respective pictures of the external world are individual affairs determined by accidents of emotional perspective. This is a subject well worth a separate study for its own sake. Often the best rememberer will experience the greatest emotional modifications of recollections *because of* & not in spite of his vivid hindsight. The very activity of the mnemonic process increases its susceptibility to suggestion.

I never confuse telepathy with occultism, as my last letter will plainly shew. When I say I think the former is *improbable,* I don't mean that it's cosmically unlikely, but merely that at present (see Wiggam, & also certain reports of recent psychological tests at various colleges) the evidence for its absence seems greater than that for its existence. The explanation given by your psychological friend is of a type frequently met with. As a layman, I cannot well attack it; but I can point out that many eminent investigators find serious flaws in it. I won't be dogmatic about your case—but I'll wager that an investigating committee of several qualified psychologists could unearth basic factors which would surprise you.

Well—I guess I'm too sleepy tonight to read "Green Tea" after all! It's longer than I had anticipated. Rain has set in—but I'm not worrying, for museum-haunting is not very continuously drenching work, & this rain may be over by morning anyhow.

Best wishes—

Yr obt Servt

H P

Notes

1. These are "There Was a Man Dwelt by a Churchyard," "Rats," "After Dark in the Playing Fields," and "Wailing Well."

2. See photo in gallery between pp. 60 and 61 in AWD, *Thirty Years of Arkham House: A History and Bibliography.*

[244] [ALS]

Jany 11, 1932

Dear A W:—

As for arguments—don't regret the thoroughness with which I consider such matters, for there is no use in believing or asserting anything unless the examination of evidence be thorough. Half-considered topics are the same as unconsidered topics—indeed, it is the habit of half-consideration which is responsible for most of the surviving delusions of the present. Regarding the behaviour of sceptics—I still insist that if a person allows a dream or "hunch" to impress him at all, he is no true sceptic. You say that in your "telepathic" case Schorer wrote 'not because of the manifestation, but because of concern for your health' . . . . . . but you had previously said that he had no reason to be alarmed about your health! If he *had* such reason, his concern undoubtedly inspired his dream. On the other hand, if he had *not* such reason, the cause of his writing *must* have been that he took his dream as a serious indication that you might be unwell. And that rules him out as a real sceptic. In a region where credulity is a good part of the local tradition, such a reaction to a dream would be unheard-of. My relatives or friends might dream in the most vivid possible way that they saw me buried or hanged or killed in a wreck—but when they awoke in the morning it would *not even begin to cross their brains* that such a phantom apparition could have any connexion with my real welfare or situation. They would consider any belief to the contrary a ludicrous superstition denoting on the one hand rustic ignorance or on the other hand decadent faddism or cult-gullibility. The very idea of writing anybody a letter on the strength of a fancied vision would seem so grotesque, naive, & unmotivated that it could not possibly be entertained or acted upon. Nor do attitudes seem any different in Boston, New York, or any other sophisticated urban centre. How things are in the remote countryside I can't say, though one might find a good deal of credulity in the decadent Wilbraham region whence I drew my "Dunwich." I doubt if hard-headed Vermont harbours much of it, though. When Yankees recovered from the superstition of the Salem Witchcraft period, they made a thorough job of their recovery! These table-movings at seances are subconsciously mechanical to a large extent, & in other cases deliberately & cleverly mechanical. "Animal Magnetism" &c. is an exploded delusion. Much of this stuff has been very ably described by Prof. Joseph Jastrow[1]—once, if not still, of your U. of Wis. As for the alleged telepathic manifestations you cite—of course the trick was that somebody played up to what you described. I've strung people along that way myself in order to shew up the falsity of their alleged visions. There was one poet who used always to be talking of the clairvoyance of his dreams, & when he would tell something about me, I would always agree to it & suggest just enough more to set him off on fresh visions. I would also pretend to confirm visions of his, & suggest enough to make him weave all sorts of extravagant nonsense. I got him to relating a strange cosmic dream—which I pretended I had shared *& continued*; & finally he began to claim he had shared my continuation, & to build onward from that. He thought he was stringing me along finely—for he probably half-believed in his own nonsense despite the 0.75 of exhibitionistic fakery in his ebullitions. Your experiments in "concentration" might have several explanations depending on exact circumstances & types of collusion which could not be known to a distant layman. It must be remembered that among people adhering to the tradition of credulity ("sceptics" in the Wisconsin sense. The very knowledge of how to proceed in traditional exercises of "telepathy" & "occultism" argues some familiarity with an insidiously biassing heritage of credulousness) there are many folk-patterns of conventional procedure—deception, (including self-deception) collusion, expectation, interpretation, &c—as potent & well-defined as anything in Frazer's "Golden Bough." Against the random reports of unscientific parlour parties we have the uniform testimony of all serious laboratory investigators (experiments in influence through mass-concentration have been common in colleges for years, & have produced uniformly negative results) that no authenticated case of "telepathy" has yet been observed by mankind. This does not prove that purely mental communication *cannot* exist, but simply that all evidence *so far* cited has been part of that same traditional system of folk-deception (so well understood by all anthropologists, yet so puzzling & incredible to the unscientific) which gives us spurious "evidence" for ghosts, vampires, poltergeists, & other stock occult paraphernalia. A man like A. E. Wiggam does not make a positive statement lightly—& you can depend upon it that the bulk of responsible thinkers have a damn good reason for taking the *really* sceptical position they do take. They have encountered all the "evidences" for impossible absurdities which you have encountered, but they use a profound sense of proportion & a keen appreciation of delusive factors in psychology & anthropology when they come to interpret that evidence & correlate it with the other observed phenomena of the external world. The only known exception is the case of your recent experience with the monstrous Yog-Sothoth (you *think* It is only a *sorcerer* . . . . but God! if you but suspected what It *really* is!!!)—the inner facts of which tally exactly & uncannily with my hideous vision in far-off Boston. Every detail is as I dreamed it—I even know that IT was actually seeking me, & my hand trembled as I hinted all I dared hint on a postcard!

If I don't type Innsmouth pretty soon, I'll send it along as it is . . . . & may Tsathoggua help you! Hope you have luck with your new things, especially "A Town is Built." Too bad you must vitiate your voodoo story with Claytonism.

I read the new W. T. whilst in Boston—Cook had a touch of malaria the third day of my stay, so we loafed about the house & idled through cheap magazines.* I agree that Wandrei's "Mbwa" is the best thing in the issue, & also accord the Level *conte cruel* a high place—though it is no more a weird tale than Faulkner's "Emily". I can't say that I place Howard's thing as low as you place it. I know it's trite, but something in it gave me a kick for all that. Maybe it was von Junzt & the Black Book. . . . I must use him, as well as Justin Geoffrey, in some future tale of mine.[3] I liked "Those Who Seek"—as I told you before when inspecting the manuscript.

---

*I saw Jacobi's tale in G. S. Not bad, but hardly in the running with "Mive".[2]

You'll find either Brobst or Strauch very interesting as a sidelight upon one of the most curious anthropological backwaters in the U.S. In some ways, the Lehigh Valley seems to share the primitive qualities (despite partial urbanisation) of the Ozarks or Cumberlands. ¶ Best wishes—H P

Notes

1. Joseph Jastrow (1863–1944), professor of psychology at the University of Wisconsin (1888–1927) and author of such works as *The Subconscious* (1906) and *Character and Temperament* (1915).

2. "The Haunted Ring," *Ghost Stories* (December 1931–January 1932).

3. REH invented von Junzt for "The Children of the Night" (*WT,* April–May 1931) and cited his book variously as *Nameless Cults* or *The Black Book.* HPL mentioned von Junzt in "The Dreams in the Witch House" (1932), "The Thing on the Doorstep" (1933), and "The Shadow out of Time" (1934–35). Justin Geoffrey first appeared in "The Black Stone" (*WT,* November 1931). HPL cited him in "The Thing on the Doorstep" (1933).

[245] [TLS, JHL]

Sauk City, Wisconsin
15 January, 1932

Dear H. P.,

Yes, of course Mark took his telepathic vision seriously enough to write; what I should have said was that he wrote because he was convinced I was ill. No, as I said before, he had no previous concern over my health. ... But he didn't dream, much as you believe he did. He saw the thing. Your determined skepticism in this one case I hold invalid. What I chiefly object to in all your comment in this last letter is your determination to list my reactions etc. with folk reactions; I deplore; and your persistence in refusing to take any assertion of mine on face value. Authenticated cases of telepathy have been recorded, I think at Columbia for one, but am not sure just where. A. E. Wiggam, for instance, is light reading to me. Well I remain totally unconvinced. But your letters are certainly most interesting on the subject, and I shall promptly use them to argue against the possibility of telepathy etc., in which I do believe, but like to argue against anyway.

I shall look forward to Innsmouth with great anticipation, and beg you to send it off as soon as you have this letter, whether it is typewritten or not. Meanwhile, I enclose a new story of Smith's, which I liked rather well, not too well, of course. No, I don't think Scribners will take either A Town is Built or the resubmitted Early Years. In fact, I was so disappointed with my submissions, that last Monday I sat down and started a new 15,000 word novelette, which I finished on Wednesday, and completely revised on Thursday, and am submitting to Scribners today. It is called Five Alone, and is the story of a family of five, queer with an inherited queerness, and overexaggerated sense of family unity which allows none of them to escape from the others. It is chiefly the story of Linda Grell, who tried to escape, but could not, and discovered it too late. I have an idea that you will like it. Last Sunday I tried my hand at a juvenile, doing a 2000 worder called A Little Girl Lost, which isn't bad but which will not sell, though it was rather fun writing.

I have meanwhile uncovered a stagnating artist in a nearby town (2 miles away only), and had him do an illustration for In the Left Wing, which is to appear in the June issue. Wright liked the illustration, and so did I; he is wondering whether he can take it now because of certain technicalities, but if he doesn't, the artist will rework it without the objectionable characteristics. He also did an excellent one for The Lair of the Star Spawn, which I hope Wright takes. He is now doing a half length life size portrait of me. Laughter in the Night, says Wright, will appear in the March issue.

I agree with you anent Jacobi's G. S. tale, but not anent Howard's tale. Old Junzt an the Black Book had just the opposite effect on me; just a pale copy of the Necronomicon. Those Who Seek was lousy in my estimation.[1]

I have not heard from Strauch, whom I wrote late in December, and will not write again. Later I will try Brobst, whose letter I thought interesting.

At Dead of Night, the new Selwyn & Blount anthology, has come; it has Prince Borgia's Mass, and is a lousy collection. I was glad to see Passing of a God[2] here, however.

as always,

August

Notes

1. REH, "The Thing on the Roof," *WT* (February 1932); AWD, "Those Who Seek."
2. By Henry S. Whitehead.

[246] [ALS]

Jany. 21, 1932

Dear A W:—

Under separate cover—as soon as I can get down to the express office—I shall be sending you a package containing two somewhat elongated horrors—Wandrei's 200-page novel, "Dead Titans Waken",[1] & my own verbose & doubtful swan-song, "The Shadow Over Innsmouth", which I have typed at last as a sort of grand finale to my present prose period. After 72 pages of that damned clicking I am about all in—too exhausted to care whether the cursed thing is any good or not. It insisted on dictating itself in just this form after endless attempts to write it otherwise—so now I'm through with it. Wright would go into convulsions about its diffuse length, but I'm not even trying it on him. The professional press & my fiction are no longer reconcilable. I have indicated a tentative circulation route on the cover—you to Klarkash-Ton, then to Melmoth & thence back to me—but if you think the damned mess is too rotten (I'm past all power of judging this thing) you can ignore the listed schedule & shoot it back to Grandpa & merciful oblivion.

As for Melmoth's chef d'oeuvre—the chief criticism I give it is that the first & second halfs are atmospherically incompatible. He began by surrendering to the popular "action" tradition, but grew cosmic & poetic after he got started into earth's bowels. In the first part bizarre horrors are introduced without adequate emotional preparation, but later on the cosmic vision gets really tremendous at times—so that I extracted a whale of a wallop from the performance as a whole, & wish I could have written it myself! However—Wandrei will come up against difficulty in placing this tale, especially in the book field. Do you suppose it might land with Wright as a serial—or in one of the scientifiction quarterlies?

By the way—before I forget it—when you get my express package (already done up, else I'd make the correction myself) would you mind taking Dwyer's name off the circulation list? On second thought I'm sending him the other copy now.

Glad to hear of your new novelette, & hope to see it in time—whether or not it finds a haven at the high altitude chosen for it. The plot sounds like the sort of thing best fitted to your creative imagination. Good luck with the juvenile, too!

And so you've discovered an artist? Hope you can get him started in W.T.—& shall be eager to see some of his headings for your tales. Does his portrait of you seem to promise well?

Sorry the S & B annual is below par. By the way—I think I'll have to buy that last year's issue with my "Rats", so would you mind telling me again (a) the exact title, (b) the exact price, & (c) the exact address of the Argus whence it is (I hope still) available?

You've probably heard from Strauch by this time. He doesn't take much literary interest in his unique backwater region because his own taste does not run to the homely—& he seems rather to dislike the local natives, with whose stock he is not allied. He certainly knows all about the local folkways & superstitions, though. Brobst would appear to belong to the local stock. It is certainly an unique phenomenon—this region of vestigial superstitions & peculiar customs, brooding for almost 250 years without assimilation to the general culture for the state & the nation. It is probably as good a field as

"Dunwich" for a study in half-decadent stagnation.

Best wishes—H P

Notes

1. The flaws referred to below remain in the published novel (*The Web of Easter Island*).

[247] [ALS]

Jany. 27, 1932

Dear A W:—

Swanson doesn't say how much he will pay for material, but promises that it will be at least *something*.[1] No vast amount—& conditioned by the way the first issue sells. I fear he can't make much headway in a field so overcrowded—but if he'll give me good printed copies of my rejected junk I'll be sufficiently satisfied. Hope you can stock him up with anything you can't place elsewhere.

I'm afraid you won't find Innsmouth much good—but Wandrei's novel will take the taste out of your mouth. I'm still recovering from that 72-page typing ordeal. It hardly seems likely that any editor would care for this—especially any Clayton hireling. You are tremendously kind to speak a good word for the old man with Bates, but I fear he's hopeless. Enclosed is a paragraph from Belknap which illustrates the sort of cheap "action" tripe needed to be popular with Handsome Harry.

Glad your artist protege is getting a foothold, & that the uninspired C C S[2] is being edged toward the wings. When I read the novel "Grand Hotel"[3] last year I noticed that a hall porter was named Senf. It's about time C C got back to the family profession! Hope your friend will get some vignette & tailpiece jobs—you might tell Wright it's about time he stopped using Brosnatch's ancient designs for Belknap's "Desert Lich" & "Were-Snake" & Seabury Quinn's "Servants of Satan" in this capacity![4] Trust you won't discourage the new artist from making a good likeness of you. You can have a background of books & exotic objets d'art if you wish to emphasise your difference from the Football Hero type.

Thanks for the Not at Night information—my order goes to the Argus in this mail. But I do think Charles Lavell was a damn cheap sport not to send us free copies after promising to do so last May. Is there anything by our gang in the latest number?

Glad Strauch replied at last. Brobst, I think, is more in sympathy with the traditions of the region—& perhaps better informed, even though he is not as intellectual a type as Strauch. He told me something I didn't know about Delaware the other day—that a group of *Moors* (whether from Spain or Morocco I don't know) settled there during the colonial period & are still a separate element in the population, being curiously called "White Indians". I am asking him more about this singular group.

Naturally you'll have to enter the high-grade magazine field by very gradual degrees, considering the competition. Some, it seems, secure a first foothold by getting things accepted by *departments* (like "The Lion's Mouth" in *Harpers*) before making the text proper. I want to see your "Five Alone" some time, whether or not it attains its lofty professional goal.

It's getting almost trite to mention that warm weather continues hereabouts. I only hope we shan't have to pay for it by a bitter February or belated spring—or both!

Best wishes—

Yr obt Grandsire

H P

Notes

1. Carl Swanson (Washburn, ND) wished to begin a magazine titled *Galaxy,* consisting in part of reprints from *WT.* It never materialized.

2. HPL apparently refers to AWD's friend Frank Utpatel and also to C. C. Senf.

3. By Vicki Baum.

4. FBL, "The Desert Lich," *WT* (November 1924); "The Were-Snake," *WT* (September 1925); Seabury Quinn, "Servants of Satan," a series of six articles about the Salem witch trials, published by *WT* in 1925 (March–August).

[249] [ASL]

Thursday [28 January 1932]

Dear A W:—

Thanks tremendously for the careful & instructive analysis of this poor old Shadow—some of the points of which seem very well based. I had myself thought of foreshadowing the blood connexion more definitely, but abandoned the idea because it would introduce suspicions of the narrator's true ancestry too early. I also thought of a subtler & more gradual introduction of the data pertaining to Innsmouth; but did not adopt it because of the undoubtedly greater length it would demand. Zadok's story could probably be made shorter by a better writer, but not by me—since I arrived at the existing form only after long & repeated experimentation. The order of presentation of the incidents would probably suffer more through change than through being let alone—though an "editorial" postscript would not be a bad idea.

I shall not, I think, submit it to any editor; but believe I will let it go the rounds of the gang as suggested. Delete Dwyer's name, though, since I have sent him the other copy. All opinions received—beginning with your valuable analysis—will be carefully filed in my weird archives, & if I ever feel able to tinker with the thing again I shall use them very gratefully in deciding on an amended structure. But as I said before, it would be out of the question to attempt any changes for several years—until, in fact, my memory is purged clean of the images & impressions which dictated the text in its present awkward form.

I am very glad you find some underlying merit in the thing, & hope Dwyer, Klarkash-Ton, & Wandrei will do the same. But to me it shows the need of taking a long vacation from the writing process—or at least, from writing in this particular style.

I am now curious to know what you will think of Wandrei's novel—my own reaction to which I think I stated in a previous letter. The latter half strikes me as containing material of tremendous power, & I certainly envy the energy & ability which produced it.

By the way—in case I ever try any more tales for my own amusement, can you tell me if Ungenennte Heidenthume is an even approximately decent German equivalent of the title "Nameless Cults"? I want to be able to make casual allusions to von Junzt's Black Book in the original. I only took German a year, & that was in 1906—the present possibly ridiculous attempt at translation being a result of blind & unintelligent groping in a meagre grammar & wholly inadequate dictionary. I thought it best to give the word "Cult" its darkest signification—the phrase as above being really, I suppose, "Unnamed Heathenisms". Any light you can shed on this matter will be of the utmost interest to an illiterate old man. I have a remote notion of some day hinting at the reason why von Junzt's great-grandson lately cut his throat after discovering certain papers in his ancestor's long-sealed Düsseldorf attic.

Well—thanks again for the thoughtful & capable analysis.

Your most oblig'd ob^{dt} Servt

H P

[250] [ALS]

Tuesday, Feby. 2[, 1932]

Dear A W:—

Bless my soul, Child, but isn't it a bit premature to set your artist friend to work on a story which will probably never be published? I certainly appreciate his willingness to take a chance on the proposition, & feel sure that the drawings will excel any others ever based on my stuff—but I hate to think of his doing the work in vain professionally, as is so likely to be the case! However—I dare say Wright might like such sketches as stock tailpieces even if the story doesn't figure in the situation. I myself, it is needless to say, shall view the sketches with the greatest interest if they come my way. Undoubtedly the choice of subjects is the best that could possibly have been made. Glad your portrait progresses well. Possibly it's your modesty which makes you think it flattering. As for the robe—aren't you afraid the public will take it as the bath-robe which athletes slip on after the close of some strenuous event? The sporting world may accept the picture as a likeness of One-Round Augie, Middleweight Champion of Southern Wisconsin, after lifting the title by a clean knockout of Kid Farnsworth of the Chicago Athletic Club. However, I presume more historically-minded spectators will see in the costume your wish to appear before posterity without the hindrance of temporary fashions likely to become obsolete—just as many an 18th century worthy, mindful of the changing fashions in coats & periwigs, posed for the artist in muslin bedroom cap & Roman toga.

About my stuff in general—I certainly appreciate tremendously the favourable opinion you express, & shall of course shew you any specimens I may turn out in future. The best thing for me to do is to disregard the outside world & let any things I may write accumulate quietly, as I did a decade ago when no possible market existed. I am always too close to the point of nervous exhaustion to be otherwise than retarded by the experience of repeated rejections. As for changes in tales—that policy would be not only highly difficult but intrinsically undesirable. While theoretically one can always save a correct copy of a MS. for later publication, in practice a pervertedly published text is often copied without any opportunity for rectification on the author's part. Thus all the "Not at Nights" have done their reprinting directly from W.T. without any notification of the respective authors.

About the Grayson material—you will be interested to know that I have owned a copy of "Adventures in Contentment" for the past decade & more. I have always thought it a delectably restful & pleasing book, & have half-intended from time to time to look up its companion volumes.[1] Glad to know that they are now all obtainable in one volume. It is interesting to learn what prime favourites they are with you—thanks for the recommendation, which will probably cause me to re-read the specimen I have, & to accelerate my quest for the others.

As for Wright v. Bates—I rather agree with you concerning their relative intelligence, though I don't think this circumstance necessarily makes Bates the better man to deal with. His very superiority makes him the more consistent in enforcing—whether he likes it or not—the Clayton policy of uniform commonplaceness; whereas Wright's irrational caprices often admit to W.T. MSS. which would never ordinarily land with a cheap editor. You'll notice that Bates's personal appreciation of "The Panelled Room" didn't gain it a berth—yet I'll bet a dollar that Wright will evntually take it as a matter of whim after repeated submissions! I have strong doubts that I'll ever be on the S.T. table of contents.

It will be interesting to see what Klarkash-Ton says about "Dead Titans Waken." Probably the text will have many reproportionings & goings-over before it reaches print, & I feel certain that the ultimate result will be very notable. Whether it will land as a book remains to be seen. I noticed the ineptness of the rural dialect, but thought I wouldn't pick any more flaws than I absolutely had to.

I am informed by the Argus that the stock of "Switch on the Light" is exhausted, but that a fresh lot is due within a week. Therefore they are retaining my dollar & promising as early delivery as possible. I doubt if I'll get the current annual. Quinn's "House of Phipps" contained some of the most anachronistic pseudo-archaism I've seen in a long while.

Thanks exceedingly for *The Midland,* which arrived yesterday. I had never seen a copy of this magazine before, though I had long known of it by reputation. Its editor was a speaker at an English Teachers' meeting in Milwaukee last November, & my friend M. W. Moe thought well of his address.[2] "Old Ladies" is a splendid piece of observation & insight, & ought to have a place in some larger unit also containing "People." Glad to hear that *Pagany* is so enthusiastic about your work, & hope you will soon be a regular contributor. Good luck with "Five Alone"—which I hope to see in MS. soon.

Cold weather struck here Sunday & persisted through Monday, but today has been one of steady moderation—first snow & now rain. It cheers one to think that next month contains the vernal equinox!

With every good wish, & the hope that your artistic neighbour will not put too much labour into the illustration of a story destined for obscurity,

I remain

Yr most obt Grandsire

H P

Later—

Yrs of Feby. 1 just blew in. Thanks for the original title of the Black Book. I feel sure that *Unausprechlichen* [*sic*] *Kulten* is the correct version!

As for Innsmouth—I am so thoroughly sick of the tale from repeated rerevisions that it would be out of the question to touch it for years. If I tried, I would only make a mess of it. Having said what I had to say, no more impetus is left. Zadok's tale could be properly shortened only by adopting a more compressed scale of detail for the *whole* of the story; a thing I have neither the inclination nor the ability to do at present. And I am still doubtful about the matter of degree in any change of stress. The best thing to do is to wait till all reports are in, & then rest for a while. Don't for Yuggoth's sake think of copying all that cursed mess. If you want a permanent copy, keep the carbon after Klarkash-Ton & Melmoth have seen it. Tell Melmoth to send it to you instead of back to me when he is through with it.

If you ever want to do a piece of free typing, you might coöperate later on in fixing up the MS. of a most unusual eccentric who got into correspondence with me about a year ago. Perhaps I've mentioned him—William Lumley of Buffalo, N.Y. He is very crude in some ways, though amazingly erudite in the lore of mediaeval magic, & possessed of a keen & genuine sense of the fantastic. He is slowly evolving a strange tale of mystical adventure to be called "The City of Dim Faces",[3] & what he has quoted of it to me sounds astonishingly promising. If it could ever be published, as I think it really might if properly revised, it would cheer the old boy to his dying day. I shall try to straighten out the text, & may type *some* of it—but I think I'll ask for charitable coöperation in the latter process. Lumley has no machine. ¶ Thanks & best wishes—H P

Notes

1. "Companion volumes" included *Adventures in Friendship* (1910), *Adventures in Understanding* (1925), and *The Friendly Road: New Adventures in Contentment* (1913). *Adventures of David Grayson* (Sun Dial Press, 1925) contains *Adventures in Contentment, Adventures in Friendship,* and *The Friendly Road,* with illustrations by Thomas Fogarty. Grayson's writings about outdoor work and leisure were published extensively in the early 1900s.

2. The editor of the *Midland* ("A Magazine of the Middle West") from its founding in 1915 until its demise in 1933 was John Towner Frederick.

3. Apparently non-extant.

[251] [TLS, JHL]

Sauk City, Wisconsin—6 February [1932]

Dear H. P.,

No, I made it perfectly clear to my artist friend that he was doing the pictures on a very slim chance indeed that renumeration [*sic*] of any kind would be forthcoming. He will have the pictures done early next week, at which time I shall mail the copies to you at once. However, I still maintain that Innsmouth should be sent to Wright, if not revised, as it is. Why not?

I daresay your attitude re writing and submitting material is okeh, but it would much better if you could dissociate the two sets sufficiently to continue writing just as you please and continue sending out things regardless of the possible effect of acceptance or rejection. It does gripe me horribly to have you manifest that disparaging attitude anent your own work, and it does also irritate me that more of your work doesn't appear in W. T., the next issue of which will certainly be 1932's best so far with In the Vault and Mrs. Lorriquer.

No, no one could possibly mistake the rich chiffon velvet, peacock blue lined robe I wear for something an athlete might put on after a battle. Work on the portrait was temporarily held up owing to Mark's appearance and the first draft of Eyes of the Serpent, now done, lousily by Mark, but still helpful as an outline for my final draft.

I am glad you know Grayson—I am very fond of him indeed. Just now I am for the first time reading Tom Jones.

I daresay you are right re Bates v. Wright. The thing I like about Bates is that if he doesn't take a ms. he tells you exactly why not, which Wright never does. I would never think of submitting a ms. twice to Bates without serious change, while I would think nothing at all of submitting the same ms. to Wright all of a dozen times without more than retyping once or twice. No, I didn't think The Panelled Room would land with Bates, but he asked to see it; so I sent it, fully expecting it back. I doubt, though, that Wright will eventually take it. As to your being on the S. T. table of contents—if you're not, it will be entirely your own fault, I believe. I still maintain that you could do an acceptable tale for S. T. with possibly a slight modification of your usual manner but without any literary deterioration.

I am glad you liked Old Ladies; it is part of Evening in Spring, and will appear in that volume as a numbered Confession. People, which was also to have formed part of it, has become A Town is Built, a separate unit now. The Midland is now holding Bishop Kroll.

I revised At Sundown and To Remember recently and sent them off to Pagany; revisions of In the Junction Station and The Sheraton Mirror went to Wright, with small hope of acceptance; revision of The Old Girls went to Frontier, which had asked for it; revisions of A Matter of Faith and The Drifting Snow remain here. A Bottle from Corezzi landed with Swanson, and I've sent him also A Visitor from Outside and The Menace from Under the Sea, two of my worst duds, but stories that will undoubtedly prove popular with the type of reader who is in the majority with W. and S. T.

I have instructed Don to shoot the carbon of Innsmouth back to me when he is finished with it, but I do not intend to keep it permanently. Thanks.

If I can help you in any way at all, I shall be glad to do so. Only say the word and let me know what to do. Meanwhile, I do hope that you will manage to find more time to create stories.

I send you herewith copies of The Drifting Snow and Five Alone. The former (and perhaps also the latter) leaves much to be desired. I think that what it needs is a general tightening up, a greater tensity, which should be easy, but doesn't appear so to me. This is the 6th of the group begun by The Panelled Room. As for Five Alone, this is the copy looked over by Associate-Professor Helen C. White, noted for her studies of the Mysticism of William Blake, et al[.], hence the often teacherish comments, with most of which I agree, however, disagreeing chiefly with her objection to the use of the construction—"she being etc.". Shoot the tales back to me when you've finished. I shall await your verdicts with great anticipation.

The March W. T. wasn't bad. I disliked the Vengeance of Ixmal, The Man

Who Played With Time, The Answer of the Dead as 2nd rate; The Thing in the Cellar and The Devil's Bride as third rate. On the whole, however, it was a well balanced issue. A new artist did the illustration for Suter's story.

Well, as always,

August

[252] [ASL]

Monday [8 February 1932]

Dear A W:—

Both of the tales are splendid—indeed, "Five Alone" is such a magnificently balanced bit of atmosphere & inevitability that I don't see how any fully awake & sober editor could possibly reject it. The steady growth of your work is surely heartening to see, & I can easily imagine what your place in the literary field will be a decade hence. About the objection to the odd constructions typified by *she walking out* (p 2) or *she perfectly natural* (p 7), I must say that I am inclined to agree with the pedagogical commentator. These constructions, whatever their abstract syntactical merits, are so conspicuously *un-idiomatic* that they tend to attract attention to themselves & thus halt the imaginative progress of the reader. An author's object should be the art which conceals art, hence obtrusive singularity is always to be shunned. However, certain other academic comments seemed to me rather pedantic. On p. 49 I see you have the speech (by Ilsa) 'She must come soon, *today yet,* or tomorrow.' I suppose you realise that this is not idiomatic English; the "yet" being a dialect redundancy. Presumably the region is Germanic, with Ilsa's generation being the first to use English exclusively, hence the expression is no doubt properly typical. Dialect is to be used when it would naturally occur—but of course not otherwise. This story is certainly a most remarkable piece of work—full of the horror (also to be noted in early New England) of exaggerated instincts in remote & lonely places. I can't think of anything that could be done to better it as a whole.

"The Drifting Snow" is also poignant & powerful. I don't know just what it could gain from a tightening up. To me much of the power hinges on the subtle & gradual way in which it builds itself up from an apparently quiet & normal setting. My only criticism touches a minor matter of chronology which you can readily change. On page 3 you have the old lady say that her father was living *ten years before*—that is, at a time when Ernest & Henry must have been at least big boys, & when she herself—as well as her brothers—was well into middle age. Yet on p. 11 you have her speaking of her father's death at a time when she & her sister were girls, & when the brothers—the boys' fathers—were themselves young, unmarried, & living at home. How come?

As for Innsmouth—I'll see what Melmoth & Klarkash-Ton have to say before clinching my resolution not to send it to Wright. At any rate, I'm glad your artist friend labours under no false expectations. I shall certainly be interested to see what he does in the way of illustration. Meanwhile I trust he will do ample justice to the exotic luxuriousness of that robed Sardanapalus—the Sultan Ahmed Dhir-Leth!

Good luck with your various ventures—surely some of those tales ought to land. If the Swanson venture survives, we will all probably have a market for things lacking a haven elsewhere. As for Wright & Bates—yes, the latter is evidently more conscious of his reasons for acceptance or rejection than is the incomparable Farny!

The March W.T. seemed very homelike with Ward & Suter back. As you say, next month ought to be rather good. When will the Swanson magazine be out? Do you know its name, price, or any further particulars?

By the way—our folklorish correspondent Brobst has just surprised me very pleasantly by announcing that he is coming to *Providence* to take a job as student nurse in a celebrated hospital for nervous & mental diseases! I shall surely be glad to see him, & hope to introduce him to the various local scenes & antiquities of which I am so fond—& which, judging from his knowledge of his own local traditions, he will probably appreciate. The hospital where he will work has its extensive wooded grounds on the delectable banks overlooking the Seekonk—just across a creek from the public reservation which has been my lifelong aestival stamping-ground!

Best wishes—H P

[253] [ALS][1]

[Postmarked Providence, R.I.,
12 February 1932]

Greetings! Just getting our friend acclimated to old Providence, but haven't been able to produce any good weather for him as yet!

Best wishes—H P

I know I'll like Providence. We are going to take in the historic sights shortly and get acquainted with some of this wonderful section's cultural advantages. Sincerely, H. B.

Notes

1. Front: Middle Campus, Brown University, Providence, R.I.

[254] [ALS]

Saturday [13 February 1932]

Dear A W:—

Yes—I know the 'she walking' type of construction is common in 18th century English, but that makes it none the less conspicuous today. As a born archaist, I myself grew up with Queen-Anne & Georgian diction, & have had the very devil of a time escaping from it. I know you are fond of unusual turns of expression, but most of these seem to harmonise with your themes & thereby escape conspicuousness. This particular archaism, on the other hand, does not seem homogeneous with the rest of your style—hence caused both the teacher & myself to be momentarily halted by it. If your style were *all 18th century,* it would not be conspicuous; for only disparity makes it so. Thus you could very well write:

> As we stopt at the *Dolphin* Inn, which stood over against the Town-Hall, I observ'd a thin antient Gentlewoman of the middle Size getting out of the *Dunwich* Post-Chaise. She walking up to the Door, a pert black Boy got out after her, burthen'd down with a great Number of Boxes and Parcels.

Swanson has just written me, asking me to ascertain from Wright the conditions governing the re-use of those tales of mine in which I did not reserve later rights—i.e., those printed prior to 1926. He speaks also of having a vague design to publish paper-covered books (price 25¢) containing small collections of the works of various weirdsters. His ambition & confidence are enviable—for he is accepting *three-year* subscriptions at reduced rates! I however, have contented myself with a year's subscription—to be deducted from my first cheque if the latter comes to more than a dollar. Hope the venture will last more than a single issue. As a title I suggested *Shadow Stories, Whispers, Macabre Tales, Bizarre Tales, Nightmares, Darkness Tales, Creepy Stories, Marvel Stories,* & half a dozen other things.

Wright will undoubtedly take most of your stories in time if somebody else doesn't do it first. Meanwhile I congratulate you on the *Prairie Schooner* episode.[1] I have just finished the new S.T., think it almost uniformly rotten except for Whitehead's "Trap" & de Rezske's "Veil of Tanit". As a third, though, one might include Barker's "Back Before the Moon" for its atmosphere.[2] The rest is just Clayton—thin, incredibly juvenile & unconvincing sensationalism of the most obviously stereotyped & synthetic order. It is leagues below the low-enough average of W.T.—for Handsome Harry's fatal intelligence spies out & rejects all too readily any item with the abhorred traces of sincere emotion or passable originality! I could never make that rag if I tried from now till Edmond Hamilton gets a new plot! "The Trap" is Whitehead's own title, but I rather like laconic, unsensational, non-tricky titles of that sort. You're right—my heavy contributions begin on p. 77. I also created the necessary distinction between scenes reflected in the mirror & objects taken bodily into it. It was H S's confusion on this point—seriously balling up the whole plot—which probably caused its many pre-revisory rejections.

Brobst was over here Thursday evening, & is a really delightful kid. Tall, thin, dark, handsome, alert, intelligent, & energy-charged—he's more vivid than his letters. He's coming over this afternoon, when I expect to take him on a trip of exploration among the colonial antiquities of Providence—which his own antiquarian interests will cause him to appreciate more than commonly. Then we'll get dinner somewhere & spend the evening here. He likes his new job. One of the patients in his ward—suffering from a mild persecution mania—is my old high-school principal.[3]

Best wishes—

H P

[P.S.] Enclosed is Klarkash-Ton's latest[4]—nothing to set the Thames on fire, though with good imagery toward the close. Those modern burial tales ought to explain why the body is not *embalmed.* This thing was written to order for Bates.

Notes

1. HPL presumably refers to the recent publication of AWD's "Atmosphere of Houses."

2. *Strange Tales of Mystery and Terror* (March 1932): Henry S. Whitehead, "The Trap" (rev. by HPL): 73–88; Eugene de Rezske, "The Veil of Tanit"; S. Omar Baker, "Back Before the Moon."

3. Charles E. Dennis, Jr., principal of Hope Street High School.

4. CAS, "The Second Interment," *Strange Tales of Mystery and Terror* (January 1933).

[255] [ALS]

Feby. 19, 1932

Dear A W:—

Congrats on "The Sheraton Mirror"! Especially since the design as well as the story landed. But damn Wright for rejecting "The Drifting Snow". I've just had an opportunity to tell that bird what I think of the dumbbell rejections of himself & his ilk—for his attitude in the matter of the new Swanson venture gave me a good opening. It seems that little Farny does not take at all kindly to the appearance of this Dakotan rival—which will, as he says, take advantage of old W.T. material to compete with W.T. itself. Accordingly he will not allow *The Galaxy* to include any of my stuff in which he holds all rights, & in addition he signifies that it will grieve & pain him if I lend comfort to the enemy by letting Swanson print the tales in which I retain rights. In other words, he wants me to do him the personal favour of forfeiting whatever Swanson would pay—in exchange, perhaps, for the good-will he has always borne me except when rejecting my MSS. & breaking his word about the book of my stuff he promised to publish in 1927! This from the guy who refused "At the Mountains of Madness". In reply, I have given him the civilised Rhode Island equivalent of the curt injunction so popular amongst the proletariat of his tempest-swept metropolis . . . . 'go jump in the lake!' I have added that if he wants to prevent his authors from selling their second rights to Swanson, he had better buy them himself! The damn'd rascal took advantage of our pristine ignorance & cabbaged all rights until we learned better & protested—& has reprinted three or four of my things without paying anything extra. 'Oy,' as the sons of Judah express it, 'he shood esk it ah favour by me a'ready!' He doesn't seem to mind Swanson's *book* plans, but the *magazine* gets his goat. Probably he'll act rather meanly toward those who allow Swanson to use reprints—but since I'm virtually withdrawing from the professional arena I'm free to thumb my nose & tell him to go to Cicero! I'm like the guy who waited to be mustered out of the army & then gave the top sergeant what he had wanted to give him for two years!

Incidentally—"Creeps by Night" is going to have a British edition,[1] & the company inform me that I shall thereby receive £2 more. Very welcome—& at present exchange rates I fancy that ought to amount to more than the usual $9.72 or whatever it was in gold standard days.

I'm enclosing Klarkash-Ton's reaction to "Innsmouth", which may interest you. You will notice that he coincides with you in recommending a shift of emphasis to the narrator's taint—though he goes beyond you in suggesting 'snappy action' for the latter half.[2] By the way—his "Seed from the Sepulchre"[3] is great stuff in places. For a writer of his prolific volume, he certainly rings the bell a surprising number of times!

Congratulations on the excellence of "Bishop Kroll"—a delightfully mellow character study. Hope you can place it advantageously if you have not already done so. I can't think of any adverse criticism—except that the ungrammatical use of *like* for *as* (p. 4, line 6) seems hard to justify unless it has some cryptical connexion with the idiom of the child. I assume that the redundant "already" in the telephone message of Pelter's housekeeper (p. 9) is an intentional touch of local dialect. I shall be eager to see your new tales—especially "The Return of Hastur" & "The Wind from the River".

Last Saturday I dragged Brobst all over the ancient hill district—showing him hidden churchyards, haunts of Poe, 1761 colony houses, vestigial rural byways, & the like. He seemed very appreciative, & we expect to make a similar trip tomorrow. He was also over Wednesday evening. He duly received your letter, & hopes he can get his reply despatched within the seigneural 14-day-limits set by that imperious chevalier, Auguste-Guillaume, Comte d'Erlette. Best wishes—Yr obt Grandsire H P

Notes

1. Dashiell Hammett, ed., *Modern Tales of Horror.*

2. CAS's letter to HPL does not survive, but he wrote the following to AWD: "I did [. . .] make what seemed to me a rather obvious suggestion about the addition of a new chapter, which could be worked in next to the last with very little verbal alteration of the

story as it stands. This chapter would be made of the narrator's broken, nightmare-like memories of being captured by the rout of monsters, who take him back to Innsmouth, but do him no vulgar harm, since they recognize his latent kinship to themselves. Without his guessing the reason at the time, they subject him to some horrible rite that is calculated to accelerate the development of the alien strain in his blood, and then let him go. I fear, though, that he won't care for the suggestion" (16 February 1932; in *Selected Letters of Clark Ashton Smith* [Sauk City, WI: Arkham House, 2003], p. 169).

3. CAS, "The Seed from the Sepulcher," *WT* (October 1933).

[256] [TLS, JHL]

chez moi/22 February [1932]

Dear H. P.,

I'm glad you liked Bishop Kroll. I myself like the character so well that I will in all likelihood use him again in other tales—providing this one goes over somewhere, as it might; I should say its chances were about equal. Meanwhile, I enclose a carbon of The Wind from the River, which I personally think better than The Drifting Snow, though perhaps this tale as well as the latter could stand greater stress on unnatural atmosphere. I don't think The Wind from the River will sell, though I hope Wright can be persuaded to take it in the end. I sent it to Bates first, not because I think he'll take it, but simply to let him know that I can do vastly superior writing than I have been doing for him, for he has a sort of respect for people who can write—curious, but true—as for instance when he proudly wrote me that Philip Hazelton (After Sunset)[1] had contributed to the slick-paper magazines, including the Saturday Evening Post, to which I replied asking him whether any of his writers had done anything highbrow and more lasting. Silence.

In all probability I shall do the revision of The Shuttered House finally, before finishing Eyes of the Serpent or starting the Return of Hastur, the plot of which I am vaguely thinking about, having decided how The Shuttered House is to be done.

Clark Ashton had already written me about the changes in The Shadow (don't you like the way in which all of us immediately assume proprietory [*sic*] rights over your work and begin criticizing it?), and I wrote him last Saturday that I didn't agree with him, save in his major point—the difference resting in the manner of making the desired change. ... As to his Seed from the Sepulchre; it is definitely not as good as it might easily have been. The orchid hunter who stumbles upon this sort of seed is stale. The story has some grand writing, yes; every Smith story has its excellent spots. But I suggested to him that if he ever did the story over, have his heroes be archaeologists going into the frozen north—following with accidental discovery of tomb with ancient mss. telling about seed of death, etc. Nothing much more there, they return home, to U. S. Finder already begins to feel strange, takes to his bed when he gets home; emaciated in a few days, strange bumps on skin etc.; meanwhile the narrator is slowly deciphering strange parchments and the story of the seeds is coming out. He solves the secret of the tomb, and rushes to his sick friend's house to tell him, and finds him there with the devilish plant sprouting all over, a luxuriant growth already, with the great flesh flower already blossoming. But to omit the anti-climactic effect of having the narrator also drawn to the flowers. I don't know how he'll take it; but it strikes me that this more or less unorthodox situation will influence editors more than his more commonplace plot. With his style, he ought to be able to make a swell story out of it, even though it's good as is.

The Prairie Schooner, one of the 8 O'Brien "best" U. S. literary magazines, has just written to ask whether, if the editorial board agree, they may not use portions of Atmosphere of Houses and Confessions iv through xi. They don't pay, but there is also a certain prestige to be gained through publication in their pages; so I shall be glad if they can use any portions.

The March S. T. is just out. I have read but two stories, The Phantom Feline or rather Feline Phantom, and Back Before the Moon, and am now going to read The Trap, and will bear in mind the influence you mentioned some time ago.[2] .. Yes, beginning on page 77 of the printed version, I can see your influence most distinctly. The tale is excellent, I think, the best in the issue, I feel sure, though I have not yet read them all. At one place Whitehead writes of Sandison's vocabulary as unusual for a boy of 15 yrs, but it isn't at all. Why did he do that, I wonder? I should by no means have called this excellent story by so prosaic a title as The Trap—rather Loki's Glass, or The Copenhagen Mirror. But if Bates took this, I can see no reason in the world why he shouldn't take your Shadow Over Innsmouth, and suggest that you send it to him; it won't hurt, anyway, to have his reaction. Go on.

Yes, Brobst wrote me that he was heading for Providence. Hope he likes it there.

well, as always,

August

Notes

1. Philip Hazelton, "After Sunset," *Strange Tales of Mystery and Terror* (November 1931).

2. *Strange Tales of Mystery and Terror* (March 1932): Gilbert Draper, "The Feline Phantom"; S. Omar Baker, "Back Before the Moon"; Henry S. Whitehead, "The Trap."

[257] [ALS]

Feby. 25, 1932

Dear A W:—

"The Wind from the River" is excellent—its atmosphere of menace starts modestly, & works itself up by very convincing degrees. I surely hope that Wright or somebody else will take it. Possibly Bates might be able to slip it over on Clayton, even if it is a bit short on hairbreadth rescues.

Your proposed changes for the "Seed from the Sepulchre" sound excellent, & I hope Klarkash-Ton will adopt them if the tale doesn't land in its present form. He is very clever in altering his work to suit requirements or conform to later suggestions.

As for Wright—I hope he can get a taste of being at someone else's mercy, for he's had authors at his mercy long enough. Belknap says that—according to a friend who knows him—Brother Farny boasts of how completely he is master of his poor scribblers in the matter of rates & terms; since their work is (or was till lately) of a sort which has no market elsewhere. I shan't do any haggling—in fact, I couldn't honourably stop Swanson from using what he wishes of my printed & right-free material, since I long ago told him he was welcome to anything of which I possessed the rights. Even a fawning offer on Wright's part would not make it fitting for me to withdraw a permission already extended to Swanson. The most I could do would be to urge a paper-bound book in preference to magazine publication. I have told Swanson how Wright regards the subject of reprinting, so that if he antagonises the former weird-tale czar he will not be doing it blindly. I'm also notifying Wandrei, Whitehead, Belknap, Klarkash-Ton & others of the situation.

The Argus has not yet sent my Not at Night, but I presume they will not forget to do so when it comes in. Sorry you aren't being paid for your story in the latest issue.[1] I believe you said there is nothing of mine in this one. Hope you'll have something included in the new "Creeps".

Revelling in my repudiation of attempted professionalism, I experimentally scribbled a new horror in three settings this week—running just over 34 pages of handwriting, & entitled "The Dreams of Walter Gilman."[2] I don't believe I'll send it around a for a long spell, but will merely hold on to it as I used to do—perhaps attempting other things in the meantime. The only thing that sets me writing is complete freedom from all restrictions & from all thought of any critical standards or readers other than myself. I am writing mostly in pencil now, for I can't get any pen that doesn't exhaust my wrist & fingers in a short while—& the very sight of a typewriter petrifies me.

I find young Brobst extremely pleasant. Last Saturday we did some of the local museums—the enclosed card illustrating one of the many treasures we beheld. What seems to fascinate him most is the ancient hidden churchyard on the steep hill not so very far from this house—a lingering bit of the bygone world hemmed in by venerable walls & roofs & shadowed by a Gothic tower built in 1810 & looking by moonlight as if it had been built in 1210 or so. You'll have to get around here some day & see some of these things!

With best wishes—

Yr most obt Servt

H P

Notes

1. There was no story by AWD in *Grim Death.*
2. Retitled "The Dreams in the Witch House."

[258] [ALS]

Feby. 29[, 1932]

Dear A W:—

I am indeed sorry to hear of your mother's illness, & hope that by this time she will be much improved. Meanwhile it is fortunate that she can have attendance as capable as that which you are affording. Congratulations on the birthday, of which I trust you may have many much happier returns.

As for Innsmouth—I can hardly say how much I appreciate the interest you have taken in the tale, & I hope you will not deem me ungrateful if after all I follow the policy of inertia which I originally outlined. I am sure that you could capably revise the tale if any second person could—yet you doubtless realise yourself that a second person's changes cannot help destroying something of the homogeneity of a piece of writing. No other person can quite duplicate the mood of the original author—so that the ultimate result of non-auctorial revision is always a little farther from the author's intention than even his first bungling version. Of course your offer of opportunities for auctorial re-revision eliminates as much as possible of this drawback—but it might conceivably lead to endless counter-revisions & a final state of deadlock, since I cannot imagine myself as acquiescing in any change in the direction of Clayton requirements. The trouble for you would be enormous—far more than I would permit myself to impose upon you despite your hyper-generous willingness to undertake it.

Nor do I think I'd better mix into any professional attempts just yet. What I need is a rest from the rebuffs & restrictions of external agencies—a rest amidst which I may or may not recover the spontaneity of uncensored personal expression which was mine before 1923 & upon the return of which any further writing of mine depends. As long as the idea of image-expressing remains mixed up with the idea of suiting this or that commercial standard, I shall continue to be literarily tongue-tied. What I must do is to get the whole loathsome picture of tradesmen & hagglers out of my head—& then I may or may not be able to write as I did in 1920. If I can write anything, I shall let it pile up as in the old days. Then some day when my nervous condition is better, I may see if some editor cares to print some of the accumulated results of my retirement without alterations. If so, well & good—if not, so be it. It is distinctly possible that I am written out, & that anything new of mine will necessarily be forced & clumsy; but only unhampered experiment after my recovery of the mood of free expression will prove that point one way or the other. I have revised the ending of the new story I told you about, & have changed the title to "The Dreams in the Witch House." Whether it's any good or not, I have not the faintest notion—but I shall let it rest unread & unattacked, & presently experiment with another story. I am facilitating the mechanical part of writing by returning to the lowly pencil of my childhood. I can't stand the typewriter or get a fountain pen that really suits, so the old graphite cylinder is the logical alternative. I've just bought a 10¢ automatic pencil at Woolworth's which seems to write easily & eliminate troublesome sharpening.

Further thanks for the new Merritt story,[1] which I shall read with interest & appreciation. Merritt has an unique atmospheric power—tremendously manifest in the original "Moon Pool"—which still survives in spots despite his disastrous concessions to the hollow popular idea. ¶ Again, expressing my boundless appreciation of your generous offer—Yr most obt Servt H P

P.S. I lately received a very pleasant letter from your friend Jacobi. Glad to see he is so well launched in the magazine world.

Notes

1. Perhaps a segment of *Dwellers in the Mirage,* which had begun serialization in the *Argosy* on 23 January 1932.

[259] [ALS]

March 4, 1932

Dear A W:—

I hope your mother is better by this time, & that you are free to wander over your favourite hills in quest of any vernal harbingers which may be sprouting or burgeoning thereon.

Glad the literary work still goes on, & that the cheques still come in. As for my own latter-day attitude toward writing & submitting—I can see why you consider my anti-rejection policy a stubbornly foolish & needlessly short-sighted one, & am not prepared to offer any defence other than the mere fact that repeated rejections *do* work in a certain way on my psychology—rationally or not—& that their effect is to cause in me a certain literary lock-jaw which absolutely prevents further fictional composition despite my most arduous efforts. I would be the last to say that they *ought* to produce such an effect, or that they would—even in a slight degree—upon a psychology of 100% toughness & balance. But unfortunately my nervous equilibrium has always been a rather uncertain quantity, & it is now in one of its more ragged phases—though I hardly fancy it portends one of the actual near-breakdowns as of 1898, 1900, 1906, 1908, 1912, & 1919. There are times when the experience of repeated rejections would mean little to me, but other times when the symbolism of the process grates harshly—& now is one of these other times. Later I may try sending again—especially after I have accumulated a stack of material & can make the submissions from stuff not so close to the actual process of writing. I feel tremendously ungrateful in not availing myself of the generous encouragement & offers you have made, & could hardly blame you if you were to wash your hands of the old man as an altogether bad job—yet I feel sure that you realise how keenly I appreciate your interest & coöperation, & how much I regret having to seem stubborn, stupid, & a prey to second childhood's whims. As for that new alleged story—I hardly know what to think of it. I have made a few changes since last writing you, & have retitled it "The Dreams in the Witch-House." I wouldn't let you waste your time typing it for the world—but I'll look it over again & see how much chance I think a second person would have of deciphering enough of the hieroglyphics to get the drift. Remember that you have no idea how illegible my corrected & re-corrected MSS. are. This epistolary scrawl is exemplary copper-plate stuff as compared with the chaos which I perpetrate in such things. Then, too, I use a pencil now—& the blurring adds to the general confusion.

I trust you will forgive Brobst for his infraction of your epistolary laws, for he really deserves much consideration amidst his present arduous job. The regimen is highly exacting—so relentless that Brobst hardly has adequate time for dressing & meals. And when his evening leisure finally does come, he is generally too fatigued to concentrate on anything requiring attention. He & a new friend of his from the hospital were over here Wednesday evening, & he told me to tell you he meant to write soon. As a matter of fact, he has written home to his parents only twice since landing in Providence! Yet he likes his job—regarding the rigid discipline in a philosophical spirit much like that of a West Point cadet.

Young Talman has just received a very notable honour—being nominated as a Trustee of the austere & important Holland Society of N.Y. He will edit the Society's official quarterly, *De Halve Maen,* & may possibly print some antiquarian notes from my pen in future—dealing with various points where the historic streams of New England & Nieuw Nederland come into contact.

With best wishes—

Yr most oblig'd, most ob^t Servt

H P

P.S. I agree that Ubbo-Sathla is the best of Klarkash-Ton's recent tales.[1] ¶ I'll have to give the Argus a reminder.

[P.P.S. on envelope:] ¶ Yrs of the 3^d just recd. I am truly profoundly sorry to 'let you down' after you have taken so many pains on my behalf—but you can bank on it that all those pains are duly registered in terms of immeasurable gratitude. ¶ You can assure Bates on the most direct authority that I have not even the shadow of a grudge against him & his magazine—except of course that I do not agree with the Clayton standard of fiction. I refrain from sending merely because I have nothing which would conform even roughly to that standard—& because my stuff will not bear the editorial changes against which Bates is unable to offer guarantees. ¶ I'm not at all sure that I'm not written out. As for forced writing—it is merely an accepted platitude that such can be any good. I've tried it in the past—& the results have never been worth saving. However—heaven knows that there are enough things I *want* to write—whether or not I *can* write them with any degree of effectiveness.

¶ Good luck with the Snake's Eyes.[2] Haven't seen the new W.T., but am glad the illustrations are better. I'm going down town today & shall get a copy. ¶ EXTRA: Pictures just came. Tell your friend they're *great!* Sorry I can't create a market for them!

Notes

1. CAS, "Ubbo-Sathla," *WT* (July 1933).
2. "Eyes of the Serpent."

[260] [ALS]

March 11[, 1932]

Dear A W:—

Some time I may submit Innsmouth to Wright—& if I ever do, I shall certainly be indebted to you for your encouragement concerning it.[1] In such a case I would of course notify you, so that your artist protege might be able to offer his delightful drawings simultaneously. But for the present I had better let MSS. pile up. Eventually I'll make you a present of that Innsmouth carbon if I don't get it printed. As for the later tale—I honestly don't believe anybody but myself could make out the MS. Thanks none the less fervently, however, for the typing offer. Somehow or other I'll manage to get it into a fairly legible form.

Wandrei has just sent a splendid tale of the sea[2]—about a MS. found in an old bottle, telling of the experiences of a seaman on a derelict. Something happened to the unknown cargo. . . . . . It gave me a great kick, my only objection being that the style of the MS. contained neologisms inconsistent with its intended date, & that certain scientific perspectives expressed by the writer were also too recent for this supposed period. I was instructed to send this on to you, but am letting young Brobst have a look at it first. When he passes it on he'll probably send the letter he has owed so long. Writing is a great problem for him nowadays; for he wants to be in good, unfatigued shape when he writes, yet is always devastatingly fagged out at the end of each gruelling hospital day. Not everyone has the excess energy which makes you such a tireless young dynamo of activity & productivity. It must be great to be a superman—but have pity on the mere mortals!

I hope in time to see the Utpatel illustrations for such old favourites as "Panelled Room" & "Miss Sarah"—& trust these will land somewhere some time. By the way—is Swanson using illustrations? If he is, he might form a good practice-field for your young friend. Hope that "Simmons" & "Wind"[3] will ultimately land in spite of doubt. "Spawn of the Maelstrom" is splendid—even though you aren't enthusiastic about it—& I'm sure Wright will take it even if Bates doesn't. Congratulations on the acceptance of "Atmosphere of Houses". Undoubtedly your other serious pieces will find a haven in time.

Sorry Snakeye is such a bore—but you'll be through with it before long. Your policy of interrupting dull work with pleasant is good if you can pursue it—but I never can arrange things that way. I can't do anything decently if I know a boresome task is hanging over my head. First of all, I have to get the worst drudgery cleaned up. No doubt Clayton will like the long story if it is so mediocre.

Last Saturday was warm & sunny, & I shewed Brobst the ancient seaport villages (once busy with commerce & whaling, but now dreaming in the shadow of their centuried roofs & tall white steeples) of Warren & Bristol on the E. shore of Narragansett Bay. Without their summer greenery they looked a bit bleak, but none the less their venerable charm was poignant & pervasive. The old wharves are idle now, except for pleasure craft, but the same lines of doorways & huddles of moss-grown gables stretch back to the sleepy common & deserted churchyards. These towns were originally in the old Plymouth Colony, & were founded after King Philip's War had cleared out the Wampanoags, whose headquarters were in this region. In 1691 the Plymouth Colony was merged into Massachusetts, & in 1747 this strip of land was awarded to Rhode Island by George II after a century-long boundary dispute. Even to this day the towns have a certain Massachusetts atmosphere about them—differentiating them from the villages of the bay's west shore.

Hope the acute cold spell of the last 3 days wasn't duplicated in Wisconsin. It's warmer today.

Best wishes—

Yr obt grandsire

H P

Notes

1. HPL in fact never did submit the story to FW (see his tart letter to FW of 18 February 1932, *SL* 4.17), but AWD did so surreptitiously in January 1933 (see letters 303 and 304). As HPL predicted, FW rejected the story (not on merit but because of

length and indivisibility).

2. "A Sea Change," published as "Uneasy Lie the Drowned," *WT* (December 1937).

3. I.e., "The Vanishing of Simmons" and "The Wind from the River."

[261] [ANS][1]

[Postmarked Providence, R.I.,
12 March 1932]

Dear August:—

Lovecraft & I visited this place this afternoon—and in its setting presented the most perfect scene I have ever encountered. I am writing this in his study, and want to let you know that I have not forgotten you, and that we speak of you frequently. Do not be angry with me for my delay in answering, but I shall send you a letter shortly. We both sent you our greatest regards.

Sincerely,

Harry

Well, well, Son—with all this [ ]ess you ought to forgive a busy & hard-working boy. We've been doing parks, museums, & colonial villages today. ¶ Had a letter from the Vanguard press this morn about a possible book—but feel sure nothing will come of it. Leeds had been speaking to them of me. Well—be good.

—Grandpa

[P.S. on front:] We were here this afternoon—great Grecian stuff.

Notes

1. Front: Benedict Temple of Music, Roger Williams Park, Providence, R.I.

[262] [ALS]

March 19, 1932

Dear A W:—

I am glad that, for once, you have had a period as pleasantly crowded as your temperament demands! This seems to have been a case of intensive exposure to the influences of an elder generation.

I shall welcome the sight of "Others"—which ought some time to be included with "Five Alone" & perhaps further material of the sort in a large volume analogous to "Evening in Spring" & "A Town is Built." Sorry the "Wind" came back, but you'll place it somewhere sooner or later. And I hope you can float your friend Utpatel to fame along with yourself!

Four books a day! Bless my soul, what assimilative energy! I have seen things by Kenneth Burke in the past, but they impressed me as rather too wilfully chaotic & theory-ridden to form serious art.[1] You will undoubtedly avoid falling into the trap of extreme radical experimentalism—"significant form", & all that.

As for the difficulty of imagining anyone too exhausted for correspondence—naturally you would have to use your purely *objective* imagination, but I should think you'd be able to picture an alien condition in view of your success in reproducing diverse characters in serious fiction. Actually, your own ability to sustain, enjoy, & positively demand a ceaseless intake & outgo of impressions is prodigiously beyond the general average—& seldom duplicated even among persons of substantial culture & aesthetic achievement. I have seen this question of rapid & persistent concentration-capacity discussed at some length, usually with the conclusion that basically different types exist—irrespective of the sheer quality of the cerebration on either side. It usually happens that prodigious concentrators become impatient with their frailer brethren, & that—conversely—persons with low energy tend (if of subjective & unphilosophical cast) to get irritated by the endless & exhaustless activity of high-pressure exponents. I think I know just one person with an energy-fund as overflowing as yours—or perhaps two. I myself, unfortunately, stand at the opposite end of the scale—though Long perhaps has even less energy than I.

As for correspondence in particular—of course, with different persons this represents a different amount of energy-expenditure. Some are naturally fluent, while other (perhaps equal or even superior in intellectual & aesthetic calibre) are not. With many—no matter how teeming their brains may be with ideas & images—there are obscure psychological inhibitions which intervene when formulated expression is demanded. Some find these inhibitions most troublesome where conversation is concerned, (Oliver Goldsmith, for example) while others view with genuine apprehension the task of setting any connected ideas & images to paper. Yet these tongue-tied & hesitant ones often produce literary work of the first quality when they actually do goad themselves into moderate spurts of sustained action. Long is a non-correspondent much worse than Brobst. It is positively painful to him to write a letter—I haven't had a full-length one from him since before Christmas—& he often postpones controversial topics for oral discussion. The average person, I judge, writes each correspondent once every month or two. I happen to have the curse of a vacuous senile fluency, hence I dash off epistolary junk with no effort; but my energy in general is so limited that I can well understand the silence of those to whom letter-writing is a real effort. Your energy is so far above the usual that you have no real basis for comparison with the average type, but added years will make you understand it in a purely objective way. There are people who dread the inflow of impressions or the exercise of their faculties just as keenly as you dread a slackening of these activities. But I agree that prompt writing has its uses in keeping a large correspondence under control. Long has no correspondent except myself, & Brobst has very few. ¶ We had the cold spell also, but it is on the wane. Spring tomorrow at 2:52 p.m.

Best wishes—H P

P.S. The Argus (who have heard from you) say they sent my book some time ago—but it hasn't showed up here. I am now apprising them of that fact. Thanks for writing them—I meant to do so, but didn't get around to it. Hope I get the book in the end.

Notes

1. Kenneth Burke (1897–1995), leading Modernist critic and fiction writer, author of *Counter-Statement* (1931).

[263] [ALS]

March 25, 1932

Dear A W:—

"The Double Shadow" certainly is great stuff. It has vivid colour & relentlessly crawling menace, & the atmospheric tension is worthy of E. A. P. I wish Klarkash-Ton could get out a book with specimens of this grade. Probably you are right in placing it above "Ubbo-Sathla"—& I suppose for that very reason it will be regretfully rejected by King Pharnaces. The resemblance to Shiel, I think, lies chiefly in the sea-cliff setting. To my mind, the style suggested good old Eddie more than anybody else. The only flaw I could pick was the possibly tautological suggestion inherent in the phrase *volumes & books* on the final page.

Sorry some of your work has failed to land—though your percentage of hits is so far above the average that you have no reason to complain. I shall be glad to see "Star-Spawn", & hope "Sheraton" appears in time for "Creeps" consideration. I'll be looking for "Wind Walker" next month. *The Prairie Schooner* will be welcome, & I probably will subscribe. By the way—one of our gang, Samuel Loveman of Brooklyn (formerly of Cleveland), is on the editorial board of a new "arty" quarterly which I think might interest you, & of which I enclose a prospectus. I have seen the first number, & it certainly looks very importantly aesthetic. I hope they can keep it up—although such ventures all too frequently die young.

Speaking of literary or near-literary decease—has Swanson told you the sad news? There ain't a-gonna be no *Galaxy!* He can't make the right financial arrangements, & the subs came in slowly—so he is forced to postpone his (& our!) fond dream. Meanwhile he speaks of experimenting with a *mimeographed* magazine or series of booklets—which does not sound extraordinarily impressive to me. By the way, I heard from the Vanguard Press again, & at their request am sending a few of my things for them to look at—"Cthulhu", "Rats", "Pickman", & "Dunwich". Other good items are loaned. I have no expectation of any favourable result, but merely make the submission as a matter of routine. No—I haven't received the book from the Argus yet, but have had a notice from them saying that it is on the way. The mistake was curious—I don't know whether I mentioned your name or not in making the original order, but if you received an unsolicited copy it would look as if there were some connexion. It's all right with me so long as I get my copy in the end.

Eight books a day! Bless my soul! Well—if you can stand it & enjoy it, who wants to check you? Glad your musical nourishment is adequate. I imagine the radio is quite a boon to those who demand aural stimulation. I've been too tired lately to read or do anything of importance, but have been reading up various minor items before giving or throwing them away.

You'll learn some day how confirmedly lackadaisical the average correspondent is—even unto the matter of answering questions. No—Sonny Belknap has no job except his writing & revision; but as in my own case, his extremely low fund of nervous & physical energy makes this absolutely all he can handle in the hours he is able to devote to work. He writes incessantly, but meets with consistent rejections from most magazines. Others in his position might turn to something else, but he doggedly adheres to a perhaps vain hope that he will eventually stumble on the formula which opens editorial gates to a certain brand of hokum. Incidentally—his latest revision job, assigned him by our old W.T. friend Henneberger, has done much to reduce him to an early grave. I can't resist enclosing his own anguished account of it for your perusal & sympathy! As for young Brobst—his curriculum is really arduous past all belief. The intensive cramming demanded is far beyond anything he ever encountered in college, & besides all this there are rigorous nursing duties. He has had to cut down all his outside hours, & cancelled two engagements with me recently in order to stay in his room & study. But as a reward he is getting some very high marks on his exercises—many 100's, & nothing below 97. He is probably wise in allowing absolutely nothing to interfere with his scholastic rating, for once he gets through this training course, he has a standing which will never let him be in need of a job. The stiffness of Butler Hospital courses, & the consequent high grade of the few who can survive them, are bywords in the medical world. Odd that little Jevish-Êi hasn't written lately—though, come to think of it, he's written me only twice since New Year's. His course, too, is very arduous & demands all his energies. Apparently he is making great strides in English; for his marks are improving, while the sample themes he enclosed last week shew a vast improvement over those he ground out last autumn. Young Grayson hasn't written me a word since I saw him in New York last July—I guess Grandpa is too dried-up an old fogy to interest the child permanently!

Weather has continued forbidding, & I fear the New England spring will be a late one. Hope I can swing some kind of a southern jaunt—it's warmth &

open air that set the old man on his feet! I don't see why people permanently inhabit any latitude north of 30°! However—I see that some parts of the South have disastrous hurricanes from which this stagnant subarctic zone is exempt.

Best wishes—

Yr obt grandsire,

H P

[Note on postcard announcing *Trend* magazine:] 50¢ per copy—$2.00 per yr. Address *Trend,* 978 St Mark's Ave., Brooklyn, N.Y.

[264] [ALS]

March 31, 1932

Dear A W:—

Thanks exceedingly for "Moss Island",[1] which is pretty effective despite prosaic lapses & a plethora of technicality. The climactic portions develop magnificently. Jacobi really has phenomenal talent, & ought to be well worth watching during the years to come.

Loveman's *Trend* article is a sort of impressionistic review of the final Proust volume.[2] I think the magazine will interest you, & perhaps you can become a contributor if it survives. No—I did not see your Proust article although I'd like to. I greatly admire Proust, although I have read only the earlier volumes. Loveman's address is *130 Columbia Heights, Brooklyn, N.Y.* His room is in one of the old houses along the lofty bluffs overhanging the East River—just across the street from the Hotel Margaret, where Joseph Pennell[3] lived. From his window he looks out over the busy waters of New York harbour, & across at the fantastically Dunsanian skyline of lower Manhattan towers. The place is a veritable museum—with Egyptian statuettes, Roman lamps, casts of Greek heads, &c. Our gang will hold a meeting there tomorrow—though I shan't be on deck. Loveman is a cousin of Amy Loveman of the Sat. Rev. of Lit., & also of the late Robert Loveman,[4] a fairly well-known Georgia poet with whom he has sometimes been confused by careless reviewers. His poetry is of very high quality—of a poignant, wistful cast—& is pervaded by a spirit which might be called Hellenistic. The longest specimen—"The Hermaphrodite"—was printed by W. Paul Cook as a small book uniform with Belknap's "Man from Genoa." I can lend you a copy if you'd care to see it; or Loveman might have one to lend or for sale, since I think Cook turned the edition over to him. If you like Loveman's poetry I can lend you a fair amount of it in manuscript form.

Sorry to hear of recent rejections, but guess the acceptances more than compensate for them. No—the Swanson downfall gave me no acute shock, for success would have been very unlikely in any case. He still talks of mimeograph ventures, but I don't attach much importance to those. I'll take a look at the

Schooner before I embark. From your description it sounds very interesting.

As for a book of my stuff—I don't think it's worth bothering very energetically about. What depressed me in the Putnam incident was not the non-appearance of the volume but the logical analysis which convinced me of the permanent inferiority of my efforts. I now think I erred (as I believe you said at the time) in sending any of the cruder specimens. Some day I may try to remove a few of the obvious crudities from things like "Dagon"—but then again I may not. As to grouping certain tales of cosmic forces in a class apart—again I fear that they fall between two stools. Whereas editors think them too uniform when separately considered, they would condemn them as too heterogeneous & perhaps even subtly contradictory if they were expressly offered as a unit. Actually, I don't think the time is yet ripe for a book of my stuff. I haven't written enough really good material to form a full-sized volume, & may never do so. For the present, it's really better to let my ill-assorted scraps remain dormant—I wouldn't have let Leeds mention me to the Vanguard if I had known of his intention.

As for my southern jaunt—eheu! A grim spectre has arisen betwixt me & the beckoning palmettos & live-oaks! Teeth! Or rather, a tooth—whose behaviour has now passed all bounds of endurance. I've made my first dental appointment, but don't know how much a siege—physical, chronological, & financial—lies ahead. In any event, though, Southern prospects look meagre! Only the ensuing weeks can tell. Glad your spring has arrived, & hope the literary echoes will be ample. Our spring is late & barren as yet, & I've had no outings so far. Best wishes—Grandpa

[On envelope:] P.S. I'm helping Whitehead prepare a new ending for a story which Bates rejected. It was about a man in 1923 who got a bruise on the head which caused him to hear strange cataclysmic sounds—that turned out to be the Tokyo earthquake. The bruise had made a sort of radio of his ears! In my new version, the bruise excites certain cells of hereditary memory & causes him to hear the destruction of one of the cities of fabulous Mu—the sunken continent of the Pacific—20,000 years ago.[5]
¶ Just read Scarborough's "Supernatural in Modern Eng. Fiction."[6] Rather good as far as it goes.

Notes

1. Carl Jacobi, "Moss Island," *Amazing Stories* (Winter 1932).

2. "Marcel Proust: 'Le Temps Retrouvé'" [review], *Trend* 1, No. 1 (March–April–May 1932): 8–9; rpt. *Out of the Immortal Night* (New York: Hippocampus Press, 2004), pp. 213–15.

3. Joseph Pennell (1857–1926), American graphic artist and illustrator, noted for landscapes and architectural scenes.

4. 1864–1923.

5. In other letters HPL refers to this story as "The Bruise." It was published, long after Whitehead's and HPL's deaths, as "Bothon" in *West India Lights* (Sauk City, WI: Arkham House, 1946).

6. Lent to HPL by J. Vernon Shea.

[265] [ANS][1]

[Postmarked Boston, Mass.,
2 April 1932]

Collective greetings from an ancient town! All hands here like "The House in the Magnolias". Will answer your epistle shortly. Munn has some great new plot ideas, which I hope to see take shape before long.

Regards—H P

I have just seen through with the bishop in Weird Tales[2] and enjoyed it much, as usual with your short stories. W. P. Cook.

Thought "Those who Seek" was the best of your work that I have seen. H. Warner Munn

Notes

1. Front: Ye Old Tyme Days in Boston.

2. Cook alludes to "The Bishop Sees Through" (*WT* May 1932).

[266] [ALS]

April 8, 1932

Dear A W:—

No—I hardly think *Trend* is worth the half-buck intrinsically, but I suppose the editors thought that a small, devoted group might come across with a fancy fee more readily than the vulgar herd would plank down an economically normal tariff. I wish it luck—& will purchase any further issues which may appear. That "story", alas, probably got by through Loveman's partiality for a promising young fellow still at a crude stage but with remarkably serious ambitions. Thompson[1] is a very bright chap about 25—I met him last year—who ran away to sea in boyhood & missed an education. Now—back on land & tied down with a wife & job—he longs to scale literary heights. Loveman got acquainted with him in a bookshop, & at once added him to a long list of literary proteges. He certainly has perseverance—& the nerve to send things even unto the American Mercury. In one of his turndowns he got a really friendly & substantial letter of advice & encouragement from crusty Aitchell himself. Gervaise Butler is another—& rather less primitive—Loveman's "find". Hope your stuff lands. Loveman has heard of you through me. It was probably at Wandrei's during your Minneapolitan period that you saw "The Hermaphrodite." Young Melmoth is quite a Loveman fan, & knew the bard quite well when in N.Y. Loveman's verse is always musical & delicate, but sometimes of course a trifle thin & repetitive of the same stock minor-key mood. A select collection would be a real contribution to American poetry. His prose, though, is too strained & empurpled by poetic leanings to be really fresh & powerful. It has lost simplicity, raciness, & even natural rhythm in a wilderness of Paterian preciosity. No—I never saw your Proustian thesis; & we couldn't have *debated* over it because I'm very much inclined to echo your view of Proust's status among XX cent. writers. I wish you could wake Little Belknap up enough to make him fight you on this topic. The young fat rascal doesn't appreciate Marcel at all, & vows that the latter is intolerably dull & unreadable! What is one to do with a child like that?

Glad to hear of the new work taking form. Bless me, but I wonder where one could get a gland treatment to generate an energy & persistence like yours! As for a book of Grandpa's maunderings—I know the present is as good a time as any; though if stress & international darkness create any demand for escape dope, I'll bank on the next generation even more than on this! I'll make all my adopted grandchildren my heirs—you & Little Melmoth & Sonny Belknap & young Jehvish-Êi & Talman & Munn & Brobst & all the bunch—& time will tell what you boys will do with grandpa's yellowed MSS. after the old man's dead & gone! No—my name won't appear on the Whitehead tale, because I shan't have written any of the text. H S offered to pay for my suggestions; but I refused because I merely gave them loosely & unformulatedly, leaving them for him to modify at will & crystallise in his own style. It was only fun to suggest without writing, & one can't charge a friend for that. May W.T. is mediocre—saved only by Klarkash-Ton, Bran Mak Morn, & M. le Comte d'Erlette. The Hamilton thing is so much like a parody on the inane essence of its genre that I absolutely refuse to believe that Hectograph Eddie wrote it seriously.

My tooth . . . . ouch, dont! [*sic*] Say, rather, *teeth* . . . . . for that goddam dental ferret has spied out four *more* cavities . . . . small ones, though. And the main agony is going to be a long & nerve-killing (*literally,* in a local sense!) process. Wednesday my right cheek was swollen like a balloon, & the whole cursed mess has me about all in. Gawd—the headache of last Wed. night!! ¶ Landscape not very vernal yet, though some gardens are shewing timid petals. May is really the first half-decent month in these polar latitudes. ¶ Blessings upon thee! H P

[P.S.] Dwyer has just lent me some weird books—an E. F. Benson collection

I never saw before,[2] "Sinister House" by Leland Hall, & "The Mortgage on the Brain", by Vincent Harper.

Notes

1. Robert Thompson of Boston.
2. E. F. Benson, *Spook Stories.*

[267] [ALS]

April 14[, 1932]

Dear A W:—

Bless me, what a vortex of activity! Glad to hear of the Oriental acceptance,[1] & hope others will ensue. Your satire is certainly inclusive enough, & I hope its pungency is commensurate with its scope!

As for W.T.—I think I understand what Talman saw in "The Thing in the Cellar", for there were vast possibilities in the idea. Still, the treatment was so ineffective that I didn't gather much of a kick. I agree that there is a certain charm about "The Last Magician". Keller could probably be a top-notcher if he had the time to buckle down primarily to fiction—but I understand he is the head of an hospital. What I like least of his are the Cornwall tales in which he tries to be funny.

Yes—come to think of it—I fear there might be some turbulent doings among an indiscriminately named board of literary heirs handling my posthumous junk! Maybe I'll dump all the work on you by naming you sole heir. The matter of compiling & placing a book would be a mere bagatelle for you—though it might possibly take a whole afternoon & cut your day's reading quota down to a dozen or so books. So you think if you got hold of Grandpa you could guarantee a book in a half-year? Well, well! That might well be if you had the cash to publish it yourself . . . . but persuading other people is another matter. No word as yet from Vanguard—but a turndown a month hence is just as good as one today, provided they don't mess up my MSS. the way those Putnam sons-of-beachcombers did.

Congratulations on the Wilkins & Post triumphs. It's an achievement nowadays even to read "The Wind in the Rosebush", for scarcely any library has a copy. I never saw it till a year & a half ago, when a nice old lady in Boston lent a copy to Munn & me. Come to think of it, I guess Mrs. Wilkins-Freeman is your own closest analogue among widely-known weird writers. She, like you, prefers subdued effects & simple manifestations; relying on atmospheric subtleties & seldom handling the cosmic or the violent. Of Post's stuff I think the only item I've ever read is "The Corpus Delecti." The Benson book I have from Dwyer is "Spook Stories". I own "Visible & Invisible" (now lent to Shea), & also have one little gem—"The Man Who Went too

Far" in a Haldeman-Julius booklet. I didn't realise that he specialised so extensively in the weird. Is "The Room in the Tower" any good? Of the other Dwyer-lent items "Sinister House" is pretty fair, though "The Mortgage on the Brain" is not so hot. Summers' "Supernatural Omnibus" certainly sounds alluring—very few of the items being known to me. But I must certainly criticise the choice of Machen's "Inmost Light"—which is damnably flat as compared with its author's best. If Summers wanted to avoid tales which are too well known, he might have used "The Red Hand" or "The Shining Pyramid".

Some day perhaps Sonny Belknap will awake to the power of Proust—but he is always impatient about detail. Your own resemblance to P. impressed me the moment I saw your serious sketches. When I was in N Y last July young Grayson was about to take his first taste of M. Marcel—but I don't know how the diet agreed with him.

Your vernal landscape must certainly be delightful. I don't think I ever heard of poplar pussies before. Spring is still late here, though I can trace budlike swellings on the branches. My tooth siege *may* be over next week—but my first 1932 outing is yet to be taken.

Best wishes—H P

Notes

1. "A Battle over the Teacups."

[268] [ALS]

Boston—April 21[, 1932]

Dear A W:—

Well, as you have by this time seen from the joint Cook-Munn-H P card, Grandpa's peregrinating again. Munn hitch-hiked down from Athol, so Cook telegraphed to see if I could come along. It was possible—& so I did; to remain until Sunday night. Weather has turned delightfully & unexpectedly warm, so that I anticipate a pleasant bit of exploring—together, of course, with much museum contemplation. Munn has grown hog-feet in the two years since I saw him last—he weighs 218 lbs now! He has some fine plots in his head, & it is possible that I may work one up for him to help him develop his style—about whose limitations he is very sensitive.

Your recent activities surely are varied enough, & I trust you have succeeded in bringing aesthetics into the railway business! Congrats on the acceptances—*Trend* surely does know a good thing, after all! The "Five Alone" acceptance is really a major triumph.

Glad to see the Magnolias blooming in S.T. I haven't had time to read the issue, but the contents looks promising. I never saw Whitehead's "Great Circle" in MS. Did I mention that Cave is a Providence man?[1] I don't know him, though. He's an uneven, careless sort of cuss, apparently.

Glad the Sheraton is definitely fixed for Sept. Congrats also on the various other acceptances. Clayton delays certainly are good omens—as witness the acceptance of Belknap's Space-Monsters[2] after a silence that got the child all worked up.

Mrs. Wilkins-Freeman certainly has a distinctive sort of mood & method, though too many tales in just that tone might possibly call for a bit of greater intensity & cosmicism as a release for imperfectly satisfied imaginative yearnings. A composite of Poe, Machen, & Blackwood, I guess, remains my absolute ideal for weird fiction. No one has ever been beyond Poe. Call him naive, crude, flamboyant, or whatever else you will—the fact remains that he put something potent & fundamental into human expression which was never there before—something too vague & ethereal for conscious definition, yet potent enough to mould a whole school of literature. And what other weirdist has ever done that? I have lately read Hanns Heinz Ewers' eloquent appreciation of Poe—lent me by Belknap—& am glad that—despite all the W. C. Brownells[3]—there are still those who, themselves of high genius, recognise the unique & profound nature of Poe's contbution to aesthetics.

I never hear of Post's "Uncle Abner"—for I ceased to care for detective stories about the time I had become familiar with the earlier series of Sherlock Holmes stuff. No—I don't like the title "*Spook* Stories". It has a suggestion of triviality. I wonder what weird items are in the second Sayer[s] omnibus? I have Machen's "Shining Pyramid" (British collection) & so has Belknap—both picked up for 50¢ as remainders.

No—I doubt if very many of the gang will ever achieve any spectacular celebrity. The redeeming thing is that not many of them desire it. But it would be a boon if some of us could improve our finances!

And so it goes. Best wishes

—Yr obt Servt

H P

Notes

1. *Strange Tales of Mystery and Terror* (June 1932): Henry S. Whitehead, "The Great Circle"; AWD and Mark Schorer, "The House in the Magnolias"; Hugh B. Cave, "Stragella."

2. FBL, "In the Lair of the Space Monsters," *Strange Tales of Mystery and Terror* (October 1932).

3. W. C. Brownell (1851–1928), a leading American critic of the day, wrote somewhat disparagingly of Poe in his study *American Prose Masters* (1909).

[269] [ALS]

Night of the Awful
Sabbat {device}
[c. 30 April 1932]

Dear A W:—

Back from Boston Sunday night—& since then wrestling with a demoniac cold. The last day of the trip was the most fruitful. We climbed Bunker Hill Monument in the morning, & in the afternoon explored the Gardner Museum of Renaissance Art. Then, in the glow of a sunset generously postponed by Daylight Time (which had just come into effect for 1932), we took in the new Georgian quadrangles at Harvard—along the river's edge, & reproducing perfectly the atmosphere of 200 years ago. As for Munn's preference for "Those Who Seek"—it was a decided & deliberate one. Probably he appreciated the historic vistas it conjured up—for it must be remembered that subject matter plays as large a part as literary quality in most persons' actual liking for a story.

So Jacobi is in touch with Cave? "Stragella" is not as bad as other things of Cave's, but it is far from the high spot of the current S.T. Howard's specimen has its points, but is strained in many places.[1] Whitehead really hits a cosmic level now & then in "The Great Circle". It gave me a real kick, & I place it near the top of his products. Sorry your Orientale didn't land the first time—but there is always hope! As for Munn—he needs to build up a spontaneous style suited to whatever subject matter he finally decides on. In the end he will probably quit the purely weird in favour of the adventure-scientifiction type. He has as yet but little command of atmosphere, so that everything of his must stand or fall by the merit of the central idea & incidents. "The Chain" is certainly his masterpiece to date.[2]

Good luck with "Town Characters" & "Others." Bates's delays in decision are much to be deplored, yet seems to follow what is a general rule in pulpdom. The editor has the helpless author at his mercy—so who can hope for better treatment? All the conditions of commercial writing are disgusting & discouraging to me—yet I don't see that anything can be done about them.

Regarding Wilkins-Freeman—yes, there is sometimes an adequate intensity, but it doesn't always get to the reader. With certain exceptions, the impression is of a sort of vague *lack of something*—one doesn't know quite what. The extreme tameness & commonplaceness of the settings, & the rather old-maidish prosaicism of the style tend to relegate the chronicled abnormalities to the realm of the purely abstract—& therefore emotionally unmoving. There is not enough to bite into—not enough to weave associative images around—& not enough unconscious poetry in the vocabulary & idiom to make the appeal more than an academically intellectual one. Yet at her best Mary E. surely could turn out some great stuff. Few admire "The Shadows on the Wall" as much as I do. As for Poe—I think his influence has been as great atmospherically as symbolically. He taught literature to put something on paper which had never been there before—dim, mystical, genius-conceived overtones of cosmic malignancy & doom which with earlier writers were merely fumbled at & ridiculously groped for. No writer has ever approached Poe in weaving certain moods. True, his range was limited; but within that range he did what no one else has ever done. I wish there could be a single writer with the sheer genius of Poe, the imaginative scope of Blackwood, & the magical prose of Dunsany!

I shall probably be among the gang in N.Y. in a fortnight or so, though southern prospects still look dubious. There have been some warmish days here, but nothing good enough to call me forth to the awakening woods & fields. Best wishes—H P

Notes

1. REH, "People of the Dark," *Strange Tales of Mystery and Terror* (June 1932).
2. H. Warner Munn, "The Chain," *WT* (April 1928).

[270] [ALS]

May 7[, 1932]

Dear A W:—

Yes—I had heard the bad news about Clayton, for Sonny Belknap wrote of the matter in a mood of picturesque despair.[1] He is wondering when his Space-Monsters (announced for next S.T.) will ever appear, & whether his other tale—The Man Who Was Sent Back[2]—will be accepted or returned. He wonders, too, whether it will be published in Astounding instead of S.T. in case of acceptance. Bates has said nothing about such details. You might let me know if you see any Belknapiana in Astounding during the coming months. Also—he wants to know if it is a fact that Clayton now pays on publication instead of acceptance, & whether there has been any departure from the 2¢ a word rate. Sorry your two tales were rejected—but of course all Clayton acceptances will now be cut in half. Good luck with the new material!

As for Swanson—this postage business is about the queerest-sounding mess I ever heard of! It doesn't seem normal for anybody to bicker over a few cents—or bother to cover up a theft of that smallness—so that I honestly think Swanson must have really lost your stamped, self-addressed envelopes & forgotten about them. Nothing but the *belief* that he is in the right could make him quibble so determinedly about a trifle. From his letters I gather that he is a naive, simple, narrow, & uncultivated soul—a frank plebeian—but I really do not get any impression of dishonesty. I lent him some old magazines a fortnight or so ago, & he was apparently very grateful for them. He even noticed the postage I paid on them & remitted the amount—

although I had had no idea of charging him for it. Too bad if he is proving insolent, but I hardly think it would pay to get excited & try to start a public campaign over the matter. There's no use in wasting energy on the swatting of small flies. He has now, he says, abandoned all publishing plans; & will return my two MSS. when he returns the loaned magazines. I don't imagine he'll be heard from very importantly in the future.

As for the current W.T.—there seemed to me nothing remarkable about it, although (as I told you last year) your "Left Wing" is a darned good story. Most of the contents seemed to me rather commonplace & traditional—marginal & unimaginative. Klarkash-Ton appears to advantage, but the La Spina thing left me cold even though I recognised a fine *chance* for horrific atmosphere in the wanderings of the hero around the forbidden wing of the accursed farmhouse. Belknap's story was better than that—with a horror of theme which even the choppy writing could not quite wreck. Sonny himself is highly dissatisfied with this tale. I wish he'd drop some of his smart theories about art & sophistication & write a really good story of the sort he now loftily condemns as naive & immature. The little rascal turned *30* a week ago Wednesday—how time does fly![3] You boys get grown up before Grandpa can realise it! R E H does tend to run themes into the ground—but for all that he rings the bell now & then. I am very fond of Whitehead's "Great Circle" in the new S.T.

Good luck with "Town Characters"—& thanks for the interesting folklore cuttings. Glad your hills are now awakened to full vernal splendour. Flowers & foliage are now in evidence in R.I.—& one day recently has been warm enough to let me get to my favourite river-bank. Details of coming trip still vague.

Best wishes— H P

Notes

1. I.e., the news was that *Strange Tales* was going from bimonthly to quarterly with the June 1932 issue.

2. Apparently retitled or unpublished.

3. Actually, FBL turned 31 on 27 April 1932. HPL believed that FBL was born in 1902 rather than 1901.

[271] [ALS]

May 14[, 1932]

Dear A W:—

Thanks for the data on the Claytonian conditions, which I have duly transcribed for Belknap's benefit. Hope your "Tree Near the Window" will land after all—through of course the retrenchment tragically lessens chances.

Swanson is certainly an enigma! I give him up! His contradictory statements about envelopes &c. surely seem to defy all laws of sense & plausible motivation—& indeed lead one to wonder just what sort of a book & magazine enterprise he would have conducted had his plans not collapsed. From circulars he has enclosed in letters, I judge that he is largely in the cheap mail-order business. Well—I hope he'll return my two MSS. & the magazines I lent him!

Yes—I certainly liked "In the Left Wing", though of course I did not compare it with those more serious tales in which you do not depend on artificial dramatic manipulation for your effect. Congratulations on the letter from Henry Holt Co.! When publishers spontaneously look you up, it's a pretty good sign that you're on the road toward arriving! Hope you'll be able to make some sort of a deal for the publication of our collected personal & reminiscent sketches.

Hope you've duly received the story I started in circulation the other day—typed by a client in payment for revisory work.[1] I don't know what you'll think of it, but it happened to be what I wanted to say at the time I wrote it some 2½ months ago. Whether I eventually try it on Wright will depend on the collective opinions of those to whom I am sending it. After you're through with it, please shoot it on to Klarkash-Ton . . . . . unless, indeed, you think it's too bad to endure general visibility.

Glad good old Canevin liked your "Magnolias"—he certainly ought to know good West Indian stuff when he sees it! Incidentally—I now have a strong hope of getting down to the scene of that undeniably powerful tale, since investigation shews the New Orleans 'bus fare to be vastly reduced of late. I must see New Orleans before civic "progress" ruins the old French market. There is so much modern stuff in the town that I probably won't like it as well as Charleston—but it's a place every genuine antiquarian must see at least once. The route thither is also fraught with historic charm—everything the other side of Washington being new to me. I shall—all being well—go through Winchester, Charlottesville, (where Poe attended the U. of Va.), Nashville, Memphis, (where I shall see the Mississippi River for the first time) Vicksburg, Natchez, & Baton Rouge. I hope to stay at least a week in N.O.—seeing if possible some of the adjacent plantation country. On the return trip I shall pause at places which interest me on the way down, & of course pay a brief visit to Belknap. Then, if I have the cash, I shall go up the Hudson to see Dwyer. Postcards will keep you pictorially in touch with my progress.

Glad you've been having some congenial ornithological glimpses. Spring is very much—& very exquisitely—in evidence here so far as the eye is concerned, but it doesn't keep warm enough to let me enjoy the outdoors. I shall be glad to get among the live-oaks & Spanish moss of more genial latitudes for a while! Each spring I seem to need a good thawing out.

Best wishes—

Yr most ob[t] Grandsire
H P

Notes

1. "The Dream in the Witch House," typed for HPL by an unidentified revision client.

[272] [ALS]

[New Orleans]
June 6, 1932

Dear A W:—

Well—this is my first breathing-spell since leaving home two weeks ago last Wednesday! When I got to New York the Longs asked me to stop for my visit at once instead of waiting till the return trip—since they had learned suddenly that the apartment was to be upheaved by painters & decorators all through June—& I acquiesced in the change. For a whole week after that I was kept incessantly busy meeting the gang—Morton, Leeds, Loveman, Kirk, Kleiner, Talman, &c. &c.—but on Wednesday evening, May 25, I finally broke away & started the trip proper by taking the night 'bus for Washington. I was under the handicap of a heavy relapse of my spring cold—induced by the unheated state of Belknap's apartment-house—& used 33 handkerchiefs in 10 days. I could not smell or taste from May 24 till yesterday!

Well—the trip has been a brilliant success so far. I caught a morning coach for Knoxville, Tenn., going through the exquisite Shenandoah Valley of Virginia, & had a veritable aesthetic orgy watching the Blue Ridge Mountains. The next day I rode across Tennessee to Chattanooga—whose hilly setting is one of the most magnificent sights I ever hope to see in my lifetime. I went up Lookout Mountain & revelled in the view, & afterward descended into the spectral caverns inside the mountain—where in a vast vaulted chamber a 145-foot waterfall thunders endlessly in eternal night. This chamber & waterfall were discovered only 2 years ago—at the end of sealed galleries whose geological formations prove them never to have been entered by mankind before. After a couple of days in Chattanooga I rode across Southern Tennessee to Memphis, where I saw the mighty Mississippi for the first time in my life. This ride involved some of the most magnificent sights of the whole trip—for most of it lay in or beside what is whimsically called the "Grand Cañon" of the Tennessee River—the magnificent bluffs forming part of the Cumberland Mountain system. Memphis is a modern town with no especial picturesqueness, but it did give me a kick to see a sunset over the Father of Waters! The next day I pushed down into the delta cotton country of Mississippi, where nothing can be seen but flat plains, niggers, & mules. In the afternoon, however, the coach reached the fine bluff country beyond the Yazoo; & I stepped off at Vicksburg to stroll around the quaint streets. In the evening—amidst golden sunset light—I pushed on to ancient Natchez, incidentally reaching the belt of far-southern vegetation, with live-oaks & Spanish moss. Natchez deserves a whole chapter to itself—for it is one of the most exquisitely fascinating places I have ever seen. In the first place, the subtropical landscape is a thing of poignant & breathless beauty—much finer than that of Louisiana, & recalling the descriptions of Chateaubriand in "Atala."[1] This last is no chance coincidence—for Chateaubriand visited in Natchez once & remembered what he saw. The country is rolling, with many picturesque ravines, & drops to the Mississippi in a perpendicular 200-foot bluff. Vegetation is lush & abundant, & the moss on the great live-oaks & cypresses creates an unforgettable picture. Most of the roads are deeply sunken below the general surface of the terrain they traverse, owing to the peculiar nature of the yellow clay. The steep walls on either side—overarched with stately trees which spread a green twilight all around—give one a sense of fantastic unreality which is hard to overcome. The town itself was founded by the French in 1716 as the military & trading post Ft. Rosalie. In 1729 all the garrison was massacred by the Natchez Indians, but a fresh start was soon made. In 1763 the treaty of Paris passed this region to Great Britain, & Fr. Rosalie became Ft. Panmure—under the jurisdiction of the new Province of West Florida. In 1779 the Spanish overran the region & held it till 1798, when it was ceded to the U.S. Natchez became a great cotton port after the Americans took it over, & from 1803 to 1820 was the capital of Mississippi. American inhabitants flocked in & built stately pillared mansions which survive to this day, the steamboats on the river ushered in a high degree of prosperity. At last, though, Vicksburg began to surpass it commercially; & the Civil War was the last straw. Now it vegetates in stately dignity like Charleston & Newport & Salem; preserving most of its fine old houses, & maintaining a continuous tradition of mellow civilisation. The town proper lies atop the great bluff like the Haute Ville of Quebec, whilst the Lower Town on the narrow shore strip—once the roaring haunt of sailors known as "Natchez-Under-the-Hill"—is abandoned to mills, niggers, & desolation. In Natchez one may find all sorts of early architecture—primitive Spanish designs, Louisiana types, Georgian approximations, & the omnipresent classic-revival specimens. The people are very courteous & urbane, & my hotel-keeper solicitously introduced me to all the leading sources of antiquarian information. In the two days I spent there I saw most of what there is to be seen, & formed a lasting admiration for the place. It takes rank with Charleston, Quebec, Salem, Marblehead, & Newburyport as one of my favourite early-American backwaters, & I certainly mean to revisit it some time. I spent both Natchez evenings reading & writing in a park at the edge of the river-bluff—watching the sun set over the might river & the fertile alluvial plains of east central Louisiana. Far below, as dusk gathered, gleamed the now few & faint lights of Natchez-under-the Hill; [*sic*] & occasionally I saw a broad Mississippi steamboat with laterally paired stacks—of the same general design as the early traditional specimens. Steamboat days on the river are by no means over, though of course the railway has cut badly into such fluvial traffic. I hated to leave Natchez—but life is long & cash is short! Finally I hopped a coach & exchanged the yellow dust of Mississippi (which is devilish hard on a dark-blue suit & black shoes) for the grey dust of a flatter & less picturesque Louisiana. I did not stop at Baton Rouge—for modernism has displaced much of the old there, & I could not stand the sight of the ugly new state capital, a semi-modernistic skyscraper put up under the auspices of that incredible clown Huey P. Long.[2] This blatant poor white now claims to belong to the main or armigerous line of Longs—of which Sonny Belknap is a scion—but I simply refuse to believe it! South of Baton Rouge the bluffs sink, & the land gets down to river level—or even below. Here the great system of artificial levees & spillways begins—& I had a chance to study the types of embankment in some detail. The levee is constantly being relocated—the earth handled by vast steam shovels. Much of this region is overrun with the tanks & refineries of oil companies—so that I am sure your "House in the Magnolias" must lie on the other side of the river! On the way to New Orleans I noted many old plantation-houses in various stages of desertion & decay—plus two, Ormond & D'Estreban, which have been gratifyingly restored. There are two distinct types of plantation house—the earlier Creole sort with raised basement, low portico, steep slant roof, & small dormers, & the later American type with vast columns & general classic-revival architecture. Both of these types coexist as far north as Natchez.

At last I came to the city itself—& here I still am! It is, of course, a modern metropolis of nearly 500,000—hence is generally not so congenial to me as Natchez—but tucked in at a bend of the river is the unchanged parallelogram of the ancient 18th century section—the "Vieux Carré"—which more than atones for all the circumambient modernity. It is impossible to overestimate the intense & compelling charm of the Vieux Carré—block on block of unbroken antiquity as expressed in old brick-&-stucco Franco-Hispanic houses with wrought-iron balconies & marvellous interior courts or patios. The town was wholly burnt down in 1788, & at once rebuilt during a period of intense prosperity & Spanish domination—hence the solid & mainly Hispanic character of the houses which survive to this day. The architecture of old New Orleans is almost unique, but its chief affinities on this continent are the styles of Charleston & Quebec. These three towns stand out as the most thoroughly ancient & exotic urban centres of North America. I am seeing the place thoroughly & gradually, & am also taking in as many neighbouring plantation-houses as possible. I've found an ideally quiet hotel—the Orleans—where an inside room & bath can be had for a dollar a day—& here I'm parked for at least a week or more. The climate of New Orleans suits me ideally. It is, I believe, even farther south than St. Augustine; & is definitely more subtropical than my beloved Charleston. Tall Washington Palms & thick, luxuriant Brazilian date palms are omnipresent, while the live-oaks, cypresses, magnolias, oleanders, Spanish moss, & luxuriant vines all unite to form a picture of tropic opulence. From the standpoint of choice greenery, Louisiana easily beats Florida. The newer American parts of New Orleans lie south of broad Canal St., & include some magnificent shady streets. The parts peopled by Creole descendants lie mostly toward the north. I have seen no French signs, & imagine that the young public-schooled generation doesn't speak much French; but the newer houses of the Creoles retain certain characteristics of older Creole architecture which make them unmistakable. Much fusion of American & Creole has taken place, yet beyond the amalgamated area many traces of the two separate elements can be discerned. I am noting as many as possible of the little local customs—some of which are apparently peculiar to the place. The fantastic above-ground cemeteries are fascinating in the extreme. In former times the newer part of the town was a network of open drainage canals running down the centre of broad streets. These canals are now roofed over & bear street-car tracks—giving rise to a broad boulevard system. One or two, though, are still open—so that I saw a sample of the way the whole city used to be. I took a long tour of the modern section in a sight-seeing bus—& have also walked through parts of it in quest of overtaken & imbedded plantation houses. But naturally, most of my time is spent in the squares & patios of the Vieux Carré. On my return trip I shall go through Mobile, Alabama—& I have not given up all hope of financing a digression to *Charleston*. I may stop off in Richmond, Washington, & Philadelphia—& in N.Y. I shall probably pause a week as Loveman's guest. Whether I get up the Hudson to see Bernard Dwyer depends on finances.

New Orleans, as you probably know, was founded in 1718 by the French-Canadian Jean-Baptiste Le Moyne, Sieur de Bienville, & rather hetergenously populated—beginning with a wave of dupes of John Law's "Mississippi Bubble".[3] It was rather crude until the 1740's, when the younger Marquis de Vandreuil (born in Quebec) became governor; but afterward developed the polished civilisation for which its better classes have been celebrated. In 1763—much against its will—it was passed to Spain, though its language & institutions remained French. The return to France & immediate sale to the U.S. in 1803 are matters of common textbook knowledge. The days of its wildest prosperity were around 1830, when the plantation system & the river steamboat trade were at their height. Its exuberant Latin heritage made it unique among American cities, & produced a type of riotous & extravagant life which will long survive in folklore. The Civil War badly checked its prosperity, but its unexcelled situation as related to economic geography has kept it the metropolis of the south. Today it is—aside from the architecture of the old section—the most modern of southern cities—so much so that I do not find it by any means so atmospherically appealing as Charleston & Richmond.

Coming to yours of the 17th ult—your reaction to my poor "Dreams in the Witch House" is, in kind, about what I expected—although I hardly thought the miserable mess was *quite* as bad as you found it.[4] I agree that the title is awkward, but think "Brown Jenkin" would be even worse. The whole incident shews me that my fictional days are probably over. At any rate, I must take that long vacation which I said long ago that I needed. I hope you didn't send the mess along to Klarkash-Ton. Just chuck it back to 10 Barnes & let it rest in peace. I can't write any more until I am wholly re-oriented to the whole subject of verbal expression. I am convinced of the essential cheapness & charlatanry of the conventional short story as a literary form, & unless I can find a substitute medium I fancy I am through. I don't think fiction is the proper outlet for any impressions I now have. The period of that kind of thing for me has come & gone.

Whether I shall continue to buy & read *Weird Tales* I don't know. I picked up the new issue from habit, but feel a vast repugnance about reading it. I think it would be better if I did not think about fiction for a while. I'm glad, though, to hear of the successes you have had in this line.

Enclosed is a prospectus of the new issue of *Trend,* which will contain your story.[5] Also a neatly printed card version of one of Loveman's appealing short lyrics. Some financial trouble has developed in connexion with the management of *Trend,* & it is possible that Loveman may drop out of the venture. Whether such a move will wreck it, remains to be seen.

If you are ornithologically inclined, you ought to come down here; for the whole region teems with gaily-coloured exotic birds of various sorts unknown in the north. They are particularly numerous in Natchez—which is not metropolitan enough to scare off most feathered visitants, as is more or less the case with New Orleans. By this time your own country must be blossoming toward its early aestivation—though in a less complete degree than the South. New England, too, will shortly be at its magical best—so that I don't feel any pangs about going home. But I shall surely dread the chilly evenings!

With all good wishes, & thanks for the candid & helpful analysis accorded my pathetic expiring gasp, I remain

Yr most oblig'd ob^{dt} Servt

H P

Notes

1. François-René de Chateaubriand (1768–1848), *Atala* (1801), a romance based in large part upon a visit that Chateaubriand had taken to wild and uninhabited regions of the American continent. HPL notes that Chateaubriand also made use of the bluffs of Natchez, MI, in his novel (see *SL* 4.41).

2. Huey P. Long (1893–1935), governor (1928–1932) and U.S. Senator (1932–35) from Louisiana, who advocated a radical scheme for the alleviation of poverty, the Share Our Wealth Plan. He was assassinated on 10 September 1935.

3. The Mississippi Bubble refers to the disastrous attempt by the Scotsman John Law

to exploit the resources of French Canada. He established a trading company at New Biloxi, MS, in 1719, and aggressively promoted the company's stock, leading to wild speculation. The stock collapsed in December 1720, and many of the colonists of New Biloxi died.

4. AWD's reaction to "The Dreams in the Witch House" does not survive, but HPL summarized it in a letter to E. Hoffmann Price (20 October 1932): "Derleth didn't say it was *unsalable;* in fact, he rather thought it *would* sell. He said it was a *poor story,* which is an entirely different and much more lamentably important thing" (*SL* 4.91).

5. "The Old Girls."

[273] [ALS]

New Orleans—
June 12, 1932

Dear A W:—

Yes—Grandpa is still hanging around New Orleans, for it's a hard city to break away from. The way to appreciate it is to stick to the ancient section & forget all about the encircling modern metropolis—& that's exactly what I'm doing. I spend all my time in the Vieux Carré, & am constantly uncovering new street vistas, perspectives of massed chimneys, gables, & balconies, & garden-garnished inner courtyards, which add to the original fascination of the place. One might make a sort of game by trying to pile up a high score of different courtyards entered. Some are manifestly open to the public & advertised as such; others have to be discovered independently, yet belong to shops & are freely open when found; still others belong to apartment or rooming houses, with their accessibility a doubtful question; whilst a few appertain to the slender stock of remaining private mansions, & are emphatically & definitely closed . . . . . unless one happens to get a glimpse through the entrance arcade when the gate is momentarily opened for visitors or tradesmen. Almost every patio differs from almost every other one in size, outline, staircase & balcony arrangement, & garden-&-fountain development; so that the sport of searching out different specimens is the very reverse of monotonous repetition. In the course of my extensive wanderings (this is my 10th full day in N.O.) I have explored an almost fabulous number of these delightful hidden paradises—being directed to some by references in books, but stumbling upon others wholly unexpectedly . . . . . a far greater delight. My chief victory over private seclusion is that involving a patio famous in every book written about N.O. in the last quarter-century, yet zealously guarded from vulgar sight by the proprietor. This is the celebrated "Patio of the Palm" at 612 Rue Royale, where a titanic Brazilian date palm springs from the soil of a small court & spreads a strange, glamorous green twilight over the whole expanse of flagstones, fountain, & prodigious water-jars. I hung around this place like a thief planning a large-scale cleanup, but was finally rewarded when a large party—evidently friends of the inhabitants—called & strolled about the patio & arcade with the gate open! One thing worth studying is the type of great fan window which usually fronts on these ancient courtyards. I think at least one of these is shewn in the folder I recently sent you.

I do all my daytime reading & writing on a bench in Jackson Square—the ancient Place d'Armes—in the lee of the old Cathedral (1794), Cabildo (1795), & Presbytere (1813). Evenings are spent in antiquarian research at the public library—for being a non-resident, I can't withdraw books from there. Just now, though, I have an encyclopaedic old book of New Orleans history & traditions lent me by the genial proprietor of my hotel—which is proving more valuable than any of the better known works at the library. Of the modern & easily obtainable volumes, nothing is better than Lyle Saxon's "Fabulous New Orleans". Read that—& digest Suydam's magnificent line drawings in it—& you can't fail to absorb much of the colour of the ancient Cresent City.

Yesterday afternoon around sunset I took the ferry across the river to the suburb of Algiers; thus navigating the Mississippi for the first time, & for the first time treading soil *west* of the Mississippi. The skyline of N.O. across the water is not as striking as one might wish. The three spires of the cathedral show up well, but the levee is so high that there is no view of the quaint gables & chimney-pots of the low-lying old houses. I suppose you know how the great levee embankments are built—the cross-section being something like this:

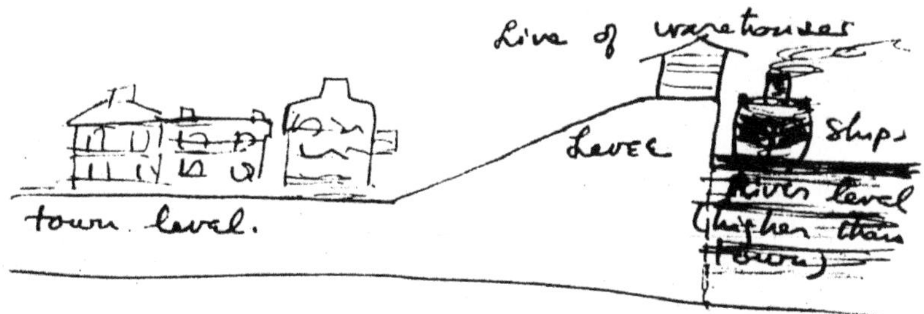

I expect to move on to ancient Mobile next Tuesday or so, & will let you know how I like that place—which is even older than New Orleans, though not so widely celebrated in song & story. After that, Atlanta, Greenville, (S.C.) Winston-Salem, Danville, & Richmond. It is from Greenville that I shall make that Charleston side-trip if I have the money . . . . which I sadly doubt more & more. After all, Charleston remains my favourite town—for it is really *living* a continuation of its tasteful ancient life. The machine age has never had a foothold there, & the antiquities have not assumed the "museum" perspective. The *whole* of Charleston is a "Vièux Carré"! But—alas—I have less & less hope of seeing it in 1932. The nearest thing to Charleston conservatism in this part of the country is Natchez. I wish I could go back there—but if I did, I'd have to cut out Mobile, which I'm loath to do. Maybe I'll find something of the Charleston spirit in Mobile.

As for writing—a good vacation, with its attendant opportunities for reorientation, won't hurt anybody. I was wise in calling a halt in 1908, for I was clearly on the wrong track then. Now the 1917–1932 period has run its course. It remains to be seen when a new period will begin, or *whether* it will begin. Some *new approach* to the mood of cosmic uncertainty & unreality which I seek to depict must clearly be worked out. Yes—Klarkash-Ton dropped a card about the "Witch-House", in which he expressed a rather bewilderingly favourable opinion. Guess I'll let it run its course & see what Melmoth & Dwyer have to say about it.

Many congratulations on the vistas opening out before you! The Holt book proposition looks excellent—for surely there is enough poignant tragedy in the Halgenau incident for a novel of any length. Once you had an entreé with a firm like Holt, you would probably find it possible to get many volumes—both novels & short story collections—published. However, I suppose this proposition will force you to delete the original "Widow Halgenau" from "A Town is Built."[1] Glad to hear of the numerous acceptances by Wright & by the high-grade magazines. I lately heard of *Contempo* from Loveman—they wanted him to do, on very short notice, a critical & biographical sketch of the late poet Hart Crane; (he was practically Crane's only remaining close friend among normal & wholesome people—Crane's mother now wants him to edit an edition of her son's collected shorter pieces) but he decided the proposition was too hurried to be feasible. The Mencken vista certainly looks promising, & I feel sure that your will make Aitchell's green-swathed & austere columns sooner or later. Glad there is good pay as well as honour in this lofty haven! Meanwhile your immediate literary programme looks dizzying in its magnitude—for what your contemplate doing before the first of next March would seem to many a veritable lifetime's labour! Thanks for the new *Trend* notice. I hope that, since last reports, Loveman & Kerr[2] have adjusted their differences of opinion on the magazine's financing; so that publication can be continued.

Among yesterday's batch of forwarded mail was a letter form the amiable & eccentric William Lumley, (I've told you about him, haven't I?) in which he expressly asks me to transmit to you his intense appreciation & admiration of your work—which he declares is getting better & better as the years go by. An interesting old boy, William—& with a streak of genuine weird sensitiveness not very far removed from a certain sort of blind, rhapsodic genius.

And so it goes. Your next epistle had better go to 10 Barnes St., so that my aunt can forward it to whatever point I next pause at for any space of time. Or it might reach me about as quickly if sent ℅ Samuel Loveman, 130 Columbia Heights, Brooklyn, N.Y.—for I don't imagine I'll have cash enough to stop anywhere for any length of time till I get to Brooklyn!

I visited a curious sort of a place last Thursday—the modern aboveground cemetery of St. Roch, in the newer Creole quarter, which looks exactly like the ancient cemeteries in every detail—tombs, wall with vaults for coffins, & all. But the most curious thing about this place is the tiny (though surprisingly tall) Gothick chapel of brick & stucco built by a French priest—Pére Theirs—*with his own hands* in the 1870's. This naive & worthy cleric, excited by one of New Orleans's numerous fever & cholera epidemics, (later eliminated through sanitation) made a vow to St. Roch (the mythical patron of plague-fighting) to build with his own hands a chapel to that demigod if none of his parishioners should be stricken during the epidemic. As chance had it, none of his parishioners did expire—hence he went forward with the execution of his vow. With a surprising native skill at engineering, the good father put up a structure of impeccable solidity, & with a certain homely grace despite occasional marks of amateur workmanship. Not many purely amateur builders could have even approached the success of the job. Since its construction, the chapel has come to be regarded by the simple Creoles as a sort of curative shrine, like Lourdes in France & Ste Anne de Beaupré in Quebec; & the walls are hung with the crutches of the "cured", as well as by odd little marble plaques with the word "Merci" or "Thanks"—votive offerings to the genius loci from grateful suppliants.

Well—best wishes!—H P

Notes

1. I.e., "Still Is the Summer Night."
2. Harrison Kerr, one of the editors of *Trend.*

[274] [ANS][1]

[Postmarked New Orleans, La.,
15 June 1932]

All hail, M. le Comte d'Erlette! Behold the convocation in session in the midst of the ancient Creole City! I didn't know Price's address, but R E Howard telegraphed him mine. A 25-½ hour session was the initial result! I feel quite transported to the bazaars of Bagdad, & the black temples of Kurdistan!
Yr obt Servt
H P

E. Hoffman Price

Notes

1. Front: Courtyard, Governor Claiborne Home, New Orleans, La.

[275] [ANS][1]

[Postmarked Richmond, Va.,
21 June 1932]

Hail, M. Le Comte d'Erlette! Back in old Richmond, home town of our good old friend Ed Poe! The place is gay with Confederate bunting—annual reunion of veterans, some not beyond their early 80's because of boyhood enlistments around 1864. Am writing this in the magnificent Japanese garden of my beloved Maymont Park—a living land of dream which you surely must see or perish in the attempt. ¶ My card-writing session with Price lasted till 6:10 a.m., & the next "evening" we parted at dawn! Some boy! A West Pointer, Arabic student, expert fencer, Oriental rug connoisseur, profound mathematician, & what not. And a royal good fellow into the bargain. Age 34—dark—moustached—handsome & spirited. ¶ Left N.O. the 18th, next day in quaint & ancient Mobile. Rather pallid after N.O. Then 2 hrs. in Montgomery—but no stops at all (except to change coaches) in the modern metropolis of Atlanta. I surely miss the gnarled live-oaks & pendent Spanish moss of the genial subtropics! Slept with 2 blankets last night. ¶ Hate like hell to move on—for Richmond has a delectably homelike atmosphere despite its urban magnitude. Next come Fredericksburg & Washington—&, I hope, Annapolis. But it's like pulling teeth to make the final plunge north. Why *do* people try to live up there? ¶ Regards—

Yr obt Grandsire
H P

Notes

1. Front: The Old Storne House and Enchanted Garden. Edgar Allen [HPL corrects to say "Allan"] Poe Shrine, Richmond, Va.

[276] [ALS]

Columbia Heights, Bklyn
June 26, 1932

Dear A W:—

Yours of the 14th awaited me when I reached Brooklyn . . . . even though you addressed it to 130 "Brooklyn Heights" instead of *Columbia* Heights. Brooklyn Heights is merely the name of the general *region;* not of a street. It represents the bluff overlooking the East River, on which Fort Sterling was built during the Revolution. *Columbia Heights* (where Joseph Pennell lived during his last years) is the street running along the edge of the bluff—from the rear windows of whose outer row of houses magnificent views of the pinnacled Manhattan skyline can be obtained. Loveman's room has such a window. Magic casements opening on the foam, &c.[1]

I'll tell honest Lumley about the coming *Pagany* item, & hope he'll get a copy. Remind me, too, when the issue is out; for I want a permanent copy of "Five Alone." I hope for the best regarding your Mencken-submitted items[2]—but as for Wright, I give him up. Don't fail to let me see the new parts of "Evening in Spring" whenever you have conveniently transmissible copies. I surely don't envy you the job of retyping the work—but am glad that only one part, rather than the whole, fills you with dread.

Glad to see your story in the new *Trend.* I don't think the printing is done gratis, for there was a good deal of dispute about the expenses of publication. Loveman has now withdrawn from the editorial board—though he may continue to contribute literary material. I think that Klarkash-Ton will also contribute. Kerr—whom I have not met—appears to be a well-meaning sort, though rather annoyingly self-satisfied & prone to be pedagogically dictatorial. So far as I know, the magazine is not yet in any great danger of foundering. Yes—Loveman mentions having been acquainted with Woolcott [*sic*].[3]

As you have learned from postcards, my trip back from New Orleans was marked by many pleasant pauses in antiquarian scenes. After reluctantly leaving Richmond, I stopped an entire afternoon in Fredericksburg—going over the familiar sights, & adding one which I had never seen before. This last was Ferry Farm, the boyhood home of Genl. Washington, & reputed scene of the cherry-tree & dollar-throwing episodes. It lies at a short distance from the village—perhaps a half-hour walk each way—& is still a seat of agriculture in the ancient manner, even though all but one of the buildings of Washington's time have long since suffered replacement. The one remaining ancient structure is a small cabin which originally served as the surveyor's office, & which is now protected by a wooden shelter. The village of Fredericksburg proper is one of the finest 18th century survivals in existence—containing whole squares of fine old brick houses dating from 1750 onward. Among other points of interest are the home of Gen. Washington's mother, the large manor-house occupied by his sister & her husband, the law offices where Pres. James Monroe practiced, &c. &c. And of course there are Civil War associations, since some of the hottest fighting of 1862 occurred here—especially at the heights just south of the settled district.

The next day—having spent the night in Washington—I visited ancient Annapolis, in Maryland. Here again is a fine old Southern town remaining in virtually its 18th condition. The large State House of 1772 occupies a grassy circle at the centre of the town, & away from it radiate streets named for members of the Royal Family—King George St., Prince George St., Duke of Gloucester St., &c. &c. Houses date from 1694 onward, & many of the old brick mansions are among the finest specimens of their kind on this continent. I had been to Annapolis only once before—in 1928. At that time I went through the grounds & buildings of the Naval Academy, but I did not repeat the process this year.

That same night I took the last 'bus to Philadelphia, & spent the next day among the well-known antiquities of that colonial metropolis & its suburbs. I took the trolley to Germantown, on the N.W. rim of the city, where a vast number of the old stone houses of the German settlers (first arriving in 1693 under the leadership of Rev. Daniel Pastorius) still survive in excellent condition. Here can be found the site of the shop of Christopher Saur, who printed the first bible ever produced in America—& the actual house of his grandson Samuel, who cast the first font of type ever cast in America. Here, too, the Dunkard & Moravian churches, all dating from before 1750; together with several ancient schoolhouses of the keenest interest. The homestead of the celebrated Wistar or Wister family is here—as well as the house to which Genl. Washington retreated during the Philad[a.] yellow fever epidemic of 1793, when Phila. was the national capital. After exploring the village (which has changed but little since 1924, when I first knew it; although it has long been a part of Philadelphia legally) I cut across westward to the mighty gorge of Wissahickon Creek, whose majestic sylvan beauty was once the subject of an essay by Poe. I do not think I have ever seen finer scenery than that afforded by this titanic ravine with its tall trees, outcropping rocks, almost perpendicular sides, & wildly rushing river. Fortunately it is a public park area, assured of preservation in its present state.

At last, however, I had to move on to N.Y., where I am staying a week as Loveman's guest—or semi-guest—having a room on the Heights a few doors north of Loveman's. Just now I'm going up to Little Belknap's for lunch—& after that I think I shall have to visit an oculist to get something out of my left eye which blew into it yesterday afternoon. Of all the goddamn luck! I don't know why my eyes tend to catch all the flying particles within a mile radius of me. Did I mention having to pay an oculist three bucks last October to perform a similar job? Hope the present episode won't wholly clean me out & spoil the residue of the trip!

Still slightly doubtful whether I can get up the Hudson to see Dwyer, but I have strong hopes—if the oculist doesn't finish me financially. I'll be home within a fortnight, I fancy, in any case. Glad you've been able to piece out your finances through canning operations. Wish I could find a source of revenue apart from pseudo-literary desecration!

Well—the gang send regards.

Best wishes—

H P

Notes

1. "Charmed magic casements, opening on the foam / Of perilous seas, in faery lands forlorn." Keats, "Ode to a Nightingale" (1819), ll. 69–70.

2. Unidentified. AWD had nothing published in the *American Mercury*.

3. Alexander Woollcott (1887–1943), American journalist, drama critic, and anthologist.

[277] [ALS]

Home—July 10, 1932

Dear A W:—

You can probably pardon this inadequate missive when I mention the melancholy circumstances under which it is composed. On July 1st—my 6th day with Loveman in Brooklyn—I received a telegram from my younger aunt saying that my semi-invalid elder aunt[1] (age 76, & the animating spirit of 10 Barnes St.) had suffered a sudden collapse & was not expected to live. At once taking a train home, I found the patient in a semi-coma; & in two days—despite the best medical & nursing care—the end arrived. The final transition to oblivion was so peaceful & imperceptible that I could not for some time believe it had actually occurred. Services were conducted Wednesday the 6th, & interment took place in ancient Swan Point Cemetery—where I shall some day be buried. The sense of loss to the two remaining members of the family—my younger aunt & myself—is tremendous; & I fear I shall be but an indifferent correspondent in the weeks to come. But such calamities are, of course, universal & inevitable. Young Brobst was here last night, & informed me that the death of his father—in Allentown—occurred last month. I was certainly in a position to extend him the most sincere & understanding sympathy.

Glad to hear of your literary progress—& sorry that Wright rejected "The Horror from the Depths." Perhaps he'll take it on the 11th or 12th submission! I can imagine the difficulty & delicacy of the task of putting "Evening in Spring" into final form, but will trust your taste & judgment to overcome all obstacles in the end. I'll welcome the sight of any parts which I have not seen—& also hope for a glimpse of "Five Alone."

Trend certainly is a bit thin & scattering for a 50¢ quarterly. Hope it'll live long enough to print your new contributions. I think the next issue will contain Klarkash-Ton's haunting "Night in Malneant",[2] which all professional pulp editors have rejected. I was glad to see your story in the second issue—which I read at Loveman's, & which I mean to procure shortly.

The eye cost me only 50¢ instead of the expected $3.00. What was in it was a long, thin cinder, & no embedding had taken place—so that it could be removed without the use of cocaine. The oculist told me that a $3.00 fee is not excessive if cocaine has to be used—as it did have to be last October. I'd like to know why I get things in my eyes about 3 times oftener than anybody else!

Thanks in advance for the cuttings you mention. "Julie Logan" was recently syndicated in the Providence Sunday Journal;[3] & I found it rather clever in parts, though marred by the usual Barrie artificiality & mannerisms.

With best wishes—
Yrs most sincerely,
H P

Notes

1. Lillian D. (Phillips) Clark (1856–1932) died 3 July.

2. CAS's "A Night in Malnéant" never appeared in a periodical and was first published in his *The Double Shadow.*

3. J. M. Barrie, *Farewell, Miss Julie Logan.*

[278] [ALS]

July 16, 1932

Dear A W:—

I surely appreciate your kind words of sympathy—& Brobst will, also, when he hears them. I expect to see him tonight. Everything hereabouts is in more or less of a state of upheaval, but signs of settling down are appearing. It is melancholy to see old, familiar arrangements change. Much old family furniture is not having to be sold or given away—just as it has been at each previous contraction of our dwindling line. However, my younger aunt & I are cramming as much as possible of my elder aunt's effects into our respective quarters. I am taking two antique tables or stands, & a good many old vases, candlesticks, lacquer boxes, paintings, & other non-bulky things. Of course it makes my room overcrowded from the point of view of perfect taste, but I had rather have my surroundings reminiscent of older & better days than merely tasteful or beautiful in an abstract way. Many talk of the joy & freedom of being without possessions, but I am not enough of a Thoreau to share their point of view. With me, contentment consists in having around me as many as possible of the things I have always been used to—furniture, pictures, & the like. I am not making any radical alteration in the arrangement of my room, since I do not wish to be violently reminded of the loss which has occurred. I am now the custodian of all the old family papers & reliques—wills, records, military & civil commissions, daguerreotypes, miniatures, & the like—many of which, so mixed was their former arrangement, I had never seen before. It will be my endeavour to keep them in better order.

I shall watch the progress of your Halgenau novel with great interest, & think the title is a very effective one. There's nothing objectionable, so far as I can see, in the repeated use of *seasons* in story titles. I'll let you know if I don't receive a copy of your "Atmosphere of Houses." I shall also be infinitely grateful for "Five Alone." I'd like to have copies to keep of some of your serious work—so that I can lend them to various persons who know you only through your W.T. contributions. E. Hoffmann Price, for example, was astonished to learn that your write delicate retrospective fiction in a subtle, unconventional vein.

Like you, I want a permanent copy of Klarkash-Ton's "Night in Malnéant". Yes—I'll make an excuse to drop Wright a line concerning your Sheraton Mirror—avoiding the appearance of log-rolling. I surely hope he'll take the Wind & Telephone later on. Knowing his vacillations, you need never abandon hope. I'll be interested to follow your new collaborated series, since I know Cantabridgian geography quite well. My younger aunt—the one still surviving—lived in Cambridge 20 years.

The other day I heard for the first time from my fellow-Rhode Islander Hugh B. Cave, who is spending the summer in Boston. He wants me to join a new organisation of pulp hack-writers (of which the gifted Arthur J. Burks appears to be the head, & which is possibly patterned upon the Authors' League) called the American Fiction Guild—but since the dues are 10 bucks per year, & since I am virtually out of the field in question, I am so far resisting this lure. However, Cave is very pleasant, & I shall probably meet him when he returns to Pawtucket (Providence's northerly neighbour) in the autumn—or before, perhaps, if I accept my friend Cook's invitation & take a Boston trip to mitigate the prevailing nerve-strain. ¶ Best wishes—

Yr obt H P

[279] [ALS]

On the Cliffs overlooking the
Boundless Atlantic-Newport
July 25, 1932

Dear A W:—

The local steamboats plying Narragansett Bay are just now engaged in one of their periodic rate wars, hence I am benefited by an unprecedentedly cheap means of reaching one of my favourite antiquarian havens—old Newport, with the winding, cobbled streets, centuried wharves, slim white steeple (1726), ancient brick colony-house (1739), stately city hall (1760), classic Redwood Library (1749), hoary Jewish synagogue (1763), & sundry vast-chimney'd mansions dating back to 1673. It usually costs from $1.00 to $1.25 for the round trip by boat (the busses soak you $1.20 *each way!*), but now it is down to *50¢*. As a result, I'm making frequent trips—just as I do to my good old river-bank—taking my black bag of working materials along & writing on the boat (2-hr. sail) & on the Newport cliffs after I get through exploring the time-mellowed town (founded 1639). I am picking up a better coat of tan than I got in all the trip to New Orleans, & am acquiring the most maritime orientation that I've had in years.

Glad to hear the news—& good luck with the Widow Halgenau! I'll let you know if the P.S. doesn't supply me within 10 days—meanwhile, many thanks for writing them. Glad *Trend* continues to take your material. I guess they'll survive a while, Loveman or no Loveman; & I'm encouraging young Strauch to send them some verses. Hope Cataract retains enough eyesight to take your better story—& that Wright may have an unexpected lucid interval regarding "The Curse of Ai".

Have heard from Cave again. He's admirably pleasant, & I feel sure I'll enjoy meeting him. He had a personal talk with Bates the other day, & says the S.T. market is somewhat more open than it has been earlier this summer. He also says that B. has a dislike of accepting anything Wright has rejected—hence advises me to look sharp to MSS. which have been to Bro. Farnsworth—since the latter has the habit of covering them with half-imperceptible red pencil marks. Also—it never does to depreciate a MS. of one's own to Bates. He's very temperamental & suggestible. I must look up Canevin's story in Adventure, which he mentioned to me some time ago. His recent W.T. thing was a bit vague, though it appealed to me because of the accurate Flatbush geography.[1] I lived in Flatbush during the first half of my two-year metropolitan sojourn. Haven't read his effort in the new S.T. Belknap warns me that his new S.T. story is shamefully mutilated by Bates.[2] It certainly does not do to send that bird any really serious work.

This Swanson surely is a curious sort of anthropological specimen, with all the elephantine causticity of the narrow & ignorant. However, he returned all my material—loaned magazines & manuscripts—honestly & civilly enough. There's no use paying any attention to primates of that calibre—hence I fancy the policy of a mature mind would be to forget all about him.

Today is certainly glorious, & this trip is about the best half-dollar's worth I've seen in a long while! I am on the eastward cliffs, with nothing but water between me & the year-old republic of Spain. Looking northeast, I can see the green shores of the Sachurst peninsula, crowned by the magnificent Gothic tower (by Ralph Adams Cram) surmounting the chapel of St. George's school. Farther east—if I wanted to walk out on the peninsula—is to be found the rock seat in the cliffs where Dean Berkeley loved to sit & read & write during his Newport sojourn of 1729–1732. The boat gives me 6 hrs. & 15 minutes here—11:30 a.m. to 5:45 p.m. I really hate to go home! Meanwhile my surviving aunt is off on a much-needed trip of relaxation to Cape Cod.

And so it goes. Best wishes—

Yr obt Grandsire

H P

Notes

1. Henry S. Whitehead, "Seven Turns in a Hangman's Rope," *Adventure* (15 July 1932); "Mrs. Lorriquer," *WT* (April 1932).

2. *Strange Tales of Mystery and Terror* (October 1932): Henry S. Whitehead, "Sea Tiger"; FBL, "In the Lair of the Space Monsters."

[280] [ALS]

River Bank [August? 1932]

Dear A W:—

Congratulations on the O. Henry Memorial mention![1] May such things come thick & fast! Meanwhile your multifarious activities, serious & commercial, continue to proceed in bewildering volume. May they all succeed. I was vaguely reminded of your delicately reminiscent work the other day when reading a volume presented to me some time ago—"Barrie Marvell", by Charles Vin[c]e. You have probably known it for ages—but if not, I'd be glad to lend it to you. The author catches the wistful wonder of early childhood in what I think to be a marvellously effective fashion.

Hope you can get an entree to a 3¢-per-word detective market. Once you have access, you can be trusted to keep 'em supplied! Cave is very clever, but probably has no great wish to become an artist. His remarkable commercial success evidently satisfies him for the nonce. Price, too, is getting into that class now that he is trying to depend financially on writing.

I've now read scraps in the new S.T., & agree that it's one of the worst yet. Sonny Belknap is worried because his cheque doesn't come—but I tell him I think the Claytons are a reasonably responsible bunch. I'm trying to think of a tactful way to speak of "Sea-Tiger" in writing H S! Klarkash-Ton's tale follows a formula used too many times before, & makes no great atmospheric contribution to it.[2]

The other day I had a compliment which left a very pleasant taste, & reminded me of my old writing days. A musician by no means unknown—Harold S. Farnese of the Los Angeles Institute of Musical Art (graduate of the Paris Conservatory & winner of their 1911 Prize for Composition)—wrote to ask if he might set music to two of my Yuggothian Fungi—"Mirage" & "The Elder Pharos."[3] Naturally, I told him to go to it—for what he said of my work in general, & of its effect on him, was highly flattering. Perhaps a pair of mediocre verses may be the means of calling two musical masterpieces into being!

Wish you could get east with your distinguished collaborator & his mother—for there's a lot to show you around here! I hope to repeat the Newport trip—probably with my guest of this week, James F. Morton, curator of the Paterson Museum. We may go all the way to Block Island, which I have never visited despite my lifelong residence here. On Saturday W. Paul Cook will be down from Boston to make it a trio.

Whitehead is still urging me to make a permanent transfer to Florida at once, while my health is still good, but I fancy the old river bank & other local reminders of my childhood & ancestry will keep me hereabouts a few years longer—until the winters begin to leave me a more complete wreck than they now do. It seems foolish to stick in a climate where only two months—mid-June to mid-August—are comfortable for me, & where half the days of winter make it impossible for me to venture outdoors, but when one has a strong geographic sense the precepts of physiological rationality often have to be set at defiance. Still—in about a decade I fear the northern winter will be definitely too much for the Old Gentleman!

I'm eager to see "Five Alone" in print as well as the prologue to "Still is the Summer Night". You are surely laying the foundations for solid literary achievement, & in the course of time all these isolated items will be consolidated into definite books—as you are now doing with "Evening in Spring."

With every good wish—

Yr most obt Grandsire

H P

Notes

1. There is nothing by AWD cited in the 1931 or 1932 volumes.

2. CAS, "The Hunters from Beyond," *Strange Tales of Mystery and Terror* (October 1932).

3. Farnese set the two sonnets from *Fungi from Yuggoth* (*WT* February–March 1931) to music, but HPL neither heard nor saw the finished work. See *SL* 4, facing p. 159, for a page from Farnese's "The Elder Pharos."

[281] [ANS][1]

[Postmarked Newport, R.I.,
5 August 1932]

Behold The Horror's abiding-place! Many of the Tcho-Tchos found harbourage in this rift after the Elder Ones obliterated Aloazar. Glorious day—& distinguished company.—Grandpa H P

Graciously deign to accept an added word of greeting from this obscure satellite of the Lovecraftian orb.

James F. Morton

Notes

1. Front: Purgatory, Newport, R.I.

[282] [ALS]

[mid-August 1932]

Dear A W:—

Thanks exceedingly for the carbon of your new novel's introduction. To my mind it is a remarkably poignant piece of writing—full of atmosphere & portentousness—& I don't think there could possibly be a better introduction to the Halgenau tragedy. I hope the novel will land—but even if it doesn't just now it probably will some time. You are undoubtedly laying a really sound literary foundation. I am returning this MS., since you will probably wish to lend it to others.

I am sending "Barrie Marvell" under separate cover. To me it seems a work of unusual charm, though you may find it lacking in subtlety. No hurry whatever about its return. Let me know if the new British anthologies are any good. Hope the new Buchan book[1] will be in the same class with "Witch Wood." And hurrah for the end of Arthur Machen's lifelong poverty![2] Wish I could land a pension of some sort to avert coming disaster. That cinema "White Zombie"[3] has been here, but according to critics it was stereotyped & worthless—hence I didn't bother to attend.

No use to send Satrap Pharnabazus "The Shunned House", for he gave it an exhaustive & definitive turn-down seven years ago. Loose sheets of the book have been salvaged, but still remain stored at Cook's sister's house without any prospect of disposal. I wish he'd get me a dozen or so sets the next time he's up there—but he always forgets it. As time passes, though, I think less & less of that story.

Sorry your new story parallelled an earlier author's work. Something odd befell a client of mine the other day—involving a story-element which *I* had intended & introduced under the impression that it was strictly original with me. The tale was sent to Handsome Harry, & he rejected it on the ground that the element in question (the act of an insect dipping itself in ink & writing on a white surface with its own body) formed the crux of another tale which he *had* just accepted.[4] Hell's bells—& I thought I'd hit on an idea of absolute novelty & uniqueness! Now I'm hoping that my client will land with Wright before the S.T. item appears, for otherwise there will be a suspicion of plagiarism from the latter.

So Wandrei is coming east, eh? The little rascal! He didn't notify any of the eastern gangsters about it! I hope he can get to Providence. There's a story by his brother in the new W.T., but I haven't had a chance to read it yet. No doubt you received the card from Morton & me—sent from Newport. Cook couldn't get around after all. Sorry that none of your clan can make the East this summer. When you do come, Grandpa will have plenty to shew you!

No—you're wrong about Florida. It is probably the most all-around healthful state in the Union. When the British took it over in 1763 they were astonished by the number of centenarians in St. Augustine. Nothing could be worse for me than cold weather—or the indoor regime which it makes mandatory. The only *continuous* feeling of vigour I've ever had was in Florida & New Orleans. Nor is the northern climate growing warmer. Warm & cold winters probably recur in cycles obscurely connected with solar radiation, but there have been no permanent changes of climate since the recession of the ice cap some 20,000 years ago.

Well—be good. Yr. obt grandsire

H P

Notes

1. John Buchan, *The Gap in the Curtain* (1932).

2. Machen had received a Civil List pension of £100 a year.

3. *White Zombie* (Halperin/United Artists, 1932), directed by Victor Halperin; starring Bela Lugosi, Madge Bellamy, and Joseph Cawthorn..

4. Hazel Heald, "Winged Death," *WT* (March 1934). It is not known what story Bates had accepted. Possibly it was a story that was accepted for *Strange Tales* but was not published in the final issue of the magazine (January 1933).

[283] [ALS]

[late August 1932]

Dear A W:—

Your programme of serious work is surely formidable, & I don't think you need to worry if you fail to come up to some preconceived standard of speed. Sorry your colleague Mrs. Latimer, whose criticisms I recall you greatly valued, did not survive. I'll be looking for "Red Hands" next Thursday, & hope to see "The Carven Image" (alas! too deeply carven by editorial mandate!) in the course of time. Good luck with the others.

As for "The Shunned House"—it was mentioned as recently as 1928, & Wright still seemed to adhere to his basis of 1925. I don't feel like hawking any products about to editors who feel as coolly toward them as does Satrap Pharnabazus, so fancy I'll let the thing rest in oblivion. My nerves need a complete freedom from contact with cheap editorial psychology! Bates's opinion of your work is typical. I give the whole damn tribe of them up!

I'm having quite a fight with Hugh B. Cave on the subject of literary motivation. When I mentioned Belknap's resentment at Bates's cuts in "Space Monsters", he came back with a rather unsympathetic rejoinder, as if an author were an ass to mind the mutilation of his products—at least, in the pulp field—& spoke of writing as a purely commercial game in which no one ought to pay too much attention to what he has written. All this, to me, was as a red rag to the proverbial bull—so I sailed into him & told him that not everybody could be satisfied to grind out colourless junk which could be slashed without harm & forgotten on the morrow. He replied with more hard-boiled arguments, & corroborated old Doc Johnson's philistine dictum by averring that no one but a genius or an idiot writes from any but a mercenary motive. Naturally, this got Grandpa going again—& in no mild vein. I used you as the classic example of one with the rare gift of writing popular stuff with your left hand while your right turns out genuine literature. At present the combat is rather a draw—for Cave seems to differ less (except emotionally) from my position, at bottom, than either he or I thought he did. He says that "Victor Rousseau"[1] is a case rather like you—an accomplished writer under his real name (whatever that is) yet a prolific fount of pot-boilers under the familiar alias. I wonder who the deuce he is? I didn't want to ask Cave to betray any confidences, so didn't ask him. Whoever he is, his worst is no worse than your worst. I suspect that Cave & I will have some heated oral arguments when he gets back to Rhode Island!

Young Melmoth the Wandrei expects to get around here next month, & I shall certainly be glad to see him. Haven't had a glimpse of him since 1929. Strauch of Allentown also hopes to be here in Septr. to see Brobst & me—making quite a social season, all in all.

Glad to hear of your new literary acquisitions. I think you'll find "Barrie Marvell" distinctly interesting. The author—Charles Vince—is absolutely unknown to me. Ever hear of him?

Well—on Tuesday I depart for Boston, Wednesday Cook & I will be seeing the eclipse from either Newburyport or Portsmouth, & Friday night—diis volentibus[2]—I shall be hopping off for Montreal & Quebec. Quite a programme—but bad weather would play the devil with all of it.

Best wishes

Your obt Grandpa

H P

[P.S.] Just recd. a copy of the new British edition of the Hammett anthology. Very prepossessing.

Notes

1. Victor Rousseau was the pseudonym of Victor Rousseau Emanuel (1879–1960), prolific American author of pulp fiction who published serious novels under his real name.
2. "If the gods are willing."

[284] [ANS][1]

[c. early September 1932]

Hail, Comte d'Erlette! Saw the eclipse Wednesday under fine conditions at Newburyport.

¶ Montreal is a fine city, but not as antiquarianly fascinating as Quebec. I move on tonight—& Quebec in the morning. Shall be home Thursday—

when I expect Strauch up from Allentown.

Regards—

Yr obt grandsire

H P

Notes

1. Front: Chateau de Ramezay, Montreal, Canada.

[285] [ALS]

Septr 12[, 1932]

Dear A W:—

Just a word of thanks for the generous & keenly-appreciated bundle amidst the prevailing rush. The cuttings were highly interesting, & the books promise to be—while I am delighted at having a permanent copy of "Five Alone." Again—most abundant thanks!

As postcards have apprised you, I saw the eclipse under ideal conditions, & had a highly pleasurable jaunt to Montreal & Quebec . . . . . in the footsteps, as it were, of your friend & his mother. Montreal is a delightful town, though its antiquities are confined to a brief strip along the waterfront. Quebec, as always, proved absorbingly fascinating. On this occasion I took a 'bus trip around the Isle of Orleans, & beheld a vast amount of absolutely unspoiled old French countryside with ancient curve-eaved cottages & white villages clustering around silver-steepled parish churches. On the homeward trip I stopped off again at Boston & took a side trip to ancient Marblehead.

I reached home just in time to welcome young Strauch, who had come from Allentown to visit Brobst & me. He is a delightful youth—slim, dark, handsome, & extremely brilliant—& I believe he will go far in the poetic field. I showed him the historic & antiquarian high spots of the town, & took him through the famous Harris Collection of Poetry in the Brown Univ. library. He is now in Boston visiting friends. I was extremely sorry he could not spend a longer time here.

Tomorrow Wandrei is due here. He intended to come last week, but got himself so sunburned that he had to cancel all engagements & call in a doctor! I hope he won't have to postpone the visit a second time!

Your "slackened" programme is more strenuous than most persons' overspeeded programmes, hence I fancy you needn't worry about it. Here's hoping the percentage of acceptances will be high. Glad the Sheraton Mirror was well received. I asked all the gang to speak an apparently casual good word for it when the right chance came.

Farnese—the man who wrote music for my Yuggothian Fungi—is urging me to attempt some sort of fantastic opera libretto or musical drama to go with his melodies, but I don't think I will.[1] Composition of that sort is beyond me—

& I'd only make an ass of myself if I tried anything so ambitious & sustained.

By the way—are you on the lookout for book bargains? Little Belknap, oppressed by the spectre of poverty, is selling his library batch by batch; & is asking me to distribute catalogue sheets (vide enc.) among my bibliophilic correspondents. Conceivably, you may find an item or two to your liking.

And so it goes. Hades, but I'll never be able to answer the letters that piled up during my absence!

Best wishes—

H P

Notes

1. Farnese's proposed that he and HPL collaborate on a musical drama in one act set on Yuggoth to have been called *Fen River*.

[286] [ANS][1]

[Postmarked Providence, R.I.,
14 September 1932]

Dear August—

Not "Five Alone", but two alone. Did I tell you I saw Fadiman at S & S's? He is expecting your novel sometime this fall. Lovecraft & I have redecided that you are destined for a great future.

Donald

Greetings, O Comte d'Erlette! Too bad you aren't here to absorb the flattering prophesies!

—Grandpa H P

Notes

1. Front: University and Manning Hall, Brown University. Card addressed by DAW.

[287] [ALS]

[late September 1932]

Dear A W:—

Melmoth the Wandrei has, alas, departed; & old age is settling down to the stagnation of hiemal imprisonment. His visit, unfortunately, could not overlap Strauch's—the latter youth having missed him by two days. Young Melmoth was delayed & handicapped by a bad case of sunburn—which prevented any ambitious pedestrianism during his stay. One day, too, was spoilt by a torrential rainstorm—which transformed most of the city to a lake & broke all weather-bureau records. I was sorry the Wanderer could not tarry longer, & hope he can get here again before he leaves the East—even though a winter visit is not likely to have many outdoor features.

Sorry that Wright has been so negligent with cheques—but all the editors seem to be irregular these days. Belknap, though, has at last been paid by Clayton—his cheques amounting to $200.00.

Yes—the trip was certainly a success in every way, even though it has left me distressingly broke. When I was young I'd have demanded more luxury—simply because that was the only sort of travel I knew about—but in later years a man of sense is glad of any chance to see what he wants to see, even though a bit of merely material discomfort be the price.

As for Farnese—I'm not turning his proposition down, but am merely telling him candidly of my total lack of experience in the dramatic field. I doubt, however, if anything can come of the idea—since no accomplished composer would wish to tack his melodies on to the creaking libretto of a novice wholly unversed in dramatic technique. It's better not to attempt anything too ambitious, & I fancy the wiser course is to let Farnese find an abler collaborator.

Your programme certainly does not look like that of a hampered & harassed man! Bless my soul, but where do you get all the excess energy? Glad some of the more serious pieces are finding appropriate placement—& abundant congratulations on the major & minor O'Brien honours.[1] Keep it up, Son! I'll wager you'll have three-starrings in the O'B. annuals right along from now onward. As for your wordage—my god, Child, but how many typewriters do you wear out per day?

Glad Schorer may find something in the Belknapian Book Bargain Bazaar—although I think Sonny Belknap is a little idiot to break up his carefully assembled library just to get a few spare dollars which are, after all, a mere drop in the bucket. If it were giving him any dependable income, it would be different—but as it is, he's only postponing a crisis a week or two more; for when the money's spent he'll be in just as bad a fix as before—& minus his books.

I'm utterly behind on all my work—travel, guests, correspondence, & a hell of a sick headache (harbinger of colder weather & indoor imprisonment!) having kept me otherwise engrossed. Price wants me to collaborate on some sort of a tale, but I haven't even had a chance to look at as yet.

Enclosed is an echo of the amateur journalistic activity which I can't quite bring myself to forego. Needn't bother to return it, since I have a godly supply of copies.[2]

With every good wish, & renewed congratulations on the O'Brien honour—Yr obt grandsire

H P

Notes

1. AWD's "Old Ladies" received a two-star rating and "Nella" a one-star rating in Ed-

ward J. O'Brien's *The Best Short Stories of 1932* (New York: Dodd, Mead, 1932), p. 336.
2. *Further Criticism of Poetry* (1932), a lengthy criticism of recent amateur verse. The ms. of the essay is titled "Notes on Verse Technique" (18 April 1932).

[288] [ALS]

Octr 11 1932

Dear A W:—

Klarkash-Ton's tale has much charm, & Satrap Pharnabazus was certainly an ass (as usual) to reject it. I hope it lands somewhere sometime. C A S has recently made a completion to the unfinished 3d Episode of Vathek which I consider marvellously clever.[1] I am hoping Wright will take it—using the Beckfordian beginning as a reprint—but I rather fear he won't. Your letter anent the Oct. W.T. is very much to the point—& I hope it will do some good. I haven't had a chance to glance either at that or at the current issue—my programme congestion being the worst in history.

The Richet article[2] is about what one would expect from the author—sincere but unconvincing. He overlooks the significant fact that only a very few reputable men of science endorse the occult—& (in view of the known facts of human credulity) adopts a false psychological principle in attaching so much importance to the belief of those few. Palladino,[3] by the way, was a notorious fake thoroughly exposed & discredited in her day. Richet is disingenuous in his statement that all denials of the occult are purely *a priori*. There are certain fundamental probabilities involved, & moreover, all positive experiment has been negative. Case after case of alleged occultism has been traced to error, deception, or unconscious falsification, while virtually every kind of "manifestation" has been duplicated by materialistic investigators & prestidigitators. Finally, there is an unanswerable argument in the lack of use made by "occultists" of their alleged power. If these people could really divine hidden things, past, present, & future, they would be able to solve the unsolved, predict real events, & profit by their ability. None has ever done so. All the major events of history are unpredicted surprises.

Glad the poetry article pleased you. Amateur journalism is slowly on the up-grade, though (not being an occultist) I can't predict how far it will ever get. No—I don't know of any executive minds among the personnel.

Hope you'll continue in your literary successes. "Farway House", "Selina Markesan", & "Still is the Summer Night" surely constitute a full-sized programme! Hope to see the entire & definitive "Evening in Spring" in the course of time.

I'll keep "Mystery at the Blue Villa"[4] in mind as a reading item. Things pile up thick & fast!

Glad you've had some good weather. It's getting too cold for Grandpa! No more outdoor reading & writing for old gentlemen, though I hope to take a few brisk walks in the woods & fields when the foliage becomes autumnally multicoloured. Then the long night of hibernation! Hell, but I wish I were starting for St. Augustine or Key West! Hope your incipient cold proves only transient. There's quite an epidemic of coryzal snuffling hereabouts.

Best wishes—

Yr most obt Grandsire

H P

Notes

1. RHB published William Beckford's "The Story of the Princess Zulkais and the Prince Kalilah" in *Leaves* No. 1 (Summer 1937): 1–16, followed by CAS's "The Third Episode of Vathek" as "Conclusion to Wm. Beckford's Story of Princess Zulkais & Prince Kalilah," 17–24.

2. Charles Richet (1850–1935), French physiologist and advocate of occultism and parapsychology. The article in question may be "Death and Its Mystery," *Living Age* No. 314 (26 August 1922): 521–24.

3. Eusapia Palladino (1854–1918) was a medium who appeared to have the power to levitate herself and to display other psychic powers. She convinced many of her psychic abilities, but was exposed as a fraud during séances held in Cambridge, England, and New York City. See H. Carrington, *Eusapia Palladino and Her Phenomena* (London: Werner Laurie, 1909).

4. By Melville Davisson Post.

[289] [ALS]

10 Barnes St.,

Providence, R.I.,

Octr 28, 1932

Dear A W:—

I have digested "Farway House" with the utmost pleasure & appreciation, & believe it fully sustains the high standards of the d'Erlette tradition. Your eye for setting, atmosphere, mannerism, & character is an enviable one, & these serious products of yours certainly indicate that you are on the road toward a genuine place in literature. It is hard to pick flaws with so excellent a performance, & anything I could say would be of the most minor sort. I might suggest that the coincidence of the doctor's arrival at the exact moment of Mrs. Bord's fatal accident is a little too extraordinary to be passed off by the suggestion of supernaturalism given—although such coincidences certainly have occurred. The only question is whether or not it is too atypical for fictional effectiveness. Lesser comments might concern the dialect. You have Thorne, a former college instructor, use *like* ungrammatically at least once, & also put a curious & foreign-sounding phrase—"You must go back to the house, *not so?*"—into the mouth of the doctor, whose first name of *Jasper* plainly indicates Anglo-Saxon origin. Also—it is hard to associate the Roman Catholic religion with a presumably Anglo-Saxon family using such given names as *Phineas* & *Abner.* These names are so overwhelmingly characteristic of the Protestant-dissenting old-American stock that their presence in a Romish family seems incongruous. Whether such an anomaly developed on Wisconsin soil you know better than I, but unless you have historical warrant for the combination, you had better change either the names or the denomination. If the Farways are supposed to be of New England stock, they must be Protestants; for Catholicism was unknown & abhorred among New Englanders up to a period long after the settlement of the West. If, on the other hand, they are a Maryland family, (except in Maryland, Anglo-Saxon Catholics were almost non-existent in America up to a generation or so ago, though there were perhaps a few in New York) or a family of non-English origin, (Irish Catholic families might bear the name of Farway) they would be extremely unlikely to give any such names as Phineas or Abner. In later generations the blending of different stocks & traditions might well give rise to apparently contradictory appellations, but Phineas is so old (an aged man even in the day of the horse & buggy) that he would necessarily go back to something like the pioneer generation. However—as I said before, these are minor, incidental points. The story itself is really splendid—vivid, convincing, & full of a certain brooding inevitability which forms the essence of real tragedy. I certainly hope this tale will land in a suitable medium. It has the real stuff in it, & I don't know of anyone else in the group who could have written so effective a thing.

I read Schorer's article[1]—& the cutting about it—with great interest. That school certainly was a curious institution, & I don't wonder that Schorer resigned his position after the first year. I doubt if many of the best military schools—like the Virginia Military Institute—can be quite as arbitrary & hypocritical as this singular establishment. Glad that the author is getting to be less dependent on his energetic colleague as time goes by!

Thanks for the Klarkash-Ton story. I haven't had time to see the final S.T. or to read the last two issues of Weird. Most who have seen the new *Strange* seem to regard it as the least worthless of all the numbers. Glad your Wind-Walker (a favourite of mine) got published before the crash.

I'll tell you shortly how Price likes "Five Alone" & "Old Ladies". His taste is by no means flawless, but it will certainly give him a jolt to discover a Derleth utterly antipodal to the one he is familiar with. He, like Cave, seems to have sold out to commercialism, & I'm trying to urge him to reserve a part of himself for genuine literary creation. However—not many could preserve a duality like yours. Wandrei is going to try it, but I doubt whether he can maintain it as he hopes. I'm anxious to see his first venture in serious, non-weird prose.[2] And by the way—little J. Vernon Shea has started up writing realistic, d'Erlettesque material of surprising excellence. I can hardly believe it is the same boy who was grinding out such impossible weird attempts only a year ago. His collegiate studies have obviously helped him vastly, & it is unfortunate that family finances will not allow him to go back this autumn. I'm advising him to send you his latest opus—"The Tin Roof"—for a critical opinion.

I shall surely be glad to see the revised version of "Evening in Spring." Yes—I think the title "Book of Little Memories" is an extremely apt one for the opening section; much more appropriate than "Confessions." As for "A Town is Built"—20,000 to 5,000 words seems rather a radical cut, but I presume you know what you're about. Possibly you will save some of the excised portions for use elsewhere. Hope the newer material duly landed with *Pagany*.

I read Morrow's book years ago, but unlike you, did not find the tales very fascinating. They seemed to me too mechanically clever—not atmospherically convincing enough. The one I remembered most was that concerning a headless living body.[3] I haven't seen any of the other new volumes you've acquired or ordered. No—I fancy the gang aren't represented at all in the new "Not at Night", for nobody's been notified, & cheques usually precede publication.

Best wishes—

Yr obt Grandsire

H P

Notes

1. Unidentified.

2. *Invisible Sun,* a mainstream novel, partly autobiographical. See further letter 304.

3. W. C. Morrow, *The Ape, the Idiot and Other People* (1897). HPL first read the collection in the fall of 1925 at the suggestion of Samuel Loveman (HPL to L. D. Clark, 27 September 1925; ms., JHL). He refers to "The Monster Maker."

[290] [ALS]

[early November 1932]

Dear A W:—

Your extremely interesting letter of the 28th ult. duly arrived, & really contains matter for research & controversy beyond the power of any doddering old layman like myself.

About the Farway family—you don't need to specify their Maryland origin, but you certainly ought to divest its members of praenomina which unmistakably suggest something else. That is my point. The names Phineas & Abner are, through historic tradition, inextricably associated with the Protestant New England Yankee; & scarcely any reader can fail to notice the glaring incongruity betwixt them & the family in which they are represented as occurring. It is an historical false note—& what is the use of deliberately lessening the perfection of a splendid piece of writing by the introduction of known false notes? Why wouldn't it be better to let the Farways be—for example—Peter & William, or John & Richard; which would be consistent with a Maryland origin? My objection is made from the point of view of historic consistency, but you will get another & even stronger set of objections (if I mistake not) from your Catholic readers, who will recognise these Yankee names—Phineas (from Grecian myth) & Abner (from the Old Testament) as utterly uncharacteristic of the punctilious papists which the Farways are represented as being. It is said—& you surely ought to know better than I—that no Catholics are allowed to be baptised with names other than those of recognised *saints*; & surely no Saints Phineas or Abner ever graced the minor pantheon of Rome! To this you will reply that the gentlemen had saintly *middle* names which they did not use—Phineas Aloysius or Abner Patrick or something like that—but in counter-response I will have to insist that such an explanation sounds somehow distinctly strained. Old records do not teem with such hybrid appellations as Adoniram Charles or Melchizidek Dennis—for any parents who felt it necessary to give their child a saint's name would not be likely to overshadow it with any austere product of Puritan archaeology. When we see names like Caleb, Cyrus, Meshek, Resolved, Asaph, Hezekiah, Abner, Benoni, Jason, Phineas, Joshua, Nahum, Nathaniel, Elisha, Elijah, &c. &c. in any part of the United States, we may safely say that the chances are 98 to 2 that they imply origin in Puritan New England—where, remembering the persecution-pyres of Bloody Mary's reign, old Gov. Endecott even cut the red cross out of England's banner rather than harbour a symbol of the "Babylonish Superstition". You can do as you like—but it's certainly a damn shame to detract from a fine piece of work by a definitely anti-historic touch which jars through constant recurrence.[1] Incidentally—it is worthy of note that Rhode Island never used the typical Puritan names to anything the extent that the more orthodoxly Puritan colonies did. They were very much in the minority here—plain old English names, & various ancestral surnames, being largely given instead. On my Rhode Island side I have one Jeremiah, one Enoch, one Eleazar, & one Asaph as scaled against any number of Thomases, Johns, James's, Stephens, Benjamins, & so on.

As for the second point—the matter of dialect—you know Wisconsin better than I, but the use of *like* for *as* or *as if* is so rare among literate persons in New England that I never knew such a solecism existed until I began reading Southern dialect pieces. Today the lower middle classes are slowly falling into it because of its prevalence in the cheap printed, cinematic, & radio matter which they imbibe, but even they did not use it to any extent until the present decade. It entered the Middle West earlier than it did New England, but would it have been a common Wisconsinism at the period of your story—

presumably around 1900? Of course, the Farways may have brought it from Maryland, which is close to the northern edge of the zone where it originated. Incidentally—the city of Charleston is almost entirely free from this & other careless Southernisms both syntactical & accentual; probably because of frequent sea communication with England, & relative separation (by febrile & malarial marsh belts) from the provincial hinterland. Concerning Dr. Grendon's borrowed idiom—only a close Wisconsin observer could properly pass on its truth to life. I know a man in Milwaukee (himself half of German ancestry) & another in Appleton, & never detected the least departure from English idiom in them. Much would depend on the doctor's age when he came to the community, I fancy. That idioms are contagious is undeniable, many loan-words & forms like the needless rising inflection of the Irish & the redundant Germanic *already* having passed into the "American vulgate" in certain parts of the country—to say nothing of the obviously negroid quality of modern Southern speech.

As for the matter of coincidence in fiction—you'll make a mistake if you try to use it as a plot element because of any new theory of yours. Just as I said before, coincidences do indeed occur; but it is so seldom that anything of any importance happens to hinge on them, that they cannot be considered as sufficiently typical for general artistic use. Whenever we meet with one in fiction it strikes us as unnatural—& of course the chances are in such a case that it has been dragged arbitrarily in by the author as a short-cut to a neat & vivid theatrical situation. The *realistic* use of coincidence would have to be confined to one or two instances of minor importance in the course of a long sweep of time—& even those instances ought not to involve any very vital consequences. The only two cases where a coincidence of vital consequences would be in order would be (a) a frankly strange story in which the coincidence itself, treated as a wonder, might form the central theme, & (b) a saga with a wide canvas, covering many generations, in the course of which a single vitally resulting coincidence might not seem so conspicuously out of place. All this, of course, refers to cases of *genuine* coincidence. Vastly more frequent, & therefore admissible in much higher proportion, are the cases of *pseudo-coincidence* in which there is either a *hidden element in common* behind the causation of the *apparently* independent coincident elements, or in which the events *did not actually happen as publicly believed*—the true facts having been edited & embellished by unconscious selective or transpository memory, or by that tendency toward half-conscious artistic fact-modelling which affects all mankind & which is exercised largely in fields where folklore & traditional credulity make the direction of the modelling seem less fallacious & incredible than it often is. Nowadays all psychologists & anthropologists realise the power of folk-beliefs, traditional story-patterns, the sheer limitations of detail-grasping, & the inevitable mutations of repetition, to create whole sets of false yet convincingly deceptive ideas about events past & present, far & near.

Typical myth-forms rise & flourish; & daily events, casually viewed without scientific analysis, are habitually interpreted in terms of them—with insidious & imperceptible twistings of the facts to suit the popular preconceived notions of what `ought to have happened', or `might very well have happened.' Memory is infinitely subject to auto-suggestion, so that a credulous person is led to exaggerate, when anything distinctive *does* happen, whatever vague ideas about such a thing (among an infinity of other things) he may have entertained at some prior time—or conversely, after ardently anticipating a thing, he may later unconsciously expand some not too dissimilar later event into an artificial & subjective identity with the original anticipated thing. Likewise, sheer inventive delusion is common—whereby the subject, having experienced a certain thing, merely imagines that he foresaw it; or, having had a sensation of anticipating something, later on comes to believe that it actually did come to pass. There are, moreover, certain very decided & often irresistible impulses toward mendacity in this province; some of them following patterns fairly well known & classifiable by psychiatrists. It is very significant that people with traditional credulities regarding discredited phenomena often report frequent encounters with such mythical things, whilst the critical & analytical investigator never encounters them. The will or willingness to believe in the impossible leads many to be deceived in cases where others, demanding corroborative evidence when the laws of nature seem to be contravened, do not find the reported marvels to be real. All of which makes it easy to see that the few actual coincidences & accidental anticipations or simultaneous thoughts which do occur in life, are—in popular belief—enormously supplemented by a body of pseudo-coincidences & pseudo-anticipations or telepathies which originates according to recognised illusion-patterns & which consequently plays a distinct part in the thought & feeling of a naive or otherwise credulous community. On this account it is of course perfectly right to record, in a realistic work of fiction, the *frequent popular belief* that some enormous coincidence, foreseeing, telepathic manifestation, or other phase of folklore magic has taken place—provided the author does not try to present it as something which *really has* taken place. While presenting the popular exterior version of what has happened, he ought also to suggest the *actual* state of things—the hidden common cause behind the apparently unrelated events of a coincidence—the type of delusion; mnemonic, reportorial, or otherwise; in an apparent case of second-sight or telepathy—& so on. He can then make convincing what would otherwise strike the rational & disillusioned reader as extravagant.

As for the specific matter in "Farway House"—possibly only the manner of presentation suggested an unlikely coincidence. If it is the custom for a district's physician to make certain rounds which cause him *always* to be relatively near any one of his patients' houses, then his dropping in within a reasonable time before or after an accident does not form so vast an improbability. That is, he is *certain* to be there, whether or not any accident occurs, within a moderate space of time from any hour that an accident would even be likely to occur. Moreover—if he knows that accidents are likely to occur at any given season, he may perhaps make a point of increasing his vigilance—thus eliminating even a suspicion of a coincidence if he chances to come upon an accident not far from the moment of its occurrence. However—in any such case a simple community predisposed to belief in such things as "divine Providence", "fate", "second-sight" & the like would undoubtedly be prone to interpret the occurrence as quasi-magical, eventually—& by su[b]tle, unconscious degrees—remodelling the account of it into a perfect fairy-tale of the sort beloved by Richet. As for your own impressions of magical or telepathic phenomena—I have outlined many times before what I deem the causes, & have suggested that they would take on a different light if you would subject them to realistic analysis—with full realisation that folklore predisposes you toward fantastic & improbable explanations, & that of rigorously scientific thinkers & psychologists, virtually none accept your underlying assumptions. A few *actual* coincidences, plus subconscious selections & transpositions of mnemonic impressions (abetted by a lack of emphatic realisation of how diametrically your traditional folklore assumptions contradict everything that is definitely known of the workings of nature) & certain cases where actual but hidden links betwixt apparently unrelated phenomena* exist, very clearly stand behind your apparent body of mystical contacts with the omniscient infinite—& you would be the first & most eager to recognise that fact if you would only shed your predisposition toward the traditional & the fantastic at the expense of the analytical & the prosaically unpicturesque. I used to have impressions of the unreal & the marvellous when I was small, credulous of the gods of Greece, & inclined to place an exaggerated value on the empirical surface aspect of my perceptions—but I exercise a sense of proportion, recognise man's infinite deceivability, & demand solid objective evidence about things now. Always remember that if the self-styled prophets, ectoplasmists, & mysteriarchs could see all things as they pretend to, they would capitalise their information & become the masters of the planet. I notice that among the biggest of inflated stocks in the Coolidge era—who are now in the bread lines, figuratively or otherwise—the percentage of "psychically sensitive" souls is not at all below the average!

As for your hypothetical case of age-guessing—you beg the question when you say (except in a purely academic fashion) that it is not impossible that an uninformed person will guess correctly the ages of 15 old ladies on

---

*as in the case of others' use of apt phrases which you are on the point of uttering. Here the general course of conversation has suggested—very naturally—the same train of images in the minds of similarly backgrounded participants—with obvious results. Cf. parallel case of Poe's M. Dupin.

sight. In cold truth, a 100% perfect score would be so rare as to be damned near impossible. If the phenomenal coincidence ever *did* occur once in the history of a community, that community* would certainly treat it as something of epochal unusualness. A naive community would insist on a magical explanation, while a sophisticated community would claim that the guesser was either a master showman with secretly obtained information or that he had acquired possession of some hitherto unknown & essentially revolutionary biological secret. In a book the feat would indeed be inadmissible, & justly so—because (aside from vaudeville acts where secret information does exist) it is something which has probably never occurred & probably never will occur. It would be no more admissible to serious, non-fantastic fiction than would be the (academically or potentially possible) despatch of a rocket to the moon. Nor would it be in the least unjust to consider the non-fantastic literary use of such a grotesque quasi-impossibility as overwhelmingly aggravated in ridiculousness & unconvincingness if any vital consequences hinged on it; because, as I have previously pointed out & as you must yourself recognise upon reflection, the number of coincidences which (coincidence upon coincidence!) happen to cover vitally determinative points is infinitely less even than that small-enough number which cover only trivial points. Vital coincidences have occurred in history, but the lives of 99 out of 100 men pass from beginning to end without any such occurrence—hence we may say that they are too essentially non-typical of life to be admissible in serious fiction (which must always have something of the universal in it) except in a very limited way (in sagas covering generations) suggested earlier in this epistle. But as I have said, *pseudo-coincidences* can be used more freely. As a last word, one may say that of course the *exact* rarity of coincidences can scarcely be insisted on mathematically. Also—that one must be careful in defining *what is meant* by an inadmissible coincidence. Certainly, the course of one's life is constantly affected by unforeseen events. If the Titanic hadn't happened to strike an iceberg, this or that person would have had a wholly different life—& so on. What makes a conicidence truly such, & therefore inadmissible in literature, is the precise dovetailing of two streams of unrelated action in which at least one of them follows a course of great exceptionalness in relation to the other. Admittedly the line of demarcation is inexact, but by applying the test of comparison with actual life we may easily recognise certain zones which are obviously admissible, & certain other zones (broad & hazy though the boundary be) which are obviously inadmissible. When a character in a family tragedy becomes an obstacle to the neat solution of certain difficulties, *how likely* is it that he will be removed conveniently by war, accident, shipwreck, or disease? When a man has secured certain papers which must be delivered at a

*i.e., that part which stopped to notice it at all. Of course, most persons glide blindly & insensitively over all the phenomena around them.

certain place at a certain time in order to determine certain important events, *how likely* is it that he will fall over a cliff into the sea (without being pushed) the night before the day of delivery? When a motorist travelling through a lonely desert countryside has a sudden heart attack, *how likely* is it that he will happen to be in front of the only doctor's office in 200 miles? You get the idea, I'm sure. An improbable coincidence is one in which two (or more) events, not commonly associated, but necessarily associated in order to produce a certain very rare event, do achieve the needed association despite the lack of any common causative element behind the separete stretches of causes which bring each to the point of contact. In the case of the stricken motorist, there can be no connexion betwixt the timing of his attack & the position of his car in relation to the house of one whom he did not know until that moment he would wish to employ. That is a sheerly accidental thing which would be *very unlikely* to occur in real life. It *might* occur, but in so small a number of cases that it would not be admissible in serious fiction. In view of the desiderate universality of fiction, I do not think the exclusion is unjust. All told, one may simplify the matter by saying that the realistic author ought to use coincidence only to that extent to which observation shews it as existing in an average slice of real life corresponding in nature & scope with the field of the projected work of fiction. This injunction can hardly arouse disagreement from any rational artist, the only ground for debate being the actual place of coincidence in real life. Close observation & analysis are needed to form any judgment on that point, & these things (all externally prescribed opinions being fundamentally impotent to alter an emotional perspective) are what each artist must exercise for himself.

Little Shea will probably send you "The Tin Roof" before long. He dropped all correspondence for a while (I didn't hear from him for 7 months) & embarked on an orgy of modern reading almost comparable to what you read in a week or I in a lifetime. College did his writing ability an enormous amount of good, & it is deplorable that paternal finance can't float him another year—or all three other years.

The completed "Evening in Spring" will certainly be a work of gratifying size—though I don't envy you the typing. Glad you have some new items under way—& imagine the "Mighty Senator" must be a highly amusing portrayal.[2] Certainly, the democratic fallacy in government produces some fearful & wonderful displays of human monstrosities! Your friend Chapple[3] unburthened himself before a Providence audience last spring, & received some rather pointed comment from both the faculty & student body of Brown University. In matters of current national politics, I have virtually no interest, because I believe that neither major party holds ideals & purposes really relevant to the permanent needs of a beastly industrial civilisation such as blind chance has forced upon the western world. Democracy is a joke in a social group so mechanised & organised that absolutely no one save a trained specialist has any genuine idea of the real nature or effect of any measure under consideration—whilst on the other hand commercial oligarchy is basically fallacious because it ignores the growing problem (aside from all depressions) of permanent technological unemployment. Moreover, such an oligarchy tends to exalt false standards of speed, quantity, & material success at the expense of genuine cultural values. What I'd like to see is a kind of modified fascism, conducted by a group whose dominant purpose is genuine equilibrium rather than excessive profit. Artificially spread-out unemployement, unemployment insurance, old-age pensions, government by commissions of experts, restriction of the franchise through very severe educational tests, (tests that would bar *me* out) replacement of the profit motive by the demand-supplying motive, education for both intelligent industry & cultivated leisure—utopian stuff, which only gawd knows how could ever be secured. All my family have been Republicans since the origin of the party, & Whigs & Federalists before that, but I'm coming to think that the Republican party represents about the most hopelessly obsolescent & least promisingly flexible organisation in the field. At the same time I don't hate Hoover as you & others do. With the outlook & convictions which his natural affiliations have given him, he has done the best he could, which is considerable. I wouldn't vote for him in the present situation, but I'd like to see him set to work under an intelligent fascist government whose policies he wouldn't be able to determine. I fancy the Democratic ticket is the best bet this year.

Glad the new Not at Night has "The Black Stone"—but it isn't a volume I'd be likely to buy.[4] As for the others you mention—don't be too generous! I have "Frankenstein", but not "Shivers, Creeps."[5] Of the contents of the McSpadden anthology, the following tales would be new to me: "Beast with 5 Fingers", "Loom of the Dead", "The Ghoul", "Widow's Mite".[6] Thanks for anything you really want to throw away, but don't dump anything you might want some time.

Congrats on your selection as one of the midwest's two young literary leaders! Wish I could get the text of the address—will it be printed? I told you you'd get there!

Best wishes—

Yr obt Grandsire

H P

Notes

1. AWD did not make the suggested revision.

2. "Lo, the Mighty Senator."

3. Possibly Joe Mitchell Chapple (1867–1950), newspaper and magazine editor and author of novels and political biographies (*Harding the Man,* 1923; *Face to Face with Our Presidents,* 1930), and popular lecturer.

4. Christine Campbell Thomson, *Grim Death*.

5. Philip Allan, ed., *Shivers* (London: Philip Allan, 1932), part of the "Creeps Library."

6. HPL refers to stories in J. Walker McSpadden's *Famous Psychic Stories* (1920): W. F. Harvey, "The Beast with Five Fingers"; E. W. Peattie, "From the Loom of the Dead"; E. W. Blashfield, "Ghoul"; and I. K. Funk, "The Widow's Mite."

[291] [ALS]

Novr. 12, 1932

Dear A W:—

Congratulations on the prospective three-starring of "Five Alone"! It was certainly amply worthy of the honour—& Price liked it much better than "Old Ladies". He was quite impressed with the hitherto unknown d'Erlette represented by three specimens, & is anxious to see more of your work. I shall probably return the completed "Evening in Spring" through him when you send it. That, I imagine, is about as representative of your serious work as any one story could be. As for the O. Henry annual—to which I am properly grateful for its inclusion of my products in its favourable lists—it is certainly not to be compared with O'Brien's. Its whole standard of selection appears to be an artificial one based on conformity to the mechanical conventions of popular commercial fiction. Young Shea says that several of the gang were mentioned last year on its lesser lists. Glad to hear of your new work—& of the landing of "A Ride Home."

As for the arguments of last time—I can't say that your rebuttal causes me to change in any way the position I expressed. However—impetuous youth will have its own way. Go ahead, & let later experience correct such minor carelessnesses & errors as you won't recognise when the old folks tell you about them now. Your work is good enough to float in spite of minor slips on rare unlifelikenesses—& after all, there's really no critic like the author ten years afterward.

Regarding *Phineas* & *Abner*—I must confess that I fail to find any relevance whatever in pre-Reformation usage. Everyone knows that nomenclature was relatively uniform before religious differences arose, & that many of the names afterward mainly appropriated by the extreme Protestant wing were originally scattered throughout the population. All this, however, has nothing whatever to do with the realigned nomenclature of two or three centuries later, especially as practiced in the New World. It is common knowledge that the Dissenting sects seized upon certain names & types of names for constant & frequent bestowal, while these became increasingly rare & finally quite obsolescent among Catholics—& to a less thorough degree among Anglicans. Of course the division was by no means a water-tight one. A large number of names—John, James, &c.—continued to be used freely in common, while one group would occasionally (freely at first, less often as the centuries passed) use some of the names characteristic of the other. Also, subtle differences in usage crept into being on the two sides of the Atlantic—thus *Michael* & *Patrick* ceased to be used by American Protestants some time before 1800, whereas they are still used by Protestants in England. But surveying the whole field broadly, it is easy to see that, in 19th century America, nomenclature had indeed fallen into certain definite group arrangements. While it could hardly be vouched that there were absolutely *no* Michaels in Protestant Vermont, & absolutely *no* Abners among the Catholic families of Maryland, (ancestral usage, extra-territorial connexions, &c. might explain certain departures) it remains an undisputed fact that Michael was an extremely rare & uncharacteristic name for a Vermonter, & that Abner was an extremely rare & uncharacteristic name for a Maryland Catholic. The artist, who depends so much on symbolism & universality, can never—as a matter of acknowledged policy—afford to deal too extensively in the freakishly exceptional unless especially motivated. It is a truism as old as the hills that real life often contains events so extravagant & so untypical of *life in general,* as to be quite valueless & unsuitable for fictional use. It may thus be safely said that when an author sets out to depict characters from a particular region, he certainly has no reason to saddle them with notably uncharacteristic names unless his plot expressly calls for such. The art of choosing such rare & misleadingly untypical names becomes inane, affected, capricious, & frivolous—because there is absolutely no reason for doing it. *Why not* choose a name that is typical? *What motive* would I have for inserting in a story about old Rhode Island people, in which names did not figure in the plot & in which I wished to convey something of the colour of the soil as unobtrusively as possible, the name of *Manuel Perez* as applied to a local native? Yet I know of one old Yankee in Providence who—for reasons best known to novel-reading parents—does bear that romantic appellation. Am I to look for stories from your pen in which Sac Prairie families blossom out with such names as Yussuf, Takamoto, Vladimir, Chang, & N'guru? If there were *any reason* for adopting an exceptional name the case would be entirely different. Lacking such a reason, the deliberate choice of something decidedly untypical & frequently misleading is certainly not to be justified by any interpretation of the rules of normal art. You evade the issue in saying that you could hardly be expected to use footnotes. Naturally there is no reason for adopting a doubtful usage & then cumbrously trying to explain it away. But there is reason to expect an artist not to adopt a doubtful usage in the first place. The fact that not many readers of the MS. have yet noticed the point is hardly a significant one. The artist wants correctness & harmony for their own sakes. With wrong names, the misleading suggestion is there; & when the work reaches the general public there cannot help being many fastidious persons with a clear historic sense who will notice it. Why make a cumbrous mess when you could use the names Peter & William & be done with the matter? What you say about non-saintly Catholic names is indeed interesting in view of opposite assertions I have heard. Am I to infer from your statement that there is absolutely no official ruling of the church touching this matter, & that the customary prevalence of saintly names is merely a matter of traditional usage? As a final observation on this matter—I presume you realise that the space I have consumed has not been for the sake of rectifying this one point. What I am really trying to get at is the general literary principle *behind* the present trivial instance. I think your work is so vital & excellent that if ought not to be vitiated by little flaws springing purely from carelessness, caprice, & youthful cocksureness. But Father Time is the boy to remedy all that!

As for dialect—as I said before, the only real criterion is the actual usage of the region depicted, observed & transcribed at first hand. All my observations were in the way of suggestions—to make you reëxamine your own memory & check up on details, as it were. Certainly, I would be the last person to pose as an authority on the usages of a region whose speech I had never investigated! There was really no *argument,* in the proper sense, in this matter; & if you're sure of your ground there's clearly nothing to do but go ahead!

Regarding the use of coincidence—you'll probably see the fallacy of your present theory later on, or have it pointed out to you by persons whose academic connexions will command your respect. Meanwhile, your actual artistic sense of life will probably partly safeguard you against the pitfalls inherent in your theory. Your instincts will balk at too much extravagance. Remember that I didn't say coincidences are *wholly inadmissible.* I said that they are admissible *only in the proportion in which they genuinely occur in real life.* You must surely agree that it is the duty of the artist to present life in its true proportions. It is deliberate & inexcusable falsification—& contrary to all principles of art—to convey a picture labelled as "real life" in which phenomena are represented as occurring habitually in a proportion in which they never do occur in objective reality. It isn't a question of whether the phenomena occur at all, but of *how often* they occur in the normal course of events. We know that the sun rises & sets—but it would be bad art to represent the sun as rising every six hours. When you plan out a story representing a certain range of time & space, it is your artistic duty to call on your first-hand knowledge of life to try to estimate about what part the element of coincidence would be likely to play in a series of events filling the given limits. The fact that one coincidence might conceivably play a part in this given quota of the event-stream would admittedly justify *one* coincidence in the story—but it wouldn't justify ten or twenty! You can easily see that most writers who rely on coincidence are abysmal pulp hacks who use the device as a short-cut to flashy plot-effects & cheap mechanical climaxes. Possibly, however, you concede all this, & are merely claiming that coincidence occurs oftener in life than it is usually considered to occur. That is a legitimate subject for serious observation & debate. ¶ As for what you consider my "too glib" use of the terms of psychology—that is merely a device to save time & circumlocution. Everybody really knew before, as a matter of plain horse sense, much that modern psychologists make precise & clear, & define in a nomenclature of increased brevity & exactness. Thus it did not take a Freud to make sensible people realise that ghost legends are the result of mistakes, inaccurate reports, instinctive lies & repetitions of habitual stories, bids for notoriety, &c. &c., or that reports of "psychic" communication are the result of people's thinking they've especially thought of something before when some later event makes that part of their general melange of ideas especially significant, &c. &c. Psychology merely codifies the results of age-long insight & supplements it with additional data. The process of shedding supernatural explanations for things has really been going on ever since man began to emerge from the total savage ignorance which gave birth to the original conceptions of "spirit", "deity", & other forms of primitive pseudo-explanation & personification. Each new age sees a little more of the myth-fabric shed. Reactions flare up, but are eventually nullified in the slow drift toward reason. Despite the deep instinct toward lying & self-deception which prompts people to perpetuate as long as they can any superstition for which they retain an attachment, there is a counterbalancing inevitability of the triumph of obvious fact which will ultimately—though with vast slowness, gradualness, & reaction-punctuated unevenness—crumble away the vestiges of superstition & religion among the minority of persons who think at all. Even now it would be illuminating to take a census of believers & non-believers in the occult, & compare the intellectual & cultural status of the two groups, each taken as a whole. I see what you mean when you speak of the fact that scientists have achieved their conclusions as a result of work conducted on the underlying assumption that irregularly reported phenomena are myths, but I do not see any ground for your belief that equally consistent conclusions could be deduced from work conducted on the opposite assumption. The fact is, that early men of science *did* conduct their research on the assumption that the marvellous was true or potentially true; discarding such an assumption only because it failed to justify itself. Thus both angles *have been tried,* & one discarded because it has been revealed as unsatisfactory & inapplicable to observed reality. If today we were to approach all the phenomena of the external world with perfect naiveté & a complete ignorance of preconceived assumptions both scientific-materialistic & traditional-spiritual—yet with a power of fact-perception enabling us to recognise relationships in the world of matter & energy & to avoid the arbitrary & baseless imaginative pseudo-explanations inevitable with primitive man—it seems likely that we would rediscover the general & particular harmonies governing motion, force, & entity, & that we would reconstruct an approximately self-consistent world much like that now commonly recognised. Of the popularly reported things which you dignify with the name of "out-of-the-ordinary" phenomena, a great number would never be observed at all, because they do not exist except in the legends of grandmothers & the folklore of faddists. A much smaller number might be observed & found to have some place in the natural order. And a still more infinitesimal number might be found to exist & defy immediate explanation, though in no way suggesting those explanations contradictory to observed fact & probability which are now advanced by "occult" dupes. As for a serious scientist working today on the assumption that reported occult phenomena are true—not only could no case be made out, but the very process is inconceivable. We have been through that phase & found it a blind alley, & it would be a waste of time to return & repeat the stumblings of our predecessors. However—if anyone were fanatical enough to do this, he would merely arrive in a roundabout way at the materialism of the present. Soberly accepting his occult data & attempting to correlate & build upon them, he would get a certain distance through ingeniously artificial logic & hypothesis—just as Ptolemy ingeniously accounted for the phenomena of the major celestial bodies, as far as the instrumentless ancients could observe them, through a wholly erroneous & now ludicrous system of non-existent "epicycles", "crystalline spheres", & the like. But just as Ptolemy's system gave way & collapsed when it had to be correlated with the growing body of actually observed facts, so would this sober occultist's artificial system collapse the moment it had to be correlated with any extension of real knowledge—since new facts have relationship only to the genuine order of things. The theorist would then find that his system was irreconcilable with observed reality, & would seek to amend it to conform. In so doing, he could not help nothing that certain basic points—the "occult" points—are incapable of reconciliation, while all the other points could be reconciled if these especial points were left out This would naturally lead to a particularly rigid testing of the recalcitrant points. If they held out under all tests, of course, they would have to be retained in spite of all their present irreconcilability. It would be necessary for mankind to discard all his existing conceptions of cosmic organisation in order to form a fresh conception capable of including them. But when the test came to be applied—as indeed it has been applied in the past—it would be found as of yore that the recalcitrant phenomena *could not* stand up under impartial investigation. Not only would it be shewn that alleged instances are mythical or erroneous, but it would be likewise shewn that a strictly material interpretation of the cosmos clearly indicates *why the myths & errors have come into being.* The recalcitrant pseudo-phenomena would be *accounted for* on a plainly verifiable basis contradictory of their reality as popularly reported. When this "debunking" process had been applied to numberless cases & types of cases & found universally operative, it would be only legitimate & sensible to infer that these cases are essentially typical of all cases where the entire structure of the universe seems to be defied by an observed appearance. There may be cases so elusive that the exact causes of the appearance cannot at present be shewn; but in view of the known conditions surrounding the vast majority of equally anomalous cases, it would be frivolous & pedantic to insist that such are essentially different, or that they form an adequate ground for a revision of cosmic conceptions to accomodate them at face value. This, we may safely say, is the road which would have to be traversed by any sober scientist starting out with the assumption that occult marvels are solid realities. The marvels would not stand up under special tests, & in the end he would have to scrap his system in favour of one resting on less assailable & contradictory assumptions. True, many parts of his revised & material theory might have flaws & errors—just as the Tychonic[1] system of the universe, while escaping some of the errors of the Ptolemaic, failed to reach the real truth; & as the original doctrine of Copernicus erred in respect to the distance & relationships of the fixed stars—but it would at least be less remote from the truth than any system resting upon demonstrable error. And thus our broad-minded scientist—repeating in himself the history of science as a heritage of transmitted effort—would come to relinquish his assumption & coincide with those who deny the occult in their basic premises. The important fact which you neglected was that the modern scientist's basis is not an arbitrarily chosen one, but one forced upon him by a total failure of the other, after persistent trials, to display any relationship to reality. By the way—you restricted the parallel to psychologists, but it cannot really be considered except in relationship to scientists as a whole, since knowledge is so interdependent. Or rather, the problem of the psychologist & that of any sort of scientific worker is essentially the same. The psychologist, in classifying the phenomena of the mind, has to distinguish between perceptions & expressions which are based on the recognition of fixed external phenomena, & those which originate through the combination of emotional & imaginative elements within the subject's mind. The invariable constancy of the former type, & the variability, absolute non-relation to reality, & subservience to increasingly recognised illusion-patterns of the latter type, are things so significant as to tell their own story—things, too, which would be recognised with equal clearness whether the investigator started out as a materialist or as an occult believer. When the psychologist explains certain religio-superstitious illusions in terms of material psychology, he is not simply trying to find explanations for obscure beliefs. The fact is, he generally gets at these conclusions quite unpremeditatedly & *from a precisely opposite direction.* He watches the human mind as it constructs false inferences from surrounding phenomena in fields quite remote from the matter of conventional faiths, & he watches also the compelling force of all sorts of early impressions in establishing fixed beliefs wholly irrespective of truth or falsity. He sees, too, the human being's infinite liability to self-deception in all fields trivial or otherwise, notes the discrepancy in evidence given by various eye-witnesses of the same event & the way in which reports become tested in certain traditional directions through repetition, & remarks that compelling urge toward conscious or half-conscious mendacity in certain fields which seems universal amongst all save a very few human types. All this data is dug out of a perfectly disinterested & unbiassed study of the human mind as an isolated object—without any reference whatever to the explanation of this or that popular belief, & without any factor involving basic assumptions of materialism or the reverse. It is only later, when the independently observed attributes of the mind are correlated & tested against the background of observed human events & practices, that the significant connexion between proved psychological action & the popular tenure of irrational & fact-contradicting beliefs is established. Only then does psychology appear as the explainer of traditional fallacy-harbouring. It is this sequence of discovery which makes the evidence of psychology so important. Once the connexion is established the psychologist may legitimately try out hypotheses & construct certain explanations based on assumption of conditions indicated by the connexion—but remember that he does not do this until such a basis is forced upon him by his previous observations. It is the case of the general scientist all over again. That some results may be erroneous, no one can well deny; & many points of view may very conceivably be altered as time passes. But in spite of the general flux & uncertainty it is still possible to find a few plain indications which we may regard as working probabilities—& these certainly do not point in the direction of occultism! As for the sporadic Cock Lane ghosts & nine-days' wonders which now & then spring up, attract eminent investigators whose statements are exaggerated by the press, & finally peter out in exposés & explanations—their own collective history is a sufficient commentary on their evidential value. Most of them follow a pretty well-recognised folklore pattern—& some are certainly clever & interesting in the extreme while the illusion is still maintained. I haven't heard much of this Theresa Neumann case, & couldn't venture an opinion on its individual features without a fuller account of the thing itself, & a verbatim text of just what Haldane, Eddington, & Einstein have said of it.[2] Also whether the Haldane in question is really acute & middle-aged J. *B.* S. Haldane—biologist & philosopher—or his conventional & dualistic father, Prof. J. S. (no B) Haldane. But it's safe to say that these men aren't letting a good show convert them to a belief in a spirit world. What they have said, & what the press has coloured their utterances to imply, are probably two widely different things. Instances of such colouring are very numerous—as witness the frantic effort of reporters to represent the late Thomas A. Edison as a believer in immortality in any conventional sense. By the way, I note that you speak of the "late" Pavlov. I had no idea the good old chap was dead. When did he die?[3]

Regarding persons who claim second-sight & ability to know distant &

future events, you are completely wrong in attempting to evade the plain evidence of my reminder that none of these persons have ever availed themselves of their claimed powers. You are in this case guilty of that sophistical over-application of the letter rather than the spirit of logic which really obscures instead of clarifying an issue. Common sense, & a general perception of the relations of things & of the natural probabilities of cause & effect, are infinitely more important than academic quibbles. The plain fact is—as easily perceivable by the unbiassed & un-fad-ridden adult mind—that our entire status is very largely determined by our universal ignorance of the future & of surrounding conditions inaccessible to the senses. Any person endowed with a perception of future events, or of the thoughts of others, (& of course our whole knowledge of the nature & workings of the cosmos indicates such perceptions as absolutely impossible) would have at his disposal unique conditions which could not fail to give him a prodigious advantage in his struggle with environment. Counting out the persons in whom such gifts would be quiescent because of an initiative too feeble to put them to use, it is clear that the bulk of real prophets & seers—if such existed—would lead lives much freer from uncertainty than the lives of the ordinary run of man. They would be complete fools if they did not turn their gifts to the foreseeing of commercial & political movements in such a way as to give them immunity from the blunders of the majority, & to lead them to unassailable security, wealth, & power. Only a person notably deficient in constructive imagination could fail to appreciate the stupendous possibilities opened up to any individual with even a rudimentary prophetic or divinational gift—& only a person notably deficient in knowledge of human nature could fail to realise how any normal individual would utilise those possibilities if they were his to command! The fact that nearly all claimants to supernatural powers & prophetic endowments are seedy, illiterate, & rather disreputable offshoots of a semi-underworld, is in sober fact a perfectly effective answer to all their claims. If they had the powers they boast of, they would be able to make something of themselves—& would be masters instead of furtive slum-dwellers dodging police & post-office inspectors. There is in all history no instance of any person's having foreseen any event, important or unimportant. Whenever any unexpected event affects a portion of mankind, it is easy to make a survey of the antecedent acts of various persons, & estimate how many did exactly what they would have done if they had known of the imminence of the event. Not in any case can it be found that anyone—save by accident, & for other reasons—did just that which a foreknowledge of the event would inevitably have caused them to do. Those who claim most loudly to be able to divine the future are often shewn to be among those whose acts before a sudden event are widely different from what they would do if really gifted with a knowledge of what was coming. All their misleading talk—afterward—of having foreseen the event is belied by the real record when it is discoverable. Now the point is, of course, that if prophecy really were a possible human attribute, it would almost undoubtedly have left a record of its past operation. No such record exists. And to say that prophecy is *possible* even if it has never yet existed, is frivolous & irrelevant for this reason: that the only cause for assuming the existence of prophecy in the first place is the claim of some that manifestations of it have occurred. Destroy that claim—as the evidence of observation does destroy it—& the very principle of prophecy becomes of gratuitous & unrelated to any conception or experience of ours that its advancement as a possibility becomes in turn a freak of childish inanity. The great trouble with occult believers is that they don't think things through in detail—& especially, that they don't appreciate the complete meaninglessness & irrelevance of assumptions unsuggested & unsupported by any trace of reputable evidence. That their attitude is largely due to the emotionally crippling force of hereditary & environmental tradition is certain—forming a strong argument for drastic changes in our methods of juvenile education. It would be a good idea to appeal to superstitious folk with diagrams & pictures illustrating the relative probabilities involved—& of course to call attention to the microscopically small numbers of all the reputable thinkers of the world who believe in the claims of the miracle-mongers. A good diagram to use on those impervious to verbal logic would be the *weighing* of the evidence touching a popularly reported miracle on a depicted pair of scales. In one pan would be the reasons in favour of believing it truly miraculous; in the other, the reasons in favour of believing it an illusion in a materialistic cosmos. Something like this:

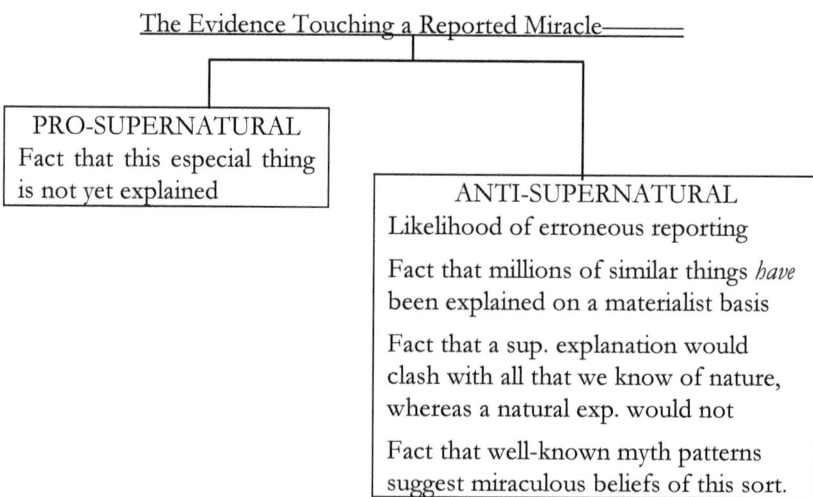

As for college & young Shea—considering the enormous good his first year did him in the way of inculcating observation, improving style, & correcting slipshod extravagances & inanities of thought, I can't feel as sure as you do that the loss of the remaining years is such a nugatory matter. He had two teachers who ripped his themes to pieces & veritably pounded sound ideas into him, & the difference of his present work from the infantile tripe he produced a year ago is radical & startling. Many have a good latent capacity which depends largely on environment for development, & if one year of college did this much, what might not another do? However, I think this first year was the most important one. It has filed off the worst defects & given the kid a start. Whether he'll keep on producing good stuff remains to be seen, but the determination he now shews is certainly a highly favourable augury.

Don't spare the new "Not at Night" from your library if you have any conceivable use for it—though of course I'll be glad to have it if it is a question of Grandpa or the ash-dump! When I said I was glad Howard's story was included, I spoke from a personal rather than a literary angle—for I concede that our Master of Massacre has by no means escaped from the crude & the conventional, despite the undeniable power of some of his suggestions of a monstrous & unhallowed antiquity. But if you were to see his letters—18 or 20 closely typed pages each time—you would perceive a remarkable character as different from the perpetrator of Conan the Reaver as the d'Erlette of "Five Alone" is from the author of "The Coffin of Lissa." God, what a man! I never knew any human being to be so deeply & passionately saturated in the life & traditions of a region as that bird is in the life & traditions of his native & ancestral southwest. He oozes its heroic & sanguinary lore at every joint, & falls into long epic or descriptive recitals which come close to pure poetry despite certain slight tritenesses in phraseology. The sustained fire behind all this is remarkable in the extreme, & I cannot help thinking of what a marvellous mouthpiece of his background he would have made if given the requisite early training. He'd do it yet if he had the leisure, for he's still comparatively young. His father, with whom he lives, is a physician. He himself follows hack-writing exclusively, although he does enough farming (I judge) to supply his own family table. He is a graduate of high-school but not of college, & regrets that he could not have been a professional athlete. In the hard life of west Texas he has been through many a knife & fist fight, & can hardly imagine what a peaceful life is. His early career was roving—knocking about oil-boom towns, travelling with carnival shows, &c. Aside from Texas & from athletics, his greatest interest is the history of ancient barbarians—one of whom he ardently wishes he were. He is unbelievably erudite in Celtic antiquities, for despite his descent from the Howards of Georgia the majority of his blood is Irish—though of colonial settlement in America. He looks—judging from snapshots—exactly like the burly, bullet-headed prize-fighter he would like to be! Altogether, there are few persons with as distinctive & clear-cut a personality as good old R E H's. He really has tremendous brilliancy, & if his attainments could be disciplined he'd do for West Texas what you're doing for Sac Prairie. I'll lend you some of his encyclopaedic letters if you think you'd enjoy a sidelight on such an unusual character.

Well—I seem to have covered a lot of space! Pardon the infliction—as well as the prosy argumentative material.

Best wishes—

Grandpa

Notes

1. Tycho Brahe (1546–1601), Danish astronomer, proposed a theory of the solar system in which the planets moved around the sun, which in turn revolved around a stationary earth.

2. Thérèse Neumann (1898–1962), of Konnersreuth, West Germany, was a stigmatist who bore 45 wounds resembling those of Christ's passion. The accounts mentioned by HPL are unidentified.

3. Ivan Petrovich Pavlov (1849–1936), Russian physiologist and experimental psychologist who received the Nobel Prize in 1904. See letters 297–98.

[292] [ALS]

Novr. 19[, 1932]

Dear A W:—

Thanks for the list of O. Henry citations—a testimony of dumbness which certainly justifies your review! Most of the items are colourless things which I have completely forgotten, but fancy placing Klarkash-Ton's "Gorgon" as low as third class . . . . . & including Belknap's pot-boiling "Horror in the Hold" at all![1] I'm glad, by the way, that you still find *Trend* a receptive medium.[2] I haven't been following it since Loveman withdrew.

Klarkash-Ton sent them some excellent material, but they finally decided it wasn't "contemporary" enough.

I shall greet both of the volumes you mention with profound gratitude. Those "Not at Nights" are surely growing into an ambitious five-foot shelf of mediocrity!

Here are some of Howard's earlier letters which dwell especially on the Southwestern frontier. If you find these promising, I'll send others. A good many are lent to Little Belknap (I'm trying to break up the child's soft urbanism by giving him a glimpse of what regular men are like!), but if the careless young scamp hasn't lost them, I'll get them back. There is certainly a vast lot of latent genius in Two-Gun Bob; & if anyone is adapted to chronicle the sage of the southwest, he's the boy. I wish you could help to bring out the poetry-suffused regional epics which I feel he has locked within him!

Congratulations on the Return of Solar Pons! Hope he proves a valuable financial ally! Best wishes for "A Town is Built" & the other specimens whose fortunes hang in the balance.

Good luck with Hjalmar & Mahmoud, of the old Maryland stock! Your official elucidation of the saints' name question is highly interesting, & settles a point upon which a vast body of misconception undoubtedly exists. It would be odd if there were actually saints named Phineas & Abner—I suppose there must be official lists of saints available somewhere.

As for coincidences—while one is perhaps not an excessive number to delineate in a chronicle covering a long period, it seems to me that I'd be careful in introducing any in a sketch of limited time-length whose place in the chronological stream was determined by other considerations. That is, it forms a *double* coincidence to have a coincidence occur in close juxtaposition with other events of sufficient importance to form the subject-matter of a story. However—it may be just as well to leave these considerations to your own instinctive artistic sense. If you go too far at any one time, you'll probably see the unlifelikeness in retrospect & be on guard against a repetition. Certainly, the case in "Farway House" isn't what one could call flagrant.

Concerning the occult—it is not with any *general scientific theory* that we have the chief difficulty in reconciling the claims of magical & quasi-magical folklore & subjective anomalies; but with *the coherent fabric of accurately observed human experience.* It is, of course, only from that coherent fabric that any theories can be made. It is no matter of scientific theory which causes us to see that no person has ever genuinely predicted an event—it is simple observation & common sense. No one, on the brink of a definite happening, has ever acted in the way a person would if the happening were foreseen. That's not formal science, but just sanity. There is no reason for believing that anything as contrary to common observation as prophecy exists. Also—it is no matter of formal science to point out that every thoroughly investigated case of "occultism" has always been found to have its basis in error, deception, magnified report, or some other explanation compatible with common experience & incompatible with the claims of the occultists.

I've just exposed an amusing case myself. A revision client in Boston—a woman of merely conventional education & no great originality—has for over a year been claiming to have had strange & accurate revelations from various seers in the Hub region. They have, she claims, told her all about her family & ancestors without any previous information. Finally she began to claim that her sibyls told her things about *me* . . . . . things, I noticed, which she herself would be apt to know through mutual acquaintances. At that state I began my exposé by casually giving out—to those mutual acquaintances—certain slightly *erroneous* statements about myself & family. And now—just as I expected—the client has begun to report interviews with Veiled Seeresses in which further revelations about me are made . . . . . revelations, needless to say, which embody the erroneous statements I set afloat! In plain fact, the lady is a damned liar—though psychology probably has a deservedly separate classification for persons who pervert truth in defence of certain fixed ideas. There exists in some individuals an unconquerable & insatiable urge to uphold certain glamourous folklore-patterns at any cost. This client is perfectly honest & reliable in ordinary matters. About Pavlov—are your sure about that date? Or is there another Pavlov in the same line? I seem to have heard accounts of him since then—of his refusal to accept the Bolshevik ideal, & of the exceptional forbearance of the Bolshevik in his case. I must see what lies behind these conflicting impressions. ¶ Best wishes—Yr obt Grandsire H P

P.S. Tried to catch the Leonid meteors Wednesday morning, but fog & a bright moon spoiled the show. In an hour's time—3:15–4:15 a.m.—I glimpsed only 5 meteors—of which 2 were really bright. Yet only 45 miles away, in Cambridge, the Harvard Observatory reported an average of one meteor per minute.

[P.P.S. on envelope:] Just got $21.61 for reprinting of Erich Zann in London Evening Standard. ¶ In a note from Whitehead I got the idea that *Astounding* is to follow S.T. into oblivion. Is this correct?[3]

¶ Speaking (as inside) of deaths—did Hugh Walpole die recently?[4] I just saw his name bordered in black in the new Am. Spectator, but haven't noticed a word of his decease anywhere else. People drop off faster than an old man can keep track of!

Notes

1. CAS, "The Gorgon," *WT* (April 1932); FBL, "The Horror in the Hold," *WT* 19, No. 2 (February 1932).

2. *Trend* had published AWD's story, "The Do-Jigger."

3. *Astounding Stories* (founded in 1930 by Clayton Magazines, Inc.) ceased publication

with the March 1933 issue but was revived in October 1933 by Street and Smith.
4. Hugh Walpole (b. 1884) did not die until 1 June 1941.

[293] [ALS]

Novr 26[, 1932]

Dear A W:—

I was just going to write you at Price's request when your of the 22nd appeared. It seems that he wants your (& Schorer's) story "In the Left Wing" for that anthology which he & others are getting up—& not knowing your address, asked me to pass the word along to you & request you to send him the text of the story if you're willing to have it appear. You'll recall that I liked that story, although you didn't yourself. He also suggests that you name any other stories of yours which you would prefer to have appear. Doubtless you'd pick something like "The Panelled Room" or "The Sheraton Mirror"—but this anthology is a hard, grim, business proposition, & something of sharp sensationalism with an obvious commercial "punch" is wanted. Final decisions on contents are made by a hard-boiled commercial critic in New York—named Lenniger—for whose Philistine judgments Price has an almost superstitious reverence. He turned thumbs down on my "Pickman's Model" (Price's choice), wouldn't even consider "The Colour Out of Space" (my choice), & finally picked "The Picture in the House" (the original *Arkham* story) as my contribution. But both Price & Mashburn are extremely fond of "In the Left Wing." Send material to *E. Hoffmann Price, 1416 Josephine St., New Orleans.*

About those books—for which appropriate advance thanks are tendered—hold 'em till I can slip you 50¢ in stamps*, which ought to cover expressage. I might not be home when they arrive, & I don't want to bother others in this establishment. In the old days my aunt would have attended to such matters. If you're low on actual spendable cash—for which stamps can't serve—just wait till you'd ordinarily be buying the stamps. No hurry whatever. If the charges are more than 50¢ just let me know. I'll appreciate the Klarkash-Ton addition—which I don't think I've read in MS.

Inasmuch as my Webster is the edition of 1891 (a mint condition copy bought by my father in the year of its issuance, but laid on the shelf while we got a "*little*"—40 years'—more use out of the dilapidated 1864 edition & put into active service only last year), the death of M. Pavlov scarcely falls within its scope. But if Pavlov passed out in 1916, then who the hell is this old guy named P—— something or other (Pavlovitch, Pavlovsky, Petrov, Petrovitch, Petrovsky . . .) who is psychologist, biologist, physician, or something, & also

---

*Eleventh hour—I've raked up enough stamps right now, hence am enclosing. But take your time about sending the stuff.

is tolerated by the bolsheviki despite his opposition to their principles? I got the impression somewhere—& so (independently) did little Belknap. That young scamp (who has gone bolshevik in the past year) was quoting the case (whatever it was) only a couple of months ago in an effort to prove the liberality of his beloved soviets. I think I saw an article on this P—— some time ago in the Times magazine. The guy—if I recall his portrait aright—was elderly & white-bearded. As for the "late" Hugh Walpole—yes, unsophisticated Grandpa fell neatly for the playful jest! But a real death notice of the sort is just the kind of thing I'd be likely to overlook in casual reading. As for the similar "decease" of certain of the editors—I fancy you are right, though perhaps one ought to wait & see what Dreiser's next novel will be like. The death of *Astounding* will cause many groans—as the death of *Strange* has already done.

Good luck with your own work. By the way—did you ever publish "The Cult of Simplicity", announced to follow "Incoherence"? If so, I'd like to see it.

As for occult stuff—my recent exposé almost exactly parallels one which I made 15 years ago, when a correspondent pretended to have dreams parallel to certain ones of my own which I had mentioned. When I described certain fake dreams, the correspondent "confirmed" all the details! As to the "grapevine telegraph" among niggers, it is pretty well agreed that *dreams & smoke columns* are responsible—both in Africa & in Haiti. This mode of signalling is traditional among the blacks. The idea of "telepathy" is not inconsistent with a realistically conceived universe—but the fact remains that no case has yet stood up under thorough & iconoclastic investigation. Mnemonic transposition is *unconscious*—& searching external research often breaks up the most honestly plausible-looking cases. I think you will find reputable scientific authorities almost solidly against the reality of any "telepathic" case hitherto recorded. As for prophecy—your anecdote is typical. Boasts of success are usually backed either by inside information or by a prophetic ambiguity capable of later interpretation in any desired direction.

I thought you'd find Two-Gun Bob interesting. If you'd care to see more of his long, half-epic letters, let me know, & I'll send some. Yes—his perspective is naturally highly provincial because of his pioneer background & roving life; but the remarkable thing is his vital response to his environment, & the exhaustless fund of emotional energy behind his pictures of glamourous old days & old ways. I'm sure you & he would find an exchange of letters interesting. His address is *Lock Box 313, Cross Plains, Texas.*

Well—best wishes, & I hope you'll send Price something for his anthology.

Your oblig'd & obt grandsire

HP

[P.S. on envelope] Sudden bad news. Whitehead died last Wednesday.[1] I knew he was in rotten health, but had no idea it was as bad as all this. He wrote breezily & optimistically less than a fortnight ago with no reference to health. Really, this gives me a damnable jolt. He was such a splendid chap in all ways—brilliant, courageous, generous, attractive, learned, & everything else admirable. This will be a frightful blow to his father—now 84.

Notes

1. Henry S. Whitehead died 23 November.

[294] [ALS]

[early December 1932]

Dear A W:—

Yes—good old "Canevin's" death is about as damnable a bit of cosmic waste as I've recently come across. The abruptness of it—despite his long illness—makes it doubly a shock. Everyone who hears of it mourns. Dwyer is quite disconsolate, while poor little Grayson—who has written me for the first time since 1931—feels as though the pillars of the world had fallen. I don't know who will administer Whitehead's affairs—possibly his father, despite the weight of 84 years. But I surely hope no notable tale will remain unpublished. He had started a series of stories about a sinister, Arkhamesque New England village called "Chadbourne". Wright is using the opening one in the Feby. issue, but the second (involving scientifiction) was lately returned by Bates after having been accepted for the doomed *Astounding*. A third—not specifically involving the supernatural & centreing around a Congregational minister—exists, but I gather it has not been submitted anywhere.[1]

Price will appreciate your shipment of tales. This Lenniger is the perfect philistine—insists on *action,* & dislikes the work of Klarkash-Ton & myself because it is *unpleasant.* He thinks a weird tale ought to leave the reader happy!

I hope I'll come on some further item regarding this Petrov-Pavlosky or whoever he is, just to settle my curiosity. Your remarks on Russian communism are exactly what I've been telling Sonny Belknap for a year—but some young folks won't listen to Grandpa! He became a rebellious proletarian about the time the critic Edmund Wilson, Jr.[2] announced his conversion to the cause—as soon as he felt that it was the proper thing for nice young men who wear clean collars & are sensitive to aesthetic niceties. I tell him he ought to go to Moscow—his experience would be broadened somewhat when the Soviets started to snatch him out of soft urban employment & set him to work in the mud on some collective farm!

Good luck with "Farway House". Yes—I think the revised version tones down the conspicuousness of the coincidence a bit, & I'm sure young Thorne will sound more lifelike without his solecisms. Later on we'll see how the readers react to Ras Tafari & Chunder Singh, the stout Maryland scions.

Too bad "The Cult of Simplicity" never got written. Possibly you'll tackle it after all if "Incoherence" goes over big. Congrats on the 50-buck prize. Not long ago the local writer—or ex-writer—C. M. Eddy Jr. sought my assistance on a mystery-ending for some contest—I wonder if it was this one? Was the story about a haunted mill with mysterious deaths by strangulation? I fixed up a long synopsis for Eddy—attributing the strangulation to the victims themselves, who raised their hands to their throats to tear away the imagined talons of others when a certain drug (as mentioned in the story) in the air produced the illusory sensation of strangulation. The yarn was a fearsome piece of crap.

As for nigger magic & telepathy—I've heard of various legends, but never knew of any which gave expert investigators any really serious food for puzzlement.

Here are three more letters from Hrobjart Havard's-sen the Reaver. Damn it, but I envy the boy his fund of energy & vigour of historical imagination! ¶ Best wishes—

Grandpa

P.S. I enclose Two-Gun Bob's picture. Please return it. He certainly looks the part!

Notes

1. The latter two stories are unidentified and may not survive.

2. Edmund Wilson, Jr. (1895–1972), a leading American social and literary critic of the twentieth century. He wrote a scathing review of HPL's work in "Tales of the Marvellous and the Ridiculous," *New Yorker* 21, No. 41 (24 November 1945): 100, 103–4, 106. In the early 1930s, Wilson forcefully supported Soviet communism.

[295] [ALS]

[mid-December 1932]

Dear A W:—

So Wright was late in hearing the sad news. Bates got word somehow, & dropped me a regretful note. Price feels quite desolated, & hopes that Wright will print some sort of obituary notice. At his suggestion I have sent a sketch of H S's career & personality—which, if he wishes, Wright can draw upon for a paragraph in The Eyrie.[1] It seems clear that the final disaster was very sudden & unforeseen. I shall perhaps never know whether he read my answer to his last letter.

Hope you'll have—or rather, hope you have had—an interesting week in the metropolitan zone. I can understand your dislike of the city proper, which parallels my sentiments toward the even worse pandaemonium called New York. Your confabulation with the W.T. gang will doubtless interesting. Kline has done wonders as a literary agent for Price—selling many tales which Lenniger could not market. I now understand for the first time his justification for existence! Haven't had a chance to read the new W.T. or any since September. Glad the February number promises to have some good stuff to keep "The Chadbourne Episode" company.

Yes—I'd imagine that H. in the M. would be most pleasing of all the tales to Lenniger. Still—zombis are dreadfully gruesome things! My own favourite, as you probably know, is Wind-Walker. But this is something for the Peacock Sultan & the Vizier Lhen-Eighur to fight about betwixt themselves.

I agree with you regarding communism, & trust that Little Belknap's addiction to it will prove short-lived. At present his saeva indignatio regarding the crumbling capitalist world is rather interfering with his aesthetic zest. He now thinks that the only true art is that of passionate rebellion . . . . it is a tragic & terrible thing when one's papa cuts down one's allowance!

Glad the Terror of the Plains proved epistolarily entertaining. When you say the word I'll shoot along some more Hrobjartiana. He certainly looks his temperament in the snap shot . . . . Ajax defying the lightning! Some day he ought to get a bit of that Southwestern colour down on paper.

Congratulations on your recent acceptances! Hope that "Frost in October" & "Woman at Loon Point" may find havens also. Too bad "Evening in Spring" didn't land—but some day a publisher will be glad enough to bring it out!

It's all right to postpone the express package till 1933—& thanks for the addition mentioned. I'll surely be glad to see the revised E. in S.—& shall, as I said, return it through M. Pierre d'Artois, alias Malik Taus. Price, by the way, says he has a new way of beating 3¢ postage with bulky MSS. He sends them *as printed matter* by express & says that he can get a rate as low as 8¢ per pound. When he submits a MS. to an editor he tells him to return it by express collect at the printed matter rate in case of non-acceptance—in fact, he prepares the return envelope with that end in view. He gives all packages the minimum valuation of $10.00. This racket might be worth investigation on your part.

Was it you or young Shea (Grandpa does get the children mixed up!) who waxed so enthusiastic about "The Fountain" by Charles Morgan? I've just secured the loan of it.

Best wishes—Yr obt ancestor H P

Notes

1. "In Memoriam: Henry St. Clair Whitehead." The notice appeared in edited form.

[296] [ALS]

Tenbarnes [after 25 December 1932]

Dear A W:—

Congratulations on your waxing fame! That article is highly interesting, & I'm sure the radio address will aid considerably in establishing you as a literary figure. Sooner or later you'll be winning Pulitzer Prizes & things of that sort. If you have any more copies of that cutting I wouldn't mind an extra—for I want to sent it around to some of the gang, & would hate to have an only copy lost or torn. Thanks exceedingly for the item.

Thanks also for the portrait of the young Sardanapalus—or the luxurious young Manchu Emperor Hsuan-Yi-Kiang, meditating on the exotic & curious pleasures of his court! That would surely make a splendid frontispiece for a thin, de luxe volume of esoteric symbolist verse on cream-coloured Japanese vellum! The arrangement is highly artistic, & the physiognomy seems better-defined than in any of the previous snaps. A good piece of portraiture applied to a worthy subject!

Your Chicago week seems to have been unusually well packed with congenial events & personalities, & I trust the strain of being a celebrity does not weigh heavily on you. The glimpses of the W.T. outfit must have been interesting—too bad King Pharnaces is so handicapped with that wretched Parkinson business. Kline is a hustling business-man, whatever his literary shortcomings may be. His success in marketing Price's stories is phenomenal—including the sale of things which Lenniger had vainly peddled. Glad that the March W.T. will contain appropriate tributes to good old Canevin. It was thoughtful of him to furnish autobiographical data—he had several times thought his life in peril, especially in the autumn of 1930, when the early stages of the gastric trouble involved acute attacks. Expressions of deep regret continue to come from all who learn of the recent sad event—Klarkash-Ton, who held the Canevin tales in particular esteem, being especially jolted.

Glad to hear of your new products & acceptances. The most impressive thing about your quantity productions is the percentage of serious material in it. Price is running up a sort of wordage record—but isn't so particular about the choice & arrangement of those words so long as they sell. By the way—without being in the least bolshevistic, Price expects to take a job as technical expert (electric welding) in Moscow next April; it having been secured for him by that young literary meteor of yesteryear, Robert S. Carr, who turned from books to business & became a power in the Soviet's American trading corporation. Regarding the anthology—"In the Left Wing" seems to be the probable choice, this being an especial favourite of Price's colleague W. K. Mashburn. I don't know what kind of a book it will be, on the whole, but its Philistine policy will certainly hurt its quality.

All right—I'll save postage on the Two-Gun Bob material. Texas would seem to be one of the must unusual parts of the country, insomuch as its level of civilisation remains distinctly tinged with the primitive—including a disregard for life & a taken-for-granted prevalence of physical violence. Conan the Reaver could hardly believe me when I mentioned the rarity of street shootings & stabbings—outside the slums—in the East. The processes of law, also, seem fabulously corrupt in Texas. Rangers & police capriciously intimidate the citizenry, & bow to the dominance of the all-engulfing oil interests, to an extent which links the traditions of Russia with those of Tammany.

It must have been little Jehvish-Êi who bubbled so enthusiastically about "The Fountain". Well—I read it, & rather concurred in his favourable opinion, albeit in the less emotional manner of old age. The language is rich & vivid, & the picture of a certain type of sensitive & reflective mind seems to me admirable. On the other hand, the philosophy is so heavily laid on that the book somewhat drags; & there is a certain mawkishness in a point of view which attaches so much mystical importance to the human emotions & personality. It is what one would expect from a devotee of the Dr. Donne period.

Thanks for the distinctive holiday greetings enclosed. Hope your holiday season is proving a festive one, & that 1933 may break all records for inspiration, acceptances, & all the other forms of good fortune.

With patriarchal blessings—

Yr obt grandsire

H P

P.S. Young Strauch, embarking on a post-graduate course at Muhlenberg centreing in Roman literature, proposes to switch his correspondence to Latin! I can see where Grandpa will have to move the Latin dictionary & two or three manuals over to the bookcase near the desk!

[P.P.S. on envelope:] Well, well! An unexpected parallelling of your metropolitan sojourn! Just got an invitation from Belknap's parents to surprise the kid by showing up for a week's visit—hence, since the 'bus fare is down to 2 bucks, I'm about to set out for the dreary jungles of Manhattan . . . starting 2 a.m. & arriving 9 a.m. Shall have two Christmas dinners—one with my aunt here this afternoon, & one at Long's tomorrow, since they chose Monday for the Yuletide observances. I'll be glad to see the gang—including our young friend Melmoth the Wandrei.

[297] [ANS][1]

[Postmarked Grand Central Annex, N.Y.,
28 December 1932]

Look here, you young rascal! So you tried to make your old Grandpa believe that Ivan Petrovitch Pavlov (1849–) died in 1916, eh? So you "aren't in the habit of making such mistakes"? Well, Sir, my other grandchild Belknap has just come to the rescue of blundering old age, & has vindicated Grandpa's original idea. *Pavlov is still living, just as I thought.* The article in the *Times* ***was*** about him. His presence among the living is attested by the N.Y. Public Library's card catalogue (entry of ***1928***) & the Encyclopaedia Britannica—13th edition, ***1926.*** Don't be so cocky again in correcting an old man—even though I *might* have been wrong just as well as right. Having a great time here in spite of rainy weather. Best wishes—Grandpa.

Greetings. I think Howard's extensive research in the matter of Pavlov rather pedantic, but it is well to be correct in such matters. Cordial good wishes. FBL Jr.

Notes

1. Front: 1:—Place D'Armes, Montréal.

1933

[298] [ALS]

Jany. 6, 1933

Dear A W:—

Well—I had a very good time in N.Y. last week, even the weather (surprisingly warm for the season) & the 'bus schedule (route now passing right by Belknap's house & letting me alight at his door without plunging into the hated maelstrom of downtown Manhattan) combining to favour me. Mr. & Mrs. Long smuggled me into the dining-room before the Child was up, & when he drowsily toddled out to breakfast he was certainly bowled over to see his aged Grandpa's withered visage above the pages of the morning *Tribune!* Later I surprised others of the gang—Talman, Kirk, Wandrei, Loveman—& on the 30th we held a meeting of the old-time sort at Sonny's I saw the old year out at Loveman's, & was presented by my generous host with a prehistoric stone Mayan idol & an early African flint implement with a craved ivory handle. I also met a friend of Belknap's whom I'd never seen before—the once successful though now hard-pressed pulp hack Neil Moran . . . . . . a very pleasant & likeable fellow, though no titan above the collar.[1] Wandrei has very snug & pleasing quarters in a warehouse district near the Hudson in the N.W. part of Greenwich Village. His psychological novel is nearly finished now. I shewed everyone the cutting of your radio fame, & all seemed duly impressed. No doubt you've duly received the card from Belknap & me in which the Great Pavlov Argument is continued. Where in hell do you suppose you ever got the notion that the old boy passed out in 1916? There is no question but that—despite your cocksureness—this impression is erroneous. No one in the gang ever heard such a report, & the documentary evidence of the recent Britannica & library cards cannot be controverted. Undoubtedly, my first impression was correct—& it *was* of Pavlov that we read in the *Times* last year. Possibly some reference work contained the given error—I recall that in 1913 a cheap encyclopaedia spoke of the "death" of John Singer Sargent in *1901,* a report which the artist would have been forced to denounce as highly exaggerated had he happened across it. I'll wager that 1916 report would give good old Ivan Petrovitch a good chuckle in spite of his 84 years. Long life to him! Belknap, Wandrei, & I did a good many of the museums—seeing the newly acquired archaic Greek Apollo at the Metropolitan, the two new Dutch rooms at the Brooklyn, & the famous Whistler painting of his mother (loan from the Louvre) at the now adequately housed (11 W. 53) Museum of Modern Art. Also some of the crazy modern junk at the Whitney Museum in 8th St.—including the blatant frescoes in the attic reading room. Ugh—thank Gawd Providence sticks to the classical tradition! I duly had the two Christmas dinners—& just for good measure the Long New Year's feast also centred in turkey. On Sunday the 1st. I saw the interior of the new Riverside Church—a genuinely impressive Gothic achievement. For years I've been watching the great tower rise on the skyline. Its inspiration is supposed to be the great Chartres cathedral, although nothing of the latter is suggested in general outlines.[2]

I hope Price's work in Moscow won't prove a complete fiasco. He doesn't expect anything wonderful, but thinks it will at least form an improvement on hack writing. Hope he won't get cheated out of the trips to Samarcand & Bokhara which seem to form the chief inducement. I'll be amused to see what the other inhabitants of 10 Barnes—mostly prim & elderly Christian Scientists—will think of me when I begin to receive frequent mail with Soviet stamps & Moscow postmarks! Probably they'll decide that I'm in league with the devil—which they already suspect since my expression of preference for the Roosevelt over the Hoover ticket last fall!

Your literary programme is as bewilderingly copious as usual, & I am glad to note the number of high-grade acceptances on it. The book rejections are nothing to be depressed about—these same readers would have an entirely different set of reactions if your name happened to be an old one on their lists. Hope 1933 will beat 1932 before it's over—not only literarily, but financially as well.

About modern reading—if I try to do any more I'm sure that Faulkner will be well represented. While at Belknap's I read Pitkin's recent "History of Human Stupidity"—which is certainly highly interesting & in places genuinely original so far as popular exposition is concerned.

Best wishes—

Yr most obt grandsire

H P

Notes

1. Neil Moran had one story in *Astounding* ("The Tooth," April 1934), but otherwise published chiefly in the detective pulps.

2. At 490 Riverside Drive between 120th and 122nd streets, overlooking the Hudson River.

[299] [ALS]

Jany. 24, 1933

Dear A W:—

So it was good old Noah who slipped you up on Pavlov, eh? Quite a parallel for the encyclopaedia which had Sargent killed off in 1901. The error is undoubtedly on Noah's side, for several reasons—including the fact that a good many of Ivan Petrovitch's books have been published since 1916, & the circumstance that nearly everyone in the gang around N.Y. recalls last year's *Times* article, which *was* about him.

Glad that you, Schorer, & Utpatel are all becoming *Trend* contributors, & that you have landed so many other items. I received the card mentioning your *Frontier* article, & have sent in a quarter for the issue containing it.[1]

Since my return home Belknap has had a bad attack of influenza, but is now comfortably convalescing. Also—on Jany. 8 Talman became the proud father of an heir to his name & estates—David Frederic Talman.

My library has had 2 or 3 accessions lately, of which the most spectacular single item is Maturin's "Melmoth, the Wanderer", in 3 volumes—a thing I've been looking for almost 20 years! It is the reprint of 1892—the last edition, so far as I know, & long out of print. This was a gift from W. Paul Cook—it having been part of the splendid library which he had before his collapse of 1930. Another gift was "The World Below", by S. Fowler Wright—fair scientifiction dealing with the world 500,000 years hence. A third item was a purchase of my own—E. R. Eddison's magnificently fantastic tale "The Worm Ouroboros", which I picked up as a remainder for 79¢.

Some good lectures hereabouts lately—on Jany. 15 a reading of James Stephens' & Walter de la Mare's poetry, & on the 18th a lecture on Schopenhauer. The series of poetry readings will later culminate the personal appearance of T. S. Eliot.[2]

By the way—I have not yet received the express package which you mentioned as being about to send on Jany. 10, so unless you changed your plan I am beginning to fear that it has suffered loss in transit. I surely hope not—but if you did send the consignments I fancy a few enquiries at the office would be in order.

So far the winter has remained remarkably mild, making my hibernation an only partial matter. Yesterday the mercury was up almost to 60°, & it does not often get below freezing. No show as yet. Hope the concluding months will not try to compensate for this benevolent start!

Best wishes—

Yr oblig'd, ob[t] Servt

H P

¶ P.S. If the shipment comes before I hear from you again, I'll drop you a line at once.

Notes

1. "A Day in March."

2. Eliot's reading was the week of 24 February. Ten years previously, HPL had decried the publication of Eliot's *The Waste Land.*

[248] [TLS, JHL]

Sauk City, Wisconsin
27 January [1933]

Dear H. P.,

I owe you a thousand apologies for my delinquency about that package of books, which I hope you have received by this time. For some inexplicable reason—probably because I wrote that the package was going out with the letter, today—I fancied that the books had been shipped and forgot all about them until I had a note from Price mentioning that you had written him to expect EVENING IN SPRING—when I peered cautiously over the edge of my table and saw to my horror that the package of books still reposed behind the table! I had a vivid picture of you wondering why the books hadn't come! However, they went out to you on Monday last, the 23rd. Perhaps I ought to be warned in time—the first cog in the machine is beginning to slip.

Do not wonder if you don't get the FRONTIER before 25th Febry, for it comes off the presses on the 20th of that month. I'm glad, though, that you sent for a copy of that issue; I anticipate your reaction to the magazine itself as well as to the story or essay, rather, which is, by the way, one of the excised portions of EVENING IN SPRING, therefore not appearing in the ms. copy of the book which came with the package.

Referring for the moment to EVENING IN SPRING—in case it appears in the ms. copy you have, I decided to drop permanently the Introductory Thesis on Four Themes.

Might I plague you again for sight of your duplicate of THE DREAMS IN THE WITCH HOUSE? I want to make myself a copy of this. When I get around to it, I'm going to copy THE SHADOW OVER INNSMOUTH, too, and ship the duplicate back to you.

I am finally at work on THE RETURN OF HASTUR. In connexion with this ms., I am using this line from THE CALL OF CTHULHU—"Ph'nglui mglw'nafh Cthulhu R'lyeh wgah'nagl fhtagn"—though my line reads "Ph'nglui mglw'nafh Hastur Be'elgs wgah'nagl fhtagn"—or, rather in line with your translation of the cult line, In his house at Be'elgs (Betelgeuse) banished Hastur waits dreaming—later I want to bring in your line for comparison to clinch a point in the narrative. I may also quote from THE CALL, THE WHISPERER IN DARKNESS, and perhaps even from THE SHADOW OVER INNSMOUTH—with due indication of origin, of course.

[Conclusion non-extant.]

[300] [ANS][1]

[Postmarked Providence, R.I.,
26 January 1933]

The package has come! Abundant thanks—& comments later. Some of these volumes are wholly unexpected—& altogether new to me. What a feast ahead! But what gives me the kick of kicks is the inclusion of "The Willows" in one of them.[2] I have wanted that book for years—& now, at last, it is mine! It is needless to say how grateful I am, & I surely hope you have not robbed your library of any volume whose absence you will ultimately regret.

Again—thanks & an old man's blessing!—Grandpa

[P.S.] I shall read "Evening in Spring" with avid interest.

Notes

1. Front: Rhode Island School of Design / Black-Figured Amphora by Nikosthenes. Greek VI Cen. B.C.

2. In John Gilbert Bohun Lynch, ed., *The Best Ghost Stories,* one of six books AWD sent HPL at this time.

[301] [ALS]

Jany 30[, 1933]

Dear A W:—

Well—I have read the revised & reproportioned "Evening in Spring", & believe that you have made a tremendous improvement over any of the original fragments & sections now embodied in it. It certainly is a natural & inevitable organic whole—explanation, general external-world background, specific local background, & finally objective events—yet leaves the way fully open for the later units of the reminiscent cycle. The proportion allotted to backgrounds is almost uniquely large, yet I do not feel that any competent critic could term it excessive or tedious. The feeling of reality & vitality never flags—& one can understand the part played by all the recorded impressions & influences in the shaping of the central figure. That figure itself is an unmistakably definite personality—with an aura of authenticity apparent even to one who, like myself, is as utterly antipodal to it in moods & interests & memories as any imaginative & landscape-loving individual well can be. If this production isn't *literature,* I'll cheerfully eat my hat! It is certainly the most substantial thing that any member of the W.T. gang has yet turned out—& I feel sure that this view will be echoed by Price despite his devotion to the most opposite types of objective writing. The MS. now goes forward to him for reading & return to you. By the way—I appreciate inclusion of the Necronomicon, R'lyeh, Erich Zann, &c. in the list of influences, as well as the retention of the Randolph Carter allusion in the "Early Years" section. If one can't be literature oneself, one can at least be mentioned in literature! About the elimination of the "Introductory Thesis"—I suppose, after all, that the plan & principle of the work are really quite obvious without it; & that the sooner the actual material is approached, the better it is. Yet I liked this section greatly, & believe that it is by no means out of place. No harm came from the delay—I presume you've received my card acknowledging the shipment. Those books—for which my thanks are never-ending—surely do form welcome additions to my library. I can't say how glad I am to have "The Willows". I'll be on the lookout for *Frontier* toward the end of February.

Enclosed is the "Witch-House"[1]—although I'm afraid it is hardly worth copying. It almost amuses me to reflect that I once thought I was on the road toward becoming able to write stories! Good luck with "Hastur"—but don't use any word sounding like "Betelgeuse" to represent a *primal* name of that distant sun (or to represent the name used by the denizens of any of its hypothetical planets), since this name is an Arabic product of the Middle Ages, & signifies "the armpit (or shoulder) of the giant (or central one)"—*Ibn al Jauzah*—Orion having been known as Al Jauzah to the astronomers of the Saracenic Caliphate—who did so much to advance the science. Since the *word* "Betelgeuse" is so wholly & recognisably a terrestrial coinage, with a known terrestrial etymology, it becomes necessary to have something *totally* dissimilar if we are to represent a non-terrestrial (or pre-Arabic terrestrial) term. In the *Necronomicon,* Abdul Alhazred would no doubt have used both the primal name—let us say *Glyn-aho*—or something of the sort—the new Arabic word *Ibt* [*sic*] *al Jauzah* (= Betelgeuse) which the astronomers around him were beginning to evolve. The point is that one can't devise a prototype-name for Betelgeuse, since the origin of the latter is known. From what you say—& if it's anything like "Wind Walker"—the new tale bids fair to be a notable production. I shall be eagerly on the lookout for it.

Talman isn't having to worry about his income yet—the Texas Co. still being generous enough to make David Frederic's future no problem—but in these times one can't always be certain about anything. I am certainly sorry to hear of your mother's illness, & certainly hope that no disastrous development will occur. After all, surgical technique is infinitely less dangerous than it used to be—so that the percentage of successful operations constantly rises. But the strain of anxiety must be tremendous while it lasts.

Congratulations on your sales—& let us hope that the rejections & postponements will eventually become sales.

Heard an excellent poetry reading by Robert Hillyer yesterday.[2]

Best wishes—

Yr oblig'd & obt grandsire

H P

Notes

1. I.e., "The Dreams in the Witch House."

2. Robert Hillyer (1895–1961), American poet, essayist, and translator. He won the Pulitzer Prize for his *Collected Verse* (1933).

[302] [ALS]

Feby 9, 1933

Dear A W:—

I lately had a letter from Harry Bates—now in Clearwater, Fla. writing a play, & in touch with Whitehead's father & friends—which sheds light on the details of H S's passing.

It seems that during the autumn his cousin from the north was replaced by the bright little "cracker" boy C. J. Fletcher (whom he had had before) as secretary & companion. On the Sunday before his death—Nov. 20—he complained of a "general malaise"—*not* connected with his stomach. His friend Miss Starr (the middle-aged lady who lent him the use of her automobile during my visit) was rather worried, & told young Fletcher to watch him carefully & telephone her if anything alarming developed. Late that night the boy heard a thud—as of a fall—in Whitehead's room, & found H S in a queer & disturbing condition—partly deprived of speech. He telephoned Miss Starr, & she went over—finding H S semi-conscious. She then telephoned Dr. Mease (prop. of the local sanatorium, & H S's regular physician), who came at once & sent for 2 other doctors. They diagnosed the case as a concussion of the brain caused by a fall. Before morning old Mr. Whitehead was notified & rushed up from St. Petersburg. H S was still semi-conscious, recognised his father, raised an arm, smiled, & said "My daddy." Those were his last words. From then until the end the doctors kept him under opiates. Fletcher, Mr. Whitehead, Dr. Mease, Miss Starr, & others were on hand & awake most of the time. Death came early on the morning of Wednesday, the 23d. It is clear that H S never had a chance to read my reply to his last letter.

H S was feeling *unusually well* until Sunday, Nov. 20th, hence I doubt if the old gastric trouble was really the direct cause of death. To me it looks like a malignly tragic *accident*—the fall in the night; which, though doubtless caused by the general weakness resulting from the old trouble, might easily have not occurred. It seems that shortly before his death H S had had all his books & household effects shipped down from the north, where for years they had been in storage. He had also just built a new sun porch on the roof of his home. It is tragic that he could not have lived to enjoy these things.

Old Mr. Whitehead (age 85), Bates says, is visibly failing under the shock—although he carries on with outward cheerfulness—the old Canevin stamina. He is quite deaf, & of late his eyes have been developing cataracts. H S's body has been placed temporarily in a St. Petersburg mausoleum, & Mr. Whitehead plans later to unite the family dust by having Mrs. Whitehead's remains brought South & arranging for three graves (including his own) side by side in the St. Petersburg Cemetery—father, mother, & only child. Thus good old Canevin will rest under the semi-tropical sun he loved so well, & beside the parents to whom he was so warmly & undeviatingly devoted.

Yours of the 3d. duly arrived. I sent "Evening in Spring" to Price some time ago, & shall be eager to hear what he things of it. As I said, it seems to me substantial & well-rounded, & I believe others will confirm that opinion. Melmoth the Wandrei said you were about to forward me his novel, & warned me not to be shocked by the more uninviting parts of it. This I shall probably not be—for although I detest all sexual irregularities *in life itself,* as violations of a certain harmony which seems to me inseparable from high-grade living, I have a scientific approval of perfect realism in *the artistic delineation of life.* If one is to transcribe a typical cross-section of existence, there is no excuse for leaving out ingredients—or for failing to depict characters who live inartistically as well as those who live artistically. Just how relevant & well-proportioned the various parts of Wandrei's novel are, I can tell better after reading it. The sanguinary finale *might* be justified by preceding events—for although the indicated mood is especially typical of adolescents, a perusal of the daily press shews that it is by no means non-existent among persons of an older chronological growth. Wandrei says he has an idea of publishing this tale pseudonymously in case of acceptance. I doubt, though, if it will land anywhere—for after all, it is its author's absolutely first attempt at large-scale realistic writing. It would, indeed, be highly extraordinary if such a first product were of perfect finish.

As to my own fiction—after a good long rest I'll take stock again. But it's always better to halt than to continue developing in the wrong direction. I'll be glad to see "The Return of Hastur", & trust that in it Betelgeuse may receive an appropriately primal & non-human name. Congratulations on the *Windsor Quarterly* acceptance[1]—which reminds me that Belknap asked me to ask you whether any of these small & select magazines (*Midland, Pagany,* &c.) pay anything. The little rascal is on the lookout for cash these days—although I seriously doubt whether his present work could make the pages of these discriminating periodicals.

I trust your mother's health is steadily improving. The new anthologies are providing interesting reading—& I'm about to lend the best one to Dwyer, who (mirabile dictu!) has never read "The Willows".

Best wishes—

Yr obt Grandsire

H P

Notes

1. "A Small Life" or "Mister God."

[303] [TLS, JHL]

Sauk City
Wisconsin
14 February [1933]

Dear H. P.

Yes, it does seem as if Whitehead's death were a tragic and avoidable accident perhaps, and it is indeed sad that he should have been snuffed out like that. Wright's In Memoriam note in the current W. T.[1] set me to looking up HSW's THE INTARSIA BOX and THE CUNNING OF THE SERPENT, the only two ADVENTURE stories of which I do not have. The company itself is unable to supply these issues, and I have not set myself to tracking them down through individual dealers in old magazines and old subscribers of ADVENTURE I hope I'll eventually be able to add these to items to my shelves. It is of course obvious that on the whole his ADVENTURE stories were far superior to his W. T. or S. T. pieces, good as many of these unquestionably were.

I have not yet dispatched Don's novel, but hope to get it out to you sometime this week. However, do not be wondering about it until you actually receive it or until I tell you I have sent it on. I read it over, but my repugnance to much of it was even greater than before, despite the fact that I was in a mood most essentially complacent and balanced. I can understand your detestation of sex irregularities in life as violations of harmony and I here fully agree with you. I had previously misunderstood you to mean protestation from a basis of morals, and on this basis I would have stood squarely opposed to you. I have known and still know many people who are sexually irregular, both homosexual men and women, and except for three cases out of perhaps 21, I have always found these people highly intellectual, fully aware of what they were doing, and in all cases quite helpless. Speaking perspectively and in the abstract, I could as easily conceive myself entering upon a monogamous homosexual relation as a heterosexual one—though perhaps practice would change that pointofview. To quibble about mere words, I should not say that perverts necessarily lived inartistically.

It does seem to me (he said in an injured tone) that you've had a good long rest. Anyway, I want to read something new from you. I'm selfish enough not to care particularly whether you want to do something new or not.

Tell Belknap that the little magazines don't pay, save for THIS QUARTER, HOUND & HORN, and a few others. But I'm pretty certain that, outside of poetry, Belknap will never make these magazines; he hasn't got it in him.

Dwyer has a treat in store for him indeed when he reads THE WILLOWS. I just recently picked up a used copy in good condition of Merritt's The Face in the Abyss for .15¢. I'll read it shortly and hope I'll like it. I haven't read a good weird for a long time, excepting the hasty re-reading of THE DREAMS IN THE WITCH HOUSE. Which reminds me to tell you that at Wright's request (I having mentioned I was re-reading your last story), I sent the ms. on to him, since he wished very much to read it. I hope you don't mind. I have recently read also Smith's tale in the March WONDER STORIES—DWELLER IN MARTIAN DEPTHS—not so hot; however, I've glimpsed it, and it will go forward to you shortly. Meanwhile, I send you a few clippings which might prove interesting to you, one of which please return—it's marked.

THE RETURN OF HASTUR has had to wait again until I finished SAC PRAIRIE NOTEBOOK II.[2] and did a few other pieces. Wright wrote to say that THE WHITE MOTH (held over 2½ yrs) would finally appear in the April W. T., THE CARVEN IMAGE in May. The literary agent, August Lenniger, wrote the other day, too, and as I suspected he would if he chose any, decided to include IN THE LEFT WING in the Price-Mashburn anthology.

Well, best, as always,

August

P. S. The mail just came in, together with a letter from Wright in which he says: "I have just written to Lovecraft, accepting THE DREAMS IN THE WITCH-HOUSE for early publication. Thank you very much for letting me see this." I did make clear to him your stand on your writing, but apparently he has simply chosen to ignore this. I hope you will not be offended by my sending him the ms., and at the same time I hope even more fervently that you'll let him keep the ms. for printing, for that will save me the job of making a typescript of the tale. I would anyway much rather have a print copy. Do write me your decision pronto, and let me know that you're not offended at my letting W. read the ms.

Notes

1. Actually, the unsigned piece was by HPL.

2. It is unknown what this item is. AWD published a piece called "Sac Prairie Notebook" but this was not published until 1945. Note that in 1941, AWD published *Village Year: A Sac Prairie Journal,* the first of several such prose collections.

[304] [ALS]

Feby. 16[, 1933]

Dear A W:—

Yes—a note from Satrap Pharnabazus yesterday apprised me that Flaming Youth had been shewing his Grandpa's stories—but I decided not to be stern & indignant. After all, $140 is $140—& the "Witch House" seems so much like part of a closed chapter that I don't believe its appearance would do much harm. Experience has taught me that I never get around to the revision of unsatisfactory tales . . . . . & if the appearance of such unutterable crap as "The Hound" (twice—Gawd help me!) & "The White Ship" has left my health relatively unimpaired, I ought to be able to survive the unveiling of this specimen. So I told Little Farny to go ahead—though I did set my foot down when he talked about reserving *radio dramatisation rights!*[1] Ædepol! Fancy a seriously written tale dragged down to the debasement of conventional illiterate shriek-mongering! No, Farnsworth, First N.A. Serial Rights only! Well—on the whole, I shall undoubtedly be thanking you when the $140 comes around. I can use it! So pray accept an old man's blessing.

I remember "The White Moth", & shall be glad to see it in print. Glad "The Carven Image" will follow. I've had no communication from Lhen-Eighur, Lord of Philistia, so possibly he has overruled Price & excluded "The Picture in the House" from the future anthological best-seller. Your "Left Wing" is good stuff—with real atmosphere—despite all that can be said of the usualness of the theme.

"The Face in the Abyss"—which I read in *Argosy* sections kindly lent by Klarkash-Ton under the title "The Snake-Mother"—is a middling specimen of Merritt-riciousness.[2] Like "The Moon Pool" it had a gradual evolution. It was first—a decade ago—a novelette under its present title, & I bought the *Argosy* containing it. Then the author decided to re-hash it—hence the "Snake Mother" of 1930 or 1931, & the book reprint under the old name. Hope you enjoy it. I hardly know whether it's better or worse than the later specimen you lent me. Merritt *could* be a marvellous atmospheric creator—vide the *original* "Moon-Pool" novelette—but commercialism has 'got' him. I've just revelled in a 7th or 8th reading of "The Willows"—& repeat my verdict that it is pretty nearly the *perfect* weird story.

Hope you find the older Caneviniana. I'd like to get a look at "The Intarsia Box", "Seven Loops in a Hangman's Noose",[3] & other items I haven't seen. Of course *Adventure* has higher technical requirements than W.T. Whether H S's contributions to it outrank his W.T. material in conception & essence, it would be interesting to speculate. I'll tell Sonny Belknap what you say of the non-remunerativeness of the "little magazines." Yes—it would take a lot of readjustment of perspective to make the kid eligible for their pages. He has—to use his favourite expression—the wrong "ideology."

No hurry about Young Melmoth's opus—hell knows I have enough to keep me busy! As for the question of erotic 'morals'—of course, there are no 'moral' values in an impersonal cosmos; but a certain sense of aesthetics, harmony, or just plain *neatness* makes one like to refrain from courses markedly opposed to social organisation, or markedly repugnant to either the hereditary feelings of the group or the natural instincts of its normal members. So far as the case of homosexualism goes, the primary & vital objection against it is that it is naturally (physically & instinctively—not merely 'morally' or aesthetically) repugnant to the overwhelming bulk of mankind—including all cultures except the few (the ancient Orient, Persia, post-Homeric Greece) in which strongly inculcated artificial traditions have temporarily overcome nature. There's nothing 'moral' in the adverse feeling. For instance—I hate both physically normal adultery (which is contemptible sneaking treachery) & paederasty—but while I might enjoy (physically) or be tempted toward adultery, I simply *could not* consider the abnormal state without physical nausea. Even excessive psychological sentimentality betwixt members of the same sex has for the average healthy person a repulsion varying from a sense of the ridiculous to a feeling of disgust—& all of this without leaving the domain of sheer unconscious, non-moral impulse. But as I said—it is the province of literature to consider *whatever is;* hence I may be less shocked than you at the Wandreian chronicle . . . . provided it seems sincere in its mode of charting reality. Of course, though, it may be artistically immature.

Speaking of novels by the young—here is E. Hoffmann's breezy reaction to the first part of "Evening in Spring". As you see, it gave him a tremendous wallop—& when you reflect on how dissimilar his type is . . . . even more dissimilar than mine . . . . you can appreciate how great a testimonial to the absolute merit of the work his response is. Please return the epistle, since I want to save those references to the Dzyan-Shamballah myth-cycle which Price has just uncovered. As you'll see, this stuff looks decidedly interesting!

Thanks for the cuttings. Old Pavvy, Noah Webster to the contrary, is surely a pretty active cadaver! I can't say that the occult stuff hits me very strongly, because it leaves out too many vital elements. I know Bergson of old.[4] He speaks of 'assumed relationships betwixt body & soul' when in truth he has not shewn any evidence for the existence of a "soul" or "mind" apart from the general processes of nature. And in considering human testimony he ignores wholly the larger psychological problem of the validity of certain statements—the urge to illusion & mendacity, the persistence of folk-myths, & the conscious or unconscious 'editing' of reports in process of transmission. He forgets that the reports of eye-witnesses of even the commonest events usually differ diametrically. Thus also with the telepathy article.[5] The author deliberately ignores all that psychology indicates regarding the origin of hallucinations, the mendacity (conscious or otherwise) & misplaced memory inherent in telepathic reports, & the fact that spectral 'experiences' never befall those reared outside atmospheres of superstition & credulity. But the sketches make interesting reading, & surely all experiment is to be recommended. ¶ Best [wishes] [corner missing]

Notes

1. See HPL's letter to FW (16 February 1933, *SL* 5.154–55).

2. *The Snake Mother, Argosy* (25 October to 6 December 1930); combined with "The Face in the Abyss" (*Argosy,* 8 September 1923) as *The Face in the Abyss* (New York: Liveright, 1931; *LL* 603).

3. Henry S. Whitehead, "The Intarsia Box" (*Adventure,* 10 November 1923) and "Seven Turns in a Hangman's Rope" (see letter 279n1).

4. Henri Bergson (1859–1941), *L'Évolution créatrice* (1907); tr. Arthur Mitchell as *Creative Evolution* (London: Macmillan, 1911).

5. AWD had sent HPL J. Arthur Hill (1872–1951), "Telephathy from the Dead" (publication unknown): [56]–58, condensed from "Fifty Years of Psychical Research," *Nineteenth Century and After* (December 1932).

[305] [ALS]

[c. 27 February 1933]

Dear A W:—

Yes—"The Face in the Abyss" is by no means bad. Merritt has an incipient magic all is own, which might have produced wonders had commercialism not intervened. Readers of "Burn, Witch, Burn" seem to report unfavourably on it. I haven't seen it. I'll be exceedingly grateful for a glimpse of "Hangman's Rope" and other Canevin items some time. I've just read "The Dweller in the Gulf", & can sympathise with Klarkash-Ton regarding the unutterable butchery practiced by those thieving kikes.[1] That spoiled ending is about the limit!

Dwyer's "Flash" is a bit sentimental & immature, but I think it shews distinct promise—considering the author's late start & limited reading opportunities. I suggested several points of improvement, & I think Dwyer would appreciate suggestions from you & all the others along the line of circulation. Price has just been added to the list.

Wandrei's novel duly arrived—although young Melmoth tells me that he finally decided not to have it sent. I'll add my comments after reading it—or rather, skimming through it, since there's no need of giving close attention to what Melmoth says is definitely *not* the final form. He plans to recast & revise extensively.

Yes—Price retyped my "Picture in the House". Indeed, I told him I wouldn't contribute anything if I had to type it. I hope he did the job accurately—he says he took especial care. He now says that Prince Lhen-Eighur has succeeded in interesting the Thomas Y. Crowell Co. in the anthology—though of course nothing may come of it.

I thought Malik Taus' comments on "Evening in Spring" would interest you. I'll pass along anything he says regarding the later sections. Congratulations on the Botkin honours![2] By the way—it turns out that Price's mystical legendry was, after all, only the stuff promulgated by the theosophists—Besant, Leadbeater, &c.[3] I thought it sounded like that. Do you know anything of the origin of that stuff? It pretends to be real folklore—at least in part (of India, I suppose)—but I have a certain sneaking suspicion that the theosophists themselves have interpolated a lot of dope. There are things which suggest a knowledge of certain 19th century conceptions.

Later

Have just completed a survey of Melmoth's novel. I think my opinion is more favourable than yours. There are, undeniably, certain disproportions—& the figure of "The Fool" is really rather mechanically theatrical—Greek chorus stuff—but on the whole I seem to see an undeniable power, unity, & inevitability.* The ending is not essentially untrue to life—vide the daily papers—although the diabolus ex machina part played by Pudge has a certain touch of unconvincingness. The Helione soliloquy you object to may be too long, but is possibly justified psychologically & artistically, as part of a stream of consciousness having an influence on the climax. As for the repulsiveness—if true to life (as I have no way of judging) it is entirely justified. Blame the age, not the artist—it is the logical outcome of the standardless "new morality" of the younger generation. No use of whitewashing the facts with reticence or sentiment. ¶ Best wishes—H P

P.S. [on envelope:] Frontier just arrived. Your sketch[4] is delightful—it has what Price aptly calls the reminiscence-inducing faculty.

Notes

1. See Steve Behrends's introduction to *The Dweller in the Gulf* (West Warwick, RI: Necronomicon Press, 1987) regarding the shoddy editing of CAS's story by the editors of *Wonder Stories.*

2. HPL refers to American folklorist Benjamin Albert Botkin (1901–1975). See AWD to HPL, letter 306. The book did not appear.

3. In letters to others on the subject, HPL mentioned the following writers suggested by Price: Annie Besant (1847–1933), *The Pedigree of Man* (London: Theosophical Publishing Society, 1904); Madame Helena Petrovana Blavatsky (1831–1891), *The Secret Doctrine* (London: Theosophical Publishing Co., 1888); C. W. Leadbeater (1847–1934), *The Inner Life* (Chicago: Rajput Press, 1911–12; 2 vols.); W. Scott-Elliot, *The Story of Atlantis and the Lost Lemuria* (London: Theosophical Publishing Society, 1925); and A. P. Sinnett (1840–1921), *Esoteric Buddhism* (Boston: Houghton, Mifflin, 1898).

4. "A Day in March."

*The artificial conversations are undoubtedly necessary parts of the reproduction of a certain atmosphere. No picture of this particular social group would be complete without them.

[306] [TLS, JHL]

Sauk City
Wisconsin

6 March [1933]
Dear H. P.,

I was glad to have your letter after an interval longer than usual; for a bit I had thought you might be ill and had begun to worry myself with the thought. Glad you liked A DAY IN MARCH. It is, as I think I mentioned before, one of the excised portions of EVENING IN SPRING. The material dressed up under the collected title of SAC PRAIRIE NOTEBOOK, portions of which Botkin took for AMERICAN JOKE BOOK, is also excluded material from EiS. All told, I think there is a goodly portion of discarded material at hand, and I believe that at least one fourth of the present first and second portions of the BOOK OF LITTLE MEMORIES[1] will be discarded in favour of material yet to be written, whether or not this form achieves book publication in or independent of FOLK-SAY V.

Other news of the week centers in the acceptance by another new magazine this year, THE WESTMINSTER MAGAZINE, a little Georgia paper printing Hergesheimer, Cabell, Anderson et al[.], of no less a story than THE PANELLED ROOM, thus vindicating my high opinion of that story. I shall see to it that you receive a printed copy of this story, which will probably appear in the Summer 1933 issue of the magazine.

However, what personally pleases me far more is the sudden culmination of the first of my irritating "dead" periods for 1933 with the gratifying conclusion of a three-day job—a new novelette, companion piece to FIVE ALONE and FARWAY HOUSE, entitled NINE STRANDS IN A WEB, to do which I discarded both the projected plots for OTHERS and SELINA MARKESAN. Like the two predecessors, this new novelette comes to 15,000 words all told, and while it does not impress me as good as FIVE ALONE, it nevertheless has I believe a sustained interest equal to FARWAY HOUSE if not stronger.

Re the discussion we had about names in FARWAY HOUSE some time back, by the way, I recently looked up Sauk County records in general and lifted several good old names borne by some of our old settlers, names which amply show that by no means all of our early settlers were German and French—look at this brief selection: Cadwallader, Ephraim, Horace, Edson, Orange, Satterlee, Roderick, Jared, Philander, Elihu, Hiram, Jesse, Jonathan, Chancey, Lyman, Dewitt, Jason, Arva, Campbell, Timothy, Sevyer (French this one), Reuben, Manlius, Jabez, Ansel (Anse), Truman, Hezekiah, Obadiah, Jasper, Adrian, Ebenezer, Philarmon, Delando (French too), Ashbury, Harmon, Orson, Enos, Elisha, Squire (given first name), Ransome, Guy—any more thoroughly English list it would be difficult to imagine. Inter-marriage has of course brought about all kinds of new names, some of which equal the famous joke name, Nosmo from the divided No Smo–king. As I did in NINE STRANDS IN A WEB, where I used such names as Anse Hubbard, Lavinia, Helen, Edson, Orson, Uriah, Jared, Lenna, and Lovien Ortell, and Satterlee Pickering (the names Lavinia and Lenna before marriage being German, von Borst, Vinnie's children Uriah and Lovien named for German ancestors, and Helen Swedish or Norwegian by birth), I am using only names which are sewn historically into the background of Sac Prairie and the county.

You will see NINE STRANDS IN A WEB as soon as I get the temporary final draft ready to dispatch.

I sent a note to Dwyer on the 13th of February, or perhaps the 20th—I don't quite remember. At any rate, I outlined to him largely the same suggestion I recorded in my recent letter to you.

That Besant, Leadbeater stuff originates undoubtedly from Indian folklore, though as you suspect, the English have unquestionably interpolated much material.

As to Don's novel—I've not retreated an inch from my stand, and what is better, I've managed to bring Don around to my point-of-view. Do you remember my writing to you while I was at Minneapolis of the superficial and false cosmic attitude of Don's group at St. Paul? Considering Don's sensitiveness and ego, I was considerably surprised to hear from him, without any urging on my part, to the effect that upon reflection he now saw eye to eye with me regarding the group in which he had been moving—in other words, they had their thumbs on a life-pulse which beat only by the energy of their own little group, and not, as necessary for the genuine artist, on the vital life-pulse of the universe. He has translated this concept to his novel, and has arrived at virtually the same conclusions to which I pointed—all of which is I believe one of the best possible signs. It will enable him to select details more carefully, more wisely, and will in the long run enable him to regard his own work with cold, practical criticism and to evaluate it properly. This accounts fully for his attitude toward his novel as it stands now. If the artist deals with material as that in Don's novel, it become necessary to impart to the work a life apart from the lives of its characters—merely excellent prose will not do, nor excellent characters, nor a combination of the two, nor yet the addition of plot and movement—it must have an urgent reality quite apart and yet stemming from the novel.

For this same postulated reason, I am unsure of EVENING IN SPRING, despite, as increasingly numerous testimonials aver, its reminiscence-inducing quality, which more vitally than anything else supplies that extra vitality, for it links the reader most strongly to the writer in the reader's own mnemonic past; therefore, I contemplate revision and more excision, so that this very element of life may be tightened.

To get what I felt about Don's novel, it's necessary to read it through carefully. A survey won't do. Certainly there is great power in portions of the ms.; I should be the last to deny this. As to the soliloquy of Helione to which I so much object. Not only do I object to the typography of this section, but to its inclusion at all, no matter how well written. I condemn your "it is possibly justified psychologically and artistically as part of a stream of consciousness having an influence on the climax"; to me, this is extremely faulty. I admit that Helione's psychology is necessary to the understanding of the actions on her part, and thus to the denouement. But the inclusion of such a chapter as this, shifting the point-of-view of what has been all along a single point-of-view novel, is inexcusable artistically because it is the mark of an artist's ability to convey all the necessary aspects from a single protagonist's view-point. It is indeed significantly simpler to jump from person to person and draw up a group, than to round out individual characters through another person's eyes, a process which becomes increasingly difficult as the number of extra characters increase. Yet this process is necessary in this kind of novel. The story is primarily and foremost of a young man's development; the artist's task is to have us develop with him, step by step, have us feel as he does, etc., from the first page to the last. A section such as this on Helione's thoughts has the effect of divorcing us from the character to whom we have been tied throughout.

That the conditions Don's description of which so revolted me are the natural outcome of the so-called standardless "new morality", I vehemently deny. Nor did Don, I believe, so portray them; if he did, I missed that point. Being myself a protagonist of this new morality, I know that no other protagonist I've met in this region or in others has exhibited any such evil results—all have been uniformly scrupulous, honest, and MORAL. It is to their credit that these new moralists have been enabled to support such strongly individual concepts and yet live socially. Of course, I don't blame the artist for portraying such conditions—not at all—nor do I blame any age for having brought them on; what I stand opposed to is the oversignificant emphasis on those conditions in this one specific case. I must confess that I was horrified (a little Puritan in me, I suspect) to think that I might have met any of these people while I was in Minneapolis; this, despite my instant knowledge of the presence of homosexuals and Lesbians in Don's circle of friends, and my own contact with many of both—a phenomenon which horrifies most people profoundly, and horrification which I can fully understand and with which I can sympathize, even though I am not in agreement with it.

I seem to have wandered considerably; so I'll stop now.

meanwhile, best, as always,

August

Later: I forgot to add that I am enclosing Whitehead's tale, THE CUNNING OF THE SERPENT, from Adventure May 20, 1925. I was sharply disappointed in this, for though a clever little story in its way, it was not weird. You need not return this, for I have no further use for it.

Notes

1. Published as "More Confessions."

[307] [ALS]

March 14[, 1933]

Dear A W:—

Your plans & prospects are interesting, as usual, & I am especially glad to hear of the distinguished harbour achieved by "The Panelled Room." The excisions from the original "Evening in Spring" are surely ample enough to make a volume by themselves—& meanwhile it is good that so many of them are achieving separate magazine publication. Congratulations on "Nine Strands in a Web"—which I hope to see in course of time.

Your researches concerning early Sauk nomenclature & ancestral origins are surely interesting in the extreme. I had of course realised that there were plenty of Anglo-American emigrants among the settlers of all parts of Wisconsin—my point being that none from New England (a source of origin strongly indicated by the names Phineas & Abner) would be Catholic. Nor would there have been time for intermarriage to have caused the incongruity, in view of Phineas's age at the period of the story. In preparing fiction of this kind, I fancy an author ought to keep for his own benefit a complete & exact table of chronology covering all persons & events. The mixed nomenclature of the later generations must surely contain some striking & unusual combinations.

Dwyer was very grateful for your remarks on "Flash". Klarkash-Ton seems to have rendered a similar verdict. As for "Invisible Sun"—I see your point regarding the superiority of a novel which has a life & vision apart from those of its characters, but don't you think that's a rather exacting standard to apply to a youth's first serious attempt? Such a standard would seem to apply to major rather than minor literature; & certainly, it would be rather overambitious to place the average youthful semi-autobiography—(the one novel which some critic has said everybody has in him)—in the major class. I'd say it was enough if the author makes his chosen material—characters & milieu—speak for itself in its own language . . . . & Young Melmoth certainly does that. As for the Helione soliloquy—if it came from a less pivotal character it might be as flagrant as you say; but H. is really more than an individual, being the summation of the disintegrative forces brought against the central figure. That Wandrei realises this is shewn by the fact that he has not further extended his shifting of perspective—whereas Helione is (at least) twice given a direct hearing. The typographical method of distinguishing unspoken thought from uttered words (followed for all characters throughout the book) may be obvious & mechanical, but I'd hardly call it a major flaw. Concerning the element of repulsiveness—I repeat that this is only a logical outcome of that repudiation of natural & age-old aesthetic attitudes concerning certain departments of life which (though neither new now moral) arrogates to itself the title of "new morality". Once the pattern of *standard-breaking* is established in the human mind, there is no limiting the extent to which it will go. If the dog-&-bitch promiscuity of the earliest "new moralists" could be excused on the ground that our normal disgust is only "old fashioned prejudice", it is not remarkable that nauseous & abnormal sodomy should make an equal claim. Next will come incest—people will clamour for "warmer, freer, more wholesome" relations betwixt brothers & sisters, parents & children—& finally bestiality . . . the frantic maenad & the black goat of the Sabbat . . . . will be justified & praised as something "honest" & "progressive". Who shall define the absolute validity of our disgust at any or all of these "new freedoms" present & future? What is the line betwixt "irrational & archaic prejudice" & a sound aesthetic standard? Echo alone answers. Unlike you, I find that most sexual letting down is also accompanied by a corresponding letdown in other spheres—honour, general taste in living, &c. It is also undeniable that a loosening of erotic standards has a strong connexion with the decay of nations & cultures. But what is to come, will come. And it does not become those who approve the beginning of the toboggan slide to be shocked at the logical extremes. It's their own circus!

Best wishes—Yr obt Grandsire—H P

P.S. Thanks for the Canevin specimen. It is clever in a routine, popular-fiction way, though of course not representing the really creative side of its author. He had a financially fortunate aptitude for evolving things in the dominant popular vein.

[308] [ALS]

March 23[, 1933]

Dear A W:—

Bless my soul, but they come thick & fast! Not only "Nine Strands", but now "Place of Hawks"! At this rate, your complete works will require an entire library building by the time your career draws to its close around the year 2000! Hope you can adjust both of the new units to your satisfaction—I shall be interested to see what they're like. Hope also that Lavell can give your selected shorts a British audience. The Sac Prairie poem ought to fit in with the rest somehow—indeed, all of your serious work seems to coalesce into a sort of longer unity. Perhaps the whole d'Erlette library of A.D. 2000 can have the single title "Sac Prairie"![1] Congratulations on the new acceptances—let us hope that all the complaisant magazines survive beyond date of publication. Your record with the serious magazines is quite impressive as Price's is with the pulps.

Well—if Melmoth the Wandrei can come up to your literary standard, it certainly won't hurt him. I could see that your critique had impressed him profoundly. Hope he can land his novel in some form or other.

As for standard-breaking—I haven't much use of the self-election of a separate class of conscious "intellectuals"; & contrary to the tenets of the late F. W. Nietzsche, I question the practicability & even the aesthetic desirability of dual codes. It seems to me that standards ought to embody the deepest of the instinctive preferences & delicacies of the race, & that their most sedulous followers ought to be those persons of superior discrimination & sensitiveness most capable of feeling and appreciating the force of tradition. If I were to pardon laxity in any, I would tend to pardon it most in the naturally coarse & ignorant, whose motives for aesthetic conduct are necessarily weakest. So-called "intellectuals" are as little likely to succeed in establishing a new permanent code as less presumptuous classes would be. Having once initiated the pattern of shifting standards, they can hardly expect the next generation of "intellectuals" to do less pioneering—& so down the scale. It is probably a very natural & inevitable process—only the condoners of step #1 ought not to feel shocked at steps #2, #3, & so on. Such a shocked feeling takes some of the force out of their scorn for the old people who don't condone step #1. As for laxity & decadence—please note that I didn't list these elements as cause & effect. Laxity is not a *cause* of decadence but merely a typical *symptom*—one of many symptoms. When a people reaches a played-out stage all its traditional moods & inhibitions—courage, honour, & so on—become relaxed along with the will to dominate & survive. The *cause* of the decline is generally obscure—often complex—& of course the exact symptoms vary in many cases. But that certain characteristic symptoms tend to exist would be a hard thing to deny. However—it takes no obscure symptoms to indicate the present definite decadence of the Western World. The process may be slow, but then, it was a long time between the Antonines & Odoacer!

Best wishes—

Your obt Servt

H P

P.S. Wright is going to reprint "The Festival" some time in the next few months.

Notes

1. The "Sac Prairie Saga," which represents the bulk of AWD's serious writings, was conceived as ultimately comprising fifty books.

[309] [ALS]

All-Fools [1 April 1933]

Dear A W:—

I surely hope you will be able to make a successful novel of "Place of Hawks"—otherwise, that you can place the four doctor-grandfather tales in their present form as a book. It would be likewise pleasant if a short story of the same cycle could make the higher levels of magazinedom. Once you secured a foothold in that exclusive domain, there would be a better chance for your later efforts. Meanwhile you seem to be rapidly becoming a titan amongst the small & select magazines—no small honour, in view of the rejections at their hands which many have reported to me. Young Shea has found them inhospitable to every offering so far submitted. Yesterday I received a circular announcing the American debut of the magazine *Story*—a very likely goal for your best work, I imagine.

As for standards—it isn't so much that I deem the masses incompetent to create or pass upon them in a conscious way, as that I very strongly doubt the competence of the so-called "intellectuals", as well, to perform that function. Matters of intellectual opinion, or matters of the clear-cut adaptation of means to definitely envisaged ends in the social-political field, are things regarding which the man of greater training & intelligence indeed has a superior right to speak. But ends & values themselves—local & nebulous & purely relative in a cosmos itself meaningless & standardless—are things of a somewhat different cast, & not to be disposed of in any intellectual way. They are outside the scope of intellect, since the only conditions they have to fulfil are those of emotional satisfaction—different for every race, nation, & age. One set is really no more or less logical than any other set. The only test of worth is the extent to which they satisfy the emotions of their holders, & act as a really effective basis of approximate agreement on which a working social pattern of objectives & methods can be reared. Their seat is not in the conscious intelligence but in the unconscious emotions. No amount of deliberate planning or cunning propaganda can alter them into any desired or predictable form, & no substitute system consciously framed can ever have the instinctive & effective authority of an original system of slow, automatic, & traditional growth. No individual or group, trying to break away from what blind hereditary tradition has bequeathed, ever achieves much real sense of harmony or repose in the new system. There is a feeling of something broken—a lack of harmony with past & background—which promotes a restlessness often expressed in further marks of aimlessness & incongruity. An unconscious aesthetic sense protests against a violation of a certain unity in the historic stream—& this whether or not the old code has any merely rational value. Of course, this disharmony & protest do not occur in cases of gradual modification extending over several generations. In a word—it is a fact that we cannot gain any *really satisfying* illusion of values & ends in life except through the engulfing effect of encountering this same illusion throughout the pages of ancestral history. When that illusion breaks, all illusions break—& a long reign of unstable equilibrium is ahead. Nor is it possible for one self-defined class to secede & pretend to establish new illusions of its own. Ties with the parent body are too well remembered. I don't think existing evidence sustains your theory that any group of "intellectuals" has evolved a single definite code. There are groups & groups & groups within groups, & codes & codes, & fractions of codes. Drink, drugs, perversion, disintegration . . . . madness, suicide, the emptiness of futility . . . . some get by, some do not . . . . But it is all very natural, & life goes on. ¶ I fear I shall have to move shortly, since my finances are in an alarming state. Hope I can get some fairly cheap quarters in a good neighbourhood. I must have ample space for my books & things. Best wishes—Yr obt Servt H P

[310] [ALS]

April 7, 1933

Dear A W:—

Ecce! Observe the latest development in Grandpa's age-long quest for a decent fountain pen! This is a *29¢* stylographic from the principal downtown Liggett's—& it writes the easiest of anything I've ever had, although it makes my script look more than commonly like hell. I've a damned good mind to go down tomorrow & buy a dozen before the special sale ceases! Irony—think of the 7-buck Watermans & Parkers that have done me dirt! I guess the principle of the stylographic point is better adapted to my hand than that of the ordinary pen. This is really too good to be true!

Good luck with all your ventures both weird & serious—& congratulations on your early start with *Story*.[1] Hope Fadiman (who wrote me once) & Lavell will soon report favourably. If young Jehvish-Êi gets in touch with you again, I think you'll find him more tractable than he used to be. That one year of college—under martinet instructors—took down his ego tremendously, & worked a veritable revolution with his style. And his *reading* is almost d'Erlettesque—it takes an old man's breath away! I think the boy will land somewhere sometime.

Looks ominously like moving hereabouts—but repeated surveys lend a palliating perspective. There are some splendid bargains on this selfsame ancient hill, so that the immediate threat of the slums seems removed. One thing I saw yesterday was almost incredible—& I may have been a fool not to snap it up at once. Gawd! A room as big as mine, 2 large alcoves, 2 south windows, running water, space for all my things, fine hill neighbourhood, & only ***$4.00*** per week! (I'm paying 9—formerly 10). The only reason I hesitated was to let my aunt make a final decision about doubling up our households in a cheap flat. Another room I saw was even more fascinating in some ways, though not so convenient for my things. 5 berries (landlady came down from 6)—& in a

Georgian house (circa 1820) in a neighbourhood full of ancient reliques of the 1750 period—fanlighted doorways, brick sidewalks, & colonial steeple in sight. Anyway—I see that I can probably get at least a fairly adequate room in a good locality for about $5.00 during the present depressional nadir. But the moving process will be hellish—it will take a full month out of my schedule.

Well—I've finished the Price collaboration at last. Gawd, what a job! Collaboration is exactly twice as hard as original writing. Sultan Malik's clear, intellectual concepts & metallic style are so unlike the maunderings of my own dreamy hat-rack that I simply couldn't do anything but virtually swamp him (though leaving his mathematical concepts & some of his purple passages in) & write a story of my own. I hope he'll like it—& that he won't alter it too much. I don't think it'll sell. It comes to 34 pages of my script—exactly the length of the Witch House. Present title—& I hope the Peacock Emir won't change it—is "Through the Gates of the Silver Key."[2]

As for standards—see how *your* beloved force of telepathy has brought the public press to *my* aid! The spirits are ungrateful! Your defense of personal & clique codes sounds admirable in theory—& of course one cannot be dogmatic one way or the other—but I saw poor Hart Crane go to pieces little by little in the years after 1922, & reserve the right to maintain an old gentleman's quizzical scepticism. If I seem to *overrate* hereditary traditions & the dominant part they play in supplying the illusions of direction, interest, & significance in the meaningless & monotonous process of existence, I feel sure that you young fellows disastrously *underrate* them. Yes, damn it, I know they have a "lessening importance in the eyes of [this year's sapient crop of fledgling] artists". Do not the nauseous boiler-factories, power stations, steam laundries, refinery smokestacks, & lopsided packing-boxes of the coming Chicago exposition prove as much?[3] But that is no indication as to the rightness or wrongness of the present leaders of fashion—artistic, psychological, or sociological. As for the restlessness of the individual—your assigned reason is plausible enough; but if anyone could (in undoubted absence of absolute cosmic standards) be other than restless after repudiating the only set of working illusions which can possibly belong to him, he would in my opinion be a very remarkable individual indeed.

And the 29-center still works! Almost exactly like a pencil—I'm certainly a stylographic convert until further notice. Talman became one long ago—but with my characteristic conservatism I didn't follow till a completely irresistible bargain lured me. I fear these things are short-lived—Talman spoke of the feed-wire tending to wear out.

Tomorrow another consultation with my aunt on the moving question. Vae pauperis! Yr obt Grandsire H P

[Note on enclosed clipping:] See how the press, without any prompting, has horned in on our debate.[4]

LET'S EXPLORE YOUR MIND— A fascinating pastime with

Albert Edward Wiggam, D. Sc., the noted Author of The Fruit of the Family Tree.

AUTHOR'S NOTE: These answers are given from the scientific point of view. Not all moral questions can be answered with absolute scientific accuracy, but no decision as to what is morally right is possible without science. Science puts the rights of organized society above the rights of individuals.

1.—Such people are in the same spiritual position as the physical position of Senator John Ingalls' mule, "Without an ancestry and without a hope of posterity." "Emancipate souls" are always persons with chronic indigestion, hysteria, or pernicious mental anemia. Emancipate them from these maladies and they become pretty decent folks. Social and moral codes are very imperfect but are better than any one can invent for himself.

2.—Yes. The fact that enlightened employers are installing psychologists, social workers, doctors, legal advisers, home economics teachers, and the like as the very life-blood of their establishments and also finding that they all pay cash dividends is one of the grandest things of this age. Such employers do not dominate; they co-operate under the most all-inclusive economic motto ever devised, "All for one and one for all."

3.—No. For nearly two hundred year Astrology has been excluded from every University, and scientific laboratory in the Western hemisphere. All the leading Protestant, Catholic, Jewish and secular encyclopedia which embody the worlds best thought and knowledge, without exception pronounce Astrology a "false superstition." Astrologers claim to "use mathematics." They borrow their mathematics from the astronomers, none of whom believes in Astrology but do not use statistical mathematics to measure the correctness of their analyses of character and prediction of events.

P.S. Clark Ashton Smith's brochure of previously unpublished weird tales will be out this month.[5] He's selling it for a quarter.

Notes

1. "A Ride Home."
2. Price's draft originally was titled "The Lord of Illusion."
3. The Century of Progress Exposition opened at the World's Fair in Chicago on 27 May.
4. The clipping (probably from the *Providence Evening Bulletin*) contained responses by Albert Edward Wiggam to a series of questions, one of which (highlighted by HPL) was: "Has the individual the right to live by a moral code of his own which is contrary to that recognized by organized society?"
5. *The Double Shadow and Other Fantasies* (1933). Contains "The Voyage of King Euvoran"; "The Maze of the Enchanter"; "The Double Shadow" (in *S&D*); "A Night in Malnéant"; "The Devotee of Evil"; and "The Willow Landscape."

[311] [ALS]

H. P. LOVECRAFT
10 BARNES STREET
PROVIDENCE, R. I.

[April 1933]

Dear A W:—

Using up my Sunday-best stationery, since (alas!) its middle line of printing will be sadly obsolete a month hence. Destination not yet decided—it depends on whether my aunt & I double up in a flat. If we do, I may be in an actual Georgian house (built 1800–1810) on the crest of the ancient hill. Otherwise, a possible harbourage is a small apartment in Benefit St. only 3 doors north of *The Shunned House.* This is in the Old Seagrave mansion, where the astronomer F. E. Seagrave lived & had his observatory until 1914.[1] I'll be able to give a future address during the week of May 1st. As to selling weird tales—I shall undoubtedly *try* to do so later on, but it would take more than that to float me at #10. I shall be lucky if I can keep afloat in the later & cheaper quarters.

Price tells me that *Astounding* has started up again under Bates—which is certainly news to me. He wants to "slant" the collaborated tale for the Clayton market—which I tell him he can do only if he leaves my name off. By the way—at last I've read up my W T file, except for the impossible serials. Cave's nigger story[2] is infinitely the best thing of his I've ever seen—I didn't know he had such a yarn in him! So you're in touch with Nard Jones. I recalled seeing a novel of his reviewed somewhere.[3]

Hope you have good luck with the book of novelettes.[4] An introduction by Zona Gale or some other Wisconsin celebrity would surely be a substantial help toward recognition & sale. I shall surely read "Nine Strands in a Web" & "Place of Hawks" with keen interest when they arrive. Retyping the earlier units of the quadrilogy will surely be a hell of a job. Haven't you any existing carbons of the original MSS.?

By the way—better wait about typing my Shunned House till you know whether the printed edition is lost or not. If it isn't, you will eventually receive a bound copy without a single typographical error.

Yes—it is amusing to speculate on what future psychologists would make of one's stories. No doubt they would find a deep significance to Klarkash-Ton's escapes from the terrestrial scene, in Two-Gun Bob's orgies of slaughter, & in my own intimations of cosmic outsideness & excursions to bygone centuries in crumbling & witch-haunted Arkham.

The stylographic still works, & has enabled me to keep my correspondence under better control than at my other recent period. I've bought another one (which works nearly as well) to hold in reserve. Undoubtedly, stylographics meet my especial needs better than straight fountains.

And so it goes. Am clearing all decks for the coming moving ordeal. If I don't survive it, remember the old man kindly! Yr obt grandsire—H P

Notes

1. Frank Evans Seagrave (1859–1934). The observatory, headquarters of the Sky-scrapers (see letter 418), is now located at 47 Peeptoad Road, North Scituate, RI. Formerly it was located at 119 Benefit Street.

2. Hugh B. Cave, "Dead Man's Belt," *WT* (May 1933).

3. Nard Jones (1904–1972) was an American novelist. His story "Nomadic Skull" appeared in *WT* (May 1933).

4. Probably *Place of Hawks.*

[312] [ALS]

[April 1933]

Dear A W:—

I couldn't very well escape that collaboration; since Price sent his original share before I could gracefully escape, & seemed so eager to go ahead that refusal would have been boorish. As it is, I delayed from September to April! Of course I retain the veto power over anything he does to my version—but at best, my opinion of the thing is none too high. I can't collaborate—any hampering element arrests my own imagination. Buy this time I believe I've conveyed that fact to the Peacock Sultan.

Glad to hear of your new weird work, & hope to see it in the course of time. What Wright rejects now, he'll doubtless accept at subsequent submissions. I shall send for the "1933" with your "Book of Little Memories". Glad it is to appear in a medium so apparently select.

Enclosed is my last remaining copy of "The Shunned House". Somebody—I can't recall who among the various persons to whom I've lent stuff—has failed to return the better & completely proofread copy. By the way—if Cook can find the edition (doubts of its fate have again arisen!) it may be bound & published by Walter J. Coates of *Driftwind.* Personally I think he's an ass to take the risk—for who the hell wants a single short story between cloth covers? He plans to advertise the thing in W.T. & in his own magazine. Well—Cook may not find the edition, & then no one need worry!

Still house-hunting—& endeavouring to find something in a decent neighbourhood large enough to hold my books, furniture, pictures, & other odds & ends. What I have in my room & alcove is enough to furnish a house, but I can't bear to part with anything more—I've done altogether too much contracting since the old home (with 19 rooms) was broken up in 1904. What you say of Sauk City rents sounds like a fable. If I thought any Rhode Island villages could compete with those, I'd gladly move out of town. The cheapest I can hope to get a decent-sized room for is $4.00 or $5.00 per week. I've just measured all my major pieces of furniture in order to estimate the possibilities of the rooms I inspect. As to the length of time taken to settle—it was 16 days before I could call 10 Barnes really finished, & this job will be worse because it calls for much contraction & elimination. With 2000 books, numberless papers, &c. &c. to classify & arrange, & with very limited energies, I shall certainly be doing well if less than a month can elapse between the first steps at #10 & the final touches at the new address. God, but I dread it! I've been in this place 7 years, & it seems like a real home—especially because my elder aunt was here. But there's no answer to grim financial necessity.

With appropriate blessings—

Yr obt Grandsire

H P

[314] [TLS, JHL]

Sauk City
Wisconsin
3 May [1933]

Dear H. P.,

Apparently the elements are conspiring against Sac Prairie, for we are still at this late date in the midst of the worst spring I can remember. With but 8½ days of clear weather in April, and thus far none in May. Miserable and driving rain, from the northeast, like snow, and though the flowers are up profusely in the woods they are late, and very very few of the trees have sent out leaves, being from two to three weeks late—an unheard of thing indeed. Oddly enough, however, all the birds came from a week to ten days earlier this year, including the whippoorwill, which came a week earlier.

I did have a few days on the hills, during which I wrote a short poem entitled Hawks Against April, which I copy here for your reaction:

Thus, wings delicately turned
Against the northeast wind,
Grace drawn upon the burned
Radiance of sun, bodies limned
Against the far-flung blue,
Darkly flecked upon the April sky
The hawks again renew
Their flight, too wisely high
For vengeful guns to roar.
Endlessly circling above the town,
They spiral, rise, they soar,
Their movements like the softest down
Athwart a summer breeze, their sight
Passing beyond the town, spurning
Roofs, their slow strong flight
One with earth's casual turning.

Which reminds me to say that I recently read your poem The Howler from the November Driftwind and rather liked it. Why not make it into a story for W. T.? You could easily enough and thereby increase your income.

I daresay Wright will print The Festival in the June, which, he wrote the other day, will also have my short, Nellie Foster. He recently rejected my revision of Passing of Mr. Eric Holm, and I've now sent him another version of Colonel Markesan.

The first number of The Windsor Quarterly, of which I send you an announcement, reached me the other day. I was much gratified with it, for it had contributions by E. J. O'Brien, J. G. Villa, Evelyn Scott, A. R. Wetjen, Samuel Putnam among others. This April issue has also my story, A Small Life, and it announces for number 2 in July, my Mister God. Numbers 3 & 4 may just possibly run in two instalments, The Early Years, or one of these issues may instead run in one installment, Farway House. At any rate, this magazine will have a great deal of my work.

Apart from revising Mass at Eight and sending it out, I have done little except work on the book ms. of Place of Hawks. I am now in the midst of Farway House, having completed Five Alone, the most difficult to retype owing to its many typings, and by the end of the week I hope to have got into Nine Strands in a Web.

The Astounding news is for some reason all balled up. I recently had a letter from Clayton saying that they were contemplating resuming A. S. with a part set off for occult and weird stories. I sent them three mss. which presently came back without comment. Since then I heard from a contributor to their Ranch Romances that the company has gone bankrupt. That is the last I know of the matter.

Yes, Cave's story in the May is quite good—it has many minor faults, of course, and the supernatural element is slight, but it is good. However, perhaps because I'm finicky about minor faults, I prefer Smith's story to Cave's in the current, and rank Don's as high as Cave's. The Carven Image and The Girl With the Green Eyes are the poorest pieces in this current issue.

Well, best of luck with moving. I hope the berth you find will be satisfactory.

best, as always,
August

[313] [ALS]

H. P. LOVECRAFT
10 BARNES STREET
PROVIDENCE, R . I.

[after 3 May 1933]

Dear A W:—

Farewell to #10! After May 15 I shall be located—together with my surviving aunt—in the upper half of a delightful Georgian house (130 years old[1]—of the sort I have always admired but never lived in) at *66 College St.* on the crest of the same ancient hill which I now inhabit, but about a half a mile farther south. The edifice stands next to the John Hay Library of Brown University, & is in a picturesque grassy court off the main highway up the hill. In the rear is a village-like garden—at a higher level than the front of the house. The fine Colonial doorway is much like the ideal one on my bookplate. There are 5 rooms & kitchenette nook & bathroom on the main (2nd) floor, plus 2 attic storerooms. I shall have a large study & a small bedroom on the south side, with my working table under a west window affording a splendid view of the outspread roofs of the lower town. The interior is as fascinating as the exterior—with colonial fireplaces, mantels, & chimney cupboards, curving Georgian staircase, wide floor-boards, old-fashioned latches, small-paned windows, six-panel doors, wing with floor at a different level (3 steps down), fascinating attic stairs, &c—just what one sees in the various ancient houses open to the public as museums. After having admired this sort of place all my life, it will be quite dreamlike to be living in one. I shall have all the space I want, & am getting 3 new bookcases & a cabinet for filing papers.

This doesn't sound much like an *economy* move, & yet it is just that—for the whole place *costs exactly what I have been paying for my one room & alcove at #10.* $40.00 per month, with steam heat & hot water piped from the adjoining college library. The house is owned by the university. Later on, when I take some pictures of the place, I'll send you prints. But it will be a hades of a job to get settled. I shall try to move in around May 15, but my aunt won't get settled till June. I am deferring all activities & obligations until June 15th. Now I hope like hell that I can manage to hang on to the new joint for a good long period. I wish I now how people manage to acquire cash!

Spring is about as backward here as at Sac Prairie, though I've taken two walks, & tried to write one afternoon on the old river bank. This northern climate is criminally wasteful—only 2 or 3 months of the 12 are really fit to live in. Your bit of verse is very appealing, & I trust it may be duly published in the course of time. Glad you liked my "Howler". I have often thought of making stories from the central ideas of several of my "Fungi from Yuggoth".

The *Windsor Quarterly* looks select & important, & I am indeed glad that you are to be a heavy contributor. I extend my sympathy regarding the typing tasks—they're more than I could undertake.

The *Astounding* situation surely is a chaos. Price & Klarkash-Ton report resumption, while Belknap—after a telephone conversation with the Clayton office—says nothing is doing. Perhaps they meant to start *Astounding* again, but went to pieces in the attempt. However, it isn't likely that Clayton could have been a market for me in any case. If they have collapsed, it will mean a bitter disappointment to Smith & Price, who have their hopes all up. Price says he means to leave New Orleans shortly—whether or not on that proposed Moscow migration, I don't know.

As for recent W.T.—one of the best things was that vampire yarn by Carl Jacobi. That had real atmosphere. Wandrei's sea story is excellent—I read it in MS. years ago. I also like your "Carven Image", & think your low estimate of it is unjustified.

Until May 15, continue to address mail to #10. I am bidding farewell to the world, refusing all jobs till after June 15, & in general preparing for the dreaded plunge—my first moving in 7 years. During the coming week I shall make trips to 66 College with a basket, carrying curios & bric-a-brac which I don't wish to entrust to the movers. Then the great plunge—& the living hell of rearranging about 2000 books. And on top of that, I must help my aunt move—a process which involves disposing of loads of stuff. Altogether, the whole spring & summer are likely to be ruined. However—when I think of the ancient & fascinating place I'm going to, I'm inclined to modify my pangs. But I'd never budge from here if I had the cash to stay on.

And so it goes.

Yr obt hble Servt

H P

Notes

1. In fact, the house (the Samuel B. Mumford House, now at 65 Prospect Street) was built c. 1825.

[315] [TLS, JHL]

Sauk City
Wisconsin
8 May '33

Dear H. P.,

So this is in all likelihood the last time I'll be addressing you at number 10! Your new home looks quite nice to me, but of course I shall be able to tell better when I do see a photograph of it. However, I have no doubt you'll prefer your new lodgings to number 10 after you are once settled. At any rate, you do have ample space for your 2000 volumes.

As to acquiring cash—write more weird tales. If he had them in a shorter length, 10,000 or under, I know Wright would use one of yours in every issue, just as he is doing with Smith. I think Clark Ashton has missed out on only one issue thus far this year. W. said he could not remember seeing The Shunned House, which I told him I am re-reading, and asked to see it. I accordingly sent it to him, making the situation clear to him regarding possible printing. However, if W. should want to use the tale and write you about it, I do hope that you'll let him—such use would not detract from the sale of the book very much. And it'll be one answer to your question—how do people manage to acquire cash!? Yes, by all means, do more stories—The Howler, for instance, would make a good 4–5,000 word short, and there need be no suggestion of writing down in any way. Some of the Fungi, too, will make good stories, just so that they are not too abstract centrally.

Apart from a new and rather good weird short, Wild Grapes, I've done nothing new since last writing you. W. has not yet made a report on the revised Colonel Markesan, though Trend surprised me this morning by taking my second poem, The Lights on the Prairie. The other day Trails took Song of the Saw-Whet Owl from Evening in Spring.

Yes, Jacobi's story was quite good. You should have seen the first draft—abysmal, yet hopeful enough. The ending is W's, neither Carl nor I likes it. His first drafts are usually bad—ditto The Cane, which is coming shortly... but his finals are fairly good.[1]

Sax Rhomer's new book of short stories, Tales of East and West is said to have a good many weird and occult stories in it as apart from mystery and detective stories,

best, as always,

August

Notes

1. Carl Jacobi, "The Cane," *WT* (April 1934); in *SNM*.

[316] [ALS]

H. P. LOVECRAFT
~~10 BARNES STREET~~
PROVIDENCE, R. I.

after May 20
66 COLLEGE ST.
[the week of 14 May 1933?]

Dear A W:—

The final plunge—with a horse-drawn moving team in consonance with the colonial nature of the haven for which it is hauled—will occur Monday or Tuesday.[1] This is my last pensive farewell to the sunlit world ere I encounter the long night of chaos. Books—bric-a-brac—printings—furniture—files of papers—gawd have mercy upon a poor old man! And no sooner will my own settlement be half-completed, than I shall have to assist in the transfer of my aunt's equally voluminous aggregation of lares & penates. My definition of an irresponsible & incurable optimist is a guy who says I'll be out of the woods before July 1st. Brobst was over yesterday, & I took him to see the new place—which he considers an eminently appropriate setting for Grandpa.

Let us hope that your idea for acquiring cash through new stories will work—I shall probably try it after emerging from the long night of chaos if I survive. My confidence, however, is none too great. Acceptances are not very frequent things with many, & Wright never displayed any inclination to use my stories *often*—even back in '25, when I flooded him with the accumulation of years. While using his beloved Quinn month after month, he would let long intervals go by without printing anything of mine, even when he had a good stock of them on hand & accepted.

As for the Shunned House—Satrap Pharnabazus' memory is on the bum. He turned it down in 1925 because it didn't begin actively enough—or something like that.[2] Hell, yes—if he'll use it now he may do so with my blessing! Yuggoth only knows when Cook will ever find the printed edition, & even if he did find it it would never be bound & on the market till long after brother Farnie had (if he took it) exercised his First North American Serial Rights.

By the way—Price has typed the Silver Key Sequel, & I'm sending the carbon on a very limited circulation round. You'll get it from Dwyer, with a request to pass on to Klarkash-Ton. Price himself—by an odd coincidence—will vacate his New Orleans quarters on the very day that I mournfully quit #10. He has acquired a second-hand Ford, & the first step of his migration will be to *St. Augustine*—where my greenest envy will attend him. He will then proceed to New York & settle there a while. I'm telling him to get in touch with Talman & Wandrei & Sonny Belknap. A trip to Providence will also be on his programme—repaying my 25½ hour call, as it were.

I hope to see "Wild Grapes" & "Col. Markesan" in print in the course of time. Congratulations on the Trend-Trails acceptances!

So "Revelations in Black" is the result of collaboration! But anyhow, Jacobi seems to have a talent worth developing. Hope to see the new Rohmer book if it contains anything really weird. ¶ And now to cart a load of bric-a-brac over to #66! Your obt Grandsire

H P

[P.S.] I am now reading my 3-volume "Melmoth" through. In its entirety, the novel undeniably drags.

Notes

1. HPL moved on Monday, 15 May.

2. FW looked at the story a second time but rejected it again. He published it only after HPL's death.

[317] [ALS]

[H. P. LOVECRAFT
~~10 BARNES ST.~~ 66 COLLEGE ST.
PROVIDENCE, R. I.]

[between 17 and 23 May 1933]

Dear A W:—

Well—Grandpa is gradually settling down at the new address,

though the monstrous task of arranging books yet looms ahead. Sunday night I completely dismantled my quarters at #10, & brought over all my desk paraphernalia in baskets. Monday the moving men were busy all day, & that night I arranged my transported desk & slept in the new place. Tuesday the movers were on the job again, & after they left I spent nearly every moment till Wednesday's grey dawn in getting my two rooms—study & bedroom—arranged . . . . . placing furniture, hanging pictures, laying rugs, &c. At odd moments I did enough to the kitchen & dining room to make the preparation of occasional meals feasible. Then came the disposal of filed papers, magazines, & other odds & ends—finding corners to fit them. This was a hell of a job even with ample cupboards & my new cabinet, but it is about done now. Yet the *worst* still looms ahead—for on the floor of what will be my aunt's living-room lie the bulk of my books in hopeless disarray! I have until the end of the month—over a week—to get them out of the way, but then the room which they occupy will have to be clear. All this work is the damn dirtiest process this side of hades—right now my shirt would make a good pirate flag if enough of the original white were left to form a skull & crossbones! But the fascination of this ancient house is, after all, adequate compensation. What a place! Everything in sight is quaintly redolent of my favourite 18th century—woodwork, small-paned windows, & all that. Having two rooms all my own, & a kitchen, dining room, & attic to overflow into, I do not need to crowd my possessions as I did at #10—hence my quarters are much more attractive than at any time since 1924. With a Georgian interior to live up to, I am exercising a certain amount of classic restraint in displaying bric-a-brac, pictures, & curios (I've always had a sort of museum complex)—& am ruthlessly banishing a vast amount of material to the attic. The latter is already taking on the aspect of the traditional New England garret, with the heterogeneous accumulations of generations!

. . . . Turning now to look around the room, I can honestly say that I'm damn satisfied. While only three of my pieces of furniture are really *18th century*, there's a goodly amount of *early 19th century* material to harmonise in all essentials with the room. Moreover—even the later items are remarkably free from Victorian extravagance; my grandparents having eschewed the worst vagaries of the age when renewing their furniture in the 1870's. And of course, in all the successive reductions after the breaking-up of the old house, I have invariably chosen the *least typically Victorian* things to save. As a result of all this, the present room certainly holds a strong amount of the atmosphere of 1795 or 1800. Only 9 feet high, with white Adam-period woodwork & mantel, appropriate paper, & no violent clashes in decoration, it certainly has a Georgian grace possessed by no other place I have ever inhabited. The keynote & high spot in the colonial fireplace & mantel—the latter adorned with real 18th century candlesticks, a pendulum clock at least a century old, & some old family vases. Above it will bring a marine view which—although painted by my mother around

or 1879—has a curious illusion of antiquity. I am having the ornate Victorian frame removed, & substituting a plain Georgian frame. On the wall beside my desk is a picture (copied in crayon by my mother from a much older painting now in the possession of cousins) of one of the homesteads occupied by my forbears at the time when the house was built. I have had it all my life—but this is the first time it has ever hung in an edifice even nearly as old as that which it depicts. (That house is still standing in Foster, R.I., & its interior is much like the interior of this joint.)[1] All told, I'm so fascinated with this place that I haven't yet felt acutely homesick for #10. One thing preventing homesickness is the fact that familiar objects cover so large a part of the encircling walls. After all, the most salient landmarks of home are those which one can carry with one. The views from the various small-paned windows are almost dreamlike—for as I have said, the house is in a semi-rustic court at the top of the great hill with a garden in the rear & on the west side. The window above my desk commands the mystical sunset. From my south bedroom window I can look along the court to the ancient houses & trees of College St., & glimpse the splendid old Unitarian steeple (1816) into the background.[2] Eastward—from the bathroom & kitchen windows, & from the east window of my aunt's bedroom—one can see the green front campus & ancient halls of Brown University. Almost all the windows command a view of some sort of green boughs, Georgian belfries, & bits of distant landscape.

The more I study this house, the more I come to believe that the two-story rear wing is not a *later* addition, but part of a *still older* house which was replaced by the existing 1800 edifice. All the architectural features bespeak greater age. The corner posts of the rooms are exposed, the window sashes have 12 instead of 6 panes, & the windows have inside shutters—all features peculiar to this part of the house. The posts & sashes certainly indicate a period anterior to 1750. Also—the chimneys & mantels in that wing are distinctly archaic. I rather envy my aunt her quaint bedroom in that section. The wing is three steps lower than the main bulk of the house. Oh, well—the 1800 part is good enough for me. The attic is fascinating—I'll have to take a picture of the old-fashioned staircase. The colonial front doorway is a fine specimen—like my bookplate, except that it is of the 1800 instead of the 1750 period. With about an hundred pictures of such doorways in my collection, it certainly gives me a kick to be actually living behind one! Pardon my boring you with all this description—but you can imagine what it means for a lifelong antiquarian to be moving into such a house for the first time. William the Conqueror thought he made quite a move in *1066*—but that had nothing on my 10–66 move! And the ironic, paradoxical part is that the move is in the interest of *economy*. It is merely *chance* that made this utterly ideal colonial home the cheapest practicable haven for my aunt & myself.

An interesting sidelight reveals the fact that, although 7 years older, I am no weaker now than in 1925. In '24, '25 & '26 I had occasion to hang a certain large painting in a heavy gilt frame, & found that the task of lifting it taxed my strength to its *absolute limit.* One feather's weight more & I couldn't possibly have managed it. Indeed, I almost collapsed under it in 1925. Well—I never thought I could manage it now—with my added years of senescence—but I gave it a try for good luck. And, strange to say, I *could* just swing it—exactly as in '24–25–26.

As for the Shunned House—Cook has found the edition, & it will appear in due time. I hardly thought Wright would want it again. As for abridgment—I'd do it *if Wright would add a note stating that the version is an abridged one, & forbidding anthologies from copying the text as printed.* But probably he wouldn't. By the way—my "Erich Zann" has achieved *still another* sale—its 5th to date—through Curtis Brown of London.[3] This time to a new cheap anthology to be issued by Denis Archer of London. Record of sales to date:

(1) W.T.
(2) Creeps by Night
(3) do. British
(4) London Evening Standard
(5) Archer anthology

The price offered for this latest sale is 5 guineas.

Price—by an odd coincidence—broke up his quarters on the same day that I did . . . . but I guess I told you that. He sent me a card from St Augustine stating that his first call would be on Single-Plot Hamilton. Hope he gets to Sac Prairie.

Sorry Satrap Pharnabazus cut your Bentley story,[4] but glad he has accepted "Markesan". Hope your new serious work goes over well. I sent a half-dollar for "1933", & am informed that I'll receive that publication during the first week in June.

I hope I can see that essay on the sup. in lit. some time. Such treatises are none too numerous.

Glad you get out regularly to your beloved hills. Spring seems to have actually arrived at last—but this goddam moving & settling keeps me tied to the house. Hell only knows when I can resume my accustomed aestival jaunts to the ancient river-bank! By the way—your two poems impress me as delightful. Ultimately, you will probably do a good deal more verse; for many of your moods are of the sort which lead naturally to it.

Sorry to learn that Strauch has lost his job. I haven't heard from him since March 14, & Brobst hasn't for a still longer period. A trip to Sac Prairie would certainly be quite an innovation for him—& I'm sure you would both enjoy the visit. He is an extremely bright, attractive, & prepossessing youth.

Two-Gun Bob has just been down San Antonio way, soaking up local colour & corn likker, & dreaming of the belligerent past. Possibly he has dropped you a line from there.

Oh, well—now for that ghastly book-sorting job! This will make the fourth time I shall have tackled it in connexion with a library of the present approximate size & nature. At my first moving in 1904 my mother attended to many of the books which are now within my own personal library. I shall have to do it all within about ten days—& may Yuggoth help me! Then the job of helping my aunt move in will ruin another half-month. Such is life. But it's some compensation to be in a genuine Georgian house. Hope you can get east & see it before long.

You'll note that I'm using Kirk charity envelopes again. Found a lot of 500 in dismantling the crowded alcove at #10. My supply may yet survive me!

Best wishes—

Your obt Grandsire—

H P

Notes

1. HPL refers to the Stephen Place–Henry Battey Farm (1769), probably built by Stephen Place, Sr. (1736–1817), on the north side of Moosup Valley Road, moved to the south side of the road in the mid-nineteenth century. (See Rhode Island Historical Preservation Commission, *Foster, Rhode Island: Statewide Historical Preservation Report P-F-1* [1982], p. 64.) Lovecraft had visited the Foster area in 1896, 1926 (see *SL* 2. 81–89, and 1929).

2. The First Unitarian Church (1816), 301 Benefit Street.

3. The proposed anthology never appeared.

4. "The Return of Andrew Bentley." FW trimmed more than 500 words from the story.

[318] [ALS]

66 College—
May 28, 1933

Dear A W:—

Scorn not the yellow of this paper—for that means history . . . . of a modest sort. In the course of adjusting stored material to this new abode I came upon a box not opened in a quarter of a century, & containing a complete file of the old *Rhode Island Journal of Astronomy,* which I issued on a hectograph from 1903 to 1907 . . . . before there was any young Comte d'Erlette in the world! Besides the file there were the odds & ends of several pads of paper which I used in "printing" the journal—& this sheet is from that residual stock. The voice of the past! I feel almost tempted to issue a 1933 number of the *R.I. Journal* on the same old paper & with the same old pen-&-ink characters!

Thanks for Sultan Malik's deteckatiff attempt—which isn't at all bad for routine work. I expect to see the Sultan ere long. As for the brogues of policemen—it is largely a literary convention now, but was sound realism when I was young.[1] For some reason or other, all Eastern police forces have attracted Irishmen as cheap restaurants have attracted Greeks, clothing shops Jews, & barber shops Italians; & up to the last generation a goodly number of the recruits were close enough to the old sod to have very eloquent brogues. Of the 4 or 5 neighbourhood policemen whom I knew well in the 1890's, all were Irish, & 2 sported magnificent brogues . . . . . equalled only by those of most of our noble dynasty of cooks. Even today the forces of the Eastern cities are overwhelmingly Irish in blood, although the predominance of the American-born generation has ironed out a good deal of the brogue. And at that, one can't say that the brogue is by any means wholly extinct. Only the other day I heard a careless motorist 'bawled out' by a voice whose infant cries were certainly uttered amidst a greener milieu than ours! By the way—I wish you had sent along the Peacock Sultan's autobiographical note. I haven't seen it.

As for the moving siege—I'm personally settled at last, although on Thursday next my aunt's moving will begin—imposing on me an auxiliary function not less arduous than that of my own upheaval. This is, therefore, merely a breathing-spell. I finished sorting my books on Wednesday, May 24, just 9 days after the mighty landslide of May 15th. That was not as long as I had anticipated—not as long as I took to settle at #10 in 1926—yet was hardly comparable to the single day in which you allege you could get moved & settled! What made this job easier than the last was the fact that I had 2 rooms to spread out in, & an attic to overflow into. It's pretty damn good to be back in a house again after 8 years of rooming! I had to get another small bookcase before I could house all my volumes—including the generous d'Erlette donation of recent months. That makes 4 new cases to give #66 an auspicious start. Another thing I've picked up is a cheap camp cot, so that (since I now have plenty of space) I can house an occasional guest. Thus when you get here on some future trip I can save you hotel bills. Price will probably be the guy to dedicate it—unless W. Paul Cook beats him. When my fat friend Morton comes in August, I'll probably take down the cot & let him use my couch—which at least won't break under him, even though his bay-window may overhand the edge!

About the Shunned House—after all, I can't bother to dicker with Satrap Pharnabazus about it. Cook has located the edition at last, & sent me a complete copy; & upon re-reading it I find the early portions so necessary to the atmosphere that I can see an abridgment would be virtually impossible. Therefore I'm telling Cook & Coates to go ahead with the book project, & letting Wright stew in his own juice. But don't bother to copy the text now. Before long you'll have a printed & bound copy for your library!

Good luck with the book MS.—& I trust the new tales & verses will also find appropriate havens. Yes—I fancy it is wise to let "Place of Hawks" form the last of the trilogy if it is stronger than its chosen companions. It will, though, have to go some to beat "Five Alone" & "Farway House."

I heard recently from little Shea, who enclosed his latest literary attempt—an intendedly realistic sketch called "The Cell". There seems to be some retrogression since his "Tin Roof"—too bad he could not keep on at the university & undergo a little more prodding from the professor who helped him so much in 1931–2. Like me, his family have had to move to cheaper quarters—& oddly enough, to continue the parallel, the move has actually given him more convenient housing. If you have occasion to write him, remember his new address—5705 Jackson St.

As for the Denis Archer anthology—the letter from Curtis Brown did not state what the title was to be. I'll let you know as soon as I find out. Hope I get a free copy! I'm glad to hear that the publisher is not a mere fly-by-night. "Erich" certainly has piled up the sales—which rather pleases me, since it is one of my own favourites. I put it next to the "Colour", even though O'Brien ignored it.

I must look up this Butts stuff.[2] As for Shiel—he is undeniably clever, but exasperatingly uneven. The florid flamboyancy of some of his prose is painful—& yet at times he becomes virtually peerless. His indubitable masterpiece—"The House of Sounds"—is a revision (made in 1908) of a vastly weaker & more effusive tale written in 1896. I saw the original (whose title I forget) once, & was certainly glad that the author saw fit to do it over. "The Lord of the Sea" rather bored me, & I never read "How the Old Woman Got Home". But "The Purple Cloud"—which I first read in 1927 & now own—is certainly magnificent; especially the first half. I also own "Prince Zaleski" . . . .

& would give a good lot to pick up the "Pale Ape" collection containing "The House of Sounds."

Some good warm days lately, though I wasn't able to enjoy them. Today is cold & rainy—indeed, the steam heat is on here. I'm glad to see that heat is furnished on these doubtful days when landlords usually leave their victims to their own devices. I shan't have to piece out with oil & gas as much as I have done elsewhere.

My weird books—including mythology & folklore—are all together now, except for such as belong in sets of standards authors. This group covers four 35-inch shelves & three 22-inch shelves—about 17 feet in all. I never thought the group would grow as large as that!

Best wishes—

Yr most oblig'd obt Servt

H P

Notes

1. HPL uses a bit of Irish brogue (for a Providence policeman's speech) in "The Haunter of the Dark" (1935).

2. Mary Butts (1890–1937), British novelist and short story writer. AWD may have suggested *Traps for Unbelievers* (London: Desmond Harmsworth, 1932).

[319] [TLS, JHL]

Sauk City
Wisconsin
31 May 33

Dear H. P.,

I write you on the first draft of what will eventually be a huge mass of stationery. The above cut when finished will be a two colour, green and black-white, and will be set lower on the page, to balance more. It is the Spring design, and as you can gather from that, I will have three other designs, one for each season. And it will cost me only the wholesale price of the paper, no more—at last some of the bread I've cast upon the waters is drifting back. It's more than welcome, believe me.

Your letter smelled ancient, and I wondered what eldritch communication came from number sixty-six. An echo from the past, indeed; to think of being communicated with on paper that was ancient before my birth! It ought to satisfy my past-nostalgia.

I include herewith Price's autobiographical note, as per your request. Please return at your convenience. I inclose also finally the carbon copies of PLACE OF HAWKS and NINE STRANDS IN A WEB, your reaction to which (in your own time) I await with keen anticipation. I am interested to know whether you will bear me out in that the longer of these two is the best of the four which go to make up the book. From you, these mss. should go to Mr. Edward L. Klein, 3141 Durrell Avenue, Cincinnati, Ohio.

I have finally finished the job of typing the book ms. and it goes out to Lieber today. I am guaranteeing any publisher a minimum sale of 500 copies providing the book is issued before Christmas and in time for Xmas sale. I have actually come to believe that at least a hundred copies can be sold right here in Sauk City, which is astonishing indeed.

I will look forward to THE SHUNNED HOUSE in bound form; indeed it will be highly welcome and a fine number to add to my select shelves of weird literature (my shelves come to 3½, but VERY select).

I fancy if Shea had wanted to get in touch with me, he would have done so before this. I fear that my sharp criticisms and positive dicta irritated him; it is a sign that he will not go very in his field if this tendency to easy irritation continues.

Shiel is, I think, one of the great living stylists, quite up to Machen, though Machen is of the old school, and Shiel is of the new, as demonstrated largely in The Lord of the Sea and How the Old Woman Got Home, two fairly ordinary books whose sheer beauty of style continues to fascinate me even over this period of two or three years since reading. He makes his language flow like limpid water. Even Machen cannot do that. You must take Machen slowly. Shiel carries you along. The tendency is noticeable already in THE HOUSE OF SOUNDS and in other stories in THE PALE APE (which I think you might be able to get through the Gotham Book Mart, 51 West 47th Street, New York City—write them, mentioning my name, and see what they can do. I got my copy for $2.00). I personally place THE PURPLE CLOUD beneath the Lord and Old Woman, though his BLACK BOX, which I have yet to read, will rank below this, with his DR. KRASINSKI'S SECRET, another very fine book. PRINCE ZALESKI has been reissued in England in a 2/6 edition, and I'll probably eventually get this to replace my old first.

Wright writes that THE RETURN OF ANDREW BENTLEY is scheduled for publication in the September issue of W. T. There will be nothing of mine in the July, for which I am sorry, but I hope that he can work something into the August. I am today getting ready a revision (shortening) of THE SHUTTERED HOUSE.

best as always,
August

[320] [ALS]

66 College St.,
Providence, R.I.,
June 5, 1933.

Dear A W:—

My aunt moved in last Thursday, & yesterday afternoon I snatched a vacational moment to get to my cherished river-bank & enjoy the rustic warmth of a belated spring. The blaze of golden sunlight on fresh green woods & blue water was magnificent—& while seated on the familiar high bluff, unchanged since my infancy, I indulged in a careful & appreciative reading of your two new stories.

Both of these tales are really splendid studies in eccentric human nature & regional colour. As a whole, they have the aura of genuine vitality about them—all the characters are truly alive & individualised—plus a sense of cosmic continuity & of the larger flow of life which is typically d'Erlettian. Price is right in attributing to such work the quality of memory-stimulation. These recallings of the past come to seem like one's own memories, & the peculiar & distinctive life of the Wisconsin valley emerges as something one almost feels one has known. You are evidently, by natural endowment, the logical laureate of the Sac countryside in general, & of its more secluded, introspective, & psychologically abnormal types in particular. A certain type of humanity—wistful, neurotic, hypersensitive, ineffectual—gains from you a vivid presentation almost without a parallel.

I think you are right in considering the longer tale the more solid, balanced, & powerful of the two. While "Nine Strands" is a tremendously fine individual study, "Place of Hawks" has a scope, variety, setting, & drama which make it the broader & more representative of the two—the more effective as fiction. These items, in conjunction with "Five Alone" & "Farway House", will certainly form a fine collection—a sort of miniature Wisconsin Comedie Humaine. Of the four, I'd say that "Five Alone" & "Place of Hawks" were tied for first place aesthetically, & that "Place of Hawks" leads from the standpoints of technique & intrinsic interest.

As for individual criticisms—oddly enough, I can't find any point to carp about in "Nine Strands." "Place of Hawks" elicited a few marginal notations yesterday, though none of these pertained to the inner essence of the tale. I'll briefly bring these points up for your consideration, letting you do about them as you like. Of course, other commentators may have covered them better than I.

First comes our old controversy about *coincidence*. Naturally, since you hold certain chimerical theories regarding the place of coincidence in life & art, you will pay no attention to what I shall say—but I wish merely to go on record. I'll give the facts for you to laugh at & disregard—& you can remember what I say when others bring up the same point. Gradually, I think, others will convince you that the indiscriminate use of coincidences & improbabilities in building up "big scenes" is a dangerously weakening device which mars the naturalness & convincingness of even the finest work. In the present case some of the accumulated coincidences on coincidences produce an effect not only theatrical but almost unconsciously comic—& dull the sense of vitality by making the dramatic mechanism irritatingly obvious. Such a *flood* of coincidences could never conceivably occur in actual life—you make Dr. Grendon a sort of magic figure like Jules de Grandin, who is always coming in contact with miraculous conditions, as if his personality attracted singular events around him! At this point you will superciliously smile & present glib & intricate arguments—but the facts remain unaltered. Don't heed me now, but wait till acute & intelligent reviewers get at you! Incidentally, though, let me give you credit for not abusing coincidence in the *worst* way this time. You depend on it for dramatic effects, but you don't make major developments of events hinge upon it. That's something! Now as for concrete instances—in the early part you have Noel's arrival unmotivatedly & unjustifiedly synchronised with the doctor's chance call on the sisters. This *could* occur, but why pick the *most unlikely of all possibilities* when it merely imparts a hampering air of unreality to the story? The reader thinks of literary mechanics when Grendon gets the telephone call about Noel on the *very day* that he has happened to look up the Pierneaus. However—this point is a mild one as compared with others ahead. The major defects begin midway in the tale, when overt events commence to pile up. For one thing—although no mention has ever been made of Dr. Grendon as an habitual sleep-talker, you have him very conveniently explain in his sleep just what is necessary to further the plot at a certain juncture. Then soon afterward you have Sevyer die on *just* the night that Grendon *happens* to be at the Pierneau house—another obviously laborious timing in the interest of theatrical mechanics. This wouldn't be so bad if it weren't the *second* unjustified coincidence in the tale—but as it is, it evokes a very dangerous impression of artificiality & unreality . . . . . . an impression all the more bewildering because the story *as a whole* is the very antithesis of the artificial & unreal. Still, let us call this second slip a minor one, too.

The thing gets flagrant & unforgivable only at the time of Noel's death. Here, where everything ought to be solemn & awesome, you suddenly spring an incredible Chinese box of interlocking coincidences so all-inclusive & obvious that the reader is brought perilously & incongruously near to the snickering-point. You have the following separate events, each the product of an absolutely unrelated set of circumstances, occurring at precisely the same time in order to create a convenient "big scene":

Casual social call of doctor—not in answer to a summons.

Delivery of telegram timed by a wholly unknown & unrelated death far away.

Death of Noel from a hemorrhage totally unconnected with either the doctor's visit or death of son.

Death of son at that period—unrelatedly—as distinguished from the exact timing of the telegram (which latter, with the death occurring when it did, might or might not have arrived just at the right second to reach the doctor's hand.)

One of these alone would not be so obtrusive. All of them together—& after the other coincidences in the story—are well-nigh intolerable. Of course the poignant power of the rest of the tale may very conceivably float it in spite of these defects, but one hates to see a writer *deliberately* trying to mar a splendid story of his own! Let us hope that more convincing critics than I can help to rid you of your single handicap.

Now for the wholly different matters—one of which is a matter of *positive knowledge* whilst the other (like the appropriateness of the names of those two old Maryland Papists Krishnamurti & Atuahalpa Farway) calls for a bit of historico-genealogical checking up.

Imprimis: you have (p. 30) the constellation of the Southern Cross mentioned as visible *in Wisconsin,* which is definitely & conclusively impossible. This is a group in the southern celestial hemisphere, only 30° from the pole, & can't possibly be seen north of the southernmost tip of Florida—& even there it would take a damn sharp eye to glimpse it. I couldn't catch it in 1931, even though I scanned what theoretically ought to have been its place amidst the vapours of the southern horizontal Key West. Practically speaking, the Cross can't be seen definitely & decently north of Mexico or the West Indies—& Wisconsin certainly knows it not. No question here—you simply can't use it unless you want to pull some deliberate nature-faking. It would be as bad as having the young crescent moon visible in the east at midnight, or something like that. Incidentally, the Southern Cross has only *four*—not five—conspicuous stars.

Point II concerns the family name *Delano*—& I'll preface it by asking whether you don't think it a bit improbable for anybody—even an extraordinarily reared person—not to know his mother's maiden name (p. 48). About the name—you have *Delano* (Anglicised form of *de Laneaux*) represented as a typical Creole name, whereas I doubt if it can exist in Louisiana. The family of Delano is of Huguenot origin & New England locale—the Anglicisation process being (like the transformation of *Apollos Rivoire* into *Paul Revere*) a peculiar result of New England's closely-knit English texture. This process would never have occurred in Louisiana, where French continued as a spoken language till almost the present century & generation. I never heard of a French name Anglicised in Louisiana. On the contrary, non-French names were often *Gallicised* there—as illustrated by the Gallicisation of the early German stock on the Mississippi above New Orleans, where names like *Troxler* became *Trosclair.* If any *de Laneaux* settled in Louisiana, the chances are that he & his posterity stayed *de Laneaux*. *Delano* is (so far as I know) purely a New England transformation, & the only known Delanos are descendants of New

England Huguenot stock. Of course, they have spread—but they wouldn't be likely to be found amidst the Catholic Creoles of Louisiana. Any transformation of the name *de Laneaux* to *Delano* could be expected only where the English influence was strong. It might have occurred amongst the Huguenots of New Rochelle, N.Y., or amongst those of Charleston. The Charleston Huguenots were about 50–50 in Anglicising their names . . . . some did & some didn't. Thus we find both *Petigrus* & *Pettigrews* springing from the same Charleston family. In New England a slow Anglicisation of French-Canadian names (etymological rather than phonetic—thus *Leblanc* becomes *White* & *Dubois, Wood* or *Forrest*) is still going on.

Well, that finishes the carping! But one inquiry: are there really any 18th century French houses left in Wisconsin? If so, I'd give my eye-teeth for a picture of one! They ought naturally to resemble Quebec rather than Louisiana types—possibly with frontier characteristics distinct from either. Have you ever seen one? The oldest French building I've ever seen is the Quebec general hospital (1620), & the oldest private house one in Rue St. Louis, Quebec (1656). 18th century Quebec types—urban, chateau, farmhouse—are quite familiar to me. I believe the American northwest had quite a bit of French architecture in the 18th century—especially Detroit & parts of Illinois & Indiana—but I understood that most was wiped out by this time. Any authentic information or description of early French architecture in Wisconsin will certainly be most welcome to me. You description in the story would of course suggest changes since the 18th century.

As per request, I'm forwarding the tales to Mr. Klein. Thanks abundantly for the glimpse. They are really great stuff—their inherent vitality & poetry get under one's skin. I delight in the occasional landscape touches. Here's hoping the book lands—& succeeds! I don't envy you the typing—ugh!

Thanks for the Price autobiography, which I return herewith. It certainly is a smooth, clever, & witty performance . . . . quite true to type. I didn't know that any of Malik Taus' service was in the Philippines . . . . . He ought to have been popular amongst the Maros!

Your new stationery certainly looks tasteful & sumptuous—& the perfected product will clearly beggar description! Let me see the set of four designs when you get your final supply. You are lucky to have an opportunity to get this material so cheaply—it makes me think of my Talman-designed bookplate. The rural seasonal designs will be infinitely appropriate for one as devoted as you to the varying aspects of nature as glimpsed from Sac Prairie's flower-starred hill. I've used up my exhumed stationery (which is no doubt contemporary with Dr. Grendon & the Grells, Farways, Ortells, & Pierneaus!) & am now back with the choice products of Frank Winfield Woolworth.

I'll be glad to see "Andrew Bentley" in September, & hope you have something in the August issue. I've just re-read "Nellie Foster", which I recall in MS. Good luck with "The Shuttered House."

As for Shiel—I suppose his best work equals Machen's stylistic average, but he can (& frequently does) write rottener than Machen ever could. I prefer even Blackwood's journalese to much of M.P.'s neo-Saltusian pyrotechnics. My "Prince Zaleski" is an old copy about to fall to pieces. I may write the Gotham mart about the Pale Ape. About a year ago I heard of somebody who got a copy for a half-dollar . . . . . it would have to be somebody other than I!

Just read a MS. of little Belknap's indicating a comeback. A dark wooded swamp abnormally teeming with frogs . . . . an idiot boy & his haggard mother & sadistic stepfather . . . . . dark tales of his own father, who had been one of those forest dwellers suspected of dealing with *Them* . . . . & finally, one of *Them* in person . . . . . . I hope the child keeps up his new streak—& if Wright doesn't take the specimen he's . . . well, at his usual level![1]

The household at #66 continues to crystallise. Saturday evening my aunt's living-room became settled, & I must confess that my own personal quarters are outdone. She has some old family pieces—really colonial—that I lack . . . . including a slat-back chair of the early 18th century. Her mantel is a triumph—old candlesticks & plates, & an old family pointing above it. Other features of the room are some oil paintings my grandfather brought from Europe in 1878, & a life-size bust of Clytië on a pedestal in a plush-hung niche. The atmosphere of my old home is recalled with a strange & poignant magic, since things have come out of long-term storage, while other items long separated are now united after 29 years. Over the staircase we are hanging an immense canvas (Rocks at Narragansett Pier) by my late elder aunt (I could curse the damn cosmos that she hasn't survived to see this layout), for which no space has previously been available since the original home disintegration of 1904. It is certainly ironic that the need for *retrenchment* should cause such a paradoxical gesture of *expansion!* Once again a home with the echoes of long-departed days . . . . & a *Georgian* one at that, which the old home wasn't!

Had my telescope out last night—pretty fair sky-vista here. Mars & Jupiter were so close together that I could get them into the same telescopic field with a 150-diameter eyepiece.

Best wishes—Yr obt Grandsire—H P

P.S. Have discovered a booklet issued by the State Educational Commission, containing a picture of Providence's ancient hill in which *this house* plainly appears! If I can get some copies I'll let you see it. It displays the whole neighbourhood as it sweeps up from ancient Market Square to the 1770 College Edifice.

Notes

1. FBL, "The Dark Beasts," *Marvel Tales* (July/August 1934).

[321] [ALS]

H. P. LOVECRAFT
66 COLLEGE STREET
PROVIDENCE, R. I.

June 10, 1933

Dear A W:—

Speaking of stationery—here's a fresh coincidence to add to your list! My aunt surprised me with this today, as a sort of adjunct to housewarming festivities. I note Stage II of the d'Erlette Gallery. Yes—I think the leaves would bear considerable improvement, but the main design is admirable.

As for those "stars" which changed their places—they were like the supposed tomcat that had kitties! In a word, they weren't *stars* at all, but *planets*. From their location during recent months I judge that they were Jupiter & Mars, perhaps in connexion with the true stars Regulus & Denebola in Leo. Stars never change their *relative* places in the sky—that is, not within any interval perceptible to mankind except after thousands of years. Recently the planets Mars & Jupiter have been very close together—last Sunday night they were in conjunction, & so close that I could get them both in the field of a telescope with an eyepiece of 150.

About de Laneaux—Delano—of course I didn't mean that the family was purely Huguenot, but simply that it was the Huguenot branch whose name became Anglicised in this especial way. Other branches may have settled in Quebec or New Orleans, but in the purely French environment of those places the name would have remained unimpaired—or even if accidentally corrupted, would not have followed the laws of English phonetics. The point merely was that the form *Delano* could not very well have evolved in *Louisiana*. It was the product of a dominantly English environment amidst which the original name seemed eccentric & difficult. All this has nothing to do with the family religion—except that it would naturally be the Huguenot branch of a French family which would emigrate to a Protestant English region where Anglicisation would be apt to occur. The *-o* termination for *-eaux* French names was a common modification in the English colonies. One of our Rhode Island pioneers, *Stephen Gano,* was originally *Etienne Ganeaux*.

As for coincidences—you surely cite an impressive number from real life; yet fail to convince me that they are *typical* enough, in large & cumulative quantities, to form convincing material in fiction. In actual existence they are scattered, & in most cases connected only with *trivial or irrelevant* events. What makes their common fictional use unconvincing is that they then centre around *vital* events in the careers of the various characters. The only way to represent life's coincidences truthfully is to shew them mainly as occurring in fields alien to the particular line of events chosen for description. For example—there might be a dozen coincidences in Dr. Grendon's life during the period covered by your story, but the chances are that not more than one or two would be connected with that especial side of his life which touched the Pierneaus. What makes these literary coincidences so suspicious is that they all cluster around a single line of events, & all promote the unfolding of the plot in the especial way the author has chosen. You'll find it in the old Gothic novels—but improved technique has frowned upon it. In "Melmoth", for example, the parricide in the monastery superintends the torture of the recreant monk & the female disguised as a novice—& soon afterward discovers that the latter (for no reason under heaven!) is his own sister. That kind of thing simply won't do today, even if it "got by" in 1820.

As for specific instances—as I said, the first one was not so bad. However, conversation indicated that Dr. G. had not been at the Pierneaus' for some time (& had not taken the boy there before)—& it is odd that this special kind of visit—the boy's first—should happen to coincide with Noel's return. As for the second—are sleep-talkers generally so accomodatingly explicit? The disjointed phrases of the average somniloquist would be of far less aid in promoting the plot! Regarding the death of Sevyer—how about the dozens of thunderstorms on nights when the doctor *wasn't* there? There is no such thing as an "equinoctial storm"—though atmospheric disturbances tend to be common & violent during the weeks of cooling weather around the general time of the autumnal equinox. Regarding the death of Noel—granting that the doctor's call was professional rather than social, it was certainly not made with any idea that the patient was in a desperate state. He might just as well not have made it that day. Assuming that he was present in the Pierneau house for half an hour on two days per week, we have a total of 1 hour per week that he was on hand. In a week, however, are 168 hours, in any one of which Noel might equally well have died. Is it less than a coincidence that his fatal seizure came during one of those brief fractions of time during which the doctor happened to be present as part of a quasi-regular schedule, & without a special summons? But of course this is not nearly as bad as the fatally facile death of the son at just the right moment to precipitate a dramatic denouement. The chances of such a theatrical event in the life of a family can scarcely be more than one in a thousand. Remember—it is not that coincidences *of some sort* don't often occur, but that coincidences *of such vital import* don't often occur.

It interests me extremely to learn that some 18th century French houses remain in Wisconsin. I don't believe the fact is commonly realised in the East, even by antiquarians of the average sort. If I ever get west, I'll certainly have to take in Prairie du Chien—& meanwhile I'll be abundantly grateful for any pictorial glimpses which the fates may throw my way. These old houses ought to be written up & made known to architectural enthusiasts in general.

This is my kind of weather—90° the other day. Besides haunting the river-bank (where I am now) I've begun exploring a rustic region north of the town which I never visited before—west of my favourite Quinsnicket woods.

Some days I've covered over 12 miles—& encountered exquisite scenery.

Your obt grandsire

H P

P.S. It is in Dunwich that the whippoorwills occur. They figure strongly as psychopomps in actual New England legend. ¶ Congratulations on the landing of your poem.

[322] [ALS]

June 22[, 1933]

Dear A W:—

The wealth of welcome Prairie du Chien material—for which I extend a limitless abundance of thanks—finds this household in a state of unlooked-for chaos. Last Wednesday my aunt, while descending the stairs to answer the doorbell during my absence, took two steps where she ought to have taken one—& as a result is laid up at the Rhode Island Hospital with a broken ankle . . . . . in a plaster cast, & with prospects of bedriddenness for 3 or 4 weeks, followed by a crutch period. This in the very midst of settling! You can imagine the effect on my programme . . . . . I am now shuttling back & forth to the hospital, & meanwhile keeping house in solitary state. Next week my aunt will probably return & have a nurse here. And just to aggravate the chronicle of disaster—I've had a note from Curtis Brown saying that my permission for the use of Erich Zann in the Denis Archer anthology arrived too late . . . . though I sent it by return mail. They add, however, that Archer may possibly want the tale later for a [*sic*] another collection.

I can scarcely express my gratitude for the delightful & revealing glimpse of Wisconsin antiquities which your postcards & later enclosures furnished. Those tombs on the hill are infinitely impressive—& wholly alter one's idea of Wisconsin as a *new* country. Your photographs finely bring out the mellow background—as do the folders & half-tones, as well as the cards. With your description—plus the map—I can manage to visualise the scene quite well. The river-bluffs must make Prairie du Chien a sort of northern counterpart of old Natchez—also on the eastern bank of the Father of Waters. The venerable houses remind one strongly of many buildings in the East—in the U.S. rather than Quebec. I don't see any of the typical French casement windows with which Quebec abounds—& of which a few specimens exist in New Orleans. The Famechon house has small-paned windows like old English & American buildings, & indeed resembles many in Providence & elsewhere. That octagonal house belongs to a well-defined American type of the 1830's & '40's. I've seen specimens as far north as Vermont & as far south as Washington, D.C.

The 1842 house shewn in the half-tone is of a type frequent in New York & New Jersey—with narrow windows above the porch. The old fur-trading post has a gable end typical of the early 19th century—much like one at the foot of this very College St! How unfortunate that the 1836 house shipped from Pennsylvania has been demolished! The frequent use of stone as a building material would seem to attest the French influence—or a Pennsylvania influence. Fort Crawford & its traditions add another leading factor to the rich background—what a pity so little is left of it! The old French cemetery with its patriarchal tree would seem to be supremely picturesque.

All the anecdotal notes are of extreme interest. I note the many surviving French names. Presumably these settlers now speak English—like the old Spaniards of St Augustine—which sets them apart from the French-Canadian wave now inundating New England. Our French-Canadians are jealously tenacious of their ancestral ways, & are among the most difficult of all foreign elements to assimilate. They are so near their homeland that they cannot acutely feel any transition, but simply spread the Quebec culture southward. They are invincibly clannish, & the towns where they predominate become as French as Quebec City itself. Woonsocket, R.I. is so solidly French that English is almost a foreign language there. The present mayor is one Felix Toupin, while Dupré, Pothier, Laliberté, Gagnon, Caderette, &c. &c. are the sort of names which predominate both in the city directory & on the rolls of the municipal government. Wherever there are mills, the French-Canadians flock in. Arctic, R.I., Central Falls, R.I., & Fall River, Mass. are other predominantly Gallic towns. Most of the speeches in the Woonsocket City Council are in French. There is a grim irony in the peace-time invasion of New England by the northern foe & whom we fought determinedly from 1689 to 1760!

Your new poems seem to me of really poignant & sensitive quality—you'll have a book of verse published yet! By the way, though—if I were you I'd investigate the prosodical value of the word *es´-tu-a-ry* before trying to rime the *unaccented* last syllable. Also—I suppose you realise that this word applies only to a *tidal* inlet. You can't engraft it on Sac Prairie.

Wright has just sent advance sheets of the Witch House, & there are some heartrending misprints—two of which made me seem woefully inane.[1] The worst misprint is that which *apparently* makes sense—but in a feeble way contrary to intention. ¶ Again expressing my limitless thanks for the antiquarian material—Yr obt Grandsire—H P

[P.S.] Trust you recd. brochure with picture of #66

Notes

1. HPL complained most of "magical love" for "magical lore" and "human element" for "known element." See *SL* 4.213–14.

[323] [TLS, JHL]

Sauk City
Wisconsin
25 June 33

Dear H. P.,

I am indeed sorry to hear about your aunt's accident, and trust that she will soon be on her feet again. I can well realize the chaos her untimely accident must have caused, and felt strongly about it when I first heard of it prior to your letter in a note from Robert Block, [*sic*] who apparently had just had it from you.

Your reaction to the Prairie du Chien material is gratifying, indeed, and I am glad you found the photographs and anecdotes interesting. At this moment, I am writing on the porch of a young friend whose home lies on what is known here as Dam Heights, being just above the power dam 4 miles above Sauk City, directly across from Black Hawk Lookout, long since celebrated by me in prose and verse (?). By an ordinary coincidence, the genial editor of the Prairie du Chien Courier and his equally genial wife, the donors of the folder on that city which I sent you, are visiting here also. I have just read your letter to them, and they found much of interest in it, being especially taken with the apparently easy way of documentation re the dates on those old houses. I have since found out that the octagonal house, which you mark as dating from the 1830's or 40's, was built by one Dr. Benedict, over 80 years ago, which would confirm your dating. The town is most interesting, as are also Dubuque Iowa and Galena Illinois, three towns to which I intend taking you if you can manage ever to get out to Wisconsin.

I am sending you herewith my latest story, ONE AGAINST THE DEAD, which stands as a protest against those critics of my novelettes on the scores of coincidences, boy-narrator, lifelessness, particularly the last two. This story is written as a direct answer to those who suggested that I get rid of the boy as a narrator. I've done it, without giving a point, and believe I have constructed a solid story to boot. I await your reaction with keen anticipation; you will find on the ms. the list of people to whom the ms. is to go. I enclose also a print copy (from the Prairie du Chien Courier) of the completed poem, Epitaph a Century After, of which I sent you the first stanza in my last letter.

Yes, I knew about estuary (which I had thought of making estu'ry), and knew about its being a tidal wave or inlet, rather, but did not wish to change it unless I couldn't get out of it. I see I can't get out of it, so changed it will shortly be.

I have sort of run away today, and am enjoying myself. I skipped out last night, leaving no word as to where I was going, but echoes of the maternal wonder reached me this noon and I was forced to communicate to say that I was for the present and until midnight incommunicado to friends who harrass me on the telephone. I shall have to follow

[Conclusion non-extant.]

[324] [ALS]

Bench in Roger Williams Park
After a call at the hospital—
June 28, 1933

Dear A W:—

Too bad your aestival stationery is delayed—but I'll be interested to see it when it comes. My aunt is getting along as well as can be expected, though the confinement to one position has caused a lameness of the back. She will probably return home next week with a nurse. Naturally I am kept extremely busy—& will be more so when the patient returns. She will not be able to get up for a month more.

Glad you have had further contacts with the Prairie du Chien editor—the Dam Heights visit must be delightful for all hands. I certainly hope I can some day make that round of historic Wisconsin & its environs! Hope your vacation from the social whirl will prove as restful as expected. It wouldn't be a bad idea to take many such!

"Michel Brisbois" shows up to advantage in printed form. The column, also, is interesting.[1] Whippoorwills are odd creatures—& (as you may recall from my Dunwich Horror) form the subject of gruesome myths in rural New-England, being regarded as malign psychopomps. About their notes—in Florida the local whippoorwhills have an ampler call than in the North, perhaps indicating their membership in another sub-species. Instead of a cluck followed by *three* notes, the prevailing cry seems to be longer & more complexly trilled—so that the small boys of Dunedin translate the message rather quaintly as "*Chuck married the widow*". These birds were especially numerous in the thickets near good old Canevin's abode at 1159 Broadway.

I have read "One Against the Dead" with keen interest & admiration; & although I don't see that you successfully refute my position regarding coincidences (*I* have no other criticism of your tales to make), I must congratulate you on producing (whether intentionally or not) a splendid *weird tale* of a very subtle sort. It would of course be sadly artificial melodrama to have everything stage-managed in such a way as to make Eleanor fall *accidentally* under the very significant circumstances—but once regard the narrative as a *weird tale,* with Haidee exacting an eye for an eye or else merely exercising a posthumous hatred, & all objections vanish. The atmosphere & tension are finely managed, & I surely hope the story will achieve publication in due course of time. By this post I am sending the MS. on to Mr. Klein. Thanks of the notice of the *Windsor Quarterly*—wish these things didn't charge such stiff prices, but probably they couldn't survive for even a brief period if they didn't. Congratulations on your entree to this publication.

By the way—did you receive that booklet with the picture of 66 College St.? I hate to have such a thing lost, yet one or two copies seem to have gone astray.

Young Bloch says you have helped him greatly. He appears to be a promising kid, though at present given to all the flamboyancies of exuberant sixteen.

Getting too dark to write now. This park is one of the finest in the country, though formal as compared with my old river-bank. I've been using it lately because the hospital (which I visit daily) lies in its direction. The squirrels here are extremely friendly—one little rascal is now on the other end of the bench on which I'm sitting. I must bring some nuts for them next time.

Regards—

H P

Notes

1. I.e., "Epitaph of a Century After" (later titled "Michel Brisbois: A Century After.") The column is unidentified.

[325] [ANS][1]

[Postmarked Onset, Mass.,
2 July 1933]

Hail, Comte d'Erlette! Am endeavouring to frustrate the Red Revolution planned by Comrade Belnapovitch, with whom I am spending 2½ days on soil that was old when Prairie du Chien was young. Had a sunny day Monday, with sinister heat-lightning in the black sky after nightfall. Home Wednesday. Now I'll try to get our young friend to sign his name. He's so economic-minded that it's hard to get him to write anything for nothing, but possibly your recent contribution to the communist paper[2] will cause him to indite the requisite monicker (not *monocle,* thank gawd—his moustachelet is bad enough without glass eyes & silken robes!) in a spirit of proletarian brotherhood. We writers must hang together! ¶ Yr obt Servt Marquis d'Echpi-Elle.

Greetings, sir. Howard appears to be a bloated capitalist, but it doesn't affect the more important aspect of his personality, fortunately. Comrade Belknapius

Notes

1. Front: Cape Cod Canal from Fire Tower. Cape Cod, Mass. [Note by HPL:] Probably this can't best your beloved hills!

2. "On the Outside."

[326] [TLS, JHL]

Sauk City
Wisconsin
3 July 33

Dear H. P.,

I am glad to learn that your aunt is progressing toward good health again. She has my sympathy in her irksome and no doubt at times painful confinement. I don't envy you the care of her while she is abed this further month at home.

Glad that you liked ONE AGAINST THE DEAD. I feel that it is a very fine piece of work, with a strong unity despite the wandering speeches of the grandparent, a device used again in IN THIS DARK HEART, on which I am now working. However, I cannot see this new story as a weird tale, though I see your point of view. There is no coincidence in this tale, though you seem to suggest that the fall of Eleanor is one; but as I understand a coincidence in fiction, particularly objectionable coincidences, it must come unexpectedly and it must give a turn to the story. Now, obviously Eleanor's fall is not a coincidence, because the reader has been told from the opening sentence that this was the night Eleanor died. Inbetweentime, I am working on a more ambitious project—a 100-line dramatic poem, entitled LISZT HEARS HIS SECOND CONCERTO: WEIMAR, 7 January, 1857. I have done 26 lines to my satisfaction and hope to have the entire poem done before long. I have also planned an informal sketch, SUGAR CAMP IN APRIL, to be done this week, and have written a 10-line memorial poem to an old lady friend who died last Tuesday of a sudden stroke. But beside that I've done nothing but work in the canning factory, making enough money to subscribe to a few magazines which I would otherwise buy at the newsstands. I figured up that the magazines I buy at newsstands cost me $21.00 more per year than the same magazines by subscription, thus the sudden rush to subscribe. I also spent a little money getting me a new book, MEN OF GOOD WILL, by Jules Romains, the first of a 16-volume novel; this book contains the first two volumes. And I bought myself a record to join my Liszt Second Concerto, the wondrously beautiful and weirdly sombre SWAN OF TUOMELA, by Sibelius, a work which has an unplumbed depth of melancholy hidden in its deep tones. If my check is sufficiently large, I'll buy Strauss's whimsical and beautiful TILL EULENSPIEGEL, my favourite Strauss tone-poem, or symphonic poem, a form invented by Liszt and perfected by Richard Strauss, though S. has done nothing so perfect as Liszt's marvellous LES PRELUDES and LES FUNERAILLES, the latter written to the memory of Liszt's friends, Chopin, Prince Lichnowsky and Count Telekey, all of whom died in the same year, 1849.

Jacobi has just send me the carbon of his latest story, SMOKE OF THE

SNAKE,[1] for criticism. I think I can manage its placement with Wright, if he does what I tell him to do with the story as it stands now. It is quite a good tale, and original enough, too. Though I fear originality doesn't count for much, for Wright rejected my FEIGMAN'S BEARD, the unusual hexerei story I did based on a tale of Brobst's.

Yes, I received that booklet you sent, and will return it in due time. Your surroundings are indeed ideal, I should say, from the antiquarian's point of view, though buildings too close to me always make me irritable and nervous.

I am glad Block thinks I've helped him. His chief tendency right now is toward imitation, he having done a palpable imitation of THE OUTSIDER recently, but I'm trying to steer him away from this, and also from the use of the Cthulhu mythology, until he is capable of doing the material justice; for W. can't be depended upon to take only good things about the Cthulhu cult. Besides Block and Jacobi, I'm whipping into shape a young lad, the young man at whose cottage I spent my last idyllic Sunday, so that he can collaborate with me. Schorer has gone too highhat to be bothered with weird tales or with my advice either for that matter.

About whippoorwills—there is a chuck-will's-widow in Illinois and sometimes in lower Wisconsin—they're all members of the goatsucker family, you know.

best, as always,
August

Notes

1. Carl Jacobi, "Smoke of the Snake," *Top-Notch Magazine* (January 1934).

[327] [ALS]

[c. 10 July 1933]

Dear A W:—

Well—my aunt is home again with a nurse, & seems to like the change greatly. In about 3 weeks she ought to be up on crutches, & then the nurse can go. Meanwhile I am kept rather closely tied.

Yes—"One Against the Dead" is a darned good story, & I hope it will encounter a favourable reception. As to the coincidence—I think I mentioned that it is not one of the most objectionable sort, though it is certainly closer to one than you realise. Let us say rather that the very dramatic setting of Eleanor's death was a *highly un-typical incident,* producing an impression of unreality & unconvincingness on the reader unless frankly taken as an attribute of a *weird tale.* I know you did not *mean* the story to be weird—but what it is will depend a good deal upon the audience.

Your new work sounds promising—especially "In this Dark Heart." Hope you'll soon be in a position to satisfy all your musical wants. I wish I had that canning factory of yours to fall back on as a life-saver!

Wright was undoubtedly an ass to reject "Feigman's Beard". Hope he'll do better with your revision of Jacobi's tale. By the way—I've never seen a good tale of Pennsylvania *hexerei* in W.T. The only one that ever appeared (to my recollection) was a flamboyant bit of melodrama too cheap for consideration.

Hope your collaborator turns out well—though I am decidedly sceptical about the value of collaboration except when an author desires to dip deeply into some technical subject too involved for convincing lay presentation. However—I believe you have a special system of using collaborators for the quantity production of popular material. Little Bloch surely is quite a kid—he'll shed the imitativeness, tautology, & flamboyancy in the course of time.

Last week came the long-heralded visit from Malik Taus, the Peacock Sultan, who rolled up in his rattling 1928 Ford Juggernaut with appropriate eclat.[1] He is really delightful, & his four days' stay was an exceedingly pleasant incident. Brobst came over twice, & on one occasion the three of us stayed up all night discussing literature & philosophy. W. Paul Cook also dropped in on his way to the N.A.P.A. Convention, though he could not stay long.

On July 2nd Price's Juggernaut enabled me to visit certain rich antiquarian regions of Rhode Island which—despite a close ancestral connexion with them—I had never before seen through lack of transportation facilities. This "Old South County" or Narragansett region west of the bay has distinctive social & historical features—it having been given over to large plantations with black slaves, quite in the Southern manner, before the Revolution—while its scenery is of unparallelled beauty. I beheld for the first time the old snuff mill where Gilbert Stuart was born, saw the vast old Robinson mansion, visited a curious deserted parsonage (built 1727) on a woodland road, enjoyed a peerless rural vista from a famous flat rock, & sought out a magnificently unspoiled colonial village—Kingston—which I had always longed to see. It was a great occasion for me, & I acquired a vast store of impressions to colour my imagination.

Some beastly cold weather lately, but I've had my oil heater repaired & manage to keep fairly comfortable. Can't go far from the house in the present state of affairs, but near-by Prospect Terrace (with its breath-taking view of the outspread lower town & of the bordering hills toward the sunset) is always a good place to write. Glad you received the booklet. Houses are not closely packed in the best parts of old Providence—lawns & gardens being very frequent.

Best wishes—H P

Notes

1. See E. Hoffmann Price, "The Man Who Was Lovecraft," *LR* 292–95.

[328] [TLS, JHL]

Sauk City
Wisconsin
17 July 33

Dear H. P.,

I finished reading THROUGH THE GATES OF THE SILVER KEY only a few moments before your letter came. I feel that your scepticism re collaboration is fully justified. This collaboration despite its brilliance in parts does not come a success for me. It may be that I am simply prejudiced; in consideration of that element, it might be wise to discount 50% of my impressions off hand. What is chiefly wrong, I think, is the atmosphere brought into the story by Price. New Orleans does not tie up atmospherically with New England. The damned Swami irritated me, even though I guessed his connexion pronto. The suggestion of the East and mysticism et al[.] is opposed to the dark brooding terror and awful mystery of the mythology of Cthulhu. Then, too, the ending is flat; it has none of the power of former endings of yours, and I cannot help bemoaning the fact that the story is being left in this form. Why not redo the end—swing into it some of the power of your words? The character of Aspinwall is ridiculously overdrawn, and I would suggest changing it if at all possible—though I see no reason for W. not to accept this script as is. I think it ought to be made still more clear (tho' I may have read hastily here) that the force of de Maurigny's [*sic*] position forces Aspinwall to come way down to New Orleans to settle the estate. Now I come to think if it, I don't think the estate could be settled in New Orleans; legally, I believe, it must be done in the state and county where the estate lies. Better make it a preliminary, paper settlement. However, despite its faults, I enjoyed the story very much. I read it on the brow of my favourite hill, looking over Sac Prairie and the valley beyond the Wisconsin to the hills lost in the summer haze, and I felt a force in the description of Carter's wanderings through the gates.

Agent Lieber returned ONE AGAINST THE DEAD, saying that he looked upon it as one of my poorest stories. Remembering that he said the same of FIVE ALONE, which I afterwards placed, I am amused; I have that same sense of having my opinion justified that I have when W. returns a good story of mine. He also rejected finally PLACE OF HAWKS, feeling that it would be a waste of time to try publishing four novelettes at this time. I feel that he is right, and will withhold the book from the market for some time, unless the Dragon Press (which is printing FIVE ALONE and possibly also PLACE OF HAWKS in its DRAGON YEAR BOOK: 1933) takes it, which is not impossible. Wright rejected my latest short, BIRKETT'S TWELFTH CORPSE, also. On July 4, we had a drowning here, which I witnessed from the bridge; it occurred at 9 o'clock that night, and I was one of three people who heard the boy call. While the others moved, I did not, preferring to assimilate all my impressions, and knowing that nothing could save the boy who was being drawn down by the current in mid-channel. The above story is one result of it; a highbrow story about a man who has an uncanny way of finding corpses in the river is another. This story is called THE CORPSE-FINDER. The story was written before the body of the boy was recovered two days later, and by an odd coincidence, the body was found precisely at the spot I had indicated in my story and by the same character! A prime coincidence, for the body might easily have been anywhere within a radius of four miles of the spit. (Jacobi lists another interesting coincidence in his last letter: having searched for two weeks for a map of Tiger Island, he casually picked up Red Book Magazine the other day and found a full page colour map in the magazine! the last place one would expect to find one.)

Added to those two stories, I managed to do another telegram short entitled, ELSIE DARLING, for possible sale to 10-Story Book, which published my last, DEATH IS TOO KIND, in their February. I also did two poems, both of which I quote for your interest. They are probably bad technically, but they might certainly be worse.

SUMMER AFTERNOON: QUAIL IN THE DEEP GRASS

They talk together gently,
Their voices breaking with low
Sweetness so sibilantly
Against the afternoon's slow
Haze. The grasses undulate
With the deft and certain grace
Of their movements.

They expatiate
Endlessly upon the lace
Of summer sounds, softly call
To one another over
Green hills, always lost in tall
Flower-bearing grass, clover,
And yellow black-eyed susans.

They
Blend their muted conversation
Gently with the casual grey
And blue of sky, no invasion
Of the day, no audience
But trees. Softly, delicately—soon
They are one with the somnolence
Of the quiet summer afternoon.

SUMMER AFTERNOON: SUNLIGHT ON OLD HOUSES

Sunlight leans so gently still
Upon old houses, patch on patch
Of shadowed light, a window-sill
Of fired yellow gold to match
The sun, a patterned moss-green roof
Against the arched trees, a bowered door
In deepest shade, held aloof
From summer's dust.

Perhaps five-score
Of years have passed them by; alone
They stand, age held in sleepless faces
Turned so blandly to the monotone
Of sound and shade and sunlit laces
Printed on the aged year-stained walls.

Sunlight soothes the years of their decline;
With soft and gentle hands it calls
The decades forth and paints them, line on line.

I am now finishing IN THIS DARK HEART and SUGAR CAMP IN APRIL, and informal narrative which is not a story. LISZT HEARS HIS SECOND CONCERTO also asks finishing, and I must do this shortly. After that, I am doing a tale which I feel sure you will like very very much; in the tradition of IN THIS DARK HEART and ONE AGAINST THE DEAD, the new tale, tentatively entitled PORTRAIT OF MY AUNT LEOCADIE, is perhaps more weird than anything previously done outside of frankly weird tales. And then a frankly weird tale, entitled WHITE SILENCE, which may and may not be a sequel to THE THING THAT WALKED ON THE WIND.

I sent Coates a group of poems for DRIFTWIND the other day; he took two, FOR ELEANOR and A HILL IN MAY, neither very good. TONE, a magazine of eclectic verse took a bad one, too, A VERBENA IN A GLASS, but are most enthusiastic about it, the editors write. I understand their first issue besides having my poem will have something of Ezra Pound's. The Anvil, a Communist magazine, took my short story, ON THE OUTSIDE.

A further note on Prairie du Chien might interest you. It has been established, I learn by consulting historical records, that the first building put up there was erected in 1695, a log blockhouse called Fort St. Nicholas. It was put up by Nicholas Perrot, representative of the French Government. This building was burned down in 1780. That there was much traffic here is evidenced by frequent mention in Indian records of "men with hats".

My canning company checks, though small (total: $26.00) plus my check for MR. JIMSON ASSISTS ($25.00), enabled me to buy the Sibelius and Strauss records I mentioned, to subscribe to The American Mercury and The London Mercury (together: $6.50, reasonable), and BOOKS. Which reminds me to mention that I picked up at a quarter the other day a copy of May Sinclair's grand THE INTERCESSOR AND OTHER STORIES (I regard THE INTERCESSOR as her BEST story); the book is in good condition. However, I have already a copy of it, which I bought new, and I had you in mind when I bought this copy. If you'll send me the postage (ten cents), I'll be glad to send the book on to you. I wdn't ask even that if I weren't so strapped just now. This volume also has THE VILLA DESIREE, which appeared in one of Cynthia Asquith's anthologies.

I enclose your pamphlet and a copy of Smith's MLOK story.[1] This is not very good, I regret to say; do not return it. Thanks for the looksee at the pamphlet. I mailed THE SHUNNED HOUSE to Block the other day, and look forward to a print copy in time.

best, as always,
August

Notes

1. CAS, "A Star-Change," as "The Visitors from Mlok," *Wonder Stories* (May 1933); rpt. as "Escape to Mlok," *Tales of Wonder* No. 15 (1941).

[329] [ALS]

The Ancient River-Bank
July 23, 1933

Dear A W:—

Since the S.K. sequel is so bad, it ought to please Brother Farnsworth . . . . though it would be just my luck to have it bad in the wrong way! I don't believe it would pay to tinker with the damned mess, for no amount of local emendation would conceal the dominant fact of heterogeneous matter. The thing isn't what I wanted to write about—& I can never get good results unless a real creative volition is behind my work. As for the estate detail—let us say that the conference was not for any binding legal step, but merely for a series of highly important preliminary discussions. De Marigny's reason for forcing all the others to come down his way was simply the arrogance of the "young intellectual" . . . . . or, come to think of it, I guess most of the Carter estate was invested in the American Sugar Refinery of

New Orleans! By the way—the name of the Orientalist is *de MARigny*—no u in it. That's an actual Creole name of great prominence.

Sorry "One Against" came back—that was really a delightful & broodingly sinister yarn. Too bad, also, that the time is not right for the book-publication of the quadrilogy. If this Dragon Year Book uses two of your novelettes in one issue it will surely be a sort of special d'Erlette number!

You certainly made literary capital of the local drowning. As for the coincidence—are you sure that the indicated spot of discovery was not some place where the currents of the river habitually wash all material floating therein? The coincidence reported by Jacobi is also interesting. Is he sure that no common element lies behind the direction of his & the *Red Book's* attention to the island in question? The same wave of public interest in a certain thing might make a person wish to see a sketch of it, & at the same time make a magazine print such a sketch. However—an absolute coincidence is by no means impossible.

Hope you'll manage to sell your "telegram short". Little Bloch sent me your "Death is too Kind", which is really decidedly clever satire. Both of your poems—"Summer Afternoon"—seem to me very fine work, being full of that selective imagery & harmony of sound typical of true poetry. You capture the spirit of things very capably through suggestion & association—which is the primary & characteristic function of the poet. Much of your prose is strongly poetic—indeed its greatest strength probably lies in that aspect of it. It is therefore not remarkable that you should experiment more & more in verse—perhaps making it one of your principal media later on. Glad so much is being placed—I'll look for your group in *Driftwind,* which I have regularly. Little Belknap will be pleased to hear of your debut in the communist press!

Thanks for the additional note on Prairie du Chien—which I'll add to my files. Old Wisconsin certainly has background! Thanks also—most abundantly—for "The Intercessor"; which ought to be a valuable item for my shelves, & for which I enclose stamps. I feel cheap in not enclosing the full quarter's worth . . . . but circumstances are what they are! Glad you were able to pick up the desiderate musical items.

Young Bho-Blôk, the Daemon Lama of Leng, duly returned "The Shunned House". Many thanks for "Mlok", about which Klarkash-Ton had told me. The *idea* is magnificent—but as you say, the mode of handling is mediocre. By the way—a very gifted & prepossessing friend of Klarkash-Ton's in Auburn is touring the east (after a trip through the Panama Canal & to Cuba) for the first time, & looking up his various friends & correspondents . . . . a young gentlewoman, a teacher of music & drawing, named Helen V. Sully. She looked up Wandrei & Belknap in N.Y., & the Longs brought her here in their car when bound for Onset last Wednesday. After seeing Prov. & Newport she has gone on to Gloucester & Quebec. On the return trip she will pass through Chicago & look up Wright—& if you can get down there (about Aug. 8 or 9—I'll let you know when she decides & notifies me), she would like very much to meet you. Try it if possible. ¶ Tomorrow & Tuesday I shall visit Belknap & his parents in Onset—accompanying them back here Wednesday. Yr obt grandsire H P

[330] [TLS, JHL]

Sauk City
Wisconsin
27 July 33

Dear H. P.,

THE INTERCESSOR AND OTHERS went off to you yesterday. The title story is May Sinclair's best,[1] in my estimation, and in this volume perhaps THE VILLA DESIREÉ comes second. The other three, which have to do with Eastern mysticism, Karma stuff, are not so pleasing to me, but there is nothing intrinsically wrong with them. Don't mention not sending a quarter; I feel cheap enough having to ask for the postage to post it out to you in the first place.

No, dear old H. P., that coincidence about the drowning is a perfectly logical one: only there's a slight variation. In my story the corpse was LODGED, but in reality it was rolling along the bottom—but at the identical spot, within a variation of 20 feet! And Jacobi's coincidence is okeh, too; he had written to me of Tiger Island before Red Book even announced the Morris serial—in other words, two months before the picture and map came out.

This past week has been a busy one for me. I've managed to break my previous speed record (12,000 words in one isolated day), by writing MURDER STALKS THE VILLAGE, a complete mystery-detective novel, 70,000 words long, in seven days flat, not counting afternoons spent across the river on my beloved hills reading, and writing poetry. I quote two of my new poems below.

SUMMER EVENING

Now the brief passion of the summer evening's afterglow
Fills the quiet dusk, one with the casual song
Of birds, the soft enriching scent of ripening corn in slow
Waving fields patterned against the earth along
The sky.
    The brittle evening star glows white and subtly green
Against the saffron emerald of this cool
Dusk, the nighthawk wheels and wildly coasts within the soothing dream
This twilight is, the suns' brief, impassioned duel
With night will soon be done, and day will fade into the mesh
Of years.

Tomorrow and tomorrow and another day
Will mark the passing, too, of the brief passion in this flesh,
Calmly, in this summer afterglow's sure way.

The other is on one of my favourite subjects, as you will long ago have noticed, the nighthawk. It is entitled, I AM AWAKENED BY A NIGHTHAWK AT DAWN.

Your's [*sic*] is a cool song, and sweet
With loneliness that sounds
Beyond the fluted notes, fleet
Against the dawn that rounds
The curved trees so sharply laced
Upon the coming day;
You have flushed the sun and faced
Advancing light's first ray.

You have taken me from dream
Into a greater dream;
You have taken me from sleep
Into the far-flung deep
Of the disquieting day.

Is it enough to say
That the way of your free song
And the erratic long
Swoop of your coasting with sound
Of wild wind in wings down-
Curved in swiftly halted flight
Is recompense for the lost night?

I am much afraid that Chicago at any time before October or late September is frankly impossible. I am pressed by much work—August will see the complete revision of the mystery novel for one thing, and at least a dozen new stories, to say nothing of countless poems and my first full-length play for four years (which I promised a society here for their presentation; so that they could save royalty payment).[2] Besides, I loathe Chicago in summer. I should be glad to see Miss Sully, but since she passes so comparatively close to Sauk City, if she would want to see me, she could just as well add the 165 miles to her itinerary and make the trip here.

Well, all best wishes. I must get back to work. The completion of the mystery novel brings my set work requirement for the period up to the total of 174,000 new words, or 24,000 over for the schedule planned up to 1 August. My title requirements, naturally because of the poems, new titles that is, reaches the total of 46 since January 1, as compared to the 52 set for the year 1933.

as always,
August

Notes

1. AWD included "The Intercessor" in *WK*.
2. AWD's "All in the Family But Sally (and She Came Close)," performed by the Young Ladies' Socality of St. Aloysius Parish, may not be the play in question, for he wrote many at this time. A note on the playbill states "This is the sixth play by August W. Derleto to be donated for public benefit."

[331] [ALS]

[late July 1933]

Dear A W:—

Thanks immensely for "The Intercessor"—which I shall peruse appreciatively at the very first opportunity. Some of May Sinclair's weird stuff is far from bad, though it tends to get entangled with moral values & psychological subtleties—& hence to lose the directness & convincingness it might otherwise possess.

You have surely been busy—& I hope that professional success may crown your detective novel. 70,000 words per week! Surely you & the late Edgar Wallace are as one!

Your poems seem to me delightful—but, in the first one, are you trying to *rhyme greeN* & *dreaM,* & *cool* & *du´-el?* If not, it would be well to avoid the appearance. If so, it simply won't do! One can't vary betwixt true rhyme & assonance in the same metrical fabric. Oh, yes—& how about the *sound* & *down* assonance in the second poem? However—these things are mere details. I repeat that both poems have the true poetic quality—capturing a definite picture & a definite mood in their apt language & imagery.

No doubt you received the Cape Cod card from Sonny Belknap & me. We had rotten weather, but heated literary & sociological discussion (what a red-hot little bolshevik the child has grown to be!) rendered the sojourn an interesting one. And what a kitten there was at the place where we stopped! (You probably know of my extreme fondness for cats.) We had one pretty good ride to Hyannis in the Long family Essex—getting a representative slice of Cape Cod scenery at its best. My favourite village on the cape is ancient, well-preserved, & white-steepled Sandwich—at which we briefly stopped. In returning Wednesday, the party could stop only briefly in Providence—but Belknap seemed to think his grandpa's new colonial quarters were pretty appropriate for the old gent!

Sorry you won't be in Chicago during Miss Sully's brief stay there—she is an extremely intelligent & prepossessing young person, & Wandrei & Sonny

Belknap nearly fought a duel (2 syllables, not rhyming with *cool!*) over the question of precedence in escorting her about New York during her sojourn in that place. Whether her predetermined tourist itinerary will permit of a side-trip to Sauk City I don't know, but I'll pass your invitation on when writing her next momentary address. She gives quite an interesting picture of good old Klarkash-Ton—who would seem to be sorely handicapped by poverty, parental dominance, & a generally uncongenial environment.

My aunt's plaster cast has now been much reduced, & she has begun to practice on crutches. In about a week more the last half of the cast can go. I shall, however, continue to be tied up; for even when the nurse is not needed I'll have to be always on hand to answer the doorbell.

I am now about to welcome a most agreeable guest—the James F. Morton whom I've often mentioned to you. We'll probably have a festive half-week. Price may very possibly pay me a second visit before going South—he now has an idea of wintering in Florida, where living is very cheap. ¶ Best wishes—Yr obt grandsire H P

P.S. The new weird magazine—Fantasy Fan, 137 W. Grand St., Elizabeth, N.J.—offers an 18 months' subscription for a dollar. Klarkash-Ton & I are contributing old stuff—no pay, but good way to get extra lending copies.

[332] [ALS]

Out on Prospect Terrace
[c. 8 August 1933]

Dear A W:—

Still awaiting a chance to read "The Intercessor". Hades, what a rush! I think that time & further experience in verse will cause you to change, all of your own accord, your indulgent attitude toward false rhymes. These things subtly affront the sensitive ear & subtract from the net value of any poem. The tendency of good technique is not to be lenient in such matters—indeed, many half-rhymes (with identical consonants but slightly differing vowels, as *grove–move, giv'n–heav'n,* &c.) formerly called "allowable" are no longer regarded as such. But I'll let time & experience (plus other criticisms you will receive) do my arguing for me. Incidentally—a really good versifier soon finds himself able to express himself in perfect rhymes without any straining or artificiality of diction. It is simply a matter of selection. It may take longer than slipshod composition, but it's worth it. The cultivated ear prefers no rhyme at all if it can't have a real one.

"Smoke on the Wind" is really great stuff—you have a positive genius for picking out significant elements. Before long you'll surely have to issue a volume of collected verse—whether or not the bum rhymes are amended!

Good luck with your murder novel & more serious work. I surely hope the commercial venture will bring you some return. Glad some cheques have come, & hope that more will follow.

Thanks infinitely for the names of the new magazines—which I'll probably bombard as soon as (or if ever) I have anything in any way suitable. At present Klarkash-Ton & I are dumping all our old junk on the non-paying *Fantasy Fan*—which is going over completely to weirdness, since its editor—Hornig—has just been made managing editor of *Wonder Stories,* & doesn't want to compete with himself in the scientifiction field.

Had a letter last week from the Knopf Co. asking to see some of my stuff with a view to possible book publication. After the Putnam & Viking fizzles I know how little such a gesture really means—yet nevertheless have shot along seven of my best or most popular—Colour, Erich Zann, Pickman, Rats, Dunwich, Strange High House, & Picture in the House. They'll come back!

James F. Morton visited me July 31–Aug. 2, & we had a great time. Took many rural walks—seeing such things as an old-time well-sweep & a drowsy village of the 1820 period—& ended up with a sail to Newport . . . . . where we explored the ancient town & sat on the rugged sea-cliffs beloved by Dean Berkeley two centuries ago when he wrote his famous "Alciphron; or, the Minute Philosopher."

I hate to see the summer go—but the evenings are so cold now that I can't write outdoors. Right now it is scarcely sunset, yet so cool that I can scarcely guide a pen. I can't form legible writing under 75° or so.

My aunt's plaster cast is off, but the doctor is making her rest before trying crutches. I shall be more tied up than ever when the nurse goes.

Am reading the excellent 2-volume life of Webster by Claude M. Fuess. Good old New England stuff!

And now to beat a retreat before I freeze!

—Yr obt grandsire

—H P.

[P.S. on envelope:] Well, well! Just had word of the revival of *Astounding Stories* (as a largely weird magazine) by Street & Smith. That sounds good! *1¢ per wd on acceptance.*

Editor is Orlin Tremaine—asst. ed, Desmond Hall. Shorts to 7500—novelettes to 15,000—no serials.

[333] [TLS, JHL]

Sauk City
Wisconsin
14 August [1933]

Dear H. P.,

The news about ASTOUNDING is good news indeed. I knew that someone had bought it, one T. R. Foley, for $100.00 from the defunct Clayton outfit. He also bought Clues; this according to the current, August, Author and Journalist. Perhaps Foley was acting as agent for S&S all the time, or else he just turned around and resold the titles to S&S. I hope it is true, for S&S will at least give a new or reissued magazine a fair chance on the stands before junking it. I understand that the receivers are trying to sell the Strange Tales title, too. Here is other news from the magazine front: "The Jay Publishing Company, 125 West 45th St. New York, is reported to be open for material to be used in a magazine of ghost stories. It may be in first or third person and in lengths up to 10,000 words, but should be fairly convincing. Rates of payment not yet announced."—This is a shoestring concern, I think. Rogers Terrill, editing Dime Mystery Book, is remaking that magazine into a book of outre horror tales, with vampire and werewolf stuff especially mentioned; the address is 205 East 42nd Street, and payment is at 1¢ per on publication. A good company to deal with.[1] I hope you have got busy and send out some of your pieces. All mine are out, even my latest, THE SNOW-THING, which came to 5000 words and is patterned closely after THE THING THAT WALKED ON THE WIND, though it is not quite as good, being a little less definite.

I daresay you are right about the poetry, but I do feel that conventionalism in this way has passed out together with poetic license. However, as you say, time will surely tell. And you must admit, despite your liking for individual poems and thoughts, that most of the material I've sent you is far from being true poetry. Here, by the way, is my latest, called LET THERE BE SINGING.

Now that the moon has come around the hill,
Let there be singing other than hyla song
From these close trees, other than whippoorwill
Call from inscrutable distance, let the long
Sweep of wind carry sound of far words
Faintly over the prairie, low and sweet,
Meshed intricately with night-song of birds
Together with music, to web the beat
Of this slow heart in dark and soothing cool
Of magic, and flush away the tiring day.

Let there be distant singing to haunt the pool
Running content along the unseen way
Of darkness; that peace may fill the channels
Yet held by day, let the faint, dram-like sound
Of distant singing seize night's panels
And wind itself around .. around ... around ....

How do you like that one? I have done one or two others in the past week, but all in all I have done very little writing owing to the presence of a guest for the past two. She, however, has finally gone, and I am relieved to be able to work at top speed again. Irritatingly enough, however, the canning factory cans corn starting this afternoon, and I must have stamp money, especially now that there are so many new magazines coming out. Yesterday I started the revision of MURDER STALKS THE WAKELY FAMILY, and have done just 25 pages of it up to this noon—which is decidedly below the average rate of speed of creation. And revision ought to go faster, as far as I am concerned.

I much fear me a volume of collected verse lies very very far in the future, even at my rate of 3–5 new poems per week. I force myself to write poetry to sharpen my prose, which is, as you know, the best kind of practise.

By all means send something to the Knopf Company. What you have sent them seems pretty representative, I think, but where was The Outsider?[2] I'll hold my thumbs for you. Some day I hope that one of the gang has sufficient prestige to force a collection of your stories on to the market; since you don't do much to get one there. I suspect I shall be the one to do it.

all best, as always,
August

Notes

1. *Dime Mystery Magazine* (December 1932–September 1938), edited by Rogers Terrill (Popular Publications), which began as a mystery magazine but switched focus to weird menace stories with the October issue. The other magazine proposed by Jay Publishing Co. never appeared.

2. HPL's first response to Allan G. Ullmann of the Knopf company on 3 August 1933 accompanied seven story mss. "The Outsider" was among a second batch of 18 tales, submitted on 16 August.

[334] [ALS]

The Old River-Bank
[c. 21 August 1933]

Dear A W:—

The enclosed two letters—which please return for reference—tell the salient facts about the renascent *Astounding*. If I ever get to writing again, this will certainly be a splendid market to try—though of course my stuff may not suit after all. The Terrill prospect sounds moderately good—but the adjective "ghost" connected with the Jay arouses thoughts of conventional limitations. Hope you're investigating all these possibilities. I have sent no MSS. out, since I doubt whether my old rejected stuff is good enough to try—while "Innsmouth" & the "Mountains" would be too long. As for Knopf—they asked to see more stuff, & I sent them a large batch including "Cthulhu", "Outsider", & other odds & ends. But I rather think no deal will develop till that far-off day you speak of, when—as a celebrity—you coerce some properly respectful firm into risking a collection by a nonentity!

Your new poem is really excellent—haunting & musical—& especially appealing at this sunset hour in the open, when dusk will soon steal over the ancient trees & underbrush & the river far below, & Venus & Jupiter will shine out close together in the west. As to the "conventionality" of true rhymes as opposed to false—I think there is something more basic than that involved. The ear, even without formal rules, is generally subtly disappointed by a false rhyme—especially if the imperfection is in the consonantal sound (which lingers last on the lips) rather than in the vowel sound. Even the "allowable rhymes" of older days involved only vowel variations. As a general thing, the ear doesn't want *any* kinship of sound if there can't be an allowable rhyme. Versifiers impatient of all restrictions would do well to adhere to rhythmical, poetic prose or blank verse.

Sorry your work has been interrupted—but you'll get chances enough. As for the canning factory—I wish to hades I had something of the sort available as a financial auxiliary! Yes—verse-writing is a splendid polisher for prose—especially poetic prose like yours—but many of your poems have a distinct value of their own. At this rate you'll have enough for a volume before you know it—for volumes aren't always of encyclopaedic magnitude.

Hornig tells me you are contributing to the Fantasy Fan. Good idea—the thing will undoubtedly be encouraging & entertaining if it lasts. I shall let all my old MSS. appear there if H. wants to print them—& shall also let him use my old historical article as a serial.

But the dusk gathers. Best wishes—

Yr obt grandsire

H P

P.S. Wandrei has just sold *Astounding* a story for $95 . . . . cheque received![1]

P.P.S. Wright has just rejected Silver Key sequel.[2]

P.P.P.S. Read "The Intercessor" the other day. As you say, the title story is the best—having a certain atmospheric power. I find I have read "Villa Desiree"[3] before—don't know where, unless it was in some anthology.

P.P.P.P.S. Am experimenting with a new story—don't know how it will turn out.

Notes

1. Probably "A Race through Time," *Astounding* (October 1933).
2. See FW to HPL, 17 August 1933 (ms., JHL):

> I have carefully read THROUGH THE GATES OF THE SILVER KEY and am almost overwhelmed by the colossal scope of the story. It is cyclopean in its daring and titanic in its execution. . . .

> But I am afraid to offer it to our readers. Many there would be . . . who would go into raptures of esthetic delight while reading the story; just as certainly there would be a great many—probably a clear majority—of our readers who would be unable to wade through it. These would find the descriptions and discussions of polydimensional space poison to their enjoyment of the tale. The story is so much more than a piece of fiction, and so far transcends not only the experiences of the readers, but even their wildest dreams, that they would have no point of contact with the ideas and thoughts presented in this opus. [. . .]
>
> It may seem strange that I reject a story which arouses my admiration as much as THROUGH THE GATES OF THE SILVER KEY; but with business as poor as it is now, I feel that we cannot risk discouraging so many readers from buying the magazine, merely by printing a story that is so utterly alien to even their wildest dreams and reveries that they are incapable of comprehending it—let alone appreciating it.
>
> . . . I assure you that never have I turned down a story with more regret than in this case.

3. May Sinclair's "La Villa Desirée" first appeared in Cynthia Asquith's *The Ghost Book*.

[335] [ALS]

Friday [1 September 1933]

Dear A W:—

I don't think much of the new story. Revision & excessive correspondence have interfered with my writing—as has also my too close contact with 'pulp' stuff. I must have more unhurried leisure, & must think less of magazines & editors, if I am ever to write anything worth reading. For the present, I'm letting "The Thing on the Doorstep" rest untyped, & am meanwhile trying to figure out just where I am weakest. As a possible restorative of the incident-handling faculty I am re-reading some of the standard weird classics (Poe, Machen, Blackwood, James) & forming analyses of their basic plots & motivations.[1] As it is, I tend to fail in everything but the weaving of atmosphere. Time will tell what I can do—but if I do get started again, I think the revived *Astounding* will form a splendid market. Glad you have sent them some good material.

Do you remember the old W.T. item, "The Brain in the Jar", by Searight & Hammerstrom?[2] Searight is now trying to get me to revise or collaborate on some fiction—he has just resumed writing after a lapse of years. So far, however, I have seen nothing of his that I care to tackle. Everything is trite, flat, & (to use F W's standby) unconvincing. He speaks of a tale of his in the Jul–Aug *Wonder*—"The Cosmic Horror."[3] Was it any good?

Your aestival stationery is delightful. What did you finally adopt as a spring design? I shall be on the lookout for your 2-colour autumnal outfit.

Glad you had a good jaunt to Prairie du Chien—but listen to this from your Grandpa! As a sort of birthday present my aunt has arranged to get someone to stay here afternoons during the coming week, so that I can have a snatch of that liberty which I have not enjoyed since June 14. Accordingly, just 24 hours from now I shall be treading the ancient pavements of *Quebec*—climbing the frowning citadel, following the bristling ramparts & cyclopean city wall, ascending & descending the jagged rocky cliffs, traversing narrow labyrinthine lanes of centuried houses & crumbling gates, & enjoying numberless breath-taking vistas of red roofs, silver spires, broad, blue river, vivid green countryside, & distant purple Laurentians. I can never tire of Quebec—which, with Charleston, stands alone on this continent. In spots, at least, the 18th century is not dead! I certainly hope the weather will be decent. In passing through Boston I shall get in touch with W. Paul Cook—whom I am due to see tonight at 5:30. At 8:45 my train leaves Boston's North Station for the great fortalice of the North! On the return journey I may try to work in side-trips to Salem & Marblehead—"Arkham" & "Kingsport."

Your new poetry all strikes me very favourably. It gets at the essence of the soil & landscape in a way that I envy. Glad to see you are to be represented in a medium as evidently exclusive as *Tone.* Only the other day a correspondent of mine—a librarian who sees all the magazines—was remarking what a fixture of the small & select publications you are getting to be!

And now to finish packing. I shall do some reading & MS. correction on the train, & shall answer some letters evenings in Quebec. I leave Quebec Tuesday at 4 p.m. Wednesday in & around Boston—Thursday on the job in Providence again.

Yr obt Grandsire H P

Notes

1. This reading resulted in "Weird Story Plots," "A List of Certain Basic Underlying Horrors Effectively Used in Weird Fiction," "List of Primary Ideas Motivating Possible Weird Tales," and "Suggestions for Writing Story" (revised as "Notes on Writing Weird Fiction"); all in *CE* 2.

2. Richard F. Searight and Norman Elwood Hammerstrom, "The Brain in the Jar" *WT* (November 1924; rpt. June 1936).

3. Richard F. Searight, "The Cosmic Horror," *Wonder Stories* (July–August 1933).

[336] [ANS][1]

[Postmarked Quebec, P.Q.,
3 September 1933]

Can Prairie du Chien tie this? Having a glorious time—weather hot & sunny, & Quebec is—Quebec! ¶ Met an odd character at hotel—blind old physician & soldier of fortune who claims to be a personal friend of Roosevelt! ¶ Saw Cook in Boston & shall again. Also looked up an old house—1637—in Bos-

ton suburbs that I'd never seen before.[2] Hope to do Salem & Marblehead on the way back.
Blessings—Grandpa

Notes

1. Front: View from Parliament Buildings, Quebec, Canada.
2. I.e., the Deane Winthrop house (1637) in the Boston suburb of Winthrop.

[337] [ALS]

Back on the Old River Bank
[early September 1933]

Dear A W:—

Well, it was a great trip. And fine weather until the very last day, when I was in Salem, Marblehead, & Boston. I got drenched while going to call on W. Paul Cook. Quebec is the most fascinating spot on this continent—you certainly ought to see it some time.

Hope your new work will all find acceptance. The *Scribner* editor's comment sounds very encouraging, & presages a time when you will become a feature of the standard as well as of the small magazines. Yes—I saw your name mentioned in connexion with *Tone* in a copy of the *Times* which I bought in Quebec.[1]

Lately had a card from Price, Belknap, & Morton—all three assembled at the latter's museum in Paterson. It must have been an interesting session—I've seen each of them separately this summer, but not all together.

I don't think I can do much for Searight. He is a pretty smooth writer just as he is, but lacks all real originality. Benevolent ghosts—attacks from other planets—the usual stuff dished up in the usual way.

I shall be watching for your autumnal stationery after the equinox. You certainly are getting well outfitted. I am always fond of seasonal pictures, & dote on the little ovals on the cover of the ancient Farmer's Almanack—spring, summer, autumn, & winter . . . the same since 1852. (The almanack was founded in 1792, & my family file goes back to 1805). If I had any seasonal stationery I'd have the pictures done in 18th century style, with scenes typical of the spirit of Thomson, Shenstone, Gray, & other Georgian bards of pastoral rusticity.

I appreciate your Wisconsin invitation, & hope I shall be able to take advantage of it before many years elapse. Sooner or later I want to see the west, where the third & fourth waves of pioneering crystallised a century ago. By the way—in Salem I saw one of the cleverest reproductions of the early settlement of 1630 that can be imagined. Bark wigwams, log & clay huts, early board huts, the first well-built houses—all types reproduced in proper size, with permanent solidity, & with a scholarly & accurate antiquarianism of the highest order. Landscape modelled with care, & with just the right native flare plus the exact garden vegetation proper to the period. Also typical 1630 blacksmith shop, salt works, saw-pit, brick-making outfit, &c. &c. Nothing else on earth could give so utterly vivid, concrete, & complete an idea of the daily life & surroundings of the first New England settlers. Its construction was supervised by the eminent architect & antiquarian George Francis Dow,[2] & it is designed to be a permanent memorial to the past. It was first opened in connexion with the Massachusetts Tercentenary of 1930. Later on, there will be moored in the harbour near it the reproduction of the old ship *Arbela* which I saw & explored in Boston three years ago.

Another marvellous recent reproduction in Salem is the exact copy of a house of 1650 or 1660 (of the "Seven Gables" type) erected by the Pequot Mills. I went over it & found it almost impossible to believe that it was less than 250 years old. This also is designed to be permanent.

On my outbound trip (as I may have mentioned on the Quebec card) I visited the ancient Deane Winthrop house (1637) in a Boston suburb. This is probably the 2nd oldest house of English origin in the U.S., & is tremendously interesting. There is a secret room in the enormous brick chimney.

But of course Quebec itself was the high spot of the trip. I circulated amongst all the familiar sights & unearthed many new things—such as the ancient Sign of Neptune on the Neptune Inn. I also visited the picturesque suburb of Sillery. On the last evening of my stay I witnessed one of the most unusual sunset effects I have ever seen—all atmospheric phenomena in that latitude being more vivid than in southern New England.

Best wishes—

Yr obt grandsire

H P

Notes

1. The "Books and Authors" column of the *New York Times Book Review* (3 September 1933): 13, discussed the appearance of the new poetry magazine *Tone,* with contributions by AWD and others.

2. George Francis Dow (1868–1936), author of *Domestic Life in New England in the Seventeenth Century* (Topsfield, MA: n.p., 1925), *The Arts and Crafts in New England, 1704–1775* (Topsfield, MA: The Wayside Press, 1927), and other books.

[338] [ALS]

[September 1933]

Dear A W:—

Congratulations on the anserine[1] heading! You surely are piling up quite a collection—& the sight of your hyemal vignette will be one of the few mitigating events of the coming aera of the frost-daemon. The present design is really delightful—the sheaves & the cloud effects set off the winged migrants splendidly.

The trip surely was delightful. As to the relative interest of Quebec & the pioneer village—I fancy the former wins when all the points are counted. In the first place the landscape setting is utterly incomparable. No other city in America has such a breath-takingly magnificent topographical background—sheer cliff, vast river with corresponding cliff on other side, outspread leagues of rolling countryside, & impressive ridge of purple mountains toward the north. Secondly—Quebec has certain architectural features of enormous picturesqueness, beauty, & imaginative appeal not to be found elsewhere on this continent—city wall, commanding citadel with cyclopean masonry, high ramparts bristling with ancient cannon . . . . . everything to remind one of the glamourous antiquities of the Old World. Third—a tremendous beauty of general layout—winding streets full of mystery, graceful red roofs & chimney-pots, massive stone edifices of the 17th century, delicate belfries & spires covered with tin & gleaming like silver in the sun, finely-arched city gates, tastefully-landscaped parks, well-chosen monuments, & (except for one unfortunate skyscraper which has, however, a traditional Norman roof) a gratifying absence of ugly buildings & industrial blights. Sir Michael Sadler of Oxford calls Quebec one of the 20 most beautiful cities in the world, & the *most* beautiful in the Western Hemisphere—using a criterion so rigid that it excludes London.[2] Added to this intrinsic *beauty* is the potent imaginative fascination which resides in vast numbers of ancient houses in their original state & relationship—preserving for our sight whole living sections of the past. The pioneer village is lovely & picturesque, but no small or single place could have as *many* points of contact with the imagination as a sizeable city with *extensive* & *developed* reliques of the past; each one *original* & not reproduced, all present in such a *variety* that a myriad different facets of historic memory are touched upon, & embodying an element of *continuous & unchanged survival* affording an incomparable sense of material linkage with the stream of the ages.

The snapshot is extremely attractive, & I am sure that your model justifies the interest you display. Yes—I agree that the posture of the hands forms the one weak point. Glad she appreciates the charms of pedestrianism on your favourite hills.

Glad to hear of your prospective regional work for *Scribners*. You'll be a feature of the big-timers before long! Hope your labours as playwright & stage director will be rewarded with popular applause. You certainly have more outlets for your energy than any ordinary person could stop to catalogue!

Your list of recent placements is surely breath-taking enough. The small magazines would probably curl up & die of deprived of your sustaining pabulum! Many correspondents, by the way, have enviously commented on that recent mention of you in the Times book section.

And still the weird magazines multiply! A recent bulletin from Klarkash-Ton heralds the appearance of a new venture to be called *Unusual Stories*—

edited by one William Crawford of Everett, Pa. No pay for contributions, however.

Glad you've had some good sessions on the hills. The approaching chill of the year's death is curtailing my outdoor reading & writing, but I manage to get a few scenic & antiquarian walks in the venerable countryside north of Providence. Last autumn I was too damnably rushed to be able to enjoy the varicoloured foliage—but this year I hope to get some glimpses. There is a bare possibility that during October I may (a) have a visit from Loveman & accompany him to Boston on a museum tour, & (b) spend a week with Sonny Belknap in the decadent cesspool of Manhattan. But both prospects are very vague.

Blessings—

Yr obt Grandsire

H P

P.S. Just read the new Astounding. Essentially mediocre & conventional—machine-made stories with no distinction in style or atmosphere. Hall was exaggerating when he spoke of having artistic standards.

[P.P.S.] Have just sent an enlargement of my weird tale history to the Fantasy Fan.[3]

Notes

1. Gooselike, in reference to the heading on AWD's stationery.

2. Sir Michael Ernest Sadler (1861–1943), British educational pioneer and master of University College, Oxford (1923–34). His remark is repeated in *Quebec: How to See It?: The Tourist's Guide* . . . (Québec, P.Q.: The Quebec Tourist Guide, n.d. [c. 1930]).

3. SHL was serialized in 17 installments in *FF*, but ceased in the middle of Part VIII.

[339] [ALS]

[early October 1933]

Dear A W:—

I shall be eager to see the spring design in its final form—as well as the soberer winter one. This autumn one is certainly tremendously artistic.

Have heard recently from the new *Unusual.* They want unconventional weird material with something of a science background. No hackneyed stuff. I've sent a couple of odds & ends & told them about my long pieces.[1] It looks as if this were a more ambitious venture than the *Fantasy Fan. Astounding* was surely a disappointment—just Claytonism over again. The other day I saw the *Dime Mystery* for the first time. Rather impossible, from what I read. I doubt if any of the new magazines could form a market for me. As to the new W.T.—my judgment is a bit more lenient than yours. I found a certain promise—an atmospheric germ, if nothing more—in "The House of the

Worm".[2] Belknap's tale had possibilities, but unfortunately spread its horror out to a weakening extent.

Glad your activities are duly progressing, & hope the artistic & remunerative items may both prosper. This *Tendency* sounds very timely & sensible—although I wish such publications would try to forego the extremes of preciosity & affectation in their titles. I see you are in, as usual, on the ground floor. What would they do without you! Your new poem sounds splendid to me—glad the photographed young gentlewoman proved such an inspiration!

The other day one F. Lee Baldwin of Asotin, Washington, wrote to propose the publication of my "Colour Out of Space" as a separate brochure.[3] I told him to go ahead if he wanted to—hence the still-future "Shunned House" may have a companion volume when or if it ever appears. More probably, something will happen to extinguish both.

Another new correspondent is one H. Koenig of N.Y., who wrote to make the old perennial enquiry about the reality of the Necronomicon, &c. It turns out that he has a marvellous library of rare spectral material (including the "Malleus Maleficarum", the "Examen of Witches",[4] &c. &c), any item of which he is gladly willing to lend! I am beginning my requests with some of Montague Summers' stuff. It seems that Koenig has been in touch with Klarkash-Ton for some time. By the way (in case I haven't mentioned it before)—I finished the enlargement of my weird fiction article & sent it to the *Fantasy Fan* for use as a serial.

Autumn is driving me more & more indoors, though I try to get a squint at the turning foliage in the woods now & then. A while ago a friend took my aunt & me for a motor ride down the west shore of the bay to ancient Wickford (the quaint & unspoiled seaport visited by Price & me last July)—which afforded some splendid scenic glimpses. This was my aunt's first real outing since her accident—tho' she now gets out in the garden, & sometimes up to the college grounds, with a cane each fair day.

Travel prospects undecided. If Loveman gets to New England I shall probably accompany him to Boston—& I may possibly pay Belknap a brief visit in N.Y. Both, however, are only possibilities.

Best wishes—

Yr obt grandsire

H P

P.S. I enclose a recent snap of 66 College. If you have a file of such things you can keep it, but other wise I'd rather have it returned some time than lost or thrown away.

Notes

1. William L. Crawford's companion publication to *Unusual Stories—Marvel Tales [of*

Science and Fantasy]—published "Celephaïs" and "The Doom That Came to Sarnath."

2. Part of this story appears to plagiarize parts of HPL's "The Call of Cthulhu." See Will Murray, "Mearle Prout and 'The House of the Worm'," *Crypt of Cthulhu* No. 18 (Yuletide 1983): 29–30, 39.

3. A typescript was prepared, but the booklet was never published.

4. Jacobus Sprenger and Henricus Institor [Heinrich Kramer], *Malleus Maleficarum [The Hammer of Witches]*, published in Germany c. 1485 as a guide to inquisitors in detecting, examining, and punishing witches. Koenig's copy probably was that tr. and ed. by Montague Summers (London: John Rodker, 1928). Henri Boguet (d. 1619), *An Examen of Witches*, tr. E. Allen Ashwin, ed. Montague Summers ([Bungay, UK]: John Rodker, 1929).

[340] [ALS]

[late October 1933]

Dear A W:—

About "The Plutonian Terror"—in spite of its mawkishness & extravagance it has one good point; a proper sense of wonder & strangeness regarding the non-human metal work found in the deserted earth. The worst fault of interplanetary writers is treating of the very fact of extra-terrestrial contacts with insufficient emotional emphasis. As for a steady decline in W T—I'd hesitate before dogmatically giving a verdict. Some of the older issues were pretty bad. With all his limitations, Wright seems to be less wholly commonplace & stereotyped in his choices than other editors in the same field. Still—one is justly impatient when one reflects on the sort of weird magazine that *could* be issued by the right person.

Hope your detective novel will find a publisher, & that a subsequent Solar Pons collection will prove practicable.[1] Trust that the delay at *Scribners* may not be an unfavourable one. And I surely hope that you can make the *Mercury*—participating in the dawn of its new editorial regime.[2] Glad the poems also continue to pile up.

This has certainly been a splendid autumn. I have taken long rural walks nearly every day, exploring sections as wild & untouched by modernity as any region in Vermont. My usual plan has been to go out some main highway by 'bus, & then strike off across country till I strike another bus-traversed highway along which I can return. Some of the odd ancient farmsteads & vivid landscape vistas that I have seen are things to remember. Had another long motor ride some time ago—traversing exquisitely beautiful & unspoiled parts of Massachusetts that I had never seen before.

The other day I helped my aunt half-way down the hill to the art museum, which has just developed an exquisite formal garden with pools, terraces, shrubs, termini, &c. in its large & picturesquely irregular inner court. There is a fascinating nich[e] & statue of Pan—& the whole thing brings up vague, pleasant reminiscences of classical antiquity.

All good wishes—
Yr obt hble Servt
H P

[P.S.] Saw a demonstration of *television* the other day at a local department store. Rather like the blurred, flickering biograph films of 1898.

[P.P.S.] Expect to visit Belknap in November.

Notes

1. AWD's first collection of Solar Pons stories, *"In Re: Sherlock Holmes,"* appeared in 1945 under AWD's own Mycroft & Moran imprint.

2. H. L. Mencken resigned as editor of the *American Mercury* with the December 1933 issue, turning the job over to Henry Hazlitt.

[341] [ALS]

[November 1933]

Dear A W:—

Congratulations on the success of your play![1] The programme seems to indicate something very interesting, & your own starring undoubtedly contributed greatly to the triumph. With authorship, direction, & acting combined, you surely had your hands full; & I am glad that a large & appreciative audience crowned your efforts.

I note your new stationery with extreme interest—the woodcut having an especially eerie charm. Is this your winter design—or is it a special late-autumn item interpolated in the series? It appeals to me especially just now, because its great round moon is exactly what I saw toward the close of my final connected series of rural walks—Oct. 31–Nov. 2. That was a delectably warm spell, & the scenery held a weird Hallowmass charm at evening. A majority of the trees still held their leaves, & the sunset hills & moon-flooded valleys seemed full of vague, elusive influences. I explored a section wholly new to me—Fruit Hill, on the city's northwestern rim—& was rewarded by as fine a series of vistas as I have ever seen. At one high point—astonishingly close to the region of continuous streets & sidewalks—there was a wholly exquisite bend of the stone-walled road from which meadows & orchards sloped down gracefully to the Woonasquatucket River—with wooded hills in the western distance, & the far-off spires & chimneys of Centredale on the north. It was here that I watched the crimson & orange sunset, & the slow climbing of the blood-red Sabbat Moon above the rock-ridged eastern hills. But cold weather lurked just around the corner, & I fear that my future walks this year will be brief & rare. Sorry you had such a poor October—*snow* is something we never get till the very end of November, & seldom get till

January. Cook—of whose sudden move to join Coates in Vermont I think I told you—recently reported a 12-inch snowfall & a temperature of 12°. It almost paralyses me to think of such things!

You are wise not to waste cash & time on pulp magazines. Aside from WT & (perhaps) *Astounding,* I have only such as are given me by sundry writers represented in them. By the way—has a second *Astounding* appeared? I don't seem to have noticed any on the stands. Glad your representation in the small magazines continues to be ample, & trust that in time you'll repeat the experience with the "quality" group. It will be interesting to see what the *Scribner* editor will have to say. I must ask Two-Gun for a look at that story based on his childhood—did I mention the huge set of snake-rattles he lately sent me? Speaking of Hawks on the Blue—an alert peregrine falcon has lately taken up his residence beneath the eaves of one of Providence's tall office buildings, & is wreaking vast havock amongst the city's pigeons. All efforts to bring him down have so far been in vain. To continue in an ornithological vein—let me congratulate you on the prize your Owl at Bay has won![2]

As for WT—the theft of an Utpatel idea, even though the idea was purchased, is certainly rather a small trick.[3] I don't see that Mrs. or Miss Brundage is any better than the Senf of other days—all right for fashion plates or tooth-paste advertisements, but without imagination. The new W T is not below the average. Sultan Malik's "Fourth Axis" could have been a great story but for the conventional "action" setting. There is a germ of originality, despite much commonplaceness, in "Shambleau", & Klarkash-Ton's offering is not without cleverness. "The Accursed Isle" has a distinct touch of genuine horror & suspense.

As possibly you know, Sultan Malik made a dash up to Chicago in his rattling Juggernaut not long ago. Wish you might have seen him—you'd have found him very interesting, despite his apparent desertion of literature for unmitigated pulpery.

Apropos of nothing—here's an historical sketch I did for Talman, who asked me to contribute something to his Holland Society organ.[4] Ordinarily, one would think an old Yankee could have nothing to offer a Dutch ancestral publication—yet I found enough links to fill 3 columns. I discover that very few persons seem to know of the Dutch hold on the Maine coast between 1674 & 1676. Of course, at the time that part of Maine was virtually a section of French Acadia—despite an English claim & a Plymouth occupation from 1629 to 1635.

Lately I saw the new magazine *Story* for the first time—sent me by young Shea. It surely does carry a phenomenally high percentage of serious material.

All good wishes—& congratulations again on that vivid woodcut!
Yr obt Servt H P

[P.S.] Wright has asked to see the Silver Key sequel again—the thing collaborated with Price.

Notes

1. Unidentified.
2. Published as "From a Nature Notebook: An Owl at Bay."
3. Margaret Brundage's cover, showing a woman, candle, ornamental disk, and skull (not illustrating any particular story), for the December 1933 *WT* is clearly based on Frank Utpatel's illustration from the August 1932 *WT* for "The Lair of the Star-Spawn" (p. 185). See letter 344n3.
4. This was "Some Dutch Footprints in New England."

[342] [ALS]

Dec. 11, 1933

Dear A W:—

Bless my soul! Before long you'll be having separate stationery for every week in the year—if not every day! The two winter designs are really delightful—obviously, the owl is a favourite motif of yours.

Well—Wright took the collaboration! What clinched the matter, I fancy, was Price's personal visit plus a highly laudatory & entirely unsolicited letter from Dwyer. Hope there'll be as little delay as possible in using—I can certainly use my end of the 140 when it gets around! Yes—keep the Dutch footprints if they're of the least interest.

Thanks immensely for the Jacobi tale. That boy has genuine power in the weird—as his "Revelations in Black" attests.[1] This story has some monstrously potent suggestions, & is handled very well—although there could be a deeper shadow of brooding alien menace. The *entity* is a bit concrete & sharply defined—a greater nebulousness, & less resemblance to terrestrial life, would add power.

As usual, I am glad to hear of your expansive progress in various provinces of the literary world. Hope nothing hampers your issuance of the detective novel—& that the plan for further books develops well. A steady book-writing programme ought to be a great financial asset—as well as an aid in acquiring literary recognition. And if you could add a musical comedy hit to your list of varied triumphs, you would certainly be on the road to economic independence!

The poetry specimen you quote strikes me as highly authentic & powerful, although the mixture of rhymes with such non-rhymes as *penalty–malady* &

disdain–disclaim halts the ear a trifle. The imagery & atmosphere are magnificent—confirming my belief in your basic classification (manifest in the tone & method of your prose as well as in your verse) as a poet. I surely hope that the published collection will materialise.

Yes—the transition of *Astounding* to the scientifiction field is attested by Sultan Malik & Klarkash-Ton as well as by Young Melmoth. I saw only the first issue, but doubt if I missed much—I read "The Daemon of the Flower"[2] in MS. Glad that Melmoth seems to have secured a steady science-tale outlet. Price is thinking of extending his hack work to the "stf" field—you could do it yourself, if you wished, though probably your present superhuman programme keeps you so busy that there would be no object in trying. As for the crowdedness of the field—I suppose a newcomer always thinks he has a chance to outdistance the others & be one of the few to survive. If *Astounding* failed under the Clayton scientifiction regime, so alas did the weird *Strange.*

Glad you're having a warmish interlude—hope it's warm enough to give you some rambles on the hills. Our October was warm, but November has averaged cold. There were some warm days in November, though—I took one the last of my full-length rural rambles on the 22nd—which would have been the 100th birthday of my maternal grandfather if he were still alive.

Best wishes—

Yr obt grandsire

H P

P.S. Had a Thanksgiving trip to Plymouth—where the festival came from. Delightfully warm day—& the ancient town displayed all its accustomed fascination. Saw an impressive sunset from Burial Hill, & then watched a great silver moon light up the waters of the harbour. Some of the old houses are now undergoing restoration. Expect to visit young Belknap for a week beginning just after Christmas (I want the festival at home) if the weather isn't too cold. Today is so damn cold that I can't go out!

Notes

1. "Revelations in Black" appeared in *WT* (April 1933). The other story is unidentified.
2. "The Demon of the Flower," *Astounding Stories* (December 1933).

[343] [ALS]

[late December 1933]

Dear A W:—

No—Grandpa still lives! A hard old bird to kill off (provided the mercury stays up around 80° indoors, & provided I can keep indoors), though easy enough to paralyse with a crowded programme!

Congratulations on your recent leaps toward fame! That article certainly looks important, & will doubtless produce chlorotic spasms of envy in such other young writers as may behold it. Hope nothing happens to impede the full detective-novel schedule, & trust that good-fortune will also make possible the appearance of "Place of Hawks" & the poetry volume. Your speed of writing leaves one quite aghast—though as a matter of fact the variability of the human species is so well known that a specimen of it ought not to cause amazement. The publication list for Dec–Jan is a fair sample of the whirling-rate of the d'Erlette vortex!

I hope Satrap Pharnabazus will let Klarkash-Ton illustrate that finally-accepted Price collaboration. I've asked him to. His turndown of Crawford's advertisement was what I call a damn cheap trick—he certainly *is* small in certain ways, as witness his ungracious attitude toward my exercise of reprinting rights a couple of years ago. But he'll probably take your two new stories in the end—he usually does. Jacobi certainly has great stuff in him, & I hope the octopus of commercialism will never engulf his talent. The present WT (or did I say so before?) is to my mind a very poor issue—Melmoth's & Two-Gun's tales being the only items worth reading. A great number of readers have commented on the cover-design steal from Utpatel's illustration of your "Star-Spawn". The worthy Mrs. Brundage would appear to be one of the foremost living exponents of the Utpatel School of art!

Beastly cold weather alternates with spells of overcoatless civilisedness. I hope the coming week will be decent, for I'm right now embarking on a visit to Sonny Belknap. I shall, I hope, also behold Melmoth the Wandrei & Jonckheer Wilfredus van Talman.

At last I've read—as a loan from Klarkash-Ton—that novel so highly recommended by you & little Jehvish-Êi—"The Lady Who Came to Stay".[1] Pretty damn good! Indeed, it gets about as far as anything of limited imaginative scope—with only the traditional household ghost as spectral furniture—possibly can. The creeping pervasiveness of the atmosphere is a thing of sheer genius, & the realistic characterisation of the ancient gentlewoman is marvellous. I can easily understand your especial fondness for the novel, since so many of your own studies centre around prim, morbid, secluded old ladies of just this sort. Has Spencer produced anything since the "Lady"? A man who could write a thing like that must have more in him. I've also just finished old Monty Summers' "Geography of Witchcraft'[']—striking source-material, & made doubly bizarre by the author's childish acceptance of the supernatural.

Having quite a Christmas here. My aunt has put up a number of decorations, but I've got a lot more hidden in my library closet, & will put them up before morning—so that when she arises she will find the old colonial fire-place in the living-room a bower of green. Trust all is festive at Sac Prairie.

With best Yuletide wishes—
Yr obt Grandsire
H P

P.S. Thanks for the Yuletide card—delightfully clever idea, & a good advertisement for the coming book!

[P.P.S.] Just read "Birkett's Twelfth Corpse" in the F F. I like it exceedingly. Just like that ass Wright to turn it down—as I suppose he did.

Notes

1. See letter 241n4.

1934

[344] [ALS]

Chateau de Longue
[c. 8 January 1934]

Dear A W:—

Well, I don't wonder the doctor has ordered you to ease up! How any mortal could have stood your pace as long as you have is a mystery to me! Take his advice—what's the use of burning the candle at both ends? Overwork & speed don't lead anywhere in particular—so why hurry?

Congratulations on your proofreading feat—& let us hope that nothing will mar the successful issuance of your novel on the 25th. I suppose proofreading is merely a light indoor sport with you . . . . yet at that one has to keep a sharp eye open for tricky, almost imperceptible errors. My biggest job in that line was the Dartmouth College history which I did (making certain revisions in the proofs) in the autumn of 1931.

Commiserations on the cold wave! I struck it here in Manhattan (where it got down to 3 below), but the omnipresent ramifications of the subway system—taking one within two or three blocks of almost anywhere underground—saved me from the need of wasting my visit in sheer hibernation. New York is the only town I could think of visiting in winter—I learned the beneficent potentialities of the subway when I lived here in 1924 & 1925. Your Sac Prairie temperatures of -22° almost transcend my imagination, though friends in Vermont & western Massachusetts sometimes report conditions almost as savage. As for walking *2 miles* in such weather—words fail me! I'd walk about a quarter of a mile & do the rest in a hearse! Two *blocks* from Belknap's up to a cinema show at 99th St. the other day (at +2) were just about enough for me—with an handkerchief over nose & mouth.

Glad you've finished "Senessen House"[1]—this series is certainly a great thing for you, especially if it paves the way for the book publication of your more serious work. I hope to gawd L & M[2] will issue "Evening in Spring". Your real fame as a big-time literary light will probably date from the appearance of that volume. Hope the anthology plan will mature—which reminds me that "Creeps by Night" has come out in a cheap edition. Your selections look good, except for the plethora of my own junk.

I haven't seen the new W T as yet, but hope it beats its immediate predecessor. Sultan Malik tells me that our collaborated attempt will appear in the July issue—which, I suppose, means pay some time in the autumn. Well—if we get pay at all we're lucky. Wandrei tells me that Satrap Pharnabazus still refuses to make good the bad cheque of some months ago. I doubt if the

Magic Carpet will be widely lamented, though it was a good market for Two-Gun Bob, the Peacock Sultan, & others who could meet its demands. The excuses anent the Utpatel steals are surely amusing enough . . . . . though in any case Utpatel ought to feel vastly complimented. It is a sign of having arrived when one's work becomes a basis of thefts![3]

Of course old Monty Summers is a profound & celebrated scholar—but he isn't the first titan of erudition to harbour residual spots of childish naivete & credulity. He knows virtually everything there is to know on the subjects he covers—but when it comes to judging evidence, & sifting traditional folklore & beliefs, he belongs with that vast army of orthodox dupes who stifle their minds & give way to emotional bias.

My home Christmas was thoroughly delightful—we even borrowed a cat to complete the atmosphere of old-time hearthside tranquility. In the early evening we went to hear some carol singing in the courtyard of a fine old Georgian mansion half way down the hill, & at midnight I took the New York coach for my present visit. So far I've had some very interesting conferences—with most of the gang, including our young friend Melmoth the Wandrei & M. de la Salle, Marquis d'Esmond, grand Siegnieur of *Astounding Stories*.[4] The latter is a distinctly likeable chap. I also met Melmoth's younger brother Howard Wandrei, & saw some of his marvellous drawings. These things fairly stupefied me with their fantastic genius—without question, the younger Wandrei is farther advanced with his pictorial art than any of the rest of the crowd (except perhaps yourself) are advanced with their literary art. It can be only a question of time before he becomes generally recognised in the larger world.

Belknap sends regards. All good wishes—

Yr obt Grandsire H P

[P.S. on envelope:] Met T. Everett Harré, the anthology man—rather interesting. He took Wandrei & me to dinner. Expect to meet A. Merritt (of Moon Pool fame) shortly.[5] Also saw Koenig, the chap who lends me weird books. Absolutely delightful fellow—blond, & looks like a boy of 20.

Notes

1. *Death at Sennessen House* was the first title of *The Man on All Fours.*

2. Loring & Mussey (New York), the publisher that issued *Place of Hawks* and AWD's early detective novels.

3. See FW to AWD, 12 December 1933 (ms., SHSW) regarding Margaret Brundage's "theft": "[Frank] Utpatel's illustration for THE LAIR OF THE STAR-SPAWN presented itself as truly symbolic of the contents of the magazine, and we suggested to Mrs. Brundage that she work out a figure along the line of the Chinaman in that illustration, with an astrological chart in the background to help out the symbolism, and adding the figure of the girl to give the suggestion of action. Mrs. Brundage copied Utpatel's figure somewhat closer than we had expected, but we accepted the cover

design because it was so excellent. Utpatel's illustration, in its turn, was deliberately copied from the style of Harvey [*sic*] Clark."

4. I.e., Desmond Hall, associate editor of *Astounding Stories.*

5. HPL met A. Merritt on Monday, 8 January.

[345] [TLS, JHL]

Sauk City
Wisconsin
10 January [1934]

Dear H. P.,

I wish I could take your and the dr's advice about easing up, but it is simply impossible. I could if it were not for the pressing burden of debts which simply must be paid, and I must at least work—I can't do any more—even though I know that the books I have already written are almost certain to eliminate the debts shortly.

The year started fairly well—except, of course, financially; it promises, except for the book, to be just as big a flop as always. Weird Tales bought a lousy poem,[1] The Fantasy Fan took Java Lights, The Tanager (a new market for me) took An Old Mill Burns, The Little Magazine took Light Again, and Outdoors (another new one) took A Day in April, A Day in May, A Day in October, and From a Nature Notebook, and wants me to do them a series of articles for every month in the year and follow the year with a department under the latter head. I shall do at least the first year's articles for them, since three are already accepted.

I did manage to write six lousy poems, one excellent poem, a mediocre short story, and the already placed A Day in May, a total of 5,000 wds, or my quota for the first week. I look forward to the revision of DEATH AT SENESSEN HOUSE, the third novel, THREE WHO DIED, and the first judge Peck short story, THE SINISTER COMPANION.

Yes, I know that Howard Wandrei's drawings are good. I saw many of them in Minneapolis. I recently had a letter from him, and just sent out my reply. He is a bit more prompt than Don in replying to letters. As you know, failure to reply irks me.

I read the galley proofs of the last half of the book—all of them, about 40 galleys, at one clip last Saturday, wearing out three checkers (I read aloud, saves time) and incidentally my throat, which is still smarting from the strain of it. Loring & Mussey have changed the date of publication from January 25 to February 15, pointing out that the News Company orders will be 2 to 300 copies more, all of which suits me perfectly well. There is a mounting possibility that L&M will issue the novelette collection, PLACE OF HAWKS, as well as the mystery novels. I have, however, absolutely no hope for EVENING IN SPRING, since it is not a trade possibility, and the beginning publisher is forced to make every one of his books pay.

The January Writers' review came out with a horrible picture of me smeared all over its front cover—and was I mortified![2] It has my article, Novels at 10,000 Words a Day! The January A&J also has a very nice editorial puff for me in a quoted letter from Barrows' Mussey of the firm, in which he expresses his appreciation to the magazine for printing a notice of them that drew my attention and brought me to them.

Well, I suppose I must get back to work. Fortunately, it is no longer so cold.

all best, as always
August

P.S. In case you are planning to buy yourself any spring books, you must get Arthur Machen's excellent new novel, macabre stuff akin to The House of Souls; it is entitled THE GREEN ROUND, and can be had from Argus Book Shop, 333 South Dearborn Street, Chicago, at $1.50. De la Mare also has a new limited edition, THE JACKET, which will presently come out in a new collection of weird shorts.[3] Thank God for the old standbys.

PPS. Wonder Stories just took three perfectly lousy poems I sent in to them. But I guess they do pay sometimes.

Notes

1. "Incubus."

2. The January 1934 issue of *Writer's Review* contained AWD's "Novels at 10,000 Words a Day" and featured a somewhat dreamy-eyed photograph of him on the cover wearing his hair coiffed high and a garish cravat; but AWD doubtless had provided the photograph to the magazine.

3. "The Jacket" appears in Walter de la Mare's *The Lord Fish,* a book of stories for children.

[346] [ALS]

Jany. 22, 1934

Dear A W:—

Home again! In fact, I've been back since Jany. 9th. All in all, I had a damned good time. Managed to take in most of the museums, & found some striking new Assyrian, Etruscan, & Greek stuff at the Metropolitan. Loveman further (I told you of the *ushabti*) enriched my own collection with a Mayan stone image & a carved wooden monkey from Bali. Also picked up some good book bargains—including the late Arthur Weigall's "Wanderings in Roman Britain", which I've wanted for years. Merritt turned out to be a delightful chap—stout, sandy, genial, & about 45 or 50. We had dinner at the

Players' Club in Gramarcy Park—Edwin Booth's[1] old residence. He is now working on a sequel to "Burn, Witch, Burn"[2]—a tale whose primary setting is the fabulous city of Ys, supposed to be sunk off the coast of Brittany. But about the most important N Y event was getting my pen fixed at the Waterman central office. I was in there 3 times, & at last have the flow adjusted to an ideal degree of freedom—so that I can glide along at lightning speed without any perceptible pressure. As you know, getting a fountain pen to work is the basic problem of my existence!

Glad to hear the news, & hope you'll be able slightly to modify, if not radically to curtail, your programme of intensive overwork. Trust the regular *Outdoors* articles won't prove exacting—you surely haven't room for many fresh responsibilities! Glad the proofreading is out of the way—though I suppose you'll later have the page proofs to go through. Damn hard work—but better than having misprints. I certainly hope L & M will take "Place of Hawks". That would form a good entering wedge for higher-grade material. It is really artistic fiction—yet of more popular interest than Evening in Spring would be. Sorry the *Writers' Review* has pictorially slandered you—but that is one of the penalties of fame.

Unusual Stories has suffered another delay & will not appear till March. Hope it won't utterly peter out before it begins. The editors of *Fantasy*—Schwartz & Ruppert,[3] who called at Belknap's during my visit—are rather sceptical of Crawford's ability to keep going on the relatively ambitious plans he has selected.

Thanks enormously for calling my attention to the new Machen item, of which I had not previously heard a word. Is it really up to the old "White People" standard? I had fancied that good old Arty had pretty well forsworn the weird—indeed, I seem to recall some utterance of his own to that effect. Glad he didn't live up to his resolution! I must see this item somehow—in fact, I may get it from the Argus when I recover a bit from my post-visit brokeness. Glad de la Mare is also still on the job. Have another bundle of loans from Koenig (a splendid chap—I met him in N Y) including Baring-Gould's werewolf classic, a collection by one Prevot entitled "Ghosties & Ghoulies", & the newer Asquith anthology, "When Churchyards Yawn". The last-named contains Machen & Blackwood items which I haven't seen before—whether really new or merely resurrected I don't know. Haven't had time to read these things—or the new W T—as yet, for work & correspondence piled up dizzyingly during my vacation, despite the forwarding of a good part of my mail.

With all good wishes—

Yr most obt Servt

H P

Notes

1. Edwin Booth (1833–1893), celebrated American actor, brother of John Wilkes Booth.

2. A. Merritt, *Burn, Witch, Burn!,* serialized in *Argosy* from 22 October to 26 November 1932; the sequel was *Creep, Shadow!,* serialized in *Argosy* from 8 September to 20 October 1934.

3. Julius Schwartz and Conrad Ruppert.

[347] [ALS]

Feby. 14, 1934

Dear A W:—

Thanks for the Jacobi story. Even his lesser work shows an atmospheric ability & sense of situation eminently to his credit. I also note the circulars, which I am slowly distributing where they'll do the most good. I may encroach on your own distributing territory now & then, but that will scarcely do much harm. It will certainly please me to do anything I can to promote the success of your book-form debut!

So the new novels are coming out of the hopper with usual speed! Sorry "Place of Hawks" will be delayed—& hope you can guarantee enough sales to ensure Christmas publication. I'll get a copy then if it's out & if I'm not stone broke. Meanwhile I hope Wakeley will sell well.[1]

Glad to hear that "The Green Round" is new—& my desire to read it increases. Hope Machen is beginning a whole new series of fantastic or macabre things. How about Blackwood—is he on the job these days? I know Dunsany is, but unfortunately he has lapsed into tameness & triviality. Never heard of "The Cadaver of Gideon Wyck" or of its author[2]—but hope it will later come my way. The Prevot book was fair—some of the little sketches could be made into powerful tales if rightly developed. Haven't got at the Asquith anthology yet. An advertisement refers to another called "Shudders", which I haven't read.[3] Glad the items are not reprints.

Young Shea lent me the two latest issues of *Story,* plus the *Story* anthology.[4] Really remarkable stuff—although this enterprise will probably develop taboos of its own as rigid as those against which it is a protest. The bulk of the tales are just a trifle barren & lacking in a vivid sense of reality. There is a tendency for them to seem like psychological studies—consciously such—rather than things which actually happened. Dwyer has lent me the interminable "Anthony Adverse", but I haven't had any opportunity to begin this all-winter reading job. It would take even you almost two hours to digest a book like that with really appreciative thoroughness!

Glad the *Outdoors* articles will fit into your programme so well. Hope *Scribner's* will take "Crows Fly High"—though the space rates of *Esquire* are likewise alluring. I saw a copy of that last month, & it certainly looks like a rather ambitious venture.

Has Melmoth the Wandrei shewed you the pictures he took during my visit? If not, I'll lend you my copies after Shea returns them.

All good wishes—

Yr obt grandsire

H P

P.S. Early spring stationery will look hopeful & cheering! I'll be eager to see your later vernal design. ¶ The Am. Poetry Journal looks promising. ¶ Coates's plan for binding & issuing my "Shunned House" has probably come to nothing. Now young Barlow may try his hand. ¶ Have sent out all of your circulars. Want to shoot along some more for distribution? ¶ Have now read the Asquith anthology. I like Blackwood's tale best.[5] Nobody can make the unreal seem real as well as Algy—& there's a lot of genius left in the old boy yet! ¶ Infamous weather lately. All low records for Providence broken last week with temperature of *17 below*. Nothing so bad since the historically hellish winter of 1778–9, when Narragansett Bay froze over. But the house heats finely.

Notes

1. *Murder Stalks the Wakely Family,* AWD's first detective novel and his first published book.

2. Alexander Kinnan Laing.

3. [Charles Birkin, ed.], *Shudders: A Collection of Uneasy Tales* (1932). But in letter 348 HPL appears to confuse this with Cynthia Asquith's *Shudders: A Collection of New Nightmare Tales* (1929).

4. Apparently Whit Burnett and Martha Foley, ed., *A Story Anthology 1931–1933.*

5. "A Threefold Lord," later reprinted in *Shocks.*

[348] [ALS]

March 11, 1934

Dear A W:—

Both of your interesting communications arrived on the same day—the four-day difference in posting being annulled by the addressing of the earlier one to "66 Barnes St" . . . . . . a puzzle finally solved by the local mail sharps. I must be getting well known—for the other day (for the first time in history) an epistle with no ampler address than "Providence R.I." found its way to my door!

I note with extreme interest your debut as a pink-tea literary lion, & trust the ordeal—with its admiring inspection & motherly questionings—was not too irritating. Thanks for the press cuttings, which surely indicate your rapid rise to fame. I'll see that the notices go where they'll do the most good—& incidentally, I hope to get a crack at the Wakeley Family myself before long.

I must see if the local library has the Mercury with the James article—which reminds me that the corresponding sketch by Klarkash-Ton in the new F F is admirably informative.[1] I shall borrow the Asquith "Shudders" from my new fount of generous loans—H. Koenig of N.Y. Hope *Story* will become more flexible as time passes, & that your tale will appear soon. Shea has subscribed, & is on the lookout.

Your literary programme leaves me as bewildered as usual—& I surely hope your new publishers will keep on demanding novels. I shall look for "Feigman's Beard" in W T. Glad you've got ahead of Lavell with the 1934 Not at Night. Is the 1933 one any good? I believe it contains Klarkash-Ton's "Isle of the Torturers".[2]

As for "Anthony Adverse"—I'll probably skim through it very lightly. Dwyer thought that certain touches of the past—New Orleans, &c.—would appeal to me. I don't take so long in reading a book once I get at it. My trouble is summoning up enough energy to get hold of the thing in the first place. Which reminds me—I've just read the new Dunsany volume—"The Curse of the Wise Woman"—& like it exceedingly. The supernatural is barely suggested, but the poetic colouring is exquisite. It is a set of boyhood memories which reminded me strongly of your own work. Dunsany may not be his old self of the early 1900's, but there's a lot left in the old boy yet! However—what has interested me most of all is Weigall's "Wanderings in Roman Britain". It set me rereading Tacitus' life of Agricola—& that led me on to a review of the "Germania". I don't wonder at Machen's absorption in the spell of Britannia Romana.

Regarding my alleged story—I'm vastly glad to hear your largely favourable opinion. Probably I'll try it on Satrap Pharnabazus before long—though I want to collect a goodly symposium of opinions first. Amusingly enough, no two commentators have agreed on any point of criticism. What each one objects to, all the others approve or pass over! I can take my choice of thinking the yarn is all perfect, or all rotten. Probably the latter. Regarding your point—the narrator *isn't* free. This is a message to the world written from Arkham Gaol. Whether the new ending you suggest would be practicable, I'll consider with care—along with other suggestions from C A S & the Peacock Sultan. It might ball things up a bit to dilute the climax with so much action-detective stuff—but we'll see. Abundant thanks, anyhow. Two-Gun Bob hasn't reported on the tale—maybe it was too tame for his sanguinary taste. No hurry about the circulation of the thing—when I get ready to bombard Wright I have a copy here.

Glad to see the vernal stationery—& wish we could have some weather to watch!* What a winter! Snowy tempest Feby. 20 tied up traffic throughout New England—& another cold spell since then. Hope things aren't quite so bad out at Sac Prairie. I'll duly pass on the press notices.

---

*March 5th carried out the idea fairly well—up to 63°, & I took a walk in the mud-covered countryside. Brooks & ponds overflowing.

Hope to gawd I can get down to Florida to visit Barlow (incidentally, of course, pausing at ancient Charleston & St. Augustine). I can tell better a month from now how my finances would stand such a strain. Haven't seen a palmetto or live-oak since the 19th of June, 1932! Price, I presume, has told you of his settlement in Pawhuska as engineering genius of a garage. He'll miss New Orleans—but it's a good idea to have a dependable source of revenue apart from writing.

Well—now to tinker with a piece of bum "poetry".

Grandpaternal blessings

—H P

Notes

1. Mary Butts, "The Art of Montagu[e] James," *London Mercury* 29 (February 1934): 306–17; CAS, "The Weird Works of M. R. James," *FF* 1, No. 6 (February 1934): 89–90.

2. Christine Campbell Thomson, ed., *Terror by Night.*

[349] [ALS]

March 29[, 1934]

Dear A W:—

Congratulations on the additional fame embodied in the *Milwaukee Journal* writeup![1] I'll pass this cutting—& the other one—along to those who will be most interested. Glad the book is taking well, & hope its successors are thoroughly assured propositions.

Your activity seems as intensive as usual, but I hope you can relax a bit when your favourite hills attain a suitable wildness. I hope the spring will not be a late one—I think I mentioned having taken one trip through the awakening woods & fields. The brooks & ponds were higher than I ever saw them before, & the broad Blackstone river was quite flooded—trees & cottage roofs emerging from the water like reliques of sunken Atlantis. Since then there has been more snow, but at last the ground is free again. Barlow has invited me down to Florida for *May* 1st, but my financial ability to accept is still problematical.

Regarding "The Thing on the Doorstep"—a closer perusal would have shewed that the episode of the Thing antedates the asylum killing in *time* though not in *order of narration.* In fact, the whole effectiveness of the climax depends on this antedating—for it is the appearance of the Thing, & the desperate message It hands the narrator, which moves the latter to perform the killing as an act of duty.

I did read "Anthony Adverse"—taking 5 days to do it. Good surface picture of late 18th & early 19th centuries, though marred by an amateurish use of coincidences, excessive mysticism & symbolism, too much heavy philosophy,

& a general letdown & slewing up during the final third. Also read A. Merritt's "Metal Monster", & can understand why he calls it his "best & worst" novel.[2] Most effective presentation of the *utterly alien & non-human* that I have ever seen—but the human characters are wooden & conventional . . . . just pulp stuff. New W T so-so. Klarkash-Ton's tale & illustration form the high spot.

Well—may your fame increase!

Yr obt Servt

H P

P.S. Belknap wants to know which of the "little magazines" (Pagany—Midland, &c) *pay* for contributions. If you could slip him—or me—a list of those you know, he would be extremely grateful. He'd also like a list of 8 or 9 or 10 of the best non-remunerative specimens.

P.P.S. [Six lines of text obliterated here.] Brobst was back in Providence for a moment on a vacation prior to having his tonsils removed. For a while he was afraid he had tuberculosis (which would mean the relinquishment of his present training & chosen career), but a more careful reading of the X-ray plates proved the fear unfounded. He will continue in Boston—after recovery from the tonsil business—till October. Is now home in Allentown till Apr. 6, when the operation will be performed in Providence.

¶ Oh, yes—& I've just read "The Green Round"—lent me by Klarkash-Ton. It is really extremely interesting—with some very potent reflections of that persistent sense of unreal worlds impinging on the real world which many imaginative persons possess. In the casualness & unexplainedness of the phenomena represented, it recalls some of Machen's queer prefaces—such as that to "The Three Impostors". Its faults are—mainly—a certain rambling diffuseness, tameness, & over-use of typical stylistic mannerisms. Also—the poltergeist manifestations tend to be somewhat hackneyed. Hardly one of Machen's greatest—but typically Machenian for all that. I'm vastly glad to have read it, & may buy a copy when I'm less broke.

¶ Price & Wright have started quite a controversy over our version of von Junzt's original title—*Unaussprechlichen* Kulten. Sultan Malik claims that *Unnennbaren* (= unmentionable) has some subtle preferability (in the way of unmistakable *evil*) over the earlier choice. Let 'em fight it out among themselves. Wish Two-Gun Bob had doped out his own original & saved us the trouble!

[P.P.P.S.] My letter in the March F F is all hashed up. For 'AN especial morbidity' read 'NO especial' &c.[3]

Notes

1. "Wisconsin Youth Writes Long Novel in Week and Sells It." *Milwaukee Journal* (10 March 1934), "The Green Sheet" p. 3.

2. A. Merritt, *The Metal Monster,* serialized in *Argosy All-Story Weekly* beginning with the issue of 7 August 1920 (rpt. Hippocampus Press, 2002). He is quoted in *FF* 2, No. 1 (September 1934): 7, as saying the novel was his best and worst.

3. The passage as printed in *FF* 1, No. 7 (March 1934), 105 reads: "It can be said that anything which vividly embodies a basic human emotion or captures a definite and typical human mood is genuine art. The subject matter is immaterial. It requires an especial morbidity to enjoy any authentic word-depiction, whether it is conventionally 'pleasant' or not. Indeed, it argues a somewhat immature and narrow prospection [*sic*] when our judgment is by the mere conventional appeal of its subject-matter or its supposed social effects. The question to ask is not whether it is 'healthy' or 'pleasant,' but whether it is *genuine* and *powerful.*"

[350] [ALS]

April 13[, 1934]

Dear A W:—

Thanks on Belknap's behalf for the list of select literary repositories, remunerative & otherwise. Hope he'll be able to follow, even tho' humbly, in your super-energised footsteps. Damn sorry to hear that *Pagany* & *The Midland* have gone under.

Hope the grand total of Wakeley [*sic*] reviews will average favourable enough to satisfy both you & the publishers.[1] Regarding the title of #2—I really think you are right in preferring "The Creeper (or Crawler) in the Halls". That has a sinister suggestion pure & simple, whereas "The Man On All Fours" possesses certain overtones of the merely grotesque & whimsical. Good luck with your third book—Ædepol, but just to count 'em makes one dizzy! Hope you can get the plays, revisions, & other miscellany out of the way in time to take a few real breaths before long! Glad to hear of the important new placements, especially that with *Scribner's.* Hope the new agent will prove helpful. The financial goal you set is surely impressive as judged by the contemporary luck of the majority.

I shall welcome "Incubus" & "Col. Markesan" when they appear. The current W T is the best for some time—with the Burks reprint, the distinctive Moore story, & the excellent specimens by Two-Gun Bob & Klarkash-Ton.

Hopes increase for a southward jaunt. I shall probably tarry a week at the villa Belnapia & then hit the road in earnest. Reports reach me of sudden peregrinations on the part of Sultan Malik—involving stops at Cross Plains & Auburn.

Your late-spring stationery impresses me as being distinctly powerful & haunting. The bits of sunset sky glimpsed through the foliage have a suggestively flame-like contour. I shall await with interest such other sub-seasonal designs as you may inaugurate during the coming months.

I've not had several rural walks in my favourite scenes, & enjoyed a couple of outdoor reading & writing sessions. However, it's only a pale imitation of the genial conditions existing around Charleston & south of there!

All good wishes—

Yr obt Servt H P

P.S. Odds in the Black Book name debate return toward *Unaussprechlichen.* Satrap Pharnabazus concedes that nothing else could be quite as malignly mouth-filling as that. It has a sinister *rhythm* about it, compared to which Sultan Malik's choice—*Unennbaren*—sounds deplorably tame.

¶ Barlow says he's persuaded his local circulating library to order Wakeley.

¶ Hopping off tomorrow night. A week at Belknap's, then a week (I hope) at Charleston, & then the main Barlovian visit. You'll receive cards.

¶ Just got April F F. Tale by Binder isn't half bad.[2] And sheets just came from Crawford—my "Celephaïs" in his home-printed magazine. Nearly done now. Glad to see your "Moscow Road"—or "The Cossacks Ride Hard", which I recall in MS.

Notes

1. Besides conventional print reviews, AWD had solicited reader comments on *Murder Stalks the Wakely Family* in his article "Novels at 10,000 Words a Day." The responses, including those from HPL, CAS, and Carl Jacobi, are mentioned in "And Did They Write!"

2. "Eando" Binder, "The Ancient Voice," *FF* (April 1934).

[351] [ALS]

Y M C A, Charleston.
April 29, 1934

Dear A W:—

As the postmark & date-line have told you, the old man has broken loose again! Had a good week in N Y with Belknap & the gang. Saw both Wandreis, & was quite bowled over by some of Howard's drawings which I had not seen before. God, but that kid has genius! Watch him—he'll get somewhere before long! Hopped off for the South Sunday midnight, & spent Monday morning in Washn—exploring the ancient Georgetown section. Richmond in the afternoon; Raleigh, N.C. in the evening. Hit my beloved CHARLESTON at dawn Tuesday. Am stopping at the Y & lapping up the colonial atmosphere of the old town as usual. What a place! The 18th century still living! And to complete the picture, the old frigate *Consititution* is in port—I went over it yesterday. Full summer down here—rich green vegetation, hot days, straw hats, & all. In Wash. & Richmond it is merely spring-like—with delicate young foliage. And when I left N.Y. it was still wintry there—with chill winds & bare boughs. There's quite a kick in passing from winter to summer in a few hours. On May 1st I move on to Savannah, & on

May 2 arrive in De Land for my visit unless plans change. Temporary address for a fortnight or so: ℅ R. H. BARLOW, BOX 88, DE LAND, FLORIDA. But I hate to leave old Charleston . . . . . no other place is quite so fascinating. The southern climate has quite put me on my feet again after the debilitation of the late horrible winter. I haven't felt better in years! Am economising very closely—keeping food down to $1.75 per week.

Thanks for the drama programme—Egad, Son, but you do grind 'em out! I'll wager this event was interesting, whatever its aesthetic status. And now another one under way!! Where do you get the energy? But I presume all this is good advertising for your novels. Glad Wakeley reviews continue dominantly favourable—& hope the sales of #2 will be sufficient to justify the sacrifice of the retitling. By the way—my prospective host will have veritable convulsions of joy when he receives the novel MS. you intend to send him. I don't believe he's ever seen a full-length novel in MS.—& one by a gifted author, which is really being published, is probably something he never dared dream of owning! Glad the sales of Wakeley continue good, & hope All Fours will equal & surpass that record.

Well—the *unassprechlichen—unnennbaren* controversy goes merrily on! Just before receiving your letter I had a note from Satrap Pharnabazus saying that *unaussprechlichen* was quite out—that it meant chiefly something *mechanically or phonetically unpronounceable*—hence I took the liberty of quoting the statements in your letter. I've no idea where Wright got the material for his cocksure statement—though I believe he refers questions of Germanic erudition to a young Austrian who works in the office.

I was extremely sorry to hear of White's suicide,[1] & wonder what could have caused it. I fancy he was odd & high-strung—he made extravagant claims regarding the amount of his work which he literally dreamed. His stuff had a certain distinctive charm—& his novel "Andivius Hedulio" is to date the only bit of Roman fiction that really reflects Roman psychology & sentiment. I recall his having told good old Whitehead about trouble with his publisher—some row which involved the holding up of the sale of the "Lukundoo" collection. Glad to hear that Benson is on the job again[2]—though some of his effusions are scarcely notable. Thanks for the warning anent "Gideon Wyck" et al.

Yes—your late spring stationery is great stuff, & I fancy you can well afford to wait a couple of months before starting in on anything new! You do keep the artists busy!

Barlow tells me that Crawford's magazine is out at last—under the title *Marvel Tales*. Glad it didn't fizzle out to nothing, & hope it will keep going. My "Celephais"—of which I had advance sheets—is afflicted with several exasperating misprints.

Had a joint card from Two-Gun Bob & Sultan Malik at Cross Plains, & fancy they must have enjoyed their personal session. Later had a card from the Peacock Sultan postmarked Juarez, Mexico. Before long he ought to be around the Klarkash-Ton region!

Well—blessings upon thee!

Yr obt Servt

H P

P.S. [on postcard:] I had the enclosed just read when a letter from Satrap Pharnabazus arrived with the following matter pertaining to the "unaussprechlichen" controversy. Looks as if our side were winning! But how ironical to have aid coming from the despised Senf!

"Senf wandered into the office yesterday, & I asked him (without explaining why I wanted to know) 'What does *unaussprechlich* mean?' 'It means "unspeakable"', he said. Then I told him why I wanted to know, & he commented, 'The fellow that said *unaussprechlich* means "unspeakable" only in the sense of "unpronounceable" couldn't have known very much about German.'

"So *unaussprechlich* it is!

"Senf is a little gnome of a man, with a marked German accent (for he was a grown man before he left Germany), & he wears a dark brown toupee which is so obviously a toupee that it fools nobody."

¶ Well—I guess Wright will use *unaussprechlichen* after all—so much for Sultan Malik's synthetic West Point German![3]

Incidentally, Wright reveals the fact that he doesn't know that The Black Book & Unaus. Kulten are supposed to be one & the same volume. Evidently he didn't read Two-Gun's *Black Stone* attentively.

Notes

1. Edward Lucas White died 30 March 1934.
2. E. F. Benson, *More Spook Stories.*
3. See letter 352.

[352] [TLS, JHL]

Sauk City
Wisconsin
3 May, 34

Dear H. P.,

I am glad to know that you're enjoying yourself, but I don't envy you in the least now that May is here and the wild cherry is white again, and there is a promise of lilacs just over the week. We have had a week of uninterrupted sunlight, and now we need rain. Last night the whippoorwills came, and I have never known a sound so welcome. As I grow older, I detest winters more and more, though I do not mind the cold so much as the necessity of staying in. I am brown as a berry, and have managed to rouse some indignation by being a one-man nudist colony on the hills only a third of a mile across the river from the village.

I am enclosing various items, the print copies of A Day in April and A Day in May, Carl Jacobi's Complete Stories tale, Crocodile,[1] and typescripts of two poems written on the first and second respectively, Spring Evening: The Indians Pass, and The Old Men Remember, which I think are among the best poems I have done, even if they are not orthodox poetry. I have attempted to put on paper a feeling for the past without being nostalgic, and believe I have succeeded.

I am now in the middle of revising THREE WHO DIED, and you may inform Barlow, together with my greetings, that I'll send him the original typescript of this book as well as that of THE MAN ON ALL FOURS shortly after I have finished it, which will be some time this month. I am also getting ready to start THE SEVEN WHO WAITED, doing the novel before the play, which will make the latter task considerably simpler.

That ass Wright is thoroughly wrong, as usual, regarding unaussprechlichen, no matter to whom he has gone. I should prefer to take the word of this community's best Germans with centuries of German culture behind them to any expert he may dig up. His definition of the word is flatly wrong.

Yes, Benson's stuff is often very uneven, I agree; still, I am glad to have a new volume by him.

Here are the two poems.

SPRING EVENING: THE INDIANS PASS

There is a wind tonight, a strong wind blowing,
And I think of the Chippewas, the Sacs, the Iroquois, like leaves before it.
From the pasture gate the urgent lowing
Of cattle, and I think, these are the sounds they made, small sounds retreating
The hills are blue now with violets, and in the valleys, hepaticas, anemones;
And there they held them, their weddings, and on the prairie, burials, their
    ceremonies.
There is music even in their names, in the sound of them—Iroquois, Sac,
    Chippewa, Yellow Thunder, Black Hawk, Spotted Eagle—like melo-
    dies made in the deep night.
Even the river, Ouisconsin, they called it. Jonathan Carver in 1766 on the
    ninth of October sat down to wrote:
"On the banks of this river there is a large town of Indians, calling themselves
    Saukies or Sacs."
And the Indians that day with their smokes across the prairie: "There is a
    paleface here. He lacks

Men, but is not afraid. He asks many questions." This from the Lookout over the prairie to the Bluff
Where the brook vanished in the sand, told in the smoke, puff on puff
Slipping from blankets. "They are a kind people, unafraid and not war-like. There are many of them here."
There is a pale moon vying with the afterglow and the wind's sound, (Death's is a long long year.)
And the leaves are before the wind like the sound of far men marching, (They went on slow feet down the valleys and the rivers, reluctant to go.)
The peepers calling April, and the whippoorwill, (The soldiers behind them, blood on their tunics, blood on their weapons to show.)
And from the village the smell of lilacs on the wind, (They took Black Hawk and he died.)
The smell of locusts drowsing down the night, (They took Spotted Eagle and he died.)
And the wind in the long mile of cottonwoods heralds the dark, and the budding catalpas.
(They walked on the buttercups, on the marigolds, on the trailing arbutus, forgetting—the Iroquois, the Sacs, the Chippewas.)

SPRING EVENING: THE OLD MEN REMEMBER

May is no quiet month; it is loud beyond others with spring,
And there are sounds, sounds, sounds. Voices of children ring
Into the dusk, and the old men, released from December ...
The old men sit against the afterglow and remember.
Birch pods bursting, dropping, softly, gently. Ten decades since the Indians padded down the lanes,
But the old men remember the sounds they made more strongly, more clearly than yesterday's rains.
The Foxes, the Sacs, the Iroquois, and to the far south the Incas, the Navajos, the Sioux;
They never saw them, but remember them now against the fading blue.
The old men are old now as the Indians. They remember yesterdays. It is a long time now since 1848,
When their fathers met each other on the cured board walks and said, "Wisconsin Territory no longer, but State!"
The pioneers are white stones in a square of land;
Some not even that, but broken and yellow in the sand.
Count d'Ervais, Colonel Brogmar, Baron Segallah—the old men remember the dead.
There is smoke in the dusk and the fragrance of wild cherry blooming, and the last sun shows red
In the west. The old men sit against the afterglow and say

To each other, "Red sky. Tomorrow will be a fine day."
Their lips shape tomorrows but they are thinking of yesterdays, and the
 sound of lilacs breaking
Gently against the wind like the far sound of men marching below the
 Mason-Dixon line, forsaking
The fields for the Union, is a stronger sound than the screams cars make on
 the streets.
Death waits for them in the sunset, and far remembrance beats
Their thinning hours. Exhausts bark, crack in the still air, and the old men
 remember the Maine,
And their still limbs, their painful limbs, their crippled limbs are running,
 running, running again.
Their eyes are lost, and they smile thinly.
"Listen, did you hear? They shot McKinley!"
They think of San Juan and start over again. Lincold [*sic*] is dead,
A gold spike on the Union-Pacific, Indians to westward, pioneers, and how red,
Raw La Follette whipped the lumber kings. The hylas and the kildeer and the
 whippoorwill are singing over waiting graves,
And the old men linger to remember, their memories like little waves washing
 down the years .. such little waves.

Let me have your reaction to these when you find time.

Meanwhile, all best wishes for the continuation of your pleasure in your southern sojourn.

as always,
August

Notes

1. Carl Jacobi, "Crocodile," *Complete Stories* (30 April 1934).

[353] [ALS]

May 19, 1934

Dear A W:—

Glad to receive yours of the 3d, with its delightful poems & interesting enclosures. I like both poems immensely—they tickle my reminiscent mood in just the right way. You surely have a knack of selecting the aptest symbols . . . . I have a weakness for the cataloguing of significant things. "The Old Men Remember" brings in many old friends familiar to me from your prose.

I guess Satrap Pharnabazus will have to give in regarding *unassprechlich* sooner or later, but it is interesting to watch him struggle! Wish you could help to set him right.

Your seasonal pieces are delightful, & I hope to see all of them as they appear. Thanks also for the Jacobi story, which is excellent of its kind. Jacobi will certainly get somewhere if he will keep his genuine literary personality free from the influence of cheap-magazine standards.

Glad your favourite hills are so attractive. Warm weather in the north is certainly delightful when it does come! I'm revelling down here—three times the vigour I ever have in the north. Stopped 8½ hrs. in Savannah, & thoroughly explored that attractive town. Not as quaint as Charleston, but delectable for all that. Florida is as much of a tonic as ever—86° the other day.

Barlow is a splendid little chap—almost as much of a prodigy as you were. Paints, writes, models, plays the piano, prints, &c. &c.—yet is only 16. His father (now absent) is a retired army colonel. The place is an attractive country-seat 14 m. west of De Land—finely landscaped but not quite finished. In the rear is a lake on which we row at sunset—when the tall Australian pines stand out against the western sky like the trees in a Japanese print. The other day Barlow killed a coach-whip snake over 7 feet long—sample of local big-game hunting. Incidentally—Barlow is having positive convulsions of joy over the MSS. you have lately sent him.

All good wishes

—Yr obt Servt H P

[P.S.] Took a trip to New Smyrna, Fla., & saw the ruins of a large Franciscan mission of 1696, & also the site (& original canal) of Dr. Turnbull's plantation of 1768.

¶ Miss Moore, author of "Shambleau", &c., has just sent Barlow a *drawing* which shows fantastic talent beyond even Rankin. Barlow is quite an incipient artist himself—though handicapped by dangerously bad eyesight. You ought to see the bas-relief of *Cthulhu* he has just made—as well as the statuette of the Hindoo elephant-god Ganesa [*sic*] which he is making for old Bill Lumley. He also has a plan for the publication or distribution of Howard Wandrei's marvellous drawings in the form of 11 × 14 reproductions by an expert professional photographer—for sale at cost. I hope H E will consent to the plan, for those weird masterpieces ought to be circulated somehow. If you're in touch with H E (who is now, as I suppose you know, on Cape Cod—℅ Alvin von Hinzmann, 543 Commercial St., Provincetown, Mass.) I trust you'll put in a good word for the scheme.

¶ Don't know when I'll be moving on—my cordial hosts keep urging me to delay my departure. Next stop, St. Augustine—although I'd try for Havana if a certain delinquent client would pay up.

¶ Through Barlow I'm now in touch with George Allan England[1]—who is in wretched health.

¶ Price is home with his mother at 5314 East 12th St., Oakland, California. He has just been to see Klarkash-Ton, & both report a great time. Price is the only W.T. colleague either Two-Gun Bob or C A S has ever seen.

¶ Shunned House sheets have come from Cook at last. When Barlow gets around to the binding I'll see that you get a copy.

Notes

1. George Allan England (1877–1936), author of *Darkness and Dawn.*

[354] [TLS, SHSW]

Sauk City, Wisconsin 22 May 1934

Dear H. P.,

Glad to have your letter, and to know that you enjoyed the excerpts. I enclose herewith A BROOK IN JUNE, just out in the current number of Outdoors. I enclose also a clipping from a recent issue of the Milwaukee Journal which may interest you. The marked portion is what I have always argued or tried to make clear in my discussions on this subject with you and others. ... Well, this month is almost drawing to a close, and spring with it, a spring than which we have had few worse, what with cold, dust, and drought, which combined to bring about abnormally short flower seasons—the lovely and delicate hepatica, for instance, had a two week season, and it should have had a five and one-half; fortunately, the rain when it did come, came soon enough to prolong by one week (the best of the month) the abnormally short 2-week season of the lilacs, one of my favourite spring flowers, though this flower should have at least a month in blossom. The locusts are out now, a wk early. The one bright spot of the spring was my discovery of a new blossom which has an incredibly lovely scent—the bloom of the wild crab-apple tree. I have had sprigs of it here on my desk all during the 15 days I took to do my fourth novel, THE SEVEN WHO WAITED, which I did directly in final draft, and which for that turned out so excellently that I have pleasure in just sitting down and rereading portions of it, which is more than I do with a lot of my poems and short stories of a more serious nature; the style of writing is matched only by Shiel's in How the Old Woman Got Home, his being better, of course. ... Not many placements in this period, however: SPRING EVENING: THE INDIANS PASS in the Yankee Poetry Chapbook, 12th new magazine for the year and the fulfilment of the quota set; AUGUST FROM A HILL to Outdoors. ... No other writing apart from the book but the August article. ... I wish I had time to copy the other two poems from the quartet of which you saw the first two, (The Ojibwa Smile and We Are Remembering Again), but I haven't for I have a lot of mechanical details to get done about shipping out this fourth book of mine. I have a strenuous program ahead of me—this 4th volume is to be dramatized and put on stage in August; the fifth book must be done by July 1, thus giving me 2 yrs to do a serious novel. And at least 3 articles, 3 stories, and 10 poems to be done in the same time . .. Enjoy yourself, all best as always,

August

[355] [ALS]

[late May 1934]

Dear A W:—

Yrs. of May 22, with its varied enclosures, proved interesting in the extreme. Your June article is delightful, & casts such a glamour over the rural landscape that one wants to hasten out & follow the Sac Prairie brook for miles along its magical course. You are such an eloquent interpreter of nature that some periodical ought to have a perpetual series of articles from you—like those of Peattie[1] in one of the Washington papers. Too bad the present spring has been, in general, such a false alarm—but glad a congenial floral discovery has afforded you compensation. From all I hear of the northern weather, I'm glad I'm out of it for the moment. Glorious here—85° to 90° right along. I feel 40 years younger, & have not a bit of the sinus trouble which constantly dogs me in the north.

Thanks for the cutting on telepathic research. Experiments such as those are certainly to be encouraged; & if their final result ever does make it appear that communication through hitherto unrecognised senses is a fact, no rational thinker will wish to dispute the conclusion.

Congratulations on the quick composition of "The Seven Who Waited", & upon the happy chance which permits it to be both qualitatively good & professionally acceptable. Barlow remarks that all your novels have titles involving *numbers*. Is that a device of your publishers? Glad the serious work also comes along. Don't let the programme get too strenuous—although you appear to revel in overwork.

I've prolonged my De Land stay to unconscionable lengths, but the hospitality of the Barlovii is irresistible. Further moves uncertain—hopes for Havana very dim, but I shall certainly spend a week in St. Augustine. If I weren't so attached to my native landscape, I'd certainly live down here!

Regards & benedictions—

H P

[P.S.] Those terror books sound interesting. Are you ordering them?

Notes

1. The nature writer Donald Culcross Peattie (1898–1964). HPL received clippings of Peattie's articles from the Washington, DC, paper from a correspondent who lived there; see letter 361.

[356] [TLS, JHL]

Sauk City
Wisconsin
4 June 34

Dear H. P.,

Perhaps you would have enjoyed our weather this past week—no one else would. Between 98 and 104 in the shade—it left me drained of all desire to do anything, affected my alimentary canal, and wrecked me in general. Today is the first passable day we've had, and yet the county is crying for rain, which we sorely need. The drought will have severe repercussions throughout the states, for speculators are forcing prices up terribly—lemons just jum[p]ed from $4.00 to $7.50 per crate, and butter in this big milk-cheese-butter state is rapidly rising in price, owing to inability of cattle to find adequate grazing land. On top of all that, the dreaded grasshoppers are beginning to leave the parched Dakotas and enter Northern Wisconsin. Twenty-five years ago, the late eternally great La Follette fought the lumber kings and warned the people of this state what depletion of our forests would mean; but the people being largely swine did not believe until too late; so here we are, with the increasingly long droughts descending upon us just as the senior La Follette said. Ignorance may be bliss, but I hope twenty million farmers die of it; those who have steadily refused to keep trees between their fields to prevent wind erosion. The last great dust storm moved four hundred million tons of top soil; since it takes four hundred years to replace lost top soil, you figure out who loses.

I am glad you are enjoying the Outdoors articles. I have just recently placed AUGUST FROM A HILL with them, and also SYRUP CAMP IN APRIL for their April 1935 issue. I am, of course, running a monthly column with them as long as long as I please.

No, I am not at the present time ordering those terror books. I may later, but now I'm too much in need of money to think getting anything. The only two new books added to my shelves were review copies—SHADOW ON THE WALL by H. C. Bailey (out June 6th), and THE PUZZLE OF THE SILVER PERSIAN by Stuart Palmer, the only other Wisconsin mystery novel writer.

I think Barlow is stretching a point by saying that all my works have titles including numbers. THE MAN ON ALL FOURS, THREE WHO DIED (which may be changed to THE TRIANGLE OF DEATH), and THE SEVEN WHO WAITED just balance MURDER STALKS THE WAKELY FAMILY, MISCHIEF IN THE LANE, and DEATH HUNTS ALONE, the last two not yet written. However, I am today starting MISCHIEF IN THE LANE, and for the three following days running down to Prairie du Chien, which is to be the setting of the new book.

My publishers, anxious to keep me entirely on their list, are promising to bring out FOUR books by me a year, two Judge Peck novels under my own name, and any serious novel under my own name extra, and two Solar Pons novels under a pseudonym. This was the result of an overture from Reilly & Lee of Chicago in my direction. L&M's latest report puts sales of MURDER STALKS at 1100. This is gratifying, being 200 over the average sale of a first mystery novel.

I wish I could persuade you to curve around into Wisconsin on your way home. If you struck Natchez, you could move upward along the old Father of Waters and into Wisconsin.

The new W. T. just reached me. It's pretty bad—only 2 good stories in the issue, THE COLOSSUS OF YLOURGNE and THEY CALLED HIM GHOST. All the others, including Howard's, crappy as hell. Including our own piece, as well. The reprint is commendable. I am looking forward to seeing THROUGH THE GATES OF THE SILVER KEY again. Tell me, did you sell THE THING ON THE DOORSTEP to Wright? It surely should place; send it in, if not.

I copy here my latest poem, SPRING EVENING: WILD CRAB-APPLE BLOOMING. You may like it:

On the prairie now the wild crab-apple tree is blooming its last, pink and
 white, no flower sweeter,
And May a month of flowers—hepaticas, anemones, violets, lilacs, locusts—
 with days passing on fleeter
Feet than any month. Nothing fragrant as the flower
Of the wild crab-apple. There is a sad hour
For its passing, beyond which it cannot remain;
And fending against that hour, only the rain.
This is the late evening for it, with the wind tearing
At its petals, and the thin year wearing
At the tree.
I can see
How its blossoms ride the wind like pale snow forgotten from December.
An old tree, so old that had it memory it could remember
The soft sounds of the Ojibwas in the damp leaf-smell of July when summer
 came to the prairie with only Indians to know.
Spring will be coming again, and the flowers again, but the slow
Year grows lonely before. Here in the last evening of the wild, sweet crab-apple,
 the reaches of my heart are not where the afterglow falls, but in shadow,
With the fading petals in the wind over the prairie, in the tall grasses, caught in
 leaves, in cobwebs in the branches and the fence-rails, and some below
The earth so soon.

The early moon
Will remember last how the white cloud on the prairie was thinned
In the night by the wind.

best, as always,
August

P.S. Frontier & Midland took SPRING EVENING: THE OJIBWA SMILE.

[357] [ALS]

De Land—
June 7[, 1934]

Dear A W:—

Glad to receive the epistle enclosed in Ar-E'ch-Bei's[1] bundle. You certainly did have some heat—more than I've ever encountered in Florida, though I doubt if I'd have found it oppressive. The hotter it is, the more energy I seem to have. Hereabouts—at this season—the mercury seems to stay around 80° or 85°. There have been warmer days—& there was one beastly cold day when I wore a bedquilt over my suit in the house, & a borrowed overcoat outdoors. Sorry you're having the twin plagues of drought & grasshoppers. Possibly some of the current results of deforestation will be a lesson to the people—though the loss of 400 years' accumulation of top soil is surely a heavy price to pay!

Glad your *Outdoors* articles are continuing. You certainly succeed in bringing out the charm of the countryside to a phenomenal degree. The Peattie articles which I mentioned (I enclose one—which you need not return) are relatively lifeless & pedantic.

Congratulations on your new publishing prospects—which I hope may enable you to get your best novels in book form. The outside offer was evidently in your favour! And so our old friend Solar Pons is to reappear—though with concealed paternity! I duly note the matter of titles. Trust you have good luck with "Mischief in the Lane"!

Your new crab-apple poem impresses me as wholly delightful—with all the reminiscent & landscape-born qualities which distinguish d'Erlettian work. Glad the previous verses have found a haven—what is *Frontier & Midland* . . . a consolidation of two of your earlier standbys?

The new W T is certainly a premier flop. That "Goeste" story is a peculiar thing.[2] Plot & revelatory climax entitle it to distinction, yet the writing is so screamingly amateurish that I don't see how it ever got accepted. I imagine that your collaboration is a resurrected minor effort—as Two-Gun Bob's feeble attempt undoubtedly is. And yet the April & May issues were both above the average. One never can tell what's coming! No—I haven't yet submitted "The

Thing on the Doorstep"—it's still going the rounds. I shall possibly let Wright see it later. He is, incidentally, going to reprint "Arthur Jermyn."

I wish indeed that I could return home by a roundabout way including Wisconsin, but finances sternly veto such an idea. Nor shall I be able to see New Orleans & Natchez, either. Straight back via the return half of my round trip ticket (though of course with stopovers) is the best I can do. Some time, though, I must invade the Middle West—it is curious how many friends I have in Wisconsin, a place I've never been near in person. When the time comes, I shall certainly appreciate your hospitable guidance over the magical hills of Sac Prairie!

Wright stubbornly refuses to heed my plea for the retention of *Unaussprechlichen Kulten,* & plans to flop tamely back to the "translated" form—simply *Nameless Cults* in English! That's one way of cutting the Gordian knot. Evidently he found that Price's *Unnennbaren* wouldn't hold water. By the way—he & I were both considerably surprised to find that the name is not used at all in the text of the Silver Key sequel!

That epistle from Brother Bill certainly is a rare museum piece! He has lately (vide enc.—which needn't be returned) been bringing up the weird versus scientific question with me; but as you see, has not obtained much satisfaction in that quarter. He seems to be an incredibly naive, ill-read, hillbillyish sort of individual—though possessed of a kind of plodding honesty. I didn't know that Klarkash-Ton & I were so instrumental in shaping the policy of *Marvel Tales!*

Ar-E'ch-Bei is enclosing an epistle of his own in this—hope you can let him have the data &c. which he wants.

Grandpaternal Blessings—

Yr obt servt

H P

Notes

1. I.e., R. H. B., or HPL's host, R[obert] H[ayward] Barlow.

2. Laurence J. Cahill, "They Called Him Ghost" (which involves a character, Charles Goeste, of Goeste Hall).

[358] [ANS, Postcard]

[Prairie du Chien, Wis.
7 June 1934]

Dear H. P.,

Here's a good picture of the juncture of the two rivers here at Prairie du Chien from the Nelson Dewey Park. I've had a good if somewhat lazy time here at PdC., though I've not neglected writing a new poem "Prairie du Chien Wis: A History in Four Panels", and the 1st chapter of "Mischief in the House." Swell old atmosphere—old French & Indian. Hills & rivers with the town bluffs beyond. August.

[P.S.] All regards to R. H. B.

[359] [ANS][1]

[No postmark; early June 1934]

Thanks for the card from Prairie du Chien. Glad you're having a good time. I'd like to see that region some day. ¶ Went to Silver Springs the other day & got a marvellous eye full. There is a placid pool at the head of the Silver River whose floor is pitted with huge abysses—visible clearly through a glass-bottomed boat—while the Silver River itself is a typical jungle stream like the Congo or Amazon. The cinema of Tarzan was taken on it.[2] I rode 5 miles down stream & back in a launch, & saw alligators &c in their native habitat. You certainly ought to see Florida some time. ¶ Ar-E'ch-Bei sends regards.

Yr obt Servt
H P

Notes

1. Front: Moonlight Scene at Silver Springs, Fla.

2. Six of the original Tarzan movies, starring Johnny Weissmuller, were filmed on location at Silver Springs between 1932 and 1942, including *Tarzan the Ape Man* (1932) and *Tarzan and His Mate* (1934).

[360] [TLS, JHL]

Sauk City
Wisconsin
15 June 34

Dear H. P.,

I am glad that the unaussprechlichen argument seems to be settled at last—it is just like Wright to stick to his weak point despite all the evidence against him, and what possessed the Sultan to stand against the original word is a mystery to me. W. too should have known better. I wd always take the word of a German before I took that of a student or scholar in matters pertaining to the language simply because there are so many fine shadings and idioms etc that it's impossible for even a most conscientious scholar to strike upon them all. ... Your Silver Springs river looks lovely by moonlight. I have never seen country like that and would doubtless enjoy it, if the heat would not be too much for me. Meanwhile, my Prairie du Chien sojourn was a fruitful one. I found a fitting setting for MISCHIEF IN THE LANE and wrote the first chapter of it. I also did a poem, PRAIRIE DU CHIEN, WISCONSIN: A

HISTORY IN FOUR PANELS, a copy of which, clipped from the Prairie du Chien weekly, I enclose for your perusal, is an attempt to delineate, in four panel-like "drops", the place of the town and its site in the history of the Northwest—Marquette for Exploration, Rolette for Fur-Trading, Streete for the Indian Question, Dousman for Empire Building. Following my return home, I wrote another poem, WE REMEMBER 1832, about Black Hawk's last battle (this much-wronged Indian Chief is a tragic figure for me),[1] and two weirds, LESANDRO'S FAMILIAR (back to the medieval Italy setting!), and THE FACTS ABOUT LUCAS PAYNE. The former I sent to Wright, and the latter to Astounding, though it will surely come back from that market. Incidentally, Wright informs me that one of my best recent shorts, WILD GRAPES, is appearing in the July issue. The July certainly will be an improvement over the June. COLONEL MARKESAN dates back to the summer of 1932; the original version was fairish, but this Wright-suggested-revision is crap of the first magnitude. And, before I forget to mention it, Wright did another of his right-about-faces and took THE METRONOME, English rights to which you will remember I previously sold to the Not at Night series. His last letter of rejection on the tale had said—"unpleasant—poorly motivated, not much story—cannot understand why you think this a good story." Crowning blow from W. T[.]'s supreme arbiter—"I thought FIVE ALONE about as good as a thing as I have seen of yours"—followed by a suggested comparison with some of my weirds. I am now trying to revise my very good little story, THE SNOW-THING (companion piece to THE THING THAT WALKED ON THE WIND) for W. T. Wright has steadfastly refused to take this, and he is more intractable regarding long pieces than he is on shorts. After his experience with some of the lousy things he's been running (Julius Long's), he returns to my rejects. ... The July Outdoors skipped my article, but it will doubtless go into the August, together with the August article.[2] The JULY NIGHT piece was crowded out by advertising and by the ad manager unknown to the editor, who seethed. ... I enjoyed the Peattie article, but it is, as you say, prosaic and sketchy, at best. Oddly enough, I never knew that the yellow-rumped and yellow-headed warbler were the same, and that they were known as the myrtle warbler; I'm not sure he's right on that point. I shall have to look it up in Chapman before I'm convinced. ... Frontier & Midland is indeed a combination of two old standbys. ... The new publishing prospects are, with the rapidity customary in my way of living, taking more tangible shape. I will sign a contract with Loring & Mussey to produce six Solar Pons novels under the nom de plume of Mason Talliaferre. The first, in plan, is tentatively entitled THE RIDDLE OF THE SINISTER COMPANION. It will be issued the first half of 1935, together with THREE WHO DIED and PLACE OF HAWKS. ... Re outdoors pieces—have you ever read Richard Jeffries' FIELD AND HEDGEROW?[3] If not, you have a rare and delightful treat in store for you. They are splendid sketches and essays, every one of which I know you would thoroughly enjoy. I am reading them very slowly, for such excellent prose cannot be gulped, so to speak. ... One of my old girls got married the other day—the only one I regretted. That makes three within a year, and leaves me feeling old. ... The heat, fortunately, has largely gone, leaving us with more or less pleasant summer atmosphere, though that season has not yet officially begun. .. Yes, the Crawford note is amusing. He has evidently set himself assiduously to finding out what you, Smith, and I thought about literature. What roused his ire was my telling him, after prolonged inanities from him, a little fictional story to the effect that a youth who asked two wise men what was the most prized possession in the world, received in answer the truth from one, and disliked him for telling it, and from the other an untruth that he liked to hear, and accordingly thought him the wiser. In effect, if I had said yes to all his stupid comments about literature, I'd have been spared all the argument. ... The linden trees are blossoming, and their aroma hangs like a cloud about them these June nights.

all best, as always,
August

Notes

1. Apparently "Black Hawk War: A Century Gone."

2. "July Night" apparently was withheld until 1935.

3. Richard Jeffries (1848–1887), prolific writer on natural history, village life, and agriculture in late Victorian England.

[361] [ALS]

[mid-June 1934]

Dear A W:—

Young Barlow—who is quite overwhelmed by your generosity in the matter of MSS & the Rankin picture—duly handed me your interesting epistle. Thanks exceedingly for the cuttings—you certainly must have made an impression on Prairie du Chien! The "History in 4 Panels" is extremely vivid & potent, & I shall preserve it amongst my Wisconsiniana.[1] Some of the figures you describe—Rolette, Dousman, &c—are familiar to me through your descriptions of a year ago, when you sent such a generous amount of Prairie du Chien material . . . . . . material still in my files. I'd like to see "We Remember 1832" some time—for I agree with you about the tragic stature of Black Hawk, in the light of all I know about him. My interest in the verses was shared by Barlow.

Glad the new novel has started well, & trust you'll have luck with the new weirds. I'll be looking for "Wild Grapes," & for "The Metronome" when it appears. If Satrap Pharnabazus doesn't eventually take "The Snow Thing" I shall ask for a glimpse of the MS.—for I don't want to miss anything even remotely allied to your splendid "Thing That Walked on the Wind."

Trust *Outdoors* will soon catch up with its schedule. If the Peattie articles are of interest I'll send more later—a correspondent in Washington gives me a batch every now & then.[2] P. may be wrong in the matter of nomenclature or classification you mention—he writes so much that an occasional slip would scarcely be remarkable. I must see the articles of Richard Jeffries some time.

Glad to hear of the book plans, & trust that Mr. Talliaferre may duplicate the successes of Comte Auguste-Guillaime. But I'm still gladder to hear of your foothold with the serious work—"Place of Hawks" & "Three Who Died."

Well—I've certainly had a great time in Florida. Rainy season on now—last week part of the road near Barlow's was washed away, & the St. John's River is phenomenally high. Now to start the slow trek northward, beginning with ancient St. Augustine.

Blessings—

Yr obt Grandsire

H P

[P.S.] Later—I held this open for Barlow to put in an enclosure, but he didn't get one written in time. Have now moved along to St Augustine—which seems just as fascinating as ever.

[P.P. S.] I wrote this in advance, but Barlow got his letter ready after all, so the postscript is for nothing!

Notes

1. AWD sent HPL a clipping of "Prairie Du Chien, Wisconsin: A History in Four Panels."

2. Elizabeth Toldridge (1861–1940), a poet living in Washington, DC, with whom HPL corresponded, steadily supplied him with newspaper clippings on various subjects.

[362] [ANS][1]

[Postmarked St. Augustine, Fla.
21 June 1934]

Well—here I am in old St. Aug at last! The Barlows brought me over in the car, & Bob spent most of the day nosing among books & papers in an antique shop. The venerable town has not changed—& I'm stopping at the same place I stopped in 1931—the Rio Vista on the bay. I have a tower room with running water for $4.00 per week—& am staying a full week. The Barlows have now gone back to De Land, & I'm drifting among the antiquities in my usual way—stopping to write in parks, &c. Am now on the bridge which extends to Anastasia Island. It's refreshing to be back among antiquities after my long sojourn in modern regions. The houses here go back to 1571, at least, & there must be dozens built before 1600. Actually, there are houses here older than any *private* house or *dwelling* in London!

All good wishes—

H P

Notes

1. Front: Oldest Frame House in U.S.A., St. George Street, City Gates in Distance, St. Augustine, Florida.

[363] [TLS, SHSW]

Sauk City
Wisconsin
25 June [1934]

Dear H. P.,

I am addressing this letter to your home address, since no doubt you will be home by the time you are ready to reply to it. I'm glad that Barlow appreciated the various items I sent him, and this week dispatched to him the first drafts of two new highbrow or serious stories, long contemplated and started but only finished last Tuesday—THE TREE and EXPEDITION TO THE NORTH. Apart from them no other writing has been done since last communicating with you. ... Acceptances as well have been minor: Tone took my poem, A PRIMER IN ECONOMIC IDEOLOGY FOR LITTLE MEN, and The Vagabond took four, SNOW, and three for reprinting, SUMMER AFTERNOON: SUNLIGHT ON OLD HOUSES, NIGHT ON THE MEADOW, and HAWKS AGAINST APRIL. ... Added to the list of forthcoming titles are A RIDE HOME in the August Story, and THE NO-SAYERS in the BROOKLYN EAGLE SUNDAY REVIEW of either June 17 or 24—if you have connections in Brooklyn, you could ascertain this, for they have sent me no copy and I am not in position to get one until I know just when the story appeared. ... Glad you liked the Prairie du Chien poem. I have had no report on it as yet, but it will probably be placed. Wright of course promptly rejected LESANDRO'S FAMILIAR and the revised SNOW-THING, as I expected him to. I'm beginning to think that he's got a prejudice against accepting anything the first time from me, since he doesn't believe that good work can be done in first draft. ... If W. doesn't eventually take THE SNOW-THING, you'll see it in ms. form. ... We have been having equinoctial storms recently, with the result that many wires are down and limbs have been torn from trees. Last night we had an especially severe wind, which tore up soil from the earth and blew it like vast clouds over and through the village. ... Something quite western, and not at all unusual. ... Meanwhile, I copy off WE REMEMBER 1832 for your perusal:

(Because he was reluctant to move from the land he had been tricked into selling, Black Hawk, with his Sac Indians, engaged in the Black Hawk war of 1832, troops having been sent against him after an incident—the murder of a pioneer family by a party of wandering Winnebagos. The site of his last major battle is at Wisconsin Heights, some miles south of Sauk City, Wisconsin; significantly, it is marked by a small marble monument.)

They were held that night by fear
Which had come upon them with the turning year.
The last soft snow mantled the trees
While they sat in their lodges remembering how the bees
Sand in the wild cherry blossoms. That night fear
Sped among them with the fleetness of a deer
In a deep forest.

"Captain March: It has come to the ear
Of this writer within the hour that on a clear
Night some time ago, a party of Indians was seen
Travelling in the general direction of the farm of one Josiah Green
On the Sac Prairie. Being followed belatedly, it was found
That the entire Green family had been killed, two on the ground
Immediately before the house, three within. You will take
Your Company and proceed at once to the break
In the hills where Black Hawk is encamped with his band.
You will proceed against them and drive them from the land
Across the Mississippi. Taylor."

The first runner broke through long before day,
And thus Black Hawk knew that soldiers were on the way.
Rousing his braves then, and the women, he told these latter to be gone
Into the south following the river to the Prairie of the Dog, to take care after dawn
Not to be seen. The braves painted in the night. This because an informant failed to specify ...
What matter it that Black Hawk himself knew that Winnebagos, specifically, one Fox Eye,
One Red Eagle, one Yellow Feather, one Three Hat, had slain in one night

A paleface family known as Green, and had then taken flight
Toward the Sac village, thus deceiving those who saw?
They fought in that darkness for a forgotten law
And lost. Black Hawk said, "Where once was a great fire and a gale,
There is nothing of us now but faint, far smoke on a pale Wind."

They died with years,
Not even fears
Left them. A hundred years later several ladies of the D. A. R., whose people had grown fat on the land,
Erected a marker in that place for Black Hawk and his band.

It could be much better, you will admit, but then it has some value as it stands.

All best wishes, as always.

August

[364] [ALS]

Home again, & on the old
River-Bank. July 16[, 1934]

Dear A W:—

I found yours of 25th ult.—together with *28* other letters—awaiting me when I reached home last Tuesday. And what Alpine accumulations of packages & printed matter . . . . & what a monolith of piled-up newspapers . . . . ! I am only about a quarter straightened out yet, & don't know when I shall ever get readjusted. Had a great week in St. Augustine—seeing all the old sights & inspecting many houses which were not open as museums on my previous visit. Also saw the recumbent skeletons in the Indian graveyard unearthed last spring. Moved north on the 28th—spending 2 days in Charleston, 1 in Richmond, 1 in Fredericksburg, 2 in Washington, & 1 in Philadelphia. In Washington I inspected the interior of the capitol & ascended the Washington monument for the first time. In Philadelphia—besides visiting ancient Germantown & the Wissahickon—I explored the brick cottage tenanted by Poe from 1842 to 1844, & opened a few months ago as a museum & shrine. When I hit N.Y. I found the Longs about to leave for Asbury Park & Ocean Grove over the week-end, & at their cordial invitation went along with them. No cash to stop in N Y, so came along home July 10 without looking up any of the rest of the gang save Loveman. It was good to see the rolling hills, giant elms, stone walls, & white steeples of ancient New England again—though northern scenery seems almost strange after my saturation with palms, live-oaks, Spanish moss, & all that goes with them. As usual, I spend all my afternoons in the open country—though there is an added attraction at home in the form of a coal-black kitten (born last month & just beginning to be playful) at the boarding-house across the back garden.

Glad to hear all the literary news. I fear that neither of my remaining Brooklyn correspondents—Leeds & Loveman—read the *Eagle,* but I could ask them to look at the files if they ever happen to be near the office. Confound Wright for his rejections! I must see "The Snow Thing" somehow—either in MS. or in print.

Your recent stories sound highly formidable! I guess I mentioned the rainy season—with overflowing streams & washed-out roads—which I struck in De Land. For the past week I've been shivering with the cold, since the chill of the northern evening finds me unprepared. Days, however, are quite tolerable. In Washington & Phila. & N.Y. I enjoyed temperatures of 96° or 97°.

Abundant thanks for the text of the Black Hawk poem—which has all the charm & soil-flavour of your other historical & reminiscent verses. You surely ought to have a volume of these things sooner or later.

Read the July W T, & believe it's one of the most uniformly mediocre issues so far—with certain exceptions. Your vine tale has its points, as has Klarkash-Ton's "Disinterment of Venus." I disliked my collaborated thing even more in print than I did in MS.—indeed, I'm not counting it among my tales at all.

Well—the twilight deepens, & it's getting too damn cold to sit out here.

Regards & blessings—

Yr obt. grandsire

H P

[365] [TLS, SHSW]

Sauk City
Wisconsin
19 July [1934]

Dear H. P.,

So your wandering is over for 1934. You seem to have enjoyed yourself, and I rather envy you the trip, though I should have been seized by qualms at being away from the typewriter for so long a time without doing anything new. And at that I haven't done much new. I did managed [*sic*] to do the entire play, THE FIVE WHO WAITED, and we mimeographed 25 copies of it in the last three days, but that, after all, is a comparatively small task, save for the mimeographing. I revised my October Outdoors article—SMOKE IN THE SKY, and another nature article and a poem, and my November piece, DUSK IN NOVEMBER, which is one of my best thus far, I think. I am enclosing herewith a copy of it, together with various other items which may interest you.—I mean to say I am enclosing a copy of my August article, AUGUST FROM A HILL, for your files—I'm still a little upset from the nervous strain of working too hard yesterday, thrashing out a very delicate love affair, and being kept up most of the night by a very low electrical storm. ... Among the other enclosures are the jacket for Benson's new book of ghost stories, containing some swell stuff, eight pieces of 13—no five, which have been in W. T. Then there is a copy of my instructions to the cast of the play, and a copy of my pamphlet assailing the village board for not repairing a sidewalk, and one of the numerous notices it got in the metropolitan press, much to the chagrin of the local government, which was not aware that I was of any importance. You need not, of course, return any of these items. Under separate cover, I am sending you a copy of Gawsworth's STRANGE ASSEMBLY, which has two pieces by Shiel and two by Machen, but nothing else of any great value.[1] If it is of any use to you, shoot me the postage.

You shall see THE SNOW-THING one of these days—as soon as I get around to sending it, and when you are settle again in the mass of work which doubtless confronts you at this time. Wright has been oddly long about reporting on my two new shorts—THE FACTS ABOUT LUCAS PAYNE and MUGGRIDGE'S AUNT, the latter of which is quite good. ... I am now getting ready to do the first Solar Pons book, THE RIDDLE OF THE SINISTER COMPANION. ... Meanwhile, the August STORY is out with my A RIDE HOME in it, and, judging by the fact that I proofed the story only two weeks ago, either the September or October SCRIBNER'S will have CROWS FLY HIGH in it. Watch for it. ... I recently had a letter from Doubleday-Doran's Crime Club suggesting that I might have something for them. It was from the same man who originally wrote me from Holt's in 32. ... There have been some new acceptances, mostly poems by the little magazines which do not pay.

All best, as always,

August

Notes

1. M. P. Shiel, "The Flying Cat" and "A Night in Venice"; Arthur Machen, "The Gift of Tongues" and "The Rose Garden."

[366] [ANS]

[Postmarked Buttonwood, R.I.,
4 August 1934]

Greetings from a convocation of daemons in an ancient setting! Will be writing you shortly—recd. the anthology, for which abundant thanks. My guest—an arch-genealogist—had just dug up a line of ancestry common to both himself & myself, extending back to 1380. No counts, but a companion & adviser to Warwick, the King-Maker.[1] Meanwhile, under our influence, local supplies of ice cream & spaghetti wane low. And scenery & antiquities get their full quota of appreciation. We're now by the shore at old Buttonwood.

A grandsire's blessing—H P

May the dark unknown append a humble word of simple greeting?
James F. Morton

Notes

1. Richard Neville, Earl of Warwick (1428–1471) was referred to as "The Kingmaker" because of his machinations in support of King Henry VI (r. 1422–61, 1470–71) and King Edward IV (r. 1461–83).

[367] [ALS]

Sunset in Roger Williams
Park: August 5, 1934

Dear A W:—

What a hectic round! Thanks for all the enclosures. That play certainly is a titanic enterprise! The August nature article is delectable—I didn't know before that you were a snake-charmer! You ought to go down to Florida & try your arts on some of the numerous ophidian population there! Benson's new book looks interesting—although some of his W.T. items were rather flat.[1] He is uneven. I believe there's one other weird collection of his which I haven't yet read. Your campaign for Better Sidewalks is surely commendable—good luck to you! The broadside is really quite a masterpiece in its way, & I don't wonder that the Madison paper commented on it.[2] In the years to come you'll probably develop into a valuable civic asset of Sac Prairie . . . . leader in all reforms & good works!

Abundant thanks for "Strange Assembly"—correct postage for which I trust I am forwarding. I shall examine & digest it with appreciation the next time I get a breathing-spell. I look forward to "The Snow-Thing", & hope Satrap Pharnabazus will act favourably on "Lucas Payne" & "Mug[g]ridge's Aunt". By the way—young Morse tells me that a new magazine, *Terror Tales,* is being established by the publishers of *Dime Mystery.* Heard anything about it?

What you say of "Dusk in November" tantalises me greatly, since I failed to find the copy you mentioned having enclosed. Hope I shall see it after all before long.

Congratulations on the high-grade acceptances! I shall try to get hold of the designated issues of *Story* & *Scribners*. Glad that the Solar Pons business is getting under way, & that Doubleday-Doran are waking up to the potentialities of your material.

Blessings & good wishes

—H P

P.S. Little Bloch has placed his first MS. with W.T.,[3] & feels that he owes much of his success to your salutary advice! Will you lend your "Innsmouth" MS. to him if I'll pay the postage? He wants to see the tale again, & my copy is wandering on a vague circuit.

[P.P.S.] Thanks for the bluff view. ¶ Did I shew you a photograph of Barlow's Cthulhu bas-relief?

[P.P.P.S.] Just recd. new F F & Marvel Tales.

Notes

1. Seven stories by E. F. Benson appeared in *WT* between July 1929 and December 1933. All but two were reprinted in *More Spook Stories.*

2. *About Sidewalks and Other Things.*

3. "The Secret in the Tomb," *WT* (May 1935). Though accepted first, it was not not Bloch's first appearance in *WT;* "The Feast in the Abbey" appeared in January 1935.

[368] [TLS, SHSW]

Sauk City
Wisconsin
6 August [1934]

Dear H. P.,

Do I gather rightly when I gather that you are taking a second vacation? It looks so. ... The above is my summer cut this year—a copy of Clair Leighton's Haymakers.[1] As you can see, the costumes are English rather than American. ... Glad you rec'd the book okeh, and I hope you enjoy it. I recently read a good new weird book, OUT WENT THE TAPER, by R. C. Ashby. I can recommend it, and while you need not buy it, you will not regret paying a rental on it from a circulating library. Another good new terror story is PLAN XVI by Douglas Browne. Best volume of new poetry this season is David McCord's THE CROWS. Loring & Mussey have begun advertising THE MAN ON ALL FOURS on the jackets of their other books. When my mother saw, "This astonishing young author etc", she snorted and said, "They don't know him!" . . . Since last writing you, my acceptances have been very minor. Wright surprised me by taking MUGGRIDGE'S AUNT, Mid-West Story took DOWN AT THE MILL and IN THE CEMETERY, two poems, The Lion & Unicorn my story, FROST IN OCTOBER, and this morning, Manuscript, Whippoorwill in the Hollow and Do They Remember Where They Lie, a poem which I quote on the next page for your reaction. ... I won the great sidewalk battle by playing my ace in the hole and writing the railroad company, which sent a representative out to agree with me, ignore the board, and repair the sidewalk. My publicity agent (yrs truly) saw that the story was prominently displayed in the Madison papers, much to the chagrin and anger of the board members. ... For the last ten days I have done nothing but write a series of poems, A SHEAF FOR MARIS, which are purely inspirational, despite the fact that I hold no brief for inspiration. Among them is DO THEY REMEMBER WHERE THEY LIE, one of the best. Here it is:

Do you remember now where they lie
In the still dust, the unnumbered thousands who have gone down
In dreams before me, do they remember how the sky
Is blue in July, do they mark in eternity the town
Where once they walked, do they remember all the little things—
How the daisies blow in August, and how in May
The lilacs drown the town in fragrance, and how the small owl brings
The summer night to loveliness? And do they
Too remember lips and eyes and hair as I remember you?
Do they remember how the slow caress, the loneliness, the lingering touch of
    hands
Assault the embattled tower of the soul and lock the blue
Depths of any close-bound heart in tight-wound bands?
Do they remember how the wind in hair, how the moonlight dark in eyes,
    how the still night
Tear with strong fingers into the far reaches of the hear,
How the long look, the slow return, the voiceless desire haunt the endless
    hours before the light
Breaks again? And do they too lock these memories apart?
Or do these thousands who have long drawn no breath
Remember only how in that last hour
All yesterdays and tomorrows went down to death?
The reaches of my heart are arid waste where long no flower

Has grown, where the striding shadows stretch their fingers
Like hills reaching from the afterglow across the prairie,
A waste where only light from cloud-hung moons lingers
In the half-dark, where but the sad screech owl will tarry
With his lonely call.
I know too well, too certainly,
Love is not all—
And yet it is enough for me.

all best, as always,
August

Notes

1. Actually, the woodcut by American artist Clare Leighton (1901–1989) is titled "Haymaking (June)" (1933).

[369] [ALS]

[after 6 August 1934]

Dear A W:—

Well—so you're varying your stationery even for the same season! The new design is extremely harmonious, though I can't quite understand just what is going on. The large shaft—or whatever it is—on the left remains a mystery to me, since it has no counterpart so far as I know in New England haymaking. I've seen mowing & hay-pitching of the old-fashioned sort—performed just as it has always been for 300 years hereabouts. In fact, I've participated in the process—whether as a help or a hindrance, only the farmer involved can say.

Haven't yet had a second to read anything, but know I shall enjoy "Strange Assembly". I'll keep "Out Went the Taper" in mind. Also "Plan XVI". Have the Aug. W.T. & the 1st issue of *Terror Tales,* but have had no time to read either. Hellish lot of revision on hand. Glad "The Man on All Fours" is beginning to get publicity. Sooner or later even your mother will be convinced that you're a great man! Glad to hear of the acceptances, even though minor. For most of the gang, they'd be major enough! Speaking of markets—Price says his agent Leninger is looking for weird stuff for some new magazine. A word to the wise . . . . . I presume you know L's address. Congrats on winning the sidewalk war—you're surely becoming a power in the community! Glad the Madison papers got all the dope.

Your new poem is great stuff. To read it, one would fancy that the symbolic, associative language of poetry was your one natural medium—& yet look at your prose! At that, though, there's a great deal of poetry in your prose.

You are a poet at bottom, as I have maintained ever since reading "Evening in Spring." Sooner or later I hope you'll have a volume of verse out.

The card from Morton & me marks a three-day visit from the Sage of Paterson (he is curator of the museum there), during which we did up many of the points of interest around Providence. On the final day we went to ancient Newport, where we saw the U.S. fleet in the harbour, explored the venerable streets, & walked along the famous ocean cliffs. Morton is now in Maine, but is going to Boston for some genealogical research. Incidentally, I shall probably be visiting near Boston a few days beginning with the 23d—having been invited by an old-time amateur journalist, Edward H. Cole. W. Paul Cook will also be on hand—he is emerging from Vermont to seek his fortune in the great city once more—perhaps Boston, perhaps New York. I'll also look up Brobst—who will, incidentally, be back in Providence in October.

I still do most of my writing in the woods & fields, though the little black kitten next door often detains me at home when I would otherwise be abroad. In 44 years of existence I've never seen a more thoroughly fascinating little devil—a dynamo of concentrated playfulness, with great yellow eyes that hold the mystery of Meroë & Ophir!

Benedictions—

Yr obt Grandsire

H P

P.S. Glad you've seen some good cinemas. I saw "Death Takes a Holiday"[1] with Belknap in N.Y., & thought the appearances of the *Shadow* in the early part were splendidly handled . . . . . an indication of what the cinema *could* do in the macabre field if it were pried loose from popular hokum. ¶ I envy you that canning factory as a financial recuperator. Can't find anything of the sort here. ¶ Your record of literary production is certainly staggering—no question about your "arriving"!

¶ Later—Have read "Strange Assembly." Some really excellent material from a general literary point of view, & one or two touches approaching the weird. The most haunting thing, perhaps, is "The Harrying of the Dead,"[2] The prize for absolute excellence would probably go to one of the realistic sketches.

¶ Have also read 3 weird books by William Hope Hodgson—"The Boats of the Glen Carrig", "The House on the Borderland," & "The Ghost Pirates"—lent me by Koenig. Do you know these? In some respects they have a peculiar & magnificent power—an ability to suggest realms & dimensions just out of reach, & sieges by hellish legions of the nameless from unsuspected, fathomless abysses of night. "The House on the Borderland" has a breath-taking cosmic reach. No comparison is possible between these fine works & Hodgson's later feeble attempt—"Carnacki the Ghost Finder"—which I read in Florida. I have prepared a note on Hodgson to be slipped into my Sup. Horror article as reprinted in the *Fantasy Fan.*[3]

[P.]P.S. A possibility arises that I may be able to follow my Boston trip with one to the ancient island of Nantucket—which I have never seen. It is said that this island preserves the Early-American atmosphere—architecturally & socially—more perfectly than any other surviving spot.

Notes

1. *Death Takes a Holiday* (Paramount, 1934), directed by Mitchell Leisen; starring Fredric March and Evelyn Venable. Based on the play *La Morte in vacanza* by Albert Casella (adapted into English by Walter Ferris, 1929).

2. By Frederick Carter.

3. The insert was to go in Chapter IX, but *FF* ceased publication before that chapter could be published. HPL's essay "The Weird Work of William Hope Hodgson" appeared in *Phantagraph* 5, No. 5 (February 1937): 5–7.

[370] [TLS, SHSW]

Sauk City
Wisconsin
8 August [1934]

Dear H. P.,

All thanks for he stamps. ... No, thanks—you can keep your Florida snakes; I am no snake-charmer, but accidentally fit into that role. I am sure the snake was far from charmed; if he got over his alarm, he was more probably thoroughly irritated, which I can well understand, knowing myself. ... I was down at Frank Lloyd Wright's again last Sunday, and saw Rene Clair's brilliantly satirical picture on success, "A Nous la Liberte".[1] Truly excellent work which clearly illustrates the importance of the director in a production. ... Also recently saw "Death Takes a Holiday", which was a disappointment after the play, which you may remember I saw in Minneapolis. ... Yes, Benson is indeed very uneven. There are, however, as I believe I said, several very good tales in this volume. ... As for Terror Tales—this is just like Dime Mystery, all detective-terror-horror stuff, nothing more. It is no market for us, unfortunately. ... Jacobi has a story in its second issue, Satan's Roadhouse, originally sold to Dime Mystery; they are not making a distinction, you see. ... Yes, you will see a print copy of DUSK IN NOVEMBER. It is one of my best outdoors pieces, I think. ... Bob asked me about INNSMOUTH, and I said I'd send it. He doesn't seem to want it just now, but "later". Which is ko with me. ... The canning factory starts work today, a season unprecedentedly early, but which promises to stretch out for six weeks or perhaps more. That is depressing, though doubtless it will help financially. ... I have just estimated that since July 21 I have done 27 poems, all of quite high calibre, 25 of which were of A SHEAF FOR MARIS, most of them sonnets. Of this sheaf, the fourth, DO THEY REMEMBER WHERE THEY LIE, probably the best, was taken by Manuscript just the other day. ... I find that I have done 87 titles thus far this year, as compared to the 75 I had set as a goal for 1934. This is quite remarkable, for it indicates that I will have done almost 200 new titles before the year is out, of which four or five will be complete novels. My financial status has improved slightly, too, which is a consolation, since it is clear that I am steadily advancing on all fronts.

All best wishes, as always,

August

Notes

1. René Clair, *À nous la liberté* (1931), a satirical comedy about two ex-convicts. One works his way up from salesman to factory owner, overseeing a highly mechanised operation in which the workers are little more than automatons. The work inspired Charlie Chaplin's *Modern Times.*

[371] [ALS]

Ancient Nantucket—
Septr 1, 1934

Dear A W:—

By this time you will have received the folder displaying the scene of my present antiquarian sojourn. I had an excellent time around Boston—visiting Salem, Marblehead, &c.—marred only by a sort of nervous collapse on Cook's part, whereby he had to return prematurely to Vermont. My host brought me home Sunday, but I merely stayed over night & lit out the next morning for New Bedford & the Nantucket boat.

And what a place is Nantucket! Absolutely the most *completely* preserved bit of the elder world in North America today. And to think I never saw it before—a place only 90 miles from my own doorstop! A perfect Yankee whaling port of a century or more ago—whole networks of cobblestoned streets with nothing but colonial houses on either side—narrow, garden-bordered lanes—ancient belfries—picturesque waterfront—*everything* that the antiquarian could desire! The only drawbacks are (a) the cold, & (b) the slight suggestion of artificiality & self-consciousness in the archaic survivals—summer-resort & art-colony stuff. I'm seeing about the whole thing in a week's sojourn. Have a 3d floor room with a splendid view of town, harbour, & sea. In the five days so far elapsed I have explored old houses, the 1746 windmill, the Hist. Soc. Museum, the venerable churches, the whaling museum, the Maria Mitchell Observatory (where I had a fine, sharp view of Saturn through the 5″ refractor), &. &c. Am traversing every inch of the centuried streets on foot, & am tempted to succumb to the local custom &

hire a bicycle for more rapid & expansive jaunts. Haven't been on a wheel in 20 years—it would bring back my youth! At the start I took a sightseeing coach trip over the entire island—beholding such things as ancient Siasconset . . . a former fishing village on the S E shore, now restored as a summer colony. The coach paused to permit of a quarter-hour stroll through the picturesque lanes of the place. The houses are tiny fisherman's huts embowered in flowering gardens—now kept in the best of shape & inhabited by appreciative tenants.[1]

Well—I shall be home on the evening of the 3d . . . . & on the next day my aunt will set out for a fortnight in Ogunquit, Maine! I can't imagine anybody wanting to go *north* at *this* time of year (I wish I were headed for Florida!), but presume she knows what she wants!

I shall be interested to see your new stationery designs—you'll probably end up by having a fresh set of 365 (or 366 for leap years) every year! The hawk motif will surely be appropriate. Thanks for the programme & poster of "Five Who Waited". You surely are getting to be a renowned dramatist & theatrical producer! Hope it was a thorough success! Glad also to read the captivating September nature article—an especially fine specimen. The reviews, too, are interesting—glad you have the chance to contribute them.

Your new verses are true poetry indeed—though I doubt whether the irregular forms can be reconciled with the conception of the sonnet. Also—*past* & *passed* do not make a *rhyme,* being *identical.* The one & only thing your poetry needs is a little technical carefulness, so that the reader will not be held up by irregularities & distracted from the subject-matter. It would be easy to add this perfection, & it wouldn't interfere in the least with your conceptions. But anyhow, the stuff is splendid. The comment by the magazine reader on the relative importance of prose & poetry is surely amusing!

Glad to hear of the new appearances in print—especially "Farway House". And I certainly hope the *American Magazine* serial proposition turns out well. Financial security is a tremendously important thing if one is to write unhampered—I wish to hades I had it!

H. Warner Munn's father has just been killed by a hit-&-run motorist. A beastly shame—there's far more of this since the repeal of prohibition. Whiskey & motor cars are a dangerous combination!

All good wishes—

Yr obt Grandsire

H P

Notes

1. See HPL's essay, "The Unknown City in the Ocean."

[372] [ALS]

Septr 8, 1934

Dear A W:—

Glad to hear all the news, & shall look forward to "Dusk in November". Congratulations on the cheque—which certainly tides you along admirably. Just as well to drop the factory work if it interferes with more important activities—indeed, I fancy a less strenuous programme in every way wouldn't be at all bad for you. It doesn't pay to overdo—that's the sort of thing that wears one out & ages one prematurely. And I surely hope that you will soon feel financially secure. Glad you're having Utpatel illustrate "Place of Hawks".[1] He has a marvellously vivid & potent style, & ought to be much better known than he is. Which reminds me that Barlow can now supply photographs of some of the Howard Wandrei drawings—$1.25 for 8 × 10; $2.00 for 11 × 14. I may have a visit from both Wandreis this month—I understand that Donald is driving east for a visiting session, & that he will subsequently bear Howard back to St. Paul. As to hit-&-run motorists—I'm almost inclined to agree with you regarding the appropriateness of capital punishment! Surely something drastic ought to be done about a form of negligence & cowardly evasion which amounts to nothing less than crime.

I'll surely appreciate a copy of the published "Farway House". Incidentally—last night, as per Koenig's orders, I mailed you those Hodgson books I spoke of—plus Barry Pain's "Stories After Dark", which I discovered in the carton after all the weeks of its presence here. In this latter volume the salient item is "The Undying Thing"—ugh! I really half-believe I ought to mention this in my article.[2] These books are Koenig's property, but in his generosity he is offering to lend them to anybody in the gang who cares to read them. Accordingly I'd suggest that you send them on—when fully through with them—to the next logical candidate for perusal . . . DUANE W. RIMEL, BOX 100, ASOTIN, WASHINGTON. Dwyer is next on the list after him.

Your two new poems—"Shy Bird" & "Flesh is Not All"—seem to me quite as poignant & authentic as the preceding ones. Some day you'll have an impressive volume of verse to your credit! Many thanks for including the transcripts.

I surely hope you can see Nantucket some time. It took quite a wrench to pry me loose last Monday, & I still find it almost impossible to believe that such a haven of the yesterdays lies only 90 miles away. Toward the end of my sojourn I covered some of the outlying sections on a hired bicycle—the first time in 20 years that I had been on a wheel. The process of riding seemed perfectly easy & familiar despite the lapse of time—& it brought back my long-departed youth with almost uncanny vividness. I felt that I ought to hurry home in time for the opening of Hope St. High School!

Just recd. the new F F. Do you know aught of this Charles Williams that Koenig writes about?[3]

Belknap reports great successes in the pulp field. Under the tutelage of Otis Adelbert Kline he is getting to be a highly enterprising young business man—but the artist of yesteryear seems lost in the shuffle!

Latest argumentative gem from Crawford: People have changed a lot in the last 30 years. They are more superficial. So oughtn't fiction to be more superficial also? !!!!!

Well—behave, & don't work too hard.

Pax vobiscum

—H P

Notes

1. The novel ultimately was illustrated with woodcuts by George Barford. See letters 385 and 386.

2. HPL listed Pain's "The Undying Thing" from *Stories in the Dark* (1901) in his "Books to mention in new edition of weird article" but did not in fact discuss it in any revised edition of SHL.

3. H. Koenig, "The Intellectual Shocker," *FF* 2, No. 1 (September 1934): 10, 15. Koenig wrote of the work of the British fantaisiste (1886–1945) Charles Williams: *War in Heaven* (1930), *Many Dimensions* (1931), *Greater Trumps* (1932), *Place of Lions* (1932), and *Shadows of Ecstasy* (1933). It is unknown which volumes Koenig lent to HPL.

[373] [ALS]

Octr. 3, 1934

Dear A W:—

No hurry about the Hodgson books—simply shoot 'em on to Rimel when you're through with them. I wouldn't have bothered you with them if Koenig had said you wished to see them. But you'll find them amply worthy of perusal. Meanwhile C A S informs me that—also at Koenig's request—he is now forwarding to you two more Hodgsoniana . . . . "Carnacki, the Ghost Finder", & "The Night Land" . . . . . which you are in turn to forward to me. Thanks in advance for the latter procedure! I read Carnacki in De Land & didn't think much of it, but since I've read the others I believe I'd like to take a look at it again to see if by any chance I did it injustice. Incidentally, Koenig has sent me two of the Charles Williams volumes which he reviews so interestingly in the Septr F F. Haven't had a chance to read them yet, & of course they may prove vastly disappointing. One never can go by another's taste. You certainly are overloaded with books for review—though all-inclusive reading is nothing new to you. Hope you'll like "The Web".[1]

Your new stationery design—trees on the slope against the sky—is magnificent—one of the best of all the series. If Utpatel prepares these, he is certainly developing a splendid technique! I am eager to see his illustrations for

"Farway House". You are surely fortunate in having so able & sympathetic an artist at hand to embellish your text.

Many thanks for "Smoke in the Sky"—an unusually captivating member of the series. You certainly do get close to the little denizens of the woodland wilds! The reviews are very graceful, & I can't detect where they have been subject to abridgment.

That Mrs. Jones has nerve to send you MSS. to correct! I told her you might know of some western regional papers prepared to accept sketches of pioneer life—such as she writes—but had no idea she would dump a lot of junk on you! Apologies & commiserations!

Congratulations on all the current triumphs—including the prospective appearance of your second book. Glad to hear of the new musical device—for I know that with you music runs a close second to literature.

All good wishes—

Yr most obt servt

H P

Notes

1. Probably Hugh Brooke's *The Web,* a novel of psychological terror.

[374] [ALS]

Octr. 27, 1934

Dear A W:—

No—the trouble I had was nothing more serious than an attack of indigestion (with which, I recall, you have yourself had a recent skirmish); but it has left me with a considerable lack of energy. I am having, because of the strain, to cut down somewhat on various activities.

Your November article is especially delightful—sunset & dusk in the open being one of my favourite spectacles. Cold weather is curtailing my outings now, though I have taken a number of rural walks through autumnal scenery. The reviews, also, are interesting. I note that you cover a volume by Elliott Merrick[1]—who is quite a close friend of one of my Vermont correspondents.

Thanks also for the Jacobi tales. He surely is a marvel of facility & versatility, & it is a pity his talent is squandered in pulp stuff. Each of these is an excellent example of its kind—the one from *Terror Tales* surely plasters on the horror thickly![2]

Glad to hear of current progress, & hope your experiments in a new technique may prove rewarding. I trust the British market may prove an increasingly available field.

I don't wonder that book-reading opportunities are few! Don't judge Hodgson from "Carnacki"—"The House on the Borderland" is the important volume. I've just managed to get through the Charles Williams books & have sent them on to Klarkash-Ton. Better let him know whether you want to see them or not. Essentially, they are not horror literature at all, but philosophic allegory in fictional form. Direct reproduction of the texture of life & the substance of moods is not the author's object. He is trying to illustrate human nature through symbols & turns of idea which possess significance for those taking a traditional or orthodox view of man's cosmic bearings. There is no true attempt to express the indefinable feelings experienced by man in confronting the unknown. The characters react to symbolic & patterned marvels according to certain traditional philosophic concepts—not in the natural, irregular fashion of actual life. To get a full-sized kick from this stuff one must take seriously the orthodox view of cosmic organisation—which is rather impossible today. Nevertheless one can enjoy those books very much in an objective way—they are full of scholarship & cleverness. You might like them immensely—as Koenig sees to have done. You'll have to decide yourself whether to have C A S forward them.

Not much news around. The days advance, & still no sign of Wandrei. Possibly he isn't coming. Dwyer has just succeeded in getting into a CCC camp. Quite a feat at 38! Moreover, he has been made editor of the camp newspaper. His present address is CCC Camp 25, Peekskill, N.Y. I'm hesitating whether or not to undertake a revision job for old de Castro—a sort of philosophic thing for which he can't pay in advance, but which has sponsoring that might ensure successful publication. One thing is certain—I can't take anything demanding haste.

All good wishes—

Yr obt Servt

H P

[P.S.] Had a great weekend with Edward H. Cole (my host of last August) Oct 19–21. He took me in his car up to West Townsend—in N. Central Mass.—where we dined at a 1774 tavern & saw the finest landscape vistas & autumn foliage that I ever beheld in my life. I had never been there before. The Wallis Brook State Forest in the region has a marvellous wooded gorge with rock waterfalls, &c. Later Cole & his wife brought me home, & my aunt & I guided them to the exquisite Narragansett Country which Price & I explored last year. Its autumnal beauty is virtually past description! We saw the old snuff mill on the Narrow River where Gilbert Stuart was born in 1755.

[P.P.S.] Barlow is taking an art course at the Corcoran Gallery in Washington.[3]

Notes

1. *From This Hill Look Down.*

2. Carl Jacobi, "Satan's Roadhouse," *Terror Tales* (October 1934). The other tales referred to are unknown.

3. Barlow studied at the Corcoran Gallery under Thomas Hart Benton, the muralist.

[375] [ALS]

Nov. 6[, 1934]

Dear A W:—

Glad the poetic muse is still on the job, & that the new book is taking its final form. It must be quite a novelty to have only one murder in a novel—& even that not a real one! Sorry the reviews are crowding out the nature article in *Outdoors*—but after all, the winter months are those which can best be skipped. Hope your cheque for "Hawk on the Blue" will arrive soon. I had a cheque from Curtis Brown the other day—$32.50, covering the last British sale of "Erich Zann". That's the *fifth* time I've been paid for this one story—wish they were all as fruitful! I'm not surprised that, with all your multifarious activities, you need a filing cabinet. I should think you'd need a whole battery of office paraphernalia, with a trained force to man it!

Glad your outings continued well through October. The exploring season is about over now—with leaves falling & temperatures approaching the freezing point. Indoor events predominate now—which reminds me that the John Hay Library next door has just been having a highly interesting exhibit of material pertaining to Poe's contemporary—the curious & fantastic Thomas Holley Chivers of Georgia.[1] And so Wandrei slipped home without calling on anybody. The reprehensible young imp!

No—I doubt whether you'd better tackle the Williams books in view of your congested programme. Too bad the Atherton volume turned out to be such a disappointment.[2] Young Baldwin of Asotin, Wash. is going to make me a present of "Creep, Shadow"—clipped from the *Argosy* & cleverly bound in leatherette by himself. I anticipate considerable pleasure in reading it, though of course aware of Merritt's limitations. Curious how tastes differ—Klarkash-Ton thought "The Night Land" much better than "Carnacki" . . . . which latter, indeed, is surely only a very mediocre echo of "John Silence". But don't judge Hodgson except by "House on the borderland" & "Glen Carrig."

Just got the new F F dedicated to C A S, & am glad to see the powerful "Primal City" in print.[3] I am quite excited over the announcement of what seems to be the first *high-grade* weird magazine ever issued—*Tales of the Uncanny*,[4] published in England & containing the work of Blackwood, Wells, Wakefield, &c. However—I suppose a good deal of this must be reprinted stuff.

And now let me thank you most profusely for "The Man On All Fours", which arrived safely with the companion items. I read it at one sitting on the night of its receipt, & found it tremendously clever & fascinating. I thought I had become quite insensitive to the appeal of the detective tale, but this one awaked long-dormant chords of response! You have certainly handled the various complex elements with the utmost skill—maintaining a well-distributed interest & keeping up a constant air of suspense & dread of impending evils . . . . even though I felt quite sure of the solution on & after page 32. It is curious how one can't help predicting a detective tale after having read several. In this case the emphasis on family insanity made one look for a mad killer—& here (p. 32) was a mention of a madman *lost in a fire* (why this *added circumstance* if not for special plot use? . . . . . ostensibly dead fire victims have popped up later in many stories!) just about the time his mother (who has obviously been shielding some one) began to be unusually queer. After that the confirmatory indications came thick & fast. "Vinnie, *he's* killed Ray" (p. 52) . . . . . crawling *man* (p. 81, confirming p. 71. Insanity of John S. unlikely) . . . . "Oh, God! What have I done?" (p. 87—idea of *responsibility*) . . . . . . music (piano) to cover suspicious sounds of someone about . . . . old lady's heavy breakfasts (p. 149) . . . . "J . . . ie, J . . . ie" (p. 151. *John* S. never seems to be called *Johnnie,* & the name is indistinctly uttered) . . . . suspicious *dust* indicates secret use of attic room (p. 143) . . . . . creeper confirmed (p. 192) . . . . footsteps *not on servants' stairs* indicate secret stairs (p. 194—all this indicating unknown hidden crawler) . . . . "even though the corpses . . . destroyed" (p. 205. element of doubt of Jimmy's death) . . . . . 'long hair, but a man' (p. 209–10. fact that crawler is not of household more *certain*—Jimmy indicated by elimination) . . . . . after p. 216 confirmatory allusions grow numerous . . . . & back on p. 172, 'odd, so far from 1st floor—moved up *four years ago*' . . . . . &c. &c. So, all told, my suspicion around p. 32 grew steadily as I read on, until I began to take Jimmy for granted. It is amusing to note that this predictability depends wholly on the technique of the standard detective novel. The same events in real life would afford much less clue, for fiction excludes many alternatives which life would allow. I recall that, toward the end of my detective-reading period, the number of predictable climaxes grew steadily greater. Incidentally, I don't think prediction really impairs the interest of a novel. In a way, it affords a distinct kind of zest—the pleasurable & superficially self-flattering conviction that one is (like the detective in the book) solving a deep mystery & getting warmer & warmer on the trail. All the joy of successful pursuit—excitement of the chase—& so on. In some cases one would feel badly let down if one's own suspicions didn't pan out.

Well—as I said—I enjoyed this tale all the way through, & believe it ought to prove a decided success. You certainly have a knack at this kind of thing! And by the way—I'll have to hand the publisher one bouquet . . . . the *title* certainly is very apt. It gets to the central mystery directly—the vague form so weirdly glimpsed. As for my usual minute flaw-picking—there's really very little to go after this time . . . . although you have Anglo-Saxons using the Continental "Ah, so?" & (I think, in another place) "not so?" despite the fact that this form is *utterly unknown* in the speech of those whose sole language-tradition is English. The idiom is one which could not occur to anybody lacking continental speech-influences. Possibly *some* living whose Continental speech-influences survive might pick it up—& yet I never heard a Wisconsin Anglo-Saxon use it . . . any more than I've ever heard a New Orleans Anglo-Saxon use the Creole idiom "you understand?" Speech-resistance is rather curious—though the redundant "already" has gained some ground among midwestern & New York City Anglo-Saxons. However—the point is doubtless a minor philological one—& I may be wrong anyhow. One thing that you'll probably hear about from others is that sentence about "the old lady *sitting grandly* in a *high-boy*" on p. 187. Since a "high-boy" is a *tall chest of drawers* (vide enclosure—which please return at your leisure), that statement would argue great elasticity, compressibility, or other attainments of a weirdly athletic nature rather strange in a dignified grandam! One may add that the name "high-boy" (or "tall-boy") is of *modern* antiquarian origin (like "banjo clock", "grandfather clock", "low boy" [for low chest of drawers used as dressing table], "gate-leg table", "Gov. Winthrop desk", &c. &c.) wholly unknown in the original heyday of the high chest of drawers. I never use the term, since to me the 18th century is a *living reality* which *modern* antiquarian terminology spoils.

And so it goes. Again let me thank you for this delightful story, which takes its place among the choicest items of my permanent collection.

Well—I'm a couple of hundred pages into "The Night Land"—but it's damned hard going. God, what a verbose mess. And yet the chronological-geographical idea & some of the macabre concepts are *magnificent!* Don't know whether I'm going to side with you or with Klarkash-Ton in the end. The pseudo-archaic English is an acute agony—a cursed hybrid jargon belonging to no age at all! That's Hodgson's weakness—you'll note a sort of burlesque Elizabethan speech supposed to be of the *18th* century in "Glen Carrig". Why the hell can't people pick the *right* archaic speech if they're going to be archaic? ¶ Well—thanks again & congratulations on a fine piece of work!

Yr obt servt

H P

P.S. I had seen the Barry Pain volume before—had sent it on to you. Please send the remaining three Hodgson books, when done, to DUANE W. RIMEL, BOX 100, ASOTIN, WASH. I shall send the rest to Dwyer for later forwarding to Rimel.

Notes

1. In December HPL heard a lecture by S. Foster Damon of Brown University on the poet Thomas Holley Chivers (1809–1858).

2. Gertrude Atherton, *The Foghorn.*

3. CAS, "The Primal City," *FF* (November 1934).

4. The magazine, edited by H. Norman Evans, published only three issues: December 1934, Summer 1937, and Winter 1937/1938.

[376] [ALS]

Caverns of Yuggoth
—Novr. 18, 1934

Dear A W:—

All I know of *Tales of the Uncanny* is what I read in *The Fantasy Fan*—the November issue dedicated to Klarkash-Ton. I thought you were a subscriber to this humble venture. But here is the brief notice in full:

> *Tales of the Uncanny,* a new English magazine, features weird yarns by such well-known authors as Algernon Blackwood, H. G. Wells, John Buchan, Hugh Walpole, Michael Arlen, H. R. Wakefield, & Somerset Maugham.

There you have it—if you want more, you'll have to write the guy who wrote the column—Julius Schwartz, 255 E. 188th St., New York, N.Y. I've been meaning to ask him for information myself, but haven't got around to it. This is apparently the sort of magazine I've always dreamed of—though possibly the best items are all reprints.

The announcements you send certainly look alluring—& I'll have to see a copy of that Cozzens book sooner or later.[1] "Last man" stories have a peculiar appeal all their own—the best so far, I think, being the first half of Shiel's "Purple Cloud."

Yes—"The Man on All Fours" surely is a delightful specimen, & no one could ever suspect the haste with which it was written. I hope to see those others of yours. Of course, it isn't likely that I could make an early prediction of the ending of all of them. Surprise endings must always be prepared for early in the book, so that the final revelation will stir a hundred vague strings of memory. Otherwise they have no real punch. Nothing is flatter or more annoying than a detective novel in which the ultimately spotted criminal is a perfectly *irrelevant* figure—either dragged in late, or absolutely removed from the play of events & suspicion in the bulk of the text. Such tales have been perpetrated more than once—& by fairly prominent authors.

The *highboy* incident surely is curious. Your local usage must be very restricted, since the ordinary meaning is universal in antique-collecting & furniture circles from Seattle to Miami & San Diego to Portland, Maine. It is, however, purely an Americanism so far as I know—quite unknown in England. It would be interesting to know just *when* it came into use—both generally & in the Sac Prairie sense. Not till late in the 19th century, I fancy. The article you describe is a typical 19th century piece of furniture not existing in colonial times. In the country at large such a thing is known as a *hall rack* or *hall stand.* I never saw one except in a front hall, & never saw the hooks removed or the table part used as a seat. Usually clothes-brushes & such transient odds & ends (things not seriously interfering with the lifting of the cover) would occupy the flat surface if a box existed—though boxes were not very common. In size such pieces were much *larger* than anything suggesting a chair—often reaching 3/4 of the way up to the ceiling. Possibly what I mean may not be exactly the same thing as a Sac Prairie "highboy".

That "not so?" business is very curious—since, as I've said, it does not seem to prevail in Milwaukee or in Appleton, Wis. This matter of speech-differences in *very limited* areas is quite notable—even Rhode Island has 7 speech-zones as recognised by the Linguistic Atlas of N. America now being prepared by Prof. Hans Kurath of Brown University. Have you heard of this colossal dialect survey—which is to cover English speech (thus excluding only Quebec French, Pennsylvania German, & Southwestern Spanish, the 3 colonially seated & surviving foreign tongues) all over the continent? It will undoubtedly reach Wisconsin in time. The present is none too soon to conduct such an enterprise, since radio, talking cinema, & a migratory population are rapidly reducing local peculiarities of accent & idiom. In the east, the only use of the continental phrase of interrogative affirmation has been the purely artificial & superficial habit of Victorian gentlemen to show off their boarding-school French by sprinkling "*n'est pas?*" or "*n'est ce pas?*" through their parlour conversation. This is now dying out—having been confined to those in school before about 1880. The fact that the phrase was never translated into English, & that it had no currency except amongst consciously cultivated females, shews how far removed this idiom is from our normal speech-habits. ¶ All good wishes—H P

P.S. I shall examine that circulated bunch of reviews with the keenest interest.

[P.P.S.] Brobst is back in Prov. He enquired about you & sent his regards.

Notes

1. James Gould Cozzens, *Castaway* (1934), a short novel about the destruction of New York City. The previous year Cozzens had published *The New Adam.*

[377] [ALS]

Dec. 4, 1934

Dear A W:—

So you don't take the F F? Well, in that case I'll enclose for your amusement the October issue—which was dedicated to me, & of which the kindly editor allotted me a prodigious number of copies.[1] No need to return it. As for *Tales of the Uncanny*—I fancy it must be a reprint magazine; at least in part, since Wells is certainly not writing any new weird fiction nowadays. However, I'd welcome even a good reprint affair—since it would give me the text of many a classic I don't own. Let me know what you find out about the venture.

I've looked over the "All Fours" reviews with great interest, & will pass along the line as suggested. I've added several names of persons who ought to be able to appreciate a good detective novel. Speaking of publicity—some of the departments of amateur journalism are looking for material, & I've given your name as one who might possibly contribute a story to one of the magazines (non-remunerative, of course) or coöperate in a poetry circle a young chap in Oklahoma is organising. Hence you may hear from one or two people on these subjects. If you'd like the added publicity, go to it. If not, feel at perfect liberty to ignore any requests.

Glad to hear of the coming book events—especially the appearance of "Place of Hawks". With the Utpatel illustrations, that certainly ought to be a winner! Hope it will sell well—I'll certainly boost it all I can!

That "Century of Creepy Stories"[2] sounds admirable, & I may try to pick it up sooner or later. It certainly would give me a lot of first-rate tales that I don't own—& a few that I've never read. Saw a review of "Castaway" recently—not very favourable, though I suspect an unimaginative temperament & philistine bias on the critic's part.

Congratulations, as usual, on the magazine triumphs. I shall look for "Crows Fly High" at the earliest opportunity. "Hawk on the Blue" is certainly destined for wide reading—from the Nile to the Ganges, & the wheat fields of Saskatchewan to the gold diggings at Koolgarlie!

Was in Boston recently—seeing W. Paul Cook, who was down from the arctic for a week. Too cold to do much—but I showed Cook the old Royall mansion in Medford (built 1737), whose interior he had never seen before. He had with him some tremendously interesting antiquarian material—old papers of the ancestors of the late Mrs. Miniter (prominent amateur journalist who 40 years ago turned down a chance to revise "Dracula"), whose literary executor he is. The items included letters from a soldier at the front in the War of 1812, letters from 49ers in California, Civil War letters, & other documents of kindred historic value. I am now keeping this material pending the discovery of suitably appreciative blood-heirs of Mrs. Miniter.

I note that you have a new stationery design. What is this—late autumn or early winter? Rather good—with the hawks (or whatever they are) against the leaden, cloud-streaked sky. Wholly in keeping with the present melancholy days.

Messages from Auburn indicate that young Melmoth has wandrei'd out to the Pacific coast, & is confabulating with Klarkash-Ton & others there. He makes the second member of the gang whom C A S has beheld in person. Advices from Washington indicate that young Barlow's eyes are somewhat improved . . . . I certainly hope they are, for the little imp has taken upon himself the task of typing my two long (& now discarded & repudiated) novelettes of 1926–7—so that he may keep the utterly worthless original MSS!

Just received from Crawford the booklet containing Klarkash-Ton's "White Sibyl" & Dr. Keller's "Men of Avalon".[3] Of these tales the former is magnificent—& the latter mawkish & mediocre. Doc Keller surely is the most *uneven* writer now at large. His yarn in the recent *Marvel Tales* was really fine![4]

Well—blessings on the Sacs & Foxes!

Yr obt h^ble^ Servt

H P

Notes

1. *FF* (October 1934). It contained "Beyond the Wall of Sleep," two sonnets from *Fungi from Yuggoth*—"The Book" (I) and "Pursuit" (II)—and an unusually lengthy segment of SHL.

2. *A Century of Creepy Stories.*

3. CAS and David H. Keller, *The White Sybil and Men of Avalon.*

4. David Keller, "The Golden Bough," *Marvel Tales* (Winter 1934).

[378] [ALS]

Dec. 22, 1934.

Dear A W:—

Commiserations on the temperature—& the stationery. However, anything aestival has its welcome side these days! Gad, what a spell New England has been through! Down to 10° or so day after day! Naturally, I was a prisoner during the worst week. Hope this business was not a sample of what the winter is going to be! Belknap invites me to Manhattan for the holidays, but I'll be damned if I could enjoy much in zero weather. Well—I trust you'll rest up a bit & avoid a repetition of the causes which brought on your attack. There is truth as well as triteness in the old gag about burning the candle at both ends!

Thanks for "January Thaw", which is full of charm, & which makes one wish for a glimpse of the woods irrespective of the season. I've always felt a certain charm in winter woods, & used to brave their climatic rigours more than I do now. This is certainly quite a publishing month for you. Brobst saw your piece in *Scribners* & was highly enthusiastic over it. I simply must get to the library & see it for myself.

Alas that *Tales of the Uncanny* turned out to be a mirage! I see that new weird pulps are appearing—*Horror Stories* (companion to *Terror Tales*) being the latest. But I doubt if any of these could be a market for me. New F F just came—Hornig has had to drop the cover . . . which is surely better than dropping the magazine! Have caught up with W T, & find the December issue infinitely better than the November. Klarkash-Ton's "Xeethra" seems to be the best item, with "The Black God's Shadow" a good second. Your story shews up finely—& the Byrne & Fleming[1] items are unexpectedly good. Bassett Morgan rings a pleasing minor variation on his single plot idea, while Two-Gun Bob hits a very fast stride in his adventure story—which is weird only by courtesy & by the laborious dragging in of a monster.

Your account of the Duke U. telepathic experiments is surely interesting, & I hope to get hold of the *Time* issue with further particulars.[2] Just what factors aside from communication with hitherto unknown senses could account for these deviations of averages remains to be seen. It is evidence which will count in the end; & if additional senses are actually indicated by a proper range of experiments & correlations, there is nothing to do but accept the supposition as a working hypothesis.

Just before my imprisonment by the cold I attended quite an impressive course of lectures connected with the local "Art Week." One of the most striking was an exhibition of rapid painting by two of the most eminent Providence artists—the landscapist H. Anthony Dyer & the portraitist John R. Frazier.[3] Each painted a picture in full sight of the audience, & the results obtained in about an hour & a half were really tremendously good. Another event was an exhibition of Japanese prints—part of 700 magnificent specimens (Hokusai, Hiroshige, & all the rest) just acquired by the local art museum. This acquisition will bring Providence into competing distance of Boston—whose Museum of Fine Arts boasts the finest collection of Japanese prints outside Japan itself. A later event was a highly interesting aesthetic experiment by Prof. Shook—the correlation of projected colours (gradations of ether waves) with music (gradations of atmospheric waves)—but unfortunately this occurred after the dawn of the frigid spell, so that I had to pass it up.

Well—I trust you'll have a pleasant holiday season, with plenty of thaws without waiting for January! I envy the Pacific Coast—Rimel & Baldwin, up in Washington, tell the most extraordinary tales of springlike phenomena, extra crops, &c. in their region . . . . yet they're nearly 5° of Latitude north of Providence!

Benedictions—

H P

P.S. Rimel wants to know if anybody can tell him the meaning of certain small red pencil dots—seemingly aimless—which appear on the pages of some (not all) of the MSS. which Wright has read & rejected. They've never appeared on my MSS.—how about you . . . . can you enlighten him?

[P.P.S.] Enclosed is new FF, which may be of interest.

Notes

1. There is no writer "Fleming" in the December 1934 *WT*, but there is a John Flanders.
2. See the unsigned article "Blind Sight," *Time* 24, No. 24 (10 December 1934): 39–41, on the telepathy experiments by Joseph Banks Rhine at Duke University.
3. Hezekiah Anthony Dyer (1872–1943); John Robinson Frazier (1889–1966).

[379] [TLS, JHL]

Sauk City
Wisconsin
27 December [1934]

Dear H. P.,

I was glad to have your letter, which came opportunely enough on Christmas day. My delay is due to the holiday season, and to various other matters [. Text obliterated by HPL] I am just finishing another huge stack of letters, but everything is down to normal again now. The temperature of which I wrote you some time ago turned into a case of small pox, extremely mild type known as variloid, which did not leave me ill for a moment nor even indisposed, but allowed me to finish the revision of SIGN OF FEAR, write two short stories, NIGHT TRAIN and ROOM TO TURN AROUND IN, my March Outdoors article, A WARNING TO THE ILL-INFORMED,[1] and several new poems. SIGN OF FEAR has now gone in to L&M, and will doubtless appear late in the summer or early in the fall of 1935, since THREE WHO DIED and PLACE OF HAWKS will easily take up the first half of the year.

As for those little red dots—yes, of course, I know all about them. Those dots are just used by W. to indicate something he wishes to recall to his attention—it may be a good descriptive phrase, it may be an error, it may be faulty punctuation, it may be the *u* in such a spelling as labour, it may be an error in time or place or a detail error. If the matter is small enough, it is sometimes possible to find another red dot above the actual point in question apart from the one at the edge of the line. I hope this clears up the matter. The dots indicate nothing more, nothing set and definite, unfortunately. It is interesting to speculate upon what W. sometimes sees, but it is impossible to find it all the time. The *our* endings usually merit them.

I have yet to read the December W. T., though I did the shorts. All thanks for the December FF, which I glanced through but did not read as yet. I was interested in the announcement of HORROR STORIES, but am doubtful of placing anything with them; they want action and gruesome mystery and really nothing supernatural or weird. Jacobi has placed with that company and is still writing for them, I think.

Glad you enjoyed JANUARY THAW. I shall be sending you WHERE THE PUSSYWILLOWS WAVE[2] soon. My March and April articles are among my best for some time.

as always

August

Notes

1. Published as "What Flieth Down the Wind?"
2. Published as "Pussy Willows."

[380] [ALS]

Dec. 30, 1934

Dear A W:—

I was about to drop you a line when yours of the 27th blew in. Howard Wandrei had just mentioned your illness, & I wondered how severe it had actually been & how complete your recovery was proving. I'm surely glad it was no worse than it was. Anything like *smallpox* sounds alarming, but I presume the variant ensured by vaccination is really nothing to be excited about. You were surely lucky to get off so easily—it would have gone harder with me, for I haven't been vaccinated since I was 2½, & all the virtue of that inoculation must be long vanished from my aged system.

So you worked through it all! Bless my soul, what a boy! Glad various publishing plans are taking shape. I shall especially welcome the appearance of "Place of Hawks"—the vivid frontispiece of which formed such an attractive Christmas card.

Rimel will be heartily grateful for your help in solving the mystery of the red dots. It is odd that none have appeared on any of my rejected MSS. Some of these latter have contained certain pencil annotations, but nothing of the sort Rimel describes.

Hope to see your next nature article in the course of time. There will be a certain note of cheer after the gulf of hyemal January is crossed—though it will for some time represent promise rather than realisation!

I doubt if anything except cheap blood & thunder material would go over with *Horror Stories*. Jacobi is certainly fortunate in his ability to suit various markets—although Sonny Belknap is developing astonishingly in that direction. You'll find the Dec. W T a marked improvement over Nov.—but bless my soul, here's still *another* issue due in a day or two! Time moves too fast for an old man to keep track of!

Trust you had a festive Yule. We had a *tree*—the first I've had in over a quarter of a century. All my old-time ornaments were of course long dispersed, but I laid in a new & inexpensive stock at my old friend Frank Winfield Woolworth's. The finished product—with tinsel star, baubles, & tinsel draped from the boughs like Spanish moss—is certainly something to take the eye! I got a set of 12 coloured lights to complete the effect.

And now I am about to take the stage-coach for Manhattan, to be once more the guest of my young grandson Belknap. It will be quite a convention this time, for Wandrei has just hit town after his long voyage from Averoigne, whilst little Bobby Barlow will be up from Washington. Expect also to see Koenig, old de Castro, & the regular gang of ancient days . . . Loveman, Kirk, Kleiner, Leeds, & so on. Hope the weather will be tolerable—frost has played its havoc of late, & for several nights the coaches have been hamper'd by the icy roads—being from 1 to 3 hours late betwixt Providence & New-York. My coach leaves tonight at 1 a.m., & is due at the Penn Station at 7:30 a.m. If the schedule holds, I shall eat breakfast at the Long board.

Has Price told you of his new plans? Instead of going to Chicago, he has an idea of buying a cheap lot at San Carlos—on the western side of San Francisco Bay near Stanford U.—& building a cheap, box-like house in the plain Moorish style. He thinks that both house & land can be made to cost less than $500—much of the construction to be done by his own hands, aided by a new & unusual building material called "Thermax". Hope he can manage it—it's the best thing he could possibly do. He is selling stories faster than he can write them down, & is about to adopt the use of the dictaphone. You boys do keep grandpa dizzy with your speed!

Brobst blew in yesterday afternoon, just after a gorgeous holiday trip to Detroit. He went all through the Ford antiquarian exhibits, & accumulated an enviable stack of booklets & postcards. He sends you his sincerest regards.

Good lecture on Mayan art this afternoon at the local museum. I try to avail myself of the advantages of a cultivated civilisation before plunging into the chaotic jungles of Manhattan.

Blessings—& Happy New Year!

Yr obt Grandsire—

H P

1935

[381] [ALS]

Home—
Jany. 12, 1935

Dear A W:—

I note with interest & suitable amazement your record of achievement for 1934. Most assuredly, you 'went over the top' in brilliant fashion! Hope the 1935 programme will be equally well realised. How you can keep to such a quantitative schedule is beyond me—but I'm glad you can! I shall be looking for your work in W T—& hope I can see "After You, Mr. Henderson" somewhere or other.

So Satrap Pharnabazus is going in for detective stuff, eh? He seems perpetually anxious to get as far away from pure weirdness as he can! Well—I fancy you can keep pace with him, whatever direction his wandering caprices may take! Good old Solar Pons may yet prove a major asset.

I shall be glad to see the coming nature articles. Looking over my stock, I find I have the instalments for April, May, June, August, Sept, Oct, Nov, & Jan. *July,* you say, did not appear. This leaves *December* a question. Could one have been omitted—or could I have mislaid one—so recently?

Thanks immensely for "The Ojibwa Smile"—which has a wealth of pageantry & philosophy within its brief compass. Glad that *Frontier & Midland* is carrying on. You surely have an exacting standard if you would accept only 27—or perhaps 35—of your many excellent poems for inclusion in a published volume! Hope you'll be able to assemble a satisfactory volume by 1936.

This reminds me that Samuel Loveman's best lyrics will probably appear in book form[1] in the near future. He has been approached by the Caxton Press of Idaho—a firm, I believe, of some standing—& has made a careful selection of his shorter material . . . . . a selection of which follows, in the case of the earlier poems, a series of verdicts laid down by the vote of our whole group—Morton, Long, Leeds, Kirk, myself, &c—a decade ago. I shall certainly welcome the appearance of this long-wished volume! Price is still investigating California real estate. His latest plan is to purchase a house already built—to which end he is investigating two new possiblities in Redwood City . . . not far from San Carlos. Possibly his temperament is shifting from the migratory to the settled. I myself incline toward the settled—that is, I want a permanent base, although I enjoy travels of wide scope & duration.

I went to visit Long Dec. 30, & had a delightful sojourn which ended last Tuesday. Barlow was up from Washington, so that the event took on quite the aspect of a convention. This was Barlow's first metropolitan visit since infancy, hence Belknap & I were kept quite busy introducing him to the various museums, galleries, bookstalls, & the like. To add to the festivity of the occasion, both the Wandrei boys—Donald from his California trip & Howard directly from St. Paul—blew in about the same time that I did. They have taken an apartment together in Greenwich Village—as, indeed, they have doubtless told you by this time. All told, we certainly had quite a roundup. At a general gang meeting Jany 3.—at Belknap's—15 persons were present, including Morton, Loveman, Leeds, Kirk, the Wandreis, Talman, Barlow, Kleiner, Long, Koenig, &c. On another occasion we met at Loveman's, & were regaled by the sight of nearly 400 Clark Ashton Smith drawings . . . . which I had not seen since 1922, & which the others (Long, Barlow, the Wandreis) had never previously seen. As for bibliothecal accessions—I picked up Lewis's "Monk" for a dollar, but little Barlow went me one better & found a fine early copy of Reynolds' "Wagner the Wehr-Wolf" for 15¢! Weather was favourable most of the time—there being only 2 days when the cold caused me extreme inconvenience.

Upon my return I found a bewildering array of tasks before me—in the midst of which I am still engulfed. Bought the Jany. W.T., but have not had time to read it as yet. It looks, from the table of contents, like a rather mediocre issue—though "The Dark Eidolon" may save it.

All good wishes—

Your most obt h[ble] Servt—

H P

Notes

1. *The Hermaphrodite and Other Poems* (1936).

[382] [ALS]

Jany 28[, 1935]

Dear A W:—

Thanks for the material enclosed. So there was no *nature* article for December.[1] The February one is full of a subtle charm—the charm of almost-hidden beginnings so characteristic of the month. I shall be glad to see the March article when it appears.

Good luck with your 1935 race against time! Hope you make all the desiderate goals. That article prepared for January '36 certainly is the acme of forehandedness! Hope that "All that Glitters" may duly develop into a successful novel.

Loveman has sent his MS. in to the Caxtons & is awaiting developments. Hope that nothing may slip up—he has been the victim of some of the most tantalising near-placements on record. Once his prose-poem "The Sphinx" was *almost* on the press when the deal fell through—& on another occasion his critical study of Edgar Saltus was similarly ditched at the last moment[2]

. . . . by a pair of scoundrels in Philadelphia who conduct the Centaur Bookshop. The Caxton outfit approached him unsolicitedly—& I venture to hope that real results will be forthcoming this time. Hope you can get a review copy & give the volume a good sendoff.

I surely hope you can get within reach of the gang some time—a visit of yours to N.Y. certainly would call out the clan! But I share your hatred of that seething dumping-ground. A fortnight of it—continuously—is just about all my nerves can stand without suffering a strain. How the Wandrei boys can take to it so spontaneously is more than I can fathom!

I note the new book-titles—& am glad "The Sign of Fear" is so well regarded by the publishers. Hope the publication schedule goes ahead as planned.

Wonder what the new *Sensations* is like?[3] But I've stopped keeping track of any pulps save *Weird.* Hope you'll be able to make the Terrill market—which pays, whatever its aesthetic limitations may be. I've just read the Jan. W.T.—& certainly, C A S is the whole thing. What a magnificent opiate nightmare "The Dark Eidolon" is!

All good wishes—

Yr most ob^t^ Servt—

H P

P.S. I've just bought 2 dark-walnut sets of drawers (at $4.44 each—at a fire sale) to supplement my filing equipment. Haven't yet decided how I'll arrange them—may superimpose one on the other, & have a single tall cabinet. This total of 10 new drawers will help to resolve the chaos of my cuttings & papers. ¶ Quite a record-breaking snowstorm Jany. 23–4—the deepest & most traffick-paralysing I can recall since 1920.

Notes

1. But the December *Outdoors* does contain the article "For December Nights."

2. Loveman had written a critical study of the work of Edgar Saltus (1855–1921) in 1924, but the publisher abandoned plans to publish the book after the manuscript had already been accepted.

3. No magazine of this title was ever published.

[383] [ALS]

#66

—Feby. 16[, 1935]

Dear A W:—

Your report of progress with the markets is surely interesting, & I hope you achieve all the new ones you have in mind. Surely, quality is preferable to quantity as a goal! I shall hail "Three Who Died" with the keenest interest & appreciation—who knows but that I may recover my childhood interest in the detective tale! "The Man On All Fours" is now lent to the Asotin boys—Rimel & Baldwin—who will undoubtedly like it & perhaps give it some publicity in the F F. Recently my aunt read this tale & liked it exceedingly—though for some reason she did not guess the outcome as soon as I did. I shall try to get "Place of Hawks" when the edition is ready—& before it is exhasted. Hope you continue to have material in W.T. Haven't had time to see the February issue yet. Enclosed, by the way, is another F F. Hornig surely is making a struggle to keep the little fellow going!

No—I send nothing to W T now. Nothing I would write would be accepted. Later, when I have 2 or 3 experimental pieces that I think good enough for display yet not too long for Satrap Pharnabazus' thumbnail tastes, I may listlessly let the cuss have a look at them before dumping them on Hornig. I'm still trying to finish that "Shadow Out of Time" in some form or other—though it insists on attaining novelette length. Possibly I shall have more energy when hot weather comes.

My new files make a very good appearance in my study—being of a dark wood & conservative design which give them the aspect of age & mellowness. When I can get the time & strength to arrange my papers in them, a vast amount of chaos will have been cleared up.

This cursed winter is turning out almost as bad as its evil predecessor—which, you may recall, was something rather picturesque in the line of malignant extremes. Mercury below +20° almost a week & a half—with myself therefore a prisoner within doors. I enclose an eloquent cutting.

Did I mention that Price has now bought a cottage on the crest of a wooded hill near Redwood City, within sight of San Francisco Bay? He moved out there late in January, & seems to like the new locale vastly. To make things perfect, a huge white tomcat strayed in & took up its abode with him after allaying the pangs of hunger with 3 saucers of milk & 2 bowls of spaghetti & diced meat. Other news—old de Castro's wife died on Jan. 23 at St. Joseph's Hospital in N.Y.

All good wishes—

Your most obt Servt—

H P

P.S. Your new stationery design is attractive.

[P.]P.S. And bless my soul, Son, but I must not forget to extend the most profound & effusive thanks for your letter to L & M anent Grandpa's stories! I don't believe they'll want them—any more than any other publisher—but I appreciate none the less vastly your kindly efforts in the matter! Egad, Sir, but your description of my stuff makes the old man feel quite important for a five-minute stretch! By the way—"The Dunwich Horror" as well as the "Colour" made O'Brien's Role of Honour. While I vastly doubt that any book of my effusions will ever appear, I would surely like to see such a thing; if only to preserve some of the tales in a less perishable form than MSS. & pulp sheets. Lending a batch of such junk is the most damnable job—& some of it always perishes. Heard from L & M yesterday, & sent them the list of tales which you suggested—this being as good an assortment as any. L & M will make the 5th consideration from book publishers my junk has had. First W T, then Putnam, then Vanguard, & then Knopf. Putnam treated my MSS. the worst of any publishers. Hope L & M will be careful of the pages—or else a lot of my yarns will have to go off the lending list. My letter was from one Barrows Mussey. Enclosed was a catalogue in which both of your coming volumes are listed.

¶ A little taste of half-decent weather—up to 51° yesterday.

[384] [ALS]

Feby. 25, 1935.

Dear A W:—

Thanks for the interesting March article. The coming of the birds surely forms a basis for some highly piquant vigils & controversies! Some day you ought to get these—& other—nature articles together in some sort of collected form. They would really make a very desirable volume.

I shall be looking for "Muggridge's Aunt", & hope you will soon have Satrap Pharnabazus well supplied with future material. He surely is a great one to object to slighly changed, re-submitted MSS! Enjoyed "The Metronome"—& seem to recall seeing it once before in MS. form. The experience with *Poetry World* surely is unique—placing your work backward in time, so to speak! "Three Who Died" will be as welcome in March as in February—after all, a fortnight isn't much as scaled against a lifetime! I've seen reviews of "I Am Your Brother",[1] & imagine it must be quite an unusual thing. Tales of family monsters locked in attics are not new, but this one appears to have unique psychological overtones. By the way—I lately read the new Dunsany volume "Jorkens Remembers Africa"—much of whose contents I had previously seen in the *Atlantic*. Not the old Dunsany—though some of the yarns are very clever of their kind.

I'll let you know anything I hear from L & M—though I really haven't the least expectancy of any favourable development. Naturally, if the miracle of publication did come to pass, I could scarcely expect free copies . . . . but this miracle isn't likely enough to set me worrying about the expense of books for presentation! As for "The Shadow Out of Time"—which I'm just finishing up now—I'm hanged if I know whether it's worth preserving or not. This is the *second* version I have completed, & I may tear it up as I did the first . . . although it is not quite as unsatisfying to me as that was. At any rate, I simply can't waste energy *typing* it until I decide whether it's worth preserving or not. If I send it as it is, the chances are that you can't make out more than half of it . . . . so what the hell? If I do decide to let you try your hand at making out the hieroglyphs, you musn't feel under any obligation to go through the whole thing. Probably the waste basket is the real ultimate destination. Most readers will complain of the *length* of the thing—but I don't yet know how the given material can be presented more succinctly. The destroyed version was short—but it didn't convey what I wished to convey. The conditions & implications brought up by the central concept left all sorts of obvious questions unanswered, while the experience in Australia remained wholly unconvincing for lack of atmospheric preparation & emotional modulation. Whether the present version is any better, remains to be seen. It is possible that I ought to tear everything up & abandon the whole idea for a year—or until I have sufficiently forgotten this version to make an altogether fresh start. And then again, it is possible that I have wholly lost the knack of fictional formulation, & ought to cease altogether from attempting stories. I'll experiment a little more, though, before finally arriving at such a conclusion. No—this is the only thing since "The Thing on the Doorstep" which I have not destroyed. Nothing recent has really *come alive*—& I certainly don't want to put forth mechanical, routine bull of the sort which messes up the pages of W T & its still worse contemporaries. By the way—if I *do* decide to let you see "The Shadow Out of Time", let me suggest that the use of a *reading-glass* will probably vastly aid the process of de-coding the apparently meaningless hieroglyphs.

Well—thanks again for the suggestion to L & M, even if (as is probable) nothing comes of it.

Benedictions—

H P

P.S. Well—after all, I'm sending the damn thing . . . . although a final reading makes me fear more than ever that the waste-basket is its one logical destination. Don't try to wade through it if it seems too utterly repellent—either chirographically or literarily. I am utterly sick of it—the very sight of it turns my stomach! If by any chance you do read it, & think it is worth saving, you might hold it—& I will send a short list of persons among whom to circulate it. I simply *can't* consider typing it . . . . though if it were any good I might strike a bargain with Barlow to perform that job.

Notes

1. By Gabriel S. Marlowe. The novel deals with a man who discovers that his mother had hidden another son in the attic of their son's home.

[385] [ALS]

March 6, 1935

Dear A W:—

Glad to learn that the mere sight of that pencil scrawl didn't give you an apoplectic shock. So you have a new artist for "Place of Hawks"? I thought Utpatel was going to illustrate that—or is an old man's memory at fault? From your description, Barford seems like an ideal person for the job. "The Long Call" will certainly make a highly acceptable volume, & I hope to see it on my shelves some day. Congratulations on the new markets—& commiserations on the revision! So you are now about to tackle the *6th* of the Peck books.[1] Bless my soul, but how the words fly! It seems only a second ago that the *first* book was out!

Don't worry about your autumnal stationery—or if it deeply troubles you, you might vernalise it by making trees of the sheaves, heading your geese north, & drawing in a ploughman!

Regarding the publicational pipe-dream—I'm not a pessimist, but merely a realist. Publishers just naturally have a habit of not issuing my effusions. What halted the Knopf outfit was lack of guaranteed sales. They wrote Wright, asking whether he could vouch for the sale of a certain number—I forget what it was—& when he couldn't, the deal was off as usual. So I'm not building dreams in the fashion of the barber's brother Alnaschar in the Arabian Nights.[2] The details of distribution don't weigh on my sense of responsibility the least bit. Sure—go ahead & write an introduction *if* there's anything to write an introduction for, although I've often wondered whether prefaces really belong in the doubtful & hesitant volumes of unknown small-timers. If they excite too great expectations, the book itself appears all the worse for its disappointing quality. But you know more about such matters than Grandpa! And if *any* preface is desired, you surely ought to be the ring-master. But, as before stated, I hardly expect that any of these matters will have a chance to come up for consideration!

As for the pencil-scrawl—gawd's blood, don't hurry about it! And if your programme gets too congested, don't hesitate to chuck it back unread or pass it along to some other victim . . . probably kid Barlow. Don't worry about the MS.—its total loss would entail no great harm, & I may junk it myself in the end.

Recently learned from the Asotin boys of the failure of the *Fantasy Fan*. February will form the final flourish. Too damn bad—for the little fellow was an invaluable forum for exchanges of ideas & suggestions among weirdists, & for giving rejected MSS. a congenial & encouraging outlet. No doubt *Fantasy Magazine* will take over a few of its features—but these can include only a small fraction, since the primary object of F M is science-fiction. Meanwhile poor Hillbilly Crawford is having his troubles—fingers smashed in press, & now his partner Eshbach has resigned. Lean times for the horror-mongers!

Haven't had time to read the March W T, but hope it's an improvement over February. Was glad, though, to see your "Metronome" in the latter. More things around here to do than one doddering old gentleman could accomplish in a year . . . the resurrected young J. Vernon Shea has just sent Grandpa a whole half-year of *Story* issues . . . . Good stuff, which I mean to read when I get the chance, in order to see what the young folks are writing. By the way—I hope you haven't forgotten that the Hodgson stuff is to go to the Asotin boys when you're through with it.

My 1935 outing season had its beginning March 2–3, when I was honoured by a visitor from your own state . . . a graduate from your own alma mater in the class of '33, one Robert Ellis Moe, son of my old friend M. W. Moe of Milwaukee, whom I've probably mentioned to you. I hadn't seen the boy since he was eleven—& bless me, how he has grown! 22 now—& with a position at Gen. Elec. Co. (he goes in for electrical engineering)—who lately transferred him to Bridgeport, Conn. . . . hence his presence in New England. He came in his 1928 Ford, & I shewed him all the antiquities of the region—not only Providence, but the quaint colonial seaports down both sides of the bay. The weather was springlike & excellent, despite considerable wind—the temperature being around 50°. It is not often that I have glimpses of the local scenery as early as this, & the novelty was very welcome. Young Moe is extremely brilliant & likeable, & seemed to appreciate the charm of the venerable countryside. He expects to get here again when the scenery is still lovelier—with the green of spring.

Of the recent local kittens, one fascinating little pickaninny is retained. Hope he'll survive longer than his lamented brother of 1934! ¶ Blessings—

H P

Notes

1. *The Narracong Riddle.*

2. In the *Spectator* No. 525 (13 November 1712), Joseph Addison tells a tale (which he found in Antoine Galland's French translation of the *Arabian Nights*) of Alnaschar, a petty merchant who deals in glassware. One day Alnaschar became so involved in a daydream about attaining fantastic wealth from his business that he inadvertently kicked over his glassware, shattering it and destroying its value.

[386] [ALS]

March 14, 1935

Dear A W:—

Thanks for the April article—excellent as usual. It really gave me quite a surprise to learn that Wisconsin has sugar-camps—I thought such things were exclusive appurtenances of the "Whisperer in Darkness" country! You're evidently becoming quite an *Outdoors* fixture—with official stationery 'n' everything! By the way—is the use of *Dorcas* as a *masculine* name, as indicated in your article, a typical Wisconsin practice? These nomenclatural twists are fascinating to observe & correlate.

I shall surely be on the lookout for "Three Who Died", & fancy it will prove even more entertaining than its predecessor. Glad the later members of the series continue the upward curve. Hope the formulation of the court-room procedure won't be too tedious a job. So Barford beats Utpatel at his own game? Fortunate you discovered just the right man at the right time. Congratulations on the endorsements—especially O'Brien's. Trust all the advertising plans may develop well, & that the sales may be such as to encourage L & M toward further serious acceptances.

Sorry "Muggridge" is postponed, but better late than never. I'll look for "Mr. Berbeck". No, damn it, that Shea shipment of *Story* begins with September. Little Jehvish-Êi observed & admired your recent tales in *Story* & *Scribners*.[1]

Don't waste too much time boosting that L & M pipe dream. Such things just don't naturally happen! Looked into the March W T, & think Searight's yarn is about the best item. I saw it in MS., & am sorry Wright cut out an introductory motto taken from the hellish & pre-human Eltdown Shards. The Stoker reprint could have been worse—& it was absolutely new to me.[2]

Providence has a new weird-science-fiction-fan—in the person of a little Jew boy with the misleading appellation of Kenneth Sterling. He recently came from N Y, & looked me up after getting my address from Hornig. An astonishingly precocious brat—with the tastes & information of a man of 30. He means to become a research biologist. Very familiar with your work, & marvels at your productivity. He's had something accepted by *Wonder*, & is bubbling over with ideas. Comes of bright stock—father a Harvard graduate, & other relatives *NY Herald-Tribune* reviewers, &c. Means to call again—hope he won't become a nuisance!

Well—the outing season seems to be under way early! I fulfilled the prophecy of the pencil postscript March 6—when the thermometer reached a maximum of 65°—by taking a 12-mile walk in my favourite countryside north of Providence. Landscape slushy & brown, but something of spring's stirring subtly in the air. In the evening Venus & the slender crescent moon made a glamourous picture in the west.

Heard a good lecture—illustrated—on the recently uncovered mosaics in St. Sophia in Constantinople the other night—by Thomas Whittemore, the bird responsible for the uncovering. That building has always fascinated me—the last major edifice created by the dying classical world. Mosaics are later—9th & 10th centuries. Another good lecture at the college was by Prof. W. F. G. Swann of the Franklin Institute—on cosmic rays.[3] Illustrated by slides & apparatus.

Just got a copy of the new 1-volume Modern Encylcopedia—$1.95.

Darned convenient—has events as late as last September. I've needed a contemporary reference-book for a long time.

¶ Extra! Since I began this epistle "Three Who Died" has come. Thanks a thousand times! It looks tremendously alluring, & I hope to give myself the pleasure of reading it very soon. In the same mail, by coincidence, there came a copy of the old Meyrink novel, "The Golem", lent by young Barlow. I certainly have a gorgeous session of reading ahead!

The younger feline generation hereabouts has narrowed down to one little nigger—Mr. John Perkins, who bids fair to carry on the best traditions of the Kappa Alpha Tau. He hisses manfully when any intruding finger is poked at him! Hope he'll live longer than his elder brother Samuel[4]—my constant companion of last summer!

Well—again thanks, appreciations, & all that.

Yr grateful grandsire—

H P

Notes

1. AWD, "A Ride Home," *Story*; "Crows Fly High," *Scribner's.*

2. *WT* (March 1935): Richard F. Searight, "The Sealed Casket"; Bram Stoker, "The Judge's House."

3. Thomas Whittemore (1871–1950), American archaeologist who devoted himself chiefly to Byzantine and Coptic art. William Francis Gray Swann (1884–1962), British physicist and director of the Franklin Institute (1927–59).

4. See HPL's poem "[Little Sam Perkins]," about a black kitten that lived only from June to September 1934.

[387] [ALS]

March 20[, 1935]

Dear A W:—

Well—I've read "Three Who Died"—& certainly enjoyed it to the limit! It's a tremendously clever piece of work, & far ahead of "All Fours" in point of construction—although the latter is a fine book, none the less, & vivid in atmosphere & narrative value. This one is a straight enigma, frankly presented as such, & I didn't get my suspicions straight till around p. 145. It wasn't till the 160's that I felt reasonably certain. This tale is much more *convincing* than its predecessor. Melodrama & the grotesque are absent, so that the case sounds as if it might have come out of the papers. The various solvers go about their work in logical fashion, & the crimes themselves are natural—implicit parts of the pattern & in no sense artificially dragged in. If there are any improbable points, they are such as do not leap out at the layman—save perhaps (p. 136) where a college student is represented as registering under a false address & with a fictitious parentage. That does sound just a bit thick—a little too convenient a device for deferring a dramatic reunion. But even this, of course, is a mere trifle in light fiction—& probably wouldn't be noticed at all except by a nosy old codger avowedly on the hunt for slips.

As to the growth of suspicion—I had no real guess till p. 50, when the veronal box was found in the jacket of Corliss's coat. Then, however, I felt that C. was the murderer of Mrs. Allison . . . . substituting 10-gr. capsules to give her an overdose. This also made me think he had probably killed Allison. A doctor can produce queer effects when he wants to, & there were some odd points. Why was Logan called in? Was Corliss's angina attack whilst on the case a sufficient reason? Or did Mrs. A. fear that something was fishy? More—Logan said Corliss was *purposely vague* with the nurse about the case. Not so good! Anyhow, a *doctor* must have murdered Mrs. A. by switching veronal capsules—10 gr. for 1 gr.—& if not Corliss, then who? Logan? Not likely. He didn't even call till after her death. My general idea here was that Corliss was trying to wipe out the whole Allison family—perhaps for an economic reason—when somehow hoist with his own petar[d]. It also seemed about 75–25 that he himself was murdered—cf. that *recently removed* label on the jar.

At p. 57 my suspicions gained intensity. So Corliss had not told of the veronal box at the inquest? Could carelessness explain this? And would he, if suspecting something wrong, have withheld his information from the coroner? No, no, Asa—you begin to look more & more like a bad egg!

Around p. 66 I began to think again of Corliss's death. Dimacher's testimony made it evident that the perles at Allison's were Corliss's *entire* stock. How come? Would carelessness explain? . . . especially in connexion with that *recently removed* label? Food for thought. Dirty work at both ends—Corliss done in by somebody with access to Allison home. Who? Henry Allison? After p. 100 Henry seems unlikely, though his illness makes one wonder of Corliss's machinations (unintentionally involving Miss Wembler) are including him.

At p. 134 everything assumed a different aspect. A sneaking double-faced past for Mrs. A, eh? Gobba! *Medical student—older* . . . . now we have a non-economic motive for a doctor's killing A . . . three guesses as to the doctor! But no motive for trying to kill Henry.

Page 145 about rounded out the plot. Corliss was certainly murdered by someone with access to Allison's. Obviously not by Jack, since Corliss had had his remedies long after J. was stricken. Attack Sept. 30. Probably not Henry. Who then but Mrs. Allison? And why—if she didn't suspect C. was murdering Allison? The Akers angle didn't seem very sound to me. After p. 150 my suspicion of Mrs. Allison grew red-hot, & the *Gobba* entry about clinched it. At the same time it now appeared that C. had a motive for killing Mrs. A. She suspected his killing—or rather, trying to kill—her husband. Would he not perceive this even if she had not told him? And would he not want her out of the way? At p. 160 the Akers letter added its bit.

166 left almost no doubt. From then on, I assumed a situation equivalent to what developed. C. poisons or inoculates A. (with Henry & Miss W. accidentally catching echoes), Mrs. A gets back at him, & he puts her out of the way. At 178 the chapter-heading "A Woman's Fingerprints" piles up the probability. This is confirmed on 195 by Metzger's letter. All over but the explaining.

After 200 the sheaf of letters confirms everything. At 219 the evidence of the typhoid's source clinches C's guilt as to Allison. At 238, of course, Mrs. A's guilt to C is clinched. At 248 C's murder of Mrs. A is clinched. And so it goes. This book prods the reader on to some real guessing, & the culprits all seem the logical ones when revealed. I didn't at any time lean to a 1-murderer theory. Minor note—you speak of Henry (p. 18) as Jack's *younger* brother, & in the *middle* thirties in 1934. Later it appears that J. was born in 1900. This makes H. *probably* around *32*. *Middle* thirties?

Well—anyhow, it's a splendid book of its type, & I only hope the later volumes sustain the same standard . . . as I'm sure they do & will. I genuinely enjoyed it, & couldn't interrupt my original sitting till it was done.

Sorry to hear of the cold, & hope it's all gone by now. Don't let any evil medicos inoculate you with strange & murderous pulmonary viruses! Congrats on acceptances—so even old lady *Atlantic* has succumbed![1] Eshbach asked me for something for the *Galleon,* but since he ruled out the weird, I had to tell him that I had nothing suitable. A tremendously attractive magazine—quite a move up from *Marvel Tales!*

As for the name *Dorcas*—is *Tabitha* also a masculine name around Sac Prairie? As you know, the two refer to the same person in Acts ix, 36–42. Dorcas or Tabitha was a benevolent lady of Joppa, who helped the poor with her needlework. Having died, she was restored to life by Peter. Surely you know that about every village in the U.S. has its church sewing circle (cf. above) called the *Dorcas Society!* Dorcas is just about as masculine a name as Mary or Martha in the world at large. I had a great-great-great-great-grandmother in the early 18th century named Dorcas Ellis. A local usage so contrary to general usage & traditional origin certainly deserves a footnote to avert the confusion of the reader. I know how confused I was when I first learned that Anne-Marie (but not, oddly enough, Marie-Anne!) was a common French *masculine* name in the 17th & 18th centuries. Another odd thing is the *José-Maria* combination borne by whiskered Spaniards.

Glad to hear that one of your old W T readers has been following your more serious work. Once in a while the worlds of pulp & literature overlap a bit!

I envy you the hiking. The temperature was up to 72° last Saturday, but I couldn't possibly arrange to get out to the tall timber. Your ornithological resources are richer than those of a densely populated region—though even here a better observer than I can find all sorts of winged pageantry. There is an old lady—whom I know slightly—who writes almost daily articles on birds for the local journal. I'll enclose a couple—in fact, I could send 'em all if you had any use for such.[2]

Marvel Tales came recently—improved format, but depressingly mediocre contents. The short tale by John Benyon [*sic*] Harris[3] seems to me the least hopeless. Hill-Billy Crawford wants me to try to get the thing on the news-stands of Providence—but I feel like an ass pestering the news agencies with such a feeble rag.

News notes—Baldwin is about to move to Lewiston, Idaho, & Rimel has some very vague hopes of a course at the U. of Montana in Missoula. If the latter event materialised, Rimel & Petaja (in neighbouring Milltown) could meet & compare notes in person.

Barlow has just lent me Meyrink's "Golem"—which looks damned promising, though I have not yet had time to read it.

Spring tomorrow at 8:18 a.m. None too soon for Grandpa!

Again congratulating you on "Three Who Died", & reaffirming the pleasure I had in its perusal,

I have the honour to subscribe my self

Your L^d^ship's most oblig'^d^, most ob^t^ Servt

H P

P.S. Seem to find only one of those bird articles. Guess they don't appear as often as I thought. But ex pede Herculem.[4]

Notes

1. The magazine published AWD's "The Alphabet Begins with AAA" (December 1935), one of AWD's early Gus Elker stories. See letter 391n2.
2. Alice Hall Walter (1869–1953), author of various books on ornithology.
3. "The Cathedral Crypt," *Marvel Tales* (March–April 1935). John Beynon Harris (1903–1969) wrote more commonly under the pseudonym John Wyndham.
4. "From the foot [we recognize] Hercules."

[388] [ALS]

6th Day of Spring [26 March 1935]

Dear A W:—

Thanks for the glimpse of the review. Do you want it back? The critic seems to enjoy an air of Olympian superiority—& to expect a good deal from a single novel! Yet on the whole it isn't a real panning. One can imagine what the same reviewer would do to one of the average conventional products of the detective fiction mill! I'll be interested to see other reviews—& will enclose anything I find in the *Prov. Journal.* The *Times* for Mar. 24 lists the volume but does not review it.

So *Tabitha* has become purely a feline name in Sac Prairie? Hereabouts it is still applied to female primates of the species *Homo Sapiens*—mostly, however, of the generation now gradually dying off. Curious how it flits from animal to animal—for it was originally an Aramaic (the corrupt or local Hebrew used in Syria in New Testament times) word signifying a *female gazelle. Dorcas* (δορκάς—from δέδορκα, perfect tense of δέρκομαι* *to flash or gleam* . . . . referring to the large, gleaming eyes of the gazelle) is the Greek word for *a gazelle or antelope,* thus forming a translation. In the Book of Acts (ix, 36) both forms are given—thus:

> "Now there was at Joppa a certain disciple named *Tabitha,* which by interpretation is called *Dorcas*: this woman was full of good works & alms deeds which she did."

Both *Tabitha* and *Dorcas* were favourite female names in early New England. The transfer of *Tabitha* to the she-cat (common here for the last century or more) represents a very interesting philological process involving *accidental* phonetic resemblance & *false* etymology. The *tabby-cat*'s designation, which originally held no especial implications of gender, comes from an *altogether different* source—the *Arabic* word *attabi,* signifying the rich *watered silk* manufactured in the *Attâbi* quarter of Bagdad. This silk was introduced into Europe through Spain (where the Moors reigned) & France, & was known in Spanish as *tabi* & in French as *tabis.* From the brindled or wave-marked surface of this silk, the name *tabby* became—in English—transferred to cats of similar marking . . . hence the name *tabby cat*—which might mean either male or female. It was not until later that the *accidental* likeness of *tabby* & *Tabitha* caused the latter name to be applied playfully to brindled cats. As soon, of course, as the transfer became popular, the term *Tabitha-cat* (&, retroactively, *tabby-cat*) shrank to cover only the ladies of the species. Curious twist of fate—a name starting with a she-quadruped (*Tabitha*—Aramaic for *she-gazelle*) ends up as designating *another* she-quadruped after passing through a human stage. Still more—here we have two utterly different *Semitic* words . . . the Aramaic word for gazelle & the Arabic name of an urban district . . . *tabitha* . . . *Attâbi* . . . . fusing together & becoming interchanged in an *Aryan* speech utterly unknown to either branch of Semites in question!

As a fanatical devotee of the felidae, I have always been interested in cat nomenclature. No doubt you know that *Tom-cat* is a comparatively recent (a century or two) designation for my favourite kind of gentleman. The original

---

*from δρακεῖν, the 2nd aorist infinitive of δέρκομαι, (referring to the flashing glance of a daemon or dragon) comes the noun δράκων [=Lat. draco], meaning a *dragon* or *serpent* or (later & by transference) *devil.* Hence, through Slavic or Roumanian sources, the word *dracu* & the proper name DRACULA. *Drak* or *dric* is an old Aryan root going back to Sanscrit—meaning to *see* or *flash.*

type-name for a he-cat was *Gilbert,* not *Thomas*—hence (from the slang or nickname form of *Gilbert*) the common Elizabethan expression *Gib-cat.* With the passage of time—& after the rise of the parallel term *Tom-cat* for a typical lusty male—the name *Gib-cat* became at least partly transferred to the pampered eunuchs of cosy & well-bred firesides. Today *Gib-cat* is almost an obsolete term—indeed, I have never heard it orally, even among rustics born early in the 19th century*.

The feminisation of such names as *Evelyn* is very curious, & the process is still going on. A good example is the surname *Shirley,* which to my mind calls up some such image as that of the Honble William Shirley, Governor of His Maj^ty's^ Province of the Massachusetts Bay in the time of George the Second. When I was young the idea of this word as a female Christian name was unheard-of in New England—or all America, so far as I know—although it had figured thus, very sparsely, in novels & plays. Then—circa 1910—it began to be noticed in a few young women . . . who *may* have been so named in the 1890's, but who possibly adopted the name through affectation. Much might be said of *affected & assumed names*—of which there are both typically patrician & typically plebeian forms. *Ivar* is a fashionable male name borne by some who were—& some who weren't—so christened. I know a sappy young pseudo-aesthete who (though of 100% English stock) is trying to Scandinavianise the name *John* to *Jon.* Among the females, there is the silly & (so far as I know, wholly artificial & assumed) use of "Kay" for *Catherine,* & the more spontaneous (since 1910 or 1915) misspelling of *May* as "Mae". This last is wholly *plebeian*—I never heard of a gentlewoman or well-born female child with this spelling. Amusingly, aging women of the lower middle class, born before the advent of the fashion, make it retroactive . . . . so that fat, grey-headed "Maes" crowd the cheap cinemas each afternoon. The cinema itself, by the way, is a fruitful source of freak names among the lower orders—hence the crop of 5 & 10 year old *Garys* &c. now in primary & grammar schools. In the middle 19th Century slang diminutives had a disgusting vogue, & ascended higher in the social scale then ever before or since—thus children of good families were named *Fred, Annie, Will, Fanny, Susie, Hattie, Frank, Carrie, Jennie,* &c. The less cultivated classes went to incredible lengths at the same period, with *Gladiola, Sadie, Mamie,* &c. Parallel affectations have developed in Great Britain—& now the South Irish are making fools of themselves by archaically Gaelicising their names—thus *Patrick Kelly* becomes *Padraic O'Ceallaigh, John Sweeney* becomes *Sean MacSwibhne,* &c. Our distinguished fellow-weirdist Two-Gun Bob has succumbed to this fashion

---

*my very early interest in antiquarianism has led me into personal contact with survivors of a surprisingly remote period. When I was 6 I visited my ancestral part of R.I. & talked of old times with a lady just turned a centenarian—born in *1796.* Thus I have actually bridged the gap to my favourite 18th century in direct conversation.

to the extent of hashing up his own middle name (*Ervin*—distinguished in Southern history for 200 years) & signing himself "Robert *Eierbihn* Howard". Another freak wave was the "romantic" period of the fabulous 'forties—the age of pale, languishing *Lenores* & *Rosabelles* & *Ermyntrudes*. Names taken or corrupted from *novels*, however, were common from the early 18th century onward . . . hence the *Amelias, Matildas, Alzadas,* &c. on ancestral charts. Occasionally, specific corruptions became narrowly local. Thus in Rhode Island the name *Roba* became *Rhoby*—& occurs twice in my own ancestry. In all this business of extravagant affectation, women seem to suffer worse than men—notwithstanding the Victorian *Egberts, Harlwyns, Percivals,* & *Athelstanes* who nowadays write their names as E. Milton Jones, H. Mason Brown, &c. &c. Another interesting tendency, indicative of the growth of sophistication & the decline of hero-worship, is the steady descent of the social ladder made by "great man" names. Up to 2 or 3 generations ago the best families were full of George Washingtons, Thomas Jeffersons, Benjamin Franklins, Zachary Taylors, James Madisons, Winfield Scotts, John Marshalls, Roscoe Conklings, Henry Clays, Daniel Websters, Stephen Douglas's, &c. Around the 80's this habit began to wane, so that the *Grover Clevelands* & Garfields & *Benjamin Harrisons* & *Ulysses Grants* were generally pretty middle-class. Later, the William McKinleys & Deweys & Theodore Roosevelts were noticeably confined to distinctly humble circles—while the present crop of young Pershings & Woodrow Wilsons & Warren Gamaliels are for the most part hill-billies & niggers! I doubt if we shall notice many Cal Coolidges or Herb Hoovers or Frank Roosevelts or Al Smiths or Jack Garners or Andy Mellons or Hughie Johnsons . . . or Huey Longs . . . among the literate & cultivated young men of 1944 or 1950!

But the old man rambles! Have just added to the filing system begun last January—getting at a bargain sale *6* small 4-drawer cabinets of papier-maché, [*sic*] with wood frame. These, tucked in various inconspicuous places, take care of a vast number of old papers, pamphlets, cuttings, &c. formerly thrown around loosely or stacked in fragile cardboard boxes. For the first time in 20 or 25 years my files have a certain approach to proper classification & accessibility.

Congrats on Acceptance 1935—XLVIII! And sympathy anent the proof-reading. Yes—spring is surely here. Took a short walk Sunday & noticed many signs of faintly awakening vegetation. But I wish I had a round-trip ticket to Charleston, & Y rent for about 2 months! ¶ Blessings—Grandpa HP

[389] [ALS]

April 13, 1935

Dear A W:—

Glad the various nomenclatural notes proved of interest. Yes—I can see where names of presidential or kindred derivation might have a distinct use as clues in detective mysteries where a chronological element is involved[.]

Congratulations on the acceptances! The list of non-d'Erletted periodicals is getting to be a very slim & unimportant one these days. Saw some of your verses in *Wonder Stories*[1] the other day . . . . & hope you can collect from them without a lawsuit.

Commiserations on the re-decoration! I know just what kind of a hell an upset house is. In 1931, when they put steam heat in 10 Barnes St., I was knocked half to hell—& the moving in '33 was still worse! As to filing—I wish you could get hold of some of the little cabinets I've just discovered. The relief in my erstwhile chaotic system is well-nigh past description! They'll go *under* tables, &c.

Yes—"Place of Hawks" certainly deserves all the proofreading L & M will let you do. Hope you'll catch all the errors in the page proofs if you've missed any in the galleys.

Just read Gustav Meyrink's "The Golem", lent me by Barlow. The most magnificent weird thing I've come across in aeons! The cinema of the same title in 1921[2] was a mere substitute using the name—with nothing of the novel in it. What a study in subtle fear, brooding hints of magic, & driftings to & fro across the borderline betwixt dream & waking! There are no *overt* monsters or miracles—just symbols & suggestions. As a study in lurking, insidious *regional* horror it has scarcely a peer—doing for the ancient, crumbling Prague ghetto what I unsuccessfully tried to do for rotting Newburyport in "The Shadow Over Innsmouth". I had never seen the novel before, but mentioned it in my article as a result of having seen the cinema. Now I perceive that I ought to have given it an even higher rating. Have you read it? If not, you ought to get on Barlow's borrowing list. The only other item of Meyrink's I've read is a story in the "Lock & Key Library."[3]

Glad the outdoor programme keeps up—It is surely cheering to be able to write *April* as a date! Hope the flooded river won't prove locally disastrous—I judge from various accounts that your region is not one frequently liable to flood disasters. Here is another of the bird articles. I never was much of a nature student—preferring broad landscape effects to details—but last December I picked up some small illustrated books on birds, flowers, trees, & butterflies which may come in handy if I ever have a chance to use them.

And here is a brief review of "Three Who Died" from the Prov. Sunday Journal of March 31. Entirely favourable, as you may see. Too bad there's a slip in nomenclature—but reviewers are a hasty & careless fraternity, who try to read too many volumes. Papers ought to spread this work out among more reviewers, & have each volume more thoroughly & accurately read. The cheapest thing about this age is its "high-pressure" fallacy—its attempts to do too much, & to do nothing thoroughly. By the way—I also enclose a brief review from the Times, which you probably have.[4]

Read Merritt's "Creep, Shadow" the other day,[5] but was rather disappointed. Essentially popular pulp romance—though there are some vivid hints of cosmic outsideness & a splendid series of climactic tableaux.

The spring hereabouts has not kept up the promise of early March. Beastly cold—rain—gales—& even a flurry of snow last Tuesday. No outings recently. May 3–4–5 I expect to visit my friend Cole in the Boston zone, & to get some glimpses of ancient Marblehead. In June it is possible that W. Paul Cook & I will do some Vermont touring—in Cook's sister's car. In July I expect to see a fellow-Wisconsinite of yours—Galpin, the chap who once roomed at 830 W. Johnson St. He was in Madison the other day for the first time since *1923*. I told him to look you up if he ever goes through Sac Prairie—he lives in his own native town of Appleton—where he was fortunate enough to get a job teaching French at Lawrence College. The coming New England trip will be his first—though he has been to Europe twice & studied in Paris.

Well—pax vobiscum.

Yr obt grandsire

H P

Notes

1. *Wonder Stories* had published three poems by AWD: "To a Spaceship," "Man and the Cosmos," and "Omega."

2. See letter 25n4.

3. Gustave Meyrink, "The Man in the Bottle" (Vol. 3).

4. Isaac Anderson, "New Mystery Stories," *New York Times Book Review* (31 March 1935): 14.

5. See letter 346n2.

[390] [ALS]

April 23[, 1935]

Dear A W:—

Speaking of fancy stationery—in going over some old junk the other day I came on a box unopened in at least 12 years. Among its contents was this yellow pad—last remnants of a stationery bargain of *1910*. Bless my soul, but how the years go! Only yesterday the death of King Edward was fresh news, Bleriot had just flown the Channel, Capt. Scott was off for the Antarctic in the Terra Nova,[1] Pres. Taft was beginning to seem a disappointment—& Loring & Mussey's star author was rendering eloquent vocal selections from a Sac Priarie cradle! Ah, me . . . little did I think that this aged claw would still be covering this ochraceous papyrus with illegible rooster-scratchings in the half-fabulous future year of *1935!*

Glad the Prov. review was new to you. Here's another bird cutting—I met old Mrs. Walter the other night at a lecture, & told her her articles were reaching a young kindred spirit out in the Sac & Fox region of the Northwest

Territory. Thanks for your May article—whose emphasis on lilacs makes me homesick for my birthplace a mile east of here. We had vast thickets of lilacs—purple & white—on either side of the carriage drive. By the way—if you're interested in folklore—New England has *two* typical local mispronunciations of the word *lilac* . . . which I will present in order of their descent in the cultural scale: *lī-lock* & *lay-lock!*

Glad there were no disastrous floods, & that floral harbingers of milder days are at hand. This is proving the damndest alleged spring hereabouts—*snow* April 17 . . . . only a flurry here, but several inches on the ground up in Sunapee, N.H. where W. Paul Cook is.

Contratulations on sundry acceptances, & on disposing of PoH proofs. Sorry the illustrations aren't quite up to your standard. Maybe Utpatel could have done better after all!

Thanks abundantly for the article on Le Fanu. I have "The House By the Churchyard"—though it is an insufferably dull & Victorian specimen. In reading it, it was all I could do to keep awake! The Estevan mellerdrammer must have been rather entertaining. Icelandic sagas? Yes, indeed, I'm intensely interested in anything about them! You are doubtless aware that R.I. persistently claims to be the "Vineland" of the Sagas, & that local historical sharks are called upon to prove that the hieroglyphs on this or that rock along Narragansett Bay are *not* the ruins of Lief Ericson, Thorfinn, or some other pre-Columbian son of Scandinavia!

Thanks for the unposed shot of Little Mussolini, Defender of Sidewalks. You certainly weren't caught at a disadvantage—as Talman caught me at the gang meeting Jan. 7. In the latter shot, I look as if about to eject a quid of tobacco from my twisted lips[2]—though in truth nothing but argumentative words were passing! By the way—if you want to see how Grandpa is aging, here's a *non*-impromptu view that you needn't bother to return. Little Bobby Barlow snapped it in De Land last June,[3] & all think the resemblance is very good—cruelly so! I suppose the Old Gent has aged still more in the 10 intervening months—but there's still some likeness left.

And now for a request. I *think* that you have a carbon copy of my "Shadow Over Innsmouth". Would you mind sending it to Hill-Billy Crawford of *Marvel Tales* as soon as possible? He wants to issue it as a booklet, & thinks he has a good opportunity to get it printed.[4] The original typescript is with L & M, but I don't want to bother them before they send the whole batch of MSS. back. I have nothing but the pencil draught, & simply could not consider re-typing. Crawford may later tackle the Mts. of Madness. I'll see that you get Innsmouth back in the end—either the MS. or the printed booklet . . . if Hill-Billy really does get it issued. In case you've forgotten the address—It is *William Crawford, 122 Water St., Everett, Pa.*

I half-expect young Moe again this coming week end. We'll probably do some antiquarian exploration in his car. The week-end after that I shall probably be visiting in the Boston zone. ¶ Best Wishes—

Yr obt grandsire

H P

P.S. Our friend Eshbach is letting down standards. He took that mawkish "Iranon" thing which you once typed for me—& 2 Yuggothian Fungi—for *The Galleon.*[5]

Notes

1. King Edward VII of England died on 6 May 1910. British aviator Louis Bleriot (1872–1936) flew from Calais to Dover on 24 July 1909. British explorer Robert Scott (1868–1912) left for Antarctica in the expedition ship *Terra Nova* on 1 June 1910. He died there around 29 March 1912.

2. See Owings and Binkin, *A Catalog of Lovecraftiana,* item no. 528 in the photo gallery.

3. See frontispiece in *SL* 5.

4. William L. Crawford (b. 1911), editor of *Marvel Tales,* published *The Shadow over Innsmouth* (1936) under the imprint of the Visionary Press.

5. *Galleon* published AWD's "Mass at Eight" in the same issue. DAW had typed HPL's story, not AWD. Eshbach also took "Harbour Whistles" for the *Galleon,* but it was not published.

[391] [ALS]

May 13, 1935.

Dear A W:—

Glad to hear of the completion of your poetry volume MS.[1] It ought to be a notable collection, & I surely hope it can find appropriate publication. I can realise how difficult it is to make final selections—Long, Loveman, & other bards I know have lost hours of sleep over similar problems. Regarding "Broadwing Soaring"—I'd be inclined to vote for admission. The idea of gathering the opinions of many critics is an excellent one. Long & Loveman, back in 1925, used to submit such matters to the vote of the entire gang at its meetings. Your triple division of the poems seems sensible & fitting—& I trust that the nature section may be filled up with new material of commensurate quality.

Thanks exceedingly for the article on magic in fiction, which interested me greatly.[2] Will appreciate the other items when they arrive. In this essay G K C seems a little naive in wondering why fictional fantasy tends toward horror & darkness. It ought to be obvious that this tendency arises from the natural constitution of the human mind, whereby associations of unreal phenomena with pain & fright & disaster are infinitely more powerful than kindred associations with favourable outcomes. Unreal portents of horror sometimes seem real & powerful, whereas unreal promises of pleasure always appear spurious, mawkish, & namby-pamby. This circumstance is, in turn, based on the essentially terrifying nature of anything unknown, uncharted, & unlooked for. The same instinct caused ancient cartographers to populate the *terra incognita* parts of their maps with dragons & daemons.

Regarding "Innsmouth"—I guess Hill-Billy can wait a bit. I'll drop young Bloch a line & see if he has it. Naturally Hill-Billy couldn't handle the tale if L & M were serious about issuing that book—but I don't regard that as a genuine possibility. The new kid in Providence—little Kenneth Sterling—has some wild-eyed publishing ideas, but in this matter Hill-Billy has the first say since the material was first promised to him. I'm going to see what he'll do with the Mts. of Madness.

From your account, the Wisconsin spring must be delightful. Well—old New England has started waking up at last, & a feathery green magic is transfiguring all the trees & shrubs, whilst the forsythias are a blaze of yellow. The damn trouble is that one has to wait so cursedly long for any decent springtide!

Outing season started again—this time, I hope, permanently. As before, the inaugurating agent was young Bob Moe, your fellow-Wisconsinite who is now living in Bridgeport. He blew in on the morning of Apr. 27, & we put in a strenuous 2 days in his Ford. Saturday we visited old Newport—seeing 2 ancient windmills; a flock of sheep with small lambkins; the home of Bishop Berkeley (1729); the Hanging Rocks where that good cleric wrote his famous "Alciphron"; the lofty cliffs; a strange rock cleft called "Purgatory" where the ocean pounds in; the house where the rebels captured Genl Prescott in 1777; & the venerable town itself . . . . with 1726 church, 1739 colony-house, 1749 library, 1760 market house, 1763 Jews' Synagogue, & private dwellings as old as 1675. Glorious hot day—82° in Providence, though not quite so good in Newport. On Sunday (temp. 80°) we went to ancient New Bedford, the quondam whaling centre, & explored the centuried waterfront. Thence to the Round Hills Estate of Col. E. H. R. Green (son of the old miser Hetty Green) in S. Dartmouth, where the old whaling barque Charles W. Morgan (built 1841) is preserved at a wharf—solidly embedded in concrete as a permanent exhibit. We went all over the vessel—which is tremendously fascinating. On the estate is also an ancient windmill moved from Rhode Island. We then explored a region—where S. Mass adjoins southeastern R.I.—which I had never seen before in my life. Splendid unspoiled countryside with rambling stone walls & idyllic white-steepled villages of the old New England type. Of the latter the best examples—Adamsville & Little Compton Commons—are both in R.I. Then back home via Tiverton (splendid marine views), Fall River, & Warren—at which latter place we stopped & ate a dinner consisting entirely of ice cream—a pint & a half (6 varieties) each. Finally back to #66—after which I guided the guest out of town & took a 4-mile rural walk before returning home. Quite a session! The next week-end—May 3–4–5—I visited a friend in the Boston zone & took 2 trips to ancient Marblehead. Cold, grey weather hampered enjoyment—though Marblehead is never uninteresting.

By the way—Hill-Billy Crawford wants me to help him find out *how book publishers get in touch with shops & have their products marketed.* Have you any idea? I'm sure I haven't! His thing would be small & paper-bound, of course.

There is a distinct possibility that I may get south after all this year—visiting Barlow in De Land after his return next month. Hope so—I long for the sight of Charleston & St. Augustine—but I can't be sure. Financial conditions will determine.

Well—don't work too hard!

Your ob^t Grandsire

H P

P.S. Bobby Barlow wishes he could get hold of the proofs of your "Place of Hawks" when you & the publishers are through with them.[3] Could such a boon be arranged for a youthful admirer?

[P.P.S.] What are *customary book royalties?* Crawford doesn't know what arrangement to make concerning the booklet he plans.

Notes

1. *HW.*
2. G. K. Chesterton, "Magic and Fantasy in Fiction," *Bookman* (London) 77 (December 1929): 161–63.
3. These proofs, sent to R. H. Barlow, are now in the HPL collection at JHL.

[392] [ALS]

June 4, 1935

Dear A W:—

Thanks for the highly interesting *Outdoors* cutting. Ants are certainly odd critters; & their achievements as herdsmen, warriors, & masters of slaves surely give them a singular cultural kinship with certain egotistical primates of the mammal kingdom! I'll have my eyes open for the new items—& many thanks for the June *Household.*[1] Hope Bobby Barlow can get his proofs. I doubt if he'd bother you about autographs except perhaps for one on the first galley or page . . . which I'm sure would be no inconvenience to you. I'll have to be getting my copy of P of H before long—& I surely hope you can dispose of the 50 allotted copies.

Thanks on Hill-Billy Crawford's behalf for the data on royalties. The other thing he wants me to find out is *how a publisher gets a book on the market**. That is, how does he get in touch with the shops, stands, & other places

*Or is it possible that no one now attempts to market material without some elaborate system of travelling agents, such as you allude to in one place?

where the book is to be sold? I suppose there are middlemen or wholesalers—but how does one get in touch with them? Hill-Billy has no source of information, & I really know nothing about the matter. Any information you can supply will be gratefully received. Of course nothing may ever come of Hill-Billy's design—but at present he has rambling notions of issuing a booklet of Moore yarns, certain science fiction items, & one of my long attempts. Glad you've had young Ludvig Prinn send "Innsmouth" along. As for the L & M pipe-dream—better have 'em send the MSS. back to me. I need copies of my stuff for lending. I am now fully convinced that no publisher would ever handle the material, & don't believe it would pay you to bring any pressure to bear. Thanks vastly, none the less, for the generous offer. Hope the tales will come back in better shape than they did from Putnam. More & more I am convinced that my days of writing are over. Incidentally—would you mind sending Bloch that pencil scrawl I sent last February? He may be able to make out part of it, & my future policy as to writing depends somewhat on a verdict regarding it. Young Ludvig Prinn may not be a top-notch critic—but I simply can't bother a really busy person with the job of deciphering the text. Probably the thing will be destroyed in the end anyhow. How are the Hodgson books coming along? Don't forget that young Duane W. Rimel, Box 100, Asotin, Wash. stands next on the list.

This has certainly been the champion springless year! I hope, however, to get down to De Land again soon—hence I may learn once more what a really good hot day is like. However—the *visual* side of spring is brilliant enough . . . vivid foliage, abundant lilacs (of which a boundless wealth can be seen from my window), & lawns of vivid emerald. Enough atmosphere to make me keenly appreciative of "Expedition to the North"—which certainly is a delectable character study. You have a knack at depicting quaint old folks, & this is one of your best specimens on the lighter side. Gus Elker is a fascinating old reprobate, & I hope to encounter him repeatedly.[2]

On May 25 I had an interesting visit from young Charles D. Hornig, erstwhile publisher of the *Fantasy Fan*. Hornig is a very pleasant & intelligent youth—reminding one slightly of Donald Wandrei, though with a vaguely quasi-Semitic turn of features. He seemed to appreciate quite keenly the archaic charm of venerable Providence—which is in some respects not unlike his own town of Elizabeth N.J. I shewed him most of the historic high spots, including the hidden churchyard on the ancient hill which I have probably described to you at one time or another. Young Sterling (who will return to N Y next month) was also on hand most of the time, making quite a convention of the event. The weather was providentially warm & sunny.

I may get started for De Land as early as June 5. Barlow gets home the 3d, & wants me to come as soon as I can make it. There are financial obstacles, but I may swing it by cutting out most intermediate stops. A day in Charleston &

one in Savannah are all I shall attempt on the Southbound trip—but returning I may manage to get a week apiece in St. Augustine & Charleston.

Did I tell you that Loveman's poems have been definitely accepted by the Caxton Printers? It's about time!

Just read the June W T—a wretchedly dull issue. The damn thing gets worse & worse! Fancy choosing some of Kline's tripe for a reprint! It amused me to see "Out of the Æons"—which I ghost-wrote—take the vote of the readers.

Well—best wishes for all your ventures.

Yr most obt hble Servt

HP

Notes

1. With AWD's "Expedition to the North."

2. Gus Elker was a recurring character in a group of stories set in Sac Prairie, WI, also featuring Great-aunt Lou and Great-uncle Joe Stoll.

[393] [ALS]

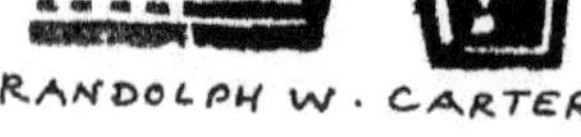

R.H. Barlow,
Box 88,
De Land, Fla.,
June 16, 1935

Dear A W:—

Observe my classy new last-week-in-spring stationery—cuts of which were designed by my artistic & enterprising host. I am especially proud of the Coffin of Lissa motif in the N.W. & S.E. corners. Other parts typify the Fungi from Yuggoth, permeated by subtle colours out of space.

Well—both of your recent communications duly reached me, together with the selection of poems for appraisal. Barlow & I have pondered well over the latter, & will endeavour to provide a series of tentative judgments—in which, of course, sheer personal bias can hardly help playing a part. I have thought it wisest to consider the whole assortment as a unit—ignoring the division into preferred & secondary poems as outlined in the MS. Amidst the crowded programme now under way down here—a programme including the clearing off of land across the lake, sundry typographical odds & ends, &c.—I fear I cannot give as detailed & analytical a set of comments as you might wish; but I'll try to record impressions as best I can. Surely there are enough other critics on the list to render my delinquencies less injurious than they might otherwise be.

To begin with, let me select the 15 poems which I like best—taken from the whole array, & preferred (so far as any preference is possible) in the order named.

1. Outposts of Nostalgia
2. The Indians Pass
3. Quail in the Deep Grass
4. Ojibway Smile
5. Wild Crab-Apple Blooming
6. Sky Bird
7. Am. Portrait 1877
8. Fox in the Winter Night
9. Do they Remember Where They Lie?
10. White are the Locusts
11. Old Men Remember
12. Door Opened
13. At Dusk the Sun
14. Hylas
15. Web of Moonlight

As for reasons for selection—it is very hard to be specific. The best poems, I feel sure, are those most rooted in your native soil & reflecting its subtle & typical symbols. "Outposts of Nostalgia" is what I call a damn good poem—something which ought to live in Wisconsin folklore. The images are clear, concrete, & apt, & the cadence of the lines is exquisite. It is a poem one wants to *chant.* I would almost suggest arranging the sentences in King-James Bible fashion, without arbitrary line-capitals . . . this being a special case demanding special treatment. Ordinarily I am an inveterate foe of e.e. cummingsism—which is palpably a sheer unmotivated affectation. Average forms of usage should be followed except in the case of poems whose structure individually verges toward metrical rhythms outside the commoner metres. When an ordinary metre—which creates certain natural expectancies—is used, those expectations ought not to be disappointed.

Other poems are notable for various reasons. "Quail in the Deep Grass" has vivid & original symbols, & "Wild Crab-Apple" gives the feel of the Wisconsin landscape admirably. "A Door Opened" has a note of genuine sadness & wistfulness which never verges on the mawkish. "White are the Locusts" is full of *pure poetry*—beauty-exaltation & depiction—as distinguished from heavy idea-conveying. The trouble with some of the more involved & ambitious poems (as I view them) is an excess of complexity, subtlety, & intellectual analysis which has a tendency to subtract from the emotional appeal & sheer beauty.

Only this point excludes from the preferred list items like "Wintered Bee", "Filled Cup". As to false rhyme (wind–limned), syllables erroneously rhymed with themselves (away-way), & occasional assonance in place of rhyme (melody-threnody)—I have discussed all this before, hence will leave a further elaboration of these points to others. I'd also recommend a greater regularity of metre in such cases as involve ostensibly regular metres. (Be Still, My Heart).

Regarding candidates for deletion—there is nothing so poor that it really needs to be cut out, but if you're anxious to reduce the bulk of the collection I might suggest the following as less important (by the standards I am using) than some of the rest:

Three Birds Flying (abrupt, obscure symbolism)
Hawks Against April (excellent, but simply not as full & effective as some others)
Doves (just a bit strained)
Dust on the Wind (heavy?)
Wintered Bee (involved, over-fancy)
Huntsman's Beacon (strained?)
Hawk on the Wind (attenuated?)[1]

Now for the classification of the poems in each section according to the individual taste of the classifier:

I.

1. Quail in Deep Grass
2. Broadwing Soaring
3. Vesper Sparrow
4. Hawks against April
5. Three Birds Flying

II.

1. Wild Crab Apple
2. Sky Bird
3. Fox in Winter Night
4. Do They Remember
5. Door Opened
6. Web of Moonlight
7. Eternity Begun
8. Night Mail
9. Filled Cup
10. Screech Owl
11. Dust on Wind
12. Be Still, My Heart

13. Doves
14. Wintered Bee
15. Huntsman's Beacon
16. Hawk on the Wind

III.

1. Outposts of Nostalgia
2. Indians Pass
3. Ojibway Smile
4. 1877
5. Old Men Remember
6. Dusk over Wisconsin
7. High Wind in Wisconsin
8. Wis. Come to Age
9. Night Portrait

IV.

1. White are the Locusts
2. At Dusk the Sun
3. Hylas Sing
4. First Scylla
5. Smoke on the Wind
6. Prairie du Chien
7. New Moon
8. We are Not Lessened
9. We are Not the First
10. Epitaph a Century After
11. Company of Ghosts
12. Violet in Autumn
13. Torrent of Spring
14. Port of Call

Well—so much for this.[2] Now to send the MS. on (after the mighty Ar-E'ch-Bei has taken a crack at it) to Mr. Lape[3]—whose judgment will, I trust, produce a series of comments more enlightening than mine. Here's hoping that the collection may, in due time, find a suitable publisher. Are L & M receptive to this idea?

Glad to hear the general news—& hope to see a Gus Elker collection some day[4] . . . . as well as the contemplated rural novel. Hope also to see "An Afternoon with Mrs. Spinnet". Barlow is grateful for the snap of Young Mussolini reviewing the Ballila, & will be additionally grateful any time you find some nice important proofs for him. Glad P of H is out—I mean to get a copy as soon as I'm recovered from my travel brokeness. Congratulations on the interest of Dodd Mead. As for that "Shadow Out of Time"—there's no real hurry, & I trust you'll manage to survive perusal. Hope it won't disappoint too badly. Barlow wants to see it, but it's promised to Bloch first. Whether I'll ever try to type it in this form is very doubtful.

Thanks vastly for "July Night"—& Ar-E'ch-Bei likewise thanks you for his copy. This is an exceptionally good instalment—with a touch of weird atmosphere which grows naturally out of the landscape. My file of these articles is getting very distinctive!

The telepathic article ought to be of considerable interest as counteracting that N.C. item. The N.C. experiments are the only reputable investigations in America which have not yielded definitely negative results. In the realm of *major* investigations, not one standard authority has the least use for the notion of non-sensory impression-transference *except* Dr. Freud *during the last 2 years.* What will develop from Freud's change of opinion yet remains to be seen. The only sensible attitude is that of complete openness to any evidence which may appear—& a rational hesitancy before deciding among conflicting presentations of apparent evidence.

Well—as you see, I'm down in my natural subtropical element. Left home June 5 & stopped nowhere except ancient Fredericksburg, Va., & my beloved CHARLESTON. The minute I struck the hot Carolina lowlands I began to feel infinitely better—really vigorous & well for the first time in 1935. Everything much the same down here, except that Bob's father & elder brother are at home. A few changes among the felidae, but High & Jack still around. Bob has a fine new pair of yellow Persians. ¶ Well—good luck with the poems! ¶ Yr obt Grandsire—

H P

Notes

1. Of these, AWD omitted only "Wintered Bee" from *HW*. The book omits more than fifteen of the other titles mentioned here and includes more than thirty-five others.

2. *HW* contains four groupings of poems: "Things of Earth"; "Maris: Beginning without End"; "Wisconsin Remembering the Twilight"; and "Sac Prairie People." HPL's suggested groupings of the poems under I–III are loosely maintained; some of the poems under IV were distributed into the first two sections, the others being dropped. There are many new poems, including "Elegy: In Providence the Spring," which AWD wrote upon HPL's death.

3. Fred Lape, publisher of *Trails: A Literary Magazine of the Outdoors.*

4. AWD's plan for such a collection was was not realized until 1996, twenty-five years after his death. See the introduction to *CM* relating to the book's delayed publication.

[394] [ALS]

% Barlow, Box 88,
De Land, Fla.,
July 15, 1935.

Dear A W:—

Yours of June 22 duly received—& thanks exceedingly for H E W's detective story. It is really clever & lifelike. H. E. may well congratulate himself on his ability to turn out saleable material of this sort.[1]

Thanks also for the new version of "Dusk Over Wisconsin"—which really seems much more powerful than the first, though that was excellent. You surely have an effective command of the spirit & pageantry of your native region!

Glad the comments on your verse collection proved helpful in conjunction with other opinions. It is only natural that verdicts from different persons (each with a separate background of tastes & associative symbols) differ widely in certain cases—but an average of 10 or 20 careful analyses is bound to suggest something reasonably absolute & definite. Hope the collection may eventually achieve publication in book form—as it probably will.

Congratulations on the new system of double novel writing! Hope both detective tales will turn out well—& that you'll soon have them sufficiently out of the way to permit of general activities.

Loring & Mussey *did* send Barlow the "P of H" proofs, & he is profoundly grateful. You'll hear from him presently—perhaps in this envelope, perhaps under separate cover. By the way—is it all right for him to use those poems of yours which he wants for a future amateur paper?

My visit continues to be extremely pleasant, & my hosts are urging me to prolong it indefinitely. This climate certainly does keep the old man pepped up! Bob's cabin across the lake is now complete, & his printing-press has been transferred thither. He is planning a number of typographical projects & is even now working on one of them. Wayne Barlow—Bob's brother—is no longer with us, since he could not get the extension of furlough from Ft. Sam Houston (where he is 2nd Lieutenant) for which he had applied. Did I tell you about the trip up Black Water Creek (a tropical river suggesting the Congo or Amazon) which we all took the Monday before Wayne's departure?

Heard from Klarkash-Ton after a long silence. His parents are better, but still very feeble. He has adopted a new hobby—sculptural carving . . . in *dinosaur bone* [a large deposit of which exists near Auburn], rhyolite, talc, & other easily workable local substances. A couple of grotesque heads sent to Ar-Ech-Bei & me are really impressive. Price & Fred Anger are about to pay their long-deferred visit to Klarkash-Ton—indeed, they may have done so ere this.

Loring & Mussey have finally made definitive the rejection which I knew they would make before I sent the damn stuff. This about finishes me with writing. No more submissions to publishers.

Marvel Tales arrived recently. What a mess! Pore Hill-Billy! About my "Shadow out of Time" MS.—Barlow is very anxious to read it—more so, I think, than Bloch—hence I think it had better come down here. It really was an imposition to expect anybody to go through it when facilities for oral elucidation were not available!

Barlow sends you his regards—& will probably insert a note of his own in this epistle before I seal it. (I mentioned this before—pardon senile repetition).

Read July W T recently—a distinctly mediocre issue, even though Hectograph Eddie does get hold of *another* old plot to run into the ground. The translation from Meyrink has a great idea—& the Moore item presents excellent dream material.

All good wishes—

Yr obt grandsire

H P

Notes

1. Possibly Howard Wandrei's "A Test Tube Full" (1 June 1935, as by Robart A. Garron), "Smot Guy" (15 June, as by H. W. Guernsey), or "Night Duty" (29 June, as by H. W. Guernsey), all in *Detective Fiction Weekly*.

[395] [ALS]

℅ Barlow, Box 88,

De Land, Florida

August 7, 1935.

Dear A W:—

Glad to hear of various successes. About the poems R H B wants—I don't think he has any on hand, but would choose from the collection you were passing around. He would want items previously unpublished.

Thanks for August nature article—graceful & well-written as usual. By coincidence (vide letter past) I read it just as a sudden rain broke over the landscape garden & sent me flying into the house . . . . & to complete the parallel, the rain soon gave place to the golden sunlight of late afternoon.

Glad you've had such an interesting letter from Two-Gun. He is certainly one of the most unusual characters in the weird circle. Klarkash-Ton is too badly harassed by the illness in his home to do much corresponding lately. His father suffered a relapse early in July, so that a proposed visit from Sultan Malik & Fred Anger had to be postponed.

Thanks for the "Shadow" MS.—which I'll send again some time if I decide to keep the story. I may be able to get opinions & typing here. Hope you'll land your nature articles in the *Monitor.*

I continue to have a great time down here, & don't know just when the return trip will come. My super-cordial hosts are urging me to remain all winter—but I'd hate to be away from my books & files that long. The effect of the climate on my health is marvellous—I feel that best I've felt since last summer. Shall probably start for home in a week.

Recently read "The Last & First Men", by W. Olaf Stapledon . . . a tremendous cosmic novel extending ahead 5,000,000,000 years & involving the successive migration of the human race to Venus & Neptune. I don't recall whether you've ever read this or not. If not, don't fail to do so. It is the only existing book about the infinite future which can be taken at all seriously.

All good wishes—

Yrs most sincerely—

H P

[P.S.] Just heard of death of Robert Nelson—author of verses in W T &c—on July 23.[1] Too bad. ¶ Saw favourable review of P of H in N.Y. Times for July 16.[2]

Notes

1. Robert Nelson, poet and correspondent of HPL, committed suicide on 22 July 1935.
2. See Edith H. Walton, "Family Skeletons," *New York Times Book Review* (16 June 1935): 7.

[396] [ALS]

St. Augustine Fla.,
August 19, 1935.

Dear A W:—

Well—I am starting north at last after a delightful & record-breaking visit. My host, too, is leaving—going to Daytona for a fortnight. Don't know how many stops on the northward route I'll be able to make—all depends on finances.

Sorry you missed the W T gang in Chicago. Reports reach me that the magazine is in rather insecure condition—deferring payment of authors from 6 to 9 months after publication. Glad you had favourable tidings at the *Outdoors* office, & hope you may become a fixture of the periodical. I read "Hawks down the Wind" with great interest, & thank you sincerely therefor. It is surely a powerful plea for your favourite winged friend, & I hope it may—printed as it will be in a magazine of wide circulation—have considerable influence.

Your contemplated change of publisher is highly interesting, & I hope you will be able to make very advantageous arrangements with the new firm. The L & M figures, as cited, are surely illuminating. However—you have reason to feel much satisfaction in being able to extract a living income from authorship at this early stage of your career—& in these times.

Barlow gave me a surprise the other day by presenting me with an accurately typed copy of "The Shadow Out of Time"! I thought he had been merely reading—not transcribing—it. Whether I shall circulate or submit the tale remains to be seen. It does not satisfy me.

Glad you own "The Last & First Men"—you'll enjoy it when you get a chance to read it. It is the only really adult book on its theme that I have ever seen. I must investigate "The Room Opposite".[1]

Am now in ancient San Agustin—revelling in ancient houses & barren streets & quaint gardens after my recent plethora of rural modernity.

Saw a *lunar rainbow*—east by the rising full moon—last Wednesday night. First time in my life.

Regards—H P

Notes

1. By F. M. Mayor.

[397] [ANS][1]

[Postmarked Charleston, S.C.,
28 August 1935]

Charleston at last! So anxious to get there that I cut out Savannah. Great to be back amidst Georgian architecture—white steeples fanlighted colonial doorways, railed double flights of steps, & so on—after nearly 3 months in a region of Hispanic background. But S.C. seems curiously *northern* after tropical Florida. Got in here 8 a.m. Monday. Leaving 8:45 p.m. Thursday—limit of my cash. Only 1-day stops in Richmond, Washington, Phila., & N.Y.—unless Wandrei lodges me in the absence of H E, who is in St. Paul. ¶ Well it has been a great trip, & I shall be glad to see my books & things & home again—and as I dread the cold of the north. ¶ Best wishes—H P

Notes

1. Front: An Old Charleston Steps, Charleston, S.C.—4.

[398] [ALS]

New York—
Septr. 7, 1935

Dear A.W.:—

Glad to hear that "Hawks down the Wind" was well received. Thanks for the Audubon address in case I decide to increase my meagre erudition on the subject. You really made a very powerful appeal.

Good luck with your Narracong & Elker work—& with "We Live in the Country" when you get at it. Glad your poetic muse is again active—"Late

Summer" strikes me as very delightful indeed, & I am sure the others must share its qualities to some extent.

W.T. certainly seems to be going to seed in many ways—which is much to be lamented in the absence of anything to fill its place. It was never anything very classical—but at least it was sometimes weird, & now & then interesting. As a hybrid combining snappy, detective, adventure, & bloody bones elements, it is quite distinctly not so hot!

Glad P of H is getting on its feet financially. The reduction of price was a wise move, since $2.00 & $2.50 is really an unreasonable figure for a novel of average length. Prices like that merely discourage buying—the reader foregoes perusal or patronises the library.

Well—I'm back in the frozen north at last, but not quite home as yet. I see that hurricanes are now devastating Florida, though places as far north as De Land & St. Augustine are not likely to suffer. I hated to leave Charleston, but had to do so in the end. Struck devastatingly cold weather in Richmond—all the energy taken out of me. However, it later grew warm, so that I arranged to enjoy many of the sights of Poe's home town. Brief pause in Washington—then a morning in Philadelphia (where I visited the botanic gardens & ancient house [1731] of the eminent naturalist John Bartram)[1] & an arrival in N.Y. in the evening . . . . Sept. 1st. I'm stopping with Donald Wandrei—using the vacant room of the family artist, who is back in St. Paul on a visit. Take my meals as usual up at Belknap's. Have seen most of the gang, & am having a very enjoyable time. Helping Loveman read the proofs of his book—which the Caxton Printers will issue next spring. Expect to return home early next week. It will surely be good to see #66 again—with my books, files, & familiar things in general.

All good wishes—

H P

Notes

1. See the discussion of the botanist John Bartram (1699–1777) in HPL's letter to Lillian D. Clark, 17–18 November 1924 (ms., JHL). HPL noted that he had visited: "the Bartram house—an eccentric, home-made stone mansion constructed by John Bartram, the botanist, with his own hands in 1731. . . . Bartram was quaintly peculiar, & his nature is reflected in the crudity & heterogeneity of his house."

[399] [ALS]

Home Again
—Septr. 20, 1935.

Dear A W:—

Upon my arrival home I found yours of Sept. 10 with interesting enclosures, as well as the previously-sent envelope of miscellaneous extracts.

Thanks in abundance for all of these. The cuttings will all go into my files. Your October article echoes some of my own impressions regarding the nocturnal landscape. Glad to see the story by H.E.—he surely has power in these brief, "hard boiled" narratives. The article on changing presentations of the spectral in fiction is really significant—& I was very glad to learn more about Leonard Cline.[1] The Icelandic article by Eddison[2] has a special appeal to me, since the far northern isle has always captivated my imagination . . . . perhaps because of my early reading of Verne's "Journey to the Centre of the Earth." Again let me thank you for this generous array of material.

Hope the visit from H E was pleasant. Sorry I couldn't see him in N Y—though it was his absence which gave me my free lodging at the Wandrei mansion! My visit was surely pleasant, as I said in my preceding note. Before I left I had seen virtually all the gang. Home Sept. 14 after a chilly coach ride. It was surely good to see ancient Providence again—though I found a stupefying mountain of letters, packages, piled-up periodicals, & other responsibilities awaiting me.

Interested to hear of the progress of your work, & hope both novels will eventually assume a form satisfactory both to you & to the publishers. Book prices form an interesting subject. Whatever the theory may be, the average citizen will be less & less disposed to pay $2.00 or more as time passes. If he can't get books at a lower figure he will either use the public libraries or do without.

Thanks for the magazine tips—hope I'll have the energy to follow them up. Yes—Two-Gun is surely turning from weirdness to sheer adventure these days. Haven't read much of the Sept. W.T.—but notice that one writer speaks of New Orleans as a fully existing city (cathedral & all!) in *1720,* whereas the site was scarcely cleared & marked out at that date.[3] Wright is certainly making a mistake in devoting so much space to detective & adventure fiction—though he seems little disposed to change that policy.

Too bad Mrs. Gilman bumped herself off[4]—I was told of it in N Y, though I haven't reached Aug. 17 as yet in my reading-up of back newspapers. My mother knew her well—since as plain Charlotte Perkins she used to be governess in the home of some friends of ours. Later her first husband was the Providence artist Stetson.[5] She always had an affected, eccentric streak of self-conscious intellectuality. Well—may she rest in peace! As for poor Huey—I regret that he had to shuffle off in so violent a way.[6] He was not without redeeming features, & might have formed a useful irritant in the complex civic struggles of the coming years. On the other hand he might have done harm—no one can tell. In any case the manner of his eradication is not to be commended.

At the present moment I'm about to hop off on a brief trip to Boston—spending the week-end with my friend Cole, & accompanying him on a motor trip into the sinister "Dunwich" country—that is, the region around Wilbraham, Mass. After my long journey this short jaunt will not be without an element of anticlimax! There is a very vague possibility that Cook may get down from Sunapee & join us.

All good wishes—

Yr most obt h^ble^ Servt

H P

Notes

1. Unidentified.

2. See letter 63n1.

3. "One Chance" by Ethel Helene Cohen.

4. Charlotte Perkins Gilman, who had cancer, committed suicide on 17 August by an overdose of chloroform.

5. Charles Warren Stetson (1858–1911).

6. Huey Pierce Long, Jr. (1893–1935), was Democratic governor of Louisiana from 1928 to 1932 and U.S. senator from 1932 to 1935, noted for his radical populist policies. He was assassinated on 8 September.

[400] [ALS]

Octr. 6, 1935

Dear A W:—

Yrs. of Sept. 24 duly recd—& many thanks for "Dusk over Wisconsin" (which I have seen & liked before) & the clever Howard Wandrei story.[1] Hope you had a pleasant visit from the artist-pulpist. Yes—Donald mentioned his marriage,[2] which I trust may prove successful & permanent. Young Brobst has also essayed matrimony—embarking simultaneously on that & a special course at Brown.

Good luck with the new books. Your series of Sauk City historical novels surely promises to be important, & I'm glad to hear that you are taking pains with the period colour. Nothing is more annoying than a tale of the past which fails to ring true. With their firm grounding in an actual scene, these novels ought to form invaluable regional documents.

Hope Wright takes "Death Holds the Post". W T is surely petering out—the Sept. issue having nothing worth much except "Vulthoom".

Curious about book prices—I know *I* won't pay 2 bucks or more a for a new book, but evidently the crowd feel differently!

As for Huey—the good he might have done is as an irritant or threat. It seems clear that the reactionary element will yield ground only under intimidation or fear, so that progress is chiefly to be secured by keeping them scared. Otherwise they hoodwink the rabble, keep themselves in power—& finally produce such misery that a violent revolution blows everything up.

Revolutions form a bad means of establishing improvements, so that judicious threats remain the sole civilised way of remodelling obsolescent institutions. Labour unions, radical agitations, bonus marches, hunger riots—these & things like them are necessary to coerce the capitalists into yielding some measure of their strangle hold. And of all such forces, what was more potent than Huey? To match his propaganda many liberal measures were enacted by the last congress. Will such happen again? True, there was the latent peril that he might have swept things his own way—but that hardly seems very strong. And if he had, he would scarcely have been as utter a disaster as anything a revolution might bring. I think fascism—certain forms of it—would probably be preferable to most of the forms which communism could take. One cannot be dogmatic on that point, but it seems to me likely. Fascism can hardly be as culturally destructive as a bigoted fanaticism which inverts values & exalts manual brawn at the expense of skill & taste. An ideal—or at least practicable—form of government might well stand midway between the two principles. What certainly cannot go on for ever is the pretence of democracy—which means no more than a false front, clumsy waste, & hidden forces behind the scenes. Better a Hitler who openly dictates than a body of tradesmen who conceal their equally arbitrary rule beneath a mask of "individualism", "free opportunity", & "constitutionalism".

Sept. 20–23d inclusive I visited E. H. Cole in the Boston zone & took several rural side-trips in his Chevrolet. Friday we explored Nahant & ancient Marblehead, & Saturday we went on a funereal pilgrimage to the remote & brooding "Dunwich" region—to sprinkle the ashes of a deceased old lady on her native soil in accordance with her lifelong wish.[3] Splendid mountain scenery, & incipiently turning leaves. Sunday we spent on Cape Cod, where the greener foliage & gentler topography gave rise to a wholly different landscape. Thus despite my long absence I ended the summer with a basically representative array of New England scenery. It is barely possible that I shall have two more trips before winter sets in—one to New Haven with my aunt Oct. 8, & later accompanying the Coles over the Mohawk Trail, & perhaps a little way into Vermont, when the autumn foliage is at its height. But this latter is wholly tentative.

You'll be sorry to hear that Clark Ashton Smith's mother died on Sept. 9. It was not unexpected, but none the less a blow for all that. Must be a great setback for Klarkash-Ton's father, who is very feeble & well along in years.[4] This parental illness has been a great strain on C A S for nearly 2 years.

October W T a trifle better than Septr. Moore & Flanders yarns good—Binder & Russell mediocre. Glad to see the Machen reprint—a tale wholly new to me, albeit a minor one. I wonder what collection it comes from?[5]

All good wishes—

Yr obt Servt

H P

P.S. I see Schorer's book got quite a review in the Times, & that it's advertised quite regularly. Bet you wrote a good bit of it![6]

Notes

1. Possibly Howard Wandrei's "Button, Button" (*Dectective Fiction Weekly*, 7 September 1935), as by H. W. Guernsey.

2. Howard Wandrei married Connie Colestock on 24 September 1935 in New York.

3. Jennie E. T. Dowe (d. 1919), amateur journalist and mother of Edith Miniter.

4. CAS's mother, Fannie (Gaylord) Smith, died 9 September 1935 at the age of 85. His father, Timeus Smith, died 26 December 1937 at the age of 82.

5. Machen's "The Lost Child" (1890; *WT*, October 1935) was included in Vincent Starrett's collection of Machen miscellany, *The Shining Pyramid* (1923; not identical to *The Shining Pyramid* [1925] owned by HPL).

6. Mark Schorer, *A House Too Old* (1935). See Harold Strauss, "The Pioneer Strain," *New York Times Book Review* (8 September 1935): 7. AWD claimed that Schorer had plagiarized his work in the novel. See Peter Ruber, *Arkham's Masters of Horror*, pp. 425–27.

[401] [ALS]

Ancient Providentium—
8 days before All-Hallows
[23 October 1935]

Dear A W:—

Your researches into early Sac Prairie history must be fascinating indeed—& I am glad that local attics still harbour so much relevant material.[1] Has the town an historical society? It would be a pity to have all this traditional accumulation dispersed through the indifference of later generations. If there isn't a museum already, there certainly ought to be one.

Glad there will be a d'Erlette-Utpatel combination in a future W T. I didn't know of any specific trouble in the aesthetic "family". An author & illustrator certainly ought to coöperate on perfectly equal terms, with no imposition or duplicity on either side.

Well, well—so you've read the "Shadow" after all! I fear Barlow's text had many errors, some of which greatly misrepresent my style—since I recall doing quite a bit of correction on my copy. It is a wonder he could decipher that pencil-scrawled MS. at all! Glad you like the thing, & appreciate the encouraging remarks you derive from it. Yes—I've noticed the tendency of my later attempts to divide into groups, though I don't know how practicable the consolidation of group-members would be. Whether future experimentation will resemble either of the recent types remains to be seen. When I get time I may try to write out a plot (Arkham stuff) which I've had in my head for a couple of years. The other day I broke my own recent anti-collaboration rule to the extent of fixing up a yarn for naive, honest old Bill Lumley, who longs to get some of his fiction into print.[2] I was going to divide the philanthropy by asking Barlow to type it, when to my disgust I realised that my MS. was too illegible for anyone but myself to read! More work for Grandpa! Well—I typed the damn thing (whose title, ironically enough, is "The Diary of Alonzo *Typer*"!) & hope old Bill will be satisfied. I'd like to see the quaint old cuss land something with Wright—though I doubt if this story will go over. More likely it will get to Hill Billy for *Marvel Tales.*

No—*I* hadn't mentioned "He Arrived At Dusk"[3] to you, but am very interested by your description of it. I must investigate Ashby & all his work.

Sorry Schorer's novel has so many defects—but anyhow, he got it into print, which is more than most aspirants can do! Possibly later work will exhibit more accuracy & maturity. However—the unauthorised use of your material surely admits of no excuse. Thanks for the November nature article—"Woodcock"—which like the others is very pleasing. You have surely became a fixture in *Outdoors!*

Klarkash-Ton has certainly had a hard time—& the continued feebleness of his father forms a formidable burden still. I wonder that he can produce any work under such discouraging circumstances! Price, at last accounts, was just about to start on a tour including Mexico & a visit with Two-Gun Bob. And incidentally, did I mention that masterly pseudo-history of the prehistoric world of Conan (Aquilonia, Koth, Nemedia, &c) which Two-Gun has prepared for *The Phantagraph*?[4]

Had an interesting trip to New Haven with my aunt Oct. 8. Sunny day, delightful ride through autumnal Connecticut countryside, & 7½ hrs. for exploration while my aunt visited a friend. New Haven is not as rich in colonial antiquities as Providence, but has a peculiar charm of its own. Streets are broad & well-kept, & in the residential districts (some of which involve hills & fine views) there are endless stately mansions a century old, with generous grounds & gardens, & an almost continuous overarching canopy of great elms. I visited ancient Connecticut Hall (1752—where Nathan Hale roomed at Yale), old Centre Church (1842—with an interesting crypt of old graves), the Pierpont house (1767), the historical, art, & natural history museums, the botanic gardens, & other points of interest.

Most impressive of all, perhaps, were the great *new* quadrangles of Yale University—each an absolutely faithful reproduction of old-time architecture & atmosphere, & forming a self-contained little world in itself. The Gothic courtyards transport one in fancy to mediaeval Oxford or Cambridge—spires, oriels, pointed arches, mullioned windows, arcades with groined roofs, climbing ivy, sundials, lawns, gardens, vine-clad walls & flagstoned walks—everything to give the young occupants that massed impression of their accumulated cultural heritage which they might obtain in Old England itself. To stroll through these quadrangles in the golden afternoon sunlight; at dusk, when the lights in the diamond-paned casements flicker up one by one; or in the beams of a mellow

Hunter's Moon; is to walk bodily into an enchanted region of dream. Nor are the Georgian quadrangles less glamourous—each being a magical summoning-up of the world of 2 centuries ago. I wandered for hours through this limitless labyrinth of unexpected Elder microcosms, & mourned the lack of further time. Certainly, I must visit New Haven again, since many of its treasures would require weeks for proper inspection & appreciation.

But even this New Haven trip did not quite end my 1935 outings. Last Wednesday morning at 6 my friend Loveman blew into town, & after a session at 66 we both started out for Boston to absorb books, museums, & antiquities. Stayed 3 days & took in quite a few things, but had no time to look up Cole or anybody else in the group. Back Friday afternoon—looked over local bookstalls & chatted at #66. In the evening I saw the guest off on the N.Y. boat.

I will at once—in response to your postcard request—look up the Sunday Journal for June 30, & hope I can find one still available. I read & cut out the review, but probably sent it to somebody—I can't remember, since I did so many things in a hurry last month when reading up all the papers since June 5th!

Have you seen young Barlow's *Dragon-Fly,* containing your lines "First Scylla"? It seems to me one of the best of the recent amateur papers, notwithstanding the editor's inexperience in typography. Hope it will prove a factor in raising N.A.P.A. standards. Edkins—whose work is so amply represented—is a fine old fellow of *68* . . . but with a peculiarly youthful temperament.[5]

Well—"Sign of Fear" duly arrived, & I must thank you exceedingly for the pleasure its reading afforded. It surely makes a neat & tasteful appearance, & nobly carries on the Judge Peck tradition. Altogether, I really believe it is your best detective product thus far. It has the substance & solidity of "The Man on All Fours" without the melodramatic overcolouring of the latter, while it equals "Three Who Died" in the rationality of the problem. The atmosphere is unusually convincing for a popular detective novel, & there is never a lack of interest. Indeed, the suspense occasioned by the suggestions of Inca background & elder signs wears remarkably well. The secret of the murderer—or would-be murderer—is guarded better than in any of the other novels . . . though amply prepared for. I had my suspicions, but could not be absolutely certain till the very brink of the revelation.

Guessing was curious. On p. 53 your emphasis on powder made me think that the puff might have held some poison. Deaths from sheer fright are rare. On p. 91 the element of *powder* again attracted notice—the indicated *exchange* of boxes suggesting that Elka's death might have been a mistake—with Cornelius as the really intended victim. Around 106–112 I became impressed with the asthmatic element, & felt sure that some asthmatic irritant in the powder was the poison. On p. 130 I had my first really definite suspicion of Elka. That sign on her blotter, indicating that the card she held was written in her room with her pen & ink, seemed very significant. There was no envelope, either. Was it not likely that, instead of *receiving* the card, she was getting ready to *deliver* it? Were there *two* streams of killing at work? At this point I thought of her unlikeable qualities, & of her indicated interest in Christopher's explorations & delvings—the latter point suggesting a possible reason for the Inca background of the hounding postals. Was she trying to get the brothers together & kill them? Pages 150 & 151 confirmed & revived this suspicion tremendously. *Elka had sent for her nephew John.* This was conclusive. But weren't Christopher & Felix also sent for? If the object was a sinister family roundup, was not Elka the obvious agent? My suspicion increased to a dominant theory (always tentative, though, in recognition of the fact that you might have a trick ending up your sleeve) on p. 179, when it was brought out *that the last threatening card was sent on the very last day Elka was alive.* This, I reflected, could be no mere coincidence! The sender was obviously in the house. What could have stopped the mailings save death? And who had died? On p. 195 the powder & pollen element strongly impressed me. I thought again of the substitution referred to on p. 91. My impression was fortified by pages 199–200, where the connexion of the shaving & powdering with Christopher's seizures is brought out. Meanwhile I began to be looking for evidence of who was at the house when the note to Felix was typed on Cornelius' machine. Page 212 gave a hint . . . among others, *Elka* was there! A similar vigil regarding the accessibility of the Bingham book was rewarded on p. 238. Among others, *Elka* was there when Cornelius had the volume. *And the notes based on it stopped when she died* . . . . the last one written at her desk . . . . After that it would have taken quite a trick to get my suspicions elsewhere—& surely enough, pp. 257–9 provided the clincher. But I was never *sure* till the actual revelation came. Damn clever stuff!

I don't know of any major weak spots which call for comment. At one time I thought the early conversation of the brothers might well be a bit more idiomatic, but that may have been a mere fleeting impression. And I don't think the device of having a death during the detective's presence is as yet hackneyed enough to be censured. Regarding the allusion to *whitening hair* on p. 67—I suppose you know that hair *cannot* whiten *in a single night.* That would involve the expulsion of the pigment from the whole length of the hairs. What *can* happen is the destruction of the sources of pigment, so that the hair *will grow out white.*

By the way—has the symbol you mention any actual mythological or folklore background (I confess I never heard of it), or is it an invention of yours? I must point out one definite mistake in your description. According to your indication (p. 116, sustained by jacket design), the "sign" is a cross surmounted by a *circumflex accent mark* [^]—yet you speak of it as a cross with a *cedilla* [̧ . . . used under a *c* (=ç) to indicate soft value] over it. *By no possible usage or liberty* can a *circumflex* be called a *cedilla.* ¶ Well—thanks & congratulations! It's a fine book, & I enjoyed it! ¶ Your obt Grandsire

H P

[Enclosure][6]

Prov. Sunday Journal—June 30, 1935

PLACE OF HAWKS
By August W. Derleth. Illustrated with wood engravings by George Barford. Hew York: Loring & Mussey. Pp. 250. $2.50.

Some day soon, as our scholars & critics keep up their lively & valuable researches into the matter of America & its uncounted ways of expression, we may get further information on America as a breeding-place for the strange & eccentric individual. Without special knowledge, anyone can start a list of evidence, beginning with your neighbourhood, your home town, & certainly including a few of the more famous rara avis [sic] in our national rolls. The accumulated names to be offered by our company of reminiscent folk will be sure to indicate the endless procession of eccentrics that march gaily through our past & present.

And a categorical study of this phase of democratic expression will be incomplete without a glance at many an American book of fiction, notably those of recent years—those in which our Faulkners, Caldwells, & (in poetry) a Jeffers, Masters, & Robinson have recorded their less conventional kind. Of this sort belong the novelettes gathered into August Derleth's first serious book (his earlier ones have been mystery potboilers). These four stories of middle western families are all concerned with the darker, madder ways of man.

They are bound together by the old doctor, grandfather of the narrator, who continued his weekly visits among his friends & farmer patients around Sac Prairie. The Grells are a family who still speak to their dead & set places at table for them, yet will not countenance young Linda's departure for marriage. The Faraways [sic] are cursed with hate & madness. Madness, too, afflicts the old lady in the Ortell family, & finally, the old maids at the Pierneau house live in the past & wish violently for a continuation of their line, not knowing his nephew to be cursed with mixed blood.

Throughout the four tales a brooding, stormy atmosphere is never relieved. Idiot boys prowl the corridors, hawks circle about the chimneys, old ladies mutter in dusky corners, & death is usually vengeful & harsh. That Mr. Derleth sustains some of these attempts is certain, but the entire impression of his "Place of Hawks" is a tentative one. His writing is often awkward & stiff, & the unmitigated similarity of mood & plot is a bit too heavy. Less able than a Faulkner or a Jeffers, Mr. Derleth's story-telling is at times quite as absurd as theirs. He has talent for characterisation & atmosphere, & when he lays both on a little less thickly, & leavens his style with more natural conversation, he may very well write a noteworthy fiction. At present he is in a promising 'prentice stage.

——W.T.S.

Have just been down to the Journal office. No copies of June 30 remaining, but I copied the review from the file. W.T.S. is Winfield Townley Scott,[7] a brilliant young poet who graduated from Brown about 5 years ago. He comes from Haverhill, Mass., & lives in a colonial house in a quaint lane on the ancient hill about half a mile south of #66. I don't know him personally. The present review seems to me just a little severe—especially from a chap who doesn't seem to know what the plural of *rara avis* is!

Notes

1. See HPL to Lee M. White, Jr., 20 December 1935: "He [AWD] will embark on a series of historical novels dealing with his native Wisconsin background. In preparation for this series he is conducting a course of antiquarian research which puts me to shame. He is going exhaustively over all the old records, newspapers, & diaries he can find in local files, libraries, & attics, & is hiring people to copy headlines & topics from the Milwaukee papers of 50 or 75 years ago. He means to know those times as intimately as if he had lived in them—& the result will be apparent when he comes to write the novels" (*Lovecraft Annual* No. 1 [2007]: 47).

2. William Lumley, "The Diary of Alonzo Typer." AWD was instrumental in securing publication of the story in *WT* following HPL's death.

3. By Rubie Constance Ashby.

4. REH, "The Hyborian Age," *Phantagraph,* February, August, October–November 1936. Published as a pamphlet (with an "Introduction" by HPL [= letter to Donald A. Wollheim, c. September 1935]) Los Angeles: LANY Cooperative Publications, 1938.

5. Ernest A. Edkins, "Fragments of a Letter to a Young Poet" and "Bizarres," *Dragon-Fly* 1, No. 1 (15 October 1935).

6. HPL copied out the review in longhand.

7. Winfield Townley Scott (1910–1968), whose essay "His Own Most Fantastic Creation" (1944) was the first major biographical piece on HPL.

[402] [ALS]

Citadel of Leng—
Nov. 10, 1935

Dear A W:—

Congratulations on the new Scribnerian prospects! It looks like a sure thing, & the opening undoubtedly forms a mighty step forward. The editor's letter shews every sign of acuteness & sober judgment, & I fancy you are now steadily advancing along that road of solid achievement & recognition which many believed from the first to be yours. Glad the novel is so well advanced—& I trust that you will for the present subordinate all other matters to the task of its completion. Of an ultimate favourable decision by Scribner's, one can entertain no serious doubt. Hope you'll land the Guggenheim Fellowship in course of time,[1] though it is certainly no easy matter. Another friend of mine (also from Wisconsin, as coincidence would have it) quite narrowly missed this boon some 2 or 3 years ago. Lack of success ought not to cause too great a disappointment. For my part, I have a double motive in hoping you get it, if this prize will cause you to honour ancient Providence with a visit! Here's hoping!

Speaking of Providence, I enclose a pair of cuttings which may be of interest. As you see, your old-time collaborator has made quite a hit with the *Journal* reviewer! I don't know the identity of "E.K.B.", though the initials quite frequently appear.[2]

Had some good news the other day from young Schwartz, to whom—at his eloquent solicitation—I last summer entrusted the "Mts. of Madness" MS. as a mere matter of unhoping routine. Now this brisk little business man staggers me by announcing that *Astounding Stories* has *accepted* the damn'd thing! At last—after 4½ years! If the information turns out to be correct, I shall be the material gainer of some 315 iron men after the deduction of Leedle Shoolie's 10% commission. I shall be glad to see this item (so contemptuously rejected by Wright) in print at last, & hope Street & Smith won't mess it up too badly. I am now (one having been lost) without any typed copy. This tale represents the most serious work I have attempted, & its prior rejection was a very discouraging influence.

Tragic news—Belknap's aunt was instantly killed in a motor accident near Miami Oct. 20.[3] Barlow has just sent Sonny the book of the latter's poems which we printed last summer as a surprise for the child.[4] F B is deeply grateful, though there is a certain aura of sadness in the coming of this gift from Florida at such a moment.

Turning to good news—a fresh piece since I began this epistle. Wandrei surreptitiously submitted my "Shadow Out of Time" to *Astounding*, & they *accepted that also!* Just got a cheque for $280.00. Holy Yuggoth, but that makes a winning streak! I have no illusions, however, about its continuance.

Nov. W.T. is distinctly above the average. Glad to see your clever "Mr. Berbeck." "The Way Home", by Paul Frederick Stern, has a remarkable strength in mood & atmosphere. A new writer to me[5]—but he'll be well worth watching. I like Sultan Malik's "Hand of Wrath" better than any of his other recent things—& good old Two-Gun is his usual sanguinary & spirited self in "Zamboula."

Those lousy bastards Loring & Mussey returned my MSS. in rotten shape—& upon examining them I find the most important item of all missing—the copy of *The National Amateur* for May, 1923, containing "Hypnos". This issue may not be replaceable, yet was one of the indispensable features of my amateur collection—issued during my presidential year & containing reports & other items of the keenest individual interest to me. I've written Mussey about it, & urged that a careful search be made—but no reply thus far. I shall, I suppose, have to advertise among the amateurs for another copy. But damn those rascals at the *other* #66—even if they did kindly soften the shock of rejection & loss with a gratuitous copy of Edwin Valentine Mitchell's "Art of Authorship"!

Just finished a new story—"The Haunter of the Dark"—though I'm not sure it's worth typing. Acting on the suggestion of someone in the Eyrie, I dedicated it to young Bloch. I'm killing him off in return for his delightful disposal of Grandpa in the "Shambler". He left the old gentleman spattered all over the room, but I leave him in neater shape—as a body sitting rigidly at a desk & gazing out a west window, with an expression of unutterable fear on the twisted features. The scene is in Providence, & the abode of the victim is #66—indeed, I've described the place a bit.[6]

Well—I trust all flourishes as usual around Sac Prairie. Am watching Journal & NY Times for reviews of Sign of Fear. ¶ Blessings—Yr obt Grandsire H P

Notes

1. AWD did in fact eventually receive a Guggenheim fellowship in 1938. He used the money awarded him to have his collection of newspaper comics bound.

2. "E. K. B." reviewed Schorer's *A House Too Old* in the *Providence Sunday Journal* 51, No. 17 (27 October 1935): sec. 6, p. 8.

3. Mrs. William B. Symmes, whose travel book, *Old World Footprints* (Athol, MA: W. Paul Cook [Recluse Press], 1928), contains a preface ghostwritten by HPL for FBL.

4. FBL's *The Goblin Tower* was a small collection of poetry published by RHB. HPL helped set the type when he visited RHB in the summer of 1935. See *SL* 5.182, 216, 218, 222.

5. Not a new writer to *WT* at all; "Stern" was a pseudonym of Paul [Frederick] Ernst (1899–1985), a regular contributor.

6. Robert Bloch, "The Shambler from the Stars," *WT* (September 1935). The story features HPL as a character. B. M. Reynolds wrote in "The Eyrie": "Robert Bloch deserves plenty of praise for *The Shambler from the Stars*. Now why doesn't Mr. Lovecraft return the compliment, and dedicate a story to the author?" (*WT* [November 1935]: 652). In "The Haunter of the Dark," the main character Robert Blake (= Robert Bloch) dies under mysterious circumstances. The story is "Dedicated to Robert Bloch." Bloch wrote yet another sequel, "Notebook Found in a Deserted House," *WT* (May 1951).

[403] [ALS]

Dec. 4—1935

Dear A W:—

Commiserations on the "Summer Night" tragedy! Yuggoth, but the typing of a quarter of a novel must have cost you a pretty penny! And yet, if you're able to utilise all your time in creative—& potentially remunerative—work, it will of course pay to have the typing done outside. The time &

energy saved will be worth more to you than the sum you pay the typist. I would certainly have to make some sort of a deal with a cheap typist (paying in revisory work, or something like that) if I were turning work out continuously. I tackled "The Haunter of the Dark" at last—& after wrestling with its 26 pages was just about all in! Incidentally, I'm circulating both carbons—one to reach you very shortly (if it hasn't come already) from Bloch. The thing doesn't amount to much, but I hope it won't bore you too badly. Haven't tried it on anything yet. It couldn't possibly go in *Astounding*, being an out-&-out *weird tale* & nothing else but. I'm circulating two carbons—the other one having gone to Klarkash-Ton, Sultan Malik, Two-Gun, & the far westerners generally. And this reminds me—I think I'll add *three* names to the circulation list of your copy, & fancy I'd better insert them right after yours. Will you, therefore, inscribe between the d'Erlette crest & the Searight shield the following addenda?

> Mrs. Natalie H. Wooley, 20 N. Early St., Rosedale, Kansas
> Richard Ely Morse, 40 Princeton Ave., Princeton, N.J.
> Bernard Dwyer, C.C.C. Camp 25, Peekskill, N.Y.

After that, Searight & all the rest as given. No hurry, but just shoot along to Mrs. Wooley when you're through with the thing. You'll notice good old Bill Lumley's name on the list. I presume you've been in touch with this quaint & appealing child of nature (who claims to be an old sailor who has witnessed incredible wonders in all parts of the world, & to have studied works of elder wisdom far stranger than your *Cultes des Goules* or my *Necronomicon*), whose admiration for your work is so vast. Well—I recently doctored up a story for Old Bill, & it has actually sold to Wright for 70 bucks! Iä! Shub-Niggurath! The Goat With a Thousand Young! Farny saw traces of Grandpa's style in the thing, & asked Old Bill about it—the latter responding with the facts literally stated. I shall let Bill keep all of his cheque (if he ever gets it), for he needs encouragement. This is his first story to be accepted by any periodical, professional or otherwise.

Yes—the Astounding acceptances (take that phrase either way!) of my tales certainly have encouraged the old man quite a bit! We shall see what happens to future attempts. Hope the readers won't pan these two novelettes too violently![1]

Glad to hear of progress on "Still is the Summer Night"—which I feel certain will land successfully. Your intensive & extensive researches into bygone folkways surely lacks nothing in thoroughness! I am reminded of a pastime in which I indulge sometimes with my aunt's aid—imagining the calendar turned back to 1898 or 1900 or 1902 or so, & conversing as one naturally would in that period . . . mentioning the shops, plays, songs, car lines, news, sights, surroundings, & daily activities then flourishing, & excluding all anachronistic idioms & allusions. When your series gets well under way, you won't leave much room for the mistake-hunters! Those old pictures must have proved interesting. I have a lot of daguerreotypes of forbears back to the 40's, & one oil painting earlier than that. Nobody among my revered progenitors was as rotten-looking as I am, yet lots of them—especially in the Phillips-Whipple-Mathewson line—had isolated features (especially around the eyes) startlingly like mine![2] Juggled genes certainly take picturesque rearrangements as they rattle down the ages! I am a sort of parody or caricature, facially, of my mother & maternal uncle.

Glad to hear of the popularity of Gus Elker in important circles, & of your comfortably mounting income. About that May '23 N.A.—don't go to any extraordinary inconvenience about it, since I might be able to get one from some amateur old-timer by advertising in a N.A.P.A. paper. Sorry to hear of your grandmother's illness, & hope it may not be as grave as you fear. I haven't had a grandparent since 1904.

Benedictions—

H P

Notes

1. Some readers objected to the appearance of these two "horror" stories in what was ostensibly a scientifiction magazine, but many did not.

2. As in "The Shadow over Innsmouth," in which the narrator is said to have the "Marsh eyes."

[404] [ALS]

Dec. 27, 1935

Dear A W:—

Glad the "Haunter" didn't put you to sleep. I shall probably let Satrap Pharnabazus have a look at it later on. All right about the added names—I sent the list to young Melmoth, who will duly insert.

Glad "Summer Night" is on its way. With your scale of production, it certainly pays to have typing done by another. Hope the Scribner editor will like the MS., & not demand too many changes. Congratulations on the acceptance of "They Shall Rise". I read your Gus Elker story in the *Atlantic* with much interest & appreciation. It is extremely sprightly & clever, & I hope the *Atlantic* will take many more of the series. The financial outlook surely is encouraging for you, & I hope that *Country Gentleman* deal will go through without a hitch.

Glad "Sign of Fear" is getting good notices. It really seems to be your best detective effort so far, & there is an originality not often found in material of this type.

Thanks for the three tales by H E.[1] He surely has unlimited skill in this medium, & manages to suit his pulp audiences without descending to the banal depths of most deteckatiff magazinists. He puts a certain tough reality into his yarns which Donald doesn't seem to get, & some day this faculty ought to start him up the ladder. It would be curious, in view of his artistic achievements, if he were to be recognised literarily before he is pictorially!

Just got something amusing from Pharnabazus—copy of "Midsummer Night's Dream" in format of pulp magazine with illustrations, announced as the first volume of "Wright's Shakespeare Library".[2] Bless me, but the old boy is going classic! 35¢ per copy. I'd invest if there weren't from 4 to 6 sets of the Bard in the house—counting the miscellany in the attic. But I have thanked Farny for the sample. He points out some amusing slips in the text—& one absent-minded note in which he called a centaur a *man with a horse's head!*

Young Sterling has been in town during the holidays, & has discussed all sorts of topics from science-fiction up. On Sunday I expect to depart on a week's visit to Little Belknap—likewise beholding Young Melmoth, H.E., old Jim Morton, Fra Samuelus, & others of the perennial group. Hope the cold weather lets up—it has been unbearable hereabouts during the last few days.

Hope you had a pleasant Yule. Once more my aunt & I had a tree, & a semicircle of modest gifts to pile around it. Among the gifts was a box of catnip for our neighbour John Perkins, who came over to chew it & roll in it. He is a monstrous mountain of black fur now—& will be a year old in mid-February.

Every good wish for a Happy New Year—

Yr most obt h^ble^ Servt

—H P

Notes

1. Possibly Howard Wandrei's "So Long, Gus!" (28 September 1935), "No Personal Danger" (19 October 1935), and "No Parking" (30 November 1935), all as by H. W. Guernsey, in *Detective Fiction Weekly*.

2. Only this volume (illustrated by Virgil Finlay) was published.

1936

[405] [ALS]

Jany. 16, 1936

Dear A W:—

Yrs. of the 1st was forwarded to me during my recent visit to Belknap. And now, after my return, I have received your card of the 9th & the delightful duo of books—for which I can scarcely express my thanks to an adequate degree! Needless to say, I am overjoyed at having a copy of "Place of Hawks"—whose parts, long familiar to me in MS., I shall take the keenest pleasure in re-reading collectively. The format & illustrations are highly prepossessing—as well becomes a volume of such literary quality. Abundant congratulations on this debut in the field of serious book-authorship! The nightmare anthology looks very alluring, & I fancy I shall derive more than one entertaining shudder from its pages. The name of Blackwood arouses high expectations despite Algy's occasional unevenness.[1] Again, pray accept my profoundest & sincerest thanks!

Thanks, too, for the H E story.[2] It surely is clever, & attests the author's power to suit pulp audiences without descending to the depths of extravagant hokum. And so Shiel has a new non-weird book out?[3] He is indeed a versatile, if uneven, cuss—& seems to be prolonging his authorship far down the avenue of years.

Glad you've had the Herm for review.[4] If the text is hashed up, the blame is partly mine—for I read the proofs 3 times last September. I saw a copy during my recent visit, & think it evokes a very good appearance. Hope you & your brother-reviewers will be favourably impressed. I think there's some damned good stuff in it. Wish S L would resume his poetical pursuits—perhaps a very cordial reception of this volume would encourage him to do so.

About the "Haunter"—I may want to let an amateur journal use it before trying it on Wright. He never used to mind the prior publication of things in those sheets of negligible circulation. For years amateurdom has been unable to handle specimens of that length, but just now a quantitative revival has led to a new demand for full-sized MSS.

My best wishes attend "Still is the Summer Night"—& I trust that all may go well with its successor. Glad you've finished "Fire in the Hollow", & hope eventually to see the revised & rearranged "Hawk on the Wind" MS. Your year's record of accomplishment attests a bewilderingly great fund of energy—especially in view of the quality of the material. Glad to see a good Utpatel illustration on the "Satin Mask"—a tale I read in MS. years ago.

My N.Y. visit was very pleasant—including the glimpses of most of the old gang, & of some new figures (Arthur J. Burks, Otto [of "Eando"] Binder, Donald Wollheim, &c.) as well. Saw good old Seabury Quinn for the first time since 1931. Attended several gatherings, including a dinner of that pulpist organisation "The American Fiction Guild". Of course Long, the Wandrei boys, Talman, little Sterling, Leeds, Kleiner, Loveman, Morton, &c. were on hand. Sorry not to get hold of Koenig & Hornig.

On two occasions—once with Sonny Belknap & again with Sonny & Young Melmoth—I visited the new Hayden Planetarium of the Am. Museum, & found it a highly impressive device. It consists of a domed round building of 2 storeys. On the lower floor is a circular hall whose ceiling is a gigantic orrery—shewing the planets revolving around the sun at their proper relative speeds. Above it is another circular hall whose roof is the great dome, & whose edge is made to represent the horizon of N.Y. as seen from Central Park. In the centre of this upper hall is a curious projection (which looks like an Hamiltonian "space ship" or like one of the armoured Martians in "The War of the Worlds") which casts on the concave dome a perfect image of the sky—capable of duplicating the outward apparent motions of the celestial vault, & of representing the heavens as seen at any hour, in any seasons, from any latitude, & at any period of history. Other parts of the projector can cast suitably moveable images of the sun, moon, & planets, & diagrammatic arrows & circles for explanatory purposes. The effect is infinitely lifelike—as if one were outdoors beneath the sky. Lectures—different each month (I heard the Dec. & Jan. ones)—are given in connexion with this apparatus. In the annular corridors on each floor are niches containing typical astronomical instruments of all ages—telescopes, transits, celestial globes, armillary spheres, &c.—& cases to display books, meteorites, & other miscellany. Astronomical pictures line the walls, & at the desk may be obtained useful pamphlets, books, planispheres, &c. I bought a planisphere apiece (25¢) for Sonny & Melmoth, so that those young rascals won't get the constellations wrong in their future stories, as they have done in the past! The institution holds classes in elementary astronomy, & sponsors clubs of amateur observers. Altogether, it is the most complete & active popular astronomical centre imaginable—though perhaps the planetaria in Chicago & Philadelphia parallel it. It seems to be crowded at all hours—attesting a public interest in astronomy which didn't exist when I was young.

Reached home Jany. 7 to confront a paralysing array of tasks—the worst tangle in a year. Programme so laden that I had to shift some of the burdens connected with the N.A.P.A. ¶ Best wishes, & once more effusive thanks for the books!

Yr obt grandsire—
H P

Notes

1. Cynthia Asquith, *My Grimmest Nightmare.* Contains Algernon Blackwood's "The Blackmailers."

2. Howard Wandrei, probably "Goods Delivered," *Detective Fiction Weekly* (28 December 1935); as by H. W. Guernsey.

3. *The Invisible Voices,* a short story collection written in collaboration with John Gawsworth.

4. AWD wrote a short notice of *The Hermaphrodite* for *Outdoors* (March 1936).

[406] [ALS]

Feby. 11, 1936.

Dear A W:—

Thanks for the February nature article, which has the charm of the all its predecessors. I rather liked the looks of M of M in *Astounding.* The illustrator drew the nameless Entities precisely as I had imagined them[1]—thus proving that he had really read the text. I'll see about the "Haunter". No—I haven't a single unpublished thing except "The Nameless City", booked elsewhere, & the novels Barlow is theoretically typing. Glad "The Shuttered House" will appear with Utpatel illustrations. I'm advising Hill-Billy Crawford to ask Utpatel for fresh designs he drew for "Innsmouth"—the latter being scheduled for issuance in booklet form ere long. Utpatel long since threw the old ones away. You'll be lucky if Farny reprints anything he has to pay for! So far all his reprints of my junk have been of tales printed before I began reserving rights. Sorry "Summer Night" has been delayed—but it'll be ripe for publication before you know it! Your programme is certainly staggering! Congratulations on the group of poems about to appear in *Voices.*[2]

I've been hopelessly struggling with a programme too large to cope with—nor has a grippe attack, which has left me weak as a rag & with very shaky eyesight, helped in the least. Young Sterling was here last month, & I helped him with a story laid in Venus—involving a maze of invisible crystal.[3] The kid grows cleverer as time passes!

Haven't had time to read either Jan. or Feby. W T, but am told that the former contains redeeming features. I see that Farny is reprinting (free) things of mine in both—rather crowding matters! I did glance a bit at the *Astounding* containing the Mts. Belknap's "Cones" wouldn't have been so bad if the little rascal hadn't dragged in a lot of extraneous stock romance.[4] The picture of an alien world, taken by itself, is really quite convincing.

Looking for a new "little magazine"? That curious roving character B. C. Black says he is about to edit (for somebody named Freese) a "literary magazine" to be called *Nuggets*—appearing March 15. Address Box 53, Upland, Indiana. He asks me for an article on the horror story—which I may or may not have the time & energy to write.

All good wishes—

Yr obt Grandsire,

H P

Notes

1. The illustrator was Howard V. Brown.

2. *Voices: A Quarterly of Poetry* (Summer 1936) under the heading "Things of Earth": Spring Evening: South Wind"; "Spring Evening: We Are Remembering Again"; "This Evening Hour"; "Forgotten Scythe"; "Old House"; and "Wisconsin Comes to Age."

3. "In the Walls of Eryx."

4. FBL, "Cones," *Astounding Stories* (February 1936).

[407] [ALS]

March 13, 1936

Dear A W:—

Hope Utpatel can arrange to do those Innsmouth drawings for Hill-Billy, for I feel sure he had caught the spirit of the tale. His work has a very distinctive power—& I am glad to note the number of your tales which he is illustrating. Incidentally, I was glad to see "The Satin Mask" with its appropriate design. I shall be on the lookout for "They Shall Rise".

Glad to hear of recent sales & placements—I'm sure you don't need to feel that you've been idle! Hope all will go well with Macmillan's. Pleased to know that "The Seven Who Waited" will have a tasteful jacket.[1]

Congratulations on your entry into Who's Who![2] Yes—your paragraph will soon come to be a long one if they list all your books, but possibly in later years you can arrange to have only certain notable ones mentioned.

You have my heartiest sympathy anent the recent cold wave. The temperatures you list sound almost fabulous in this region—& clearly shew that I could never survive a Wisconsin winter. Our worst was +4.8°, & for the most part the thermometer hung around +20°. What made the spell so bad was the fact that it seldom got above 25° or so. Bays & rivers froze as they seldom do, & Nantucket was twice isolated from the mainland. A considerable break in the cold came around Feby. 16—when rain & melting put Rhode Island into a quite picturesquely flooded condition. I'm not feeling quite as rotten as in Jan. & early Feb., but won't be good for much till some really warm outdoor weather comes. My programme is so overcrowded that the elimination of tasks is imperative. What complicates it additionally is the illness of my aunt—with a grippe attack far worse than mine. I am chained to the house as a combined nurse, butler, & errand-boy, & don't see any immediate let-up. However—it's worse on my aunt than it is on me! She may have to have a session at the hospital presently.[3]

Others, though, have more genuine tragedies. On Feby. 13 the fiancé of C. L. Moore—a mighty winter sportsman—was instantly killed while cleaning his rifle. Miss M. is quite disorganised by the shock, & has just been to Florida with her mother. They stopped at Bobby Barlow's on the way south, & expect to make an ampler visit there next summer. Bob was glad to meet the distinguished author of "Shambleau" in person, though he wished it could have been under less melancholy circumstances.

A magazine note of interest—though I don't suppose it affects you, since you don't write science fiction—is the sale of *Wonder Stories* by Hugo the Rat to the Margulies group—Standard Magazines, 22 W. 48th St., N.Y. City. Belknap—who is in very solidly with the Margulies outfit & likes their type of dealing—will doubtless be delighted by the change. I had a letter from Margulies asking to see material of mine, but doubt if he would care for anything of the sort I write.

Under separate cover I am sending an amateur magazine which may be of some interest—with a review of Belknap's "Goblin Tower".[4] Edkins—the editor—is one of the finest specimens of the old-school amateur journalist now living, & I feel intensely proud in having persuaded him to get back to activity. He was a star member of the N.A.P.A. in the 80's & 90's. Although 68 years old, he has all the interest & zest of a boy. In his review he tries to be fair, although I fear he doesn't quite do justice to the *massed* effect of some of Belknap's weird poems.

Temperature last Tuesday was 64° . . . & 62° on Wednesday. We can't expect that right along at this time of year, but it's welcome when it does come!

All good wishes—
Yr obt Servt
H P L

Notes

1. This must have been speculative, for the book did not appear until 1943.
2. Albert Nelson Marquis (ed.), *Who's Who in America*, vol. 19 (Chicago: A. N. Marquis Company, 1936), p. 718.
3. Annie Gamwell in fact was to have a mastectomy for breast cancer.
4. [Ernest A. Edkins], "*The Goblin Tower*," *Causerie* (February 1936): 2–4.

[408] [ALS]

April 9, 1936

Dear A W:—

Just a line to assure you of my continued existence, though my correspondence has lost all semblance of regularity under the pressure of existing conditions. My aunt went to the hospital on March 17, & is now sufficiently recovered to migrate to a convalescent home—where she will probably be for a fortnight more. The tasks falling upon me have been wholly beyond my power to perform, & virtually all my usual activities have perforce been abandoned. All revision jobs returned untouched except one (a text book on English usage)[1] on which I was most kindly granted a time-extension. I have very little energy, & have to rest for long periods each day. Damn this northern climate! My eyes give out occasionally without warning—producing a sort of vortex-like vision which summarily calls a halt to the day's labours.

Glad to hear of the springlike weather in Wisconsin. Our almost premature spring was followed by a colder spell—which has added to my exhaustion. Some trees & shrubs are heavily budded—they today certainly holds no woodland beckonings!

Hill-Billy Crawford has just sent proofs of the Utpatel drawings—which are really splendid. Though not avowedly a weird specialist, U. possesses a true sense of the fantastic which none of the W T regulars—except perhaps Rankin—can even approximate. In my opinion he will go far in the artistic field, & I certainly feel fortunate in having his work in "Innsmouth". Sorry Hill-Billy's change of mind caused needless work on a woodcut.

I am surely sorry to hear of the many recent deaths in your family—though you are really lucky to retain grandparents so long. My paternal grandmother died long before I existed, & my paternal grandfather before I could see him. I recall my maternal grandmother, and was less than 5½ when she died. My maternal grandfather—the most congenial associate of my youth—died when I was 13½.[2]

Glad to hear of the new purchases, & to see my old favourite "They Shall Rise" in print with an excellent illustration. Hope plans for the non-pulp work will materialise successfully, & that "Wind Over Wisconsin" blows favourably. Too bad the Guggenheim plan didn't pan out—but I fancy requirements are almost hypercritically exacting. Another Wisconsin friend of mine—Alfred Galpin of Appleton—tried in vain some years ago on the basis of musical work.

Hope the recent floods didn't inundate Sac Prairie. In these parts some disastrous submersions occurred—though Providence (like most seaports) escaped. Streets were under water 4 miles south of here.

Young Sterling—the science fiction fan who was in Providence last year—has been seriously ill in N.Y. with an abscess of the lower colon. Had to have an operation, blood-transfusion, & intra-venous nourishment. He is now, however, pulling around all right at the Mt. Sinai Hospital.

Thanks immensely for the offer of "Prince Zaleski". However, I have a tattered copy (most of the leaves loose) slowly disintegrating on my shelves, so you can use your judgment as to whether I'm the most worthy recipient of your extra.

Price may come east next month for a brief business trip, & if so he expects to get to Providence. I shall surely be glad to see him.

Klarkash-Ton is sending around a loan exhibit of his miniature sculpture. Would you care to be on the lending list? I expect to receive it by express from Loveman shortly.

All good wishes—

Yr opprest & obt Grandsire,

H P

Notes

1. See letter 417.

2. HPL refers to Helen Algood Lovecraft (1821–1881); George Lovecraft (1818?–1895); Robie Alzada Place Phillips (1827–1896); and Whipple Van Buren Phillips (1833–1904).

[409] [ALS]

May 7, 1936

Dear A W:—

Well—Grandpa is still alive . . . just about so! I probably mentioned my aunt's transfer to a convalescent home on April 7—& to this news I may add that on the 21st she returned to 66. Her recovery is steady but slow—& she still requires a certain amount of coöperation in household administration. My own programme is beyond reclamation—so that I am almost desperate enough to make a bonfire of all my files, obligations, & unanswered epistles! April was hellishly cold, but now there has come a milder period. Some days (but not today) are warm enough to permit of my writing outdoors on Prospect Terrace—& in general I have a trifle more strength than I did last month. Barlow has invited me South, but I don't believe I'll be able to accept. I wish I could, for a week of Charleston or Florida weather would bake some life into my old bones!

I surely will be grateful for the coherent copy of "Prince Zaleski". Mine is also the 1st edition—but old Jim Morton absolutely ruined it a decade ago by stuffing it into a brief case with some other material when I lent it to him. Not that it was in especially good shape before. Now—after 2 or 3 more lendings—it is what one might term a loose-leaf edition!

Thanks vastly for the two nature articles, which I appreciated greatly. "Retreat to Nature" is especially fine, & ought to be preserved in some collection of your essays.

When my stack of unread borrowed books is a little less lofty I'll try to get a look at the Garland volume you mention.[1] I've seen other tomes with the same arguments, but can't say that they've seemed very convincing to me. "Proofs" of marvels & miracles are always vague or second-hand—& when tracked down seem to dissolve like the accounts of the Hindoo rope trick. My reasons for distrusting reports of occult phenomena might be grouped roughly under some half-dozen headings—essentially as follows:

(1.) Believers wholly ignore the tremendous body of anthropological knowledge which shews how legends & folk beliefs are constantly created & persistently diffused in complete defiance of facts. Most of the supernatural events reported never happened at all. Other accounts represent amplifications & distortions of events which were not supernatural. Mere erroneous reporting & judicious "editing" explains a good part of the plausible tales which are circulated. This principle is admirably illustrated by the numberless *other* silly errors habitually entertained by immense numbers of persons of every kind—absurd historical, scientific, economic, philosophical, & miscellaneous beliefs which persist in spite of sound scholarship, & which ought to shew how easy it is for fallacy to have the widest & most serious acceptance.

(2.) Believers likewise ignore the tremendous myth-making capacity of the human mind. No eminent psychologist—who understands our complex mental processes & obscure motives—has ever believed in the supernatural. Volumes could be written on *motives for harbouring & promoting supernatural delusions*—motives which involve escape, ego-assertion, mental indolence, self-vindication in instinctive believers, religious mania, & dozens of less obvious considerations. The average ignorant person feels compelled, in order to obtain mental ease, to produce "evidence" for the supernatural. *Conscious though almost involuntary mendacity* is a larger factor in occult reports than is commonly realised.

(3.) Sheer *error unchecked by a knowledge of how completely irrational occultism is* accounts for a vast number of tales. A simple person is impressed by a coincidence or hallucination or bit of transposed memory which presents a puzzle. *To him,* an occult solution is as natural as a rational one, since he does not realise how utterly, basically, & antipodally all assumptions of the supernatural conflict with everything we really know of the universe. Therefore he accepts the mythical interpretation at once, because it is usually vastly simpler than the real explanation could possibly be.

(4.) It is significant that all tales of the occult are based on archaic prototypes which were evolved when nothing was known of the composition of the cosmos. Virtually all these myths obviously postulate an universe of the ancient legendary kind—with the heavens tributary to the earth, mankind at the centre of things, the archaic dualism of matter & "spirit" existent, external, transient, & deceptive appearances real, popular eschatology a fact, relative things absolute, human values, emotions, & personality cosmically important, &c. &c. &c. The tales become irrelevant & absurd when considered in the light of time, space, matter, & energy as known today. When modern charlatans try to drag contemporary science into their fakeries they produce an amusing spectacle—radically mistaking & misinterpreting the science they adopt, & blithely blending it with the most utterly contradictory concepts of ancient folklore. Hence the circus of "vibrations", "ectoplasm", "animal magnetism", &c.

(5.) No evidence of the supernatural has ever been detected by any person not emotionally or traditionally inclined toward irrational belief. The high percentage of religious, egotistical, emotional, ignorant, eccentric, inferior, culturally orthodox (i.e., trained in the humanities instead of the sciences), senescent, & downright senile types [all types attaching high importance to emotional appearances, & hostile to cool objective vision & impersonal scientific analysis] among believers cannot be ignored. It would be silly to accept any theories or beliefs repudiated by the bulk of first-rank physicists, biologists, psychologists, anthropologists, astronomers, philosophers, &c. Moreover, we may justly ask why, if occult phenomena *do* occur, they *never* manifest themselves except to persons already inclined to believe in them! Such precise *selectiveness* is too significant to overlook.

(6.) Whenever rational investigators have organised to investigate an allegedly supernatural occurrence to the very bottom, a natural explanation has been found. Moreover, virtually every known "supernatural" manifestation—including "mind-reading"—is constantly reproduced on the vaudeville stage by coldly mechanical & materialistic performers.

However—I shall read the Garland volume with the keenest interest when I get the chance, just as I have read similar volumes by Chevreuil, Flammarion, Jung-Stilling,[2] & others in the past.

Glad your literary opportunities continue to multiply, & that you will have another tale in *Scribner's*.[3] Your new plan with the novel—revision as you go—is probably wise; although you may later on wish to make changes in the early parts to harmonise with newly-introduced & unforeseen elements in the subsequent sections. Congratulations on the editorship of the Wisconsin anthology![4] Harrison's anthologies are sometimes regarded more or less as rackets, but a certain number of them undoubtedly do represent bona fide ventures—with really well-selected material. I am sure that no one could do your native state better justice than yourself!

I was glad to see "They Shall Rise" (an old friend in MS. form) in print, & do not believe it is by any means as bad a story as you think. Both March & April W Ts were definitely above the dismal average—Jacobi's & Bloch's stories being worthy companions for yours in the latter issue. Haven't had a chance to read the May as yet, although I got it the other day. And so old Satrap Pharnabazus is calling for some spicy sex stuff to match his covers, eh? Well—once in a while there may be room for a weird story! I wish somebody *would* found a rival magazine, but fear there isn't much hope for it.

Your mention of springtime rambles a month ago convinces me that your season must have advanced ahead of ours—for which I envy you. I haven't been able to take any real walks as yet, but my aunt & I were treated to a delightful motor ride in southeastern Massachusetts last week. The full vernal glory of flowers & leaves has developed only within the past few days—but just at this moment the R.I. landscape is surely a joy to the eye. Glad to hear that you've taken to astronomical observation—in which pursuit a good field-glass is certainly nothing to be despised! Have you ever studied Garrett P. Serviss's "Astronomy with an Opera Glass"? That classic—which has guided the amateur observers of 2 generations & more—ought to be full of helpful hints for you. If you haven't a copy I'd be glad to send you mine for a long-term loan. By the way—if you want a shot at the Andromeda nebula you can get one now by making your observations in the morning before dawn. Andromeda is high in the sky by 3 a.m.

I'll see that a copy of "Innsmouth" comes your way when (or if ever) Hill-Billy Crawford completes his edition. Only about a quarter of it appears to be set up. I like Utpatel's illustrations extremely, & fancy they will be about the most important part of the volume. In a few days "The Shadow Out of Time" will appear in *Astounding*—hope it gets as good illustrations as "Mts of Madness" did. The new *Phantagraph* came the other day, with the opening instalment of Two-Gun Bob's "Hyborian Age". Two-Gun sent me a new snapshot of himself last month. He's grown a drooping moustache, & in a 10-gallon hat looks exactly like a western cinema sheriff. Which reminds me to thank you for the very pleasing new snap of yourself. ¶ Patriarchal blessings—

H P

Notes

1. Hamlin Garland, *Forty Years of Psychic Research.*

2. HPL owned Jung-Stilling's *Theory of Pneumatology.*

3. "The Old Lady Has Her Day."

4. AWD and Reymond E. F. Larsson, eds., *Poetry out of Wisconsin.* The anthology included poetry by HPL's friends Alfred Galpin and Maurice W. Moe.

[410] [ALS]

June 5, 1936

Dear A W:—

Events move slowly. A little warm weather now & then, hence a slight increase in the old man's energies. Aunt improves slowly, albeit set back by the strain of an imperative dental siege. My own programme is hopeless—only wholesale neglect & repudiation will ever clear it up. Simply haven't the strength to dispose of existing & incoming tasks in the number of hours I can remain awake & unexhausted.

Glad to hear of your constant progress & achievements—& thanks in advance for "Zaleski". Hope no unduly cold nights came to blast the expectations of Sac Prairie orchards. Haven't had a chance yet to read May W T—but shall look for "The Telephone in the Library" (did I ever see this in MS.?) in the June issue. Glad you have a good astronomical hand book—but if you ever care to borrow the Serviss volume it's at your disposal. No—you probably couldn't have seen Sirius very well as late as May, since it sets then about 8 o'clock (Standard Time), only an hour after the sun. By the time the twilight would be deep enough to show it, it would be too close to the horizon (lost in thick vapours) to be seen. You could have seen Procyon, Castor, & Pollux in the evening dusk—but not much of Orion. Betelgeux sets not long after Sirius. Capella would have been bright in the northwest—with Vega visible in the N.E. by the time darkness was complete. Jupiter—in opposition June 10—rises earlier & earlier each evening. Have you a good almanack to go by? Another great help is a revolving *planisphere*—a disc representing the sky which turns through a frame with an opening to show the heavens visible at any given hour on any given day. I think I mentioned these as being on sale at the Hayden Planetarium in N.Y. for a quarter. If you aren't already supplied, you ought to send for one. A knowledge of the apparent motions of the sky—moon, planets, constellations, &c.—is valuable to any author, giving him excellent atmospheric material & saving him from many embarrassing boners. (like Venus in the east in the evening, or a thin crescent moon high in the sky at midnight, or Orion & Scorpio visible at the same time, &c. &c.) Later this knowledge ought to be supplemented (for the sake of one's own sense of orientation to the universe) with some elementary facts about the real size, dimensions, distances, nature, motions, &c. of the various heavenly bodies & systems of bodies.

Speaking of astronomy—I lately stumbled on about the most interesting genealogical discovery I ever made . . . . when I unexpectedly learned for the first time *that I am a great-great-great-great-great-great-great-great-great-grandson of the Elizabethan astronomer who introduced the Copernican theory into England!* For one who has always been an amateur devotee of celestial science, this was certainly quite a find! Ordinarily I'm not much of a genealogist, being content to take what existing charts tell me & let it go at that. The other day I ran into a caller of my aunt's—an old lady related to us in the Field & Wilcox lines—& she mentioned how proud I ought to be of our common forbear, *the astronomer John Field or Felde*. That had me quite floored, since our charts carried the Field line back only to the original Providence settler John Field, who died in 1686, & I knew damn well that *this* bird was no star-gazer! Well—it soon turned out that the ancestry of this settler has been known for ages among genealogists, though I had no inkling of it. The 16th Century astronomer (whose 1557 ephemeris contained the first English account of the Copernican system, & who has been called "The Proto-Copernican of England") was the Prov. colonist's *own grandfather*—hence *my* 9-times-great-grandfather. It surely gave me a kick to get a real man of science in my pedigree—which as a general thing is lousy with clergymen but short on straight thinkers. [But I'll be hanged if this new discovery hasn't added *one more* damn divine to the bunch—for it seems that the Providence settler's maternal grandfather was the Rev. John Sotwell, Vicar of Peniston in Yorkshire!] Later I looked up the standard Field genealogy (by F. C. Pierce, 1901) at the Hist. Society & found out all about the line. It comes from one Sir Hubertus de la Feld [of the family of Counts de la Feld, seated near Colmar in Alsace], a follower of William the Conqueror who took lands in Lancashire in 1069; the Prov. Stock springing from the Yorkshire branch centreing around Sowerby, Ardsley, & Thurnscoe in the West Riding. I've copied a lot of notes, & now have my Field lineage straight back—in exactly 20 generations—to Roger de la Feld of Sowerby, baron in 1240. But it's the *astronomer* who interests me—& about whom I hope to enlarge my knowledge. I have a triple allotment of Field blood, being descended from no less than three grandchildren of the Providence settler.

Hope your abandonment of the weird field will concern only the "pulpier" part of it. Wish Margulies would accept your suggestion for a good weird magazine, but from all accounts his publications tend toward the cheap, the sensational, & the "action"-infested. Trust the anthology matter will develop favourably.

Sooner or later I'll get around to the Garland book—but the old fellow's honest belief that he has personally met "supernormal" things by no means rules out all the points I brought up. The trickiness, inaccuracy, & capricious bias of our apparent perceptions & memories are always emphasised when "eye-witness" accounts of actual occurrences, or memories of certain real or supposed events, are carefully compared & rigidly examined. As for your own view—you *can't* rule out* the principle embodied in my first point, because it is constantly operating to perpetuate old delusions & create new ones. Deep & implicitly accepted folk-beliefs arise every year from the flimsiest errors or from nothing at all. Press despatches set the gullible agog with all manner of marvels—& many of these find a permanent lodgment in folklore (helping to create a mass mood favourable to occult stories) simply because nobody bothers to investigate & explode them. A classic example is a *subsidiary* product of the "Indian rope trick". This "trick" is itself sheer folklore—*no one has ever seen it performed*—but in the 19th century it was accepted as genuine sleight-

*i.e., you can't distinguish what comes under this head (as reported by others) & what doesn't.

of-hand & tentatively explained in various ways. The favourite theory was *mass hypnotism;* & it was said that many persons had *photographed* the "trick" *& found nothing but the performer in an inert pose* on the developed plates, thus proving the hypnotic nature of the performance. Well—the truth is that *this story was just as much a folklore illusion as the "trick" itself*—albeit one of spontaneous contemporary growth. No one had ever photographed the "trick"—because no such "trick" ever existed except in imagination & legend! Track down half the "cases" reported in Flammarion &c., & you'll find them more or less of this nature. Others will form various sorts of misinterpretations of actual natural happenings. A few will be lies—conscious or unconscious. In most cases the *traditional nature* of such "manifestations" makes their character obvious. My second point is valid because the human mind has just as strong incentives for faking the so-called "supernormal" as for faking the traditionally supernatural. Point three holds because we know physical laws to be dependable in all ways perceptible to mankind. The alleged principle of "indeterminacy" applies only to minute electronic motions—& is in itself no *real* absence of cause & effect, but only a case where *predictable* causation is absent. That barber shop coincidence about the clock is surely very interesting. Such occur now & then, though it doesn't do to let important fictional developments hang on them. As for marvels—of course we cannot say that all the physical laws of the cosmos are yet discovered. We may yet recognise phenomena at present not thought to exist. But when people claim things which we never see ourselves, & which clearly seem to violate physical laws that always work, we are justified in demanding a lot of proof!

I note your new stationery—which is very attractive indeed. Is the gifted Utpatel responsible for the sturdy ploughman? The green hill background is highly effective.

All good wishes—

Yr obt Grandsire

H P

[411] [ALS]

The Antient Hill

—June 20, 1936.

Dear A W:—

Your recent activities are surely as bewilderingly numerous as of yore. 220 books since last September—*besides* your writing! Such figures sound, to an ordinary mortal, like various interstellar distances stated in miles! Hope the anthology will develop smoothly. 1736 is a pretty early beginning . . . . who was the pioneer bard—an Indian or a French settler?[1] Hope the improved form of the "Summer Night" will repay your pains. Congratulations on recent sales & placements—& confound Wright for his increasingly dilatory financial tactics!

Anent the constellations—it's surely odd that your maps haven't steered you to Vega, which was high in the sky at the time of your early-June observations. Are you sure you had the map right-side up? Because Vega was far *above*—not *below* Cassiopeia . . . . & indeed still is. In early June Cassiopeia is virtually scraping the northern horizon in the early evening, hence there couldn't very well be anything below it save the trees & spires & chimneys of Sac Prairie! Here is the way the northern stars & the neighbours were in early June:

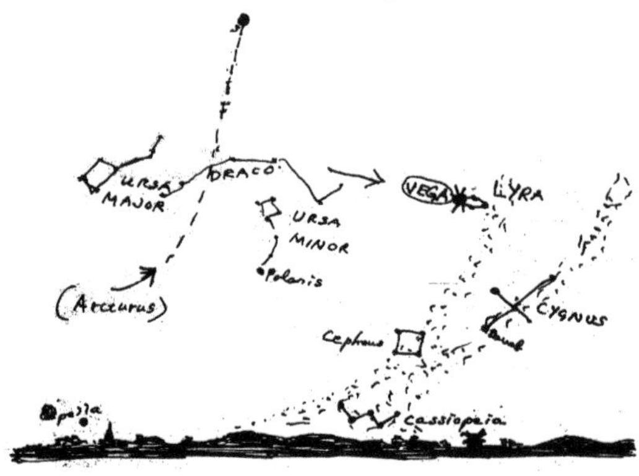

Everything is now, of course, shifted westward at the same hour. Capella has set, Vega is *very* high—climbing toward the zenith—& Cassiopeia's "W" is tilted upward as it climbs away from the horizon. Arcturus—beyond the zenith—is beginning to descend toward the west. Turning to the *southern* sky—Libra is not very easy to find, since it has no bright stars. But if you draw a line from Antares to Spica, Libra will be about midway along it—the first bunch of stars beyond the kite-like outlines of Scorpio. Scorpio itself is an easy & conspicuous group—you can't miss it as it crawls along the southern horizon with its deep-red star Antares. It (Antares) crosses the meridian about 10 p.m. (11 p.m. Daylight-Saving Time) in late June. In Florida one sees Scorpio soaring quite high in the southern sky. The bright star in the east or S.E. during later June evenings is Altair, in Aquila. Meanwhile Sagittarius follows Scorpio toward the meridian—skirting the southern horizon in an especially rich region of the Milky Way. This group is full of interesting clusters which will repay field-glass observation. Do your local papers have monthly articles like the enclosed, treating of astronomical phenomena? I used to write a similar monthly article for Providence's lesser paper.[2]

Which reminds me to thank you for the nature article. I'll wager the old mill & its pond were picturesque in their day!

Effusive thanks in advance for "The Lost Valley"!! If an old man's memory be dependable, this volume contains one of Algy's very best yarns . . . perhaps "The Wendigo". Am I right? About the stationery—Utpatel certainly knows his stuff! That's a clever idea regarding the alteration of the landscape to produce an autumnal scene. Hope you act on it.

Had a titanic file-cleaning in early June—or perhaps I mentioned that. Also corrected printed text (3 copies each) of M. of M. & Shadow—finding the former sickeningly mangled. Likewise read up old W T issues. Two-Gun Bob's work—both the serial & "Black Canaan" is certainly notable. He understood how to suggest infinite fear & menace. Glad to see "Tel. in Library" in print. Bloch is coming along well, & I hope he'll escape the most hackneyed pulp formulae. By the way—young Hornig is in San Francisco on a newspaper job secured for him by good old Abe Merritt. Hope he succeeds. On his way out he stopped in Indianapolis to call on Miss Moore, who liked him very much. The Pacific coast is getting to be quite a weird centre—young Kuttner's rise adding to its lustre in that respect.

But the main news of the day is very sad—& forms the reason for that ominous *past tense* used above in connexion with R E H's splendid work. For if a recent depressing & staggering report be correct, good old Two-Gun is no more—having ended his own life.[3] It still sounds incredible to me—& I wish I could hear a report contradicting it. I had a long, normal letter from R E H written May 13. He was worried about his mother's health, but otherwise seemed perfectly all right. If the news is indeed true, it forms weird fiction's worst blow since the passing of good old Canevin in 1932. Scarcely anybody else in the gang had quite the driving zest & spontaneity of Brother Conan. Crom, what a year of disaster is 1936! It is hard to say just what made Two-Gun's yarns stand out so, but the real secret is that *he was in every one of them.* Even when he made outward concessions to the Mammon-guided editors & commercial critics he had an inner force & sincerity which broke through the surface & put the imprint of his personality on everything he wrote. I can't understand the tragedy, for although R E H had a moody side expressed in his resentment against civilisation (the basis of our perennial & voluminous epistolary controversy) I always thought that this was a more or less *impersonal* sentiment—like Sonny Belknap's rage against the injustices of a capitalistic world. He himself seemed to me pretty well adjusted to his environment. Well—weird fandom certainly has occasion to mourn!

Turning to less melancholy topics—I'm going to see if I can impose on your good nature a bit . . . . . albeit in a matter which may appeal to your local loyalty as a Son of the Badger. You've heard me mention my gifted young friend (35 next November, but always young to an old man!) Alfred Galpin of Appleton, Wisconsin—a musical student under the late Vincent d'Indy, an instructor in French at Lawrence College, a fellow-graduate of your own alma mater (he roomed at 830 W. Johnson whilst in Madison), & (lucky little rascal) a resident of his birthplace at 726 E. College Ave., Appleton. Well—the enclosed epistle from him (which please return) speaks for itself. The young sage has written a first novel of the detective breed, & with all the confidence of youth expects it to land at once & with immediate payments![4] Just a question of where to send it—what publisher to honour with the credit of bringing out a future classic! Now since my knowledge of book-publishing arrangements is infinitesimal as compared with your own, it occurs to me that you might do this brilliant fellow-Wisconsinite a darned good turn by dropping him a line of advice based on your ample experience. I'll wager the book is *good*; for that kid excels in whatever he attempts, & is marvellously well-grounded in literature (old & new) of the most solid sort. Would you call Loring & Mussey (the bastards who lost or stole my May '23 *National Amateur*, pox rot 'em!) still a good firm for a beginner to tackle, or would you recommend boldness in approaching some standard publisher? As for the way to fasten a 225 p. MS.—you just leave the sheets loose, don't you, or just put a large elastic band around the whole business? If you don't want to bother to write Galpin directly, you can simply spill any convenient tips in your next bulletin to Grandpa. But I think you'd like Alfredus the Great—he was an infant prodigy in his day, & has one of the most astonishing intellects I've ever encountered. I always thought he'd be a critical & philosophical writer something like Remy de Gourmont or Mencken; but around 1924 he got sidetracked on music, & has ever since been striving to become a composer . . . . not wholly without success, since some very respectable orchestras have used compositions of his. He once set some of Belknap's and Loveman's verses to music.[5]

Another issue of Edkins' *Causerie* is out, this one with a review of Loveman's book.[6] I'll try to throw a copy your way. Meanwhile E A E himself is in the Evanston Hospital pulling out of a serious kidney operation. The criticism is in the main acute & fair, though Edkins blames Loveman unduly for what he calls his "defeatist" attitude toward life. Actually, a poet's attitude toward life doesn't matter one god damn—so long as he crystallises & transmits, with suitable grace & power, whatever mood or attitude he *does* happen to have.

And so it goes. Any tips you can devise for Galpin will be appreciated. And I'm damned if I can yet believe the bad news about ol' Two-Gun!

Ever yr oblig'd & obt Grandsire—

H P

Notes

1. *Poetry out of Wisconsin* contains no such poem.

2. HPL published astronomy articles in the Providence *Tribune* (morning, evening, and Sunday editions) from 1906 to 1908, now gathered in *CE* 3.

3. HPL had learned from C. L. Moore that REH committed suicide on 11 June.

4. Galpin had written a novel first entitled *Death in D Minor* and later *Murder in Montparnasse*. It was never published. See HPL to Alfred Galpin (20 June 1936), in *Letters to Alfred Galpin* (New York: Hippocampus Press, 2003): 223–24.

5. He also composed an "Elegy" for HPL for solo piano.

6. Edkins reviewed Loveman's *Hermaphrodite and Other Poems* in *Causerie* (June 1936).

[412] [ALS]

July 9, 1936

Dear A W:—

No further details regarding the R E H report—but I'll add any news which comes between now & mailing-time. It certainly is a damnably melancholy thing if true. Conceivably, good old Two-Gun had a definitely gloomy & brooding temperament—of which his rancour against civilisation was merely an outgrowth. Now that one thinks of it, he never displayed the quality of *humour,* except in a bitter, ironic way. And as for his drinking—it always seemed as if he took to liquor in the Nordic rather than the Latin-Mediterranean way—that is, seeking oblivion or dulled sensibilities as opposed to sharpened sensibilities. But in any case it's a devilish shame if such a vigorous personality is cut off at the age of thirty. His long letters shewed what was in him—& what would have come out some time—& his stories were the most consistently vital of all the voluminous pulp products. Certainly, this is the worst knockout blow since the loss of Whitehead.

Good old Monty James's passing is a shock, too—albeit less close than the loss of a star correspondent. Your announcement was the first I knew of the matter, & I'm very grateful for the cutting. One more real master gone—although I don't think James had quite the same convincing power that Blackwood & Machen have. But he certainly could produce fascinating stuff—& "Count Magnus" & "The Treasure of Abbot Thomas" stand among the greatest existing things of their kind. His antiquarianism always fascinated me. Few other moderns could equal him in reproducing the style of 18th century prose. Chesterton, too, is a vast loss. Indeed, 1936 seems to me peculiarly a year of disaster! George Allan England has just died—at 59.[1]

Glad your constellation knowledge is getting coördinated. What you need for a quick & easy grasp of the various groups is a revolving planisphere—which you can set to show the precise area of the sky visible at any hour on any night of the year. I was lucky enough to get hold of one when about half through the task of uranographical acquisition. Lacking a planisphere, the way to find groups at hours later than the common evening ones is to use *advance* maps on the basis of 1 month for 2 hours. Thus if a July map gives the sky for 10 p.m., use an August map for midnight & a September one for 2 a.m. In general, the sky shifts 15° each hour *on a given night,* while *at the same hour* it shifts 30° each month. Did you see the nova—now fading—on the border of Cepheus & Lacerta?[2] I missed it because of cloudiness. As for the planets—you *may* see Jupiter's satellites (but not his disc) with an 8-power field glass, but you can't hope to catch Saturn's rings without at least a small telescope having powers of 25 or more. I have a 3″ telescope which was never very good, & which the years (no doubt disturbing the alignment of lenses through the denting of the brass) have done nothing to improve.[3] It has eye-pieces of 100 & 50, but nowadays it doesn't seem to stand the high power as well as it used to. The lower the power with a given object glass, the brighter & clearer (albeit *smaller*) the rings. Nowadays I content myself with the 50. I got the instrument in 1906, having previously had a 2½″ glass.

Thanks for slipping the information to Galpin, who will assuredly be abundantly grateful. His verve in expecting an instant sale on his own terms is certainly refreshing—but I presume that's the sort of mood which makes people accomplish things!

Thanks likewise for the valued additions to my library—plus the loan. I hope your hurry for the return of the latter is not excessive, since I am already hemmed in by mountains of unread borrowed books. But perhaps I'll take the liberty to slipping it in ahead of some others—since the order of returning does not always have to be guided by dates of lending.

Your current nature article seems to me exceptionally fine—poetry in substance if not in form. I'd never have suspected the June–July juggling! Thanks. Glad the revision of the novel goes on apace. Thoroughness pays in the end. The anthology certainly sounds like a full-time job, but I'm sure you'll produce brilliant results. Usual congratulations on current sales.

I'm very grateful for the glimpse of the two new poems, both of which seem to me extremely good. Your Sac Prairie series will evolve into a new Spoon River Anthology before you're through with it![4]

Two of the most historic old mansions on the hill are now open as public museums, & I inspected both last week. Here's a folder about one of them . . . . which doesn't overrate it in the least. Old J. Q. A. was right—I endorse his dictum after having looked over a very fair number of exteriors & interiors all the way from Quebec to St. Augustine & New Orleans. Of course, I haven't seen Mexico—but then, neither had J. Q. A.![5]

Schwartz has some plan for reprinting stuff of mine in England. In connexion with this I sent "Doorstep" & "Haunter" to Wright for his official rejection, & he *accepted* both!

Warm day at last. 92°. Thank gawd—I live again!

Yr obt Grandsire—

H P

P.S. Just had word from Two-Gun's father. Sad report is all too true. R E H shot himself when he learned that his mother's illness was fatal. Double funeral. Must be unbearable for poor old Dr. Howard—wife & splendid only child gone at one blow. R E H's melancholy streak must have gone deeper than we thought. Most take the loss of the elder generation more philosophically.

P.P.S. Just received a splendid elegy on R E H from Barlow.[6] Didn't know the kid was such a poet!

[Enclosure: Brochure: Historic John Brown House]

Notes

1. M. R. James died on 12 June, G. K. Chesterton on 14 June, and George Allan England on 26 June.

2. A nova appeared in the Crown of King Cepheus in June 1936.

3. Annie Gamwell gave this telescope and apparently HPL's planisphere to AWD following HPL's death. They in turn went to Hugo Schwenker, AWD's boyhood friend, and are now in the possession of The August Derleth Society.

4. AWD's *Hawk on the Wind* (1938), *Man Track Here* (1939; dedicated to Edgar Lee Masters), *Here on a Darkling Plain* (1940), *Wind in the Elms* (1941), *Rind of Earth* (1942), *Selected Poems* (1944; intro. Edgar Lee Masters), *The Edge of Night* (1945), and *Collected Poems: 1937–1967* (1967) all contain sections entitled "Sac Prairie People," poems written in the manner of the free verse monologues in *Spoon River Anthology* (1915) by Edgar Lee Masters (1869–1950). AWD's poems, however, are in the third person. *In a Quiet Graveyard* (1997) collects the various poems as well as many unpublished items.

5. One was the John Brown House (1786–88), 52 Power Street; now home of the Rhode Island Historical Society. John Quincy Adams (cited in the enclosed brochure) stated in his diary that it was "the most magnificent and elegant private mansion that I have ever seen on this continent." The other house was the Edward Carrington House (1810; 1812), 66 Williams Street. John Corliss built the original two-story part of the house in 1810. Margarenthe Dwight, a descendant of Carrington, gave the house and many of its furnishings to the Museum of Art, Rhode Island School of Design as a museum showing the influence of the China trade in New England. It has been a private residence since 1931.

6. "R. E. H.," *WT* (October 1936); rpt. *Eyes of the God: The Weird Fiction and Poetry of R. H. Barlow,* ed. S. T. Joshi, Douglas A. Anderson, and David E. Schultz (New York: Hippocampus Press, 2002), p. 148.

[413] [ALS]

The Ancient Hill
—July 29, 1936.

Dear A W:—

I read Exhibit A in the Wright case with much interest, & how it indicates that old Farny is being scared into a less irresponsible financial policy. We shall see whether or not that sap shows any trend toward reversal. As for the phrase "payment on publication"—I presume F W regards it merely as a conventional form like "Yr obedient Servant". After the example of Gernsback, the words themselves are not to be taken literally.

I envy you your 103° temperatures, though it has been pretty good here off & on. The 90° weather lasted long enough to get me quite definitely on my feet—setting my digestion right & abolishing a good part of the nervous exhaustion. I could accomplish as much in a day as in a whole week prior to the warm spell. Congratulations on the reducing! Possibly I told you about how I knocked off 50 lbs. in 1925. I now hover around 140. But the drought surely is a tragedy. Here there has been rain, though I believe the Middle West is less fortunate.

Sorry that the Galpinian opus isn't a 100% masterpiece. Holy Yuggoth, but I didn't think you'd agree to *read* it, with all the other things you have to do! But I'm sure Galpinius is appropriately grateful.

More proofs of "Innsmouth" have come from Crawford's printers. Granted ample longevity, I may see the issuance of the volume.

Took a Newport boat trip the other day, rambling through the ancient town & doing some writing on the rocky cliffs. Got a good coat of sunburn, now peeling off with an interestingly leprous or decompositional effect.

July 18–19 I had an enjoyable visit from a couple of fellow-Wisconsinites of yours—my old friend M. W. Moe (poet-teacher . . . of Milwaukee) & his gifted son Robert (the latter—now of Bridgeport, Conn.—the youth who was here with his car in the spring of '35). It was my first sight of M W M in 13 years, & I fancy he found me more changed than I found him. Bob brought him in his car, & we covered quite a bit of scenic & historic ground in the all-too-brief span of 2 days. Weather favoured us greatly, for we had warmth & sun throughout—whereas the very next day was cold & rainy, with Grandpa heavily blanketed & shivering over an oil heater!

Have you seen Peltier's comet as yet? A badly tree-&-roof-screened northern horizon has prevented observations from 66, but one evening I saw the object through the Ladd Observatory's 12-inch telescope.[1] Just a tiny disc with fanlike luminous haze spreading from it.

By the way—what are the best magazines (mostly non-remunerative "little magazines", I suppose) to which to send a non-commercial story of the "slice-of-life" or character-study type—the sort commonly found in *Story?* A correspondent of mine (Frederic J. Pabody, 1367 E. 6th St., Cleveland, O.) is experimenting in fiction of this sort, & has just had a tale rejected by *Story*. He doesn't know where to send it next—& neither do I! If he doesn't get encouragement somewhere, I fear he'll go commercial & take to devising "O. Henry endings" "slanted" at the so-called "slicks".

Latest local news is pleasant—consisting of nothing less than Barlow's arrival in Providence for a stay of indefinite length.[2] Some property adjustments about the De Land place are occurring, & Ar-E'ch-Bei thought this would be a good time to pay the Old Gentleman a visit & make his headquarters in ancient New-England for a while. I surely am glad to see him—& I forgive him the moustache & side-whiskers he has grown. He grew a full beard last spring, but parted with the bulk of it because of the public attention it attracted. Hope I can persuade him to get rid of the residue—although my non-success in abolishing Belknap's moustachelet makes me pessimistic.

But Ar-Ech-Bei's whiskerage is more successful than Sonny's! Barlow has taken a room at the boarding-house across the garden, & will certainly be a most congenial neighbour. He is full of literary plans—including that of a high-grade mimeographed magazine of distinctive material.[3] Before long you'll probably hear from him—with a request for your history of weird fiction since 1890. I'm glad Ar-Ech-Bei blew in yesterday instead of the day before, for up to that time I was about knocked out by the cold spell. 88° or 90° yesterday—which put me on my feet once more.

All good wishes—

Yr obt Grandsire

H P

Notes

1. Brown University's observatory, on Doyle Avenue in Providence.
2. Barlow visited HPL in Providence from 28 July to 1 September.
3. Barlow published only two issues of *Leaves.*

[414] [TLS, SHSW]

Sauk City
Wisconsin
3 August [1936]

Dear H. P.,

I am much afraid that Exhibit A in the Wright case means very little. To date he has sent me, only after urging, only $29 of the $80 due me on the April story, and he still owes me including that sixty no less than $220, now that Death Holds the Post is out in the August–September issue, for, as you've doubtless noticed, he has gone back to predating his issues again. I wonder what, if anything, he saves, since he must save something or he wouldn't do it. If his accounts are reckoned by the year, by dates, then he saves the price of the magazine, which probably amounts to about $1000, including payment for material used. And he certainly owes more than that to his authors for used material. At any rate, it will be interesting to see what he will do about paying. He may be sure that the A&J[1] people, once they have been notified, will keep on the watch. ... I went off on a four day vacation last week-end, beginning Wednesday, and returned home on Saturday evening to find a stack of letters sufficiently high to keep me busy most of Sunday and part of this morning, before the mails for today start coming. I also found that The New Republic, issue of August 5 now out, is using my poem, Evenings in Wisconsin, and that the August issue of Scribner's announced fiction by August Derleth in its September issue, which means that they are using The Old Lady Turns the Other

Cheek, since that is the only one they have left, though they have another under consideration now. ... Yes, I greatly fear that Galpin's book needs extensive revision, and I believe he now realizes that, too. I had to warn him about airing his personal prejudices: pro-Wagner in Music, anti-Semitic racially, etc. in a book designed purely for entertainment, since that would arouse reader-antagonism, the net result of which involved me in a long and pleasant correspondence with friend Galpin which is even now continuing. He seems an interesting and pleasant fellow indeed, and I may some day meet him, if we can arrange it. .... I still hope to see Innsmouth myself before I decline into senility, which often seems not very far off. ... Speaking or writing of sunburn, I took on a positive lobster colour and was somewhat pained by over-exposure to sunlight on the lake 75 miles north, where we holidayed. But fortunately I do not burn badly and never peel, the lobster colour duly changing to a deep satiny brown, which makes me look more like an Indian than anything else. ...... You mention that Moe is a poet-teacher: do you have copies of any of his poems? He is definitely eligible to inclusion in the Wisconsin poetry anthology, and since we do not want to miss anyone, I should like to see some from Galpin, think we will use a short lyric entitled November, which pleases me. .... Or, failing the poems, can you send me Moe's address? .... Peltier's comet has succeeded in the sky-map you so kindly enclosed to get sight of it soon. Last night the moon was far too bright to see it, and obscure vision of all but first and second magnitude stars. ..... I can recommend to your attention a new horror novel: The Undying Monster, by Jessie D. Kerruish, just published by Macmillan, or rather, to be out by the time you have this note. ..... I found it a very good piece of work, ranking with Dracula in type, though with not its force nor power, and yet deserving of serious attention from the horror-mongers. .... You ask for a list of little magazines to which your friend Pabody might send his story. The most receptive of these is published in his own Ohio: MANUSCRIPT, 17 West Washington St., Athens, Ohio; then there are FANTASY, 950 Heberton Avenue, Pittsburgh, Pa.; THE TANAGER, Grinnell, Iowa; AMERICAN PREFACES, Iowa City, Iowa; LITERARY AMERICA, 175 Fifth Avenue, New York City. These are the best of the lot. I wish him luck. .... Glad to hear of Barlow's advent; hope he will enjoy himself there, and wish I might myself be there. Some day, perhaps. ... The heat continues, though it is overcast today, and close, so that we may hope for rain, though I am not sanguine enough to do so.

All best, always,

August

Notes

1. *Author and Journalist.*

[415] [ALS]

The Ancient Hill
—Aug. 22, 1936.

Dear A W:—

Sorry W T finances still seem unpromising, & hope you'll get all of your 220 in the end. I noticed the change in dating,[1] but hardly fancy old Farny would dare to gyp his subscribers by handing them an 11-issue "year". I trust the A & J outfit will lend their influence toward making him toe the mark. Congratulations on *Scribners* & *New Republic* contributions.

Galpin is enthusiastically appreciative of your help with his novel, & is preparing a new structure on the fragments of the old. His latest letter forms quite a d'Erlette panegyric, & he hopes to see you the very next time he is able to invade the Madisonian terrain. I think you'll like him. He's an incredibly lean chap 6′ 2″ tall, & with a rather scholarly aspect. Will be 35 next November, & has been a philosopher & aesthete of sorts from infancy. Was quite a high light in amateur journalism from 1917 to about 1922. Glad Galpinius coughed up some early poems—he contributed to amateurdom under various pseudonyms such as Consul Hasting, A. T. Madison, Julius Zuricher, Albert Frederick Willie, Anatol Kleinst, &c. &c. &c. As for something by good old Mocrates—I haven't anything in detached form, but will ask him to ship you a cargo of his best. He's a bard of very modest pretensions, but sure knows his technique. Address: *M. W. Moe, 1810 West Wisconsin Ave., Milwaukee, Wis.*

Hope you caught Peltier's comet—which according to current reports lost its tail before fading into obscurity. I enclose a few odd cuttings on the subject.

Thanks for the tip anent "The Undying Monster", which I hope I shall come across. Thanks, too, for the list of "little magazines" to quote to Pabody. He'll certainly be profoundly grateful.

Glad to see "Down River in August". You surely are becoming a fixture of *Outdoors*—& show great ingenuity in finding new things to say about the landscape as seasons repeat themselves.

Another favour solicited for an aspiring struggler—an old lady who wants to place a saccharine tale of a haunted house (involving a conventional lunatic & a happy marriage at the end) in some magazine. Is there any *rural* publication which would consider accepting such an 1875 relique with or without pay? The thing is not really crude from the standpoint of a half-century ago. You might mention any possible medium to me—or drop a kindly line to the author, Mrs. M. E. Sutton, 505 W. 167th St., New York City. Thanks in advance for any name you can conveniently furnish.

Old Adolphe de Castro—the one-time friend of Bierce & creator of endless reams of fictional junk & learned charlatanry—blew into town Aug. 5 after a trip to Boston for the melancholy purpose of scattering his wife's ashes in the sea in accordance with her ante-mortem request. I shewed the old boy around a bit, & he, Barlow, & I wrote rhymed acrostics on Poe whilst seated on a tomb in the hidden hillside churchyard just north of here[2]—where long ago the bard of Nis & Aidenn used to roam when on visits to Providence.

Speaking of impromptus—enclosed are a triad of modernistic character sketches which Barlow wrote the other day without any effort or premeditation whatsoever. He pretends to despise them, but I rather think he'd like to see them in one of the little magazines which you so kindly listed for Pabody. What do you think of them? Would you encourage R H B to revise & submit them, & to pursue further endeavours along the same line? He could grind out this stuff endlessly if there were any demand for it. It seems rather in the *Story* line.

Barlow & I went to Newport Aug. 15—seeing both the ancient town & the lofty sea-cliffs, & having rather a pleasant sail despite temperatures lower than I like.

Thanks exceedingly for having the *Household Magazine* with your appealing story sent me.[3] This periodical, I fear, is a bit too enlightened for the old lady above-mentioned. She needs something closer to the soil & the naive yokelry of gawd's country.

Aug. 20—my 46th birthday—Barlow & I made a trip to ancient Salem & Marblehead, pausing in Lynn to pick up young Sterling (now recovering from his operation & about to enter Harvard next month) & another friend. The old towns seemed as impressive as usual—you surely must see them some day.

Well—I hope this enclosed R H B stuff doesn't form a nuisance. Don't bother to comment too minutely on it.

Yr obt Grandsire—

H P

P.S. Would you mind lending Barlow (℅ H P L) the MS. of "Evening in Spring"? He has heard much of it, & is extremely anxious to read it.

Notes

1. *WT* was a combined issue for August–September.

2. Adolphe de Castro, "Edgar Allan Poe," *WT* (May 1937); R. H. Barlow, "St. John's Churchyard," and HPL, "In a Sequester'd Providence Churchyard Where Once Poe Walk'd," *Science-Fantasy Correspondent* (March–April 1937). HPL's poem was reprinted in *WT* (May 1938) as "Where Poe Once Walked: An Acrostic Sonnet." Maurice W. Moe later wrote a poem of his own and published it, along with HPL's, RHB's, and de Castro's, in a mimeographed booklet, *Four Acrostic Sonnets on Poe* (1936).

3. "That Wedding of Annie's."

[416] [TLS, SHSW]

Sauk City
Wisconsin
26 August [1936]

Dear H. P.,

I read Barlow's stuff with a good deal of interest, but must regretfully report that while it has the promise it is as yet pretty unformed, and not likely to see publication. Also, it is extremely difficult to read, owing to the fact that RHB is not up on paragraphing, etc. Structurally, the pieces are pretty bad. I Hate Queers has the most promise, but before the really chief characters are introduced, we get 4 pages of tripe about people who do not concern the leads at all. Nobody would take a story like that, though the best bet for Barlow's emergence into little magazine print would be Manuscript, 17 West Washington, Athens, Ohio. I have made a few marks here and there in one or two of the stories, though I did not contribute the usual amount of marginal notes owing to close typing. School of Art is so far from a story that it can rightly be classed as exposition or description, while Birthday is what is known as a static sketch. The use of long-winded, platitudinous expressions annoys, but despite all this I should think there is definitely hope that RHB may make something out of such material as this. Let him drop at once any air of sophistication he may have. Affectations may serve a purpose to one's self, but not in print.

F&R have just issued Alexander Laing's (Cadaver of Gideon Wyck) DR. SCARLETT, an adventure-mystery with distinctly real overtones of the supernatural. Well worth your attention: I understand F&R and Laing will bring out a series.

As soon as my duplicate comes back, I'll lend Barlow EVENING IN SPRING. I met Galpin in Madison [a] week ago and found him a very pleasant chap indeed, far older than he looks. We have been having some acidulous exchanges on Hitler: he pro, I anti: Russia I more or less pro: he anti, and some lengthy discussions on music. He tried to inveigle me into coming upstate with him, but it was no go: I still have the 2nd draft of Still Is the Summer Night to complete—70 pages to go at this writing, and almost finished., The final draft will not be so agonizing. Despite having jerked 30 pages in a lump, the ms. is 400 pages long, 30 more than the original. I want to get this off to Scribner's 10 September, and go on immediately to the final draft, though if the way I feel about each successive draft is any index, I shall probably never admit any such thing as a final draft, certainly not one with which I am completely satisfied. And then there is the poetry anthology, which is nearing completion, which has been announced for Nov 2, though I doubt whether it will be ready by the first of October. Thanks for Moe's address; I'll write him at once.

Yes, I saw Peltier's comet, once just past Cassiopeia, and again in Aquarius, but after that moonlight made it invisible even with glasses. I note already now late at night the winter stars—the Seven Brothers, and Aldebaran show low in the east around eleven o'clock. For a long time the sky has been too hazy for mush [*sic*] astronomical observation, owing to dust and smoke clouds, but of late we have had storms and heavy drenching rains 8 night out of ten, with the result that the stars have come beautifully bright and clear again.

As for Mrs. Sutton's saccharine tale: I don't know any market off hand. She might try the Family Herald, St. James Street, Montreal, Quebec, Canada; Brit, Williamsport, Pa; National Home Monthly, Bannatyne and Dagmar Sts., Winnipeg Can. All pay on publication, some small rate.

[Note by HPL:] The Household Magazine, Topeka, Kansas. (Arthur Copper, Pub.)

No, RHB's tales are far from the Story line: Story's are crisp and clear, Barlow's are jumbled. I Hate Queers might be revised to some good end, but much of it would have to be cut, and some staple point-of-view maintained throughout. He shifts point-of-view constantly, which is very confusing and not good creation. Frankly, the stuff shows sloppy writing: I can easily believe that he just dashed it off.

Glad you liked the Household tale: the 4th Scribner's tale comes out tomorrow.

All best, always,

August

[417] [ALS]

The Antient Hill
—Sept. 23, 1936

Dear A W:—

Barlow appreciated your criticisms immensely, & will doubtless be guided by them in future attempts. He is now, of course, in a purely experimental stage—scarcely knowing what he wants to write, or whether he wants to write at all . . . as distinguished from painting, printing, bookbinding, &c. My own opinion is that writing best suits him—but I think he does better in fantasy than in realism. A recent atmospheric sketch of his—"The Night Ocean"[1]—is quite Blackwoodian in its power of dark suggestion. However—it's just as well to let the kid work the realism out of his system. At the moment he seems to think that the daily lives & amusements of cheap and twisted characters form the worthiest field for his genius. Plainness in style will develop with maturity. I've passed along the tip about *Manuscript,* and the promise of *Evening in Spring.*

Thanks for the recommendation of *Dr. Scarlett*—which I hope I'll have a chance to read when I get the time. Interested to hear that you've at last met the mighty Galpinius, & can imagine what spirited arguments you had. He always was a great chap for opinions! Sorry you couldn't get to Appleton as per his suggestion. Additional thanks for the names of naive markets for Ma Sutton's 1875 period pieces. I'll pass 'em on with acknowledgments.

Commiserations on your crowded programme—though you're doubtless used to such congestion. Here's hoping that "Still is the Summer Night" does well at Scribner's.

Glad you caught the comet before its final vanishment. Yes—today's advent of autumn is all too plainly proclaimed by the late-evening appearance of the winter constellations. Fomalhaut creeps toward the meridian, Taurus & Auriga are up before and midnight, & great Orion begins to light up the small hours. Pretty soon the active part of the year will be over for Grandpa! I notice, by the way, the melancholy flight of the ducks over the harvest fields in your seasonal stationery.

Wandrei, I see, is home again in St. Paul—& I trust he'll settle there permanently. I still maintain that New York is a loathsome dunghill, & that the best place for anybody is the native heath to which he is attached & adjusted by a million invisible threads. Barlow started west Sep. 1. Address—℅ GEORGE H. GEIGER, 104 Third Ave., Leavenworth, Kansas.

Had a very interesting letter the other day from Virgil Finlay the illustrator. He seems to be an extremely pleasant as well as brilliant chap.

Morton was here Sept. 11–12–13, going hence to the Harvard Tercentenary exercises. I am wallowing feverishly in a revision job which I had to neglect while R H B was here, & have just finished a 60-hour stretch without sleep—since a rush has developed toward the end.[2] James Ferdinand & I had a pretty good time—getting away with 2 quarts apiece of ice cream at noon on the 12th, & also absorbing a pint apiece more in the evening after a heavy spaghetti dinner. That's what we call reducing. Old Jim is now revelling in the honour of a crossword puzzle championship won at the Boston convention of the Puzzler's League. He'll get a silver loving cup 'n' everything. Barlow had a good time in N Y with Long, Sterling, & Howard Wandrei. En route west he lost a ten-spot, but his ma telegraphed him funds in Chillicothe, Ohio. In Indianapolis he stopped for a highly enjoyable call on Miss Moore.

Glad to hear you took a couple of good ol' Moe's pomes—including the churchyard acrostic.[3] Moe has had quite a nerve-&-heat breakdown, but is now pulling around slowly. His son was here Sept. 19–20—in town to call on a congenial young gentlewoman & taking a graduate philosophy course at Brown.[4] With this attraction in town, ancient Providence bids fair to see more of young Moe! Speaking of the churchyard acrostic epidemic—young Kuttner has added to the plethora with a fine specimen—more nearly poetry than a good many of the earlier ones. Not in sonnet form, but in an irregular dactylic-anapaestic metre.[5] Wonder who'll be the next to carry on the tradition? By the way—did I tell you that old de Castro sold his churchyard acrostic to W T? It would never have occurred to Barlow or me to send in the fruits of such an idle half-hour's pastime! After old Dolph sold his, we *did* send ours in—but Farny turned 'em down because he he [*sic*] had already taken one on that theme. If you ask me, Old Dolph's was the lousiest of the lot!

Autumnal blessings—

Yr obt Grandsire—

H P

Notes

1. Lightly revised by HPL.

2. The work was for Anne Tillery Renshaw's manual *Well Bred Speech* (1936). Much of HPL's work—including whole chapters that he wrote—was not used in the published version. The material survives at JHL.

3. "Invocation," "A Psalm of Trust," and "In a Providence Churchyard."

4. Little is known about Eunice French., but HPL wrote to a correspondent: "The youthful philosopheress—one Eunice French—is quite a phenomenon . . . a prodigy right in the class with you & Alfred Galpin & Leedle Meestah Stoiling. She graduated at Vassar last June, & is a veritable encyclopaedia of all human knowledge—to say nothing of being an advanced musician, expert in piano & 'cello" (letter to RHB, 30 September 1936; ms., JHL).

5. Kuttner's "Where He Walked," was published with the Poe acrostics by HPL, RHB, Adolphe de Castro, and Maurice W. Moe in David E. Schultz's "In a Sequester'd Churchyard," *Crypt of Cthulhu* No. 57 (St. John's Eve 1988): 26–29.

[418] [ALS]

The Ancient Hill

—Oct. 24, 1936

Dear A W:—

Well—I've got around at last to reading the Garland book, as I trust its safe return has attested. Many thanks for the loan. Like other chronicles of its kind, it surely presents a fascinating array of data—including much of a nature meriting careful investigation, correlation, analysis, & reflection. Garland is to be congratulated on resisting the spiritualist conclusion, even though he falls for the faked photographs of the continental "ectoplasm" devotees, & for the Boston medium so many times exposed by different committees of experts. The record as it stands is certainly a superficially impressive one, & could be understood best in connexion with a close study of Garland's own psychology . . . as checked up by the evidence obtainable from other witnesses of the varied marvels. Some things are very curious—such as the peculiarly *set traditions* of all this marvel-mongering—the inevitable table, rappings, plates, trumpet, darkness, &c. &c. Once in a while one or two of these hereditary stage-properties will be dispensed with—but usually they are all there. Curious, too, that these things are never seen by unbiassed observers of the first rank of acuteness. William James found really convincing "psychic" phenomena hard to run across[1]—but they jes' nachelly pour in on Brother Hamlin! It is significant that nothing ever develops which is not in the mind or imagination of either "medium" or "sitter". Obviously, the performer (sincerely deluded or otherwise) acts as an hypnotic agent on the spectators, causing them to receive certain suggestions & impressions of words uttered or acts performed or sights seen. Much remains to be discovered about the suggestibility of the human imagination, & this "occult" business deserves minute examination. The question as to (a) how much actual mechanical wonder-working objectively takes place in any given "seance", & (b) how the more baffling of these objective wonders are effected, is worthy of the most careful consideration & research. We certainly never learn from reports *just what really did occur,* & yet a certain amount of mechanical "magic" exists without question in these demonstrations. Of the nature of that magic, the investigations & the duplicating feats of the late Houdini give at least an opening clue. I saw him do on the stage of the Providence Opera House only a fortnight before his death things impossible according to the known laws of the physical world. That is—things *apparently* impossible. We must remember things like this before declaring that a seance contains a true miracle. Can we postulate a wholly unexplainable residue? That is for the future investigator to decide—bringing into play all that modern psychology knows of human suggestibility, false & transposed memory, the growth of folk myths from pure fiction, & the hitherto underestimated forces which make for fanatical propaganda & bold mendacity in favour of the supernatural. Senile drivel of the Lodge, Crookes, & Doyle[2] variety can be ruled out. Of the less absurd so-called evidence for the supernatural put forward—including much of Garland's, Chevreuil's, & Flammarion's—we may say that it is (a) outwardly impressive, & (b) in *any* case of the highest *psychological* importance. The importance of this class of demonstration in all our attempts to explain *human emotions & beliefs* is overwhelming—& it is acutely unfortunate that these "miracles" have not received an infinitely wider & closer study. Every "occult" manifestation *which has had the benefit of concerted investigation by the highest authorities* has been found to be (a) a mistaken impression or mechanical imposture, (b) a wrong interpretation of some natural phenomenon, or (c) a myth which never occurred in the first place—or which represents the radical mis-reporting of anything which did occur. For obvious reasons, only a few of the millions of reported occult phenomena have had the benefit of such thorough investigation. Is it not then necessary to enlarge the field & see what the best of scientific observation can do to classify the myriad alleged phenomena which still remain mysterious by default? Are there new physical & biological principles to be discovered, or will the existing laws of matter, psychology, & anthropology elucidate all the baffling appearances? Meanwhile thanks again for the loan of this provocative volume.

Speaking of the bizarre—I had an interesting note the other day from an apparently scholarly chap in San Francisco—by name, Stuart Morton Boland—who announces himself as a librarian who has been all over the world studying esoteric elder parchments like the Necronomicon in various places such as Budapest, Madras, Bombay, &c. He thinks there may be some substratum of truth behind my references to the Necro, & will accordingly be disappointed when he finds that Grandpa is a callous materialist. But I'm being very courteous in my disillusionment; since he seems to be an extremely pleasant sage, & has promised to send me some mysterious objects which he obtained at the cryptic pre-Nahuan Pyramid of the Sun at Teotihuacan during a recent trip to Mexico. The latter will surely be welcome, since my private "museum" already contains 5 Central-American items—2 early Mayan images, an earthen Aztec image, an Aztec bowl, & an earthen Aztec calendar-stone.

Your new stationery is really splendid—with that mellow Harvest or Hunter's Moon looming up behind the withering foliage. It is autumn to the life, & holds all the touches of wistful magic which helps to redeem that melancholy season. Hope you'll be able to get the other seasons captured equally well in corresponding designs.

Meanwhile good luck with "Still is the Summer Night". You are surely getting steeped in Wisconsin foundations, & I hope some day to read the results thereof. Trust the revised poetry collection will gradually crystallise & find an appropriate publisher, & am glad the short story work goes on. I shall look for "Glory Hand" in W T.

Thanks for the tips on new weird items—of which I had previously heard of only one, the Blackwood volume.[3] I saw a review of this which indicated that it contained some material previously published, but I presume much is new. I hope to see all three volumes in the course of time, & shall be very grateful for accounts of their contents. Haven't had a chance to read Nov. W T, but went through the Oct. issue some time ago. The Eshbach story is hopeless tripe, but Bloch & Kuttner do pretty well. Moore item is average, & "House of Duryea" has a clever ending. On the whole a mediocre number, though somewhat better than its predecessor. I also read Two-Gun Bob's final Conan tale—which seemed not much above the routine level, though of course superior to most pulp junk. Sorry to learn of the death of Harriet Monroe[4]—one by one the landmarks vanish. But she surely leaves solid work behind her.

Glad you've finally seen the nebulae in Lyra & Andromeda. Don't count too heavily on the clusters in Auriga unless you can get hold of something more powerful than a field-glass. They are distinctly borderline cases for 8-power. The enclosed sketch shews where you'll find the three main clusters if you find them at all. However, even with a small glass there are certain vague misty indications of these clusters. Indeed, the presence of the Milky Way causes the whole expanse of Auriga to be more or less glittery with hints of star-dust. The higher in the sky Auriga is, the better you'll be able to catch faint objects in it. It is really a winter constellation.

Hope you finally take Moe's acrostic—which is certainly vastly improved by the amendment. I was sure you'd find Galpin interesting, & hope he'll prove a competent instructor in the art of raising traditional "yarbs". His pro-fascism is not to be marvelled at in view of his past Menckenian attitudes, but this new anti-Semitism of his is really curious. He never used to have it (our good friend Loveman is of Jewish origin, & Galpin was a prime booster of his work), & I fancy it must be an outcome of his latter-day Germanophilia—which tends to forget the older Germanic main stream while centreing around the present eccentric regime. The general Jewish question has its perplexing cultural aspects, but the biologically unsound Nazi attitude offers no solution. It *is* unfortunate when the art & scholarship of a nation tend to become centred in a group of alien cultural source, whose emotions do not represent the nation's emotions; but the only sound ways to fight this evil are encouragement of the alien group's assimilation, & increasingly stimulated efforts to arouse authentic expression from the dominant population. What is more, it is silly to *belittle* even the admittedly hybrid art of Judaeo-Germans or Judaeo-Americans. It may not represent genuine German or American feeling, but it at least has a right to stand on its own feet as a frankly exotic or composite product—which may well excel much of our own art in intrinsic quality. Still more—it is equally silly to insist that the mere element of *blood* as distinguished from *culture* makes art necessarily hybrid. The typically English compiler of "The Golden Treasury" was ½ Jewish![5] It will be a vast task to work out a real modus vivendi between the essentially hostile Aryan & Semitic cultures, & nobody will ever be quite satisfied with the result. The Jews will resent the weakening of their culture as it gradually becomes absorbed in that of the west, & the Aryans will continue to resent the persistent residue which resists absorption. But whatever permanent difficulties there are, almost any line of solution is better than the arbitrary & unscientific one which the Nazis have chosen, & which bids fair to be more or less copied by other fascist groups. A fascist Spain will probably be anti-Semitic—though the rebels did not scruple to call in the aid of the traditionally hated Moors! Hell, what a world! The future of government certainly is dark & confused. Nobody knows what the devil to do, & nobody could clear the way toward doing it if he did know. Old-time plutocratic capitalism will never work again; but how to get a decent brand of socialism which *will* work, preserve traditional values, resist reactionary pressure, & secure intelligent legislation amidst the welter of ignorant, emotional, & capricious voters, is more than any layman can say. One would prefer a gradual evolution like that going on in the Scandinavian countries—but will the frantic pulling-back of stubbornly acquisitive elements (with "old-time freedom" as their rallying-cry) permit of any real forward move without a violent coup d'etat? And could a coup d'etat be managed without the slipping in of some tyrannical & arbitrary group like that imagined in Lewis's "It Can't Happen Here"? I give it up! Modern politics is too much for an old man!

About a 60-hour sleepless stretch—I couldn't manage such a thing except at rare intervals, & under the stress of some vast incentive or inescapable compulsion. In the recent case, compulsion was present. At other times—as when I take long day-&-night 'bus trips without doing more than a brief doze—the element of pleasant incentive predominates. I usually sleep about 7 hours out of the 24, though the hours I choose for such repose vary greatly. I work best at night, & always hate to interrupt a stretch of continuous work if I find myself in a good mood.

Harking back to astronomy—the other night I attended a meeting of the local organisation of amateur astronomers—"The Skyscrapers", which functions more or less under the auspices of Brown University—& was astonished at its degree of development. Some of the members are almost serious scientific observers, & the society is contemplating the purchase of a well-known observatory (the Seagrave Observatory—whose private owner & director died recently) with an 8″ refractor in the western part of the state. It has separate meteor, variable star, moon, planet, comet &c. sections, which hold meetings of their own & report to the general society as units; & enjoys the use of the college observatory. Surprisingly systematic work is done—largely in the variable star & meteor fields—& the enthusiasm of the 70 or 80 members seems to be immense. It brings back my early astronomical interests so vividly that I'm half-tempted to apply for membership! At the recent meeting there was an address on early Rhode Island astronomy, & the reflecting telescope of Joseph Brown—used to observe the transit of Venus on June 3, 1769 & owned by the college since 1780 or so—was exhibited. It is really curious how radically the general public's interest in astronomy has increased since my day. When I was young no layman seemed to give a damn about the universe & its mechanism & phenomena!

Oct. 20 & 21 were phenomenally warm, so that I was able to add to my outdoor period—supposedly over. I took an exploring walk down the east shore of the bay & discovered some splendid woods I never saw before. Other rural excursions have extended well into October—though of course outdoor reading & writing could not be kept up. Lately I've taken to haunting a wooded hill—Neutaconkanut—on the western rim of the town (& visible in the distance from my window) whence a series of marvellous views of the outspread city & adjacent countryside & blue bay can be obtained. I had ascended it before, but have only recently examined & appreciated the exquisitely mystical sylvan scenery—curious mounds, flower-starred meadows, & hushed hidden valleys—beyond its crest. It will henceforth be a favourite goal of mine.

Pres. Roosevelt was here Oct. 21, & I had some fine glimpses of him. He spoke from the terrace in front of the State House. All good wishes—

Yr Obt Grandsire H P

P.S. Note a new address (another uncle's) for Barlow—℅ H. M. Langworthy, 810 W. 57th St. Terrace, Kansas City, Mo.

[P.P.S.] Hope your severe cold is now wholly a thing of the past.

Notes

1. William James (1842–1910), "What Psychical Research Has Accomplished," in *The Will to Believe* (1897). James also published several papers in the *Proceedings* of the American Society for Psychical Research.

2. For Lodge, see letter 13n2. Sir William Crookes (1832–1919), British chemist and physicist. His most important work was in the investigation of the conduction of electricity in gases. He developed the Crookes tube (mentioned in "The Shunned House") and in it produced cathode rays for the first time. He also wrote *Researches into the Phenomena of Modern Spiritualism* (Manchester, UK: "Two Worlds" Publ. Co., 1904). Sir Arthur Conan Doyle became an avowed spiritualist after the death of his son in World War I.

3. *Shocks.*

4. Harriet Monroe (1860–26 September 1936), poet and editor. She was the founder of *Poetry: A Magazine of Verse* in October 1912 and its editor until her death. The magazine was primarily a vehicle for the Imagism, Impressionism, and *vers libre* movements, but early on it had published a few poems by CAS.

5. I.e., Francis T. Palgrave (1814–1897).

[419] [ALS]

The Ancient Hill
—Nov. 18, 1936.

Dear A. W.—

Surely your autumnal design has amply repaid the labour expended upon it. It has a very curious & pervasive charm—conveying something of the same sensation that its actual scenic prototype might convey. I'm glad, by the way, that you had a resplendent October in Wisconsin—for ours was a great disappointment (as perhaps I mentioned in my preceding epistle) so far as foliage was concerned. We had no frost till Oct. 26; but heavy rains removed much leafage earlier in the month, whilst some trees remained green anomalously late—then losing their leaves almost at once. It was the dullest autumn within my memory—though elsewhere in New England gorgeous effects were reported. However—apart from the matter of foliage, the season lacked nothing in fascination. It had for me an added charm because—as I think I said before—I discovered so many splendid woodland regions close at hand which I had never previously seen or heard of. It surely gives an old man a renewed illusion of youth & of adventurous expectancy to come upon something fresh & unexpected when he had thought all such things were past! Since my last letter I have opened up one more realm of fascinating terra incognita—the region west of the Neutaconkanut Hill which I previously mentioned, & the western slopes of that eminence itself. On Oct. 28 I penetrated a terrain which took me half a mile from any spot I had ever trod before in the course of a long life. I followed a road which branches north & west from the Plainfield Pike, ascending a low rise which skirts Neutaconkanut's western foot & which commands an utterly idyllic vista of rolling meadows, ancient stone walls, hoary groves, & distant cottage roofs to the west & south. Only 2 or 3 miles from the city's heart—& yet in the primal rural New-England of the first colonists! Just before sunset I ascended the hill by a precipitous cart-path bordering an ancient wood, & from the dizzy crest obtained an almost stupefying prospect of outspread countryside, gleaming rivulets, far-off forests, & mystical orange sky with the great solar disc sinking redly amidst bars of stratus clouds. Entering the woods, I saw the actual sunset through the trees, & then turned east to cross the hill to that more familiar cityward slope which I have always known. Never before had I realised the great extent of Neutaconkanut's surface. It is really a miniature plateau or table-land, with valleys, ridges, & summits of its own, rather than a simple hill. From some of the hidden interior meadows—remote from every sign of nearby human life—I secured truly marvellous glimpses of the remote urban skyline—a dream of enchanted pinnacles & domes half-floating in air, & with an obscure aura of mystery around them. The upper windows of some of the taller towers held the fire of the sun after I had lost it, affording a spectacle of cryptic & curious glamour. Then I saw the great round disc of the Hunter's Moon (2 days before full) floating above the belfries & minarets, while in the orange-glowing west Venus & Jupiter commenced to twinkle. My route across the plateau was varied—sometimes through the interior, but now & then getting toward the wooded edge where dark valleys slope down to the plain below, & huge balanced boulders on rocky heights impart a spectral, druidic effect as they stand out against the twilight. I did not begin to cover the full extent of the plateau, & can see that I have a field for several future voyages of discovery. Finally I came to more familiar ground—where the grassy ridge of an old buried aqueduct gives the illusion of one of those vestigial Roman roads in Arthur Machen's Gwent country—& stood once more on the well-known eastward crest which I have gazed at since the age of three. The outspread city was rapidly lighting up, & lay like a constellation in the deepening dusk. The moon poured down increasing floods of pale gold, the glow of Venus & Jupiter in the fading west grew intense. Then down the steep hillside to the car line (too cold for enjoyable walking when there's no scenery to compensate for shivers!) & back to the prosaic haunts of man.[1]

As for Garland & the occult—I'll be readier to adopt the so-called "open-minded" attitude (which so lightly disregards the conflict of all these fugitive folklore reports with everything taught by solid research concerning the way in which the forces of nature operate) when the subjects of psychological influence & of the instinct for pro-supernatural mendacity have been more thoroughly explored & correlated with the marvellous tales of the seance-initiates. There is room for profound research in the one field of escapist propaganda-mania—an instinct which I have repeatedly encountered & occasionally exposed. I'll look up that telepathic business when I get hold of the current *Harpers*.[2] I've heard of the Duke University experiments—& also of those conducted at some Pacific Coast university (U. of Cal. or Stanford—I don't recall) which flatly contradict them. In any case the whole subject deserves the continued researches of students specially fitted for such investigations—students who are prepared to observe, detect, record, & interpret all conditions & events from the sole standpoint of available evidence.

Glad to hear of the various successes, & trust the final acceptance of "Still is the Summer Night" is now to be reckoned among them. Your current reading is as impressive as usual, & I don't wonder that it excludes such junk as W T & its fellow-pulps. I haven't had time to look at the December issue—except to note with pain that Finlay's excellent illustration more or less belies the text of the "Haunter". I hope before long to get access to the new Blackwood, Machen, & de la Mare items[3]—even though I fail to rise to the height of ownership.

Later

Got hold of *Harpers* & read the telepathic article with great interest. The results of those experiments do look extraordinary, & would seem to demand some very definite consideration & comment from physiologists, psychologists, physicists, & others into whose territories the implications of the tests apparently extend. It will be interesting to see what replies are elicited, & what details of the experiments & interpretations of the "law of probability" are brought out. The integrity & dependability of the experimenters are certainly unassailable—indeed, the whole thing differs widely from the sort of seances with jumping trumpets, ectoplasmic arms, & self-playing pianos which Garland reports. Meanwhile I still await with interest the second article of the series,[4] in which some attempt at an explanation of the results is promised.

Concerning politics—I find myself in thorough agreement with the position outlined in your last letter . . . . & judging by the election returns, quite a few others hold more or less similar views! The *extent* of the landslide delighted me, although I had begun to look for something in that direction. The feeble arguments, obvious hokum, absurd accusations, & occasionally underhanded tactics of the Republicans reacted against them—while some obscure instinct of common sense seemed to keep the extreme radicals from wasting their votes on obviously hopeless tickets. It amuses me to see the woebegone state of the poor ostriches who constitute Providence's exclusive clique, & away from whose past-drugged ideology it is impossible to pull my aunt. Around election-time I came damn near having a family feud on my hands! These complacent old birds actually thought their beloved Langhorne or Lampton (or whatever his name was) had a chance! However, the immediate university element wasn't so stupid. Indeed, one of the professors said just before the election that his idea of a rotten sport was a man who would *take* one of the pro-Langtry (or whatever his name was) bets offered by the white-moustached constitution-savers of the Hope Club easy-chairs![5]

The other day I received, in the course of its circulation, your extremely fine sketch "Goodbye, Margery", which I read with keen interest & attention. I recalled its prototype in "Evening in Spring", & believe that the present version represents a distinct advance. The style has all that haunting, dreamlike, reminiscent quality which one associates with your best work, & the frequently recurrent image of the lonely street lights & trees helps greatly to intensify the impression. There are, of course, some who might find a touch of preciosity in prose as close to poetry as this—but I would not concur in such a criticism. To my mind this dreamlike reminiscence forms a legitimate genre in itself—& one which you handle with peculiar aptitude. The tale is delicate—involving fragile & elusive emotional elements—but powerful & sincere; & it leaves a residue of very convincing feeling. It ought to be acceptable almost anywhere—except in the wretched commercial "pulps" & "slicks". Are you planning to publish it separately, or does it form a sample of a general overhauling of "Evening in Spring"? Or both? I promptly sent the manuscript along to young Albrecht Dürer,[6] who I am sure will share my appreciation of it.

The new "fan" magazine—*Science-Fantasy Correspondent*—is out at last, &

is certainly a credit to its youthful editors.[7] Not a misprint so far as I can see! Hill-Billy Crawford has also finished my "Innsmouth" book at last—with 33 bad misprints, but with a detailed errata-sheet to offset them. He'll have a hard time getting rid of the edition—but I warned him in the first place. ¶ All good wishes—

Yr most obt. grandsire—

E'ch-Pi-El

Notes

1. AWD incorporated much of this paragraph into the "posthumous collaboration" "The Lamp of Alhazred" (1957).

2. E. H. Wright, "The Case for Telepathy," *Harpers* 173 (November 1936): 575–86.

3. Algernon Blackwood, *Shocks;* Arthur Machen, *The Cosy Room* or *The Children of the Pool;* Walter de la Mare, *The Wind Blows Over.*

4. E. H. Wright, "The Nature of Telepathy," *Harper's* 174 (December 1936): 13–21.

5. In the presidential election of 1936, the Democrat Franklin D. Roosevelt defeated the Republican Alf Landon and third-party candidate William Lemke.

6. I.e., Howard Wandrei.

7. Willis Conover and Corwin F. Stickney.

[420] [ANS][1]

[Postmarked Providence, R.I.,
24 November 1936]

A thousand thanks for the Blackwoodian collection which has just reached me as an advance agent of Yuletide! Since you know of the superlative esteem in which I hold Blackwood—as perhaps the only writer who has ever treated the deep-seated human illusion of unreality with adequate analytical seriousness—you can imagine the extent & genuineness of my gratitude. I fear that other tasks will be neglected whilst I succumb to the irresistible lure of these pages. I read "Chemical" in another anthology, but "Full Circle" (the other marked story) will be entirely new to me. My Blackwood library is increasing—thanks very largely to yourself. I now have "John Silence", "The Lost Valley", "Shocks", "Julius LeVallon", "Jimbo", & "The Willows" in an anthology. I wish it were easy to get hold of "Incredible Adventures" & "The Centaur". Both have vanished from the Prov. Public Library. Again, my sincerest & profoundest gratitude.

—Yr obt Servt
H P

Notes

1. Front: Brown University, Van Wickle Gate and University Hall, Providence, R.I.

[421] [ALS]

The Ancient Hill—
Dec. 16, 1936.

Dear A. W.—

Your chromatic experiments with the Hunter's Moon in your stationery are surely ingenious. The same scene in winter, with snow & a cold, bluish-white moon, wouldn't be at all bad—though it might be too much to expect a perfect parallelling of the present design's success. I envy you the Wisconsin autumn—of which your article indicates that you made good use. That wild island so close at hand must be extremely fascinating, & ought indeed to make a good setting for the opening of your novel. Quite a coincidence that you've begun finding hitherto unvisited places near home just as I've started on a similar course of discovery! I enjoyed the article greatly, & thank you very much for sending it along.

Meanwhile, sincere congratulations on the Scribnerian acceptance despite the programme of added labour which it would seem to impose on you. It certainly forms a decisive step forward, & its effect on your prestige cannot but be excellent. Hope the anthology won't prove too burdensome before you are rid of it. Eventually I hope to see a published "Evening in Spring" containing all your semi-poetic reminiscent material. And in the interim I am glad to hear of all the story sales to markets high-grade & otherwise. Editorship of a book of Garland's poems would be a distinction, but a distinction with a high cost in time & labour. I fancy you'd be wiser in declining the honour—for after all, you're getting a very decent quote of prestige as it is, through the much more important channel of direct achievement on your own hook! As for trying to float a volume of Grandpa's weird tales some day—naturally I shall have blessings rather than objections to offer, but I wouldn't advise the expenditure of too much time & energy on the project. I'm afraid such a thing would be a mere remainder-counter flop even if it did get into print! But thanks for the idea, none the less! I shall keep an eye open for the new Machen volume, & must meanwhile reiterate my grateful delight in the Blackwood collection which so opportunely arrived. This latter surely is the most welcome addition my library has had in some time.

I shall indeed be interested to see what the general scientific response to the Rhine telepathic experiments turns out to be.[1] All such things call for careful investigation—& experiments of the Rhine type ought if possible to be correlated in some way with that different set of experiments lately conducted in several places, concerning so-called "brain waves" or variations in the electrical radiations of cerebral cells corresponding to variations in cerebral activity. I read the second Harpers article with great interest, although its conclusions (or the way they were put) make the matter seem rather more fantastic than it did before. The author is anxious to prove that the alleged transmission of knowledge is neither sensory in the ordinary significance of the term nor related to wave motion; but in his statements he postulates virtually impossible conditions—i.e., "non-material" receipt of impressions, as if there were some mystical essence in the cosmos & in human consciousness apart from the forces manifest as electrons, atoms, energy, & matter. It won't do to relapse into mythological concepts—that gets one nowhere. If the human mind—a material organism—received the cell-altering electric charge constituting a new impression in any of these cases, it received it in a material way. There was a link of some sort—call it what you like (electron-stream, lines of force, &c. &c.)—betwixt perceiver & object (or mental concept in another) perceived. But before we credit the evidence fully, we must of course reëxamine & reinterpret it. That many of the participants came from families in which legends of strange marvels are current*, sheds a curious light on their predisposition & bias. Of course, a perfectly impartial superintendent & interpreter of the experiments would render such a bias immaterial—but all the same, one must be on guard. If, however, the evidence *is* to be accepted, it seems to indicate (a) that a single cognitive faculty apart from *known* sensory perception exists (rarely & faintly) in man, (b) that this faculty is independent of distance, (c) that it is *exerted* by the perceiver rather than merely passively exercised, (d) that its successful exercise is closely connected with the exerciser's mental & physical state, & (e) that it is hereditary. The assertion that it seems to be an evolved rather than a primitive faculty is backed by no visible evidence. Well—all this ought to call for a lot of thought, expert analysis, & authoritative comment. ¶ Best holiday wishes—

Yr. obt Grandsire—

H P

P.S. Your Christmas card forms a delightful combination of poetry & pictorial art. ¶ Under separate cover I'm sending with my compliments a copy of "Innsmouth", corrected as far as possible, and a damn poor job for all that!

Notes

1. J. B. Rhine (1895–1980) established the Duke University Parapsychology Laboratory in 1935 for the scientific study of psychic phenomena.

---

*The writer overlooks the proved erroneousness or charlatanry of virtually all deeply investigated reports of the sort.

1937

[422] [ALS]

The Antient Hill—
Jany 17, 1937.

Dear AW:—

Glad "Innsmouth" safely arrived—but what a mess poor Hill-Billy made of the format! Here's a list of additional errata which I hope you'll correct in the book—discovered by the eagle eye of one of the kid "fan mag" editors.[1]

News anent "Summer Night"" is gratifying despite the arduous nature of wholesale proofreading. Hope the portraits turn out well—& that they'll prove an asset in spreading the rising author's fame. I anticipate great pleasure in the reading of this work. Meanwhile I trust the next of the series will prove equally successful—justifying the widespread & coöperative research. Evidently these books are going to reflect Wisconsin's *real* past, rather than any vague & boner-riddled fabric of guesswork & half-knowledge, as is all too common in historical novels! You were wise, I think, in turning down the Garland proposition. Glad to hear of the new W T acceptances, & hope to get hold of the *Story* containing "Old Huckleberry".

I trust your Yuletide was suitably festive & gift-bestrown. Ours here was commendably cheerful—including a turkey dinner at the boarding-house across the garden, with a congenial cat meandering among the tables & finally jumping up on the window-seat for a nap. We had a tree in front of the hearth in my aunt's living-room—its verdant boughs thickly festooned with a tinsel imitation of Florida's best Spanish moss, & its outlines emphasised by a not ungraceful lighting system. Around its base were ranged the Saturnalian gifts—which included (on my side) a hassock tall enough to let me reach the top shelves of my bookcases, & (on my aunt's side) a cabinet of drawers for odds & ends, not unlike my own filing cabinets, but of more ladylike arrangement & aspect. Of outside gifts (aside from "Shocks")[2] the most distinctive was perhaps that which came quite unexpectedly from young Conover, the editor of the new "fan mag" (which is, by the way, about to absorb Schwartz's *Fantasy*) in Cambridge Maryland . . . . daown awn de Eastern Sho'. For lo! when I had removed numberless layers of corrugated paper & excelsior, what should I find before me but the yellowed & crumbling fragments of *a long-interred human skull!* Verily, a fitting gift from a youthful ghoul to one of the hoary elders of the necropolitan clan! This sightlessly staring monument of mortality came from an Indian mound not far from the sender's home—a place distinguished by many archaeological exploits on the part of the enterprising editor & his young friends. Its condition is such as to make its reassembling a somewhat ticklish task—so that I may reserve it for the ministrations of some expert mender like Bobby Barlow upon the occasion of a future visit. Viewing this shattered yield of the ossuary, the reflective fancy strives to evoke the image of him to whom it once belonged. Was it some feathered chieftain who in his day oft ululated in triumph as he counted the tufted scalps sliced from coppery or colonist foes? Or some crafty shaman who with masque & drum called forth from the Great Abyss those shadowy Things which were better left uncalled? This we may never know—unless perchance some incantation droned out of the pages of the Necronomicon will have power to draw strange emanations from the lifeless & centuried clay, & raise up amidst the cobwebs of my ancient study a shimmering mist not without power to speak . . . or to communicate ideas after the fashion of our friend Prof. Rhine. In such a case, the revelation might be such that no man hearing it could any longer live save as one of those hapless entities 'who laugh, but smile no more'![3]

The first half of our winter was phenomenally warm, so that my hibernation was considerably postponed. My health, however, has been rotten—an early exposure to cold having revived a curious winter tendency to badly swollen feet. To this is conjoined a digestive trouble & general weakness which may have some kinship to the prevailing grippe. However, I manage to totter forth (in old shoes suitably cut & stretched) for brief neighbourhood walks whenever the weather is warm enough, & suppose I'll eventually pull through this winter as I've pulled through 46 other damn winters in my day. But it gets to be cursed monotonous. Why in hell did people ever found permanent settlements north of Lat. 30°?

Good luck & best wishes—

Yr ob[t] Grandsire

H P

Notes

1. See Lovecraft to John J. Weir, 31 December 1936 (ms., private hands): "There are about 50 errors in Crawford's edition of my 'Innsmouth'. I found about 35, but the eagle-eyed [Corwin] Stickney spotted (too late, alas, for the printed list of errata!) many that I had overlooked." HPL wryly speculated to correspondents that even the errata list had errors. (It did.)

2. After HPL's death, his aunt Annie Gamwell informed AWD that he had taken the Blackwood book to the hospital to read during his stay.

3. Poe, "The Haunted Palace," l. 48.

[423] [TLS, SHSW]

22 January [1937]

Dear H. P.,

I send along: 1) the newest Outdoors piece; 2) a tear-sheet ad listing the contents of one of the very best anthologies of its type to have come my way; 3) application blanks for a HM fellowship, which I urge you to try for at least—mayhap a study of the supernatural in literature—show them your ms. and suggest revision, lengthening, and bringing up to date, additional research, etc.—might interest them sufficiently to merit their attention. Paul Brooks of Houghton Mifflin suggested that I send these out to persons whom I thought to literary promise. .... I sympathize with you in regard to the weather. I hardly know what I would do had I the cold allergy you suffer under. The weather here has been miserable and as unprecedented as last's, for, while we do not have the excessive snow and cold of last year, we have a far more dangerous health condition: fluct[u]ating weather temperatures from 35 and even 50 above to 10 below; the latter is of course far healthier, but the fluctuations in temp, and the resultant snow, sleet, rain has [*sic*] created ice over everything, trees and earth alike, so that the going is difficult, and has moreover increased danger from influenza and pneumonia. I myself suffered for a week with a kind of malaise, during which my body was doubtless fighting off some infection, successfully, as it turned out, since I went immediately upon a healthy diet: fruit, and fruit juices: toast; and black tea. I can recommend it to you if you take cold or anything akin. .... I have your additional errata for THE SHADOW OVER INNSMOUTH, which is now being read by Ben Abramson of the Argus Book Shop,[1] who thinks he may buy and sell some copies of the opus. I wish him all luck, and have offered to do a brief monograph on the book. I have also notified Ben of my intention to sometime see to press a collected and selected edition of your short stories. I have told Ben that while The Shadow is representative of what you can do, still it is not rep. of your best. .... The portraits for STILL IS THE SUMMER NIGHT turned out splendidly indeed, and one will be used on the back of the jacket. I saw the cover of the book the other day, a sample sent me; it is in every detail my design, save the briefly noted changing of my name from smaller letters to large on the book's face. It is handsome and striking and not garish; it is likewise durable. The book will come, as I think I told you, to 356 pages in print. It has a handsome title page indeed, and I feel that it is by and large the best effort of mine yet to see print. The entire sales force of Scribners is enthusiastic about the book, which their publicity department tells me is a very concrete asset, for these are the men who sell the books to the dealers, and they can sell so much more if they believe in a book themselves. The book will be published in March, though I will have advance copies in two weeks time.[2] The date given me is March 5, but this is tentative, and it is possible that the book will be set to a somewhat later day—two weeks or so. As far as I am concerned, it is immaterial to me when it comes, for I am now familiar with the physical appearance it has, and am besides wrapped up in WIND OVER WISCONSIN, though I have not yet been able to return to that novel. Instead, I got busy and took down and wrote new notes for a book which has been lurking in my mind for some time, tentatively called: VILLAGE YEAR: A SAC PRAIRIE NOTEBOOK or JOURNAL, with the result that I now have some 40,000 words of this opus written, and all the old notes transcribed, ready for additional writing as the journal moves. This book will be ready for press a year from know, together with WIND OVER WISCONSIN. Scribners will issue in the fall, also, providing I revise it, a new Judge Peck. Also, Ritten House of Philadelphia will bring out HAWK ON THE WIND, my book of poems, containing 55 titles. .... I wrote two articles for Reading and Collecting,[3] revised the Gus Elker tale, PREVAILING WESTERLY, at Scribner[']s request, and wrote a new weird, MONCATI TOOK A PICTURE, (rejected today by Wright), and a new Gus Elker, A BIRD IN THE BUSH, which I hope to sell to Household. Atlantic cropped up again with renewed request for a new story, and I daresay I will have to get at that before I get to WIND OVER WISCONSIN. I wouldn't, but I need the money badly just now, and so must work. .... My yuletide was adequately gifted with a new desk, a chair to go with it, a little money and candy, and a new jacket. .... Handsomest Xmas tree in the village was furnished by me to three spinster friends: a fair-sized branch of well-budded alder, which they hung tastily [*sic*] with just silver tinsel. It was very handsome. ..... Perhaps that Indian whose skull you have may have been a wandering Sac, mayhap a character in WIND OVER WISCONSIN? Who shall say? ...... Well, I reckon this is enough for one letter. I hope and pray it finds you in good health again; I know full well how annoying such petty things may be. ... All best, always,

August

Notes

1. Ben Abramson of the Argus Bookshop in Chicago published HPL's *Supernatural Horror in Literature* and AWD's *H. P. L.: A Memoir* in 1945.

2. A copy had been sent to HPL, but though likely received was not read before his death.

3. "A Master of the Macabre" (see Appendix), subsequently revised to reflect HPL's death two months later, and "A Note on Arthur Machen."

[424] [TLS]

The Antient Hill—
[17 February 1937]

Dear A.W.:—

Behold the old man reduced to the hated clicker—a lesser evil in view of the general weakness (an attribute of my present varied grippe-like maladies) which makes my script shaky, laboured, and indecipherable in any substantial quantity. Glad to see the February OUTDOORS article—which almost makes the winter woods seem attractive. It probably takes a sharper eye than mine to catch all the bits of colour you chronicle, but the general charm of certain forests in winter (they have to be dense ones, and not mere clumps of thin, scraggly trees which let in the disillusioning sunlight) has always more or less impressed me. In my youth I occasionally rambled through such, though the ordeal of such extended trips in the cold season is a bit too much for me now. The very near forests are usually of a thinnish sort which need foliage in order to be glamourous—though, come to think of it, those Squantum Woods which I discovered last October ought to bear out your article reasonably well. If I weren't so damn laid up I'd try a walk down there some warm day soon.

Thanks for the advertisement of "The Haunted Omnibus",[1] which with its 60 bizarre illustrations must be quite a notable item. I find that I have read most of the material included, but wouldn't mind owning this grim gallery for all that. Regarding the Houghton-Mifflin fellowship blank—extreme thanks for the compliment of sending it! Actually, I don't believe it would be wise for me to make any promises or assume any obligations in my present state of uncertain health and depleted energies (I've had to sidetrack a speculative proposition of Talman's[2] for lack of strength to do one single thing more than I'm doing)—for nothing is more ignominious than biting off more than one can chew. I can't do anything very long without resting on the couch—I get dizzy and weak, and lack power of concentration—and could never contract for a research proposition involving the hunting up of all sorts of books which I don't own. I always said I'd like to do a second edition of Sup. Horror in Lit., but now I know I never shall. It would take more tracking down of books that I don't know, more reading, and more goddam typing, than I could ever handle except in some land of perpetual 90° temperatures. But thanks just the same for sending the blank—the compliment of which I surely appreciate!

Commiserations on your own spell of bad health, which I trust is by now wholly over. Your diet sounds sensible—I am myself going in for mild things, and having some sort of fruit each morning. Our winter has continued to average warm—above 32° most of the time, an usually over 40° (never anywhere near zero—in fact, it almost never gets down there in Providence)—a circumstance which has helped me vastly by enabling me to get out for short afternoon walks. In a really cold winter I would be wholly deprived of outdoor air and exercise, and would be so much the worse therefor. But all the same I shall be damned glad when mid-May brings some civilised and endurable temperatures!

Thanks enormously for shewing "Innsmouth" to the Argus proprietor—and for volunteering a review in case he decides to handle some copies. It's up to him to decide whether or not this slipshod tome would stand grouping with more illustrious neighbours "Along the North Wall".

Congratulations on the good outcome of the portraits, and on the appearance of STILL IS THE SUMMER NIGHT and its dust wrapper. This pleasing exterior, plus the enthusiasm of the publishers, ought to cooperate finely with its intrinsic merit in making a success of it. You'll doubtless be a rather famous figure by the time "Wind Over Wisconsin" comes out! Hope "Village Year" and the detective item will also develop smoothly. Bless me, but what a young dynamo of activity you are! And the poetry volume, too! The various reviews will have to issue a "Special d'Erlette Number"!

Hope all the magazine projects will mature successfully. I liked your "Glory Hand" in the Feb. WT, which gave a decidedly original twist to the "Beast with Five Fingers" motif.

Congratulations on the Yule acquisitions—and on your triumph in tree-selection. Yes—that skull I received may well have been that of a Sac from the Prairie, since the wide wandering of individual Indians is well proved by the discovery of artifacts far from their source.

Had a request not long ago for a freshened-up version of some old astronomical articles of mine,[3] and as a result I've been trying to brush up on the heavens a bit after 20 or 30 years. The progress of astronomy has left me absurdly behind—but certain books are valuable in helping one cover the lost decades. Our public library—weak on astronomy until a couple of years ago—has spruced up and provided a surprisingly ample array of contemporary treatises, and I have four of them out now. As an introduction for the novice, nothing seems to beat the short manual by Bartky, while Stokeley's [*sic*] "Stars and Telescopes" rounds out the picture well. The eminent F. R. Moulton's "Consider the Heavens" seems tedious reading at first, but ultimately presents the best of all pictures of the cosmos as a whole—as conceived by astronomers at present. Of formal text-books, that by J. C. Duncan (3d ed. 1935) is by all odds the best I've yet found. One can glide over the mathematical parts without losing the general thread. Another thing of interest to the constellation student is the little magazine called THE MONTHLY EVENING SKY MAP ($1.50 per annum) published by the 86-year-old Leon Barritt, 244 Adams St., Brooklyn, N.Y. This shews the morning and evening sky for each month in middle northern latitudes, the evening sky for the southern hemisphere (invaluable for anybody writing about Australia or South Africa or South America), and various other things of interest. A damn good value. I think I shall subscribe—and if you'd care to see a sample copy I'll send one. Thirty years ago I bought a large planisphere from Barritt—the so-called "Barritt-Serviss Star and Planet Finder", with a graduated ecliptic and thumb-tacks for planets. An accompanying booklet gave the right ascension of each planet at short intervals for about a decade ahead, so that one could simply stick the tack on the ecliptic at the right place and be all set. Time passed, the booklet became obsolete, and I didn't know what had become of Barritt and his firm. For a while I used the Nautical Almanack in setting the planets, but after I ceased to buy the almanack I simply let the thing slide. Now—after a full generation—I discover that the old coot is still going strong at 86, and conducting his business at full blast—even on an increased scale, for he issues this little magazine and acts as agent for telescopes, books, and all sorts of astronomical devices. So at last I'm getting another planet booklet (up to 1947) and blowing the dust off the old planisphere. I'm surely glad I didn't throw the device away (or rather, give it away), as I might well have done, since I have other planispheres which shew merely the stars. Funny how early interests crop up again toward the end of one's life. Another old specialty of mine—chemistry—gave me a salute the other day when I found out that one of the "fan mag" kids—young Bordley of Maryland[4]—is a red-hot chemical enthusiast with a well-equipped laboratory.

Wright lately gave me the Finlay originals of the headings of my two recent stories, and I found them infinitely better than the reproductions. The "Doorstep" one is really quite a fantastic triumph in its way.

Has Rimel shewed you the silhouette (linoleum block) he made of Belknap from study of several differently-angled snapshots?[5] Not at all bad, as Sonny himself agrees. Hope he'll have as good luck with his next victim—which is yourself. I've lent him all the best snaps of you which my files yield up.

Obeisances and benedictions—

Yr obt Grandsire,

H P

Notes

1. Ed. Alexander Laing.

2. Wilfred B. Talman had approached William Morrow & Co. about the possibility of publishing a weird novel to be written by HPL. See *SL* 5.338–40, 343–50, 420–21.

3. Charles Blackburn Johnston, the Barlows' handyman in DeLand, Florida, now "connected" with Stetson University and its astronomical society, asked HPL for a series of "elementary articles on the heavens for the local paper" (see *SL* 5.422). HPL

resurrected his series, "Mysteries of the Heavnens" (1915) for that purpose, but never revised the articles.

4. Thomas Kemp Bordley, friend of Willis Conover.

5. Rimel had made a linoleum cut of HPL to accompany F. Lee Baldwin's, "H. P. Lovecraft: A Biographical Sketch," *Fantasy Magazine* 4, No. 5 (April 1935): 108–10, 132. The cut of FBL apparently was not published.

Appendix

One for the Black Bag

My dear sir:

Having lately come across a copy of the *Dragnet* for the first time, and noting your desire for opinions from readers, I am compelled to express my pleasure at the excellent quality of the publication.

In the February issue, to my mind, two stories stand out as of especially distinctive merit. One of these—"The Black Bag"—handles the elements of suspense and surprise with a skill and assurance not often met with in popular magazine fiction; and somehow achieves a naturalness which causes the rather free use of coincidence to pass unnoticed.

The other—and perhaps the better technically—is "The Adventure of the Black Narcissus" by August W. Derleth. The extremely fine craftsmanship of this tale creates a sense of constantly impending revelation and never-flagging interest; whilst the denouement comes with such a mingled inevitability and shock of surprise that we feel not only dramatically satisfied, but moved with a conviction of reality which no mere theatrical claptrap could supply. There is an element of unusual proportion and sanely consistent verisimilitude which does not clash at all with the rapid and brilliant movement and the expert knitting of plot-developments. I sincerely hope that Mr. Derleth is a permanent member of your writing staff, for his "Solar Pons" seems eminently qualified to take rank with the standard detectives of fiction.

With best wishes for your group of publications, I am

Yours very truly,

H. P. LOVECRAFT,
10 Barnes Street,
Providence, R. I.

The Weird Tale in English Since 1890 [excerpt]

V.—LOVECRAFT, SHIEL, MACHEN, BLACKWOOD

To the cosmic horror group belong four names—Mr. Howard P. Lovecraft, Mr. Matthew Phipps Shiel, Mr. Arthur Machen, and Mr. Algernon Blackwood—and each of these is supreme. Of these only one is American, and it is not surprising to note that his work strikes me as most directly influenced by Poe. Mr. H. P. Lovecraft's horror stories have not been published in book form, beyond the appearance of three of them in collections. Outstanding among his stories are three, which have so far seen only magazine publication in *Weird Tales*; these are *The Outsider,"* *The Rats in the Walls*, and *The Music of*

Erich Zann. Of these stories, *The Outsider* seems supreme; yet it is extremely difficult to designate any one better than another, for his work is quite uniform, falling below par occasionally, and sometimes reaching heights of fascinating Dunsanian fantasy, as in *The Strange High House in the Mist.* Mr. Lovecraft's method, so closely akin to Poe's, is to swing boldly out into the unknown, to capture it and bring it back to us. In this he succeeds admirably; whether it be the story of the accursed cult of Cthulhu, the inconceivable tale of the horror that descended upon Dunwich, or the narrative of the incredible thing that modeled for Pickman—Mr. Lovecraft is consistently convincing. Since *The Outsider* is out of print at the present writing, the quotation of large excerpts is not amiss. The story concerns a ghoul who rises from his long sealed grave and ventures into the outside world; he is unaware that he is a ghoul, and when he appears at a house party, frightening the guests out of the house, he sees himself in a mirror, but looks upon the apparition as that of the monster which has frightened the guests. When recognition comes, he flees into the night. In method the story is distinctly Poe; not until the very last line is the reader fully aware of the identity of the ghoul, who tells the story himself. I quote at random from the beginning of *The Outsider:*

> Unhappy is he to whom the memories of childhood bring only fear and sadness. Wretched is he who looks hack upon lone hours in vast and dismal chambers with brown hangings and maddening rows of antique books, or upon awed watches in twilight groves of grotesque, gigantic, and vine-encumbered trees that silently wave twisted branches far aloft. . . . I know not where I was born, save that the castle was infinitely old and infinitely horrible; full of dark passages and having high ceilings where the eye could find only cobwebs and shadows.

From this, the unfortunate ghoul makes his escape, and wanders out into the countryside. He enters the house where the party is in progress; here is his description of the "monster" that frightened the guests, from which he himself turns in loathing:

> . . . it was a compound of all that is unclean, uncanny, unwelcome, abnormal, and detestable. It was the ghoulish shade of decay, antiquity, and desolation; the putrid, dripping eidolon of unwholesome revelation; the awful baring of that which the merciful earth should always hide. God knows it was not of this world—or no longer of this world—yet to my horror I saw in its eaten-away and bone-revealing outlines a leering, abhorrent travesty on the human scrape; and in its moldy, disintegrating apparel an unspeakable quality that chilled me even more. . . . Nearly mad, I found myself yet able to throw out a hand to ward off the fetid apparition which pressed so close; when in one cataclysmic second of cosmic nightmarishness and hellish accident, my fingers touched the rotting outstretched paw of the monster beneath the golden arch.

And now for the revelation, which the author manages cleverly to conceal until the end; this is accomplished without any device whatsoever, and appears perfectly natural.

> But in the cosmos there is balm as well as bitterness, and that balm is nepenthe. In the supreme horror of that second I forgot what had horrified me, and the burst of black memory vanished in a chaos of echoing images. In a dream I fled from that haunted and accursed pile, and ran swiftly and silently in the moonlight. When I returned to the churchyard place of marble and went down the steps I found the stone trap-door irremovable; but I was not sorry, for I had hated the antique castle and the trees. Now I ride with the mocking and friendly ghouls on the night-wind, and play by day amongst the catacombs of Nephren-Ka in the sealed and unknown valley of Iladoth by the Nile. I know that light is not for me, save that of the moon over the rock tombs of Neb, nor any gayety save the unnamed feasts of Nitokris beneath the great Pyramid; yet in my new wildness and freedom I almost welcome the bitterness of alienage.
>
> For although nepenthe has calmed me, I know always that I am an outsider; a stranger in this century and among those who are still men. This I have known ever since I stretched out my fingers to the abomination within that great gilded frame; stretched out my fingers and touched *a cold and unyielding surface of polished glass.*

The idea of telling the story from the point-of-view of the ghoul is, while not entirely new, here in its best form. *The Outsider* achieves a cosmic effect through the potency of the author, whose cumulative narrative moves evenly along to the utterly revealing climax of the last line. However excellent *The Outsider* may be, it is *The Rats in the Walls* which achieves the most utterly gruesome effect of any short story in the language; indeed, the closest approach to this story is Dr. James' excellent *Count Magnus.*

The Rats in the Walls concerns the sole survivor of the old line of de la Poer, who returns to England after the late War, buys up the old de la Poer estate, Exham Priory, and sets about rebuilding it, despite ugly rumours current in the neighbourhood. His neighbour, Captain Norrys, an antiquarian, urges him to the restoration, and supports him generally. The work finished, de la Poer takes up his abode in Exham Priory. For a time all goes well; then his sleep is disturbed by a sound as of many rats running in the walls—but the walls are new, save for ancient masonry in the center—and the curious antics of his cat, Nigger-man. At the same time, he is beset by a curious dream of a dæmon swine-herd in a hellish grotto, symbolic of some strange horror of the past, which he vaguely feels is connected with his ancestors. about whom he hears horrible rumours. He remembers a relative who had taken up voodoo-worship in his own time, and on research he finds strange stories of his ancestors, among them the one who fled to America, after murdering his family, and changed his name to Delapore, from which the narrator has converted it back to de la Poer.

There are strange stories of awful orgies that happened long years past, and there are tales of the terrible habits of the de la Poers, and even now de la Poer is a name to inspire the simple country folk with fear and hatred. And there is one story of a vast exodus of rats from the Priory; coming after the last de la Poer had fled to America, leaving the Priory to its ghosts. De la Poer determines to trace the sound of the rats, which seems to proceed from the top of the house to the bottom, and far below. He sets about this, and deep dungeons and strange passages are discovered. But there are no rats. At length, de la Poer, together with Norrys, Thornton, a psychic investigator, and others discover vats, in which are nothing but bones, reaching down to a great depth, suggestive of the kind of rites performed by the old de la Poers. The story has an horrible climax; de la Poer, maddened by the sound of the rats that can never be seen, and influenced by heredity, attacks and partially devours Captain Norrys. I quote the end of this most gruesome of all weird tales:

> Something bumped into me—something soft and plump. It must have been the rats; the viscous, gelatinous. ravenous army that feast on the dead and the living . . . . Why shouldn't rats eat a de la Poer as a de la Poer eats forbidden things? . . . . The war ate my boy, damn them all . . . . and the Yanks ate Carfax: with flames and burnt Grandsire Delapore and the secret . . . . No, no, I tell you, I am *not* that dæmon swineherd in the twilit grotto. It was *not* Edward Norrys' fat face on that flabby, fungous thing! Who says I am a de la Poer? He lived, but my boy died! Shall a Norrys hold the lands of a de la Poer? Its voodoo, I tell you . . . . that spotted snake . . . . Curse you, Thornton, I'll teach you to faint at what my family do! . . . . 'Sblood, thou stinkard. I'll learn ye how to gust . . . . wolde ye swynke me thilke wys? . . . . *Magna Mater! Magna Mater! . . . . Atys . . . . Dia ad aghaidh 's ad aodaun . . . . agus bas dunach ort, agus leat-sa! . . . . Ungl . . . . nngl . . . . rrlh chchch . . . .*
>
> That is what they say I said when they found me in the blackness after three hours; found me crouching in the blackness over the plump-half-eaten body of Captain Norrys, with my own cat leaping and tearing at my throat. Now they have blown up Exham Priory, taken my Nigger-Man away from me, and shut me into this barred room at Hanwell with fearful whispers about my heredity and experiences. Thornton is in the next room, but they prevent me from talking to him. They are trying, too, to suppress most of the facts concerning the priory. When I speak of poor Norrys they accuse me of a hideous thing, but they must know it was the rats; the slithering, scurrying rats whose scampering will never let me sleep; the daemon rats that race behind the padding in this room and beckon me down to greater horrors than I have ever known; the rats they can never hear; the rats, the rats in the walls!

Even the gruesomeness of the decay of M. Valdemar, or of the fleshless faces of Count Magnus' victims cannot compare with this awful picture which the author limns before us. *The Rats in the Walls* is an incomparable piece of work.

The Music of Erich Zann is the story of a student in Paris who hears the cosmic music of an old musician, listens first in interest, then in fear and growing horror to the eerie music from beyond the garret window of Zann's room and to that awful music from the viol in the old man's hands, coming forth even after the cosmic forces have taken his life. The student flees, and never again, despite years of search, can he find the house in the Rue d'Auseil where he heard the music of Erich Zann; nor will he ever know the significance of this music, nor why, when he looked from the window expecting to see the moon and the stars and the lights of Paris, he saw nothing but a vast blackness where furious winds were blowing and from which came the cosmic music of the spheres.

Mr. Lovecraft's medium is the first person almost always; certainly his most effective stories are done in first person, as the above three will bear witness. His capacity for making the reader feel the forces from beyond, from outside, is unequalled in America today; in the command of his English he stands alone as well. Most of his tales are of cumulative horror, relying upon a piling up of incidents, perhaps at first apparently meaningless or everyday, but emerging at last as horribly significant. In his general method he is first cousin to Poe, save that from Lovecraft all symbolism is absent.

A Master of the Macabre

It is a sad and ironic commentary on the reading public and publishers in general that the first book by an American writer who is a master of the macabre with every right to be placed among Shiel, Blackwood, James, Machen, and de la Mare should have been issued by an obscure publisher, that, moreover, it should be incompetently proofed and badly printed, and that the title chosen from among the available works should not be the best, even though it is a horror tale of a high order. But whatever the Visionary Publishing Company did not do, it succeeded in creating a Literoddity which will be long sought after by students and lovers of the macabre in fiction, when it published in April, 1936, H. P. Lovecraft's *The Shadow Over Innsmouth,* illustrated with woodcuts by Frank Utpatel.

Howard Phillips Lovecraft, one of the last members of a family that had been in America four centuries, died March 15 of this year in Providence, Rhode Island, at the age of forty-six; at that time he had been writing for publication for over twenty years. But until the Visionary venture of last year, he had achieved nothing beyond magazine publication and inclusion in anthologies, among them T. Everett Harré's *Beware After Dark,* the well-known Christine Thomson *Not at Night* series, and Dashiell Hammett's *Creeps By Night.* When the first of his manuscripts came to the desk of Edwin Baird, then editor of *Weird Tales,* the editor waved it aloft with loud hosannas and sent it post-haste to press as the kind of material for which he longed but seldom received. Thus began, inauspiciously enough, Lovecraft's introduction to a wider reading public than the amateur press journals in which his work had previously appeared. *Weird Tales,* under Baird's editorship and under that of his successor, Farnsworth Wright, has published more stories by H. P. Lovecraft than all other magazines together, including among them many a title long since enshrined in the memory of his devoted readers—*The Outsider,* that haunting graveyard tale which might have been written by Poe; *The Rats in the Walls,* the most memorable horror narrative I have ever read; the often-reprinted *The Music of Erich Zann;* and most of the tales comprising what is loosely referred to as "the Cthulhu mythology" of Lovecraft's creation: an entire mythos of legendary gods and evil forces from outside, touching only occasionally upon this everyday world of ours; this he built up from a few hints deriving originally from Poe's *Narrative of A. Gordon Pym,* and Bierce's *An Inhabitant of Carcosa,* and, just prior to Lovecraft's literary beginnings, further elaborated by Robert W. Chambers in that writer's little-known volume, *The King in Yellow.* In one of his letters, Lovecraft says: ". . . all my stories, unconnected as they may be, are based on the fundamental lore or legend that this world was inhabited at one time by another race who, in practising black magic, lost their foothold and were expelled, yet live on outside, ever ready to take possession of this earth again . . .", which will be recognized as being basically. similar to the Christian mythos regarding the expulsion of Satan and the constant power of evil. In another letter, he adds, "All my tales are based on the fundamental premise that common human laws and interests and emotions have no validity or significance in the vast cosmos-at-large. . . . Only the human senses and characters have human qualities. These must be handled with unsparing *realism (not catchpenny romanticism),* but when we cross the line to the boundless and hideous unknown—the shadow-haunted *Outside*—we must remember to leave our humanity and terrestrialism at the threshold."

Despite the fact that the bulk of Lovecraft's tales saw the light of day in pulp magazines, he was not without recognition in his lifetime. It is significant that many a contemporary writer has borrowed facets of his mythology for use; some critical acclaim has come to him by way of his anthology appearances; and Edward J. O'Brien gave many a star to his stories, triple-starring *The Colour Out of Space* and *The Dunwich Horror,* two of his finest tales, which appeared almost a decade ago. The O. Henry Memorial Prize collections have likewise listed Lovecraft titles year after year.

The Shadow Over Innsmouth, while not representative of Lovecraft's best work, is yet eminently worthy of notice. It is the tale of a traveler's being drawn to shunned Innsmouth on the Massachusetts coast, and of what an unearthly horror he finds to send him fleeing in terror for his life. But that is not all; the mounting crescendo of frightful horror is not enough, for the tale ends with a shocking anti-climax all along subtly hinted at but never quite revealed. The narrative is told in the first person, as are the majority of Lovecraft's stories. It begins prosaically enough, and yet almost immediately there becomes apparent a sinister undercurrent. The actual visit to Innsmouth discloses a strange air not so much of desertion as of secret, nocturnal habitation, and the aspects of the citizens do not reassure the narrator; they were "repellent-looking", they had an odd "fish-like odor", they seemed to be suffering from some strange infliction, and had what the narrator comes to term "the Innsmouth look". Then the scene stirs to life, the sinister undercurrents well forth, the narrator's odd fear and loathing crystallize into tangible horror, and, after listening to an incredible narrative from an old native, he finds confirmation on every hand, finds himself unable to escape Innsmouth by the regular channels, and is at last forced to flee for his life with an unspeakable horror at his heels. But he escapes, he comes free, he awakes from his terror-induced swoon to a "gentle rain", and the reader has just time to draw a breath of relief before the shocking revelation of the anti-climax bursts upon him.

Lovecraft himself had no very high opinion of his work. Perhaps those publishers who requested sight of his stories are in part responsible; certainly a careless editor can too easily fail to recognize the merit that a fellow craftsman cannot escape seeing. He had become inured to being told that the public will not buy short stories; he had read often enough about publishers' reluctance, the trend of the times, the fickle public. One of the largest American publishers offered to publish a collection if Lovecraft could guarantee that a first edition would be sold out. Any reader of his stories could have assured that without hesitation, but Lovecraft could not. The publisher had made a tactical error, and Lovecraft recalled his manuscript. Since then, he had sent his collection to no one, and hesitated to respond even to the urging of his closest friends.

There is now in preparation a comprehensive collection of the writings of H. P. Lovecraft, and a first volume, *The Outsider,* including the bulk of his short stories and his masterly study, *Supernatural Horror in Literature,* may appear before the year is out. A second omnibus, to follow next year, will contain his best poems and various prose pieces, and finally, a third, *Selected Letters,* will certainly establish him as a letter writer perhaps without equal in our time. Until these books appear, a slightly wider audience may know what hint of an unknown, unexplored fund of macabre tales lies behind *The Shadow Over Innsmouth.*

H. P. Lovecraft, Outsider

> "As for the proper course for a young writer—I would say that it is to forget all about time and place, to assimilate all that is soundest throughout the literature of his ancestors, and to express what he has to say in that manner which his background-knowledge impels him to regard as most powerful and artistic. That is what I have tried to do. . . .

There is no question but that realism must form the groundwork for any first-rate piece of writing, no matter how far from reality the author may push any one line of development. Unless the writer knows how to describe and vivify the every-day scene around him, he will never know how to describe and vivify anything. But although he must begin at home, there is of course no obligation for him to stay there."

—*H. P. Lovecraft*

He is dead now: on March 15th, in his forty-seventh year: and I doubt whether there is often aroused by any one man's passing so spontaneous a grief among all who knew him—not alone for the qualities of the man but for the curious position he held in the world of contemporary letters. About his life there is little to say save that he was born, his constant ill health made him virtually a recluse, and he died. About too many writers there is even less to say. But in the comparatively short period of his major writing—scarcely two decades—he gradually assumed a position unique among his fellow writers as the outstanding American exponent of the macabre tale. And at the same time, to those to whom he wrote, he became a correspondent without equal, a letter-writer who might have sprung full-bodied from eighteenth century England.

Because of his early ill health, H. P. Lovecraft became an omnivorous reader; he read everything upon which he could lay his hands; and out of that voluminous reading grew his lasting respect for the manners and customs of the eighteenth century. "Indeed," he wrote on one occasion, "the eighteenth century is the key to my whole personality. I was born two hundred years too late, and never feel quite at home for lack of a powdered periwig and velvet small-clothes." Not only did he unconsciously make an effort to conduct himself as he might have done had he lived two centuries earlier, not only did he surround himself with eighteenth century objects, but his prose, his poetry, and above all his letters took on a leisureliness which sets them distinctly apart from all others. His enforced seclusion lent to him a perspective more farsighted than he might otherwise have had; thus he was able in his correspondence to take a long view of present-day phenomena, and whether he wrote of Mussolini, of Poe in Providence, of Proust, of proletarian literature, of the cinema, he maintained an absolutely impartial point-of-view, as if, indeed, he were writing from a vantage point two centuries removed. And gradually there grew up around him a circle of correspondents, most of whom he had never seen, a circle which can be likened only to a literary salon, a transplanting of a past phenomenon into a contemporary mould.

From Greek mythology and the *Arabian Nights,* from Poe, Baudelaire and Dunsany, he derived his admiration for the weird. He had already in his teens edited an amateur journal of astronomy and had early been caught in the fascination of outside spaces, and not much later he became affiliated with the United and National Amateur Press Associations, groups of young editors and. writers who preceded the little magazines and reviews in point of time but strove to serve much the same ends, save with a more journalistic bent. At about this time he began to write; already having tried his hand with moderate success at eighteenth century versification, he now began to construct fantasies, dream-fabrics which he later saw bore some resemblance to the work of Lord Dunsany, with which he was not then familiar. From pure fantasy, Lovecraft went on to terror and horror, and presently he was writing such remarkable tales as *The Outsider, The Rats in the Walls, The Music of Erich Zann, The Colour Out of Space, The Whisperer in Darkness,* and *The Dunwich Horror,* two of which appeared on Edward J. O'Brien's Roll of Honor, and all of which were listed at various times in both O'Brien and O. Henry Memorial volumes, as were many others of his stories.

After a time there became apparent in his tales a curious coherence, a myth-pattern so convincing that after its early appearance, the readers of Lovecraft's stories began to explore libraries and museums for certain imaginary titles of Lovecraft's own creation, so powerful that many another writer, with Lovecraft's permission, availed himself of facets of the mythos for his own use. Bit by bit it grew, and finally its outlines became distinct, and it was given a name: the Cthulhu Mythology: because it was in *The Call of Cthulhu* that the myth-pattern first became apparent. It is possible to trace the original inception of this mythology back through Robert W. Chambers' little-known *The King in Yellow* to Poe's *Narrative of A. Gordon Pym* and Bierce's *An Inhabitant of Carcosa;* but in these stories only the barest hints of something *outside* had appeared, and it was Lovecraft who constructed the myth-pattern in its final form. In his stories then he merged fantasy with terror, and even his poetry took on certain symbols of the mythos, so that presently he was writing: ". . . all my stories, unconnected as they may be, are based on the fundamental lore or legend that this world was inhabited at one time by another race who, in practising black magic, lost their foothold and were expelled, yet live on outside ever ready to take possession of this earth again . . .", a formula remarkable for the fact that, though it sprang from the mind of a professed religious unbeliever, it is basically similar to the Christian mythos, particularly in regard to the expulsion of Satan from Eden and the power of evil.

Lovecraft himself had no very high opinion of his work. "The only thing I can say in favour of my work is its sincerity," he wrote not long before his death. He was himself aware of its faults and limitations; he knew better than anyone else how insidiously the commercialism of pulp requirements affected his tales; he made no effort to widen his scope, though in his thousands of letters are embodied many an essay, formal and informal, including some fascinating whimsies, such as his fanciful biography of *Ibid.* Of his work only so long ago as 1931, he wrote: "It is excessively extravagant and melodramatic, and lacks depth and subtlety. . . . My style is bad, too—full of obvious rhetorical devices and hackneyed word and rhythm patterns. It comes a long way from the stark, objective simplicity which is my goal . . ." But if anything, this is, despite its sincerity, evidence of his excessive modesty.

His record of publication is not large—some fifty titles, chiefly in *Weird Tales,* and anthology representation in Dashiell Hammett's *Creeps By Night,* and T. Everett Harré's *Beware After Dark,* among others. He was published abroad, ranging from *The London Evening Standard* to the *Not at Night* anthologies of Christine Campbell Thomson. His closest successors to his unofficial title of master of the macabre were among his best friends: Clark Ashton Smith, and the late Henry S. Whitehead. His only equal was Edith Wharton—Gertrude Atherton, Irvin S. Cobb, Dubose Heyward, and some few others having done too little in the field for all the excellence of what they had written. His only book is the badly printed and bound *The Shadow Over Innsmouth,* published in April, 1936.

Now that he is dead, there are signs of awakening interest in his work. Neither his prose nor his poetry will ever attain the status of world recognition, but his genius will be recognized, his work will be appreciated by that comparatively small but widespread public who read Machen, de la Mare, Dunsany, Blackwood, and Montague Rhodes James, and as the years pass, it will become more evident, all questions of merit aside, that H. P. Lovecraft was a literary outsider in his time.

I salute not only his curious genius, but his magnificent spirit, as a writer, he stands among the best in his field, however limited that may be; as a man, he had no contemporary equal, for even as Oliver Alden was the last puritan, so Howard Phillips Lovecraft was the last gentleman.

H. P. L.—Two Decades After

Twenty-one years after H. P. Lovecraft's untimely death at 47, he seems still so alive to those of us who, like myself, knew him for many years as correspondent and friend, that it seems incredible that more than two decades should have gone by since the last one of his crowded holograph letters came to hand. Time, which has softened the grievous shock of his loss, has in no way lessened him in heart or mind or diminished his stature in that small niche given to the macabre in American letters.

In these two decades, Lovecraft has become known and read far more widely than he had ever dreamed he might be—though I doubt that he ever really envisioned any wide reading audience, for he was not by nature vain or even particularly sure of himself as a writer, and he was always far too dissatisfied with his accomplishments, being acutely and painfully conscious of how far he had yet to go to reach his goals. ("It almost amuses me to reflect that I once thought I was on the road toward becoming able to write stories," he writes in a letter dated January 30, 1933, accompanying a manuscript copy of *The Dreams in the Witch-House,* and, almost three years later, November 10,

1935: "Just finished a new story—*The Haunter of the Dark*—though I'm not sure it's worth typing.")

His work has since been widely published—not only in America, but in England, France, Spain, Portugal, South America, and in the Scandinavian countries; it has been anthologized—indeed, there is scarcely a major Lovecraft story which has not found its way into an anthology; it has reached out to radio audiences; and it has even earned the accolade of academic approval, for some of the fiction has made its way into various textbooks. What a contrast to Lovecraft's mild elation at learning that *The Colour out of Space* had won for him a Roll of Honor rating in Edward J. O'Brien's *The Best Short Stories of 1928!*—for which he supplied a classically comprehensive biographical paragraph:

> "Was born of old Yankee-English stock on August 20, 1890, in Providence, Rhode Island. Has always lived there except for very brief periods. Educated in local schools and privately, ill health precluding university. Interested early in color and mystery of things. More youthful products—verse and essays—voluminous, valueless, mostly privately printed. Contributed astronomical articles to press, 1906–18. Serious literary efforts now confined to tales of dream-life, strange shadow, and cosmic 'outsideness,' notwithstanding sceptical rationalism of outlook and keen regard for the sciences. Lives quietly and eventlessly, with classical and antiquarian tastes. Especially fond of atmosphere of Colonial New England. Favorite authors—in most intimate personal sense—Poe, Arthur Machen, Lord Dunsany, Walter de la Mare, Algernon Blackwood. Occupation—literary hack work including revision and special editorial jobs. Has contributed macabre fiction to *Weird Tales* regularly since 1923. Conservative in general perspective and method as far as compatible with phantasy in art and mechanistic materialism in philosophy."

It is curious, but wholly understandable—Vincent Starrett foresaw it when he wrote that Lovecraft was "his own most fantastic creation!"—that the man Lovecraft was continues to loom on the horizon of his friends' awareness as well as on the perimeter of his readers' consciousness increasingly as time goes by. The Lovecraft "cult," happily, has faded and gone—the work on the one hand, and the man on the other alone remain, to be seen more clearly and known a little better and more honestly without the beclouding fog of uncritical admiration, which is so often the lot of briefly popular writers in the field of entertainment.

A small but substantial amount of Lovecraft's fiction remains in the front rank of macabre literature in English. No critic has improved upon H.P.L.'s own criticism of his stories—"The only thing I can say in favour of my work is its sincerity. It is excessively extravagant and melodramatic, and lacks depth and subtlety. . . . My style is bad, too—full of obvious rhetorical devices and hackneyed word and rhythm patterns. It comes a long way from the stark, objective simplicity which is my goal . . ."

He did achieve that simplicity in his letters—those stimulating, intelligent communications which were the product of an active, informed mind. He was forever throwing out challenging opinions, ideas, concepts in them; above all, he was provoking his correspondents to think independently. "As for standards," he wrote typically on All-Fool's day of 1933, "it isn't so much that I deem the masses competent to create or pass upon them in a conscious way, as that I very strongly doubt the competence of the so-called 'intellectuals' as well, to perform that function. Matters of intellectual opinion, or matters of the clear-cut adaptation of means to definitely envisaged ends in the social-political field, are things regarding which the man of greater training and intelligence indeed has a superior right to speak. But ends and values themselves—local and nebulous and purely relative in a cosmos itself meaningless and standardless—are things of a somewhat different cast, and not to be disposed of in any intellectual way. They are outside the scope of intellect, since the only conditions they have to fulfill are those of emotional satisfaction—different for every race, nation, and age."

He would have made an admirable teacher, had his own limitations not quite sensibly bidden him to submit to a more reclusive life in which he could give his vivid imagination more rein and free his fancy to produce the tales by which he will be remembered long after those of us who knew him are gone. Quietly, unintentionally, his influence among his correspondents was profound; for many of us, isolated all over America, he provided a needed link to an alert mind, aware of many facets of knowledge, a man who eschewed violence in his opinions and avoided setting forth unalterable dicta, whose primary concern was a meeting of minds on a purely intellectual plane.

Now, two decades after his death, no one would have been more astonished than he to realize that his work had achieved a place as permanent as any work in an essentially minor literary genre, and that his own corner among the best American writers in the category of the macabre—Poe, Hawthorne, O'Brien, Bierce, Crawford, Robert W. Chambers, Mary E. Wilkins-Freeman, James, Edith Wharton, and a handful of others—was secure.

Glossary of Frequently Mentioned Names

Abramson, Ben (1898–1955), Chicago bookseller, proprietor of the Argus Book Shop. Publisher of the magazine *Reader and Collector,* AWD's *H. P. L.: A Memoir* (1945) and HPL's *Supernatural Horror in Literature* (1945).

Anger, William Frederick (b. 1921), weird fiction fan and late correspondent of HPL.

Bacon, Victor E. (1905–1997), amateur journalist, editor of *Bacon's Essays* which published work by HPL and CAS, and Official Editor of the United Amateur Press Association (1925–26).

Baird, Edwin (1886–1957), first editor of *WT* (Mar. 1923–Apr. 1924), who accepted HPL's first submissions to the magazine. Also editor of *Real Detective Stories.*

Baldwin, F[ranklin] Lee (1913–1987), weird fiction fan and late associate of HPL. He had intended to publish "The Colour out of Space" as a booklet, but never did so.

Barlow, R[obert] H[ayward] (1918–1951), author and collector. As a teenager he corresponded with HPL and acted as his host during two long visits in the summers of 1934 and 1935. In the 1930s he wrote several works of weird and fantasy fiction, some in collaboration with HPL. HPL appointed him his literary executor. He assisted AWD and DAW in preparing the early HPL volumes for Arkham House. In the 1940s he went to Mexico and became a distinguished anthropologist. He died by suicide.

Bates, Harry (1900–1981), editor of *Strange Tales* and *Astounding Stories.*

Bishop, Zealia Brown (Reed) (1897–1968), HPL's revision client. HPL ghostwrote "The Curse of Yig" (1928), "The Mound" (1929–30), and "Medusa's Coil" (1930) for her based on her slim plot synopses.

Blackwood, Algernon (1869–1951), prolific British author of weird and fantasy tales whose work HPL greatly admired when he read it in 1924.

Bloch, Robert (1917–1994), author of weird and suspense fiction who came into correspondence with HPL in 1933. HPL tutored him in the craft of writing during their four-year association.

Brobst, Harry K[ern] (b. 1909), late associate of HPL who moved to Providence in 1932 and saw HPL regularly thereafter.

Brosnatch, Andrew, *WT* artist.

Brundage, Margaret (1900–1976), *WT* artist.

Bullen, John Ravenor (1886–1927), amateur poet from Canada. HPL edited his poems, *White Fire* (1927), for posthumous publication.

Bush, (Rev.) David Van (1882–1959), prolific author of inspirational verse and popular psychology manuals, many of them revised by HPL.

Cave, Hugh B[arnett] (1910–2004), prolific author of stories for the pulp magazines. Lived for a time near HPL in Pawtuxet, RI. They corresponded briefly but never met.

Clark, Dr. Franklin Chase (1847–1915), HPL's uncle and a physician who also translated some of the Latin classics. He helped HPL considerably on his early prose and verse.

Clark, Lillian D[elora] (1856–1932), HPL's maternal aunt. She married Dr. Franklin Chase Clark in 1902. From 1926 to her death she shared quarters with HPL at 10 Barnes Street.

Clayton, William, founder of the Clayton Publishing Company, which published several pulp magazines, including *Strange Tales of Mystery and Terror* and *Astounding Stories.*

Coates, Walter J[ohn] (1880–1941), editor of *Driftwind.*

Cole, Edward H[arold] (1892–1966), longtime amateur associate of HPL, living in the Boston area.

Conover, Willis (1921–1996), weird fiction fan who edited *Science-Fantasy Correspondent* (1936–37) and was a late correspondent of HPL.

Cook, W. Paul (1881–1948), publisher of the *Monadnock Monthly,* the *Vagrant,* and other amateur journals; a longtime amateur journalist, printer, and lifelong friend of HPL. He first visited HPL in 1917, and it was he who urged HPL to resume writing fiction after a hiatus of nine years. In 1927 Cook published the *Recluse,* containing HPL's "Supernatural Horror in Literature."

Crane, Hart (1899–1932), eminent American poet who met HPL sporadically in Cleveland (1922) and New York (1924–26, 1930). HPL admired his work, especially *The Bridge* (1930), on which HPL saw him at work in 1924. He died by suicide.

Crawford, William L[evy] (1911–1984), editor of *Marvel Tales* and *Unusual Stories* and publisher of the Visionary Publishing Company, which issued HPL's *The Shadow over Innsmouth* (1936).

de Castro, Adolphe (Danziger) (1859–1959), author, co-translator with Ambrose Bierce of Richard Voss's *The Monk and the Hangman's Daughter,* and correspondent of HPL. HPL revised his "The Last Test" and "The Electric Executioner."

de la Mare, Walter (1873–1956), British author and poet who wrote occasional weird tales much admired by HPL for their subtlety and allusiveness.

Dunsany, Lord (Edward John Moreton Drax Plunkett) (1878–1957), Irish writer of fantasy tales whose work notably influenced HPL after HPL read it in 1919.

Dwyer, Bernard Austin (1897–1943), weird fiction fan and would-be writer and artist, living in West Shokan, NY; correspondent of HPL.

Eshbach, Lloyd Arthur (1910–2003), editor of a little magazine (not devoted to the weird) entitled the *Galleon.*

Farnese, Harold S. (1885–1945), musical composer and sporadic correspondent of HPL. It was he who provided AWD with the spurious "Black Magic" quotation attributed to HPL.

Finlay, Virgil (1914–1971), one of the great weird artists of his time and a prolific contributor of artwork to the pulps; late correspondent of HPL.

Galpin, Alfred (1901–1983) of Appleton, WI. Amateur journalist, French scholar, composer, and protégé, then longtime friend, of HPL.

Gamwell, Annie E[meline] P[hillips] (1866–1941), HPL's younger aunt, living with him at 66 College Street (1933–37).

Gamwell, Edward F[rancis] (1869–1936), HPL's uncle. For a time he was editor of the *Cambridge* [MA] *Tribune.* He married Annie Gamwell in 1897, but the couple had separated by 1916.

Gernsback, Hugo (1884–1967), editor of *Amazing Stories, Wonder Stories,* and other pioneering science fiction pulps.

Grayson, Allan D., poet and friend of Henry S. Whitehead.

Guiney, Louise Imogen (1861–1920), a once noted Massachusetts poet and essayist. HPL claims that his family stayed with her at her home in Auburndale during the winter of 1892–93, but this has not been confirmed.

Henneberger, J[acob] C[lark] (1890–1969), founder of *College Humor* (1922f.) and the original publisher of *WT.*

Hersey, Harold (1893–1956), science fiction editor and publisher. He edited the *Thrill Book* (1919) and took over the editorship of *Ghost Stories* during its final years (1930–31).

Hodgson, William Hope (1877–1918), British author of weird fiction whose work had fallen into obscurity until it was rediscovered in the 1930s, largely through the efforts of H. C. Koenig.

Hornig, Charles D[erwin] (1916–1999), editor of the *Fantasy Fan* (1933–35) and associate editor of *Wonder Stories*.

Howard, Robert E[rvin] (1906–1936), prolific Texas author of weird and adventure tales for *Weird Tales* and other pulp magazines; creator of the adventure hero Conan the Barbarian. He and HPL corresponded voluminously from 1930 to 1936. He committed suicide when he heard of his mother's impending death.

Janvier, Meredith (1872–1936), bookseller in Baltimore.

Keller, David H. (1880–1966), physician, psychiatrist, and popular science fiction author.

Kirk, George [Willard] (1898–1962), member of the Kalem Club. He published *Twenty-one Letters of Ambrose Bierce* (1922) and ran the Chelsea Bookshop in New York.

Kleiner, Rheinhart (1882–1949), amateur poet and longtime friend of HPL. He visited HPL in Providence in 1918, 1919, and 1920, and met him frequently during the heyday of the Kalem Club (1924–26).

Koenig, H[erman] C[harles] (1893–1959), late associate of HPL who spearheaded the rediscovery of the work of William Hope Hodgson.

Kuttner, Henry (1915–1958), prolific author of science fiction and horror tales for the pulps and a late correspondent of HPL (1936–37). HPL introduced Kuttner to C. L. Moore, whom he would later marry.

Leeds, Arthur (1882–1952?), an associate of HPL in New York and member of the Kalem Club. He was the author (with J. Berg Esenwein) of *Writing the Photoplay* (Springfield, MA: The Home Correspondence School, 1913; rev. ed. 1919).

Leiber, Fritz, Jr. (1910–1992), late associate of HPL who became one of the leading figures in science fiction and fantasy.

Lenniger, August, pulp author and literary agent.

Long, Frank Belknap (1901–1994), fiction writer and poet and one of HPL's closest friends and correspondents. Late in life he wrote the memoir, *Howard Phillips Lovecraft: Dreamer on the Nightside* (1975).

Lovecraft, Sarah Susan (Phillips) (1857–1921), HPL's mother. She married Winfield Scott Lovecraft in 1889 and settled in Dorchester, MA, but returned with her son to her family home in Providence when her husband was institutionalized at Butler Hospital in 1893. From 1904 to 1919 she lived alone with HPL at 598 Angell Street. She spent her last two years at Butler Hospital.

Lovecraft, Winfield Scott (1853–1898), HPL's father. He attended an unspecified military college, then eventually became a salesman for the Gorham (Silversmiths) Co., based in Providence. He suffered a seizure in Chicago in 1893 and was placed in Butler Hospital, where he died of paresis (the term then used to denote syphilis).

Loveman, Samuel E. (1887–1976), poet and longtime friend of HPL and DAW as well as of Ambrose Bierce, Hart Crane, George Sterling, and Clark Ashton Smith. He wrote *The Hermaphrodite* (1926) and other works.

Lumley, William (1880–1960), eccentric late associate of HPL for whom HPL ghostwrote "The Diary of Alonzo Typer" (1935).

Machen, Arthur (1863–1947), Welsh author of weird fiction. He corresponded sporadically with AWD.

Marlow, Harry R., amateur journalist and printer, former president of the National Amateur Press Association.

McNeil, Everett (1862–1929), prolific author of historical and adventure novels for boys; member of the Kalem Club.

Merritt, A[braham] (1884–1943), writer of fantasy and horror tales for the pulps. His work was much admired by HPL in spite of its concessions to pulp formulae. His late novel, *Dwellers in the Mirage* (1932), may have been influenced by HPL.

Miniter, Edith (1867–1934), amateur author who also professionally published a novel, *Our Natupski Neighbors* (1916) and many short stories. She hosted HPL at her home in Wilbraham, MA, in the summer of 1928.

Moe, Maurice W[inter] (1882–1940), of Appleton and Milwaukee, WI. Amateur journalist, English teacher, and longtime friend and correspondent of HPL.

Moore, C[atherine] L[ucile] (1911–1987), late associate of HPL who later married Henry Kuttner and became a leading figure in science fiction and fantasy.

Morse, Richard Ely (1909–1986), poet, librarian, and late correspondent of Lovecraft.

Morton, James Ferdinand (1870–1941), amateur journalist, author of many tracts on race prejudice, free thought, and taxation, and longtime friend of HPL.

Munn, H[arold] Warner (1903–1981), prolific contributor to the pulp magazines, living near W. Paul Cook in Athol, MA.

Olinick, George O. (1888–1957). Early *WT* illustrator.

Orton, Vrest (1897–1986), a late member of the Kalem Club. He was for a time an editor at the *Saturday Review* and later the founder of the Vermont Country Store. He compiled an early bibliography of Dreiser, *Dreiserana* (1929).

Petaja, Emil (1915–2000), science fiction fan and late associate of HPL's; later a prolific author and editor.

Phillips, Whipple Van Buren (1833–1904), HPL's maternal grandfather. A wealthy industrialist, he established the Owyhee Land and Irrigation Company in Idaho. He provided strong guidance to HPL in the absence of HPL's father. His death in 1904 and the subsequent mismanagement of his estate forced HPL and his mother to move from 454 Angell Street to smaller quarters at 598 Angell Street.

Poe, Edgar Allan (1809–1849), pioneering American author of weird fiction.

Price, E[dgar] Hoffmann (1898–1989), prolific pulp writer of weird and adventure tales. HPL met him in New Orleans in 1932 and corresponded extensively with him thereafter.

Quinn, Seabury (1889–1969), prolific author of weird and detective tales to the pulps, notably a series of tales involving the psychic detective Jules de Grandin.

Rankin, Hugh Doak, illustrator for *WT.*

Ruppert, Conrad (1912–1997), publisher of the *Fantasy Fan* (1933–35).

Rimel, Duane W[eldon] (1915–1996), weird fiction fan and late associate of HPL, who revised some of his early tales.

Schorer, Mark R. (1908–1977), schoolmate of AWD in Sauk City and an early collaborator. His father managed the canning factory in Sauk City where AWD worked for ten years to supplement his writing income. He is noted for his biography *Sinclair Lewis: An American Life* (1961).

Schwartz, Julius (1915–2004), editor of *Fantasy Magazine* who acted as HPL's agent in marketing *At the Mountains of Madness* to *Astounding Stories.*

Senf, C[onstantine] C. (1873–1949), illustrator for *WT.*

Shiel, M[atthew] P[hipps] (1865–1947), British author of weird fiction.

Smith, Charles W. ("Tryout") (1852–1940), longtime amateur journalist, editor of the *Tryout,* and friend and correspondent of HPL.

Smith, Clark Ashton (1893–1961), prolific California poet and writer of fantasy tales. He received a "fan" letter from HPL in 1922 and corresponded with him until HPL's death.

Starrett, Vincent (1886–1974), American bookman who corresponded briefly with HPL in 1927.

Sterling, George (1869–1926), American poet and early mentor of CAS. Author of *The Testimony of the Suns* (1903) and *A Wine of Wizardry* (1909).

Sterling, Kenneth (1920–1995), young science fiction fan who came into contact with HPL in 1934. He later became a distinguished physician.

Stickney, Corwin F., copublisher with Willis Conover of *Science-Fantasy Correspondent* (1936–37), later titled *Amateur Correspondent* (1937f.), edited by Stickney alone.

Strauch, Carl Ferdinand (1908–1989), friend of Harry Brobst and correspondent of HPL. Later a distinguished professor and critic.

Sully, Helen V. (1904–1997), friend of CAS who visited HPL in Providence in 1933, then saw DAW and others in New York.

Talman, Wilfred Blanch (1904–1986), correspondent of HPL and late member of the Kalem Club. HPL assisted Talman on his story "Two Black Bottles" (1926) and wrote "Some Dutch Footprints in New England" for Talman to publish in *De Halve Maen,* the journal of the Holland Society of New York. Late in life he wrote the memoir *The Normal Lovecraft* (1973).

Utpatel, Frank (1908–1980), artist friend of AWD who illustrated some of AWD's work for *WT* and later did many jackets and interiors (primarily woodcuts) for Arkham House; late correspondent of HPL.

Wandrei, Donald (1908–1987), poet and author of weird fiction, science fiction, and detective tales. He corresponded with HPL from 1926 to 1937, visited HPL in Providence in 1927 and 1932, and met HPL occasionally in New York during the 1930s. He helped HPL get "The Shadow out of Time" published in *Astounding Stories.* After HPL's death he and AWD founded the publishing firm Arkham House to preserve HPL's work. For their joint correspondence, see *Mysteries of Time and Spirit* (Night Shade Books, 2002).

Wandrei, Howard (1909–1956), younger brother of Donald Wandrei, premier weird artist and prolific author of weird fiction, science fiction, and detective stories; correspondent of HPL.

Weir, John. J. (1922–1977), late correspondent of HPL and editor of the fanzine *Fantasmagoria.*

White, Helen Constance (1896–1967), AWD's English professor at the University of Wisconsin. See AWD's essay "An Appreciation."

Whitehead, Henry S[t. Clair] (1882–1932), author of weird and adventure tales, many of them set in the Virgin Islands. HPL corresponded with him and visited him in Florida in 1931. HPL wrote a brief eulogy of Whitehead for *WT.*

Wollheim, Donald A. (1914–1990), editor of the *Phantagraph* and *Fanciful Tales* and prolific author and editor in the science fiction field.

Wright, Farnsworth (1888–1940), editor of *Weird Tales* (1924–40). He rejected some of HPL's best work of the 1930s, only to publish it after HPL's death upon submittal by AWD.

Bibliography

A. Works by H. P. Lovecraft

Books

The Ancient Track: Complete Poetical Works. Edited by S. T. Joshi. San Francisco: Night Shade Books, 2001.

The Annotated Supernatural Horror in Literature. Edited by S. T. Joshi. New York: Hippocampus Press, 2000.

At the Mountains of Madness and Other Novels. Edited by S. T. Joshi. Sauk City, WI: Arkham House, [1985]. [*MM*]

Collected Essays. Edited by S. T. Joshi. New York: Hippocampus Press, 2004–06. 5 vols. [*CE*]

Commonplace Book. Edited by David E. Schultz. West Warwick, RI: Necronomicon Press, 1987; in *MW*. [*CB*]

Dagon and Other Macabre Tales. Edited by S. T. Joshi. Sauk City, WI: Arkham House, [1986]. [*D*]

The Dunwich Horror and Others. Edited by S. T. Joshi. Sauk City, WI: Arkham House, [1984]. [*DH*]

From the Pest Zone: The New York Stories. Edited by S. T. Joshi and David E. Schultz. New York: Hippocampus Press, 2003.

The Horror in the Museum and Other Revisions. Edited by S. T. Joshi. Sauk City, WI: Arkham House, [1989]. [*HM*]

Letters from New York. Edited by S. T. Joshi and David E. Schultz. San Francisco: Night Shade Books, 2005.

Lord of a Visible Work: An Autobiography in Letters. Edited by S. T. Joshi and David E. Schultz. Athens, OH: Ohio University Press, 2000.

Letters to Alfred Galpin. Edited by S. T. Joshi and David E. Schultz. New York: Hippocampus Press, 2003.

Miscellaneous Writings. Edited by S. T. Joshi. Sauk City, WI: Arkham House, 1995. [*MW*]

Mysteries of Time and Spirit: The Letters of H. P. Lovecraft and Donald Wandrei. Edited by S. T. Joshi and David E. Schultz. San Francisco: Night Shade Books, 2002.

Selected Letters. Edited by August Derleth, Donald Wandrei, and James Turner. Sauk City, WI: Arkham House, 1965–76. 5 vols. [*SL*]

The Shadow over Innsmouth. Everett, PA: The Visionary Publishing Co., 1936.

The Shunned House. Athol, MA: Recluse Press, 1928 (printed but not bound or distributed until 1959–61). In *MM*.

Stories

"The Alchemist." *United Amateur* 16, No. 4 (Nov. 1916): 53–57. In *D*.

"Arthur Jermyn." See "Facts concerning the Late Arthur Jermyn and His Family."

At the Mountains of Madness. Astounding Stories 16, No. (Feb. 1936): 8–32; 17, No. 1 (Mar. 1936): 125–55; 17, No. 2 (Apr. 1936): 132–50. In *MM, SPC.*

"The Beast in the Cave." *Vagrant* No. 7 (June 1918): 113–20. In *D*.

"Beyond the Wall of Sleep." *Pine Cones* 1, No. 6 (Oct. 1919): 2–10. *Fantasy Fan,* 2, No. 2 (Oct. 1934): 25–32. In *D, OSM.*.

"The Call of Cthulhu." *WT* 11, No. 2 (Feb. 1928): 159–78, 287. In *Beware After Dark! The World's Most Stupendous Tales of Mystery, Horror, Thrills and Terror,* ed. T. Everett Harré. New York: Macaulay, 1929, pp. 223–59. In *DH*.

The Case of Charles Dexter Ward. In *MM, NYP.*

"Celephaïs." *Rainbow* No. 2 (May 1922): 10–12. *Marvel Tales* 1, No. 1 (May 1934): 26, 28–32. In *D*.

"The Colour out of Space." *Amazing Stories* 2, No. 6 (Sept. 1927): 557–67. In *DH, NS.*

"Cool Air." *Tales of Magic and Mystery* 1, No. 4 (Mar. 1928): 29–34. In *DH*.

"Dagon." *Vagrant* No. 11 (Nov. 1919): 23–29. *WT* 2, No. 3 (Oct. 1923): 23–25. In *D*.

"The Descendant." In *D*.

"The Doom That Came to Sarnath." *Scot* No. 44 (June 1920): 90–98. *Marvel Tales of Science and Fantasy* 1, No. 4 (Mar.–Apr. 1935): 157–63. In *D*.

The Dream-Quest of Unknown Kadath. In *MM.*

"The Dreams in the Witch House."' *WT* 22, No. 1 (July 1933): 86–111. In *MM, S&D.*

"The Dunwich Horror." *WT* 13, No. 4 (Apr. 1929): 481–508. In *DH*.

"Facts concerning the Late Arthur Jermyn and His Family." *Wolverine* No. 9 (Mar. 1921): 3–11. *WT* 3, No. 4 (Apr. 1924): 15–18 (as "The White Ape"). *WT* 25, No. 5 (May 1935): 642–48 (as "Arthur Jermyn"). In *D*.

"The Festival." *WT* 5, No. 1 (Jan. 1925): 169–74. *WT* 22, No. 4 (Oct. 1933): 519–20, 522–28. In *D*.

"From Beyond." *Fantasy Fan* 1, No. 10 (June 1934): 147–51, 160. In *D, WoT.*

"The Haunter of the Dark." *WT* 28, No. 5 (Dec. 1936): 538–53. In *DH*.

"He." *WT* 8, No. 3 (Sept. 1926): 373–80. In *D*.

"Herbert West—Reanimator" (as "Grewsome Tales"). *Home Brew:* 1, No. 1 (Feb. 1922): 84–88 ("From the Dark"); 1, No. 2 (Mar. 1922): 45–50 ("The Plague Demon"); 1, No. 3 (Apr. 1922): 21–26 ("Six Shots by Moonlight"); 1, No. 4 (May 1922): 53–58 ("The Scream of the Dead"); 1, No. 5 (June 1922): 45–50 ("The Horror from the Shadows,"); 1, No. 6 (July 1922): 57–62 ("The Tomb-Legions,"). In *D*.

"The Horror at Red Hook." *WT* 9, No. 1 (Jan. 1927): 59–73. In *You'll Need a Night Light,* ed. Christine Campbell Thomson. London: Selwyn & Blount,

1927, pp. 228–54. In *D.*

"The Hound." *WT* 3, No. 2 (Feb. 1924): 50–52, 78. *WT* 14, No. 3 (Sept. 1929): 421–25, 432. In *D.*

"In the Vault." *Tryout* 10, No. 6 (Nov. 1925): [3–17]. *WT* 19, No. 4 (Apr. 1932): 459–65. In *DH.*

"The Lurking Fear." *Home Brew* 2, No. 6 (Jan. 1923): 4–10; 3, No. 1 (Feb. 1923): 18–23; 3, No. 2 (Mar. 1923): 31–37, 44, 48; 3, No. 3 (Apr. 1923): 35–42. *WT* 11, No. 6 (June 1928): 791–804. In *D.*

"The Music of Erich Zann." *National Amateur* 44, No. 4 (Mar. 1922): 38–40. *WT* 5, No. 5 (May 1925): 219–34. In *Creeps by Night: Chills and Thrills,* ed. Dashiell Hammett. New York: John Day Co., 1931, pp. 347–63. In *Modern Tales of Horror,* ed. Dashiell Hammett. London: Victor Gollancz, 1932, pp. 301–17. *Evening Standard* (London) (24 Oct. 1932): 20–21. *WT* 24, No. 5 (Nov. 1934): 644–48, 655–56. In *DH.*

"The Mysterious Ship" [juvenilia]. In *MW.*

"The Nameless City." *Wolverine* No. 11 (Nov. 1921): 3–15. *Fanciful Tales* 1, No. 1 (Fall 1936): 5–18. In *D.*

"Nyarlathotep." *United Amateur* 20, No. 2 (Nov. 1920): 19–21. *National Amateur* 43, No. 6 (July 1926): 53–54. In *MW.*

"The Outsider." *WT* 7, No. 4 (Apr. 1926): 449–53. *WT* 17, No. 4 (June–July 1931): 566–71. In *D.*

"Pickman's Model." *WT* 10, No. 4 (Oct. 1927): 505–14. In *By Daylight Only,* ed. Christine Campbell Thomson. London: Selwyn & Blount, 1929, pp. 37–52. *WT* 28, No. 4 (Nov. 1936): 495–505. In *The "Not at Night" Omnibus,* ed. Christine Campbell Thomson. London: Selwyn & Blount, [1937], pp. 279–307. In *DH.*

"The Picture in the House." *National Amateur* 41, No. 6 (July 1919 [*sic*]): 246–49. *WT* 3, No. 1 (Jan. 1924): 40–42. *WT* 29, No. 3 (Mar. 1937): 370–73. In *DH.*

"Polaris." *Philosopher* 1, No. 1 (Dec. 1920): 3–5. *National Amateur* 48, No. 5 (May 1926): 48–49. *Fantasy Fan* 1, No. 6 (Feb. 1934): 83–85. In *D.*

"The Quest of Iranon." *Galleon* 1, No. 5 (July–Aug. 1935): 12–20. In *D.*

"The Rats in the Walls." *WT* 3, No. 3 (Mar. 1924): 25–31. *WT* 15, No. 6 (June 1930): 841–53. In *Switch On the Light,* ed. Christine Campbell Thomson. London: Selwyn & Blount, 1931, pp. 141–65. In *DH, SNM.*

"The Shunned House." In *MM, WK.*

"The Silver Key." *WT* 13, No. 1 (Jan. 1929): 41–49, 144. In *MM.*

"The Statement of Randolph Carter." *Vagrant* No. 13 (May 1920): 41–48. *WT* 5, No. 2 (Feb. 1925): 149–53. In *MM.*

"Strange High House in the Mist." *WT* 18, No. 3 (Oct. 1931): 394–400. In *D.*

"The Thing on the Doorstep." *WT* 29, No. 1 (Jan. 1937): 52–70. In *DH.*

"The Tree." *Tryout* 7, No. 7 (Oct. 1921): [3–10]. In *D.*

"The Very Old Folk." *Scienti-Snaps* 3, No. 3 (Summer 1940): 4–8. In *MW.*

"The Whisperer in Darkness." *WT* 18, No. 1 (Aug. 1931): 32–73. In *DH*.

"The White Ship." *United Amateur* 19, No. 2 (Nov. 1919): 30–33. *WT* 9, No. 3 (Mar. 1927): 386–89. In *D*.

Revisions and Collaborations

Barlow, R. H. "The Night Ocean." *Californian* 4, No. 3 (Winter 1936): 41–56. In *HM*.

Bishop, Zealia. "The Curse of Yig." *WT* 14, No. 5 (Nov. 1929): 625–36. In *Switch On the Light*, ed. Christine Campbell Thomson. London: Selwyn & Blount, 1931, pp. 9–31. In *The "Not at Night" Omnibus*, ed. Christine Campbell Thomson. London: Selwyn & Blount, [1937], pp. 13–29. In *HM*.

de Castro, Adolphe. "The Last Test" [orig. "A Sacrifice to Science"]. *WT* 12, No. 5 (Nov. 1928): 625–56. In *HM*.

———. "The Electric Executioner" [orig. "The Automatic Executioner"]. *WT* 16, No. 2 (Aug. 1930): 223–36; *HM*.

Heald, Hazel. "The Horror in the Museum." *WT* 22, No. 1 (July 1933): 49–68. In *Terror by Night*, ed. Christine Campbell Thomson. London: Selwyn & Blount, (1934), pp. 111–41. In. *The "Not at Night" Omnibus*, ed. Christine Campbell Thomson. London: Selwyn & Blount, (1937), pp. 279–307. In *HM*.

———. "Out of the Aeons." *WT* 25, No. 4 (Apr. 1935): 478–96. In *HM*, *S&D*.

———. "Winged Death." *WT* 23, No. 3 (Mar. 1934): 199–215. In *HM*.

Houdini, Harry. "Under the Pyramids." *WT* 4, No. 2 [May–June–July 1924]: 3–12 (as "Imprisoned with the Pharaohs"; as by "Houdini").

Lumley, William. "The Diary of Alonzo Typer." *WT* 31, No. 2 (Feb. 1938): 152–66. In *HM*.

Price, E. Hoffmann. "Through the Gates of the Silver Key." *WT* 24, No. 1 (July 1934): 60–85. In *MM*.

Sterling, Kenneth. "In the Walls of Eryx." *WT* 34, No. 4 (Oct. 1939): 50–68. In *D*.

Talman, Wilfred Blanch. "Two Black Bottles." *WT* 10, No. 2 (Aug. 1927): 251–58. In *HM*, *SNM*.

Whitehead, Henry S. "The Trap." *Strange Tales of Mystery and Terror* 2, No. 1 (Mar. 1932): 73–88. In *HM*.

Essays

"An Account of a Trip to the Antient Fairbanks House, in Dedham, and to the Red Horse Tavern in Sudbury, in the Province of the Massachusetts-Bay." In *CE* 4.

"Books to mention in new edition of weird article . . ." In *CE* 5.

"Commonplace Book." In *CE* 5.

"A Descent to Avernus." *Bacon's Essays* 2, No. 2 (Summer 1929): 8. In *CE* 4.

A Description of the Town of Quebeck, in New-France. In *CE* 4.

Further Criticism of Poetry. See "Notes on Verse Technique."

"A List of Certain Basic Underlying Horrors Effectively Used in Weird Fiction." In *CE* 2.

"List of Primary Ideas Motivating Possible Weird Tales." In *CE* 2.

"In Memoriam: Henry St. Clair Whitehead." *WT* 21, No. 3 (Mar. 1933): 391 (unsigned). In *CE* 5.

"The Materialist Today." *Drift-Wind,* 1, No. 1 (Oct. 1926): 6–9]; rpt. *The Materialist Today.* North Montpelier, VT: The Driftwind Press, 1926. In *MW, CE* 5.

"Mysteries of the Heavens Revealed by Astronomy." *Asheville* [NC] *Gazette-News,* 16 February–17 May 1915. In *CE* 3.

"Notes on Verse Technique." Published as *Further Criticism of Poetry.* Louisville, KY: Printed on the Press of George G. Fetter Co., 1932. In *CE* 1.

"The Poetry of John Ravenor Bullen." *United Amateur* 25, No. 1 (Sept. 1925): 1–3, 6. In *CE* 2.

"Preface." In *White Fire* by John Ravenor Bullen. Athol, MA: The Recluse Press, 1927 [actually Jan. 1928], pp. 7–13. In *CE* 2.

"Sleepy Hollow To-day." In Sterling A. Leonard and Harold Y. Moffett, eds. *Junior Literature: Book Two.* New York: Macmillan, 1930, 1935, pp. 545–46 (an excerpt from "Observations on Several Parts of America"). In *CE* 4.

"Some Dutch Footprints in New England." *De Halve Maen* 9, No. 1 (18 Oct. 1933): 2, 4. In *MW, CE* 4.

"Suggestions for Writing Story." In *CE* 5.

"Supernatural Horror in Literature." *Recluse* No. 1 (1927): 23–59. Rev. ed. in *Fantasy Fan* (Oct. 1933–Feb. 1935).In *D, CE* 2.

"The Unknown City in the Ocean." *Perspective Review,* Winter 1934 (Fourth Anniversary Number): 7–8. In *CE* 4.

"Vermont—A First Impression." *Driftwind* 2, No. 5 (Mar. 1928): [5–9]. In *MW, CE* 4.

"Weird Story Plots." In *CE* 2.

"The Weird Work of William Hope Hodgson." *Phantagraph* 5, No. 5 (Feb. 1937): 5–7. Incorporated into "Supernatural Horror in Literature."

"The Work of Frank Belknap Long, Jr." *United Amateur* 23, No. 1 (May 1924): 1–4 (unsigned). In *CE* 2.

Poems [all poems are in *The Ancient Track*]

"The Ancient Track." *WT* 15, No. 3 (Mar. 1930): 300.

"Ave atque Vale: To Jonathan E. Hoag, Esq.: February 10, 1831–Oct. 17th, 1927." *Tryout,* 11, No. 10 (Dec. 1927): [3–4].

"The East India Brick Row." *Providence Journal* 102, No. 7 (8 Jan. 1930): 13.

"An Epistle to the Rt. Honble Maurice Winter Moe, Esq. of Zythopolis, in the Northwest Territory of HIS MAJESTY'S American Dominion."

"Festival." *WT* 8, No. 6 (Dec. 1926): 846 (as "Yule Horror").

Fungi from Yuggoth.

I. "The Book." *Fantasy Fan* 2, No. 2 (Oct. 1934): 24.
II. "Pursuit." *Fantasy Fan* 2, No. 2 (Oct. 1934): 24.
X. "The Pigeon-Flyers." *WT* 39, No. 9 (Jan. 1947): 96.
XI. "The Well." *Providence Journal* (14 May 1930): 15.
XII. "The Howler." *Driftwind* 7, No. 3 (Nov. 1932): 100.
XIII. "Hesperia." *WT* 16, No. 4 (Oct. 1930): 464.
XIV. "Star-Winds." *WT* 16, No. 3 (Sept. 1930): 322.
XV. "Antarktos." *WT* 16, No. 5 (Nov. 1930): 692.
XIX. "The Bells." *WT* 16, No. 6 (Dec. 1930): 798.
XX. "Night-Gaunts." *Providence Journal* (26 Mar. 1930): 15. *Interesting Items* No. 605 (Nov. 1934): [6] (as "Night Gaunts"). *Phantagraph* 4, No. 3 ([June] 1936): 8.
XXI. "Nyarlathotep." *WT* 17, No. 1 (Jan. 1931): 12.
XXII. "Azathoth." *WT* 17, No. 1 (Jan. 1931): 12.
XXIII. "Mirage." *WT* 17, No. 2 (Feb.–Mar. 1931): 1975.
XXVII. "The Elder Pharos." *WT* 17, No. 2 (Feb.–Mar. 1931): 175.
XXIX. "Nostalgia." *Providence Journal* (12 Mar. 1930): 15. *Phantagraph* 4, No. 4 (July 1936): 1.
XXX. "Background." *Providence Journal* (16 Apr. 1930): 13. *Interesting Items* No. 592 (Sept. 1932): [1]. *Galleon* 1, No. 4 (May–June 1935): 8. *The Lovecrafter* 47, No. 1 (20 Aug. 1936): 1 (as "A Sonnet").
XXXI. "The Dweller." *Providence Journal* (7 May 1930): 15. *Phantagraph* 4, No. 2 (Nov.–Dec. 1935): 1935: [3].
XXXII. "Alienation." *WT* 17, No. 3 (Apr.–May 1931): 374.
XXXIII. "Harbour Whistles." *Silver Fern* 1, No. 5 (May 1930): [1]. *L'Alouette* 3, No. 6 (Sept.–Oct. 1930): 161. *Phantagraph* 5, No. 2 (Nov. 1936): 1.
XXXVI. "Continuity." *Causerie* (Feb. 1936): 1.

"In a Sequester'd Providence Churchyard Where Once Poe Walk'd." *Science-Fantasy Correspondent* 1, No. 3 (Mar.–Apr. 1937): 16–17. *WT* 31, No. 5 (May 1938): 578 (as "Where Poe Once Walked: An Acrostic Sonnet"). In *Four Acrostic Sonnets on Poe* (1936), ed. Maurice W. Moe.

"The Messenger." In B. K. Hart, "The Sideshow." *Providence Journal* (3 Dec. 1929): 14. *WT* 32, No. 1 (July 1938): 52.

"Nathicana." *Vagrant,* [Spring 1927]: 61–64.

"The Poe-et's Nightmare." *Vagrant* No. 8 (July 1918): [13–23].

"The Outpost." *Bacon's Essays* 3, No. 1 (Spring 1930): 7. *Fantasy Magazine* 3, No. 3 (May 1934): 24–25. *O-Wash-Ta-Nong* 3, No. 1 (Jan. 1938): 1.

"Psychopompos: A Tale in Rhyme." *Vagrant* No. 10 (Oct. 1919): 13–22.

"Quinsnicket Park." *Badger* No. 2 (June 1915): 7–10.

"Recapture." *WT* 15, No. 5 (May 1930): 693. (Later sonnet XXXIV of *Fungi from Yuggoth.*)

"To Zara: Inscribed to Miss Sarah Longhurst—June 1829." As by "Edgar Allan Poe." Included in a letter by HPL to Maurice W. Moe, [Aug.] 1922 (*SL* 1.164–65).

Letters

Letter to "The Eyrie." *WT* 3, No. 1 (Jan. 1924): 86, 88.

"One for the Black Bag." *Dragnet* 2, No. 3 (Apr. 1929): 372.

Letter to Farnsworth Wright (5 July 1927). *WT* 11, No. 2 (Feb. 1928): 282.

Letter to Farnsworth Wright (22 Dec. 1927). In *LVW* 203–5.

"Retain Historic 'Old Brick Row.'" *Providence Sunday Journal* (24 Mar. 1929): A5.

B. Works by August Derleth

Books

Atmosphere of Houses. Muscatine, IA: Prairie, 1939.

Collected Poems: 1937–1967. New York: Candlelight Press, 1967. Shelbourne, Ont.: Hawk & Whippoorwill, 1995. [*CP*]

Colonel Markesan and Less Pleasant People (with Mark Schorer). Sauk City, WI: Arkham House, 1966. [*ColM*]

Consider Your Verdict: Ten Coroner's Cases for You to Solve. New York: Stackpole, 1937 (as by "Tally Mason").

Country Growth. New York: Charles Scribner's Sons, 1940. [*CG*]

Death at Senessen House. See *The Man on All Fours.*

Dwellers in Darkness. Sauk City, WI: Arkham House, 1996. [*DD*]

Hawk on the Wind. Philadelphia: Ritten House, 1938. [*HW*]

Here on a Darkling Plain. Philadelphia: Ritten House, 1940. [*HDP*]

In a Quiet Graveyard: Poems of Sac Prairie People. Ed. Peter Ruber and George A. Vanderburgh. Shelbourne, Ont.: Hawk & Whippoorwill, 1997. [*QG*]

In Re: Sherlock Holmes—The Adventures of Solar Pons. Sauk City, WI: Mycroft & Moran, 1945. [*SH*]

The Man on All Fours. New York: Loring & Mussey, 1934.

Mischief in the Lane. New York: Charles Scribner's Sons, 1944.

Murder Stalks the Wakely Family. New York: Loring & Mussey, 1934.

Not Long for This World. Sauk City, WI: Arkham House, 1948. [*NLW*]

Place of Hawks. Illustrated with wood engravings by George Barford. New York: Loring & Mussey, 1935. (*LL* 235). In *Wisconsin Earth.* [*PH*]

Sac Prairie People. Sauk City, WI: Stanton & Lee, 1948 [*SPP*]

Selected Poems. Introduction by Edgar Lee Masters. Prairie City, IL: Press of James Decker, 1948. [*SP*]

Sign of Fear. New York: Loring & Mussey, 1935. (*LL* 236)

Someone in the Dark. Sauk City, WI: Arkham House, 1941. [*SD*]

Something Near. Sauk City, WI: Arkham House, 1945.[*SN*]

Still Is the Summer Night. New York: Charles Scribner's Sons, 1937.

Still Small Voice: The Biography of Zona Gale. New York: Appleton-Century, 1940.

The Chronicles of Solar Pons. Sauk City, WI: Mycroft & Moran, 1973. [*CSP*]

The Man on All Fours: A Judge Peck Mystery Story. New York: Loring & Mussey, [1934]. (*LL* 234)

Man Track Here. Philadelphia: Ritten House, 1939. [*MTH*]

The Mask of Cthulhu. Sauk City, WI: Arkham House, 1958. [*MC*]

The Memoirs of Solar Pons. Sauk City, WI: Mycroft & Moran, 1951. [*MSP*]

The Narracong Riddle. New York: Charles Scribner's Sons, 1940.

The Seven Who Waited. New York: Charles Scribner's Sons, 1943.

The Survivor and Others. Sauk City, WI: Arkham House, 1957.

Three Who Died. New York: Loring & Mussey, 1935. (*LL* 237)

Village Year: A Sac Prairie Journal. New York: Coward-McCann, 1941. In *Wisconsin Earth.*

Wind in the Elms. Philadelphia: Ritten House, 1941. [*WE*]

Wind over Wisconsin. New York: Charles Scribner's Sons, 1938.

Wisconsin Earth: A Sac Prairie Sampler. Sauk City, WI: Stanton & Lee, 1948. Westport, CT: Greenwood Press, 1971.

Wisconsin in Their Bones. New York: Duell, Sloan & Pearce, 1961. [*WB*]

Books Edited

The Night Side: Masterpieces of the Strange and Terrible. New York: Rinehart & Co., 1947. [NS]

Night's Yawning Peal: A Ghostly Company. New York: Pellegrini & Cudahy; Sauk City, WI: Arkham House, 1952. [*NYP*]

The Other Side of the Moon. New York: Pellegrini & Cudahy, 1949. [*OSM*]

Poetry out of Wisconsin. Ed., with Raymond E. F. Larsson. New York: Henry Harrison, 1937.

Sleep No More: Twenty Masterpieces of Horror for the Connoisseur. New York, Toronto: Farrar & Rinehart, 1944. [*SNM*]

The Sleeping and the Dead: Thirty Uncanny Tales. Chicago: Pellegrini and Cudahy, 1947. [*S&D*]

Strange Ports of Call: Twenty Masterpieces of Science Fiction. New York: Pellegrini & Cudahy, 1948. [*SPC*]

Who Knocks? Twenty Masterpieces of the Spectral for the Connoisseur. New York: Farrar & Rinehart, 1946. [*WK*]

Worlds of Tomrrow: Science Fiction with a Difference. New York: Pellegrini & Cudahy, 1953. [*WoT*]

Stories

"A Bird in the Bush." *Progressive Farmer and Southern Ruralist* 53, No. 5 (May 1938). In *CM.*

"Across the Hall." *WT* 15, No. 6 (June 1930): 810–12.

"The Adventure of the Black Narcissus." *Dragnet* 2, No. 1 (Feb. 1929): 69–75. In *SH.*

"The Adventure of the Broken Chessman." *Dragnet* 3, No. 4 (Sept. 1929): 347–60. In *MSP.*

"The Adventure of the Late Mr. Faversham." *Dragnet* 4, No. 3 (Dec. 1929): 338–50. In *SH.*

"The Adventure of the Limping Man," *Detective Trails* 1, No. 2 (Dec. 1929): 195–210. In *SH.*

"The Adventure of the Missing Tenants." *Dragnet Magazine* 4, No. 1 (June 1929): 67–76; rev. *CSP.*

"The Adventure of the Retired Novelist." In *SH.*

"After You, Mr. Henderson." *Strange Stories* 3, No. 3 (June 1940): 98–102, 112. In *NLW.*

"The Alphabet Begins with AAA." *Atlantic Monthly* 156, No. 6 (Dec. 1935): 734–39. In *CG, CM.*

"An Afternoon with Mrs. Spinnet." See "Mrs. Spinnet."

"The Ancestor." In *The Survivor and Others.*

"Atmosphere of Houses." *Prairie Schooner* 6, No. 2 (Spring 1932): 162–68. Another installment in *River* 1, No. 2 (Apr. 1937): 47–49. Excerpts incorporated in *Evening in Spring.* See also *Atmosphere of Houses.*

"Bat's Belfry." *WT* 7, No. 5 (May): 631–36.

"A Battle over the Teacups." *Oriental Stories* 2, No. 3 (Summer 1932): 417–20.

"Birkett's Twelfth Corpse." *Fantasy Fan* 1, No. 4 (Dec. 1933): 53–55. In *NLW.*

"Bishop Kroll." *Literary Monthly* 1, No. 3 (Feb. 1934): 3–14.

"The Bishop Sees Through." *WT* 19, No. 5 (May 1932): 714–16, 719–20.

"Book of Little Memories." See "More Confessions."

"The Bridge of Sighs." *WT* 18, No. 2 (Sept. 1931): 260–62. In *NLW.*

"The Captain Is Afraid." *WT* 18, No. 3 (Oct. 1931): 391–93.

"The Charing Cross Horror." See "The Tenant at Number 7."

"The Coffin of Lissa." *WT* 8, No. 4 (Oct. 1926): 551–53. In *You'll Need a Night. Light,* ed. Christine Campbell Thomson. London: Selwyn & Blount, 1927, pp. 182–86. In *Not at Night!,* ed. Herbert Asbury. New York: Macy-Masius (The Vanguard Press), 1928, pp. 108–12.

"Confessons." *This Quarter* 4, No. 3 (Mar. 1932): 451–57; and *Contempo* (21 Feb. 1933): 8.

"The Cossacks Ride Hard." *Marvel Tales* 1, No. 1 (May 1934): 21–25.

"Crows Fly High." *Scribner's Magazine* 96, No. 6 (Dec. 1934): 358–62. In *CG, CM.*

"Dawn." *Tryout* 11, No. 5 (May 1927): [16]–[18].

"Death Is Too Kind." *Ten Story Book* 31, No. 8 (Feb. 1933): 20–22.
"Death Walker." See "The Thing That Walked on the Wind."
"The Deserted Garden." *WT* 13, No. 3 (Mar. 1929): 333–36.
"The Devil's Pay." *WT* 8, No. 2 (Aug. 1926): 204–6.
"A Dinner at Imola." *WT* 13, No. 4 (Apr. 1929): 478–80. In *NLW*.
"The Do-Jigger." *Sauk City Pioneer Press*, Plains Edition (2 Oct. 1930). *Trend* 1, No. 4 (Jan.–Mar. 1933): 122–24.
"The Drifting Snow." *WT* 33, No. 2 (Feb. 1939): 77–84. In *NLW*.
"Elsie, Darling." *Redwood Monthly* 2 (Apr. 1936): 7–10.
"Expedition to the North." *Household* 35, No. 6 (June 1935): 4, 37–39. In *SPP, CM*.
"Factory Afternoon." *New Day* 9, No. 40 (6 July 1935): 5.
"The Facts about Lucas Payne." See "Memoir for Lucas Payne."
"Farway House." Accepted for *Medallion* but not published there.
"Feigman's Beard." *WT* 24, No. 5 (Nov. 1934): 636–40. In *NLW*.
"Five Alone." *Pagany* 3, No. 3 (Summer 1932): 14–44. In *PH*.
"Frost in October." *Lion & Unicorn* 1, No. 1 (Oct.–Nov. 1934): 21–24. *New Stories* 2, No. 3 (June–July 1935): 209–13. In *CG*.
"Glory Hand." *WT* 29, No. 2 (Feb. 1937): 231–36. In *SD*.
"Goodbye, Margery." *American Prefaces* 3, No. 2 (Nov. 1937): 19–20. Published as the final section of *Evening in Spring*.
"Hawk on the Blue." *London Daily Express* No. 10,733 (4 Oct. 1934): 12. *Hinterland* 1, No. 2 (Oct.–Nov. 1936): 56–58. In *CG*.
"He Shall Come." *Manuscripts* 1, No. 3 (Dec. 1929): 209–13. In *NLW*.
"House on the Highway, The." *WT* 13, No. 6 (June 1929): 838–40.
"Incident in a Roman Camp." See "Old Mark."
"In the Moonlight." See "The Moon Is Fair Tonight."
"In This Dark Heart." *Decade* 1, No. 2 (July–Aug. 1939): 24–26.
"Ithaqua." *Strange Stories* 5, No. 1 (Feb. 1941): 40–47. In *SN*.
"Just a Song at Twilight." *WT* 16, No. 2 (Aug. 1930): 269–73. In *NLW*.
"The Lady Who Wouldn't Stay Dead." See "The White Moth."
"The Lamp of Alhazred." *Magazine of Fantasy and Science Fiction* 13, No. 4 (Oct. 1957): 44–53. In *The Survivor and Others*.
"Lesandro's Familiar." *WT* 27, No. 5 (May 1936): 622–25. In *NLW*.
"Light Again." *Little Magazine* 1, No. 2 (Feb.–Mar. 1934): 13–15. In *SPP*.
"The Lilac Bush." *WT* 15, No. 2 (Feb. 1930): 265–67. In *NLW*.
"Lo, the Mighty Senator." *Characters* 1, No. 3 (May–June 1934): 81–84.
"Mass at Eight." *Galleon* 1, No. 4 (May–June 1935): 9–14.
"The Matchboy." *Western Rustler* 1, No. 3 (Sept. 1929): 23–24.
"A Matter of Sight." *WT* 15, No. 1 (Jan. 1930): 115–17. In *NLW*.
"Melodie in E Minor." *WT* 13, No. 2 (Feb. 1929): 255–56.
"Memoir for Lucas Payne." *Strange Stories* 2, No. 1 (Aug. 1939): 72–76. In *DD*.
"A Message for His Majesty." *Strange Stories* 2, No. 3 (Oct. 1939): 75–78.

"The Metronome." *WT* 25, No. 2 (Feb. 1935): 245–48. In *Terror by Night,* ed. Christine Campbell Thomson. London: Selwyn & Blount, [1934], pp. 151–58; *SN.*

"Mister God." *Windsor Quarterly* 1, No. 2 (Summer 1933): 166–70.

"Moncati Took a Picture." See "The Second Print."

"The Moon Is Fair Tonight." *Little Magazine* 1, No. 1 (Dec. 1933–Jan. 1934): 11–12.

"More Confessions." *1933: A Year Magazine* No. 1 (June–Dec. 1933): 26.

"Mr. Berbeck Had a Dream." *WT* 26, No. 5 (Nov. 1935): 630–35. In *NLW.*

"Mr. Jimson Assists." *Magic Carpet* 3, No. 2 (April 1933): 250–52, 254–56.

"Mrs. Bentley's Daughter." *WT* 16, No. 4 (Oct. 1930): 461–64. In *NLW.*

"Mrs. Spinnet." *Detroit Free Press All-Fiction Magazine* (1940). In *CG.*

"Muggridge's Aunt." *WT* 25, No. 5 (May 1935): 633–37. In *SD.*

"Nellie Foster." *WT* 21, No. 6 (June 1933): 782–85. In *NLW.*

"Night Train." *Decade* 11, No. 4 (1953): 12–16.

"Nine Strands in a Web." A section of *PH.*

"The No-Sayers." *Brooklyn Eagle Magazine of Features* (12 Apr. 1935): 4–5, 12. In *CG.*

"Now Is the Time for All Good Men." *Scribner's Magazine* 98, No. 5 (Nov. 1935): 195–98. In *SPP.*

"An Occurrence in an Antique Shop." *WT* 13, No. 1 (Jan. 1929): 70–72.

"The Old Girls." *Trend* (June–Aug. 1932): 41–43.

"Old Huckleberry." *Story* 9, No. 53 (Dec. 1936): 23–31. In *CG.*

"Old Ladies." *Midland* 19, No. 1 (Jan.–Feb. 1932): 5–9. Rewritten and included in *Evening in Spring* as "Take Arms!"

"The Old Lady Has Her Day." *Scribner's Magazine* 100, No. 1 (July 1936): 35–39.

"The Old Lady Turns the Other Cheek." *Scribner's Magazine* 100, No. 3 (Sept. 1936): 146–49. In *WB* (as "The Other Cheek").

"Old Mark." *WT* 14, No. 2 (Aug. 1929): 266–72.

"An Old Mill Burns." *Tanager* 9, No. 2 (Jan. 1934): 21–34.

"On the Outside." *Anvil* No. 2 (Sept.–Oct. 1933): 21–22.

"One Against the Dead." In *SPP.*

"The Panelled Room." *Leaves* No. 1 (Summer 1937): 65–70. *Westminster Magazine* 22, No. 3 (Autumn 1937): 35–45. In *SD.*

"The Passing of Eric Holm." *Strange Stories* 2, No. 3 (Dec. 1939): 101–4 (as by "Will Garth"). In *DD.*

"The Peace of the Cardinal Archbishop." *Outlander* No. 3 (Summer 1933): 33–36.

"Place of Hawks." One section of *PH.*

"The Portrait." *WT* 15, No. 4 (Apr. 1930): 463–65.

"Prince Borgia's Mass." *WT* 17, No. 1 (Aug. 1931): 107–10. In *At Dead of Night,* ed. Christine Campbell Thomson. London: Selwyn & Blount, 1931, pp. 145–50. In *NLW.*

"The Return of Hastur." *WT* 33, No. 3 (Mar. 1939): 66–84. In *SD, MC.*
"The Return of Sarah Purcell." *WT* 28, No. 1 (July 1936): 92–97. In *NLW.*
"A Ride Home." *Story* 5, No. 25 (Aug. 1934): 67–73. In *CG.*
"Room to Turn Around In." *Literary America* 3, No. 2 (Feb. 1936): 908–12.
"The River." *WT* 9, No. 2 (Feb. 1927): 252–54.
"St. John's Wood." See "The Tenant at Number 7."
"The Satin Mask." *WT* 27, No. 1 (Jan. 1936): 25–34.
"Scarlatti's Bottle." *WT* 14, No. 5 (Nov. 1929): 680–82.
"The Second Print." *Strange Stories* 1, No. 2 (Apr. 1939): 45–49 (as "Lord of Evil" by "Tally Mason"). In *NLW.*
"The Shadow on the Sky." *Strange Tales of Mystery and Terror* 1, No. 3 (Jan. 1932): 384–89. In *NLW.*
"The Sheraton Mirror." *WT* 20, No. 3 (Sept. 1932): 330–37. In *SD.*
"The Shuttered House." *WT* 29, No. 4 (Apr. 1937): 432–40. In *SD.*
"The Sleepers." *WT* 10, No. 6 (Dec. 1927): 829–31.
"A Small Life." *Windsor Quarterly* 1, No. 1 (Spring 1933): 51–54.
"The Snow-Thing." See "Ithaqua."
"Something from Out There." *WT* 43, No. 2 (Jan. 1951): 50–58.
"The Splinter." *Tryout* 11, No. 3 (Mar. 1927): [7–12].
"Still Is the Summer Night." *Literary Arts* 1, No. 1 (Feb.–Mar. 1934): 5–7. (Unrelated to novel of same title.)
"The Strauss Waltz." *Characters* 2, No. 1 (Jan.–Feb. 1935): 1–3.
"The Telephone in the Library." *WT* 27, No. 6 (June 1936): 710–19. In *SD.*
"The Tenant." *WT* 11, No. 3 (Mar. 1928): 322–26. In *NWL.*
"The Tenant at Number 7." *WT* 12, No. 5 (Nov. 1928): 690–92.
"That Wedding of Annie's." *Household* No. 9 (Sept. 1936): 2–3, 18. In *CM.*
"These Childless Marriages." *10 Story Book* 31, No. 5 (May 1932): 25–26, 28.
"The Thing That Walked on the Wind." *Strange Tales of Mystery and Terror* 3, No. 1 (Jan. 1933): 18–26. In *SN.*
"Things We Know Not Of." See "Old Mark."
"Those Who Seek." *WT* 19, No. 1 (Jan. 1932): 49–56. In *NLW.*
"Town Characters." *Literary America* 2, No. 5 (May 1935): 373–80.
"The Tree." *Decade* 3, No. 6 (Mar.–Apr. 1942): 14–17.
"The Turret Room." *WT* 10, No. 3 (Sept. 1927): 365–66.
"Two Black Buttons." *Dragnet* 4, No. 1 (Oct. 1929): 429–39.
"Two Gentlemen at Forty." *10 Story Book* 30, No. 1 (July 1931): 25–27, 42–44.
"The Vanishing of Simmons." *WT* 21, No. 2 (Feb. 1933): 266–72.
"The Whistler." *WT* 15, No. 5 (May 1930): 682–84.
"The White Moth." *WT* 21, No. 4 (Apr. 1933): 540–44. In *NLW.*
"Widow Halgenau." See "Still Is the Summer Night."
"Wild Grapes." *WT* 24, No. 1 (July 1934): 85–88.
"The Wind from the River." *WT* 29, No. 5 (May 1937): 586–95. In *SD.*
"Wraiths of the Sea." *Mind Magic Magazine* 1, No. 2 (July 1931): 17–18.

Collaborations with Mark Schorer

"The Black Castle." *WT* 9, No. 5 (May 1927): 675–77, 719.

"A Bottle for Corezzi." *Strange Stories* 2, No. 3 (Dec. 1939): 30–36 (as by "Mark Schorer").

"The Carven Image." *WT* 21, No. 5 (May 1933): 599–606. In *ColM.*

"Colonel Markesan." *WT* 23, No. 6 (June 1934): 750–60. In *ColM.*

"Death Holds the Post." *WT* 23, No. 2 (Aug.–Sept. 1936): 222–33.

"The Elixir of Life." *WT* 8, No. 1 (July 1926): 126–28.

"The Evil Ones." See "The Horror from the Depths."

"Eyes of the Serpent." *Strange Stories* 1, No. 1 (Feb. 1939): 52–68. In *ColM.*

"The Figure with a Scythe." *Tryout* 11, No. 2 (Jan. 1927): [5-8] (as with "Mary R. Schorer").

"The Horror from the Depths." *Strange Stories* 4, No. 2 (Oct. 1940): 14–31 (as "The Evil Ones"). In *ColM.*

"The Horror from the Lake." See "The Horror from the Depths."

"The House in the Magnolias." *Strange Tales of Mystery and Terror* 2, No. 2 (June 1932): 220–31. In *ColM.*

"In the Left Wing." *WT* 19, No. 6 (June 1932): 772–83. In *ColM.*

"The Lair of the Star-Spawn." *WT* 20, No. 2 (Aug. 1932): 184–94. In *ColM.*

"Laughter in the Night." *WT* 19, No. 3 (Mar. 1932): 409–13. In *ColM.*

"The Marmoset." *WT* 8, No. 3 (Sept. 1926): 361–64.

"A Matter of Faith." *WT* 24, No. 6 (Dec. 1934): 765–70.

"The Night Rider." *WT* 9, No. 1 (Jan. 1927): 47–48.

"The Occupant of the Crypt." *WT* 39, No. 12 (Sept. 1947): 62–70. In *ColM.*

"The Pacer." *WT* 15, No. 3 (Mar. 1930): 395–402. In *Swicth On the Light,* ed. Christine Campbell Thomson. London: Selwyn & Blount, 1931, pp. 115–29. In *ColM.*

"Red Hands." *WT* 20, No. 4 (Oct. 1932): 549–33. In *ColM.*

"The Return of Andrew Bentley." *WT* 22, No. 3 (Sept. 1933): 335–46. In *ColM.*

"Riders in the Sky." *WT* 11, No. 5 (May 1928): 621–24.

"Spawn of the Maelstrom." *WT* 34, No. 3 (Sept. 1939): 84–94. In *ColM.*

"The Statement of Eric Marsh." See "The Lair of the Star-Spawn."

"They Shall Rise." *WT* 27, No. 4 (Apr. 1936): 437–49. In *ColM.*

"Town Characters." *Literary America* 2, No. 5 (May 1935): 373–80.

"The Vengeance of Aï." *Strange Stories* 1, No. 2 (Apr. 1939): 71–78 (as by "Mark Schorer"). In *ColM.*

"A Visitor from Outside." In *Arkham's Masters of Horror,* ed. Peter Ruber. Sauk City, WI: Arkham House, 2000, pp. 430–43.

"The Woman at Loon Point." *WT* 28, No 5 (Dec. 1936): 597–606. In *ColM.*

Poems

"American Portrait: 1877." *Commonweal* 21, No. 23 (5 Apr. 1935): 648. In *SP, CP.*

"At Dusk the Sun." *Galleon* 1, No. 5 (July–Aug. 1935): ii.

"Be Still, My Heart" (= "O My Heart"?). *Berkeley Poetry Magazine* 1, No. 1 (Apr. 1937): 27.)

"Black Hawk War: A Century Gone." *Nebulae: Verse of Today* 2, No. 2 (July 1935): 3.

"Broadwing Soaring." *New Writers* 1, No. 2 (Feb. 1936): 22. In *HW.*

"Charlie Techmann." In *HW, SP, CP, QG.*

"Do They Remember Where They Lie?" *Manuscript* 1, No. 5 (Oct. 1934): 35.In *HW, CP.*

"Doves" (= "Spring Evening: Doves"). *Literary America* 4, No. 2 (Winter 1936): 153. ("Spring Evening: Doves." *American Poetry Magazine* 21, No. 6 (Mar.–Apr. 1941): 5. In *HW, SP, CP.*

"Dusk over Wisconsin." *Frontier and Midland* 16, No. 1 (Autumn 1935): 59. In *HW, SP, CP.*

"Dust on the Wind." *Voices* No. 81 (Apr.–May 1935): 5–6. In *HW.*

"Epitaph of a Century After." *Prairie du Chien Courier* (1933). *American Poetry Journal* (Feb. 1934): 14. In *WE* as "Michel Brisbois: A Century After."

"Evenings in Wisconsin." *New Republic* 87 (5 Aug. 1936): 372. In *HW* (as "Evenings") and *CP.*

"Filled Cup." See "Over the Filled Cup."

"First Scylla." *Dragon-Fly* No. 1 (15 Oct. 1935): 27.

"Flesh Is Not All." *New Writers* 1, No. 1 (Jan. 1936): 22.

"For Eleanor." *Driftwind* 8, No. 5 (Nov. 1933): 156.

"Forgotten Scythe." *Voices* No. 86 (Summer 1936): 9. In *MTH.*

"Fox in the Winter Night." *Voices* No. 81 (Apr.–May 1935): 6–7. In Albert Emerson Brown, ed. *The Verse-Land Anthology: One Hundred Poems by Verse-Land Poets.* Otsego, MI: Verse-Land Press, 1935, vol. 1, p. 40. In *HW, SP.*

"From a Nature Notebook: An Owl at Bay." *Trails* 2, No. 4 (Autumn 1933): 9–10.

"Hawk on the Wind." *Literary America* 4, No. 1 (Fall 1936): 79. In *HW, WE, SP, CP.*

"Hawks Against April." *American Poetry Journal* (Aug. 1933): 28. In *HW, SP.*

"High Wind in Wisconsin." *Voices* No. 81 (Apr.–May 1935): 6. In *HW.*

"A Hill in May." *Driftwind* 8, No. 11 (May 1934): 351.

"Huntsman's Beacon." *Shards* 5, No. 2 (Spring 1937): 13. In *HW.*

"Hylas Sing." See "Nocturne: The Hylas Sing."

"Incubus." *WT* 23, No. 5 (May 1934): 600.

"In the Cemetery." See "Spring Evening: In the Cemetery."

"Indians Pass." See "Spring Evening: The Indians Pass." In *SP, CP.*

"Late Winter Morning: Outposts of Nostalgia." In *HW, SP, CP.*

"Let There Be Singing." *Kosmos* 1 No. 1 (Nov.–Dec. 1933): 29.

"Lights on the Prairie." See "Twilight on the Prairie."
"Man and the Cosmos." *Wonder Stories* 6, No. 8 (Mar. 1935): 1381.
"Maris: Night Portrait." *Shards* 5, No. 2 (Spring 1937): 15. In *HW*.
"Michel Brisbois." See "Epitaph of a Century After."
"Nella." *Pagany* 3, No. 1 (Winter 1932): 134–9.
"New Moon: February." *Shards* 5, No. 1 (Winter 1937): 11. In *HDP*.
"Night Mail." *Driftwind* 9, No. 12 (June–July 1935): 383. In *HDP*.
"Night on the Meadow." *Medallion* 1, No. 1 (May 1934): 20.
"Night Portrait." See "Maris: Night Portrait."
"Nocturne: The Hylas Sing." *Kaleidograph* 7, No. 7 (Nov. 1935): 6.
"Nocturne: Torrent of Spring." *Westward* 4, No. 9 (Sept. 1933): 16. In *SP, CP*.
"The Ojibwa Smile." See "Spring Evening: The Ojibwa Smile."
"Old House." *Voices* No. 86 (Summer 1936): 9–10.
"Omega." *Wonder Stories* 6, No. 6 (Nov. 1934): 691.
"On Finding a Violet in Autumn." *Fantasy* 4, No. 4 (Spring 1935): 30. In *MTH*.
"Outposts of Nostalgia." See "Late Winter Morning: Outposts of Nostalgia."
"Over the Filled Cup." *Voices* No. 81 (Apr.–May 1935): 7–8. In *HW*.
"Prairie du Chien, Wisconsin: A History in Four Panels." Appearance in the *Prairie du Chien Weekly* not found. *Centaur* 1, No. 3 (Dec. 1934): 14–17 (as "Prairie du Chien: A History in Four Parts").
"A Primer in Economic Ideology for Little Men." *Welcome News* 11, No. 1 (Apr. 1938): 46.
"Quail in the Deep Grass." See "Summer Afternoon: Quail in the Deep Grass."
"Screech Owl Calling." *Voices* No. 81 (Apr.–May 1935): 4–5. In *HW*.
"Shy Bird." *Shards* 2, No. 4. (Nov. 1935): 12. In *HW, SP, CP*.
"Sixteen Years on Death." *Tryout* 11, No. 4 (Apr. 1927): [19]–[20].
"Smoke on the Wind." See "Summer Afternoon: Smoke on the Wind."
"Song of the Saw-Whet Owl." *Trails* 3, No. 3 (Summer 1934): 13.
"Spring Evening: In the Cemetery." *Mid-West Story Magazine* 1, No. 11 (Oct. 1934): 17.
"Spring Evening: South Wind." *Voices* No. 86 (Summer 1936): 7.
"Spring Evening: The Indians Pass." *Yankee Poetry Chapbook* (Autumn 1934): 19–20. In *SP, CP*.
"Spring Evening: The Ojibway Smile." In *HW, SP, CP*..
"Spring Evening: The Old Man Remembers." *Voices* No. 81 (Apr.–May 1935): 3–4. In *HW, SP,* and *CP* as "Spring Evening: The Old Men Remember."
"Spring Evening: We Are Remembering Again." *Voices* No. 86 (Summer 1936): 7–8.
"Spring Evening: Wild Crab-Apple Blooming." *Shards* 2, No. 4 (Nov. 1934): 12. In *HW, SP, CP*.
"Summer Afternoon: Quail in the Deep Grass." In *HW*.

"Summer Afternoon: Smoke on the Wind." *Tone* No. 2 (1 Dec. 1933): 29.
"Summer Afternoon: Sunlight on Old Houses." *Vagabond* 19, No. 2 (Oct. 1934): 4. In *HW*.
"Things of Earth." *Voices* No. 86 (Summer 1936): 7. In *HW*.
"This Evening Hour." *Voices* No. 86 (Summer 1936): 8–9.
"Three Birds Flying." See "Three Doves Flying." In *HW, SP, CP*.
"Three Doves Flying." *New Republic* 87 (1 May 1935): 334.
"To a Spaceship." *Wonder Stories* 5, No. 8 (Mar. 1934): 914.
To Remember [August W. Derleth] and *Salute Before Dawn* [Albert Edward Clements], Windsor Pamphlet No. 2. Hartland Four Corners, VT: Windsor Quarterly Publications, 1933, pp. 7–12.
"Torrent of Spring." See "Nocturne: Torrent of Spring."
"Twilight on the Prairie." *American Fireside* 1, No. 5 (Sept.–Oct. 1936): 12.
"A Verbena in a Glass." *Tone* No. 1 (1 Sept. 1933). [5].
"Vesper Sparrow." *Vespers* 2, No. 4 (Sept. 1935): [11]. In *MTH*.
"Violet in Autumn." See "On Finding a Violet in Autumn."
"We Are Not Lessened." *Poetry World* 6, Nos. 9/10/11 (Apr.–May–June 1935): [5].
"We Are Not the First." See "Spring Evening: We Are Remembering Again."
"We Remember 1832." See "Black Hawk War: A Century Gone."
"Web of Moonlight." *Manuscript* 2, No. 3 (May–June 1935): 67. In *HW*.
"Whippoorwill in the Hollow." *Manuscript* 2, No. 1 (Feb. 1935): 33–37.
"White Are the Locusts." *Kosmos* 3, No. 1 (Aug.–Sept. 1934): 30.
"Wild Crab-Apple Blooming." See "Spring Evening: Wild Crab-Apple Blooming."
"Wintered Bee." *Prairie Schooner* 10, No. 3 (Fall 1936): 226. In *MTH*.
"Wisconsin Come to Age." *Voices* No. 86 (Summer 1936): 10.

Drama

The Business Called Life (with Mark Schorer).
The Five Who Waited.

Essays

About Sidewalks and Other Things. [1934.] (Copy in HPL papers, JHL.)
"An Appreciation." *Demcourier* 12, No. 2 (March 1942): 8–9. Regarding Helen C. White, AWD's English professor.
"A Day in March." *Frontier and Midland* 13, No. 3 (Mar. 1933): 189–91.
"And Did They Write!" *Writer's Review* 2, No. 8 (May 1934): 28–30.
"The Case for the Intelligentsia." *Midwestern Conference* (Apr. 1931): 5–6, 40–42 (Part I: "The Cult of Incoherence").
"H. P. Lovecraft: Outsider." *River* 1, No. 3 (June 1937): 88–89.
"H. P. L.—Two Decades After." *Fresco* 8, No. 3 (Spring 1958): 9–11.
"A Master of the Macabre." *Reading and Collecting* 1, No. 9 (Aug. 1937): 9–10.

"The Monocle of My Great-Grandfather." *Space* 1, No. 7 (Nov. 1934): 77–78.
"A Note on Arthur Machen." *Reading and Collecting* 1, No. 12 (November 1937): 5–7.
"Novels at 10,000 Words a Day." *Writer's Review* 2, No. 4 (Jan. 1934): 3–4. In Roberts, *A Derleth Collection.*
"Plight of the *Midland.*" *Commonweal* 15 (17 Feb. 1932): 439–40.
"The Weird Tale in English Since 1890." <1930> *Ghost* No. 3 (1945): 5–32.

Reviews

Review of *Susan Shane* by Roger Burlingame. *Wisconsin Literary Magazine* 26, No. 2 (Jan. 1927): 29–30 (as by "AWD").
Review of *Song of Life* by Fannie Hurst. *Wisconsin Literary Magazine* 26, No. 3 (Mar. 1927): 31–32 (as by "AWD").
Review of *Gallions Reach* by H. M. Tomlinson. *Wisconsin Literary Magazine* 27, No. 2 (Dec. 1927): 38 (as by "AWD").
Review of *Salammbo* by Gustave Flaubert, ill. Mahlon Blaine. *Wisconsin Literary Magazine* (April 1928): 37–38 (as by "AWD").

Writings in Outdoors *(period of correspondence only)*

"A Day in April." 2, No. 2 (Apr. 1934): 19, 34.
"A Day in May." 2, No. 3 (May 1934): 14.
"A Brook in June." 2, No. 4 (June 1934): 18, 31.
"August from a Hill." 2, No. 6 (Aug. 1934): 10, 34.
"Good Books You Should Own." 2, No. 6 (Aug. 1934): 17 (unsigned; by AWD?).
"Mill-Pond in September." 2, No. 7 (Sept. 1934): 31, 34.
"Good Books You Should Own." 2, No. 7 (Sept. 1934): 32.
"Smoke in the Sky." 2, No. 8 (Oct. 1934): 11, 21, 29, 34.
"Good Books You Should Own." 2, No. 8 (Oct. 1934): 30.
"Dusk in November." 2, No. 9 [as 11] (Nov. 1934): 20–21.
"Good Books You Should Own." 2, No. 9 [as 11] (Nov. 1934): 34.
"For December Nights." 2, No. 10 (Dec. 1934): 4–5, 18.
"Good Books You Should Own." 2, No. 10 (Dec. 1934): 34.
"January Thaw." 2, No. 11 (Jan. 1935): 24–25.
"Good Books You Should Own." 2, No. 11 (Jan. 1935): 34.
"Pussy Willows." 2, No. 12 (Feb. 1935): 18.
"Good Books You Should Own." 2, No. 12 (Feb. 1935): 19.
"What Flieth Down the Wind?" 3, No. 1 (Mar. 1935): 14–15.
"Good Books You Should Own." 3, No. 1 (Mar. 1935): 34.
"Syrup Camp in April." 3, No. 2 (Apr. 1935): 20–22.
"Good Books You Should Own." 3, No. 2 (Apr. 1935): 32.
"Where the Lilacs Grow." 3, No. 3 (May 1935): 16.
"Good Books You Should Own." 3, No. 3 (May 1935): 29.

"Afternoon in June." 3, No. 4 (June 1935): 10, 20.
"Good Books You Should Own." 3, No. 4 (June 1935): 31.
"July Night." 3, No. 5 (July 1935): 14–15.
"Good Books You Should Own." 3, No. 5 (July 1935): 34.
"Pike Country." 3, No. 6 (Aug. 1935): 22–23.
"Good Books You Should Own." 3, No. 6 (Aug. 1935): 34.
"Hawks Down the Wind." 3, No. 7 (Sept. 1935): 22–23.
"Good Books You Should Own." 3, No. 7 (Sept. 1935): 29.
"Night in October." 3, No. 8 (Oct. 1935): 27.
"Good Books You Should Own." 3, No. 8 (Oct. 1935): 34.
"Wood Cock in the Marshes." 3, No. 9 (Nov. 1935): 15.
"Good Books You Should Own." 3, No. 9 (Nov. 1935): 27.
"Fireside in December." 3, No. 10 (Dec. 1935): 24–25.
"A Robin in January." 3, No. 11 (Jan. 1936): 23.
"Good Books You Should Own." 3, No. 11 (Jan. 1936): 34.
"February Afternoon." 3, No. 12 (Feb. 1936): 28–29.
"Good Books You Should Own." 3, No. 12 (Feb. 1936): 33.
"Good Books You Should Own." 4, No. 1 (Mar. 1936): 34.
"Retreat to Nature." 4, No. 2 (Apr. 1936): 14.
"Good Books You Should Own." 4, No. 2 (Apr. 1936): 33.
"Good Books You Should Own." 4, No. 3 (May 1936): 33.
"An Exercise in Botany." 4, No. 3 (May 1936): 34.
"Sunfish in the Millpond." 4, No. 4 (June 1936): 12.
"Good Books You Should Own." 4, No. 4 (June 1936): 33.
"Night in July." 4, No. 5 (July 1936): 16.
"Good Books You Should Own." 4, No. 5 (July 1936): 33.
"Down River in August." 4, No. 6 (Aug. 1936): 28–29.
"Good Books You Should Own." 4, No. 6 (Aug. 1936): 33.
"Good Books You Should Own." 4, No. 7 (Sept. 1936): 33.
"Along September Starways." 4, No. 8 (Oct. 1936): 27. 31.
"Good Books You Should Own." 4, No. 8 (Oct. 1936): 33.
"Log of the Camping Life." 4, No. 9 (Nov. 1936): 24–25.
"Good Books You Should Own." 4, No. 9 (Nov. 1936): 33.
"Where the Wahoo Grows." 4, No. 10 (Dec. 1936): 28–29.
"Good Books You Should Own." 4, No. 10 (Dec. 1936): 33.
"Good Books You Should Own." 4, No. 11 (Jan. 1937): 22, 33.
"Color in February." 4, No. 12 (Feb. 1937): 36.
"Good Books You Should Own." 4, No. 12 (Feb. 1937): 41.
"Night Wind." 5, No. 1 (Mar. 1937): 20–21.
"Good Books You Should Own." 5, No. 2 (Apr. 1937): 24.
"In Defense of Idling." 5, No. 3 (May 1937): 14–15.
"Good Books You Should Own." 5, No. 3 (May 1937): 33.
"Good Books You Should Own." 5, No. 4 (June 1937): 33.

Works that appear to be unpublished or nonextant, or that may have been retitled.

"All That Glitters."
"At Sundown." Ms. PH.
"Beyond the End."
"The Black Powder." (See "The Case of the Black Powder.")
"Body of the Moon."
"Book of Little Memories."
"Calling to the Stars." Verse.
"The Case of the Black Powder." Ms. PH.
"The Chicago Horror."
"The Child."
"Coleman's Shoulder." Ms. PH.
"Company of Ghosts." Verse.
"The Corpse-Finder."
"The Dance of Death."
"A Day in May."
"Death in the Crypt." (Same as "The Occupant of the Crypt"?)
"Death of an Old Man."
"The Door." Ms. PH.
"Door Opened."
"Down at the Mill." Verse.
"The Early Years." Ms. PH.
"East India Lights."
"Eternity Begun." Verse.
"Fire in the Hollow."
"The Garden of the Dead." (Same as "The Deserted Garden"?)
"The Gold." Ms. PH.
"The Grotto."
"Hawks Down the Wind."
"The Head of the House of Macht." Ms. PH.
"Houses at Night."
"The Hunt." Ms. PH.
"The Inversion of Hay."
"I Am Awakened by a Nighthawk at Dawn."
"In the Junction Station."
"In the Pool."
"Java Lights." Ms. PH.
"July Macabre."
"Lanterns over the Marshes." Verse.
"The Laughter."
"The Leaves Fall." Ms. PH.
"The Lights on the Prairie." Verse.
"A Little Girl Lost." Ms. PH.

"Liszt Hears His Second Concerto: Weimar, 7 January, 1857."
"The Long Call."
"The Lost Continent."
"The Lost Path."
"The Man from the Islands." (Same as "The Man from Dark Valley"?)
"Mater Dolorosa."
"The Menace from the Stars."
"The Menace from Under the Sea."
"The Mill Wheel."
"Moscow Road." (Same as "The Cossacks Ride Hard"?)
"The Nature of the Evidence."
"165 Bascom Hall."
"Others."
"A Panorama to the West."
"People."
"The Piece of Parchment."
"Pomegranates." Ms. PH.
"Port of Call." Verse.
"Portrait of My Aunt Leocadie."
"Prevailing Westerly." A Gus Elker story. Ms. PH.
"A Question of Habit."
"Rain in October."
"Rebirth."
"The Rector Sits Alone."
"Retreat to Nature."
"The Sand." Ms. PH.
"Selina Markesan."
"The Seventeenth of February."
"Senessen House." Variant title of "Death at Senessen House." (See *The Man on All Fours.*)
"Shadows." Ms. PH.
"The Sinister Companion."
"Small Town in Autumn."
"Snow." Verse.
"Spring Death."
"Sugar Camp in April." (An essay?)
"Summer Evening." Verse.
"Symphony." (Same as "Symphony in Gold"?)
"Symphony in Gold."
"A Town Is Built." Mss. (two) PH, ms. SHSW.
"The Tree Near the Window."
"The Undead."
"Walking in the Moonlight." (Same as "In the Moonlight"?; ms. PH).

"We Live in the Country."
"When the Leaves Fall." (Same as "The Leaves Fall"? ms. PH).
"White Silence."
"The Wind." Ms. PH.
"Wind at Night." Verse.
"The World Is Mad." Ms. PH.

C. Items Published in *Weird Tales*

Lists all appearances by HPL and AWD, and stories mentioned by them in their correspondence.

8, No. 5 (November 1926)
The Peacock's Shadow — E. Hoffmann Price
The Dog-Eared God — Frank Belknap Long, Jr.

8, No. 6 (December 1926)
The Metal Giants — Edmond Hamilton

9, No. 1 (January 1927)
Drome [1/5] — John Martin Leahy
The Last Horror — Eli Colter
The Night Rider — August W. Derleth
The Horror at Red Hook — H. P. Lovecraft

9, No. 2 (February 1927)
The Man Who Cast No Shadow — Seabury Quinn
The Atomic Conquerors — Edmond Hamilton
Drome [2/5] — John Martin Leahy
The Church Stove at Raebrudafisk — G. Appleby Terrill
The Unearthly — Don Robert Catlin
The River — August W. Derleth

9, No. 3 (March 1927)
The City of Glass — Joel Martin Nichols, Jr.
The Blood Flower — Seabury Quinn
Evolution Island — Edmond Hamilton
The White Ship — H. P. Lovecraft
Drome [3/5] — John Martin Leahy

9, No. 4 (April 1927)
Drome [4/5] — John Martin Leahy

9, No. 5 (May 1927)
The Master of Doom — Donald Edward Keyhoe
Drome [5/5] — John Martin Leahy

The Black Castle	Mark R. Schorer & August W. Derleth
10, No. 1 (July 1927)	
The Return of the Master	H. Warner Munn
The Mystery of Sylmare	Hugh Irish
The Edge of the Shadow	R. Ernest Dupuy
10, No. 2 (August 1927)	
The Bride of Osiris [1/3]	Otis Adelbert Kline
The Man with a Thousand Legs	Frank Belknap Long
Two Black Bottles	Wilfred Blanch Talman
10, No. 3 (September 1927)	
The Turret Room	August W. Derleth
The Bride of Osiris [2/3]	Otis Adelbert Kline
10, No. 4 (October 1927)	
The Dark Lore	Nictzin Dyalhis
The Time-Raider [1/4]	Edmond Hamilton
Pickman's Model	H. P. Lovecraft
The Red Brain	Donald Wandrei
The Bride of Osiris [3/3]	Otis Adelbert Kline
10, No. 3 (November 1927)	
The Time-Raider [2/4]	Edmond Hamilton
The Shadows	Henry S. Whitehead
10, No. 6 (December 1927)	
The Infidel's Daughter	E. Hoffmann Price
The Canal	Everil Worrell
Bells of Oceana	Arthur J. Burks
The Sleepers	August W. Derleth
The Time-Raider [3/4]	Edmond Hamilton
11, No. 1 (January 1928)	
The Garret of Madam Lemoyne	W. K. Mashburn, Jr.
The Giant World [1/3]	Ray Cummings
In Amundsen's Tent	John Martin Leahy
The Golden Whistle	Eli Colter
The Time-Raider [4/4]	Edmond Hamilton
The Bone-Grinder	Wilford Allen
11, No. 2 (February 1928)	
The Call of Cthulhu	H. P. Lovecraft
The Curse of Alabad, Ghinu and Aratza	Wilfred B. Talman

11, No. 3 (March 1928)
The Eighth Green Man — G. G. Pendarves
The Tenant — August W. Derleth

11, No. 5 (May 1928)
Riders in the Sky — Mark R. Schorer & August W. Derleth
Sonnets of the Midnight Hours: — Donald Wandrei
1. The Hungry Flowers [v]
2. Dream Horror [v]

11, No. 6 (June 1928)
The Lurking Fear — H. P. Lovecraft
The Philosopher's Stone — August W. Derleth
Sonnets of the Midnight Hours: 3. Purple [v] — Donald Wandrei

12, No. 1 (July 1928)
The Three-Storied House — August W. Derleth
The Space-Eaters — Frank Belknap Long, Jr.
Sonnets of the Midnight Hours: 4. The Eye [v] — Donald Wandrei

12, No. 2 (August 1928)
Sonnets of the Midnight Hours: 5. The Grip of Evil Dreams [v] Donald Wandrei

12, No. 3 (September 1928)
The Owl on the Moor — Mark R. Schorer & August W. Derleth
Sonnets of the Midnight Hours: 6. As I Remember [v] — Donald Wandrei

12, No. 4 (October 1928)
The Werewolf's Daughter [1/3] — H. Warner Munn
Carnate Crystal — Mayo Reiss
Sonnets of the Midnight Hours: 7. The Statues [v] — Donald Wandrei
The Conradi Affair — August W. Derleth & Carl W. Ganzlin
The City of Lost Souls — Genevieve Larsson
Ol' Black Sarah [v] — Bernard A. Dwyer

12, No. 5 (November 1928)
Sonnets of the Midnight Hours: 8. The Creatures [v] — Donald Wandrei
The Last Test — Adolphe de Castro [Lovecraft]
The Werewolf's Daughter [2/3] — H. Warner Munn
Tenant at Number 7 — August W. Derleth

12, No. 6 (December 1928)
Beyond Power of Man — Paul Ernst
Statement of Justin Parker — August W. Derleth
Sonnets of the Midnight Hours: 9. The Head [v] — Donald Wandrei
The Werewolf's Daughter [3/3] — H. Warner Munn

13, No. 1 (January 1929)
The Silver Key — H. P. Lovecraft
An Occurrence in an Antique Shop — August W, Derleth
The Chemical Brain — Francis Flagg
Sonnets of the Midnight Hours: 10. The Red Specter [v] — Donald Wandrei

13, No. 2 (February 1929)
The Ghosts of the Gods — E. M. Hill
The Star-Stealers — Edmond Hamilton
The Devil-People — Seabury Quinn
Highwaymen — W. Benson Tooling
The Vengeance of the Dead [1/2] — Eli Colter
The Brass Key — Hal K. Wells
The Ghost Ship — Arlton Eadie
A Witch's Curse — Paul Ernst
The Three — Louise Van de Verg
Pope Joan — Alvin F. Harlow
The Isle of Lost Souls [3/3] — Joel Martin Nichols, Jr.
Sonnets of the Midnight Hours: 11. Doom [v] — Donald Wandrei
Melodie in E Minor — August W. Derleth
An Adventure in Anesthesia — Everil Worrell
The Tall Woman — Pedro Antonio de Alarcon
Crete [v] — Robert E. Howard

13, No. 3 (March 1929)
The People of Pan — Henry S. Whitehead
The Immortal Hand — Arlton Eadie
The Deserted Garden — August W. Derleth
The Rat — S. Fowler Wright
The Sea Horror — Edmond Hamilton
The Hounds of Tindalos — Frank Belknap Long
The Phantom Farmhouse — Seabury Quinn
Sonnets of the Midnight Hours: 12. A Vision of the Future [v] — Donald Wandrei

13, No. 4 (April 1929)
A Dinner at Imola — August W. Derleth
The Dunwich Horror — H. P. Lovecraft

13, No. 6 (June 1929)
The Last of the Mayas [1/2] — Arthur Thatcher
The House on the Highway — August W. Derleth

14, No. 1 (July 1929)
The Wishing-Well — E. F. Benson

The Death Touch	Cheater L. Saxby
The Last of the Mayas [2/2]	Arthur Thatcher
Forbidden Magic [v]	Robert E. Howard
14, No. 2 (August 1929)	
Old Mark	August W. Derleth
14, No. 3 (September 1929)	
The Hound	H. P. Lovecraft
14, No. 4 (October 1929)	
Skull-Face [1/3]	Robert E. Howard
14, No. 5 (November 1929)	
The Curse of Yig	Zealia Brown Reed [Lovecraft]
Skull-Face [2/3]	Robert E. Howard
Scarlatti's Bottle	August W. Derleth
14, No. 6 (December 1929)	
Skull-Face [3/3]	Robert E. Howard
The Inheritors	August W. Derleth
15, No., 1 (January 1930)	
The Curse of the House of Phipps	Seabury Quinn
The Life-Masters	Edmond Hamilton
A Matter of Sight	August W. Derleth
15, No. 2 (February 1930)	
Thirsty Blades	Otis Adelbert Kline & E. Hoffmann Price
The Comet-Drivers	Edmond Hamilton
The Black Monarch [1/5]	Paul Ernst
Behind the Moon [3/3]	W. Elwyn Backus
The Lilac Bush	August W. Derleth
The Horror on Dagoth Wold [v]	Frank Belknap Long, Jr.
The Fearsome Touch of Death	Robert E. Howard
A Ghost	Guy de Maupassant
15, No. 3 (March 1930)	
The Ancient Track [v]	H. P. Lovecraft
The Black Monarch [2/5]	Paul Ernst
The Pacer	Mark R. Schorer & August W. Derleth
15, No 4 (April 1930)	
On Icy Kinarth [v]	Frank Belknap Long, Jr.
The Portrait	August W. Derleth

The Shut Room	Henry S. Whitehead
The Black Monarch [3/5]	Paul Ernst
The Signal-Man	Charles Dickens
15, No. 5 (May 1930)	
The End of the Story	Clark Ashton Smith
The Land of Lur	Earl Leaston Bell
The Black Monarch [4/5]	Paul Ernst
Light-Echoes	Everil Worrell
The Whistler	August W. Derleth
The Footprint	G. G. Pendarves
Recapture [v]	H. P. Lovecraft
15, No. 6 (June 1930)	
The Black Monarch [5/5]	Paul Ernst
16, No. 2 (August 1930)	
Just a Song at Twilight	August W. Derleth
The Last Test	Adolphe de Castro [Lovecraft]
16, No. 3 (September 1930)	
Fungi from Yuggoth:	H. P. Lovecraft
1. The Courtyard [v]	
2. Star-Winds [v]	
16, No. 4 (October 1930)	
The Bride Well	David H. Keller
Mrs. Bentley's Daughter	August W. Derleth
Fungi from Yuggoth: 3. Hesperia [v]	H. P. Lovecraft
16, No. 5 (November 1930)	
Fungi from Yuggoth: 4. Antarktos [v]	H. P. Lovecraft
16, No. 6 (December 1930)	
Something from Above	Donald Wandrei
Fungi from Yuggoth: 5. The Bells [v]	H. P. Lovecraft
17, No. 1 (January 1931)	
Fungi from Yuggoth:	H. P. Lovecraft
6. Nyarlathotep [v]	
7. Azathoth [v]	
The Horror from the Hills [1/2]	Frank Belknap Long, Jr.
Passing of a God	Henry S. Whitehead
17, No. 2 (February/March 1931)	
Fungi from Yuggoth:	H. P. Lovecraft

7. Mirage [v]
8. The Elder Pharos [v]
The Horror from the Hills [2/2] — Frank Belknap Long, Jr.

April/May 1931, 17, No. 3
Fungi from Yuggoth: 10. Alienation [v] — H. P. Lovecraft

17, No. 4 (June/July 1931)
The Venus of Azombeii — Clark Ashton Smith
Hill Drums — Henry S. Whitehead
The Outsider — H. P. Lovecraft

18, No. 1 (August 1931)
The Whisperer in Darkness — H. P, Lovecraft
Prince Borgia's Mass — August W. Derleth

18, No. 2 (September 1931)
The Footfalls Within — Robert E. Howard
Satan's Stepson — Seabury Quinn
Deadlock — Everil Worrell
The Bridge of Sighs — August W. Derleth

18, No. 3 (October 1931)
Black Terror — Henry S. Whitehead
The Captain Is Afraid — August W. Derleth
The Strange High House in the Mist — H. P. Lovecraft

18, No. 4 (November 1931)
Subterranea — W. Elwyn Backus
The Tale of Satampra Zeiros — Clark Ashton Smith
The Black Stone — Robert E. Howard
Doom Around the Corner — Wilfred Blanch Talman

18, No. 5 (December 1931)
The Haunted Chair [1/3] — Gaston Leroux

19, No. 1 (January 1932)
The Monster of the Prophecy — Clark Ashton Smith
Those Who Seek — August W. Derleth
The Malignant Invader — Frank Belknap Long, Jr.
The Haunted Chair [2/3] — Gaston Leroux
Mive — Carl Jacobi

19, No. 2 (February 1932)
The Devil's Bride [1/6] — Seabury Quinn
Night and Silence — Maurice Level

The Thing on the Roof — Robert E. Howard
The Tree-Men of M'bwa — Donald Wandrei
The Haunted Chair [3/3] — Gaston Leroux

19, No. 3 (March 1932)
The Vengeance of Ixmal — Kirk Mashburn
The House of the Living Dead — Harold Ward
The May Who Played with Time — A. W. Bernal
The Answer of the Dead — J. Paul Suter
The Devil's Bride [2/6] — Seabury Quinn
The Thing in the Cellar — David H. Keller
Laughter in the Night — August W. Derleth & Mark Schorer

19, No. 4 (April 1932)
In the Vault — H. P. Lovecraft
Mrs. Lorriquer — Henry S. Whitehead
The Devil's Bride [3/6] — Seabury Quinn

19, No. 5 (May 1932)
The Vaults of Yoh-Vombis — Clark Ashton Smith
The Terror Planet — Edmond Hamilton
The Last Magician — David H. Keller
The Horror from the Mound — Robert E. Howard
The Devil's Bride [4/6] — Seabury Quinn
The Bishop Sees Through — August W. Derleth

June 1932, 19, No. 6
The Devil's Pool — Greye La Spina
In the Left Wing — August W. Derleth & Mark Schorer
The Brain-Eaters — Frank Belknap Long, Jr.
The Devil's Bride [5/6] — Seabury Quinn
The Weird of Avoosl Wuthoqquan — Clark Ashton Smith

July 1932, 19, No. 5
The Devil's Bride [6/6] — Seabury Quinn

August 1932, 20, No. 2
The Lair of the Star-Spawn — August Derleth & Mark Schorer

20, No. 3 (September 1932)
The Sheraton Mirror — August W. Derleth
Over Time's Threshold — Howard Wandrei

20, No. 4 (October 1932)
Red Hands — August W. Derleth & Mark Schorer

20, No. 6 (December 1932)
The Lives of Alfred Kramer — Donald Wandrei

21, No. 2 (February 1933)
The Chadbourne Episode — Henry S. Whitehead
The Cats of Ulthar — H. P. Lovecraft
The Vanishing of Simmons — August W. Derleth

21, No. 3 (March 1933)
In Memoriam: Henry St. Clair Whitehead — [H. P. Lovecraft]

21, No. 4 (April 1933)
Revelations in Black — Carl Jacobi
The White Moth — August W. Derleth

21, No. 5 (May 1933)
Dead Man's Belt — Hugh B. Cave
Spawn of the Sea — Donald Wandrei
The Girl with the Green Eyes — Mary Elizabeth Counselman
The Carven Image — August W. Derleth & Mark Schorer
The Beast of Averoigne — Clark Ashton Smith

21, No. 6 (June 1933)
Nellie Foster — August W. Derleth

22, No. 1 (July 1933)
The Horror in the Museum — Hazel Heald [Lovecraft]
The Dreams in the Witch-House — H. P. Lovecraft

August 1933, 22, No. 2
An Elegy for Mr. Danielson — August W. Derleth

September 1933, 22, No. 3
The Return of Andrew Bentley — August W. Derleth & Mark Schorer

22, No. 4 (October 1933)
The House of the Worm — Mearle Prout
The Plutonian Terror — Jack Williamson
The Black, Dead Thing — Frank Belknap Long
The Festival — H. P. Lovecraft

22, No. 5 (November 1933)
Shambleau — C. L. Moore
Lord of the Fourth Axis — E. Hoffmann Price
The Holiness of Azédarac — Clark Ashton Smith
The Accursed Isle — Mary Elizabeth Counselman

23, No. 3 (March 1934)
Winged Death — Hazel Heald [Lovecraft]

23, No. 4 (April 1934)
The Death of Malygris — Clark Ashton Smith

23, No. 5 (May 1934)
Incubus [v] — August W. Derleth

23, No. 6 (June 1934)
The Haunter of the Ring — Robert E. Howard
The Colossus of Ylourgne — Clark Ashton Smith
They Called Him Ghost — Laurence J. Cahill
Colonel Markesan — August W. Derleth & Mark Schorer

24, No. 1 (July 1934)
Through the Gates of the Silver Key — H. P. Lovecraft & E. Hoffmann Price
Wild Grapes — August W. Derleth
The Disinterment of Venus — Clark Ashton Smith

24, No. 3 (September 1931)
A Cloak from Messer Lando — August W. Derleth

24, No. 5 (November 1934)
Feigman's Beard — August W. Derleth
The Music of Erich Zann — H. P. Lovecraft

24, No. 6 (December 1934)
A Witch Shall Be Born — Robert E. Howard
The Vengeance of Ti Fong — Bassett Morgan
Black God's Shadow — C. L. Moore
The Graveyard Duchess — John Flanders
Xeethra — Clark Ashton Smith
The Werewolf's Howl — Brooke Byrne
A Matter of Faith — August W. Derleth & Mark Schorer

25, No. 1 (January 1935)
The Dark Eidolon — Clark Ashton Smith

25, No. 2 (February 1935)
The Metronome — August W. Derleth

25, No. 3 (March 1935)
The Sealed Casket — Richard F. Searight
The Judge's House — Bram Stoker

25, No. 4 (April 1935)
Out of the Eons — Hazel Heald [Lovecraft]

25, No. 5 (May. 1935)
Muggridge's Aunt — August W. Derleth
Arthur Jermyn — H. P. Lovecraft

25, No. 6 (June 1935)
The Cup of Blood — Otis Adelbert Kline

26, No. 1 (July 1935)
The Avenger from Atlantis — Edmond Hamilton
Jirel Meets Magic — C. L. Moore
The Violet Death — Gustav Meyrink

26, No. 3 (September 1935)
Vulthoom — Clark Ashton Smith
One Chance — Ethel Helene Coen

26, No. 4 (October 1935)
The Cold Gray God — C. L. Moore
The Mystery of the Last Guest — John Flanders
In a Graveyard — Eando Binder
The Amulet of Hell — Robert Leonard Russell
The Lost Club — Arthur Machen

26, No. 5 (November 1935)
Shadows in Zamboula — Robert E. Howard
The Hand of Wrath — E. Hoffmann Price
The Way Home — Paul Frederick Stern
Mr. Berbeck Had a Dream — August W. Derleth

26, No. 6 (December 1935)
The Hour of the Dragon [1/5] — Robert E. Howard

27, No. 1 (January 1936)
The Satin Mask — August W. Derleth
The Hour of the Dragon [2/5]
Robert E. Howard
Dagon — H. P. Lovecraft

27, No. 2 (February 1936)
The Hour of the Dragon [3/5] — Robert E. Howard
The Temple — H. P. Lovecraft

27, No. 3 (March 1936)
The Hour of the Dragon [4/5] — Robert E. Howard

27, No. 4 (April 1936)
The Face in the Wind — Carl Jacobi
They Shall Rise — August W. Derleth & Mark Schorer
The Hour of the Dragon [5/5] — Robert E. Howard
The Druidic Doom — Robert Bloch

27, No. 5 (May 1936)
Lesandro's Familiar — August W. Derleth

27, No. 6 (June 1936)
Black Canaan — Robert E. Howard
The Telephone in the Library — August W. Derleth

28, No. 1 (July 1936)
Red Nails [1/3] — Robert E. Howard
The Return of Sarah Purcell — August W. Derleth

28, No. 2 (August/September 1936)
Red Nails [2/3] — Robert E. Howard
Death Holds the Post — August W. Derleth & Mark Schorer

28, No. 3 (October 1936)
Isle of the Undead — Lloyd Arthur Eshbach
The Opener of the Way — Robert Bloch
Doom of the House of Duryea — Earl Peirce, Jr.
The Tree of Life — C. L. Moore
Red Nails [3/3] — Robert E. Howard
R.E.H. [v] — R. H. Barlow
The Secret of Kralitz — Henry Kuttner

28, No. 4 (November 1936)
Picknan's Model — H. P. Lovecraft

28, No. 5 (December 1936)
The Haunter of the Dark — H. P. Lovecraft
The Woman at Loon Point — August W. Derleth & Mark Schorer

29 No. 1 (January 1937)
The Thing on the Doorstep — H. P. Lovecraft

29, No. 2 (February 1937)
Glory Hand — August W. Derleth

29, No. 3 (March 1937)
The Picture in the House H. P. Lovecraft

D. Works by Others

Dates in angular brackets indicate first publication.

Adams, Samuel Hopkins (1871–1958). *The Piper's Fee.* New York: Boni & Liveright, 1926.

Alden, Abner (1758?–1820). *The Reader: Containing the Art of Delivery, Articulation, Accent, Pronunciation,* [etc.]. <1802> 3d ed. Boston: Printed by J. T. Buckingham for Thomas & Andrews, 1808. (*LL* 16)

Allen, Hervey (1889–1949). *Anthony Adverse.* New York: Holt, Rinehart & Winston, 1933.

———. *Israfel: The Life and Times of Edgar Allan Poe.* New York: George H. Doran Co., 1927. 2 vols. (*LL* 18)

Arlen, Michael (1895–1936). *Ghost Stories.* London: Collins, [1927]. (*LL* 41)

Asbury, Herbert (1891–1963), ed. *Not at Night!* New York: Macy-Masius (The Vanguard Press), 1928. (*LL* 46)

Ashby, Rubie Constance (1899–?). *He Arrived at Dusk.* New York: Macmillan, 1933.

———. *Out Went the Taper.* New York: Macmillan,1934.

Asquith, Cynthia (1887–1960), ed. *The Ghost Book.* London: Hutchinson, 1927. New York: Charles Scribner's Sons, 1927.

——— [et al.] *My Grimmest Nightmare.* London: George Allen & Unwin, 1935. (*LL* 45)

———, ed. *Shudders: A Collection of New Nightmare Tales.* London: Hutchinson; New York: Charles Scribner's Sons, 1929.

———, ed. *When Churchyards Yawn: Fifteen New Ghost Stories.* London: Hutchinson, 1931.

Atherton, Gertrude (1857–1948). *The Foghorn.* Boston: Houghton Mifflin, 1934.

———. "The Striding Place." *Speaker* (20 June 1896). In *The Bell in the Fog and Other Stories.* New York: Harper, 1905.

Aubrey, Frank ([pseud. of Francis Henry Atkins] 1840–1927). *A Queen of Atlantis: A Romance of the Caribbean Sea.* London: Hutchinson, 1899.

Austin, F. Britten (1885–1941). *On the Borderland.* Garden City, NY: Doubleday, Page, 1923. (*LL* 51)

Bailey, H[enry] C[hristopher] (1878–1961). *Shadow on the Wall.* New York: Doubleday, Doran, 1934.

Baring-Gould, S[abine] (1834–1924). *The Book of Were-Wolves: Being an Account of a Terrible Superstition.* London: Smith, Elder, 1865.

Barrie, J[ames] M[atthew] (1860–1937). *Farewell, Miss Julie Logan: A Wintery Tale.* London: The Times, 1931; New York: Charles Scribner's Sons, 1933.

Bartky, Walter (1901–?). *Highlights of Astronomy*. Chicago: University of Chicago Press, 1935.

Baum, Vicki (Hedwig Baum, 1888–1960). *Grand Hotel*. Tr. Basil Creighton. Garden City, NY: Doubleday, Doran, 1931. Tr. of *Menschen im Hotel* (1929).

Beckford, William (1759–1844). *Vathek*. <1786> Introduction by Ben Ray Redman, illustrated by Mahlon Blaine. New York: John Day Co., 1928. (*LL* 75)

Beeding, Francis ([pseud. of Hilary Aidan St. George Saunders] 1898–1951). *The House of Dr. Edwardes*. Boston: Little, Brown, 1928.

Begbie, Harold (1871–1929). *On the Side of the Angels: The Story of the Angels at Mons—An Answer to "The Bowman."* London: Hodder & Stoughton, 1915.

Belloc, Hilaire (1870–1935). *The Haunted House*. Illustrated by G. K. Chesterton (1874–1936). New York & London: Harper & Brothers, 1928.

Benoit, Pierre (1886–1962). *Atlantida*. Tr. Mary C. Tongue and Mary Ross. New York: Duffield, 1920.

Benson, E[dward] F[rederic] (1867–1940). *More Spook Stories*. London: Hutchinson, 1934.

———. *Raven's Brood*. Garden City, N.Y.: Doubleday, Doran, 1934.

———. *The Room in the Tower and Other Stories*. <1912> London: Alfred A. Knopf, 1929.

———. *Spook Stories*. London: Hutchinson, 1928.

———. *Visible and Invisible*. New York, George H. Doran, 1923 or 1924. (*LL* 79)

———, and Brander Matthews (1852–1929). *Two Masterly Ghost Stories*. Girard, KS: Haldeman-Julius, n.d. (*LL* 80). Contains: "The Man Who Went Too Far."

Béraud, Henri (1885–1958). *Lazarus*. Tr. Eric Sutton. New York: Macmillan, 1925. (*LL* 81)

The Holy Bible: Containing the Old and New Testaments. Translated out of the Original Tongues, and with the Former Translations Diligently Compared and Revised, by His Majesty's Special Command. Edinburgh: M. & C. Kerr, 1795. n.p. (*LL* 85)

Bierce, Ambrose (1842–1914?). *Can Such Things Be?* <1893> New York: Boni & Liveright (Modern Library), 1918. (*LL* 87) [Contains: "An Inhabitant of Carcosa," "The Death of Halpin Frayser."]

———. *The Devil's Dictionary*. <1906, 1911> New York: A. & C. Boni, 1925.

———. *In the Midst of Life: Tales of Soldiers and Civilians*. <1891> Introduction by George Sterling. New York: Modern Library, [1927]. [Contains: "A Horseman in the Sky."]

———, and Adolphe Danziger [de Castro] (1859–1959). *The Monk and the Hangman's Daughter; Fantastic Fables; [etc.]*. <1892; 1899> New York: A. & C. Boni, 1925. (*LL* 90)

Birch, A. G. *The Moon Terror.* And Stories by Anthony M. Rud, Vincent Starrett, and Farnsworth Wright. Indianapolis: Popular Fiction Publishing Co., [1927]. (*LL* 93)

Birkhead, Edith. *The Tale of Terror: A Study of the Gothic Romance.* New York: E. P. Dutton, 1921. (*LL* 94)

[Birkin, Charles, ed.] *Shudders: A Collection of Uneasy Tales.* London: Philip Allan, 1932. [*LL* 802]

Blair, Hugh (1718–1800). *Lectures on Rhetoric and Belles Lettres.* <1783> With a Memoir of the Author's Life. To Which Are Added, Copious Questions; and an Analysis of Each Lecture, by Abraham Mills. Philadelphia: J. Kay, Jun., & Brother; Pittsburgh: J. I. Kay & Co., 1829. (*LL* 102)

Blackwood, Algernon (1869–1951). *The Centaur.* London: Macmillan, 1911.

———. *The Dance of Death and Other Tales.* London: Herbert Jenkins, 1927. New York: Lincoln MacVeagh/Dial Press, 1928.

———. *Day and Night Stories.* London: Cassell, 1917. New York: E. P. Dutton, 1917.

———. *Dudley and Gilderoy: A Nonsense.* London: Ernest Benn, 1929. New York: E. P. Dutton, 1929.

———. *The Empty House and Other Ghost Stories.* London: Eveleigh Nash, 1906. New York: Donald C. Vaughan, 1915. New York: Knopf, 1917.

———. *The Extra Day.* London: Macmillan, 1915.

———. *Full Circle.* London: Elkin Mathews & Marrot, 1929.

———. *The Garden of Survival.* New York: E. P. Dutton, 1918.

———. *Incredible Adventures.* London: Macmillan, 1914. New York: Macmillan, 1914. [Contains: "A Descent into Egypt."]

———. *Jimbo: A Fantasy.* New York: Macmillan, 1909. (*LL* 95)

———. *Julius LeVallon: An Episode.* London: Cassell, 1916. New York: E. P. Dutton, 1916. (*LL* 98)

———. *John Silence—Physician Extraordinary.* London: Eveleigh Nash, 1908. Boston: John W. Luce, 1909. London: Macmillan, 1912. New York: Vaughan & Gomme, 1914. New York: Knopf, 1917. New York, E. P. Dutton, [1920]. (*LL* 96, 97)

———. *The Listener and Other Stories.* London: Eveleigh Nash, 1907. New York: Vaughan & Gomme, 1914. New York: Knopf, 1917. [Contains: "The Listener," "The Willows."]

———. *The Lost Valley and Other Stories.* London: Eveleigh Nagh, 1910. (*LL* 99) [Contains: "The Wendigo."]

———. *Shocks.* New York: E. P. Dutton, 1936.

———. *Strange Stories.* London: William Heinemann, 1929.

———. *Ten Minute Stories.* London: John Murray, 1914. New York: Dutton, 1914.

———. *Tongues of Fire and Other Sketches.* London: Herbert Jenkins, 1924. New York:, Dutton, 1925.

———. *The Wave: An Egyptian Aftermath.* London: Cassell, 1916. New York: E. P. Dutton, 1916.

Blashfield, Evangeline Wilbour (d. 1918). "The Ghoul." In J. Walker McSpadden, *Famous Psychic Stories.*

Bloomfield, Robert (1766–1823). *The Farmer's Boy: A Rural Poem.* Ornamented with Elegant Wood Engravings by A. Anderson. 5th American ed., from the 6th London ed. New York: Printed by Hopkins & Seymour, and Sold by G. F. Hopkins, 1803. (*LL* 106)

Bromfield, Louis (1896–1956). *The Strange Case of Miss Annie Spragg.* New York: Frederick A. Stokes, 1928.

Browne, Douglas G. (1884–1963). *Plan XVI.* Garden City, NY: Doubleday, Doran [for the Crime Club], 1934.

Brownell, W[illiam] C[rary] (1851–1928), *American Prose Masters: Cooper–Hawthorne–Emerson–Poe–Lowell–Henry James.* <1909> New York: Charles Scribner's Sons, 1923.

Buchan, John (1875–1940). *The Gap in the Curtain.* London: Hodder & Stoughton. 1932.

———. *The Runagates Club.* Boston: Houghton Mifflin, 1928. (*LL* 129)

———. *Witch Wood.* Boston: Houghton Mifflin, 1927.

Bulfinch, Thomas (1796–1867). *The Age of Fable; or, Beauties of Mythology.* <1855> Edited by J. Loughran Scott. Rev. ed. Philadelphia: D. McKay, [1898]. (*LL* 130)

Bullett, Gerald (1894–1958). *The Street of the Eye and Nine Other Tales.* London: John Lane/The Bodley Head, 1923; New York: Boni & Liveright, [1924].

Burnett, Whit (1899–1973), and Martha Foley (1900–1977), ed. *A Story Anthology 1931–1933: Thirty-Three Selections from the European Years of "Story," the Only Magazine Devoted Solely to the Short Story.* New York: Vanguard Press, 1933.

Busson, Paul (1873–1924). *Die Wiedergeburt des Melchior Dronte.* <1924> Tr. by Prince Mirski and Thomas Moult as *The Man Who Was Born Again.* New York: John Day Co., 1927. (*LL* 140)

Cabell, James Branch (1879–1958). *The Cream of the Jest.* New York: Robert M. McBride, 1917.

———. *The Eagle's Shadow.* New York: Doubleday, Page, 1904.

———. *Figures of Earth: A Comedy of Appearances.* New York: Robert M. McBride, 1921.

———. *Jurgen: A Comedy of Justice.* New York: Robert M. McBride, 1919.

———. *The Line of Love.* New York: Harper & Brothers, 1905.

Caine, Hall (1853–1931). *The Woman Thou Gavest Me: Being the Story of Mary O'Neill.* London: Heinemann, 1912. Philadelphia: J. B. Lippincott, 1913.

Carroll, Lewis ([pseud. of Charles Lutwidge Dodgson] 1832–1898). *Alice's Adventures in Wonderland.* <1865>

Carver, Mrs. *The Horrors of Oakendale Abbey: A Romance.* <1797> Frankford, PA: J. F. Gilbert, 1812.

A Century of Creepy Stories. London: Hutchinson, [1934].

Chambers, Robert W. (1865–1933). *In Search of the Unknown.* New York: Harper & Brothers, 1904. (*LL* 166)

———. *The King in Yellow.* Chicago: F. Tennyson Neely, 1895. (*LL* 167) [Contains: "The Yellow Sign" (in *SNM*)]

———. *The Mystery of Choice.* New York: D. Appleton & Co., 1897.

———. *The Maker of Moons.* New York: D. Appleton & Co., 1896.

———. *The Slayer of Souls.* New York: George H. Doran, 1920.

Chancellor, John. *The Dark God.* New York: Century Co., 1929.

Cline, Leonard (1893–1929). *The Dark Chamber.* New York: Viking Press, 1927. (*LL* 183)

Coates, Robert M. (1897–1973). *The Eater of Darkness.* <1926> New York: Macaulay, 1929.

Collins, Gilbert (1890–?). *The Valley of Eyes Unseen.* London: Duckworth, 1923. New York: Robert M. McBride, 1924.

Collins, Wilkie (1824–1889). *The Woman in White.* <1860>

Cozzens, James Gould (1903–1978). *Castaway.* New York: Random House, 1934.

———. *The Last Adam.* New York: Harcourt, Brace, 1933.

Cram, Ralph Adams (1863–1942). *Black Spirits and White: A Book of Ghost Stories.* Chicago: Stone & Kimball, 1895. [Contains: "The Dead Valley."]

Crawford, F. Marion (1854–1909). *Wandering Ghosts.* New York: Macmillan, 1911. London: T. Fisher Unwin, 1911 (as *Uncanny Tales*). [Contains: "The Upper Berth."]

Cyclopaedia of Arts and Sciences, by A Society of Gentlemen. London: W. Owen, 1764. (*LL* 214). HPL owned Vols. 1, 2, and 4.

D'Annunzio, Gabriele (1863–1938). *The Flame of Life.* Tr. Kassandra Vivaria [pseud.]. Boston: L. C. Page, 1900.

Davis, William Stearns (1877–1930). *A Friend of Caesar: A Tale of the Fall of the Roman Republic, 50–47 B.C.* New York: Macmillan, 1900.

de Castro [Danziger], Adolphe (1859–1959). *Portrait of Ambrose Bierce.* New York: Century Co., 1929.

de la Mare, Colin, ed. *They Walk Again: A Collection of Ghost Stories.* New York: E. P. Dutton, 1931.

de la Mare, Walter (1873–1956). *Broomsticks and Other Tales.* London: Constable, 1925.

———. *The Connoisseur and Other Stories.* London: Collins, 1926. New York: Alfred A. Knopf, 1926. (*LL* 228) [Contains: "All Hallows."]

———. *Ding Dong Bell.* London: Selwyn & Blount, 1924.

———. *The Jacket.* [not found]

———. *The Lord Fish.* London: Faber & Faber, [1933].

———. *On the Edge*. London: Faber & Faber, 1930. [Contains: "A Recluse."]

———. *The Return*. <1910> New York: Alfred A. Knopf, 1922.

———. *The Riddle and Other Stories*. <1923> New York: Alfred A. Knopf, 1930. (*LL* 229) [Contains: "Seaton's Aunt" (*NS*) "The Tree."]

———. *The Wind Blows Over*. New York: Macmillan, 1936.

Dell, Floyd (1887–1969). *Moon-Calf: A Novel*. New York: Alfred A. Knopf, 1920.

Dennis, Geoffrey (1892–1963). *Harvest in Poland*. New York: Alfred A. Knopf, 1925.

Dickens, Charles. *Barnaby Rudge*. <1841> New York: A. L. Burt, [1902?]. (*LL* 242)

———. *Christmas Stories*. <1843–45>

———. *David Copperfield*. <1849–50>

———. *A Tale of Two Cities*. <1859> New York: A. L. Burt, [1904?]. (*LL* 251)

Doke, Joseph J. *The Secret City: A Romance of the Karroo*. Toronto: Hodder & Stoughton, [1913?].

Dostoevski, Feodor (1821–1881). *The Brothers Karamazov*. Tr. Constance Garnett. New York: Macmillan, 1912.

———. *Crime and Punishment*. Tr. Constance Garnett. New York: Macmillan, 1914.

Doyle, Sir Arthur Conan (1859–1930). *Adventures of Sherlock Holmes*. London: George Newnes, 1892.

———. *The Captain of the Polestar and Other Tales*. London: Longman, 1890. [Contains: "J. Habakuk Jephson's Statement," "John Barrington Cowles," "The Ring of Thoth."]

———. *Danger! and Other Stories*. London: John Murray, 1918.

———. *The Green Flag and Other Stories of War and Sport*. London: Smith, Elder, 1900.

———. *The Hound of the Baskervilles*. London: George Newnes, 1902.

———. *The Last Galley: Impressions and Tales*. London: Smith, Elder, 1911.

———. *The Maracot Deep and Other Stories*. London: John Murray, 1929.

———. *Memoirs of Sherlock Holmes*. London: George Newnes, 1893.

———. *The Return of Sherlock Holmes*. London: George Newnes, 1905.

———. *Round the Fire Stories*. London: Smith, Elder, 1908.

———. *Round the Red Lamp*. London: Methuen, 1894. [Contains: "Lot No. 249."]

———. *The Sign of Four*. London: Blackett, 1890.

———. *A Study in Scarlet*. London: Ward, Lock, 1888.

———. *Tales of Adventure and the Medical Life*. London: John Murray, 1922.

———. *Tales of Long Ago*. London: John Murray, 1922. (*LL* 261)

———. *Tales of Pirates and Blue Water*. London: John Murray, 1922.

———. *Tales of Terror and Mystery*. London: John Murray, 1922.

———. *Tales of the Ring and Camp.* London: John Murray, 1922.
———. *Tales of Twilight and the Unseen.* London: John Murray, 1922. (*LL* 262) [Contains: "Lot No. 249."]
———. *The Valley of Fear.* New York: George H. Doran, 1914.
Drake, H[enry] B[urgess] (1894–1963). *The Shadowy Thing.* <1925> New York: Macy-Masius, 1928.
Dreiser, Theodore (1871–1945). *An American Tragedy.* New York: Boni & Liveright, 1925. 2 vols.
Duncan, John Charles (1882–?). *Astronomy.* New York: Harper & Brothers, 1926; 3rd ed. 1935.
Dunsany, Lord (Edward John Moreton Drax Plunkett, 18th baron) (1878–1957). *Alexander and Three Small Plays.* London: G. P. Putnam's Sons, 1925.
———. *The Blessing of Pan.* London: G. P. Putnam's Sons, 1927. (*LL* 270)
———. *The Book of Wonder* <1912> [and *Time and the Gods* <1906>]. New York: Boni & Liveright (Modern Library), [1918]. (*LL* 271)
———. *The Charwoman's Shadow.* New York: G. P. Putnam's Sons, 1926.
———. *The Curse of the Wise Woman.* London: William Heinemann; New York: Longmans, Green, 1933.
———. *A Dreamer's Tales and Other Stories* [*A Dreamer's Tales* <1910> and *The Sword of Welleran* <1908>]. New York: Boni & Liveright (Modern Library), [1917], [1919], or [1921]. (*LL* 273)
———. "The Electric King." *Harper's Magazine* 161, No. 3 (August 1930): 268–79. In *The Travel Tales of Mr. Joseph Jorkens.* London, New York: G. P. Putnam's Sons, 1931.
———. *The Last Book of Wonder.* Boston: John W. Luce, 1916. (*LL* 278) [Contains: "The Secret of the Sea."]
———. *Mr. Jorkens Remembers Africa.* London: William Heinemann, 1934. New York: Longmans, Green, 1934 (as *Jorkens Remembers Africa*).
———. *Alexander and Three Small Plays.* London & New York: G. P. Putnam's Sons, 1925.
Durant, Will (1885–1981). *The Story of Philosophy: The Lives and Opinions of the Greater Philosophers.* Garden City, NY: Garden City Publishing Co. (A Star Book), 1927. (*LL* 284)
Eddison, E. R. (1882–1945). *Styrbiorn the Strong.* London: Jonathan Cape, [1926].
———. *The Worm Ouroboros: A Romance.* Illustrated by Keith Henderson. New York: A. & C. Boni, 1926. (*LL* 291)
Eliot, T. S. (1888–1965). *The Waste Land. Dial* 73, No. 5 (Nov. 1922): 473–85. (*LL* 238) New York: Boni & Liveright, 1922.
Ewers, Hanns Heinz (1871–1943). *Edgar Allan Poe.* Berlin: Schuster & Loefler, 1905. Tr. Adele Lewisohn. New York: B. W. Huebsch, 1917.
———. *The Sorcerer's Apprentice.* Tr. Ludwig Lewisohn. New York: John Day Co., 1927.

Faulkner, William (1897–1962). *These 13.* New York: Jonathan Cape & Harrison Smith, 1931.

Fielding, Henry (1707–1754). *The History of Tom Jones.* <1749> New York: Modern Library, 1931.

Fleckner, James Elroy (1884–1915). *Hassan: The Story of Hassan of Baghdad and How He Came to Make the Golden Journey to Samarkand.* New York: Alfred A. Knopf, 1922.

Fletcher, J[oseph] S[mith] (1863–1935). *The Time-Worn Town.* New York: Alfred A. Knopf, 1924.

Forbes, Esther (1891–1967). *A Mirror for Witches.* London: William Heinemann, 1928. Boston: Houghton, Mifflin, 1928.

Forster, E. M. (1879–1970). *The Celestial Omnibus and Other Stories.* New York: Alfred A. Knopf, 1923.

Fort, Charles (1874–1932). *The Book of the Damned.* New York: Boni & Liveright, 1919.

———. *Lo!* New York: C. Kendell, 1931.

———. *New Lands.* New York: Boni & Liveright, 1923.

Frank, Waldo (1889–1967). *Chalk Face.* New York: Boni & Liveright, 1924.

Frazer, Sir James George (1854–1941). *The Golden Bough: A Study in Magic and Religion.* <1890–1915> New York: Macmillan, 1930.

Freeman, Mary E[leanor] (Wilkins) (1852–1930). *The Wind in the Rose-bush and Other Stories of the Supernatural.* New York: Doubleday, Page, 1903. (*LL* 333) [Contains: "The Shadows on the Wall" (in *WK*), "The Lost Ghost."]

French, Joseph Lewis (1858–1936), ed. *Ghosts, Grim and Gentle.* New York: Dodd, Mead, 1926.

———, ed. *Masterpieces of Mystery.* Garden City, NY, Doubleday, Page, 1920. 4 vols. (*LL* 335)

Fuess, Claude Moore (1885–1963). *Daniel Webster.* Boston: Little, Brown, 1930. 2 vols.

Funk, Isaac Kaufman (1839–1912). "The Widows Mite." In J. Walker McSpadden, ed., *Famous Psychic Stories.*

Garland, Hamlin (1860–1940). *Forty Years of Psychic Research: A Plain Narrative of Fact.* New York: Macmillan, 1936.

———. *A Son of the Middle Border.* New York: Macmillan, 1917.

Gautier, Théophile (1811–1872). *Mademoiselle de Maupin.* <1835> New York: Boni & Liveright (Modern Library), [1918]; Modern Library, 1925. (*LL* 345)

Gawsworth, John ([pseud. of Terence Ian Fytton Armstrong] 1912–1970), ed. *Strange Assembly.* London: Unicorn Press, 1932. (*LL* 42)

Gerould, Katherine Fullerton (1879–1944). *Vain Oblations.* New York: Charles Scribner's Sons, 1914.

Gilman, Charlotte Perkins (1860–1935). "The Yellow Wall Paper." *New England Magazine* (Jan. 1892). Boston: Small, Maynard, 1899.

Gorman, Herbert S. (1893–1954). *The Place Called Dagon.* New York: George H. Doran, 1927.

Gourmont, Remy de (1858–1915). *A Night in the Luxembourg [Une Nuit au Luxembourg].* <1906> Tr. Arthur Ransome. Boston: John W. Luce, 1912.

Grayson, David ([pseud. of Ray Stannard Baker] 1870–1946). *Adventures in Contentment.* <1907> (*LL* 61)

Haggard, H. Rider (1856–1925). *She: A History of Adventure.* <1887> (*LL* 385)

———, and Andrew Lang (1844–1912). *The World's Desire.* London: Longmans, Green, 1890.

Hall, Leland (1883–1957). *Sinister House.* Boston: Houghton Mifflin, 1919.

Hall, Radclyffe (1886–1943). *The Well of Loneliness.* London: Jonathan Cape; New York: Covici-Friede, 1928, with an introduction by Havelock Ellis.

Hammett, Dashiell (1894–1961), ed. *Creeps by Night: Chills and Thrills.* New York: John Day Co., 1931. Contains HPL, "The Music of Erich Zann," pp. 347–63; DAW, "The Red Brain," pp. 423–40. (*LL* 394)

———, ed. *Modern Tales of Horror.* London: Victor Gollancz, 1932. (*LL* 395)

Hamsun, Knut (1859–1952). *Growth of the Soil.* <1921?> Tr. from the Norwegian by W. W. Worster. New York: Grosset & Dunlap, 1926.

Hardy, Thomas (1840–1928). *Tess of the D'Urbervilles.* <1891>

Harper, C. Armitage, ed. *American Ghost Stories.* Boston: Houghton Mifflin, 1928.

Harper, Vincent. *The Mortgage on the Brain: Being the Confessions of the Late Ethelbert Craft, M.D.* New York: Doubleday, Page, 1905.

Harraden, Beatrice (1864–1936). *Ships That Pass in the Night.* New York: G. P. Putnam's Sons, 1894.

Harré, T. Everett (1884–1948), ed. *Beware After Dark! The World's Most Stupendous Tales of Mystery, Horror, Thrills and Terror.* New York: Macaulay, 1929. Contains HPL, "The Call of Cthulhu." (*LL* 397)

Harvey, W[illiam] F[ryer] (1885–1937). *The Beast with Five Fingers.* London: J. M. Dent; New York: E. P. Dutton, 1928.

———. "The Beast with Five Fingers." In J. Walker McSpadden, *Famous Psychic Stories.*

Hauff, Wilhelm (1802–1927). *Tales.* London: George Bell & Sons, 1886.

Hawthorne, Julian (1846–1934), ed. *The Lock and Key Library: Classic Mystery and Detective Stories.* New York: Review of Reviews Co., 1909. 10 vols. (*LL* 400)

Hearn, Lafcadio (1850–1904). *Fantastics and Other Fancies.* Ed. Charles Woodward Hutson. Boston: Houghton Mifflin, 1914.

———. *Kwaidan: Stories and Stodies of Strange Things.* <1904> Boston: Houghton Mifflin, 1930. (*LL* 412)

———. *Some Chinese Ghosts.* Boston: Roberts Brothers, 1887.

Hecht, Ben (1894–1964). *Erik Dorn.* New York: G. P. Putnam's Sons, 1921.

Hemingway, Ernest (1889–1961). *The Sun Also Rises.* New York: Scribner's, 1926.

Hodgson, William Hope (1877–1918). *The Boats of the "Glen Carrig."* London: Chapman & Hall, 1907.

———. *Carnacki, the Ghost-Finder.* London: Eveleigh Nash, 1913.

———. *The House on the Borderland.* London: Chapman & Hall, 1908.

———. *The Ghost Pirates.* London: Stanley Paul, 1909.

———. *The Night Land.* London: Eveleigh Nash, 1912.

Hogarth, William (1697–1764). *The Complete Works of William Hogarth.* Introductory Essay by James Hannay. London: Printing & Publishing Co., 1890. 2 vols.; 150 plates. (*LL* 426)

Hogg, James (1770–1835). *The Private Memoirs and Confessions of a Justified Sinner.* <1824> London: A. M. Philpott, 1924.

Horler, Sydney (1888–1954). *The Screaming Skull and Other Stories.* London: Hodder & Stoughton, 1930.

Housman, Laurence (1865–1959). *All-Fellows and The Cloak of Friendship.* <1896, 1905> New York: Harcourt, Brace, [1923].

Howells, William Dean (1837–1920), ed. *The Great Modern American Stories.* New York: Boni & Liveright, 1920.

———, and Henry Mills Alden (1836–1919), ed. *Shapes That Haunt the Dusk.* New York: Harper & Brothers, 1907.

Hudson, W[illiam] H[enry] (1841–1922). *Green Mansions.* <1904> New York: Modern Library, 1916.

Huysmans, J[oris]-K[arl] (1848–1907). *Against the Grain [A Rebours].* <1884> Tr. John Howard, introduction by Havelock Ellis. New York: A. & C. Boni, 1930. (*LL* 454)

———. *Down Stream [A vau-l'eau] and Other Works.* Chicago: P. Covici, 1927.

———. *Down There [Là-Bas].* <1981> Tr. Keene Wallis. New York: A. & C. Boni, 1924.

———. *En Route.* <1895> Tr. C. Kegan Paul. New York: E. P. Dutton, 1920.

Ingram, Eleanor M. (1886–1921). *The Thing from the Lake.* Philadelphia: J. B. Lippincott, 1921.

Jackson, Charles Loring (1847–1935). *The Gold Point and Other Strange Stories.* Boston: Stratford Co., 1926. (*LL* 466)

Jacobs, W[illiam] W[ymark] (1863–1943). "The Monkey's Paw." In *The Lady of the Barge.* New York: Dodd, Mead, 1902.

James, M[ontague] R[hodes] (1862–1936). *Abbeys.* With an Additional Chapter on "Monastic Life and Buildings" by A. Hamilton Thompson. London: The Great Western Railway, 1925.

———. *The Collected Ghost Stories of M. R. James.* London: Edward Arnold, 1931.

———. *Ghost-Stories of an Antiquary*. London: Edward Arnold, 1904. (*LL* 468) [Contains: "Count Magnus" (in *SNM*), "The Treasure of Abbot Thomas."]

———. *More Ghost Stories of an Antiquary*. London: Edward Arnold, 1911. (*LL* 469) [Contains: "The Tractate Middoth," "Casting the Runes."]

———. *A Thin Ghost and Others*. London: Edward Arnold, 1919. (*LL* 470) [Contains: "An Episode of Cathedral History."]

———. *A Warning to the Curious*. London: Edward Arnold, 1925. (*LL* 471) [Contains: "A View from a Hill" (in *S&D*)]

James, Henry (1843–1916). *The Two Magics: The Turn of the Screw; Covering End.* <1898> New York: Macmillan, 1911. (*LL* 467)

Jefferies, Richard (1848–1887). *Field and Hedgerow.* <1889> London: Longmans, Green, 1900.

Johnson, Samuel (1709–1784). *A Dictionary of the English Language.* <1755> 12th ed., corr, & rev. with Considerable Additions from the 8th ed. of the Original. Montrose, 1802. (*LL* 479)

Joyce, James (1882–1941). *Ulysses.* <1922>

Jung-Stilling, Johann Heinrich (1740–1817). *Theory of Pneumatology, in Reply to the Question, What Ought to Be Believed or Disbelieved concerning Presentiments, Visions, and Apparitions, According to Nature, Reason, and Scripture.* Translated from the German, with Copious Notes, by Samuel Jackson. London: Longman, Rees, Orme, Brown, Green & Longman, 1834. (*LL* 488)

Kerruish, Jessie Douglas (1884–1949). *The Undying Monster: A Tale of the Fifth Dimension.* New York: Macmillan, 1936.

Kingsley, Charles (1819–1875). *Hypatia; or, New Foes with an Old Face.* <1889> London: J. M. Dent; New York: E. P. Dutton (Everyman's Library), 1925.

Kittredge, George Lyman (1860–1941). *Witchcraft in Old and New England.* Cambridge, MA: Harvard University Press, 1929.

Knowles, Vernon (1899–1968). *Here and Otherwhere.* London: R. Holden, 1926.

———. *The Street of Queer Houses and Other Stories.* New York: Boullion-Biggs, 1924. London: W. Garder, Darton & Co., 1925.

Kosztolányi, Dezsö (1885–1936), *A véres költö.* <1921> Tr. as *The Bloody Poet: A Novel about Nero.* With a prefatory letter by Thomas Mann. Tr. from the German by Clifton P. Fadiman. New York: Macy-Masius, 1927.

Krutch, Joseph Wood (1893–1970). *Edgar Allan Poe: A Study in Genius.* New York: Knopf, 1926.

———. *The Modern Temper. A Study and a Confession.* New York: Harcourt, Brace, 1929.

Laing, Alexander Kinnan (1903–1976). *The Cadaver of Gideon Wyck.* New York: Farrar & Rinehart, 1934.

———. *Dr. Scarlett: A Narrative of His Mysterious Behavior in the East.* New York: Farrar & Rinehart, 1936.

———, ed. *The Haunted Omnibus.* New York: Farrar & Rinehart, 1937.

Lawrence, D[avid] H[erbert] (1885–1930). "The Rocking-Horse Winner." *Harper's Bazaar* No. 2565 (July 1926): 97, 122, 124, 126. In Cynthia Asquith, ed. *The Ghost Book.*

Leblanc, Maurice (1864–1941). *The Three Eyes.* Tr. Alexander Teixeira de Mattos. New York: Macauley, 1921. New York: A. L. Burt, n.d.

Le Fanu, J[oseph] Sheridan (1814–1873). *All in the Dark.* <1866> London: Downey & Co., n.d.

———. "Green Tea." *All the Year Round* (23 Oct.–13 Nov. 1869). In *In a Glass Darkly.* London: Richard Bentley, 1872.

———. *The House by the Churchyard.* <1863> London: Macmillan, 1899. (*LL* 523)

———. *Uncle Silas: A Tale of Bartram-Haugh.* <1864>

Leith, W. Compton ([pseud. of O. M. Dalton] 1866–1945). *Sirenica.* <1913> With an Introduction by William Marion Reedy. Portland, ME: Thomas Bird Mosher, 1927. (*LL* 523)

Level, Maurice (1875–1926). *Tales of Mystery and Horror.* Tr. Alys Eyre Macklin. New York: Robert M. McBride, 1920. (*LL* 529)

———. *Those Who Return [L'Ombre].* Tr. B. Drillien. New York: Robert M. McBride, 1923. (*LL* 530)

Lewis, Matthew Gregory (1775–1818). *The Monk: A Romance.* <1796> London: Brentano's, [1924]. (*LL* 531)

Lewis, Sinclair (1885–1951). *Elmer Gantry.* New York: Harcourt, Brace, 1927.

———. *It Can't Happen Here.* Garden City, NY: Sun Dial Press, 1935.

Long, Frank Belknap (1901–1994). *The Man from Genoa and Other Poems.* Athol, MA: Recluse Press, 1926.

———. *The Goblin Tower.* Cassia, FL: Dragon-Fly Press, 1935.

Loveman, Samuel (1887–1976). *The Hermaphrodite: A Poem.* Athol, MA: W. Paul Cook, 1926. (*LL* 549)

———. *The Hermaphrodite and Other Poems.* Caldwell, ID: The Caxton Printers, 1936. (*LL* 550)

———. *The Sphinx: A Conversation.* [North Montpelier, VT: W. Paul Cook, 1944.]

Lynch, John Gilbert Bohun (1884–1928), ed. *The Best Ghost Stories.* Boston: Small, Maynard & Co., [1924]. (*LL* 558)

MacDonald, George (1824–1905). *Lilith: A Romance.* New York: Dodd, Mead, 1895. (*LL* 567)

Machiavelli, Niccolò (1469–1527). *The Prince.* <1513> London: Philip Allan, 1925.

Machen, Arthur (1863–1947). *The Children of the Pool and Other Stories.* London: Hutchinson, 1936.

———. *The Cosy Room and Other Stories.* London: Rich & Cowan, 1936.

———. *Far Off Things.* <1922> New York: Alfred A. Knopf, 1923. (*LL* 570)

———. *The Green Round.* London: Ernest Benn, 1933. Sauk City, WI: Arkham House, 1968.

———. *Hieroglyphics: A Note upon Ecstasy in Literature.* <1902> (*LL* 571)

———. *The Hill of Dreams.* <1907> (*LL* 572).

———. *The House of Souls.* <1906> New York: Alfred A. Knopf, 1923. (*LL* 573) [Contains: "The White People."]

———. *The London Adventure: An Essay in Wandering.* New York: Alfred A. Knopf, 1924. (*LL* 574)

———. *The Shining Pyramid.* London: Martin Secker, 1925. (*LL* 576)

———. *The Three Impostors.* <1895> New York: Alfred A. Knopf, 1930. (*LL* 578)

———. *Things Near and Far.* New York: Alfred A. Knopf, 1923. (*LL* 577)

Manhood, H[arold] A[lfred] (1904–1991). *Nightseed and Other Tales.* New York: Viking Press, 1928.

Mann, Thomas (1875–1955). *Death in Venice.* <1912> Tr. Kenneth Burke. New York: Knopf, 1925.

Markham, Virgil (1899–?). *Death in the Dusk: Being Alfred Bannerlee's Own Revision and Enlargement of His Journal Notes from the Evening of October 2nd, 1925, to the Breaking Off, October 9th: Together with the Conclusion of the Narrative Later Supplied by Him; and the Communication of April 17th, 1926.* Now First Arranged and Edited by Virgil Markham. New York: Alfred A. Knopf, 1928.

Marlow, Gabriel S. *I Am Your Brother.* London: Collins, 1935.

Marsh, Richard (1857–1915). *The Beetle.* London: Skeffington, 1897. (*LL* 595)

Masefield, John (1878–1967). *Poems.* New York Macmillan, 1925.

Matthews, Brander (1852–1929). "The Rival Ghosts." In *Tales of Fantasy and Fact.* New York: Harper & Brothers, 1896. Rpt. in Joseph Lewis French, ed., *Masterpieces of Mystery.*

Maturin, Charles Robert (1782?–1824). *Melmoth the Wanderer.* <1820> London: Richard Bentley & Son, 1892. 3 vols. (*LL* 599)

Mayor, F[lora] M[acdonald] (1872–1932). *The Room Opposite and Other Stories of Mystery and Imagination.* London: Longmans, Green, 1935.

McCord, David Thompson Watson (1897–1997). *The Crows.* New York: Charles Scribner's Sons, 1934.

McKenna, Stephen (1888–1967). *The Oldest God: A Novel.* Boston: Little, Brown, 1926.

McSpadden, J. Walker (1874–1960), ed. *Famous Psychic Stories.* New York: Thomas Y. Crowell Co., 1920. (*LL* 584)

Merrick, Elliott (1905–1997). *From This Hill Look Down.* Brattleboro, VT: Stephen Daye Press, 1934.

Merritt, A[braham] (1882–1943). *The Moon Pool.* New York: G. P. Putnam's Sons, 1919.

———. *Seven Footprints to Satan.* New York: Boni & Liveright, 1928.

Meyrink, Gustav (1868–1932). *The Golem.* <1915> Tr. Madge Pemberton. London: Gollancz; Boston: Houghton Mifflin, 1928.

Middleton, Richard (1882–1911). "The Ghost Ship." In *The Ghost Ship and Other Stories.* <1912> London: T. Fisher Unwin, 1923.

Mitchell, Edwin Valentine (1890–?). *The Art of Authorship.* New York: Loring & Mussey, 1935.

The Modern Encyclopedia: A New Library of World Knowledge. Ed. A. H. McDannald. New York: Grosset & Dunlap, 1935. (*LL* 613) First published by W. H. Wise & Co. (New York), 1933 (rev. 1935).

Morand, Paul (1888–1976). *Black Magic.* Tr. from the French by Hamish Miles; illustrated by Aaron Douglas. New York: Viking Press, 1929. (*LL* 620)

Morgan, Charles (1894–1958). *The Fountain.* New York: Alfred A. Knopf, 1932.

Morris, Lloyd R. (1893–1954). *The Rebellious Puritan: Portrait of Mr. Hawthorne.* New York: Harcourt, Brace, 1927.

Morrow, W[illiam] C[hambers] (1854–1923). *The Ape, the Idiot and Other People.* Philadelphia: J. B. Lippincott Co., 1897.

Moulton, Forest Ray (1872–1952). *Consider the Heavens.* Garden City, NY: Doubleday, Doran, 1935.

Neale, Arthur (1873–1933), ed. *The Great Weird Stories.* New York: Duffield, 1929. (*LL* 637)

The New England Primer; or, An Easy and Pleasant Guide to the Art of Reading. <1760?> (*LL* 643)

Norris, Frank (1870–1902). *McTeague: A Story of San Francisco.* <1899> Garden City, NY: Doubleday, Page, 1924.

Oliphant, Mrs. [Margaret] (1828–1897). *Stories of the Seen and Unseen.* Boston: Little, Brown, 1900.

Onions, Oliver (1873–1961). *The Painted Face.* London: Heinemann, 1929.

Pain, Barry (1864–1928). *Stories in the Dark.* London: Grant Richards, 1901.

Palmer, Stuart (1905–1968). *The Puzzle of the Silver Persian.* London: Crime Club/William Collins, 1935.

Palgrave, Francis T. (1814–1897), ed., *The Golden Treasury: Selected from the Best Songs and Lyrical Poems in the English Language.* <1861> (*LL* 671)

Parker, Richard Green (1798–1869). *Aids to English Composition, Prepared for Students of All Grades.* Boston: R. S. Davis; New York, Robinson, Pratt & Co., 1844. (*LL* 673)

Pater, Walter (1839–1894). *Marius the Epicurean: His Sensations and Ideas.* <1885> New York: Boni & Liveright (Modern Library), [1921]. (*LL* 677)

Peattie, Elia Wilkinson (1862–1935). "The Loom of the Dead." In J. Walker McSpadden, ed. *Famous Psychic Stories.*

Pemberton, Clive. *The Weird o' It.* London: Henry J. Drane, 1906.

Perutz, Leo (1884–1957). *The Master of the Day of Judgment.* Tr. Hedwig Singer. London: Elkin Mathews & Marrot, 1929. New York: Charles Boni, 1930. Tr. of *Der Meister des Jüngsten Tages* (1923). (*LL* 687)

Pitkin, Walter B. (1878–1953). *A Short Introduction to the History of Human Stupidity.* New York: Simon & Schuster, 1932.

Phillips, Mary Elizabeth (1857–1945). *Edgar Allan Poe: The Man.* Chicago: John C. Winston Co., 1926. 2 vols.

Phillpotts, Eden (1862–1960). *The Grey Room.* New York: Macmillan, 1921.

———. *The Red Redmaynes.* New York: Macmillan, 1922.

Pierce, Frederick Clifton (1855–1904). *Field Genealogy.* Chicago: W. B. Conkey, 1901.

Poe, Edgar Allan (1809–1849). *The Narrative of Arthur Gordon Pym of Nantucket.* <1838>

———. *Tales of Mystery and Imagination.* Illustrated by Harry Clarke. <1919> New York: Tudor Publishing Co., 1933. (*LL* 701)

Post, Melville Davisson (1869–1930). "The Corpus Delecti." <1896> In Julian Hawthorne, ed. *The Lock and Key Library.*

———. *The Mystery at the Blue Villa.* New York: D. Appleton, 1919.

———. *Uncle Abner, Master of Mysteries.* <1918> New York, London: D. Appleton, 1928.

Powys, John Cowper (1872–1963). *Wolf Solent.* New York: Simon & Schuster, 1929.

Prevot, Francis C. *Ghosties and Ghoulies.* Chelsea, UK: Chelsea Publishing Co., 1933.

Priestley, J. B. (1894–1984). *The Old Dark House.* New York: Harper & Brothers, 1928.

Radcliffe, Ann (1764–1823). *The Italian; or, The Confessional of the Black Penitents.* London: T. Cadell & W. Davies, 1797.

———. *The Mysteries of Udolpho.* <1794> London: George Routledge & Sons, [1882]–[192-]. (*LL* 718)

———. *The Romance of the Forest.* London: T. Hookham & J. Carpenter, 1791.

Railo, Eino. *The Haunted Castle: A Study of the Elements of English Romanticism.* New York: E. P. Dutton, 1927.

Ransome, Arthur (1884–1967). *The Elixir of Life.* London: Methuen, 1915.

Renard, Maurice (1875–1939), and Albert Jean. *Blind Circle [Le Singe].* Tr. from the French by Florence Crewe-Jones. Chicago: White House, 1928.

Reynolds, George W. M. (1814–1879). *Wagner, the Wehr-Wolf.* London: J. Dicks, 1848, 1857, 1872.

Richardson, Leon Burr (1878–1951). *History of Dartmouth College.* Hanover, NH: The Stephen Daye Press, 1932. 2 vols.

Rohmer, Sax ([pseud. of Arthur Sarsfield Ward] 1883–1959). *Bat Wing.* New York: McKinlay, Stone & Mackenzie, [1921].

———. *Brood of the Witch-Queen.* <1918> New York: A. L. Burt, 1926. (*LL* 920)

———. *The Green Eyes of Bast.* New York: A. L. Burt, [1920].

———. *Grey Face.* Garden City, NY: Doubleday, 1924.

———. *The Romance of Sorcery.* New York: E. P. Dutton, 1914.

———. *Tales of East and West.* London: Cassell, 1932.

Romains, Jules (1885–1972). *Men of Good Will.* Tr. W. B. Wells and Gerald Hopkins. New York: Alfred A. Knopf, 1933–46. 14 vols. Translation of *Les Hommes de bonne volonté.*

Saintsbury, George (1843–1933), ed. *Tales of Mystery.* New York: Macmillan, 1891. [Containing extracts of Ann Radcliffe, *The Mysteries of Udolpho;* Matthew Gregory Lewis, *The Monk;* and Charles Robert Maturin, *Melmoth the Wanderer.*] (*LL* 755)

Saxon, Lyle (1891–1946). *Fabulous New Orleans.* New York: Century Co., 1928.

Sayers, Dorothy L[eigh] (1893–1957), ed. *The Omnibus of Crime.* <1928> Garden City, NY: Garden City Publishing Co., 1931. (*LL* 761)

———, ed. *The Second Omnibus of Crime.* <1931> New York: Coward-McCann, 1932.

Scarborough, Dorothy (1878–1935). *The Supernatural in Modern English Fiction.* New York: G. P. Putnam's Sons, 1917.

Schorer, Mark (1908–1977). *A House Too Old.* New York: Reynal & Hitchcock, 1935.

Scott, Sir Walter (1771–1832). *Letters on Demonology and Witchcraft.* <1830> London: George Routledge & Sons, 1884. (*LL* 771)

Seabrook, William B[uehler] (1887–1945). *The Magic Island.* New York: Harcourt, Brace, 1929.

Serviss, Garrett P[utnam] (1851–1929). *Astronomy with an Opera-Glass.* <1888> 8th ed. New York: D. Appleton & Co., 1906. (*LL* 780)

Shelley, Mary (1797–1851). *Frankenstein; or, The Modern Prometheus.* <1818> New-York: H. G. Daggers, 1845. (*LL* 793)

Shiel, M[atthew] P[hipps] (1865–1947). *The Black Box.* New York: Vanguard Press, 1930.

———. *Dr. Krasinski's Secret.* New York: Vanguard Press, 1929.

———. *Here Comes the Lady.* London: Richards Press, 1928.

———. "The House of Sounds." In *The Pale Ape and Other Pulses.* London: T. Werner Laurie, 1911; in *SNM.*

———. *How the Old Woman Got Home.* New York: Macy-Masius (The Vanguard Press), 1928.

———. *The Invisible Voices* (with John Gawsworth). London: Richards Press, 1935.

———. *The Last Miracle.* <1906> London: Victor Gollancz, 1929.

———. *The Lord of the Sea.* <1901> New York: Alfred A. Knopf, 1924. (*LL* 798)

———. *Prince Zaleski.* Boston: Roberts Brothers, 1895. (*LL* 800) <AWD refs a rpt. of 1933>

———. *The Purple Cloud.* <1901> New York: Vanguard Press, 1930. (*LL* 800)

———. *Shapes in the Fire.* London: John Lane, 1896. [Contains: "Vaila."]

Sienkiewitz, Henryk (1846–1916). *Quo Vadis.* Tr. Jeremiah Curtin. Boston: Little, Brown, 1896.

Sinclair, May (1863–1946). *The Intercessor and Other Stories.* New York: Macmillan Company, 1932.

———. *Uncanny Tales.* New York: Macmillan, 1923. London: Hutchinson, 1923.

Sinclair Upton (1878–1968). *The Jungle.* <1906>

Smith, Clark Ashton (1893–1961). *The Double Shadow and Other Fantasies.* Auburn, CA: Auburn Journal Press, 1933). (*LL* 810)

———. *Ebony and Crystal: Poems in Verse and Prose.* Preface by George Sterling. Auburn, CA: [Auburn Journal,] 1922. (*LL* 811)

———. *Odes and Sonnets.* Preface by George Sterling. San Francisco: Book Club of California, 1918. (*LL* 812)

———. *Sandalwood.* Auburn, CA: Auburn Journal, 1925. (*LL* 813)

———. *The Star-Treader and Other Poems.* San Francisco: A. M. Robertson, 1912. (*LL* 814)

——— and David H. Keller. *The White Sybil* [CAS] *and Men of Avalon* [Keller]. Everett, PA: Fantasy Publications, 1934. (*LL* 817)

Sokoloff, Boris (1893–?). *The Crime of Dr. Garine.* Introduction by Theodore Dreiser. New York: Covici-Friede, 1928.

Spencer, R[obin] E[dgerton] (1896–1956). *The Lady Who Came to Stay.* New York: Book League of America, 1931.

Spengler, Oswald (1880–1936). *Der Untergang des Abendlandes.* <1918–22> Tr. by Charles Francis Atkinson as *The Decline of the West.* London: George Allen & Unwin, 1922–26. 2 vols.

Spurrell, H[erbet] G[eorge] F[laxman]. *Out of the Past.* London: Greening, 1903.

Stapledon, [William] Olaf (1886–1950). *Last and First Men.* London: Methuen, 1930.

Steele, Wilber Daniel (1886–1970). "The Woman at Seven Brothers." *Harper's Magazine* 136 (December 1917): 101–10. Rpt. in C. Armitage Harper, ed., *American Ghost Stories;* in *WK.*

Stein, Gertrude (1874–1946). *Three Lives.* <1909> New York: A. & C. Boni, 1927.

Stine, Wilbur N. (1863–1934). *Amos Meakin's Ghost.* Philadelphia: Acorn Press, 1924.

Stockton, Frank R. (1834–1902). "The Transferred Ghost." In *The Lady or the Tiger? and Other Stories.* New York: Charles Scribner's Sons, 1884.

Stoker, Bram (1847–1912). *Dracula.* <1897> Garden City, NY: Doubleday, Page, 1925. (*LL* 848)

Stokley, James (1900–?). *Stars and Telescopes.* New York: Harper & Brothers, 1936.

Summers, Montague (1880–1948). *The Geography of Witchcraft.* London: Kegan Paul, Trench, Trübner & Co.; New York, Knopf, 1927.

———, ed. *The Supernatural Omnibus.* London: Victor Gollancz, 1931. Garden City, NY: Doubleday, Doran, 1932.

———. *The Vampire: His Kith and Kin.* London: Kegan Paul, Trench & Trübner, 1928.

———. *The Vampire in Europe.* London: Kegan Paul, 1929.

Tacitus, P. Cornelius (56?–115?). *The Works of Cornelius Tacitus.* With an Essay on His History and Genius, Notes, Supplements, &c., by Arthur Murphy. New ed. New York: Bangs, Brother & Co., 1855. (*LL* 860)

Taine, John ([pseud. of Eric Temple Bell] 1883–1960). *The Greatest Adventure.* New York: E. P. Dutton, 1929.

Tarkington, [Newton] Booth (1869–1946). *The Plutocrat.* Garden City, NY: Doubleday, Page, 1927.

Thacher, James (1754–1844). *An Essay on Demonology, Ghosts and Apparitions, and Popular Superstitions.* Also an Account of the Witchcraft Delusion at Salem, in 1692. Boston: Carter & Hendee, 1831.

Thackeray, William Makepeace (1811–1863). *The History of Pendennis: His Fortunes and Misfortunes, His Friends and His Greatest Enemy.* <1850> Edited by Robert Morss Lovett. New York: Charles Scribner's Sons, 1917. 2 vols. (*LL* 988)

———. *Vanity Fair.* <1847–48>

Thomson, Christine Campbell (1897–1985), ed. *At Dead of Night.* London: Selwyn & Blount, 1931. Contains AWD's "Prince Borgia's Mass."

———, ed. *By Daylight Only.* London: Selwyn & Blount, 1929. Contains HPL's "Pickman's Model." (*LL* 876)

———, ed. *Grim Death.* London: Selwyn & Blount, 1932. (*LL* 877)

———, ed. *Gruesome Cargoes.* London: Selwyn & Blount, 1928. (*LL* 878)

———, ed. *Not at Night.* London: Selwyn & Blount, 1925. (*LL* 879)

———, ed. *More Not at Night.* London: Selwyn & Blount, 1926. Contains AWD's "Bat's Belfry."

———, ed. *Switch On the Light.* London: Selwyn & Blount, 1931. Contains AWD's and Marc R. Schorer's "The Pacer."(*LL* 881)

———, ed. *Terror by Night.* London: Selwyn & Blount, 1934. Contains AWD's "The Metronome."

———, ed. *You'll Need a Night Light.* London: Selwyn & Blount, 1927. Contains HPL's "The Horror at Red Hook" and AWD's "The Coffin of Lissa."(*LL* 882)

Thomson, James (1700–1748). *The Seasons; with The Castle of Indolence.* <1730; 1748> New-York: Published by W. B. Gilley, . . . Clayton & Kingsland, Printers, 1819. (*LL* 883)

Toksvig, Signe [Kristine] (1891–1983). *The Last Devil.* New York: John Day Co., 1927.

Tolstoy, Leo (1828–1910). *Anna Karenina.* <1875–77>

Tyson, J[ohn] Aubrey (1870–1930). *The Barge of Haunted Lives.* New York: Macmillan, 1923; orig. *All-Story Magazine* (Nov. 1908–Apr. 1909).

Van Vechten, Carl (1880–1964). *Peter Whiffle: His Life and Works.* New York: Alfred A. Knopf, 1922. New York: Modern Library, 1929.

Vaughan, Robert Alfred (1823–1857). *Hours with the Mystics.* <1856> New York: Charles Scribner's Sons, 1893.

Vince, Charles (1887–?). *Barrie Marvell: His Dreams and Adventures.* Boston: Little, Brown, 1923. (*LL* 910)

Wakefield, H[erbert] Russell (1890–1964). *Others Who Returned: Fifteen Disturbing Tales.* New York: D. Appleton, 1929. (*LL* 912) [Contains: "The Cairn," "'Look Up There!,'" "Blind Man's Buff."]

———. *They Return at Evening.* New York: D. Appleton, 1928. (*LL* 913) [Contains: "'He Cometh and He Passeth By'" (in *SNM*), "The Red Lodge," "The Seventeenth Hole at Duncaster" (in *WK*), "'And He Shall Sing.'"]

Walpole, Horace (1717–1797). *The Castle of Otranto.* <1764> (*LL* 916)

Wandrei, Donald (1908–1987). *Dark Odyssey.* St. Paul, MN: Webb Publishing Co., [1931]. (*LL* 917)

———. *Ecstasy and Other Poems.* Athol, MA: Recluse Press, 1928. (*LL* 918)

———. *The Web of Easter Island.* Sauk City, WI: Arkham House, 1948.

Webster, John (1578?–1632?). *The White Devil and the Duchess of Malfy* [*sic*]. <1612; 1623> Edited by Martin W. Sampson. Boston: D. C. Heath, 1904. (*LL* 929)

Webster, Noah (1758–1834). *An American Dictionary of the English Language.* <1828> Revised and Enlarged by Chauncey A. Goodrich and Noah Porter. Springfield, MA: G. & C. Merriam, 1864. (*LL* 930)

———. *Webster's International Dictionary of the English Language.* Now Thoroughly Revised and Enlarged under the Supervision of Noah Porter (Springfield, Ma: G. & C. Merriam, 1891. (*LL* 932)

Weigall, Arthur (1880–1934). *Wanderings in Anglo-Saxon Britain.* London: Hodder & Stoughton, 1927.

———. *Wanderings in Roman Britain.* London: Butterworth, 1926. (*LL* 933)

Wells, H[erbert] G[eorge] (1866–1946). *The Island of Doctor Moreau.* London: Heinemann, 1896. Rpt. in *Amazing Stories* (Oct.–Nov. 1926).

———. *The Outline of History.* <1921> Garden City, NY: Garden City Publishing Co., 1929.

———. *Thirty Strange Stories.* New York: Arnold, 1897.

———. *The Time Machine and Other Stories.* New York: Hold, 1895. London: Heinemann, 1896.

———. *Twelve Stories and a Dream.* London: Macmillan, 1903. [Contains: "A Dream of Armageddon."]

———. *The War of the Worlds.* New York: Harper & Brothers, 1898.

Werfel, Franz (1890–1945). *Goat Song.* Tr. Ruth Langner. Garden City, NY: Doubleday, Page, 1926. A translation of *Bocksgesang* (1921).

Wharton, Edith (1862–1937). *Tales of Men and Ghosts.* London: Macmillan; New York: Charles Scribner's Sons, 1901.

———. *Here and Beyond.* New York: D. Appleton, 1926.

White, Edward Lucas (1866–1934). *Andivius Hedulio: Adventures of a Roman Nobleman in the Days of the Empire.* New York: E. P. Dutton, 1923. (*LL* 942)

———. *Lukundoo and Other Stories.* New York: George H. Doran, 1927. (*LL* 943)

———. *The Song of the Sirens and Other Stories.* New York: E. P. Dutton, 1919. (*LL* 944)

———. *The Unwilling Vestal: A Tale of Rome under the Caesars.* New York: E. P. Dutton, 1918.

White, Gilbert (1720–1793). *The Natural History of Selborne.* <1789> New York: Harper & Brothers, 1842. (*LL* 945)

Whitehead, Henry S. (1882–1932). *Pinkie at Camp Cherokee.* New York: G. P. Putnam's Sons, 1931.

Wiggam, Albert Edward (1871–1957). *The Marks of a Clear Mind; or, Sorry But You're Wrong About It.* New York: Blue Ribbon Books, 1933.

Wilde, Oscar (1854–1900). "The Canterville Ghost." *Court and Society Review* (23 Feb.–2 Mar. 1887).

———. *De Profundis.* <1905>

———. *Fairy Tales and Poems in Prose.* New York: Boni & Liveright (Modern Library), [1918]. (*LL* 954).

———. *The Happy Prince and Other Tales.* London: D. Nutt, 1888.

———. *A House of Pomegranates.* London: J. R. Osgood, McIlvaine, 1891. [Contains: "The Fisherman and His Soul."]

———. *The Picture of Dorian Gray.* <1890> New York: Boni & Liveright (Modern Library), 1918. (*LL* 956)

———. *Poems.* New York: Boni & Liveright (Modern Library), [19—]. (*LL* 957) [Contains: "The Sphinx" and "The Ballad of Reading Gaol."]

Wilder, Thornton (1897–1975). *The Bridge of San Luis Rey.* New York: Boni, 1927.

———. *The Cabala.* New York: A. & C. Boni, 1926.

Williamson, Henry (1895–1977).*The Beautiful Years.* London: William Collins, 1921. Rev. ed. London: Faber & Faber, 1929. (*The Flax of Dream,* Volume 1.)

———. *Dandelion Days.* London: William Collins, 1922. Rev. ed. London: Faber & Faber, 1930. (*The Flax of Dream,* Volume 2.)

———. *The Dream of Fair Women.* London: William Collins, 1924. Rev. ed. London: Faber & Faber, 1931. (*The Flax of Dream,* Volume 3.)

———. *The Lone Swallows and Other Essays of the Country Green.* London: William Collins, 1922. New York: E. P. Dutton, 1926.

———. *The Old Stag.* London: G. P. Putnam's Sons, 1926.

———. *The Pathway.* London: Jonathan Cape, 1928.

———. *The Peregrine's Saga and Other Stories of the Country Green.* London: William Collins, 1923.

———. *Tarka the Otter: His Joyful Water-Life and Death in the Country of the Two Rivers.* London: G. P. Putnam's Sons, 1927.

———. *The Village Book.* New York: E. P. Dutton, 1930.

Wolfe, Thomas (1900–1938). *Look Homeward, Angel: A Story of the Buried Life.* New York: Charles Scribner's Sons, 1929.

Wright, Dudley (1868–1949). *Vampires and Vampirism.* London: W. Rider & Son, 1914.

Wright, S. Fowler (1874–1965). *The World Below.* New York: Longmans, Green, 1930. (*LL* 974)

Wyllarde, Dolf (d. 1950). *Stories of Strange Happenings.* London: Mills & Boon, 1930. (*LL* 975)

Yardley, Edward. *Supernatural in Romantic Fiction.* London: Longmans, Green, 1880.

E. Secondary

Cockcroft, T. G. L. *Index to the Weird Fiction Magazines: Index by Title.* Lower Hutt, New Zealand: T. G. L. Cockcroft, 1962.

Collins, Tom, ed. *Is* No. 4. Meriden, CT: Spectator Amateur Press Society, October 1971. Special August Derleth issue.

Cook, W. Paul. "A Plea for Lovecraft." *Ghost* No. 3 (May 1945): 55–56.

Derleth, August. *H. P. L.: A Memoir.* New York: Ben Abramson, 1945.

———. "Lovecraft as a Formative Influence." In H. P. Lovecraft. *Marginalia.* Ed. August Derleth and Donald Wandrei. Sauk City, WI: Arkham House, 1944, pp. 355–61.

———. "Lovecraft as Mentor." In H. P. Lovecraft and Divers Hands. *The Shuttered Room and Oher Pieces.* Sauk City, WI: Arkham House: 1959, pp. 141–70.

———. *100 Books by August Derleth.* Sauk City, WI: Arkham House, 1962.

———. *Thirty Years of Arkham House: A History and Bibliography.* Sauk City, WI: Arkham House, 1970.

Dyke, Bill. *Remembering Derleth: All About Augie: 1909–1971.* Sauk City, WI: August Derleth Society, 1988.

Everts, R. Alain, et al., ed. *Etchings and Odysseys* No. 6. Madison, WI: Strange Company, 1985. Special August Derleth issue.

Joshi, S. T. *H. P. Lovecraft: A Life.* West Warwick, RI: Necronomicon Press, 1996.

———. *Lovecraft's Library: A Catalogue.* 2nd ed. New York: Hippocampus Press, 2002.

———. *Sixty Years of Arkham House.* Sauk City, WI: Arkham House, 1999.

———, and David E. Schultz. *An H. P. Lovecraft Encyclopedia.* Westport, CT: Greenwood Press, 2001. New York: Hippocampus Press, 2004.

Litersky, Dorothy M. Grobe. *Derleth: Hawk and Dove.* Aurora, CO: National Writers Press, 1997.

Moskowitz, Sam. "I Remember Derleth." *Starship* 18, No. 1 (Spring 1981): 7–14.

Olson, Dwayne H. "The Papers of Howard Wandrei: An Overview." *Scream Factory* No. 18 (1996): 74–79.

Owings, Mark, and Irving Binkin. *A Catalog of Lovecraftiana: The Grill-Binkin Collection.* Baltimore: Mirage Press, 1975.

Parnell, Frank H., with Mike Ashley. *Monthly Terrors: An Index to the Weird Fantasy Magazines Published in the United States and Great Britain.* Westport, CT: Greenwood Press, 1985.

Price, E. Hoffman. *Book of the Dead—Friends of Yesteryear: Fictioneers and Others (Memories of the Pulp Fiction Era).* Ed. Peter Ruber. Sauk City, WI: Arkham House, 2001.

Roberts, James P., ed. *Return to Derleth: Selected Essays.* Madison, WI: White Hawk Press, 1993.

———, ed. *Return to Derleth: Selected Essays, Volume Two.* Madison, WI: White Hawk Press, 1995.

[———, ed.] *A Derleth Collection.* Sauk City, WI: Geranium Press, 1993.

Ruber, Peter, ed. *Arkham's Masters of Horror: A 60th Anniversary Anthology Retrospective of the First 30 Years of Arkham House.* Sauk City, WI: Arkham House, 2000.

Squires, John D. *M. P. Shiel and the Lovecraft Circle: A Collection of Primary Documents Including Shiel's Letters to August Derleth, 1929–1946.* Kettering, OH: The Vainglory Press, 2001.

[Unsigned.] "A 'Special' Halloween Letter to Knock the Socks Off H. P. Lovecraft Fans!" *August Derleth Society Newsletter* 15, No. 3 (Autumn 1994): 1–2.

Wilson, Alison M. *August Derleth: A Bibliography.* Metuchen, NJ: Scarecrow Press 1983.

Wright, Farnsworth. Letters to August Derleth. Mss. State Historical Society of Wisconsin.

Index

CPSIA information can be obtained
at www.ICGtesting.com
Printed in the USA
BVHW090214021118
531864BV00001B/37/P

9 781614 980612